Chronologies of Modern Terrorism

Chronologies of
Modern
Terrorism

Barry Rubin and Judith Colp Rubin

M.E.Sharpe
Armonk, New York
London, England

Cover images provided by Getty Images and the following (left to right):
Central Press/Stringer/Hulton Archive; Roger Viollet; Stringer; Alex Wong.

Library of Congress Cataloging-in-Publication Data

Rubin, Barry M.
  Chronologies of modern terrorism / Barry Rubin and Judith Colp Rubin.
    p. cm.
  Includes bibliographical references and index.
  ISBN 978-0-7656-2047-7 (hardcover : alk. paper)
  1. Terrorism—History—Chronology. 2. Terrorism—History—20th century. 3. Terrorism—History—
21st century. 4. Radicalism. I. Rubin, Judith Colp. II. Title.

HV6431.R84 2007
363.32502′02—dc22   2007039657

Printed in the United States of America

Contents

Introduction

Terrorism is a controversial issue and defining it can be confusing. Terrorism is the deliberate tactic and strategy of killing civilians or government officials and detroying a country's infrastructure by groups seeking political power. As a political tool, terrorism has a number of aspects that have remained remarkably consistent during its 200-year-long history as a consciously formulated aspect of ideology. These include:

- A belief that terrorism will encourage broader mass support for a movement by increasing popular contempt for the target and by inspiring a belief that a target government cannot defend itself and thus can be easily defeated.
- A calculation that terrorizing an enemy will force him to flee or give up. Terrorist attacks are thought to be capable of destroying the functioning of a government, economic system, or society.
- A belief that if other less extreme means of bringing change have been frustrated, terrorist action at least brings a sense of revenge.
- Confidence that the shock value of terrorist action can bring wider interest in and support for the cause.

What is especially striking is the fact that terrorism has not been a very successful strategy in bringing significant change compared to such alternatives as mass organizing, mutual concessions to achieve a peaceful resolution, democratic competition, constructive socio-economic development, or even warfare against national military forces. That is the reason conventional Marxism

rejected terrorism. It is also the reason that terrorists themselves have often been considered not only morally reprehensible but also incomprehensible by observers who believe their efforts will inevitably fail. The problem, of course, is that, rightly or wrongly, the terrorists do not agree with that assessment.

This book attempts to provide the historical background of modern terrorism and provide a representative chronology of terrorist acts from the mid-twentieth century to recent times. Four basic types of entries are included:

- The main events of historical conflicts that resulted in many terrorist acts.
- The history of groups that became practitioners of terrorism, in some cases beginning before they chose such terrorism as a tactic.
- Key developments in counterterrorist activity. The response of targeted states and groups will give the reader a sense of how the wars against terrorists were fought and why terrorist groups succeeded or—in most cases—failed.
- Specific incidents of terrorism, including shootings, assassinations, bombings, kidnappings, and the like. Such incidents constitute the largest number of entries. From the wide variety of actions in many times and places, the reader can follow its changing scope and intensity.

It should be mentioned that governments have committed many actions that could be equated with terrorism, most notably the Fascist and Communist regimes of the twentieth century, but such acts are better considered in the category of state repression, a factor that makes no judgment about their relative justness. The possession of state power leads to acts that differ both qualitatively and quantitatively—jailing, torture, confiscation of assets, imprisonment, exile, and the like. Instances of state repression could clearly fill another book as voluminous or more so than this one. For these reasons, they are not included here. At the same time, some of the terrorist acts described in this book may have received secret government support, and many more likely received a government's tacit approval in overt or covert operations against enemies or rivals.

Classifying Terrorist Groups

Terrorism can be divided into two basic categories. Social revolutionary terrorism seeks to transform a society according to some ideological plan. Social revolutionary terrorism reached an apex in Russia during the half century leading up to the 1917 Bolshevik Revolution, which established a Communist regime in place of the czarist empire. Similarly, contemporary Islamist terrorists fight to establish Islamist governments in target states. Nationalist terrorism is the effort of an ethnic or religious community to take over a state or to gain independence from one. Nationalist terrorism reached its most comprehensive form in Ireland in the late 1800s and early 1900s, during that country's long struggle against British rule. More recently, for example, the Tamil people in Sri Lanka have used terrorism in their struggle to gain autonomy and concessions from the majority Sinhalese.

In addition, the practice of terrorism can be divided into several clear eras. Terrorism became a distinct doctrine in the French Revolution of the 1790s, justified as a way to transform society by destroying or intimidating rivals and mobilizing supporters. During the late 1800s, the ideologies of anarchism and Marxism included terror as part of their arsenal of tactics in bringing about social revolution.

In the mid-1800s, Russian oppositionists developed the idea of the professional revolutionary who would devote his life to revolution above any personal interests, family life, or moral considerations. Many held that glorious revolutionary aims justified a wide range of violent actions, including bombings, hostage-taking, and assassinations. Also

during this period, anarchists carried out assassinations of leaders and public officials in the hope of eradicating government altogether.

In the late 1960s and the 1970s, new revolutionary movements arose, shaped by a generation that believed older radical forces, including Communist parties and Arab nationalist regimes, had failed. In many places, terrorist groups emerged from these movements. In Europe, there were social revolutionary movements in Italy and Germany and nationalist revolutionary upsurges in Ireland and among the Basques of Spain. In the United States, terrorist acts were committed by social revolutionaries hoping to foment revolution and by African-American and Puerto Rican nationalist groups.

In Latin America, almost every country had a Marxist-Leninist social revolutionary group that used terrorism as a part of its strategy. Asia also had such movements, notably in the Philippines and India. But there were also nationalist movements among ethnic groups in India (notably Sikhs) and among Muslims focusing on Kashmir. Within Africa, terrorism became an important factor, most notably in Rwanda, where it helped cause a campaign of populist genocide.

The Middle East became a particular hotbed of terrorism in the 1960s in part because states were energetic sponsors of such activities to attack or subvert their neighbors. The most prominent target was Israel, the Jewish state established in 1948. Among the main state sponsors of aggression at various times were Egypt, Iran, Iraq, Libya, and Syria; Saudi Arabia and Kuwait were among the main financiers. On the Middle East's eastern frontier, Afghanistan and Pakistan followed similar policies.

In North America and Europe (excepting the nationalist movements among the Basques of Spain and in Northern Ireland), terrorist groups—always quite small—were largely eliminated by the 1980s. In Latin America there was some decline, although revolutionary terrorism continued in Colombia and especially in Peru. In Africa, terrorism remained a sporadic phenomenon.

In Asia, in Sri Lanka and especially in Kashmir, conflicts involving terrorism continued at relatively higher levels than elsewhere, in the latter case fueled by Islamist-inspired terrorism exported by Afghanistan under the Taliban regime and by Pakistan. This new wave of terror also inspired terrorist acts in the southern Philippines, Indonesia, Thailand, and occasionally China.

From the 1980s onward, Islamist ideology seized center stage in the world of terrorism. At first, the main emphasis was the direct taking of power through Islamist revolutions, notably in Algeria, Egypt, and Lebanon. These insurgencies were mainly defeated, though they did not come to an end.

Failure to take power in these instances led to the development of a new variety or at least strategy of Islamist terrorism, Jihadism, which targeted the West—especially the United States—rather than Arab regimes and Israel. The Jihadist attacks on the United States on September 11, 2001, appeared to show the way for future terrorist movements, but they also provoked a strong counterattack by the United States and by many of its allies in Western Europe. Osama bin Laden's al-Qaeda movement survived but suffered serious damage. Security in the West increased, and many terrorist cadres were arrested. Even Jihadist groups began to concentrate more on carrying out a long-term terrorist war in Muslim nations, for example, in Saudi Arabia and in Iraq, after the fall of Saddam Hussein.

Organization

Chapter 1 outlines the origins and early development of modern terrorism, from the French Revolution to the success of the Russian Revolution in 1917. The remaining chapters focus on terrorism in different parts of the world, providing chronologies for separate regions.

Chapter 2 looks at social revolutionary terrorism in Europe and the United States. This is the purest continuation of nineteenth-century terrorism, administering violent shocks on a country to try to break down its system. Violence by revolutionary social groups in these regions was sporadic and never seriously threatened the governments or societies of these mature states, but it often received extensive publicity through media news coverage, which sometimes succeeded in giving terrorist acts large symbolic significance even when the number of people affected was small. Among the most prominent groups were the Black Panthers and the Weather Underground in the United States; the Red Army Faction, or RAF, in Germany (also known as the Baader-Meinhof Gang); and the Red Brigades in Italy.

Chapter 3 looks at Western nationalist groups that have resorted to terrorism. The general integration of Western societies greatly reduced the potential for nationalist movements compared to earlier eras, but significant violence occurred over long periods in Ireland and in Spain. In Ireland, terrorism began as a tactic against British rule and played a role in the establishment of the Irish Free State in 1921. It soon broke out again in disputes about the status of Northern Ireland, which remained under British tutelage with the support of its largely Protestant population. From the mid-1960s to the mid-1990s, hundreds of civilians were killed by the anti-British Irish Republican Army (IRA) and pro-British Protestant groups. In Spain, some Basques in the country's northwest region sought greater autonomy from the central government. The extreme terrorist wing of the Basque movement carried out a long series of terror attacks, primarily targeting Spanish government officials, but also killing Basque leaders who opposed the violence and favored a negotiated settlement. Terrorist violence also afflicted Turkey, where Kurds in the eastern provinces carried on a terrorist campaign against the Turkish government, seeking an independent Kurdish state.

In Latin America, covered in chapter 4, radical movements were almost exclusively social revolutionary. During the 1960s and 1970s, they developed a new revolutionary strategy in which elements of twentieth-century guerrilla warfare were combined with nineteenth-century terrorist tactics. Depending on the time, group, and country, emphasis was placed on urban or rural areas. This strategy failed repeatedly but was revived from time to time. Revolutionary leaders often identified the United States as the main culprit in their countries' troubles and targeted representatives of U.S. business and government for retribution. Terrorist activity culminated in the creation of the Shining Path (Sendero Luminoso), the organization in Peru that gained control of parts of that country and threatened at one point to overturn its government before being at least partly defeated. Latin American regimes reacted to terrorist threats with special vigor. Thousands of revolutionaries and their sympathizers disappeared, presumably killed by government forces or by "death squads," who wore no uniforms but often received secret government support.

Chapter 5 presents terrorist activity in Asia and Africa. Many radical groups took their inspiration from Maoist techniques used during the Chinese

Communist revolution. Where Mao's movement had a strong social revolutionary component, however, many of these later Asian and African movements concentrated on local issues and were more nationalist than social revolutionary. India, in particular, faced challenges from a number of ethno-religious minorities seeking independence or broad autonomy. Among these groups were Sikhs in northwest India, Muslims in Jammu and Kashmir, and a variety of tribal peoples on the country's northeastern border with Bangladesh. Just off India's coast in Sri Lanka, terrorism was a part of a long, brutal campaign by the Tamils to gain autonomy from the majority Sinhalese. Muslims in the southern Philippines, through what constituted both an Islamist and nationalist revolt, also sought autonomy.

In Africa, terror tactics were often part of violent conflicts between tribal groups. In Rwanda, when a group of radicals of the Hutu people gained power in 1994, Hutus went on a rampage against the Tutsis, who had dominated the government in the past. Nearly a million Tutsis and moderate Hutus were killed. Elsewhere in Africa, terrorist tactics were adopted by the Lord's Resistance Army, an extreme Christian group, in Uganda.

In the latter half of the twentieth century and the first years of the twenty-first, the most important development in terrorist activity was the rise of Islamist groups as advocates and practitioners of nationalist terrorist philosophy in the Middle East. The final three chapters of the book describe Islamist terror in three different settings and periods.

Chapter 6 discusses terrorism in the Middle East. With the establishment of the Jewish state of Israel in 1948, Palestinian nationalists sought to overturn this outcome and replace Israel with a Palestinian Arab state. Terrorism was a central part of their strategy. And as the nationalist group, the Palestine Liberation Organization led by Fatah, and Arab nationalist-led states experienced defeats, Islamist ideology spread both among Palestinians, in the form of the rise of Hamas, and in Arab countries.

Chapter 7 follows the development of the Islamist movement, which became an incubator for terrorist activity. Islamists first gained political power in Iran, where they helped to overthrow the monarchy with a regime led by Ayatollah Ruhollah Khomeini.

At nearly the same time, the Communist government of neighboring Afghanistan was besieged by an Islamist opposition. The Soviet Union sent troops to support the regime and was drawn into a long, bitter war with Afghan partisans. Afghanistan became the battleground on which militant Islamists learned to fight. Later, Afghanistan would welcome terrorist organizer Osama bin Laden to set up training camps for his al-Qaeda organization. By the 1990s, Islamist thought and terrorist tactics were fueling Muslim radicals against Indian rule in Kashmir, Chechen nationalists seeking independence from Russia, and separatist Muslims in the Philippines. Al-Qaeda began a series of attacks against Western nations, including the planting of a bomb in an underground garage of the World Trade Center in New York City in 1993.

The threat of Islamist terrorism received full worldwide recognition only after September 11, 2001, when al-Qaeda suicide teams hijacked four U.S. passenger airliners and crashed three of them into landmarks in New York City and Washington, D.C. The image of two of the World Trade Center towers, 107 stories tall, in flames brought cheers from radical Muslims and anti-Americans around the world. About 3,000 people died in the attacks.

Chapter 8 begins with the 9/11 attack and provides a chronology of later Islamist attacks. It also traces the response of the United States and its allies. Weeks after the attack, the alliance invaded Afghanistan, removed the Taliban government, and began pursuing bin Laden and his lieutenants. In April 2003, the United States invaded Iraq, naming that nation and its president, Saddam Hussein, as targets in the "War on Terror." Once again, the attack succeeded in removing the regime from power, but establishing an effective replacement government was a more difficult task. In the meantime, Islamist radicals flocked to Iraq to adapt their insurgency and terrorist skills to a war against the United States. Iraq became a training ground for terrorist insurgency just as Afghanistan had been during the Soviet-Afghan war.

Thus, the structure of the book facilitates examination of the phenomenon of terrorism by region, historical period, and type of movement. Readers can also use the book to search for specific events, trace the path of terrorism in individual countries, or look at the role of individual groups. Given the broad range and volume of material covered, the intention is to facilitate and encourage further research.

We would like to thank Yeru Aharoni, Joy Pincus, Carmen Galvan, and Sarah Cattan for research assistance on this project.

Chronologies of
Modern
Terrorism

The Early History of Terrorism as Ideology and Strategy

Political violence has always existed in history at very high levels and throughout the world. What is newer, however, is the conscious use of deliberately organized and ideologically justified terrorism by nonstate actors as a political philosophy and as a strategy for seeking to gain political power rather than merely as a by-product of political struggle.

Among the key factors in the birth of this kind of coherently planned and justified terrorism were developments also central to the broader shaping of modern politics. One critical issue, for example, was the growth of mass politics. Only after the bulk of the citizenry became active in determining who would rule a country and after organized revolutionary movements were formed to seek power through a systematic strategy did it become worthwhile to deliberately kill ordinary civilians.

Up to that point, a period which coincides roughly with the French Revolution, only a small ruling elite participated in struggles for power. Ordinary people might be oppressed, tortured, or killed for immediate gain, but the battles among the nobility made up politics and determined which people and policies would hold power. As a result, except during full-scale war, bloodshed tended to be limited to the elimination of royals or nobles—those who held power and were seen as obstacles by those seeking to achieve control, or those challenging or conspiring against the incumbents. For example, Mary, Queen of Scots was executed by Queen Elizabeth I for her conspiracies with French and Spanish forces to seize the English throne. Or, to go back further, Julius

Caesar was assassinated by a group of Roman senators seeking to block his bid for total power.

A second key factor in the development of terrorism was the rise of modern ethnic nationalism. In the past, the goal of regimes was to conquer and rule additional peoples, not to eliminate them altogether. Massacres certainly took place, especially of defenders or residents of a territory who had refused to surrender. This act might be due to an immediate thirst for revenge or a demonstration to others of the fate awaiting them if they did not give up. In that sense, such behavior closely resembled modern terrorism. In general, though, empires wanted more subjects, as taxpayers or slaves, regardless of their language, religion, or customs.

Still, only when a self-conscious national-ethnic community bound together by a common loyalty and political direction coalesced would it have an incentive to physically eliminate a competing group. In conflicts between such groups, both sides might be affected because a side that might otherwise have surrendered or offered only token opposition to more forgiving challengers would also fight harder. In addition, nationalist propaganda was developed that could demonize an enemy and declare it worthy of extinction. At the same time, nationalism created an audience of citizens who might applaud and be inspired to activity by terrorist acts, whereas previously they would have been indifferent to this kind of appeal. Modern nationalism became one source for the politics of terrorism.

The other, conscious social revolutionary aspirations, was also a product of the modern period. A social revolutionary movement created coherent radical political ideologies which justified rebellion and the punishment of its enemies; disciplined political-revolutionary organizations; and created individuals who devoted their lives to the cause—professional revolutionaries. The punishment of a set of classes or categories of citizens was now rationalized as a necessary part of humanity's forward march. Murder of another group became a strategy for gaining or keeping power.

Terrorism functioned in a number of ways in this regard. At the extreme, it involved the actual elimination of a group so that it could no longer hold or seek power. Instead of merely wiping out an entire royal family and then feeling securely in power, the Communists and Nazis felt it necessary to destroy large groups, such as rich peasants or Jews.

At the same time, the very ruthlessness of the terrorist's mission might so threaten some enemies as to push them into an escalating mutual race toward repression. If a large group was supporting revolution, the response could be to target a whole section of the population, trying to terrorize into quiescence a group seen as threatening. Such killing, however, might also inspire mass uprisings.

For the revolutionaries themselves, the temptation would be to believe that they would win if their enemies could be shown to be too weak to defend themselves. Often, single acts of terrorism became powerful propaganda in themselves, publicizing the existence and ideas of the revolution, encouraging sympathy for the revolution, and intimidating its opponents.

This is not to suggest, of course, that modern politics revolves around terrorism. There were many political movements, even revolutionary ones, that did not use terrorism as a central strategy. Nationalist groups, more often than not, sought to achieve their goals through other means, including what might be called "conventional violence." But terrorism now became a way—seen as illegitimate by most, but justified by a sizable minority—to seek political power.

Modern terrorism had significant forerunners long before the French Revolution, especially in struggles involving religion. For example, in 1572 high-ranking Catholic noblemen in France began a large-scale massacre of French Protestants with the aim of wiping them out. An estimated 10,000 people were killed. Spain acted as a state sponsor of revolution in Britain, using British Catholic surrogates in plots to assassinate Queen Elizabeth and place a Catholic on the throne. Yet these actions were to a large extent the product of state activities and dynastic quarrels, closer to traditional uses of political violence.

Thus, the French Revolution is the best point at which to commence the history of terrorism. There, for the first time ever, terrorism was at the core of a comprehensive political philosophy and strategy to gain and retain power. Many of the critical elements of terrorism are clearly expressed and implemented during the French Revolution: the deliberate instilling of fear, the elimination of entire social groups (first the aristocracy, then the Girondin moderates, then rivals among the radicals themselves), the use of terror against others as a way of mobilizing one's own supporters, and incitement to murder as a means of political expression and to achieve utopian goals.

It was no accident that the very word "terrorist" was coined in 1793 by the revolutionary activist journalist Gracchus Babeuf. It was the revolutionary leader Jean-Paul Marat who proposed to "place terror as the lord of the day," a strategy that, his colleague Pierre-Paul Royer-Collard explained, was "the only way to arouse the people and force them to save themselves." In denying that terrorism was the act of a despotic government, the radical leader Maximilien Robespierre claimed that it was essential for establishing a virtuous regime. But the tendency of terrorism to spread and to poison the movement using it is illustrated by the fact that Babeuf and Robespierre themselves were guillotined, victims of the terror regime they instituted and justified.

The French Revolution produced a lasting legacy of both democratic potentiality and revolutionary romanticism. Yet it is easy to forget that the movement itself was an abject political failure. In less than a decade it had collapsed, due less to foreign intervention than to internal disorder, and terrorism greatly contributed to those problems. An emperor, Napoléon, took power, established his own noble class, and led the country into 15 years of bloody and wasteful wars. France's political turmoil was not resolved and democracy firmly established until more than 80 years after the revolution.

Yet as an idea the French Revolution triumphed internationally, having more intellectual influence than its more successful American counterpart where terrorism was never even advocated, much less practiced. The nineteenth century was rife with political upheaval in Europe as democratic movements battled monarchies, Socialist groups challenged capitalism, and nationalist causes rejected the rule of diverse peoples by empires. In most cases, terrorism was not endorsed or used as a weapon, even in the face of vicious repression by state authorities.

In the search for a successful formula for making revolution, however, the extremist fringes of these movements did believe terrorism was a workable strategy and a beneficial tactic. The new ideas generated by the French Revolution and Socialist theorists provided a basis for justifying such behavior, especially since the forces for change were so regularly defeated and often repressed when trying to use other approaches.

A typical, though especially blunt, example of such reasoning was provided by the German-American radical Karl Heinzen, who said in 1848: "If you have to blow up half a continent and cause a bloodbath to destroy the party of barbarism, you should have no scruples of conscience."

But why should terrorism be expected to bring about such change? It appealed to those who had two basic types of hope: those who believed political violence would discredit and demoralize the rulers and those who believed it would win over and mobilize the masses. In the former case, terrorists did not use political violence as blackmail, threatening a ruling class with violence in order to force it to grant reforms. Rather, their goal was the destruction of the existing order. For them, assassination was intended to paralyze the governmental apparatus, making it impossible for the regime to function and thus supposedly bringing about its downfall.

Even more important was the intended mass appeal of such violence. Terrorists believed that the "propaganda of the deed" would inspire others to follow suit, showing that the well-placed gunshot would have more influence than 10,000 pamphlets. Encouraged by seeing that their rulers were so vulnerable and that the system's destruction was possible, the masses would supposedly rise up and support the revolution, or at least applaud and sympathize with the revolutionaries.

By the 1880s, however, most Western European countries—and especially Britain, France, Italy, and Germany—had attained a measure of democracy. Trade unions and Socialist parties were grow-

ing in power and influence; living standards were starting to rise. The prospects for Socialist revolution seemed low. In these countries, sub-nationalist issues had been largely resolved, with the notable exception of Ireland, which offered the first use of terrorism on behalf of a nationalist movement. Terrorism was practiced mainly by small groups of anarchists, for whom only the elimination of government itself was acceptable.

It is not surprising, then, that the next great theater of terrorist operations became Russia. There, Marxist and populist revolutions, national conflicts, and frustration at the intractability of the political and social orders all came together. Heinzen's standpoint would find many adherents, most notably with the world's first modern terrorist organization, the group called People's Will. Most of the group shared the anarchist view that the Russian state should be destroyed and that the land belonging to the government and the nobility should be handed over to the peasants.

Rejecting Marxism, which usually—but not always—preached the superiority of mass organization over individual acts of violence, members of People's Will claimed that they were merely enacting the people's will. The organization and its descendant, the Social Revolutionary Party, held a romantic socialist-anarchist philosophy focused on arousing the peasantry. Assassinating czarist officials was seen as a central element in their strategy. Summarizing three of the most important strategic rationales for terrorism, the party's program announced in 1880: "Terrorist acts will show the government is not invincible, raise morale [among its enemies], and instill a revolutionary fervor."

In a story often repeated in the history of terrorism, their actions would be counterproductive for the people they claimed to champion and even for their own expressed aims. The wave of assassinations they unleashed—especially the killing of Czar Alexander II in 1881—would actually destroy the hopes for peaceful reform in Russia. Rather than delivering a rural utopia, their labors would help destroy the independence of their beloved peasantry, enslaving them to the Communist regime's nationalization of all land.

Indeed, that same Soviet regime, which relived so many aspects of the French Revolution, also explicitly extolled the use of terror as a means of retaining control over the state. Not only those who would restore the old regime but also liberals,

Social Revolutionaries, anarchists, and members of the Communist Party would be tortured, sent to concentration camps, and murdered in extraordinary numbers. Peasants who opposed collectivization and members of ethnic minorities also suffered greatly from such depredations.

As in the case of its French predecessor, the revolutionary regime would be debased and ultimately weakened by its dependence on terrorism and its waste of human resources—even the death of many who had devoted their lives to the Communist cause. Indeed, the history of the Soviet Union once again proved that Robespierre was wrong when he ridiculed the idea that "terror was the activating principle of a despotic government."

The second powerful totalitarian ideology of the twentieth century, fascism, went even further in basing itself on terror over its own citizens and those whom it would conquer. In Fascist Italy, Nazi Germany, and their imitators elsewhere in Europe, terror was also justified on the basis of a utopian dream. There, however, it added the feature of explicitly advocating the extinction of other ethnic or national groups deemed "inferior races," as opposed to, in the Soviet model, classes deemed enemies of the state.

Whatever differences existed among all these ideologies, the basic concepts of terrorism as a strategy and tactic remained in place: the physical extinction of opponents, the rationale for large-scale murder, the intimidation of others, and the mobilization of support from one's own target audience. A critical principle was that those purveying terrorism had to believe, rightly or wrongly, that it would be popular among those it would recruit as supporters.

This book classifies the actions of regimes such as the USSR and Nazi Germany as examples of state repression rather than as terrorism. Yet the role their ideas and actions played in fostering revolutionary terrorism elsewhere in the world should not be underestimated. In general, nineteenth-century terrorism had focused on ruling groups, especially officials. The twentieth century's contribution to terrorism was to transform the tactic of terrorism into a strategy. In this context, terrorism can be used systematically against civilians for many reasons, including their religion, ethnicity, or class. They might also be targeted because they supported the government or existing society, belonged to competing revolutionary groups, or were simply not supportive enough of the group committing terrorism.

July 1586

Anthony Babington, a Catholic in England involved with the Spanish government, writes a letter to the imprisoned fellow Catholic Mary, Queen of Scots asking her to approve a plan to assassinate Queen Elizabeth I to pave the way for Mary's succession to the throne. The plotters were under government surveillance and Babington and other conspirators are executed on September 20, 1586; Mary herself is executed on February 8, 1587. The Babington affair is one of several unsuccessful assassination attacks against Elizabeth I that furnish one of the earliest examples of state-sponsored terrorism.

November 5, 1605

A plot by a British Catholic, Guy Fawkes, and several others to blow up the House of Parliament with kegs of gunpowder in an attempt to kill King James I and his Protestant allies is discovered and thwarted. The plot was also to have included kidnapping the king's children and starting a revolt in the English Midlands. Several men are arrested and executed for the Gunpowder Plot. Fawkes is hanged on January 31, 1606.

September 2–6, 1792

Three years after the revolution in France overthrows the monarchy, the September Massacres take place in Paris when crowds break into prisons and slaughter many prisoners. These massacres signal the beginnings of organized terror in which real or imagined enemies of the revolution are murdered. At first, the targets are aristocrats and their supporters, but later those killed include moderate revolutionaries and even radical rivals of the militant forces in power.

1793   Gracchus Babeuf, a French political agitator and journalist, coins the word "terrorist" in his newspaper, *The Tribune of the People.*

1793–1794   The period known as the Great Terror or Reign of Terror in France is the first conscious and systematic use of such concepts as "terror," "terrorism," and "terrorists." Terror is justified as a strategy by the revolutionary rulers of France as a way of retaining power, destroying their enemies, fighting intervention, and mobilizing the people. Since terror is said to bring about good political ends, it is extolled as a method leading to the people's welfare and virtue.

January 21, 1793   King Louis XVI of France is guillotined in front of a cheering crowd, having been convicted of high treason by the National Convention, the constitutional and legislative assembly of France in this period.

April 6, 1793   The Committee of Public Safety is created by the National Convention. This committee of 12 men directs the Reign of Terror, taking control of trials and executions.

July 13, 1793   Jean-Paul Marat, a member of the radical Jacobin faction in France is assassinated in his bathtub by Charlotte Corday. Corday is a supporter of the Girondins, the more moderate faction. Her action sets off a wave of revenge killings by the Jacobins of both Girondins and members of their own faction on charges of treason.

July 17, 1793   Four days after Marat's death, Charlotte Corday is guillotined for his murder.

August 2, 1793   Maximilien Robespierre, a leader of the Committee of Public Safety, the effective government of France during the Reign of Terror, says, "The terrifyingly swift sword of the law should hang over the heads of all the conspirators, striking terror in the hearts of their accomplices and of all the enemies of the fatherland."

August 30, 1793   A Jacobin, Pierre-Paul Royer-Collard, invokes Marat's revolutionary precept to legitimize the proposal to "place terror as the lord of the day" as "the only way to arouse the people and force them to save themselves."

September 5, 1793   The French National Convention votes to implement terror measures to repress alleged counterrevolutionary activities. During the next seven months, 35,000 to 40,000 people are killed.

December 25, 1793   Robespierre, in the speech "The Principles of the Revolutionary Government," invokes the good of the people as the paramount reason for terror.

February 5, 1794   Robespierre says: "It has been said that terror was the activating principle of a despotic government. We want to establish an order of things such that a universal tendency toward the good is established and the factions find themselves suddenly hurled on to the scaffold."

March 1794   Marie-Jean Hérault de Séchelles, a member of the National Convention and the Committee of Public Safety, who was prominent in shaping the Reign of Terror, is guillotined.

March 17, 1794	Jacques-René Hébert, one of the leaders of the *sans-culottes*, militant supporters of the French Revolution, is guillotined along with 17 of his followers.
March 30, 1794	Georges-Jacques Danton, an advocate of a relaxation of emergency measures, particularly the Reign of Terror, and his followers are charged with conspiracy to overthrow the government. The trial is a mockery, and Danton is guillotined.
July 26, 1794	In a speech to the National Convention, Robespierre calls for an end to the use of terror as a result of the many new enemies he has created.
July 27, 1794	The French National Convention ousts Robespierre and has him arrested.
July 28, 1794	Robespierre is guillotined in front of a cheering crowd, for sending thousands of others to a similar fate during the French Revolution. As a result, the Reign of Terror comes to an end in France.
1795	Edmund Burke, Anglo-Irish politician and statesman, is one of the first writers to use the word "terrorist" in English. In his *Reflections on the Revolution in France,* he writes of "those hell-hounds called terrorists [who] are let loose on the people."
July 21, 1795	The Companions of Jehu, a movement started in the south of France to oppose the French Revolution, is crushed by General Louis-Lazare Hoche at Quiberon, France. The Companions of Jehu had planned an uprising to coincide with invasions by Britain and Austria.
November 1795	Babeuf is reported by the police to be openly preaching "insurrection, revolt, and the constitution of 1793." The French Constitution of 1793 was ratified by the National Convention but never applied, and then supplanted by the French Constitution of 1795.
May 10, 1796	Babeuf is arrested with many of his associates, including Augustin Alexandre Darthé and Philippe Buonarroti, two former members of the National Convention.
September 7, 1796	An unsuccessful attempt is made by 500 or 600 Jacobins to rouse soldiers at Grenelle, France, to rise up and help release Babeuf.
April 6, 1797	Babeuf is condemned to death and guillotined the next day.
May 24, 1798	Irish nationalists rebel against British forces; the nationalists believe that French troops are going to invade Ireland.
December 24, 1800	An assassination attempt on Napoléon Bonaparte, as he is on his way to the opera, fails in Paris. Royalist plotters kill 52 bystanders.
March 21, 1801	Russian Czar Paul I is murdered at St. Michael's Palace in St. Petersburg by a band of dismissed officers headed by a former lieutenant general in the Russian army.

July 23, 1803   Robert Emmet, an Irish nationalist rebel leader, leads an uprising that fails to take Dublin Castle and collapses into general rioting. During the disorders, the Lord Chief Justice of Ireland is murdered in his carriage.

September 19, 1803   Emmet is convicted of treason and is executed the next day.

1811   The Luddite movement spreads rapidly throughout England. The Luddites are a group of English workers protesting against the changes brought by the Industrial Revolution. Losing their jobs to more efficient machines, they respond by destroying them.

May 11, 1812   British Prime Minister Spencer Perceval is assassinated in the lobby of the House of Commons. The assassin, John Bellingham, wanted compensation for his wrongful imprisonment in Russia due to a bankruptcy for which he was an assignee. He is hanged in public a week later.

1813   Due to Luddite activities, "machine breaking" is made a capital crime and 17 men are executed this year.

January 29, 1820   The Cato Street conspiracy forms in Great Britain, following the death of King George III. The revolutionary group plans to kill all cabinet ministers to take advantage of the political situation and overturn the Six Acts. The Six Acts comprise new legislation that claimed any meeting for radical reform was "an overt act of treasonable conspiracy."

May 1, 1820   Five members of the Cato Street conspiracy group are hanged at Newgate Prison. Five other death sentences are commuted to exile from Britain.

December 1825   In St. Petersburg, Russia, a group of military officers stages a revolt against Czar Nicholas I. These rebels are liberals who feel threatened by the new ruler's conservative views. During this revolt, the military governor of St. Petersburg, General Mikhail Miloradovich, is shot and killed. The rebels are eventually defeated by the czar's forces. But as a result of this revolt, Nicholas I implements a variety of new regulations to prevent the spread of the liberal movement in Russia.

July 1830   Louis-Auguste Blanqui, a French political activist, takes part in political demonstrations against King Charles X of France (the French monarchy was restored in 1814). Blanqui holds the belief that socialist revolution should be carried out by an elite group of conspirators, which brings him into conflict with every French regime during his lifetime, and he spends half his life in prison. Advocating direct revolutionary action, Blanqui is among the first to conceive of the idea of being a professional revolutionary.

1843   William Weitling, a labor leader in the United States, espouses ideas on mobilizing the criminal underworld in a revolutionary struggle.

1848   A series of revolutions and nationalist insurrections take place in France, Germany, Italy, and other countries. In France, this results in the establishment of the Second Republic, a successor to the revolutionary republic of the 1790s.

1848	Karl Heinzen, a radical active in both Germany and the United States, argues that while murder is forbidden in principle, this prohibition does not apply to politics. In his essay "Der Mord" (Murder), he proclaims that all means are valid to hasten the advent of democracy. He writes: "If you have to blow up half a continent and cause a bloodbath to destroy the party of barbarism, you should have no scruples of conscience. Anyone who would not joyously sacrifice his life for the satisfaction of exterminating a million barbarians is not a true republican."
1848	Karl Marx, an influential German political philosopher and social theorist, in his article "The Bourgeois and the Counter-Revolution," writes approvingly of the French proletariat of 1793–1794 and the Great Terror. Marx writes that it is a good, "plebian way of smashing the enemies of the bourgeoisie, doing away with absolutism, feudalism, and philistinism."
July 29, 1848	In Tipperary, Ireland, an unsuccessful nationalist revolt against British rule is put down by the police.
November 5, 1848	Karl Marx writes, "There is only one way to shorten the murderous death agonies of the old society, only one way to shorten the bloody birth pangs of the new society . . . only one means: revolutionary terrorism."
December 2, 1848	Charles-Louis-Napoléon Bonaparte, the nephew of Napoléon I, wins the French presidential election.
1849	Fyodor Dostoevsky, a Russian writer, is arrested and imprisoned for engaging in revolutionary activity against Czar Nicholas I. The czar mistakenly believes that the Petrashevsky Circle, of which Dostoevsky is a member, engages in subversive revolutionary activity. The czar closes down the organization and arrests its members.
November 16, 1849	Dostoevsky is sentenced to death for anti-government activity linked to a radical intellectual group. After a mock execution in which Dostoevsky faces a staged firing squad, his sentence is commuted to a number of years of exile performing hard labor at a Katorga prison camp in Siberia.
1851	Charles-Louis-Napoléon Bonaparte overthrows the French republic.
1852	Bonaparte takes the title Napoléon III, becoming emperor of France.
1856	The Fenian movement in Ireland and the United States is created with the aim of achieving Irish independence from Britain by force. It becomes known variously as the Fenian Brotherhood, the Fenian Society, the Irish Republican Brotherhood, and the Irish-American Brotherhood.
May 10, 1857	The Sepoy Mutiny begins in Meerut, India, to drive the British colonial rulers from the subcontinent. As part of this effort, British civilians are massacred by the insurgents in several places, though the insurgency is ultimately put down with equal violence.
January 14, 1858	Felice Orsini throws a bomb at Napoléon III, killing and injuring members of

his entourage. Orsini is an Italian nationalist who believes Napoléon III to be the main obstacle to Italy's unity and independence.

March 13, 1858   Orsini is executed by guillotine.

June 20, 1858   The last rebels of the Sepoy Mutiny surrender in Gwalior, India.

October 16, 1859   John Brown, an American who believes in the immediate end to slavery in the United States, leads 21 men in an attack on the federal armory at Harpers Ferry, Virginia. The attack fails and does not begin the uprising of African-American slaves Brown was hoping to ignite.

December 2, 1859   John Brown is hanged.

July 14, 1861   Oscar Becker, a law student from Leipzig, tries unsuccessfully to kill Prince Wilhelm I at Baden in Germany. At his trial, Becker states that his motive was a desire to punish the Prussian ruler for not unifying Germany.

1865   The Molly Maguires are established in the United States. They are a secret organization of Irish-Americans in coal mining districts of eastern Pennsylvania. Their name comes from a woman who led an extralegal, anti-landlord organization in Ireland during the 1840s, and their membership is drawn from the Ancient Order of Hibernians, an Irish-American fraternal society. The movement rises to combat oppressive working and living conditions. Since the police and justice systems are entirely controlled by the mine owners, the Molly Maguires often resort to murder or intimidation of the police, mine agents, and superintendents.

April 14, 1865   John Wilkes Booth assassinates President Abraham Lincoln at Ford's Theatre in Washington, D.C. Booth and his co-conspirators believe they are helping the South, but with Lincoln's death the possibility of peace with magnanimity dies. Booth is killed while trying to evade capture. Four of his associates are eventually captured and hanged on July 7.

April 4, 1866   Dmitry Karakazov, a 26-year-old student, fires his pistol at Czar Alexander II as he enters his carriage after a walk in his summer garden in St. Petersburg. The terrorist misses and is seized immediately.

May 7, 1866   Prince Otto von Bismarck, prime minister of the Kingdom of Prussia, is wounded by shots fired by a student named Ferdinand Blind. Blind was influenced by Orsini, an Italian revolutionary who tried to kill Napoléon III. Blind later hanged himself in prison.

1867   A Fenian plan to launch a nationalist uprising in Ireland is foiled by the arrests of the group's leaders.

April 7, 1868   D'Arcy McGee, a member of the Canadian parliament, is assassinated in Ontario by a Fenian sympathizer who is hanged for the crime. McGee had denounced the Fenian brotherhood in America, which was advocating that Irish revolutionaries take over Canada forcibly and hold it hostage in order to attain Ireland's independence.

Terrorism as Political Strategy

Whereas the French Revolution introduced the "solution" of terrorism for its political problems and later theorists justified the use of terrorism to advance social revolution, it was the Russian radical Sergei Nechayev who developed the first comprehensive plan for an underground revolutionary group focusing on a terrorist strategy. He also created the concept of the professional revolutionary, an individual deliberately shaped to be the pitiless deliverer of "social justice" in the form of murder.

In Italy, Germany, France, and America, individual anarchists had carried out assassinations, but they had little impact except to horrify the general public and discredit their own cause. The Irish Fenians were the first nationalist group to employ terrorist tactics. But Nechayev's ideas and actions did the most to develop the theory and practice of organized terrorism. In Russia, Nechayev's writings led to the organization of the Land and Liberty group. Later, a splinter group of Land and Liberty, known as the People's Will, became the first organization that sustained terrorist activities over many years.

In its earliest years, Land and Liberty attacked officials who had mistreated radicals or were especially unpopular. Later it became more indiscriminate. What especially excited the group's members about terrorism was that it could be carried out by small, concealed groups. They lacked the patience of the long-term organizing advocated by Marxists—who had enjoyed little success in Russia during the years of its greatest activity—and also argued that their country lacked the urban proletariat considered necessary for that type of revolution.

The successes of Land and Liberty and its offshoot, the People's Will, also became, in a way that would be repeated by later terrorist movements, their undoing. Given their small numbers and the high priority the Russian government gave to finding the assassins, the groups repeatedly lost their most effective leaders. Political assassinations simply led to more of the same, without the political progress terrorists believed would come. The Social Revolutionary Party, which owed much to the People's Will, later became one of the main opposition parties in Russia, but only after abandoning much of its terrorist activities and concentrating on organizing the peasantry.

Around the turn of the nineteenth century, Macedonian, Armenian, Serbian, and other nationalist movements took up terrorism as a strategy. Perhaps the single most influential terrorist attack in history was that of the Serbian Black Hand, which assassinated Archduke Franz Ferdinand, the crown prince of the Austro-Hungarian empire in Sarajevo, then a provincial capital in the empire. This action led directly to the outbreak of World War I, demonstrating the multiplication effect, which was one of terrorism's most dangerous features.

The Black Hand also introduced another important factor for the future: the terror-sponsoring state. The group was a creation of Serbian intelligence, which was seeking to gain control over land in Austria-Hungary inhabited by ethnic Serbs. Much of the attraction for Serbia—and its successors as state sponsors of terrorism—was that an enemy could be attacked and responsibility denied. In fact, the Austro-Hungarian government knew that Serbia was responsible for the assassination of Archduke Ferdinand, and it presented that government with an ultimatum that would have destroyed that country's independence. Other nations that would soon declare war on Austria-Hungary and on one another, however, either refused to believe the accusations against Serbia or sided with Serbia for political reasons.

1868   Sergei Nechayev, a radical Russian political activist, first appears in St. Petersburg in an era of student protests against the government, which refuses to make reforms to modernize the country to become less backward in comparison to Western Europe. Meanwhile, Mikhail Bakunin, a militant anarchist from Russia, becomes active in the First International, an association of radicals, where his doctrine has great influence, competing with the ideas of Karl Marx. He advocates the violent overthrow of existing states and institutions as a necessary step to achieving freedom.

1869   Nechayev briefly leaves Russia, becomes friends with Bakunin, and participates in the publication of a number of proclamations. Nechayev founds the organization People's Tribunal in Moscow. He advocates murder as an essential tool of revolution. Nechayev and Bakunin collaborate on a book entitled *Catechism of the Revolutionary,* which appears in Russia. *Catechism* is the first publication to advocate the use of large-scale terrorism as a revolutionary strategy. It defines a revolutionary as "a doomed man without private interests, affairs, sentiments, ties, property, or even a name."

May 26, 1869   The last public hanging in Britain is of Fenian bomber Michael Barrett. He had previously been arrested for illegally discharging a firearm.

1871   In the chaos following France's disastrous defeat in the Franco-Prussian War, Emperor Napoléon III is overthrown. In Paris, socialist and pro-democratic forces gain control of much of the city, forming the Paris Commune. The Commune is overthrown with great brutality by the French government.

1871   Fyodor Dostoevsky publishes his book *The Possessed,* which depicts young revolutionaries as brutal nihilists for whom the end justifies the means. The main political character is based on Nechayev and on the true story of a revolutionary group that murders one of its own members as a suspected traitor.

June 21, 1871   In the United States, four members of the Molly Maguires—Alexander Campbell, John Donohue, Michael Doyle, and Edward Kelly—are hanged at the Carbon County Prison in Pennsylvania for the murder of two mine bosses.

1875   The Molly Maguires reach the height of their power when they manage to organize a union and to call a strike. Franklin Gowen, president of the Reading Railroad, which has extensive mining interests, hires the Pinkerton National Detective Agency to infiltrate the union. The power of the Molly Maguires is finally broken by the spying activities of James McParlan, a Pinkerton detective. Ten members of the Molly Maguires are hanged. Some historians argue, however, that the group was not involved in assassinations, and that this charge was fabricated by the companies and McParlan.

1878   The Land and Liberty group, a Russian clandestine revolutionary group, forms and publishes a manifesto in which the following goals are set out: the confiscation of the landlords' land; the expulsion and often the complete annihilation of government officials; and the establishment of "Cossack circles"—autonomous communes with elected, rotating executives decided by the people.

January 25, 1878 Vera Zasulich, a member of Land and Liberty, hears that one of her comrades, Alexei Bogoliubov, has been badly beaten in prison. Seeking revenge, Zasulich travels to the local prison and shoots General Fyodor Trepov, the police chief of St. Petersburg.

May 11, 1878   Emil Hoedel, who has connections to the German workers' movement, attempts and fails to take the life of the German Emperor Wilhelm. Substantial evidence suggests the attempt was planned by Emil Werner, the leader of the German section of the Jura Federation in Switzerland, one of the strongest organizations in the anarchist movement.

June 2, 1878

After a failed attempt to kill the German emperor, Dr. Carl Nobling shoots himself. Nobling is an anarchist who believes the state is the true enemy of the people and that property has to be abolished and replaced by communal associations.

August 16, 1878

Sergei Stepnyak-Kravchinsky, a member of Land and Liberty, shoots and kills the head of the Russian political police, General Nikolai Mezentsov, marking the beginning of overtly violent opposition to the czar. Stepnyak-Kravchinsky escapes to Western Europe to write novels glorifying the era's terrorists.

November 17, 1878

Giovanni Passanante, an anarchist, attacks King Umberto of Naples. The king wards off the blow with his saber but his prime minister, Benedetto Cairoli, is severely wounded.

1879

Russian Prince Pyotr (Peter) Kropotkin launches the periodical *La Révolte* in Switzerland, in which a typical editorial proclaims the necessity of terror, of "permanent revolt" not just by oral and printed propaganda but also "by the dagger, the rifle and dynamite."

April 2, 1879

An attempt by Land and Liberty member Alexander Solovyov to assassinate Czar Alexander II fails. Solovyov fires five times at the monarch as he takes his habitual walk on the grounds of the Winter Palace in St. Petersburg, but all the bullets miss, and the police escort captures Solovyov at once. He is tried and publicly hanged later that spring.

August 1879

The People's Will (Narodnaya Volya) group forms with the objective of overthrowing the czarist regime. At the very first formal meeting, they pass a resolution that their top priority is killing the czar.

1880

The program of the Executive Committee of the People's Will is first published in the organization's journal, summarizing the targets and goals of political assassination: "Terror will be used against the most harmful members of the regime; it will be used to dispose of spies; it will be invoked in retaliation for the government's most heinous acts. Terrorist acts will show the government is not invincible, raise morale, and instill a revolutionary fervor."

1880

Nikolai Morozov, a member of the People's Will, writes a pamphlet entitled "Terroristicheskaya Borba" (The Terrorist Struggle). He writes, "All that the terrorist struggle really needs is a small number of people and large material means. . . . The future will show if the contemporary terrorists will live up to their standards. We are, however, deeply convinced that the terrorist movement will overcome all the obstacles in its way; the triumph of the cause will show all the antagonists that the terrorist movement fully satisfies the conditions of contemporary reality, which put this form of struggle in the forefront."

1880

G. Tarnovski, a member of the People's Will, writes a pamphlet entitled "Terrorizm i Rutina" (Terrorism and Routine). In it he writes: "Terrorists, the defenders of the people, have the right to ignore the public conscience which 'always denies' the defense of the people. . . . Terrorism directs its blow against the real perpetrators of evil . . . the position of the representatives of autocracy is completely changed by the presence of terrorism as a system."

1880   Andrei Ivanovich Zhelyabov, the architect of the People's Will strategy, draws the conclusion that "history moves frighteningly slowly, one has to give it a push." Speaking at a conference in Kharkov, Ukraine, Zhelyabov propounds the idea that the regime must be attacked again and again until it is forced to grant political freedom; then it would be possible to engage in peaceful propaganda activities.

1880   Prince Pyotr Kropotkin, one of Russia's foremost anarchists, writes "The Spirit of Revolt," which argues that a few courageous men dissatisfied with words can change a political situation dramatically through violence.

February 5, 1880   A bomb explodes at the Winter Palace, killing 11 and wounding 56 soldiers who are on guard, but sparing Czar Alexander II. The penetration of the palace by Stephen Khalturin, a Land and Liberty member, shows the skills of that group.

August 16, 1880   Another attempt on the czar's life fails. This one is organized by Andrei Ivanovich Zhelyabov and involves blowing up a bridge in St. Petersburg.

March 1, 1881   Czar Alexander II, while traveling in a closed carriage from St. Michael's Palace to the Winter Palace in St. Petersburg, is watched all along the route by members of the People's Will. A first set of bombs misses the carriage and instead lands among his Cossack guards. The czar is unhurt, but he insists on getting out of the carriage to check the condition of the injured men. While Alexander is standing with the wounded Cossacks, another terrorist, Ignatei Grinevitski, throws his bomb. Czar Alexander is killed instantly, and the explosion is so great that Grinevitski himself is also killed.

March 8, 1881   Nikolai Rysakov, who threw the first bomb at the czar, delivers what later becomes known as the Rysakov Confession, describing terrorism as a merely defensive instrument, designed to build up and develop revolutionary strength and the legend of an unstoppable revolution. He blames the inevitability of terror on the Russian system, claiming, "It was not we who prepared the ground for terror."

April 3, 1881   Andrei Zhelyabov, Nikolai Rysakov, and three other members of the People's Will are executed for involvement in the assassination of the czar.

June 1881   Johann Most, founder of *Die Freiheit* (Freedom), an English-based anarchist journal calling for violence to overthrow all governments, publishes an article praising the assassination of Czar Alexander II of Russia. Most is arrested and sent to prison in London for 18 months. After his release, he moves to the United States, where he continues to publish *Die Freiheit*.

May 6, 1882   At Phoenix Park, Dublin, Lord Frederick Cavendish, British secretary for Ireland, and Thomas Henry Burke, his undersecretary, are stabbed to death by members of the Invincibles, a terrorist splinter group of the Fenian movement.

November 1882   Sergei Nechayev dies in prison of tuberculosis.

1883   Sergei Stepnyak-Kravchinsky, the Russian who had previously killed the head of the Russian political police, General Mezentsov, writes *Underground Russia* in London. He concludes, "The Terrorist . . . is noble, terrible, irresistibly fascinating, for he combines in himself the two sublimities of human grandeur: the martyr and the hero."

September 1883

In a memo, the Irish-American Fenians declare, "We cannot see our way to an armed insurrection in Ireland this side of some great foreign war with England . . . [I]n the meantime we shall carry on an incessant and perpetual warfare with the power of England in public and in secret."

1884

Johann Most, the anarchist editor of *Die Freiheit,* publishes a book in German called *The Science of Revolutionary Warfare,* in which he combines tips on how to make and use everything from poison to letter bombs with advice on how to behave if arrested with hand grenades or nitroglycerine concealed under one's clothing: "It is vital . . . to remain calm and collected."

June 14, 1884

Seven peasants, alleged to be among 15 convicted members of La Mano Negra (The Black Hand), an anarchist organization in Andalucia, Spain, are executed for crimes committed at the end of 1882, and the first months of 1883. Some believe that La Mano Negra was fabricated by the government to help crack down on revolts in southern Spain.

December 1884

William Lomasney, a Fenian, is killed by his own bomb when trying to blow up London Bridge. It was the second terrorist attack by Lomasney, who had been born in the United States and fought in the Union army during the Civil War. On October 30, 1883, he detonated bombs on two trains in London which wounded more than 70 people.

1885

Errico Malatesta, an Italian anarchist, moves to Buenos Aires, where he starts publication of *La Questione Sociale* and is involved in the founding of the first militant workers' union in Argentina, the Bakers Union. His leadership provides strong anarchist influence on the Latin American workers' movements for years to come.

March 5, 1886

Charles Gallo, a young anarchist, from his vantage point in the visitors' gallery of the Paris stock exchange, throws a bottle of vitriol at the stockbrokers and clerks below, and then wildly fires three revolver shots at them. He fails to harm anyone. At his trial, when being led off to 20 years' hard labor, he shouts "Long live revolution! Long live anarchism! Death to the bourgeois judiciary! Long live dynamite!"

May 3, 1886

In the United States, a workers' protest at the McCormick Harvester plant in Chicago demanding a shorter workday turns into a riot. Police fire into the crowd, and one demonstrator is killed.

May 4, 1886

At Haymarket Square in Chicago, Illinois, a protest denounces the events at the McCormick Harvester plant. While police are trying to disperse the crowd, a bomb explodes. Seven police are killed, and 70 people injured. Labor radicals are blamed. As a result, four are hanged, one commits suicide in prison, and three are jailed for life (although their sentences are later commuted).

1887

As a member of the People's Will, Jozef Pilsudski, future founder of the Polish republic after World War I, is arrested and sentenced to exile in Siberia for five years.

March 1, 1887   In Russia, Alexander Ulyanov, the elder brother of Vladimir Lenin, is arrested along with comrades from the People's Will after the discovery of plans to kill Czar Alexander III. The conspirators never come near their target, since the police arrest the plotters after intercepting a letter.

April 1887   Italian anarchist Errico Malatesta and about 30 others start an insurrection in the province of Benevento, Italy, taking the villages of Letino and Gallo without a struggle. The revolutionaries burn tax registers and declare the end of the king's reign. After leaving Gallo, however, they are arrested by government troops and held for 16 months before being acquitted.

May 5, 1887   Alexander Ulyanov is hanged for planning the murder of Czar Alexander III.

1889   Errico Malatesta publishes an anarchist newspaper called *L'Associazione* in Nice, France, until he is forced to flee to London.

1892   Sergei Stepnyak-Kravchinsky writes, "The terrorists cannot overthrow the government, cannot drive it from St. Petersburg and Russia; but having compelled it, for so many years running, to neglect everything and do nothing but struggle with them, by forcing it to do so till for years and years, they will render its position untenable. Already the prestige of the Imperial Government has received a wound which it will be very difficult to heal. An emperor who shuts himself up in prison from fear of the terrorism is certainly not a figure to inspire admiration."

July 23, 1892   Alexander Berkman, a Russian writer and activist, fires two gunshots into Henry Frick, a wealthy Pennsylvania industrialist, in his office in Pittsburgh. Frick, who had been targeted because he had used armed strikebreakers to deal with striking workers in the Homestead steel plant in Pennsylvania, which resulted in the death of ten men, survives and Berkman spends the next 14 years in prison until being pardoned.

1892   Escaping from police custody in France, François Ravachol, an advocate of terrorism, attacks the home of a judge and a government attorney, killing no one but causing considerable property damage. He argues that killing the representatives of the bourgeois order, the proletariat's worst enemies, is a positive value in itself.

October 23, 1893   The Internal Macedonian Revolutionary Organization (IMRO) is established in Salonika. Led by Damien Gruev, its goal is autonomy for Macedonia under the slogan, "Macedonia for the Macedonians." It is the first organization to link the achievement of nationalist goals with a terrorist strategy. From 1898 to 1903, the IMRO wages a campaign of revolutionary terrorism against the ruling Turkish government.

December 9, 1893   Auguste Vaillant, a French anarchist, hurls a bomb from a balcony at the Chamber of Deputies in Paris. No one is killed. Vaillant goes to his death exclaiming, "Long live anarchy! My death will be avenged!"

February 12, 1894   Emile Henry, long known to the French police as an anarchist militant, places a bomb in the crowded Café Terminus near the St. Lazare railway station in Paris. As a result, 20 people are injured, of whom one later dies.

February 15, 1894   French anarchist Martial Boudin makes an unsuccessful attempt to destroy the Royal Greenwich Observatory in London, England, with a bomb.

March 15, 1894   Jean Pauwels, a Belgian anarchist, accidentally blows himself up at the Madeleine Church in the heart of Paris while transporting a bomb. He is later deemed responsible for two previous explosions in February.

June 4, 1894   After delivering a speech at a public banquet in Lyons, French President Marie-François-Sadi Carnot is stabbed to death by an Italian anarchist named Sante Geronimo Caserio.

1896   The Northern Union of Socialist Revolutionaries is formed in Russia. It is the forerunner of the Socialist Revolutionary Party, which will replace the People's Will as the main terrorist group.

August 26, 1896   Members of the Armenian Revolutionary Federation seize the Ottoman Bank in Constantinople, with its largely French and British staff, to draw the attention of European countries to their cause. During a struggle with Turkish soldiers, ten terrorists and Turkish soldiers are killed. The government's response leads to a three-day massacre in which thousands of Armenians are killed.

June 22, 1897   A British health official and an army lieutenant are killed in Poona, India, as they leave celebrations for the sixtieth anniversary of Queen Victoria's coronation. The Chapekar brothers, two Indian nationalists, are tried; one of them, Damodar, is hanged for the murder.

August 8, 1897   At the baths of Santa Agueda in the Basque provinces, Spanish Prime Minister Antonio Cánovas del Castillo is shot and killed by an Italian anarchist.

September 10, 1898   Luigi Luccheni, an Italian anarchist, kills Empress Elizabeth, the wife of Franz Joseph, emperor of the Austro-Hungarian Empire, in Geneva, Switzerland, by stabbing her with a shoemaker's awl. Luccheni had intended to kill the French Duke of Orleans, but he had already left the area.

1900   The Social Revolutionary Party is founded in Kharkov, Ukraine. It relies on terrorist tactics and carries out hundreds of political assassinations. The group demands that all land be confiscated from the nobility and distributed among the peasants. The Socialist Revolutionaries are greatly influenced by the tactics used by the People's Will. They have a terrorist wing named the Socialist Revolutionary Combat Organization.

January 5, 1900   Irish nationalist leader John Edward Redmond calls for a revolt against the British.

April 4, 1900   An anarchist shoots at the Prince of Wales during his visit to Belgium at the birthday celebrations of the king of Belgium. The prince is not wounded.

July 29, 1900   King Umberto I of Italy is shot three times and killed by the anarchist Gaetano Bresci in Monza. Bresci is captured and put on trial, where he is defended by the anarchist lawyer Francesco Saverio Merlino.

August 29, 1900   Gaetano Bresci is sentenced in Milan to hard labor at Santo Stefano prison on Ventotene Island, where numerous anarchists had been sent over the years. He is found dead in prison less than a year later. The death is attributed to suicide, but he was almost certainly murdered by the guards.

1901   Gregory Gershuni, a socialist and a founder member of the Workers' Party for the Liberation of Russia, becomes head of the Socialist Revolutionary Combat Organization and is responsible for planning the assassination of Minister of the Interior Dmitry Sipyagin.

1901   In *Iskra,* his party's newspaper published in London, Lenin writes: "In principle we have never rejected terror nor can we reject it. Terror is one of those military means that can come in handy and even be even necessary at a certain moment of a battle, when the troops are in a certain shape under certain circumstances." While accepting terror as a tactic, however, Lenin rejects it as a strategy, arguing that mass organization and agitation will prove more effective.

1901   Victor Chernov, a founder of the Socialist Revolutionary Party, forms and edits the Socialist Revolutionary journal *Revolutionary Russia.*

February 1901   An expelled student, P.V. Karpovich, assassinates Russian Minister of Education N.P. Bogolepov. This sets off a whole new wave of terrorism in Russia.

September 6, 1901   U.S. President William McKinley is standing in a receiving line at the Buffalo Pan-American Exposition when Leon Czolgosz, a follower of anarchist Emma Goldman, strikes aside the hand the president offers and fires two shots with a handgun. The president dies on September 14.

October 29, 1901   Leon Czolgosz, the assassin of U.S. President William McKinley, is executed by electrocution.

April 28, 1902   Social Revolutionary Stephan Balmashov assassinates Russian Minister of the Interior Dmitry Sipyagin and N.M. Bogdanovich, the governor of Ufa, at the Mariinsky Palace, St. Petersburg.

April 29, 1903   In Salonika, Macedonian nationalists associated with the Internal Macedonian Revolutionary Organization (IMRO) cause simultaneous explosions at the Ottoman Bank, the principal gas main of the city, and the casino, signaling the start of a season of violence against the Ottoman government. Nationalists run through the streets throwing bombs into the entrances of cafes, bars, and restaurants frequented by Europeans in order to stir up feelings against the Ottoman government. The ploy fails and the terrorists are decimated by arrests. The Macedonian rebellion culminates in the St. Elijah Day Uprising in August.

May 4, 1903   Goce Delcev, a founder of IMRO, dies in a skirmish with Turkish police near the village of Banitza in the Serres region while preparing an uprising in Macedonia.

June 11, 1903   King Alexander Obrenović of Serbia and his wife are shot in Belgrade by a group of conspirators led by Dragutin Dimitrijevic, later to become the founder and leader of the Black Hand, a Serbian nationalist group.

August 2, 1903	The St. Elijah Day Uprising, led by IMRO, occupies the city of Krusovo in the Ottoman Empire and establishes a Macedonian republic there. The revolutionaries are defeated and dispersed ten days later by Ottoman authorities. More than 200 Macedonian villages are burned, there are thousands of casualties on both sides, and 70,000 persons are left homeless.
1904	In Russia, Evno Azef replaces Gregory Gershuni as head of the Socialist Revolutionary Combat Organization. Soon afterward, Gershuni is arrested by the police based on information supplied by Azef, who is a secret informer for the security police. Gershuni is imprisoned, but escapes in 1905 and flees abroad. He dies of tuberculosis in Switzerland in 1908.
1904	Errico Malatesta moves to London, where he writes several important pamphlets, including "L'Anarchia."
June 16, 1904	Eugen Schauman shoots and kills Nikolai Ivanovich Bobrikov, the czar's governor-general of Finland, then turns the gun on himself. Schauman, a government clerk, leaves letters saying he is punishing Bobrikov for his crimes as a repressive official.
July 28, 1904	Russian Minister of the Interior Vyacheslav Plehve is assassinated by a bomb thrown by Egor Sazonov, a member of the Socialist Revolutionary Party. The Socialist Revolutionary Fighting Section immediately put out a proclamation saying, "The death of Plehve is but one step forward on the path to the liberation of the people." Plehve was a leading opponent of reforms in Russia and a supporter of suppressing minority groups.
1905	The Bengali author Aurobindo Ghosh writes *Vawani Mandir*. In this book, he explains the plans and programs of the Bengali revolutionary terrorist group he hopes to form to fight British rule. (Ghosh later leaves the nationalist movement and becomes a widely admired yoga master and philosopher.)
January 22, 1905	In St. Petersburg, a crowd of unarmed peaceful demonstrators marches to present a petition to the czar but many of the marchers are gunned down by Imperial Guards. The event has been organized by Father George Gapon, a paid agent provocateur of the Okhrana, the czarist internal security police. This day becomes known as Bloody Sunday, and the response to the incident sets off a full-scale revolution which the czarist government puts down only with great difficulty.
February 4, 1905	I.P. Kaliaev, a member of the Socialist Revolutionary Combat Division, murders Grand Duke Sergei Alexandrovich, governor-general of Moscow and the czar's uncle.
September 1905	Vladimir Lenin writes in *Proletari*, a Bolshevik journal, "The bomb is no longer the arm of the undisciplined terrorist. It now becomes an essential part of the arming of the people."
September 30, 1905	Frank Steunenberg, the former governor of Idaho, is assassinated by a bomb that is set off when he opens the door to his house. The assassin is a former miner, Harry Orchard, a member of the Western Federation of Miners. It is later understood that three union bosses masterminded the attack in revenge for Steunenberg's role in crushing an 1899 strike.

October 13, 1905   The 1905 Revolution begins in Russia. By the time it ends, on December 3, the czar promises a constitution. During this revolution, terrorist groups organize plots against the lives of czarist officials and raids on banks and government institutions.

November 28, 1905   Irish nationalist Arthur Griffith founds Sinn Féin (We Ourselves) in Dublin. Its goal is independence from Great Britain for all of Ireland. By 1918, Sinn Féin members will occupy 73 of Ireland's 106 parliamentary seats.

1906   Lenin writes that the revolutionary party needs terrorist violence at present in order to "destroy the government, police and military machinery." But all such activity must be under the party's control.

1906   The Maximalist group splits off as the more extreme wing of Russia's Social Revolutionary Party (SRP). It engages in assassination attempts as well as thefts to finance the movement.

1906   In India, the *Jugantar* is founded as a revolutionary Bengali weekly with a message that "If it be lawful for an individual to use physical force for self-preservation, why should it be unlawful for a nation to do the same. If it not be a sin to commit manslaughter in order to defend one's self against thieves . . . why should it be a sin to kill a few men in order that a nation might become free."

March 1906   Father George Gapon, the secret police agent who helped foment the January 1905 march in St. Petersburg that led to the massacre of the marchers, leaves Russia to live in Geneva where he joins the SRP. Another party member, Pinchas Rutenberg, discovers Gapon is sending messages to the Russian minister of the interior. Convinced that Gapon is a spy, SRP leader Evno Azef (himself a secret informer) gives orders for him to be murdered. He is found dead in a cottage outside St. Petersburg, where he had planned to meet Rutenberg.

April 1906   Disguised as policemen, the Maximalists push their way into Prime Minister Pyotr Stolypin's house during a reception and throw several bombs. Stolypin is not harmed, but 24 people are killed and 22 others wounded in the blasts.

May 6, 1906   Social Revolutionary assassins seriously wound the governor-general of Moscow, Admiral Dubasov. On the same day they also assassinate the governor-general of Ekaterinoslav in the Ukraine.

1907   Lokmanya Tilak, an Indian leader, begins organizing anti-British uprisings. He and his colleagues are deported by the British to Burma for one year.

1907   Joseph Conrad, a Polish-born British writer, completes a novel entitled *The Secret Agent*. The story is woven around the actual attack on the Greenwich Observatory in 1894. In the novel, Verlac, a Russian anarchist also working for the police, is instructed to undertake an action that will discredit the revolutionaries.

June 25, 1907   Joseph Stalin organizes the first major Bolshevik terrorist act. In Tiflis, his men attack and rob a State Bank carriage, causing bloodshed and getting away with 340,000 rubles.

February 1, 1908   King Carlos of Portugal and his son, Crown Prince Luis Felipe, are shot dead in the streets of Lisbon. The two regicides are members of a secret political society, presumably anarchist.

April 12, 1908   The Polish viceroy of Galicia, Andrzej Potocki, is assassinated by a Ukrainian nationalist, Myroslav Sichynsky, in protest against the killing of Ukrainian peasants. Sichynsky escapes to the United States and then to Canada.

1909   Leon Trotsky writes critically that terrorist work is too focused on a single moment of attack, overestimates personal heroism, and requires such secrecy that it is at direct odds with "agitational and organizational activity among the masses."

July 1, 1909   Sir William Curzon Wyllie, the political secretary to the secretary of state for India, is killed in London by Madan Lal Dhingra, an Indian nationalist.

August 17, 1909   Madan Lal Dhingra is hanged in the Pentonville jail.

November 13, 1909   Two bombs are thrown into the carriage in which the British Viceroy Lord Minto and his wife are driving in Ahmedabad, India. They both escape unharmed, but the driver of the carriage is killed.

1910   Emma Goldman, a Lithuanian-born anarchist who emigrated to America, writes *Anarchism and Other Essays*.

October 1, 1910   Two bombs explode at the printing plant of the *Los Angeles Times* during a campaign by the newspaper's workers to establish a union. At least 20 people are killed and 17 others injured. James and John McNamara, brothers active in the trade union movement, are arrested and eventually plead guilty, even though labor leaders claim that the McNamaras were framed for an act committed by other union radicals.

1911   Emma Goldman publishes an essay entitled "The Psychology of Political Violence." Goldman equates propaganda of the deed (terrorism) with the elemental forces of nature. "To the earnest student, it must be apparent that the accumulated forces in our social and economic life, culminating in a political act of violence, are similar to the terrors of the atmosphere, manifested in storm and lightning."

1911   Leon Trotsky writes that terrorism creates great trouble among the working class. "If all we have to do to achieve our aim is to arm ourselves with revolvers, why then should we engage in the class struggle? If we can intimidate the rulers by the noise of some explosion, what need is there of a party?" In another article he explains, "Individual terrorism in our eyes is inadmissible precisely for the reason that it lowers the masses in their own consciousness, reconciles them to incompetence, and directs their glances and hopes toward the great avenger and emancipator who will some day come and accomplish his mission."

May 1911   Ten men in Serbia create the Black Hand secret society with official backing. Serbia becomes the first modern state sponsor of terrorism against another country. Early members include Colonel Dragutin Dimitrijevic (*see* 1903) and the chief of the Intelligence Department of the Serbian General Staff, Major

Voja Tankosic. The main objective of the Black Hand is the creation, by means of violence, of a Greater Serbia. Its manifesto says: "To realize the national ideal, the unification of all Serbs. This organization prefers terrorist action to cultural activities; it will therefore remain secret." Dimitrijevic, also known as Colonel Apis, establishes himself as the leader of the Black Hand.

September 1, 1911
Russian Minister of the Interior Pyotr Stolypin is assassinated by Dmitry Bogrov, a member of the Socialist Revolutionary Party. Bogrov is hanged ten days later.

1912
Vladimir Burtsev, a revolutionary scholar, exposes Evno Azef, the head of the Socialist Revolutionary Combat Organization, as a government informer and agent provocateur. Azef escapes to Germany and dies in Berlin in 1918.

November 1, 1913
The Ghadar, a movement organized by expatriate Indians (mainly in North America) committed to throwing the British out of India by terrorist means, starts a weekly newspaper. The first issue of *Ghadar* proclaims, "The time will come when rifles and blood will take the place of pen and ink."

June 28, 1914
Austrian Archduke Franz Ferdinand, heir to the throne of Austria-Hungary, and his wife, Sophia, Duchess of Hohenberg, travel to Sarajevo to view maneuvers by the Austro-Hungarian army. At around 10 a.m., the motorcade carrying them has a narrow escape when a bomb thrown by Nedjelko Cabrinovic, a member of the Black Hand, fails to cause any damage. After a visit to the mayor, the archduke's car takes a wrong turn and is fired upon with two shots from a pistol by Gavrilo Princip, also a member of the Black Hand. Both Franz and Sophia die from their wounds. The assassination creates an international crisis, which leads directly to World War I.

March 9, 1916
Mexican warlord Pancho Villa and his men cross the U.S. border and raid the town of Columbus, New Mexico. They steal horses and guns, and kill 15 Americans. Villa resents U.S. support for Venustiano Carranza, leader of the rival Constitutionalists in the Mexican Revolution, and feels cheated by American arms' merchants.

April 24, 1916
The Irish Republican Army (IRA) stages an uprising in Dublin demanding an independent state. About 3,000 men take part. Their hope is that Britain's involvement in World War I will prevent the country from reacting effectively to repress the revolt.

April 29, 1916
Faced with British troops, Patrick Pearse, leader of the IRA uprising, realizes that the revolt has failed and now can lead only to the death of civilians. He orders the rebels to surrender.

May 3–12, 1916
Some 3,000 suspects are arrested and 15 leaders executed as a result of the uprising in Ireland. Among them is the already mortally wounded James Connolly, an Irish Socialist Republican, who faces the firing squad in a chair because he is unable to stand.

May 1917
Dragutin Dimitrijevic, the leader of the Black Hand, is tried on charges of plotting against the Serbian government and executed.

Terrorism in the Age of Totalitarians

While one revolution, the French, began modern political terrorism, the Russian Communist and German Nazi revolutions changed its course. Each of these revolutions resulted in powerful totalitarian regimes, but also gave birth to a whole spectrum of movements, some sponsored by the regimes, and others independently inspired by their ideology and successes.

Despite many differences, these movements put the highest priority on the use of political violence to intimidate enemies and to mobilize support for themselves. Terror was not something to be hidden, at least from their own supporters, but celebrated as protecting virtue and seeking social righteous-

ness. Indeed, their rationales were remarkably parallel to those of the French revolutionaries.

There are two important points here for the history of terrorism. First, the powerful new regimes and the movements they sponsored or encouraged provided new ideological justifications for terrorist groups around the world. Second, states began to sponsor terrorism systematically in other countries through state-directed agents or independent clients. The legacy in years to come would be a wide variety of revolutionary groups, some leftist, some rightist, and others whose ideas were so mixed that they could not be placed on that ideological spectrum.

October 26, 1917	In St. Petersburg, pro-Bolshevik soldiers take over key locations and capture the Winter Palace. The All-Russian Congress of Soviets meets and transfers power to the Soviet Council of People's Commissars, with Lenin as its chairman. The resulting Soviet regime becomes an inspiration for revolution and a state sponsor of terrorism.
November 24, 1917	A bomb thought to have been planted by anarchists kills nine police officers in Milwaukee, Wisconsin.
December 11, 1917	Lenin calls on his Bolsheviks to start "revolutionary terror against the saboteurs and the striking functionaries" who threaten his new regime.
December 20, 1917	Lenin establishes the Cheka, a Soviet state security organization, as the first official arm of Bolshevik terror, placing it under Feliks Dzerzhinsky.
1918	In Macedonia, Toomov and Bazhdarov, two members of IMRO, write *The Revolutionary Movement in Macedonia.* The group's terrorist violence is intended to persuade the great powers that their interests can be preserved only by meeting the organization's demands.
January 1, 1918	Lenin, returning from a conference, is shot at in his car. The car is damaged and the windshield is shattered, but Lenin escapes unhurt.
June 4, 1918	Trotsky claims that although Russia is now plunged into a civil war, "The Russian revolution has so far not known terror in the French sense of this word."
June 20, 1918	The Bolshevik regime is challenged when V. Volodarsky, the commissar of propaganda and agitation and chief editor of the *Red Gazette*, is murdered by Grigory Semyonov, a Socialist Revolutionary Party member.
June 24, 1918	The Central Committee of the Left Socialist Revolutionaries decides to organize a wave of terrorism against "the leading representatives of German imperialism," which is occupying Russian territory as a result of World War I.

June 26, 1918   Lenin protests to Grigory Zinovyiev, head of the Comintern, the Soviet organization created to supervise foreign Communist parties, over the lack of prompt retribution for the death of Volodarsky: "We are placing ourselves in an embarrassing situation; in our resolutions. . . . [w]e threaten with mass terror, but when it comes to action, we apply brakes to the entirely correct initiative of the masses."

July 6, 1918   Two young men who announce themselves as members of the Cheka are received by Count Willhelm Mirbach, the German ambassador to Russia at his home in Moscow. They claim they have come to warn him of a conspiracy against his life. Pretending to look for a paper in his pocket, one of them draws a revolver and shoots the ambassador. The two assassins escape through a window. The murderers Yakov Blumkin and Nicolai Andreyev do belong to the Cheka, but are also secret members of the outlawed Socialist Revolutionary Party. By killing the German, they hope to revive hostilities between Russia and Germany in order to bring down the Bolshevik government.

July 7, 1918   Boris Savinkov, leader of the Combat Division of the Socialist Revolutionary Party, and his men take over the city of Yaroslavl in Russia. After bitter fighting, the rebels surrender 12 days later.

July 17, 1918   Czar Nicholas II, his wife, and their five children, who have been detained by the government since March, are executed by a detachment of Bolsheviks in Ekaterinburg in central Russia. The family physician and three servants are also killed. In Moscow, Lenin and his associates approve the execution, possibly after it occurs.

July 30, 1918   A young sailor from Kronstadt, Germany, Boris Donskoy, in protest of German occupation of the Ukraine, throws a bomb that kills German Field Marshal Von Eichorn.

August 1918   Lenin claims it is not the Communists who are responsible for terror; it is "the bourgeoisie of the entire world" who forced the Soviet side to answer terror with terror. "Here is where the source of terror lies. . . . Those who sermonize us against terror are naught but agents—a weapon, witting or not, in the hands of those imperialist terrorists who are strangling Russia with their blockades. . . . But their cause is hopeless." The Mensheviks, Socialist Revolutionaries, and capitalists, hatching their plots to regain power, Lenin writes, "try to tell the Soviet government to stop using terror."

August 9, 1918   To a local Communist leader in Nizhni Novgorod, Lenin writes urgently that a White Guard uprising is evidently in preparation in that city and that it must be thwarted by "mass terror at once." On the same day, Lenin telegraphs his commissars at Penza and Vologda to launch "a merciless smashing" and "a ruthless mass-terror against the kulaks [rich peasants], the priests, and the White Guards."

August 17, 1918   Moisei Uritsky, a Bolshevik revolutionary leader, is killed by a Social Revolutionary student, Leonid Kanegeiser.

August 20, 1918   In his *Letter to American Workers,* Vladimir Lenin repeats his argument that no revolution or civil war could be waged without terror. "The British bourgeois forget their year 1649, the French their 1793. Terror was just and legitimate when the bourgeoisie used it to its own advantage against the feudals. Terror became monstrous and criminal when the workers and the poorest of peasants dared to apply it against the bourgeoisie! Terror was just and legitimate when used to replace one exploiting minority by another exploiting minority. Terror became monstrous and criminal when it began to be used in the interests of the overthrow of every exploiting minority, in the interests of the really great majority—of the proletariat and the semi-proletariat, of the working class and the poorest peasantry."

August 30, 1918   Lenin speaks at a meeting of factory workers and inveighs against the enemies of the revolution. As he leaves the plant and starts to get in his car, the Socialist Revolutionary Fanya Kaplan goes up to him and fires three bullets, two of which strike him, one in his shoulder, the other in his neck. In response the Bolsheviks execute Kaplan and shoot 500 prisoners in Petrograd (formerly called St. Petersburg) and 60 in Kronstadt.

September 5, 1918   The Council of People's Commissars issues the decree "Concerning the Red Terror" authorizing the Cheka to send "class enemies" to concentration camps and shoot those involved in counterrevolutionary activities.

October 1918   A leading Cheka official, Martyn Latsis, writes "Red Terror" in the *Cheka Weekly,* telling secret police personnel, "We are destroying the bourgeoisie as a class." The issue determining punishment is not what a prisoner's political views are but " . . . to what class does he belong? What is his origin? What is his education or profession? It is these questions that ought to determine his fate."

November 1918   Trotsky acknowledges that "certain comrades say our actions are too harsh, too devoid of mercy," but concludes that Bolshevik survival depends on the "Red Terror."

November 7, 1918   Lenin, addressing a meeting of Cheka personnel in Moscow, says that the excesses of terror need to be reduced, but it must continue as a revolutionary weapon.

November 20, 1918   Lenin cautions his party that terror and repression are not sufficient, at least for dealing with the petit bourgeoisie, and persuasion must also be used.

January 1919   The Irish Republican Army launches a guerrilla war against British authorities in Ireland, attacking isolated police stations and gaining control over large rural areas.

January 5, 1919   Socialist demonstrations in Berlin turn into an attempted Communist revolution with the Spartacist League, an extreme left-wing Marxist group, at the forefront.

January 15, 1919   Rosa Luxembourg, a leader of the German Communist Party, is kidnapped, tortured, and murdered by soldiers of the right-wing Freikorps in Berlin, as are hundreds of other Communists in the suppression of the revolt.

January 15, 1919   Karl Liebknecht, another leader of the German Communist Party, is abducted by Freikorps soldiers and brought to the Eden Hotel in Berlin, where he is tortured and interrogated for hours before being executed.

April 28, 1919   Gavrilo Princip, the assassin of the Archduke Franz Ferdinand, dies of tuberculosis at Teresienstadt.

June 2, 1919   Anarchists are suspected of setting off a series of bombs in eight cities in the United States, including Washington, D.C., where a bomb partially destroys the home of Attorney General A. Mitchell Palmer. The events set off a Red Scare, in which the U.S. government raids the offices and homes of suspected radicals (known as the Palmer Raids) and takes many into custody.

December 1919   As foreign socialists criticize Lenin for using terror, he replies that such measures are needed against counterrevolutionary plots at home and justified by anti-Communist terror abroad, citing the killings in Germany as an example.

1920   Leon Trotsky writes *Terrorism and Communism* in reply to Karl Kautsky, a Socialist theoretician, who attacked Lenin under the same title. "The terror of czarism was aimed at the proletariat," Trotsky writes. "The gendarmerie of czarism throttled the workers who were fighting for a socialist order. Therefore it was pernicious terror. But we Communists shoot landlords, capitalists, and generals who are striving to restore the capitalist order. This is beneficial terror." Trotsky jeered at Kautsky: "Do you grasp the distinction? For us Communists it is quite sufficient."

March 13, 1920   The Kapp Putsch is an extreme right-wing attempt to take power in Germany. Led by Wolfgang Kapp, a rabid nationalist, a number of ex-soldiers take Berlin without firing a shot. As a result, Socialist leaders, including Prime Minister Friedrich Ebert and Minister of Interior Gustav Noske, flee to Stuttgart. However, a general strike by government supporters ends the putsch after five days.

April–May 1920   Lenin writes a critique of terrorism as a tactic for organizing a revolution in "Left-Wing Communism: An Infantile Disorder."

September 16, 1920   In New York City, a horse-drawn cart explodes on Wall Street near the New York Stock Exchange just after noon, as workers pour onto the street for their lunch break. The bombing kills 34 people and leaves more than 200 others injured. Anarchists are suspected of carrying out the attack.

November 21, 1920   Eight groups of the Dublin Brigade, an Irish nationalist organization, kill 12 British secret service officers in their homes. The next day, known as Bloody Sunday, several hundred British soldiers go to Croke Park in Dublin, where 10,000 people are watching a game of soccer, surround the field, and open fire on the crowd. They kill 17 people and wound 50 others.

November 28, 1920   The Irish Republican Army sets fire to 15 warehouses in Liverpool, England.

March 8, 1921   Spanish premier Eduardo Dato is assassinated while leaving the Parliament building in Madrid. He is murdered by Luis Nicolau, Pedro Mateu, and Roman Castenellas, members of an anarchist group, the National Labor Confederation (CNT). They were angry at Dato for imprisoning and killing many trade unionists.

May 25, 1921   The Dublin Brigade sets fire to the Customs Office in Dublin, Ireland, destroying all the municipal records.

August 26, 1921	Matthias Erzberger, head of the Catholic Center Party in Germany, who is hated by right-wing nationalists for having signed the armistice to end World War I, is assassinated while walking in the Black Forest. The killers, naval officers Heinrich Schulz and Heinrich Tillessen, flee to Hungary. The government declares martial law.
March 1922	Lenin, at the Eleventh Party Conference, announces a more moderate economic policy, but continues to support state terror: "Here is where we need a purge through terror—trial on the spot and unconditional execution."
June 4, 1922	German Social Democratic Deputy Karl Gareis, who threatened to expose local rightist military groups, is killed in Munich.
June 22, 1922	Sir Henry Wilson, a staunch Irish Protestant, is shot dead in London by two IRA members, Reginald Dunne and Joseph O'Sullivan, who also shoot two policemen before they are arrested. They are both sentenced to death.
June 24, 1922	German Foreign Minister Walter Rathenau is killed by two right-wing army officers.
August 22, 1922	The president of the Irish Provisional Government and commander-in-chief of the army, Michael Collins, is killed in an ambush by hard-line IRA members angry at the signing of the Anglo-Irish treaty which gained Irish independence but left the six northern provinces with Protestant majorities under British rule.
November 24, 1922	Popular author and Irish Republican Army member Robert Erskine Childers, accused of leading anti-treaty terrorist activities, is executed by an Irish Free State Firing Squad.
December 7, 1922	Sean Hales, a deputy in the lower house of the Irish Parliament, is killed, and the vice chairman of the lower house is severely wounded by the IRA as they are on their way to a parliamentary session.
December 14, 1922	Gabriel Narutowicz, the president of Poland, is assassinated after only two days in office. As a Socialist, he had been heavily criticized by the National Democratic Party and was shot by Eligiusz Niewiadomski, a fanatical supporter of that group.
February 1923	Trotsky writes that terror is necessary as this was the only effective way to intimidate the petit bourgeoisie.
March 9, 1923	Lenin suffers his third stroke, rendering him bedridden and unable to speak. He is forced to give up leadership of the country. Stalin begins to consolidate his own hold on power.
April 1923	The commander-in-chief of the IRA, Liam Lynch, dies fighting against British forces.

May 10, 1923	A Russian opposed to the Communist revolution assassinates the well-known Soviet diplomat V.V. Vorovsky in Lausanne, Switzerland.
July 20, 1923	Pancho Villa, one of the foremost generals of the Mexican Revolution and famous for his 1916 raid on U.S. territory, is assassinated in Parral, Chihuahua, by his political rivals.
November 8–9, 1923	Adolf Hitler leads the abortive Beer Hall Putsch through which he hopes to use his SA "Brown Shirts" militia to launch a march on Berlin. The ringleaders are arrested.
January 21, 1924	Lenin dies of a massive stroke at the age of 53.
April 1, 1924	Hitler is sentenced to five years in jail for his participation in the Beer Hall Putsch. However, he serves only nine months.
June 10, 1924	Giacomo Matteotti, a Socialist leader and fearless opponent of the Fascists, is kidnapped and murdered by them in Italy.
April 1925	Communists, perhaps at Moscow's order, try to assassinate Czar Boris III of Bulgaria by placing a bomb in the Sveta Nedelya Cathedral during a religious service. The king survives, but 124 people, including most of his cabinet, are killed.
May 7, 1925	Boris Savinkov, a Russian Socialist Revolutionary leader, who organized terrorist opposition to the Bolshevik regime, is murdered in the Lubyanka prison in Moscow.
1926	A Bengali novel called *Pather Dabi* by author Saratchandra Chattopadhyay is published, describing sympathetically the strategy and spirit of terrorist revolutionaries.
May 26, 1926	Simon Petlyura, a nationalist Ukrainian leader who massacred Jews at the end of World War I, is assassinated in Paris by Sholom Schwartzbard, a Jewish student whose family was murdered in the pogroms. Schwartzbard is tried by a French court and found not guilty.
July 10, 1927	Kevin O'Higgins, vice president of the Irish Free State, is assassinated in Dublin by the IRA.
July 24, 1927	The Iron Guard, an ultra-nationalist, anti-Semitic, Fascist movement in Romania, is founded by Corneliu Zelea Codreanu.
November 12, 1927	Trotsky is expelled from the Communist Party of the Soviet Union, leaving Joseph Stalin with undisputed control of the Soviet Union.
April 12, 1928	Bomb attacks by Italian anarchists against the king of Italy in Milan leave 17 bystanders dead.
July 17, 1928	Leon Toral assassinates Álvaro Obregón Salido, president of Mexico, in a restaurant. Toral, a Roman Catholic seminary student, opposes Obregón's anti-clerical platform.
January 1929	Ante Pavelic and Gustav Percec create the Croatian Ustasha, a right-wing nationalist organization, which will carry out terrorist attacks on Jews and Serbs.
January 1930	Bhagwat Charan writes *The Philosophy of the Bomb,* a manifesto published by a small left-wing Indian group, the Hindustan Socialist Revolutionary Army,

which opposes Mohandas Gandhi's policy of nonviolence in seeking India's independence from Britain.

May 6, 1932   Paul Gordulof, a Russian émigré, shoots French President Paul Doumer in Paris at the opening of a book fair. Doumer dies the next day.

May 18, 1932   Naval officers in Tokyo, rejecting civilian control of the government, assassinate Japanese Prime Minister Tsuyoshi Inukai. The killing ends parliamentary rule in Japan, preparing the ground for Japan's foreign aggressions and eventually its involvement in World War II.

July 17, 1932   Armed Communists attack a National Socialist demonstration in Altona in northern Germany, leaving 18 dead. The event becomes known as the Bloody Sunday of Altona. Outrage at the attack weakens the Weimar government and strengthens the National Socialists (Nazis). Many other political street fights follow.

January 30, 1933   German President Paul von Hindenburg appoints Hitler as chancellor.

February 15, 1933   In Miami, Florida, Giuseppe Zangara attempts to assassinate President-elect Franklin D. Roosevelt but instead hits Chicago, Illinois, Mayor Anton J. Cermak, who dies on March 6. Zangara's motive may have involved anarchist ideas or insanity; others believed that he was a Mafia hit man sent to kill Cermak, not Roosevelt. Zangara is later executed in the electric chair in the Florida State Penitentiary.

February 27, 1933   The German parliament building (Reichstag) burns down. Marinus van der Lubbe, a mentally disturbed Dutch Communist, is arrested. He is tried, found guilty, and executed. The act was probably committed by the Nazis to provide a pretext for seizing power, but van der Lubbe had previously advocated violent action and may have been guilty.

February 28, 1933   Hindenburg and Hitler declare a national emergency and suspend civil liberties. Hitler quickly makes himself the country's unfettered dictator.

October 1, 1933   Austrian Chancellor Engelbert Dollfuss, who had banned the Nazi Party, is seriously injured in an assassination attempt.

December 10, 1933   Romania's Liberal Prime Minister Ion Duca bans the Iron Guard.

December 30, 1933   As Duca is returning to Romania after a meeting with the country's vacationing king in Greece, he is assassinated by the Iron Guard.

May 1934   The Bulgarian army stages a coup which leads to the abrupt end of the Macedonian nationalist group IMRO and the arrest of its members.

June 30, 1934   On Hitler's explicit instructions, a number of former officials and some prominent Nazis are murdered. Those killed include General Kurt von Schleicher, Gregor Strasser, and Captain Ernst Röhm. In this "Night of the Long Knives," the top leadership of the SA, the Nazi storm troopers, is purged and restricted to pre-military training and ceremonial parades.

| **July 1934** | As a reward for its role in the purging of the SA, the SS, the Nazi paramilitary troops, are officially recognized as independent of the SA and are given responsibility for the SA concentration camps. |

July 25, 1934   Austrian Nazis in Vienna murder Austria's chancellor Engelbert Dollfuss, preparing the way for Hitler's eventual takeover of that country.

October 9, 1934   Croat Fascists assassinate King Alexander of Yugoslavia, then on a state visit to France, and French Foreign Minister Louis Barthou. King Alexander had supported an alliance of states that threatened to stop Hitler's expansionism.

December 1, 1934   In the Soviet Union, Politburo member Sergei Kirov is shot dead at the Communist Party headquarters in Leningrad (formerly called St. Petersburg) by Leonid Nikolayev. It is widely thought that Stalin ordered this murder to eliminate a popular potential rival and provide an excuse for launching a massive purge in the party leadership.

February 26, 1936   Government offices in Tokyo are invaded by 1,400 Japanese soldiers. They demand that General Kazushige Ugaki be arrested and that General Sadao Araki be made head of the Kwantung Army. They also demand the deaths of top civilian officials.

February 29, 1936   Emperor Hirohito orders the Japanese army to arrest the conspirators in the Tokyo government offices and 19 of them are executed in July.

1937   The League of Nations formulates the Convention for the Prevention and Punishment of Terrorism, which says such acts are crimes against humanity which should be condemned by all states. It is accepted by 24 countries but ratified by only one and thus never comes into force. The convention defines terrorism as all "criminal acts directed against a state and intended or calculated to create a state of terror in the minds of particular persons, or a group of persons in the general public."

May 23, 1938   The leader of the Ukrainian Nationalists, E. Konowalets, is killed in Rotterdam by a bomb. His death is thought to have been ordered by Stalin.

November 9–10, 1938   A government-organized wave of anti-Semitic attacks sweeps Germany, with attacks on Jews and their property throughout the country on November 9, and continues into the following day. Streets in Jewish areas are littered with broken glass from destroyed shops and houses, giving the events the name Kristallnacht (Night of Broken Glass).

November 29, 1938   While Corneliu Zelea Codreanu and 17 members of the Iron Guard are being transported from one Romanian prison to another, all are killed, apparently by order of Romania's king.

September 21, 1939   Members of the Iron Guard assassinate the new Romanian prime minister, Armand Calinescu, to avenge the death of Corneliu Zelea Codreanu.

November 8, 1939   Hitler narrowly escapes an assassination attempt while celebrating the sixteenth anniversary of the Beer Hall Putsch.

1940   The Lehi, a terrorist group, is founded by Zionist leader Avraham Stern in British Palestine. It considers British rule of Palestine an illegal occupation and concentrates its attacks mainly against British targets in Palestine. The group is also known as the Stern Gang.

May 24, 1940   Trotsky survives a raid on his home in Mexico by alleged Stalinist assassins.

August 20, 1940   Stalinist agent Ramón Mercader attacks Leon Trotsky in his home outside Mexico City, driving the pick of an ice axe, whose shaft had been drastically shortened, into his skull. Trotsky dies the following day.

Social Revolutionary Terrorism in Europe and North America

Ever since the first chop of the guillotine in France, revolution and terrorism have gone hand in hand. Amid the peaceful protests of the 1960s and 1970s in the United States and Europe were those who believed their goal of establishing a utopian society and opposing what they labeled oppressive capitalist governments justified any type of violence. These were always small groups, albeit perhaps with larger numbers of sympathizers, yet the multiplier effect of terrorism gave them disproportionate impact and publicity.

In the United States, only two major organizations, the Black Panthers and the Weathermen, staged attacks, and these were relatively minimal ones. Terrorism did not pose any significant threat to American society. But in Europe, where the tradition of violent revolution was much stronger, the sting of terrorism was more deeply felt. In Italy, the Red Brigades and Ordine Nuovo claimed several victims. In Germany, many top businessmen were assassinated by the Red Army Faction, or RAF, also called the Baader-Meinhof Gang. In Greece, the Revolutionary Organization 17 November successfully targeted Americans on a number of occasions before being rounded up.

In Europe, social revolutionary terrorism was usually more specifically targeted than its nationalist equivalent. There were random victims but attacks were usually aimed at specific individuals and institutions. Of course, there were exceptions, such as in Italy: Ordine Nuovo's bombing of the Piazza Fontana in Milan, killing 16 people

and wounding 90, and the bombing by the Armed Revolutionary Nuclei of a Bologna train station that killed 85.

Although the duration of terrorist campaigns and the number of attacks in Europe did not compare to those in the Middle East and Asia, they were often romanticized by a large sector of the intellectual class. There was a revolutionary vacuum because the Communist parties were widely perceived as being part of the system, which, in the minds of many, these movements came to fill. Yet there was also another dimension to this vacuum. Much of the terrorism came after the peak of the radical movements of the 1960s, when it was already clear that they were not going to achieve power or even gain mass support. As so often has happened, terrorism resulted less from frustration over oppression as from frustration with a failed revolutionary movement.

Most of this terrorism came from the left, but there were also some rightist attacks, which sometimes—as in the case of the Oklahoma City bombing—were the deadliest and began to occur with a greater frequency. This might be partly a matter of definition. After all, in the 1930s, Fascist movements—the German Nazis, Italian Fascists, and Romanian Iron Guard, to name the most significant examples—had used a great deal of political violence in seeking power.

By the late twentieth century, however, Western societies had evolved to the point where they embodied many of the characteristics sought by nineteenth- and early twentieth-century social revolutionaries. Elements on the extreme right could easily believe that they were alienated enough to seek social transformation by violent means. As communism had failed for the left, so had fascism failed for them. Thus new groups arose that often took on cult elements and different causes.

At this end of the spectrum, those committing violence in Europe and America did so in the name of Christian fundamentalism, opposition to abortion, white supremacy, and fear of an excessively powerful U.S. government. The century's most destructive extreme right-wing terrorist was Timothy McVeigh, who exploded a bomb at the Alfred P. Murrah Federal Building in Oklahoma City, Oklahoma, killing 168 and wounding 800 others. McVeigh was inspired by *The Turner Diaries*,

a novel written in 1978 that was filled with white supremacist, anti-government hatred.

Finally, individuals acting as terrorists could have more impact. A century earlier, the lone gunman, motivated by a personal grievance or anarchism, could commit a single act of attempted assassination before being captured or killed. Now, through technology and better strategies, it was possible for one man to wage a long-running campaign. The most notable such example was the Unabomber, a recluse living in a Montana cabin, who was vehemently anti-technology. The perpetrator of one of the most remarkable campaigns, which terrorized an entire nation for several months in 2001, was the person who sent mail laced with anthrax to many prominent American individuals and institutions. That person has never been identified.

January 30, 1956	African-Americans in Montgomery, Alabama, begin a boycott of local white merchants, protesting local laws forcing African-Americans to ride in the back of city buses. The house of the boycott leader, the Rev. Martin Luther King, Jr., is firebombed. King and his family escape unharmed. Local white supremacist groups are suspected. As the campaign for civil rights continues, many other leaders and supporters will be victims of violence.
1962	The Port Huron Statement, the political manifesto for the Students for a Democratic Society (SDS), is adopted by its 60 founding members. It criticizes the American political system for failing to achieve international peace or to solve myriad social ills. The Port Huron Statement also calls for a fully "participatory democracy," which would empower citizens to share in the social decisions that directly affect their lives and well-being. The SDS focuses its efforts on helping to promote the civil rights movement and improving conditions in urban ghettoes and initially prefers nonviolent tactics. This event initiates the "New Left," which would result in the formation of several new terrorist groups.
June 12, 1963	Medgar Evers, the Mississippi field secretary for the National Association for the Advancement of Colored People (NAACP), is shot and killed outside his home in Jackson, Mississippi. Evers was working on a program to register African-Americans to vote. The assassin is identified as Byron De La Beckwith, a member of a local chapter of the Ku Klux Klan (KKK), a white supremacist organization. Local authorities decline to prosecute De La Beckwith, but he is finally convicted in 1994, more than 30 years later.
September 15, 1963	At 10:19 on this Sunday morning, a bomb explodes at the Sixteenth Street Baptist Church (an African-American congregation) in Birmingham, Alabama. The church has been a meeting place for civil rights groups. Four girls participating in Sunday school are killed. The bombing causes national outrage, and federal law enforcement agencies take new steps against white supremacist terrorism in the South. Four KKK members are identified in the bombing, but

their prosecutions are delayed for years. One will die before being prosecuted, one will be convicted in 1977, and two others in 2001 and 2002.

November 22, 1963   President John F. Kennedy is assassinated in Dallas, Texas, during a presidential motorcade there. It appears that the assassin was Lee Harvey Oswald, a former Marine who had defected for a time to the Soviet Union and who had become involved in some left-wing causes after returning to the United States. Controversy remains, however, over the identity of the assassin or assassins.

June 21, 1964   Three young civil rights volunteers from the North visit the ruins of Mt. Zion United Methodist Church in Neshoba County, Mississippi. The church, which had served as a meeting place for a campaign to register African-American voters, had been burned down by the local Ku Klux Klan four nights earlier. The young volunteers are arrested by local authorities, then released by prior arrangement to waiting KKK members. The three—two white and one African-American—disappear. Their bodies are found on August 4. Federal authorities charge 19 Ku Klux Klan members in their deaths, and seven are convicted in 1967. The incident prompts a further increase in anti-terrorist activity by federal prosecutors.

1965   As the United States becomes increasingly involved in the war in Vietnam, the anti-war movement, spearheaded by the Students for a Democratic Society (SDS), grows. The SDS organizes a national march in Washington, D.C. From this point on, the movement grows increasingly militant in its opposition to the Vietnam War, employing such tactics as demonstrations and occupation of administration buildings on college campuses.

February 21, 1965   African-American activist Malcolm X is assassinated in New York City in a dispute between Black Muslim groups. Malcolm was an important leader in the Nation of Islam movement, but broke away from it, becoming more radical politically. He emphasized the need for African-Americans to gain control of their own destiny. His speeches and writings helped begin the "black power" movement that influenced the Black Panthers and other radical groups.

October 1966   The Black Panther Party is formed in Oakland, California, by Huey Percy Newton and Bobby Seale. The group views the United States as a racist and capitalist state. Its goals include freedom for all imprisoned blacks, exemption of black people from military service, and full employment of the black population.

May 2, 1967   Twenty-six Black Panthers are arrested in Sacramento when they arrive heavily armed to visit the state legislature of California.

June 2, 1967   The shah of Iran pays an official visit to Berlin, leading thousands of students to take to the streets to protest his repressive regime. As marchers begin to disperse, the police surprise them with a new technique called "The Liver-Sausage Method," in which the crowd is stuffed long and tight on the sidewalk between the barricades and buildings. The police then form a wedge and rush the middle of the "sausage." The demonstrators naturally rush sideways—the sausage exploding at its ends—and into the flailing truncheons of hundreds more waiting police. At one point the police grab one protester, whom they believe to be a ringleader. Detective Sergeant Karl-Heinz Kurras points his gun at the protester's head, and the guns goes off, possibly accidentally, killing Benno Ohnesorg, who is attending his first protest. The growing leftist movement gains a martyr, and the date itself is later commemorated in the naming of terrorist group Movement 2 June, which is founded in 1971.

October 17, 1967

Huey Newton, co-founder of the Black Panthers, and another Black Panther member get into a firefight with police in Oakland, California. Two officers are killed, and Newton is seriously wounded. He is indicted in November and goes on trial in July 1968. In September 1968, he is sentenced to two to 15 years in prison for his involvement in the shoot-out.

April 4, 1968

The Rev. Martin Luther King, Jr., who has received the Nobel Peace Prize for his nonviolent protests against racial discrimination, is assassinated by a sniper at a motel in Memphis, Tennessee, where King is leading a protest campaign on behalf of the poor. The assassination causes riots to break out in African-American neighborhoods of major U.S. cities. A drifter named James Earl Ray is captured and later convicted of the killing, but many doubters, including King's family, believe unknown conspirators carried out the assassination.

April–May 1968

About 40,000 students on nearly a hundred campuses across the United States demonstrate against the Vietnam War and against racism in activities sponsored by the SDS. At Columbia University in New York, the administration building and other campus buildings are occupied by nearly 1,000 angry students, who set up barricades and establish "revolutionary communes" in the buildings. After the police storm the buildings with the administration's consent, the majority of students at Columbia join in a boycott of classes that shuts down the university. More than 700 protestors are eventually arrested.

The Era of Western Social Revolutionary Terrorism

The New Left era of radicalism in the West during the 1960s spawned a new era of social-revolutionary terrorism more widespread than anything that had happened since the era of anarchist-socialist terrorism between 1880 and 1910. This fact can be attributed to a number of factors beyond those that led to an upsurge in nonterrorist radicalism at that time.

First, the perceived failure of the Soviet Union, Communist parties, and Marxism-Leninism created a search for alternative revolutionary strategies and ideologies. New models included China and Cuba, proponents of guerrilla warfare. Because rural guerrilla activity or trying to mobilize the masses through organizing was impossible in Europe and America, Western proponents—paralleling but exceeding contemporary Latin American or Vietnamese models—adapted

with far more emphasis on assassination, kidnapping, and bombing.

Second, the terrorists had no connection with actual workers or even average people in their societies. They came largely from wealthy or better-off families or at least from people shaped more by years as students than any experience with work. The German terrorist movement had more mental patients than proletarians as members. The social revolutionary terrorists—in contrast to those with a core element of religion (Islamists) or nationalism—had no idea how to appeal to the masses. The old concept of the "propaganda of the deed" was attractive as a way of projecting their own self-image and desire to become revolutionary heroes rather than as a reference to a rational strategy.

Third, the failure of the New Left movement to bring about political change (or even short-range social change) in any Western country also engendered a desperation in which more militancy seemed to be the answer for some to their frustration. That is why the Western era of social terrorism gathered steam in the 1970s and into the 1980s as the political movements disintegrated.

It should be emphasized that terrorist movements usually involve small groups of people, and this was especially true for these New Left groups. This was another attraction of terrorism. A few dozen—or even at times a dozen—people could have a dramatic national impact while political movements numbering their adherents in the tens of thousands were virtually invisible and totally ineffective.

April 2, 1968	Andreas Baader, a leftist student activist, his girlfriend Gudrun Ensslin, Horst Sohnlein, and Thorwald Proll plant time bombs in the Kaufhaus Schneider department stores in Berlin and in Frankfurt am Main, which cause extensive damage. It is their attempt to start a world revolution. Two days later, police arrest them. They are sentenced to three years' imprisonment, but are released on June 13, 1969, pending review of their cases. When the court demands that they return to prison one month later, Sohnlein complies but the other three flee to Paris and later to Italy. On April 3, 1970, in Berlin after picking up some hidden guns, Baader and Astrid Proll, Thorwald's sister, are arrested.
April 11, 1968	Joseph Bachmann, a right-wing carpenter, shoots and wounds Rudi Dutschke, leader of the Ausser Parlamentarische Opposition (APO, the Extra-Parliamentary Opposition), a leftist student political movement, in Berlin. The attack sparks massive student riots in Berlin. Bachmann is convicted of the shooting in 1969 and commits suicide in prison the next year. Dutschke, who never fully recovers from his injuries, dies in 1979.
August 22–29, 1968	The U.S. Democratic Party meets in Chicago to nominate a candidate for president. (President Lyndon B. Johnson has declined to run for a second term, and the party is torn between pro-war and anti-war factions.) A coalition of radical groups, including the SDS and the Black Panthers, plans major demonstrations against the war, hoping to influence the nation and the convention. In response, Chicago mayor Richard Daley mobilizes thousands of local police and calls up National Guard units to control demonstrators. In a series of confrontations, some televised live by news organizations in Chicago, as many as a thousand are injured and nearly 700 are arrested. In December, a government-sponsored report on the riots criticizes law enforcement, characterizing the Chicago disorders as "a police riot." Nonetheless, in March 1969 the federal government indicts eight protest leaders, including Tom Hayden of the Students for a Democratic Society (SDS) and Bobby Seale of the Black Panthers, on charges of inciting a riot.
1969	Ordine Nuovo (New Order), a radical Fascist group, is founded among others in Italy by Pino Rauti, as an alternative to the Italian Social Movement, a Fascist group established after World War II by supporters of the dictator Benito Mussolini. The Red Brigades (Brigate Rosse) is founded by Renato Curcio, among others, in Italy with the goal of sparking a Marxist revolution.
February 7, 1969	An attempt to bomb the motorcade of U.S. President Richard Nixon during a state visit to Berlin is thwarted. Two terrorists, Dieter Kunzelmann and Rainer Langhans, are arrested. They are founders of a notorious terrorist group, Kommune I, in Berlin in 1966, who now claim membership in the West Berlin

Tupamaros, a group named for a terrorist group in Uruguay that has committed several kidnappings and assassinations.

June 1969

In the United States, the SDS holds its last convention, dividing into many factions. One splinter, calling itself the Action Faction, publishes an essay detailing its ideological beliefs that ends with a quotation from the Bob Dylan song "Subterranean Homesick Blues": "You don't need a weatherman to know which way the wind blows." The group eventually becomes the Weathermen and later the Weather Underground Organization (WUO).

October 8, 1969

In the Weathermen's first major protest, called Days of Rage, several hundred members and supporters use clubs and chains to vandalize shops and cars on Chicago's Gold Coast, an exclusive area of shops and apartments. Six members are shot and 68 are arrested.

December 1969

In the United States, the Weathermen decide to go underground and begin a terrorist campaign. The organization changes its name to the Weather Underground Organization (WUO).

December 4, 1969

Local leaders of the Black Panther Party in Chicago, Fred Hampton and Mark Clark, are killed by Chicago police in a raid on Hampton's apartment. According to the federal grand jury's findings, only one of the 90 bullets fired came from the apartment. All surviving Panther members are arrested for "attempted murder of the police and aggravated assault." On December 6, the Weather Underground bomb several police vehicles in Chicago to retaliate for the killing.

December 12, 1969

A powerful bomb explodes in a crowded bank on the Piazza Fontana in Milan, killing 16 and wounding 90 others. The same day, three bombs blow up in Rome, causing several injuries. Two anarchists—Giuseppe Pinelli and Pietro Valpreda—are arrested in connection with the bombings. Three days later, Pinelli mysteriously falls out of a window at police headquarters; Valpreda remains in jail for years awaiting trial and serves more time after he is convicted of pursuing "subversive activities." In 1985, however, he is acquitted of all charges for lack of evidence. Italian authorities eventually attribute the bombings to the neo-Fascist group Ordine Nuovo, whose aim was apparently to discredit leftist and anarchist groups. Members of the group are convicted of participating in the bombing, but later acquitted on appeal.

February 1970

A young psychiatrist at Heidelberg University in Germany, Dr. Wolfgang Huber, is fired for his unorthodox therapy methods. In response, his patients, mostly students, occupy the hospital director's office and he agrees to keep Huber on. Huber's thesis is that his patients' sickness is the product of capitalist society and the only way to cure them is to foment a Marxist revolution. Huber's patients organize themselves into the Socialist Patients Collective (SPK). In 1971 the SPK officially disbands, but many of its former members later join the Red Army Faction (RAF), also known as the Baader-Meinhof Gang.

February 16, 1970

The Weather Underground bombs San Francisco's Golden Gate Park police station, killing one officer and injuring others.

March 6, 1970

A townhouse in New York's Greenwich Village is destroyed in an explosion. Three members of the Weather Underground—Ted Gold, Diana Oughton, and Terry

Robbins—are killed, and the remains of a WUO bomb-making factory are discovered in the rubble. Two other members—Cathy Wilkerson, whose father owned the house, and Kathy Boudin—escape after the explosion and go into hiding.

April 2–3, 1970 Twelve Weathermen are indicted by a federal grand jury for conspiring to cross state lines with the intention of inciting the October 1969 Days of Rage.

April 15, 1970 Linda Evans and Dianne Donghi, Weather Underground members, are arrested by the FBI. Another leader, Kathy Boudin, who escaped the explosion in the New York townhouse, joins the Black Liberation Army, a tiny group of radicals, with whom she plans prison escapes and bank robberies.

May 4, 1970 Ohio National Guardsmen kill four students during an anti-war demonstration at Kent State University in Kent, Ohio. On the same day, Mississippi state highway patrolmen investigating a student protest fire into a women's dormitory at Jackson State College, killing two students and wounding 11 others. The deaths of nonviolent college protesters increase tensions between anti-war youth and supporters of the Nixon administration.

May 14, 1970 Well-known left-wing journalist Ulrike Meinhof collaborates with others to help convicted terrorist Andreas Baader escape from jail in Berlin. Meinhof and Baader, along with Gudrun Ensslin and Horst Mahler, begin what they name the Red Army Faction (RAF) but that outraged German newspapers call the Baader-Meinhof Gang.

May 21, 1970 The Weather Underground issues the "Declaration of a State of War," written by Bernardine Dohrn. In the remainder of the year, the WUO carries out at least six bombings, primarily in California and in New York City.

Late May 1970 The RAF in Berlin releases its manifesto, which opens: "Let the Class Struggle unfold! Let the Proletariat organize! Let the Armed Resistance begin!"

June 9, 1970 The Weather Underground claims responsibility for bombing the New York City police headquarters, in revenge for the killings of the Black Panthers in December 1969 and of anti-war demonstrators at Kent State University in May.

July 1970 Ordine Nuovo bombs the Rome–Messina train, killing six people and wounding 100 others.

July 23, 1970 Thirteen Weather Underground members are indicted by a federal grand jury on charges of conspiring to engage in acts of terrorism and sabotage against police stations and other institutions.

September 12, 1970 With the assistance of the Weather Underground, Harvard University professor and promoter of psychedelic drugs Dr. Timothy Leary escapes from a California jail, where he is serving a sentence for possession of marijuana. Together with his wife, Leary is smuggled to Algeria, and they eventually move to several other countries.

September 29, 1970 The Red Army Faction (RAF) robs three Berlin banks to obtain money to finance its operations.

October 8, 1970   Police in Berlin capture RAF leaders Horst Mahler, Monika Berberich, Brigitte Asdonk, and Irene Görgens. In spring 1971, Mahler, Görgens, and Ingrid Schubert are tried for their involvement in Baader's escape from prison in May. Mahler is acquitted; Görgens and Schubert are convicted. Görgens is sentenced to six years in prison and Schubert to four.

December 1970   Weather Underground member Caroline Tanner is arrested by the FBI in Pittsburgh, and fellow member Judith Alice Clark is arrested by the FBI in New York.

RAF members Eric Grusdat, Karl-Heinz Ruhland, Ali Jansen, and Ulrich Scholze are arrested in different German cities for involvement in the September 29 bank robberies. Jansen, who has shot a policeman, is sentenced to ten years in prison.

1971   The Revolutionary People's Struggle (called the ELA from its initials in Greek) is formed in Greece to overthrow the military dictatorship that has ruled since 1967, and to establish a Marxist regime. It remains a nonviolent group until 1974, when it takes up terrorist methods such as bombing government, business, and U.S. military facilities.

The Movement 2 June, an anarchist organization, is established in Germany by former members of Kommune I and other radical leftists. The group takes its name from the date in 1967 when a German university student, Benno Ohnesorg, was killed by police during Berlin protests against the state visit of the shah of Iran.

Mid-February 1971 Siegfried Hausner and Carmen Roll of the Socialist Patients Collective (SPK) attempt to bomb a train carrying West Germany's president, but arrive after it has left the Heidelberg station.

April 1971   Police discover an abandoned Weather Underground bomb factory in San Francisco. Bombings continue at a reduced pace.

June 24, 1971   Police stop a group of SPK members for a routine check in Heidelberg. The SPK members run away, and one of them wounds a policeman. The homes of many SPK members are raided and the remaining members go underground, many of them joining the RAF.

July 8, 1971   Two Berlin radicals, Thomas Weissbecker, connected to the RAF, and Georg von Rauch are in a Berlin court, having been charged with beating a journalist. Von Rauch is convicted and Weissbecker acquitted, but in the confusion after von Rauch's sentence is announced, the men, who resemble each other, switch places and von Rauch walks out of the courtroom. Weissbecker announces that he is the one who should have been released. Confused and embarrassed court personnel let him go.

July 15, 1971   RAF members Petra Schelm and Werner Hoppe try to escape after being stopped at a police roadblock in Hamburg while driving a stolen BMW. Hoppe is arrested; Schelm is killed.

July 21, 1971   Dieter Kunzelmann is arrested in Berlin for his bombing activities in West Berlin. He is sentenced to nine years in prison.

September 25, 1971   Two police officers try to arrest RAF members Margrit Schiller and Holger Meins on the autobahn in Freiburg. Both officers are wounded and the terrorists escape.

October 22, 1971   Schiller is captured by Hamburg police. A shoot-out with RAF members attempting to rescue her leaves one officer injured and another dead. In February 1973, Schiller is released from prison, and promptly goes back underground.

Winter 1971   The exploits of the RAF prompts formation of a special section of Germany's federal law enforcement agency to oversee Germany's anti-terrorism efforts.

December 1971   Movement 2 June member Rolf Pohle and RAF member Marianne Herzog are captured by German police. When Georg von Rauch and Bommi Baumann are pulled over by a Berlin police officer, von Rauch begins shooting. The police officer shoots von Rauch dead, but Baumann escapes.

December 22, 1971   RAF members Klaus Junschke, Ingeborg Barz, and Wolfgang Grundmann raid a branch of the Bavarian Mortgage and Exchange Bank in Kaiserslautern. A police officer, Herbert Schoner, walks in on the raid and is shot dead.

1972   The Turkish Communist Party/Marxist-Leninist (TKP/ML) is founded by Ibrahim Kaypakkaya with its armed wing called the Turkish Workers' and Peasants' Liberation Army (TIKKO). Many extreme leftist groups are formed in Turkey during this era.

February 2, 1972   A bomb explodes in West Berlin's British Yacht Club, killing an elderly German boat-builder, Irwin Beelitz. Movement 2 June claims responsibility, saying the attack was in support of the Irish Republican Army (*see* chapter 3).

February 21, 1972   Members of the Red Army Faction (RAF), in full carnival-mask regalia, raid a bank branch in Kaiserslautern. Later that day, member Ingeborg Barz, who had been in the group for about three months, telephones her mother in Berlin, indicating that she will leave the group soon and return home. She is never seen alive again and is thought to have been killed by Baader for trying to leave. In July 1973, her remains are reportedly found in woods outside Munich, though many dispute the police identification.

March 2, 1972   Augsburg police try to arrest Thomas Weissbecker, loosely connected to the RAF and Movement 2 June and perpetrator of the prison switch with Georg von Rauch. He is killed and his companion, Socialist Patients Collective (SPK) member Carmen Roll, is arrested.

March 15, 1972   Karl-Heinz Ruhland, the German auto shop worker turned terrorist turned informer, is sentenced to four-and-a-half years in prison for his participation in the RAF.

March 29, 1972   Till Meyer, a Movement 2 June member, is arrested in Bielefeld. In December, she is sentenced to three years in prison for the attempted murder of a policeman, but on November 13, 1973, she escapes from Castro-Rauxel prison.

May 11, 1972   Baader, Gudrun Ensslin, Holger Meins, and Jan-Carl Raspe detonate three pipe bombs outside the U.S. army officers' club near Frankfurt am Main, killing

Lieutenant Colonel Paul Bloomquist. RAF members, calling themselves the "Petra Schelm Commando," after member Schelm, who was killed by police the previous year, claim responsibility in a communiqué demanding the end to the U.S. mining of North Vietnamese harbors.

May 12, 1972   Baader, Meins, and Ensslin plant a car bomb to explode in a government parking lot in Munich, destroying 60 cars. The RAF claims responsibility as the "Tommy Weissbecker Commando," after member Weissbecker, who was killed two months earlier by police.

May 12, 1972   Angela Luther and Irmgard Moller of the RAF sneak into the Augsburg Police department and leave two pipe bombs, which explode and injure five policemen.

May 15, 1972   Baader, Raspe, and Meins put a car bomb in the Volkswagen of Judge Wolfgang Buddenberg, who had signed most of the arrest warrants for RAF members, in Karlsruhe. Buddenberg's wife, Gerta, is the first one to drive the car, and she is permanently injured by the blast.

May 19, 1972   Meinhof, Siegfried Hausner, Klaus Junschke, and Ilse Stachowiak place six bombs in the Hamburg offices of the Springer Press. Three of them blow up, injuring 17 people.

May 19, 1972   The Weather Underground plants and explodes a bomb at the Pentagon, headquarters of the U.S. Department of Defense, in Washington, D.C. There are no injuries.

May 24, 1972   Irmgard Moller and Angela Luther of the RAF drive two cars equipped with 50-pound bombs onto the campus of the Campbell Barracks of the U.S. Army Supreme European Command in Heidelberg and detonate them in a parking lot, killing two U.S. soldiers and one civilian. According to the group's communiqué this is "in response to American bombings in Vietnam."

June 1, 1972   Andreas Baader, Jan-Carl Raspe, and Holger Meins of the RAF are captured in Frankfurt following a gun battle with police.

June 8, 1972   Gudrun Ensslin of the RAF is captured in Hamburg after a clothing boutique salesclerk notices a gun in her jacket pocket.

June 9, 1972   RAF member Brigitte Mohnhaupt and Movement 2 June member Bernhard Braun are captured in Berlin.

June 15, 1972   RAF members Ulrike Meinhof and Gerhard Muller are captured in Hanover.

July 7, 1972   New RAF member Hans-Peter Konieczny is captured in Offenbach. In return for his release, he aids in the capture of other gang members, Klaus Junschke and Irmgard Moller.

July 13, 1972   Lawyer and RAF member Jorg Lang, who had brought Konieczny into the group, is arrested in Germany on suspicion of supplying the group with apartments.

Late 1972   Andreas Baader, while testifying at Horst Mahler's trial, announces a hunger strike for all RAF prisoners.

May 8–June 29, 1973	The RAF prisoners conduct a second hunger strike, which lasts two months.
May 18, 1973	Ibrahim Kaypakkaya, leader of the Turkish Communist Party and (TKP/ML) and its armed wing, TIKKO, dies in Diyarbakır prison, after being captured by Turkish forces.
July 7, 1973	Movement 2 June member Gabi Krocher-Tiedemann is arrested after a shoot-out in Berlin and on December 12 he is sentenced to eight years' imprisonment for the attempted murder of a policeman.
August 1973	Movement 2 June member Inge Viett escapes from her Berlin prison cell by sawing through the bars with a smuggled saw.
September 28, 1973	The Weather Underground bombs the offices of ITT, a major U.S. telecommunications company, in New York and in Rome, as a protest against the anti-Socialist coup carried out in Chile (where ITT has very large interests).
1974	Timothy Leary is arrested at the Kabul, Afghanistan, airport and extradited to the United States. He cooperates with the FBI's investigation of the Weather Underground in exchange for a reduced sentence. On April 21, 1976, he is released from jail by California Governor Jerry Brown.
1974	Female members of the Revolutionary Cells (RZ) attack the German Federal Constitutional Court the day after its decision supporting only limited abortion rights although there are no injuries. The RZ, another successful left-wing terrorist group in Germany, was formed in Frankfurt am Main during 1972–1973.
February 13, 1974	The trial for bombing Berlin's British Yacht Club by members of the Movement 2 June begins with Verena Becker, Wolfgang Knupe, and Willi Rather as defendants. Supporters riot outside the courtroom. Becker is convicted.
April 18, 1974	In Italy, Red Brigades (BR) kidnap Italian Attorney General Mario Sossi in Genoa. He is released on May 23.
May 1974	Eight activists are killed in Brescia, Italy, when a hand grenade is thrown into an anti-Fascist march. Neo-Fascist activists are suspected.
June 1974	Two neo-Fascists from the Italian Social Movement (MSI) are shot and killed in Padua, the Red Brigades' first murders.
June 4, 1974	Ulrich Schmucker of Movement 2 June is shot dead in a Berlin park by members of the group which accused him of being an informant.
July 1974	The Weather Underground issues a manifesto entitled "Prairie Fire," urging serious discussion of its radical politics as well as continued violence. At the same time, the group is beginning to fragment. After a few further bombings in the next 15 months, most attacking U.S. corporations, the group's terrorist campaign ends.

September 1974   Red Brigades leaders Renato Curcio and Alberto Franceschini are arrested and jailed in Italy. Curcio escapes the following year after a jailbreak led by his wife, Margherita Cagol, but is recaptured 11 months later.

October 2, 1974   The five primary members of the Red Army Faction (RAF), Andreas Baader, Ulrike Meinhof, Gudrun Ensslin, Jan-Carl Raspe, and Holger Meins, are indicted for dozens of crimes, including murder. The prisoners continue their hunger strike. Prison officials begin force-feeding Ensslin and Meins.

November 9, 1974   Holger Meins dies from his hunger strike, and the next day demonstrations take place in Frankfurt, Cologne, Hamburg, Berlin, and Stuttgart.

November 10, 1974 Gunter von Drenkmann, president of Germany's Superior Court of Justice, is assassinated in his Berlin home as he is celebrating his sixty-fourth birthday. The attack is apparently a botched kidnapping by Movement 2 June in response to the death of Meins.

Mid-November 1974 German police conduct nationwide raids. Two Protestant church figures, the Rev. Cornelius Burghardt and Undine Zuhlke, a social worker and wife of a prominent minister, are arrested and accused of smuggling a letter from an RAF member out of prison. Burghardt and Zuhlke are released on November 29.

November 29, 1974 Meinhof is sentenced to eight years' imprisonment for her part in assisting Baader's escape from jail (*see* May 14, 1970). Mahler is given an additional four years on top of the sentence he is already serving, for a total of 12 years, and Becker is acquitted.

1975   The revolutionary organization 17 November is established in Greece. A radical leftist group, it is named after the November 1973 student uprising in Athens protesting the military regime.

February 27, 1975 Peter Lorenz, the Christian Democrat Union (CDU) andidate for mayor of West Berlin, is kidnapped by members of Movement 2 June. Angela Luther, who has been underground for three years, is identified as one of the kidnappers. The next day, Movement 2 June demands immediate release of six terrorists: Horst Mahler, Verena Becker, Gabriele Krocher-Tiedemann, Ingrid Siepmann, Rolf Heissler, and Rolf Pohle, in addition to two protesters, in exchange for releasing Lorenz. The two protestors are released and five of the six terrorists are given free passage to Yemen. Horst Mahler refuses to be released. On March 4, Lorenz is set free.

April 24, 1975   Six RAF terrorists, mostly former members of the Socialist Patients Collective (SPK), take over the West German Embassy in Stockholm. Taking 11 hostages and setting explosives, they demand the release of all RAF defendants. Two hostages are shot before a wiring short causes the dynamite to explode prematurely, killing one terrorist, Ullrich Wessel. All of the other terrorists and hostages survive despite severe injuries, and the terrorists are captured without a fight. Terrorist Siegfried Hausner dies of his injuries on May 5. The lawyer Siegfried Haag becomes leader of the "second generation of the RAF," which is dedicated to freeing the first generation's leaders from prison.

June 5, 1975   Italian authorities discover the farmhouse where the Red Brigades are hiding a hostage. In the raid, they free the hostage and kill Margherita Cagol, an important Red Brigades member and wife of Renato Curcio, a founder of the organization.

June 23, 1975   Klaus Croissant and Hans-Christian Ströbele—members of the RAF—are arrested, and Croissant's Stuttgart offices are raided.

August 19, 1975   The RAF defendants are finally officially charged: Gudrun Ensslin, Andreas Baader, Ulrike Meinhof, and Jan-Carl Raspe are jointly charged with four murders, 54 attempted murders, and a single count of forming a criminal association.

September 1975   Most of the Movement 2 June leadership is in jail, charged with the kidnapping of Peter Lorenz and the bank raids.

December 21, 1975   In a carefully planned attack, an international group led by Ilich Ramirez Sanchez (known as "Carlos the Jackal") storms a conference of the Organization of the Petroleum Exporting Countries (OPEC) in Vienna, Austria. They take participants hostage and demand that a political statement be read on radio stations throughout the Middle East. Three men are killed in the attack—an Austrian policeman, an Iraqi guard, and a Libyan official. Authorities provide the terrorists with a chartered jet, and they take off with 42 hostages, including ministers from 11 OPEC members. The hostages are eventually released in Algeria.

     Carlos the Jackal, born in 1949, was perhaps the most notorious individual terrorist in the world in the 1970s. Born in Venezuela, he came from a wealthy family with Marxist sympathies. As a teenager he lived in London, and he attended university in Moscow. There he befriended Palestinian students and later joined the Popular Front for the Liberation of Palestine (PFLP), a terrorist group (*see* chapter 6). Before the OPEC kidnappings, he had made his reputation by directing a car bombing in Paris in 1972 that injured more than 60 people, and later had a hand in the grenade attack on the well-known Paris cafe Les Deux Magots. The OPEC attack became his most famous operation.

December 23, 1975   Richard Welch, an employee at the U.S. Embassy in Athens, Greece, is murdered in Athens by 17 November, the radical leftist organization. He is the first of four U.S. diplomats to be killed by the group.

January 13, 1976   After months of pre-trial courtroom maneuvers, the trial of RAF members (or the Baader-Meinhof Gang, as they are still called) begins in Stuttgart, where the RAF prisoners are held in the Stammheim prison. It comes to be known as the Stammheim trial. The defendants admit to membership in an urban guerrilla group and take "political responsibility" for the bomb attacks.

January 18, 1976   Italian police capture Renato Curcio, a founder of the Red Brigades.

March 1976   RAF members Gerhard Muller and Irmgard Moller are sentenced to four and a half years in prison for committing terrorist acts.

May 9, 1976   RAF co-founder Ulrike Meinhof is found hanging in her Stammheim cell window, and her death is declared suicide.

Mid-May 1976   There are demonstrations protesting the "murder" of Meinhof held in cities throughout the German Federal Republic, the largest in Frankfurt and Berlin. Bombs explode in Nice and Paris, France, and at the U.S. Air Base in Frankfurt.

June 8, 1976   The Red Brigades murder state prosecutor Francesco Coco and two bodyguards in Genoa.

June 27, 1976   Four terrorists—two from the Popular Front for the Liberation of Palestine (PFLP) and two from the German group Revolutionary Cells (RZ)—hijack an Air France plane with 258 passengers en route from Tel Aviv to Paris via Athens, and divert it to Entebbe, Uganda, where they are protected by Ugandan dictator Idi Amin. The terrorists are led by Carlos the Jackal and Wilfred Böse and Brigitte Kuhlmann, members of the RZ. The hijackers demand the release of several dozen terrorists imprisoned in Israel and four other countries, including six members of the RAF and Movement 2 June. On July 1, the hijackers release all the non-Israeli hostages and offer to release the crew, who opt to stay with the plane. Two days later, as the deadline for the terrorist threat to blow up the plane approaches, an elite Israeli commando unit storms the plane and kills the terrorists and 45 Ugandan soldiers. Also killed in the rescue mission are the leader of the Israeli assault force, Yonatan Netanyahu, and one of the Israeli hostages.

July 7, 1976   Monika Berberich of the RAF escapes from Lehrterstrasse maximum-security prison in Berlin with Movement 2 June members Inge Viett, Gabrielle Rollnick, and Juliane Plambeck. They beat up a guard, scale a wall, and disappear. Berberich is captured just two weeks later, on July 21.

July 8, 1976   Gerhard Muller, a former RAF member arrested with Ulrike Meinhof, testifies against the defendants in the Stammheim trial in exchange for a reduced sentence. Muller describes the structure of the RAF in great detail.

July 21, 1976   Rolf Pohle, who specializes in acquiring arms for terrorists like the RAF, is captured in Athens and extradited to Germany after German Chancellor Helmut Schmidt threatens the Greek government with massive economic sanctions if it fails to turn him over.

1977   Action Directe, an urban guerrilla group, is formed in France by two left-wing groups: Groupes d'Action Révolutionnaire Internationalistes (GARI; in English, Revolutionary Internationalist Action Groups) and Noyaux Armés pour l'Autonomie Populaire (NAPAP; in English, Armed Core Groups for Popular Autonomy). Its aim is to bring to power a Marxist-Leninist regime.

February 1977   RAF member Kay-Werner Allnach is convicted of belonging to a criminal gang but is acquitted of more serious charges due to lack of evidence.

April 1977   The Red Brigades in Italy carry out terrorist attacks almost daily, often targeting security services, magistrates, and prison wardens, and intimidating judges and juries in order to stop trials of terrorists.

April 7, 1977	German Federal Prosecutor General Siegfried Buback is murdered, along with two others, near his home in Karlsruhe. "The Ulrike Meinhof Commando," named for the dead co-founder of the RAF, claims responsibility in revenge for the deaths of Holger Meins, a leading RAF member, who died during a hunger strike in 1974, and Siegfried Hausner, who died in prison.
April 28, 1977	Andreas Baader, Gudrun Ensslin, and Jan-Carl Raspe are found guilty of four murders and over 30 counts of attempted murder. At the end of a two-year-long trial, they are sentenced to life imprisonment.
July 30, 1977	RAF members Brigitte Mohnhaupt and Susanne Albrecht assassinate Jurgen Ponto, the latter's godfather and chairman of the Dresdner Bank, in his Frankfurt home.
August 25, 1977	Members of the second generation of the RAF use a defective homemade rocket launcher in a failed attempt to destroy the Federal Prosecutor's Office in Karlsruhe.
September 5, 1977	Hanns-Martin Schleyer, a leading industrial manager, board member of Daimler-Benz, and notorious former Nazi, is kidnapped from his car in Cologne by RAF terrorists. Three police guards and his chauffeur are killed. The kidnappers demand the release of RAF prisoners. Negotiations continue all month. This is the first day of the intensive period of terrorism later known as "the German Autumn." During this period, a major counterterrorism campaign is conducted, including large-scale telephone tapping.
October 13, 1977	A Lufthansa Boeing 737 bound for Frankfurt from Mallorca is hijacked by four Palestinian terrorists shortly after takeoff and diverted to Rome's Fiumicino Airport. There are 91 hostages, almost all of whom are German vacationers. The hijackers demand the release of 13 Palestinian terrorists in German and Turkish prisons plus $15 million. They force the plane to land on October 14 in Bahrain for refueling before heading to Dubai. Joint statements are issued by the Palestinians hijackers and the RAF kidnappers who are holding Hanns-Martin Schleyer. On October 16, the Palestinian hijackers have the Lufthansa plane flown to Aden. The Palestinians' leader, "Martyr Mahmud," kills the pilot, Jürgen Schumann. The next day the plane flies to Mogadishu, Somalia. The hijackers demand that the German government fly Andreas Baader, a co-founder of the RAF, and the other prisoners to Mogadishu or they will blow up the plane. At night, a plane carrying the crack German counterterrorist team along with two British army Special Air Service soldiers lands at the airport. They storm the plane, rescuing the hostages, killing three hijackers, and seriously wounding the fourth, Souhaila Sami Andrawes Sayeh. She is sentenced in Somalia to 20 years in prison, but in January 1978 Palestinian terrorists force her release. After moving to Oslo in 1991, she is caught and extradited to Germany, where she is sentenced to 12 years in prison, but is released after serving half her sentence due to bad health.
October 17–18, 1977	Baader, Raspe, and Ensslin commit suicide in jail, while Irmgard Moller attempts suicide but fails. She succeed in killing herself on November 13.
October 27, 1977	Baader, Ensslin, and Raspe are buried in Stuttgart, marking the end of the first generation RAF or Baader-Meinhof Gang.

December 1977	Klaus Croissant, the RAF lawyer, is extradited from France to Germany to face charges of supporting a terrorist organization.
1978	The Revolutionary People's Liberation Party/Front (DHKP-C), best known as Dev Sol, is formed in Turkey as a splinter faction of the Turkish People's Liberation Party. Dev Sol has a Marxist-Leninist ideology and aims to overthrow the Turkish regime.
March 16, 1978	The Red Brigades kidnap former Italian Prime Minister Aldo Moro, together with five of his bodyguards in Rome. The bodyguards are killed, and the kidnappers offer to free Moro in return for the release of their members who have been arrested for terrorism. Moro is found dead 55 days later.
May 10, 1978	In the aftermath of the Moro killing, the Italian government arrests and convicts hundreds of people for involvement in terrorist groups and actions. So strong is the reaction that some Red Brigades leaders blame their chief, Mario Moretti, for initiating the Moro kidnapping.
May 25, 1978	A man later known as the Unabomber plants a bomb in a Chicago parking lot addressed to an engineering professor in Troy, New York. The bomb is ultimately referred to the police, and an officer is slightly injured when it explodes as he is trying to disarm it. The Unabomber will plant or mail more than a dozen more bombs in the next 16 years, targeting engineering and computer science professors, corporate executives, and leaders of companies that consume natural resources. Three men will be killed, and several others severely injured. The anonymous bomber claims to support and represent environmentalists and others who oppose the effects of industrialization and technology.
Summer 1978	Through Mario Moretti, the Red Brigades establishes links with the Palestine Liberation Organization (PLO). The PLO proposes an alliance with the Red Brigades and the German RAF to carry out attacks on "Zionists" in Europe. Abu Iyad, a Fatah leader second only to Yasir Arafat, offers the European groups weapons and training in exchange for cooperation in staging attacks. Four such operations take place.
January 9, 1979	A 67-year-old Spanish Supreme Court judge is murdered on his way to his office in Madrid. Judge Cruz Cuenca is walking near a large department store on a busy street in Madrid when he is shot in the head. His murderers claim to belong to the left-wing group named GRAPO (the First of October Anti-Fascist Resistance Group).
1980	The Movement 2 June disbands, and its remnants join forces with the RAF. The leaders of Action Directe, Jean Marc Rouillian and Nathalie Ménigon, are arrested in France. They are released in 1981 in a general amnesty.
August 2, 1980	The Armed Revolutionary Nuclei, an offshoot of the Italian right-wing group Ordine Nuovo, bombs a Bologna train station using a suitcase packed with over 40 pounds of explosives. Eighty-five people are killed, and 200 others are wounded.

December 1980

In the Red Brigades, a new faction emerges calling itself the Guerrilla Party of the Metropolitan Proletariat (P-GPM) under the leadership of Giovanni Senzani.

December 3, 1980

Bill Ayers and Bernardine Dohrn, two of the Weather Underground's main leaders, turn themselves in to U.S. authorities after living in hiding for more than a decade. They have two children and have raised and adopted the child of WUO member Kathy Boudin, who remains at large.

April 1981

Red Brigades members kidnap Ciro Cirillo, one of the Christian Democratic Party's (CDP) most admired personalities from Naples. He is later released with the help of the local Mafia for a high ransom.

May 24, 1981

Four gunmen from Dev Sol (DHKP-C), the Turkish terrorist faction founded in 1978, hijack a Turkish Airlines plane en route from Istanbul to Ankara. They order the pilot to land at the small military airfield at Burgas, Bulgaria. The hijackers demand $500,000 and freedom for 47 prisoners in Turkish jails. They threaten to kill five American banking executives among the 112 passengers aboard and to blow up the plane if their demands are not met. Twenty-four hours later all passengers are eventually freed in a rescue assault.

August 31, 1981

The RAF detonates car bombs at the Ramstein Air Force Base, headquarters of the U.S. Air Force in Europe, injuring 20. Ramstein is near Kaiserslautern in southwest Germany.

September 15, 1981

The RAF fire Soviet-made RPG-7 rocket grenades at the armor-plated car of General Frederick J. Kroesen, the commander of U.S. Army forces in Europe. He and his wife sustain minor injuries.

October 20, 1981

The Weather Underground reappears when its members hijack a Brinks armored car in Nanuet, New York, killing one Brinks guard. Police intercept the stolen van, and two policemen are killed in the shoot-out. Kathy Boudin, who had lived in hiding since surviving the explosion of a townhouse in New York City in 1970, is caught and convicted of being an accessory to the murders. She serves 22 years in jail, gaining release on parole in September 2003.

December 17, 1981

U.S. Army Brigadier General James L. Dozier, senior U.S. official at NATO headquarters in Verona, Italy, is abducted from his apartment by Red Brigades terrorists. On January 28, 1982, Italian elite police units free Dozier from a "people's prison" in Padua, capturing his five kidnappers. A severe crackdown follows in which most of the group's leaders are arrested. Many turn informer, leading security forces toward further arrests.

1982

The Army of God, a U.S. organization committed to using violence to stop abortions, is founded.

January 4, 1982

Red Brigades sympathizers blow out a portion of a prison wall in Rovigo, freeing several group members. One prison guard is killed, and six others are wounded.

January 10 and 16, 1982

Italian police conduct raids on Red Brigades hideouts in Rome and Biella. Surface-to-air missiles, anti-tank weapons, and explosives are confiscated.

January 18, 1982   Police in Rome foil a Red Brigades raid at a political party convention on January 28 in which the group planned to kidnap or kill as many as 100 political leaders.

August 1982   The French government bans Action Directe (AD) following a series of attacks. In 1984, the group will align itself with the Red Army Faction centered in Germany.

November 15, 1983   U.S. Navy Captain George Tsantes, together with his Greek driver, is gunned down by the 17 November group as he rides to work in Athens.

February 15, 1984   Leamon Hunt, a U.S. citizen who is chief of the Multinational Force and Observers Group (MFO) peacekeeping force in Sinai, is assassinated in Rome in a joint operation of the Red Brigades and the Lebanese Armed Revolutionary Faction (FARL). In 1984, three FARL members are arrested for the attack and in November 1987, Red Brigades member Rosa Fresa Lambetti is also arrested for involvement in it.

March 1984   The Red Brigades divides into two splinter groups. The larger is the Communist Combatant Party (BR-PCC), and the smaller is the Union of Combatant Communists (BR-UCC).

April 1984   Four imprisoned leaders of the Red Brigades-PCC, Curcio, Moretti, Ianelli, and Bertolucci, publish an "open letter" in which they reject the armed struggle as pointless, stating "The international conditions that made this struggle possible no longer exist." Despite this manifesto, the Red Brigades-PCC will continue to carry out violent acts.

December 18, 1984   In the RAF's first action since May 1982, a car bomb is planted at a school for NATO officers in Oberammergau, but is discovered and defused. Several days later, RAF prisoners begin a hunger strike, demanding the right to meet together in jail. These events revitalize the group.

January 1985   During the month, RAF supporters carry out many small bombings in support of the demands of the RAF prisoners.

January 15, 1985   General Rene Audan, head of international arms sales at the French Ministry of Defense, is shot dead at his Paris home by terrorists from the Action Directe and RAF.

February 1985   RAF members murder Ernst Zimmerman, chairman of the industrial motor manufacturer MTU, and his wife in their suburban home in Munich. The RAF prisoners end their hunger strike.

March 1985   Ezio Tarantelli, economics advisor to the Italian government, is killed by the Red Brigades in Rome.

June 6, 1985   An RAF bomb explodes at the Frankfurt airport in Germany, killing three people.

August 8, 1985   The RAF and Action Directe claim responsibility for bombing the U.S. Air Base in Frankfurt, killing two passersby. To gain access to the air base, the RAF kidnaps and kills an American soldier, Edward Pimental, in order to obtain his ID card.

December 11, 1985 — Hugh C. Scrutton, the owner of a computer rental store in Sacramento, California, stops on his way to lunch to remove what looks to be a road hazard in the parking lot behind his store. The object, actually a bomb filled with nail fragments, explodes and kills Scrutton. The bomb was placed by the Unabomber.

February 1986 — The Red Brigades-PCC murderers Lando Conti, the ex-mayor of Florence, and tries unsuccessfully to kill former Prime Minister Bettino Craxi.

July 9, 1986 — Karl Heinz Beckurts, president of the German industrial corporation Siemens, and his driver are killed when Beckurts's limousine hits a bomb planted by the RAF outside his home in Strasslach, Germany.

August 2, 1986 — RAF member Eva Haule and supporters Luiti Hornstein and Chris Kluth are arrested. On August 13, two more supporters, Barbel Perau and Norbert Hofmeier, are arrested in Duisburg. The following day there is a third arrest in Duisburg. This is part of a new campaign to bring criminal charges against those giving the RAF political support and assistance.

October 10, 1986 — The RAF assassinates Gerold von Braunmühl, political director of the German Ministry of Foreign Affairs, at his home in Bonn.

November 17, 1986 — The head of the Renault car company, Georges Besse, is assassinated in Paris by Action Directe.

February 21, 1987 — The main Action Directe members, Jean Marc Rouillian, Nathalie Ménigon, Joëlle Aubron, and Georges Cipriani, are arrested in an isolated farmhouse. They are sentenced to life imprisonment, but Joëlle Aubron is released in 2004 for health reasons.

March 12, 1987 — Licio Giorgieri, a senior Italian Air Force general, is murdered by the Red Brigades-UCC in Rome.

April 16, 1988 — Roberto Rufillini, Italian senator and academic and government advisor, is assassinated by Red Brigades-PCC members.

June 28, 1988 — Captain William E. Nordeen, a defense attaché at the U.S. Embassy in Athens, is killed by a car bomb detonated by remote control. The 17 November group claims responsibility.

September 1988 — The arrest of most of the Red Brigades-PCC members and the group's further ideological reconsideration bring an end to the era of high-intensity terrorism in Italy.

September 20, 1988 — The RAF fails in an attempt to assassinate Hans Tietmeyer, a German representative to the International Monetary Fund (IMF) and the World Bank in Bonn.

February 1, 1989 — RAF prisoners begin a hunger strike to end solitary confinement and to gain recognition as political prisoners. This demand gains wide popular support in leftist and liberal circles.

November 11, 1989	Alfred Herrhausen, president of the Deutsche Bank, is killed when his car hits a bomb outside his home in Bad Hamburg, West Germany. RAF claims responsibility.
1990	A raid by Greek officials on a safe house of ELA, the terrorist group founded in 1971, uncovers a weapons cache and evidence of direct contacts with other Greek left-wing militant groups such as 1 May and Revolutionary Solidarity.
September 26, 1990	Dev Sol (DHKP-C) gunmen assassinate the former deputy director of the Turkish National Intelligence Agency in Istanbul.
February 7, 1991	Dev Sol (DHKP-C) terrorists shoot and kill a U.S. civilian contractor as he is getting into his car to travel to work at Incirlik Air Base in Adana, Turkey.
March 12, 1991	U.S. Air Force Sergeant Ronald Stewart is killed by a remote-controlled bomb in an Athens suburb. The 17 November group claims responsibility.
April 4, 1991	In Berlin, the RAF assassinates Detlev Korsten Rohwedder, president of the Treuhandanstalt, an organization working to integrate the East German economy with that of West Germany.
August 19, 1991	Dev Sol (DHKP-C) claims responsibility for the fatal shooting of a British businessman in his Istanbul office.
October 7, 1991	Çetin Görgü, assistant press attaché at the Turkish Embassy in Athens, is killed in an attack on his car. The 17 November group claims responsibility.

End of an Era

By the 1990s, European revolutionary groups, which were mostly the product of the political ferment of the 1960s and 1970s, were fading. In France, terrorism had barely gotten started during this era, while in the United States terrorists succeeded in perpetrating only scattered actions. In Germany and especially Italy, the problem was much more serious. Still, by the mid-1980s, the main groups—the Red Brigades in Italy and the Red Army Faction (known to many as the Baader-Meinhof Gang) in Germany—had been largely destroyed.

Although sporadic social revolutionary terrorism took place in Western Europe thereafter, it was mainly a "one-generation" phenomenon, carried out by people shaped by a very specific set of experiences at a particular point in time. Even the largest of these New Left groups in Europe found it impossible to replace their founders and early leaders when they were killed or imprisoned.

Another characteristic of these groups was their total isolation from popular support. True, a larger group (usually leftists and liberals, but sometimes radical conservatives) sympathized with the terrorists, because they shared their revolutionary beliefs or thought them well intentioned and persecuted. Such supporters made it easier for the terrorist groups to survive briefly by providing logistical support such as hiding places and money, but fell far short of supporting a long-term struggle.

In fact, the groups were widely unpopular; their violent actions brought condemnation from the overwhelming majority of the population. They had made a principal mistake for any terrorist or revolutionary group: appearing to act against the masses' interests rather than to champion those interests. Some groups pretended that the masses secretly appreciated their efforts, but it was difficult to find real evidence of support.

As a result, the new terrorist organizations looked for substitute revolutionary supporters—women, alienated youth, various social minorities, or oppressed peoples in developing nations—but none was successful at building a durable movement. The basic truth was that Western societies were post-revolutionary, and that radical movements remained rooted in the thinking of the nineteenth century. In trying to repeat the Bolshevik or other revolutionary experiences, new terrorist groups proved Marx's dictum that history repeats itself, the first time as history and the second as farce. Unfortunately, as in all terrorist stories, many people suffered terribly for the illusions of such groups.

April 1992	Red Army Faction (RAF) leaders announce a cease-fire and renounce terrorism, demanding in return the release of imprisoned terrorists, improved treatment for remaining RAF inmates, and German government flexibility on a variety of social issues.
November 23, 1992	Three Turkish girls are killed and nine others injured in an arson attack in Mölln, in northeastern Germany. Violence against "guest workers," especially Turks, is attributed to neo-Nazi German nationalists.
March 27, 1993	The RAF breaks its cease-fire and undertakes its first terrorist operation in two years by blowing up an empty prison complex with at least 400 pounds of explosives.
March 29, 1993	An arson attack on the house of a Turkish family in Solingen, Germany, results in the death of five, including three children, and seven injuries. Neo-Nazis are responsible.
April 1993	Red Brigades founder Renato Curcio, who has been in jail since 1976, is allowed to enter a work release program.
June 27, 1993	German police pursue RAF members Birgit Hogefeld and Wolfgang Grams. Hogefeld is captured; Grams dies during the chase, apparently committing suicide to avoid capture.
September 19, 1993	17 November terrorists explode a bomb on a bus in Greece, killing one policeman and injuring 13 others.
1994	Red Zora, a German feminist urban guerrilla group allied with the Revolutionary Cells (RZ), sets fire to trucks belonging to a company that supplies groceries to refugee facilities on the premise that the firm was "making money off refugees." They also carry out an arson attack on the Frankfurt subway system, protesting higher fares and "racist" practices among ticket controllers.
1994	German courts grant early release to two RAF members: Irmgard Moller, who served 22 years of a life sentence for a car bomb attack that killed three U.S. soldiers in 1972, and Ingrid Jakobsmeier, who served two-thirds of her sentence for participating in attacks against the U.S. military in 1981.
January 10, 1994	A small bomb explodes outside the NATO Defense College in Rome. The Red Brigades claims responsibility on behalf of a group calling itself the Combatant Communist Nuclei (NCC).
January 24, 1994	Former Bank of Greece Governor Michalis Vranopoulos is gunned down with his driver-bodyguard in a central Athens street by the 17 November group.

July 4, 1994	A 17 November member assassinates the acting deputy chief of mission of the Turkish Embassy in Athens.
August 14, 1994	Ilich Ramirez Sanchez, known as Carlos the Jackal, hunted for years by a host of law enforcement and intelligence agencies, is captured in Khartoum, Sudan. Soon afterward, he is transferred to France under heavy security. There he is tried for the murder of two French policemen and of the Palestinian terrorist-turned-Israeli agent Michel Moukharbal in 1975. On December 23, 1997, he is sentenced to life in prison.
December 1, 1994	Irmgard Moller of the Red Army Faction (RAF) is released after 22 years in prison.
December 10, 1994	New York advertising executive Thomas Mosser opens a package in his kitchen, setting off a fatal explosion from a bomb made by the Unabomber, who has targeted Mosser for his public relations firm's work for Exxon, the company whose tanker spilled oil in Alaska's Prince William Sound.
1995	The Nuclei Territoriali Antimperialisti (NTA) is formed in Italy as an extreme left-wing organization seeking a Marxist revolution in Italy. The NTA is opposed to Italy's free-market capitalism and perceived imperialism. It also advocates class struggle and the replacement of Italy's current governmental structure by the rule of the proletariat. The group is estimated to have around 20 members.
1995	Although German officials say the RAF has largely disintegrated, they worry about successor organizations assuming its role. The emerging Anti-Imperialist Cells (AIZ) mount several bombing attacks against German interests in 1995, claiming responsibility for a series of nonfatal bombing attacks on the homes of conservative politicians.
1995	Alparslan Türkes is allowed to reconstitute his ultra-nationalist party MHP, which has connections with terrorist groups. The party takes part in the Turkish elections, gaining 8.5 percent of the vote.
April 19, 1995	At 9:02 a.m., a truck bomb explodes outside the Alfred P. Murrah Federal Building in Oklahoma City, Oklahoma, just as the building's hundreds of workers are arriving. One hundred sixty-eight people are killed, and nearly 600 others are injured. Timothy McVeigh will be convicted of the bombing and be executed for the crime in June 2001. It is claimed that McVeigh was inspired by *The Turner Diaries*, a white supremacist, anti-government book written in 1978. Terry Nichols, who met McVeigh when they were in the U.S. Army, will also be convicted of participating in the bombing and be sentenced to life in prison.
April 24, 1995	A package mailed by the Unabomber to the California Forestry Association explodes when opened, killing Gilbert B. Murray, the timber lobbying group's president.
April 24, 1995	The *New York Times* receives a letter from the Unabomber. Billing himself as "the terrorist group FC," he promises to stop sending bombs if a long enclosed

article is printed in a national periodical. The Unabomber also demands that three yearly installments be published to clarify material in the treatise and rebut criticisms of it. On September 19, the *Washington Post* prints the Unabomber's manifesto.

September 1995   A German court sentences RAF member Sieglinde Hofmann to life imprisonment for assisting in five murders and three attempted murders, including the unsuccessful 1979 bomb attack on NATO Commander Alexander Haig in Belgium.

October 1995   Johannes Weinreich, former RAF member and alleged deputy to Carlos the Jackal, is indicted in Berlin for transporting explosives into Germany later used to bomb the French cultural center. Weinrich had been extradited to Germany from Yemen. At the same time, Germany releases several former RAF terrorists who have served from 11 to 20 years of their sentences.

October 1995   On the basis of a French warrant, Italian police arrest former RAF member Christa-Margot Fröhlich. A German national, she is wanted for complicity in a 1982 Paris attack carried out by Carlos the Jackal (Ilich Ramirez Sanchez), which killed one person and injured 63 others.

February 1996   German authorities arrest Bernhard Falk and Michael Steinau, two suspected members of the leftist group Anti-Imperialist Cell (AIZ).

April 3, 1996   Theodore Kaczynski, a former professor at the University of California at Berkeley living as a recluse in a one-room cabin without electricity in Montana, is arrested and charged with possession of bomb components. He is the Unabomber. On May 4, 1998, following a plea bargain, Kaczynski is sentenced to four consecutive life terms plus 30 years.

April 18, 1996   On the first anniversary of the Oklahoma City bombing, the U.S. Congress passes a bill boosting the ability of law enforcement authorities to fight domestic terrorism. The Antiterrorism and Effective Death Penalty Act imposes limits on federal appeals by death row inmates and other prisoners and makes the death penalty available in some international terrorism cases. It also bars fundraising by foreign terrorist groups and allows the deportation of alien terrorists without the need to disclose classified evidence against them.

July 27, 1996   A bomb explodes at the Centennial Olympic Park during the Summer Olympic games in Atlanta, killing a woman and wounding 111 other people. The bomb was hidden in a knapsack and detonated at the base of a concert sound system. The assailant is Eric Rudolf, who later explains that he targeted the Olympics as part of an anti-abortion protest.

November 1996   After two years of hearings, the German courts convict RAF member Birgit Hogefeld on three counts of murder—including the 1985 murder of a U.S. soldier and the subsequent bomb attack at the U.S. Rhein-Main Air Base—and four counts of attempted murder. She is sentenced to life in prison.

May 28, 1997   Greek ship owner Costis Peratikos is killed by the 17 November group as he leaves his office in the port of Piraeus. The group issues a manifesto claiming that Peratikos was targeted because he allegedly misused a large government bailout and threatened to close down his shipyard, which would have forced the layoff of 2,000 employees.

January 29, 1998   An off-duty police officer is killed and a clinic worker injured in a bombing of the New Woman All Women Health Care Center in Birmingham, Alabama, by Eric Rudolf because the center performs abortions.

April 1998   The RAF announces its "self-dissolution" following more than two decades of struggle against the German government. Meanwhile, German courts continue to adjudicate cases against RAF members for terrorist acts committed in the 1980s.

October 22, 1998   Barnett Slepian, an obstetrician/gynecologist, is assassinated in the kitchen of his Amherst, New York, home, by a gunman who shoots him through a window. His assailant is James Charles Kopp, who targeted Slepian because he performed abortions. Kopp is later arrested in France and extradited to the United States, where he is convicted and sentenced to life in prison.

March 5, 1999   The Turkish Workers' and Peasants' Liberation Army (TIKKO) detonates a bomb in Cankiri as the governor of that province drives by, killing four. Eight are injured, including the governor. Eleven suspects in the case are convicted in June 1999 for the attack.

April 27, 1999   A bomb planted by the Revolutionary Nuclei (an offshoot of the Revolutionary People's Struggle or ELA) explodes near the entrance to the Athenaeum Intercontinental Hotel in Athens, killing one woman and injuring one man. The hotel was hosting an economic conference at the time, attended by economic leaders from other parts of Europe. An anonymous caller warned of the attack, allowing the hotel to evacuate its guests and employees. The caller said the bombing was a protest against NATO bombings then being carried out in Serbia.

May 20, 1999   The Red Brigades-PCC claims responsibility for the assassination of Italian Labor Ministry advisor Massimo D'Antona near his home in Rome.

June 4, 1999   Two members of the Turkish group Dev Sol (DHKP-C) are killed by police as they attempt to attack the U.S. consulate-general in Istanbul with rockets and guns.

September 1999   Austrian police kill suspected German RAF terrorist Horst Ludwig-Mayer and arrest his accomplice Andrea Klump. Klump is extradited to Germany for membership in the outlawed RAF and for possible complicity in several of its actions.

October 12, 1999   TIKKO terrorists open fire at random in Suluova, Amasya Province, Turkey, killing one person.

2000   Revolutionary Proletarian Initiative Nuclei (NIPR), a leftist extremist group, appears in Rome. The group, which identifies with the ideology of the Red Brigades and adopts its logo of a five-point star with a circle around it, has about 12 members.

2000   Italy's counter-terrorism efforts focus primarily on the Red Brigades-PCC which assassinated Labor Ministry advisor Massimo D'Antona in 1999. Leaks from the investigation complicate the arrest and interrogation of several suspects, however. One much-publicized suspect is released because of lack of evidence, but remains under investigation. On April 2, 2003, Nadia Lioce, a member of the Red Brigades, is officially charged with D'Antona's murder.

January 2000　　Johannes Weinreich, a former RAF member and lieutenant to Carlos the Jackal, is convicted of murder and attempted murder during an attack in 1983 on a French cultural center in West Berlin.

June 9, 2000　　British military attaché Stephen Saunders is killed while driving his car in Athens. In a 13-page communiqué, the 17 November group takes responsibility for the crime, justifying it as retribution for the role of the British government with NATO in air raids in Kosovo.

July 6, 2000　　Two fire bombs are found in the offices of the Italian Confederation of Trade Unions (CISL). The Revolutionary Proletarian Nucleus claims credit, saying the office was targeted because it signed an agreement with businesses allowing easier firing of employees.

September 15, 2000　　Members of the Nuclei Territoriali Antimperialisti (NTA), the Italian terrorist group formed in 1995, detonate two bombs at the offices of the Foreign Trade Institute and the Central European Initiative in Rome.

November 2000　　RAF member Andrea Klump goes on trial on charges of participation in a failed attack on the NATO base at Rota, Spain, in 1988.

November 12, 2000　　The Revolutionary Nuclei claim responsibility for four bomb blasts in Athens, which target branches of the U.S. Citibank, Britain's Barclays bank, and the studio of a Greek-American sculptor. No one is injured.

December 2000　　Germany's Foreign Minister Joschka Fischer testifies at the trial of acquaintance Hans-Joachim Klein. Klein is charged with three murders in connection with the infamous 1975 attack on OPEC ministers in Vienna led by Carlos the Jackal.

2001　　The leading industrialized democracies, known as the Group of Eight (G-8), produces an Action Plan for improved counter-terrorism coordination among the members.

January 3, 2001　　A Dev Sol (DHKP-C) operative walks into a police regional headquarters in Istanbul and detonates a bomb strapped to his body, killing a policeman and injuring seven others. This is the first, but not the last, time the group carries out a suicide attack.

April 10, 2001　　The NIPR, the Italian terrorist group that first appeared only in 2000, claims responsibility for a bomb attack on a building that houses a U.S.-Italian relations association and the Institute of International Affairs in Rome, saying the blast is to protest recent attempts to limit the right of workers to strike.

September 10, 2001　　A Dev Sol (DHKP-C) suicide bomber attacks a police booth in a public square in Istanbul, killing two policemen, mortally wounding an Australian tourist, and injuring more than 20 others.

September 17 or 18, 2001   Five letters are mailed from Princeton, New Jersey, to different media organizations contaminated with the deadly anthrax virus. Neither the individual or group responsible nor the motive for these attacks has been identified.

September 19, 2001   A letter addressed to the actress Jennifer Lopez containing a Star of David and a bluish powder arrives in the mail room of the supermarket tabloid *The Sun* in Boca Raton, Florida. Robert Stevens, a photo editor at the newspaper, sniffs some of the powder and falls ill. He is found to have been exposed to the deadly anthrax virus. On October 5 he dies as a result of contracting inhalation anthrax.

October 6–9, 2001   Two more anthrax letters are mailed, targeting U.S. Senators Thomas Daschle and Patrick Leahy. Both are intercepted before the senators are exposed.

October 22, 2001   Two United States Postal Service workers in the Washington, D.C., area die from pulmonary anthrax contracted from handling contaminated mail.

October 31, 2001   Kathy Nguyen, a New York City hospital worker, dies of inhalation anthrax. It is not clear where she contracted the disease.

November 21, 2001   Ottilie Lundgren, 94, of Oxford, Connecticut, is diagnosed with inhalation anthrax. The source is most likely contaminated mail, although no anthrax was detected in her home. She is the fifth and final person to die of the disease.

February 2002   Italian terrorist group NIPR claims responsibility for an explosion on Via Palermo adjacent to the Interior Ministry in Rome.

March 19, 2002   The Red Brigades-PCC assassinates Professor Marco Biagi, a Labor Ministry advisor and one of the authors of controversial labor reforms. He is gunned down outside his Bologna home as he is cycling home from work. Investigators discover that Biagi is shot by the same gun that was used in 1999 to kill D'Antona. On March 21, the Italian prime minister, Silvio Berlusconi, vows to press ahead with controversial labor market changes in defiance of the killing.

July 18, 2002   Greek law-enforcement officials finally dismantle Greece's most notorious terrorist group, 17 November. Having identified 17 November's "signature" gun following the arrest of Savvas Xiros on June 29, Greek police arrest the group's suspected leader, Alexandros Giotopoulos. By the time he is put on trial in July 2003, 19 suspects are charged with 23 murders. The trial ends on December 8 with the conviction of 15 members and the acquittal of four. Giotopoulos is given 21 life terms—the longest sentence in Greek history—and Dimitris Koufodinas receives 13 life terms. Four other members are sentenced to as many as ten life terms, although they will likely spend a maximum of 25 years in prison. Due to a 20-year statute of limitations in Greek law, group members cannot be sentenced for the first four killings they committed.

November 5, 2002   Argentine police, together with the local office of Interpol, capture Leonardo Bertulazzi, former head of logistics of the Red Brigades.

January 2003   The Turkish Communist Party/Marxist-Leninist (TKP/ML) announces that it is changing its name to the Maoist Communist Party (MKP). The group's armed unit TIKKO changes its name to the People's Liberation Army (HKO).

March 2, 2003   During a shoot-out between police and Red Brigades terrorists on a train traveling between Rome and Florence, a terrorist and a policeman are killed. Activist Nadia Desdemona Lioce is captured. She is tried and convicted on charges relating to several assassinations and sentenced to life in prison.

May 20, 2003   A member of Dev Sol (DHKP-C), is killed in Ankara, Turkey, when a bomb that she had attached to her body explodes in the lavatory of a cafe.

June 24, 2004   A bomb detonates aboard a passenger bus in Istanbul, killing four people, including the bomber, and injuring at least 15 others. Dev Sol (DHKP-C) claims responsibility for the attack, but says the bomb detonated prematurely.

July 1, 2005   A suicide bomber from Dev Sol (DHKP-C) is killed by Turkish security officials in Ankara after he attempts to enter a building where Prime Minister Recep Tayyip Erdogan has offices.

3

Nationalist Terrorism in Europe and North America

Nationalist tensions in Europe had been a prime cause of political violence for many centuries. Conflicts between countries over territory and even hegemony on the continent continued throughout the twentieth century. But after World War I there were few nationalist battles left within European states. Germany, France, and Italy had been forged into coherent states and sub-nationalism disappeared except for footnotes. The breakup of the Austro-Hungarian empire also eliminated many pre-1918 issues. The old Russian empire, after the Communist revolution, proclaimed itself a state in which all ethnic groups were equal. And if this were not true, any expression of dissent was harshly repressed.

There were still some ethnic conflicts in which a group sought national self-determination by succession from an existing state. Yugoslavia, a virtual confederation of ethnic groups—Macedonians, Croatians, Serbians, Albanians, and others—frequently saw political violence as a result of this situation which at times involved terrorism. But most national groups could also claim a homeland elsewhere in Europe.

This factor has frequently become an issue in international politics, sometimes involving terrorism. The existence of German minorities in such countries as Poland and Czechoslovakia was a rationale for the expansionism of Nazi Germany. The secret sponsorship of a seemingly independent nationalist group in Austrian-ruled Bosnia-Herzegovina was a ploy of Serbian intelligence which led to World War I. There were some other groups whose location became the occasion for ethnic conflict, as with the Hungarian-inhabited but often Romanian-ruled region of Transylvania.

In Europe, though, the existence of a long-running conflict producing a nationalist terrorist organization seems to require a never-fully-integrated group having two features: no national homeland and dissatisfaction by at least some members with the state where they lived. Within Western Europe, the two cases that best meet these criteria have been the Irish and the Basques.

Other scattered terrorist actions occurred stemming from fringe nationalist extremists, notably the Quebec Liberation Front (FLQ) demanding an independent state in Canada. But none of these were sustained.

Ireland's Terrorist Troubles

The Irish story of terrorism is a multi-layered one in a way perhaps unique in the world regarding terrorism. Ireland was a Celtic, Catholic society ruled for many centuries by an Anglo-Saxon/Norman Protestant colonial power which incorporated it more tightly than any other territory in its far-flung British empire. Yet much of the same can be said of Wales and Scotland, where nationalist political violence has never taken place in modern times.

In Ireland, political violence began as sabotage by Irish peasants against English landlords. During the nineteenth century, Irish activists sought independence by peaceful means, by terrorist methods, and through alliances with Britain's foreign enemies. Within Britain itself, there was considerable sympathy at least for Irish self-rule, as long as peaceful strategies were pursued. The failed 1916 Easter uprising was followed by a guerrilla war in which Britain was no longer willing to pay the price. At last in 1937, Ireland became an independent country, albeit without the six northern provinces, which remained under British rule.

The second phase of fighting was a civil war between two groups in Ireland—the nationalists, who accepted the compromise with Britain, and the more radical parties, who rejected it. The moderates prevailed and a considerable proportion of the radicals accepted the situation, but the Irish Republican Army (IRA) preserved the radical position, carrying out occasional outbursts of terrorist violence in the ensuing decades.

The third era in the drama of terrorism really begins in the mid-1960s, at a time of internal conflict in Northern Ireland. The Protestants, who strongly favored continued ties with Britain, were mostly descendants of Protestant Scottish immigrants. The central issue in the 1960s' conflict was to obtain equal rights for the minority Catholics, but this quickly slid into the more traditional issues of Irish nationalism and unification with Ireland.

Both sides formed militias that were ready to use terrorism against each other's population. In this two-sided terrorist battle, militants considered the killing of individuals on the other side—often ordinary citizens—a normal part of the conflict, and it continued for 30 years. For the IRA, terrorism was both a tradition and the product of political frustration. There was no way that a Catholic minority could force Britain to leave or the Protestants to give up.

Like much terrorism elsewhere, terrorism in Ireland had little political effect except to damage the society and economy of Northern Ireland. The majority on each side supported their communal leaderships but was not going to be driven to revolutionary action. Recognizing the impasse, most Catholic terrorist groups accepted a cease-fire in 1994. The level of violence fell sharply and another round of the long-running conflict came to an end.

1966	A long period of violence begins in British-ruled Northern Ireland between Protestants and Catholics. The Northern Irish Protestants, known as Loyalists because they favor continued close ties with the United Kingdom, form the paramilitary Ulster Volunteer Force (UVF) to fight the Irish Republican paramilitaries. These forces are known as Republican because they favor breaking ties with the United Kingdom and becoming part of the Irish Republic. The Red Hand Commandos is a Loyalist paramilitary group associated with the UVF. During this year, three civilians are killed, two Catholic men and an elderly Protestant woman by the UVF/Red Hand Commandos.
August 1968	Meliton Manzanaz, chief of secret police in the Basque city of San Sebastian, is assassinated outside his house by Euskadi Ta Askatasuna (ETA) members. This is the first successful terrorist attack engineered by the ETA. Six ETA members are sentenced to death for the killing.
1969	In Northern Ireland, 19 people—including 15 civilians, a policeman (a member of the Royal Ulster Constabulary), two IRA members, and a UVF member—die this year.
1969	During the year, the paramilitary organization known as the Provisional Irish Republican Army (PIRA), most often referred to as the IRA, is formed. The IRA's goal is to drive the British out of Northern Ireland by force. The organi-

zation is a splinter group of the Official IRA (OIRA), which descends from the original IRA that fought to establish the Irish republic decades earlier.

1969   The Grey Wolves are formed as the youth wing of the Turkish Nationalist Movement Party (MHP). The Grey Wolves become involved in criminal and terrorist activities and try to foment revolution in the Soviet territory of Azerbaijan.

1970   The death toll in Northern Ireland is 29 in this year. Among the dead are 19 civilians, two Ulster policemen, and six IRA members.

October 5, 1970   Members of the Quebec Liberation Front (FLQ) kidnap British Trade Commissioner James Richard Cross in Quebec.

October 10, 1970   The FLQ kidnaps Canadian Vice Premier and Minister of Labor Pierre Laporte, demanding that the Canadian government release 13 FLQ prisoners and let them go to Algeria or Cuba. They also ask for $500,000 in gold, the name of an informer who led to the discovery of an FLQ hideout a few months earlier, and the reinstatement of post office workers in Quebec who had been fired. The government offers only safe passage abroad in exchange for the release of Laporte and James Richard Cross, who had been kidnapped a few days earlier. Laporte is murdered, and his body is discovered in the trunk of a car on October 18. On December 3, the kidnappers release James Richard Cross. The following year, on December 28, 1971, the kidnappers are captured; three are sentenced to life imprisonment.

October 16, 1970   Following the wave of FLQ violence in Quebec, the Canadian government authorizes security forces to arrest 500 suspected FLQ terrorists. Following the crackdown, FLQ terror stops.

1971   Violent deaths in Northern Ireland soar to 180 in this year. The victims include 94 civilians, 23 Republican, and three Loyalist group members.

February 9, 1971   Five civilians, including two BBC engineers, are killed by a land mine while driving near Trillick in Tyrone, Northern Ireland. Their Land Rover is mistaken by the IRA for a British army vehicle.

August 25, 1971   A Protestant man is killed when an IRA bomb explodes at offices in Belfast, the capital of Northern Ireland. A warning is made by telephone, but the device explodes as 600 employees are evacuating the building. Thirty-five people are injured in the attack, including a pregnant woman, with at least two incurring severe injuries.

October 9, 1971   A Protestant woman is killed and 19 people are injured when a UVF bomb explodes in the Fiddler's House, a Catholic-owned bar in the predominantly Catholic Falls area of Belfast.

November 2, 1971   Three Protestant civilians, two men and one woman, are killed and 30 people are injured in an IRA bomb attack on the Red Lion Bar in Belfast. Three men enter the bar with the bomb and tell everyone they have ten seconds to evacuate. The explosion occurs after six seconds, leaving the majority of customers caught in the blast. While the primary target of the terrorists is an Ulster police station next to the pub, that building remains undamaged.

December 4, 1971   Fifteen people are killed and 16 injured when UVF terrorists detonate a bomb in a Catholic bar in Belfast. The Tramore Bar, more commonly known as McGurk's, is totally destroyed. In 1976, Robert Campbell confesses to driving the car that delivered the bomb to the pub and receives 16 life sentences.

December 11, 1971   Four people, a Protestant man, a Catholic man, and two Protestant infants, are killed, and 19 are injured in a bomb explosion in a furniture showroom in a predominantly Protestant area in west Belfast. No organization claims responsibility, but it is generally thought to be the work of the IRA as a reprisal to the McGurk's bombing the previous week.

December 17, 1971   One man is killed and five injured in a bomb attack on a bar in the predominantly Catholic area of west Belfast. It is thought that three UVF men enter the Star pub and then exit after leaving the bomb on the doorstep, where it explodes.

1972   The total number of people who die this year in the troubles in Northern Ireland is 497, including 259 civilians, 108 British soldiers, 26 members of the Ulster Defense Regiment (UDR, a special unit of the British army established in 1970, staffed by residents of Northern Ireland), and 17 Ulster policemen. Of the paramilitaries who are killed, 74 are Republicans and 11 are Loyalists.

1972   The Ulster Defense Association (UDA) is established when several small Loyalist groups merge to counteract the strengthening of the IRA. UDA's main aim is to protect the Protestants and Loyalists, but they also carry out terrorist acts against the Catholic side. The paramilitary Ulster Freedom Fighters (UFF) carry out attacks with the tacit support of the UDA. Since there is no official connection, the UDA is able to remain a legal organization.

January 30, 1972   Thirteen Catholic men are shot dead by the British army's Parachute Regiment following a civil rights march in Derry in what becomes known as Bloody Sunday. The killings serve as an impetus to the IRA, which gains in strength after this incident.

January 31, 1972   In one of a series of Republican attacks following Bloody Sunday, an IRA bomb explodes in central Belfast outside the British Home Stores, killing one Catholic man and injuring two others.

February 22, 1972   Six English civilian workers and one British soldier are killed and 17 injured in an Official IRA car bomb attack on the Parachute Regiment's headquarters in Aldershot, Hampshire, in southern England. An Irish man who lives in London is convicted of the murders and sentenced to life imprisonment in November.

March 4, 1972   Two Catholic women are killed and 70 people injured in an IRA bomb in a restaurant in Belfast city center. The Abercorn Bar, which is completely destroyed in the attack, is crowded with young people when a bag, left at a table, explodes.

March 20, 1972   Eight are killed—four Protestant civilians, two Ulster police officers, one UDR officer, and a British soldier—and 150 injured when an IRA car bomb explodes near Belfast city center.

May 13, 1972   One person is killed and 63 injured when Loyalists detonate a car bomb outside a Catholic-owned bar in west Belfast.

May 28, 1972   Eight Catholics are killed, including four civilians, when an IRA bomb explodes prematurely in the Short Strand area of east Belfast. Two of the dead are found to have traces of explosives on their hands, suggesting they had been handling the bomb before the blast.

July 12, 1972   A hooded man enters a pub and kills two men, a Catholic and a Protestant, in predominantly Protestant Portadown in County Armagh. A terrorist from the Ulster Defense Association/Ulster Freedom Fighters (UDA/UFF) is caught and later sentenced to life imprisonment.

July 21, 1972   Nine people are killed and an additional 130 severely injured when 22 bombs detonate around Belfast on Bloody Friday. Thirty years after the event, the IRA issues an official apology.

July 31, 1972   A total of nine people, including five Catholics and four Protestants, are killed, and another 30 are injured in three bomb explosions in Claudy, in predominantly Catholic County Derry. The IRA is likely responsible.

August 22, 1972   Nine people—five Catholic civilians, one Protestant civilian, and three IRA terrorists—are killed and six are injured when a bomb, being taken through customs at a checkpoint in Newry, County Down, explodes prematurely. The IRA issues a statement claiming responsibility.

September 14, 1972   Three people are killed and 50 injured in a UDA/UFF car bomb attack on the Imperial Hotel in the predominantly Catholic area of west Belfast.

September 26, 1972   Two Catholic men are killed and 17 are injured when an Ulster Volunteer Force (UVF) car bomb goes off outside a bar in Smithfield, near central Belfast.

December 20, 1972   Four Catholic men and one Protestant man are killed and four people are injured in a UDA/UFF shooting spree which takes place in a bar in predominantly Catholic Waterside in County Derry. After the two assailants enter the bar and begin firing machine guns indiscriminately at customers, they escape in a stolen car and are never caught.

1973   Two hundred sixty-three die in the Northern Ireland conflict this year, including 133 civilians, 59 soldiers and 13 Ulster police officers. Thirty-seven Republicans and 12 Loyalists are also among the dead.

January 27, 1973   One of the first Armenian terrorist acts against Turkish citizens occurs in Los Angeles, California, when Turkish Consul General to the United States in Los Angeles Mehmet Baydar and his deputy, Bahadir Demir, are murdered by Armenian-American Gurgen (Karakin) Yanikian. Yanikian is arrested and sentenced to life imprisonment, but is paroled on December 31, 1984, and dies shortly afterwards.

May 15, 1973   A Protestant man is killed when he triggers an IRA booby-trap device, which was left in a derelict building near where he is working as a laborer. It is thought that warnings issued to the Ulster Constabulary had been an attempt to lure the security forces to the scene.

May 31, 1973   A Catholic man is killed when a bomb is thrown into a Catholic-owned bar in the center of Belfast. The UVF is responsible for the bombing, which is one of three Loyalist attacks on Catholic bars that night.

June 12, 1973   Six elderly Protestants, four women and two men, are killed when an IRA car bomb explodes in predominantly Protestant County Coleraine. Two men are found guilty of the murders at a trial in January 1974; one is sentenced to eight years' imprisonment and the other is given six life sentences.

December 20, 1973   Luis Carrero Blanco, 70, is killed in Madrid by a bomb placed under his car. Blanco was a longtime associate of Spanish dictator Francisco Franco and was serving as prime minister in the Franco government. The ETA claims responsibility for the assassination, whose purpose is to avenge the killing of nine Basque militants by the government.

1974   Violence in Northern Ireland results in a death toll of 304. The dead include 206 civilians, 45 soldiers, seven Ulster Defense Regiment (UDR) members, five Ulster police officers, 24 Republican paramilitaries, and six UDR Loyalists.

February 3, 1974   Twelve people are killed—nine of them soldiers—and 14 are injured in an IRA bomb explosion on a bus in England. The vehicle is transporting soldiers and their families from Manchester to an army camp and a Royal Air Force (RAF) base near Darlington.

May 17, 1974   Thirty-three people are killed in the Irish Republic in what comes to be known as the Dublin and Monaghan bombings, the worst atrocity there to date and the greatest loss of life in a single day of the conflict. Three car bombs explode in busy streets in Dublin during the evening rush hour, causing 26 deaths and 140 injuries. Ninety minutes later, a car bomb blast outside Greacen's Pub in Monaghan, near the border with Northern Ireland, kills seven more people.

The attacks coincide with a strike by the Loyalist Ulster Workers' Council in Northern Ireland, which is aimed at ending a power-sharing agreement between Loyalist and Unionist politicians, which had been agreed to in November 1973. The power-sharing agreement collapses on May 28. Nineteen years later, in 1993, the UVF would admit sole responsibility for the bombings in Dublin and Monaghan. There had long been speculation that British forces had played a role in the planning of the attacks.

June 9, 1974   A Catholic teenage girl is killed and 13 people are injured, including her father and two siblings, when a UDA/UFF bomb explodes outside a greyhound track on the outskirts of Belfast. A UFF operative admits that the organization is responsible but claims that the bomb detonated prematurely.

September 16, 1974   A prominent Protestant magistrate is murdered by the IRA at his home in east Belfast. A senior Catholic judge who recently advised a jury against a guilty verdict in a case against Ulster Volunteer Force (UVF) members is killed by the IRA in almost identical circumstances at the same time in south Belfast.

October 5, 1974   Five people are killed, including four soldiers and one civilian, and 57 are injured when an IRA bomb explodes at a pub in Guildford, England. Three men and one woman, known as the "Guilford Four," are convicted in 1975 of carrying out this attack, and of the bombing of a pub in Woolwich one month later. Fifteen years later, in 1989, the four will be released after a review shows that they were convicted on the basis of coerced confessions and misleading evidence by authorities. No one else will be charged with the crime.

November 20, 1974   A Catholic man is killed and two people are injured when two UVF gunmen enter a pub in the predominantly Protestant district of Larne and open fire with a submachine gun. The attack is in retaliation for an attack on a leading Loyalist in Larne on the same day. In May 1975, four men are given life sentences for the shooting spree.

November 21, 1974   Twenty-one people are killed and over 160 are injured in IRA bomb attacks on two pubs in Birmingham, England. The first explosion takes place at the Mulb, killing ten and injuring dozens. A few minutes later, another bomb goes off at the nearby Tavern in the Town, killing 11. The legal proceedings against those who come to be known as the Birmingham Six are one of the most controversial in English legal history. Following the attacks, six men of Irish origin are arrested, and on August 15, 1975, they are each sentenced to life imprisonment. They always maintain their innocence and claim that they had signed false confessions after being brutalized by police officers. Their first appeal, in January 1987, is rejected, but on March 14, 1991, their convictions are overturned by the Court of Appeal and they are released after 16 years in jail. The case is considered a grave miscarriage of justice. The real bombers are never prosecuted.

December 8, 1974   A splinter group called the Irish National Liberation Army (INLA) is formed by expelled members of the Official IRA. Their aim is to establish a unified Communist state in Ireland. In advancing its aim to unify Ireland and Northern Ireland, the group perpetrates attacks against Protestants of Northern Ireland. In 1998, after coming under suspicion in the horrendous bombing in Omagh, INLA declares a cease-fire. Despite abiding by the cease-fire, the organization remains armed.

December 17, 1974   In downtown London, a man is killed when an IRA bomb explodes at a telephone exchange. Three other bombs explode in London that day with no injuries. No one is found responsible.

Armenian Nationalist Terrorism

Like Irish nationalist terrorism, its Armenian equivalent has a long pre–World War I history, interrupted and then revived in the context of modern radicalism. During the late nineteenth century, Armenian nationalism strove to recreate the ancient Armenian state out of the Ottoman Empire. Like Irish national feeling, a religious factor—the Christian Armenians versus the Muslim Ottomans—played a role in the Armenian movement. There was also the element of state sponsorship, with Czarist Russia providing some support to weaken its Ottoman rivals.

During World War I, in which Russia was fighting the Ottomans, the Russians gave backing to Armenian insurgents. Amidst bloody communal fighting and fear that the Czarist army's advance might be met with a supportive Armenian rising, the Ottoman government, led by the nationalistic Young Turks, decided to deport the Armenian population of Anatolia. Their property was despoiled and during the deportations hundreds of thousands of Armenians were murdered. Most of the survivors became refugees. Armenian groups continued the nationalist movement in exile during the following decade but with very little effect.

During the radical upsurge of the 1970s, and with help from Arab states and radical Arab movements opposed to Turkey, an Armenian terrorist group developed. It targeted mainly Turkish diplomats. With the loss of its Beirut base in 1982 and the killing of key leaders, the movement largely collapsed. Ironically, it was the fall of the Soviet Union which allowed the creation of an independent Armenia, satisfying Armenian national aspirations.

1975	Among the 207 fatalities of the Northern Ireland dispute in this year, 174 are civilians, 15 are soldiers, seven are Ulster Defense Regiment (UDR) members, and 11 are Ulster police.
1975	The Armenian Genocide Justice Commandos (JCAG) is founded in Beirut by the Tanak Party and the Armenian Revolutionary Federation (ARF). It is an Armenian nationalist revolutionary organization seeking to reestablish an independent Armenian state within the territory occupied by the former Republic of Armenia during World War I that is now part of eastern Turkey. JCAG is primarily nationalistic and its members are very Westernized nationalists who value Western and world public opinion highly, and therefore take pains to avoid harming non-Turkish nationals.
January 20, 1975	The Armenian Secret Army for the Liberation of Armenia (ASALA) is founded by Hagop Hagopian and Hagop Tarakciyan. It operates mainly out of Beirut. ASALA's primary objectives are to demand reparations from the Turkish government for the World War I–era killings of Armenians, which Armenians generally call an act of genocide, and to establish an independent Armenian state from northeastern Turkish territory. In contrast to the JCAG, ASALA also promotes Marxist-Leninist ideology and is aligned with international terrorist groups of similar leanings, including the Irish Republican Army (IRA), Italian Red Brigades (BR), and Kurdistan Workers' Party (PKK).
February 9, 1975	The mayor of the Basque town of Galdacano, Victor Legorburu Ibarreche, is shot to death and two police guards are wounded by four unidentified youths from ETA.
February 9, 1975	Two Catholic teenagers are killed in an Ulster Defense Associaton/Ulster Freedom Fighters (UDA/UFF) gun attack on a church adjacent to the predominantly Protestant area of north Belfast. They are leaving St. Bride's Church following the end of the service when two men approach and shoot them at close range. A congregant strikes one of the attackers with his collection box and is subsequently shot in the nose. No one is prosecuted for the killings.
April 12, 1975	Six Catholics are killed in an Ulster Volunteer Force (UVF) attack on a bar in east Belfast. A man places the bomb in the Strand Bar and jams a piece of wood across the door in order to prevent people from getting away. A man is charged with the murders and tried in September 1975, but is acquitted due to lack of evidence.

April 17, 1975   Three Catholics are killed when a UVF bomb explodes at a house in Killyliss, County Tyrone. The woman and her two brothers arrive at the cottage and trigger the blast by opening the door. The UVF claims responsibility, but no one is ever charged.

July 31, 1975   Three members of the well-known Irish music group Miami Showband are killed and two other members injured in a botched attempt by the UVF to frame them as IRA affiliates transporting a bomb. The band is driving towards Newry from Banbridge after a performance when they are stopped at a mock roadblock by a UVF gang disguised as military personnel. As they are lined up and questioned, two terrorists plant a bomb in the van, set to explode after they continue their journey. However, the device goes off prematurely when they close the door, killing the two instantly. Following the explosion, three band members are shot to death. The two remaining band members survive, one hiding in a ditch until the terrorists leave the scene. Two UVF men, who are also members of the UDA, are convicted of the murders on October 15, 1976, and sentenced to 35 years' imprisonment.

August 13, 1975   Five Protestants are killed and 60 are injured in an IRA bomb and gun attack on a bar in a predominantly Protestant area of west Belfast. Two men pull up outside the Bayardo Bar and one opens fire on two men standing outside. The second man then places a bomb at the entrance and then the two drive away. In May 1976, three men are convicted of carrying out the attack and sentenced to life imprisonment.

September 5, 1975   A British man and a Dutch woman are killed when an IRA bomb explodes at the Hilton Hotel in Park Lane, London. Four members of the IRA's Balcombe Street Gang are later convicted of manslaughter for the bombing, as well as for six other murders.

October 2, 1975   Eight civilians and four UVF terrorists are killed in a day of unprecedented violence across Northern Ireland. Four Catholics are shot to death at Casey's Bottling Plant in Millfield, west Belfast. A Protestant man is shot in east Belfast. A Catholic man is killed by a booby-trap bomb attack at his photographer's shop in north Belfast. A Catholic man is killed in a bomb and gun attack on a bar in County Antrim. A Protestant woman dies in a bomb attack on a bar in Killyleagh, County Down.

October 22, 1975   The Turkish Ambassador in Vienna, Daniş Tunaligïl, is shot dead by three Armenian terrorists at the embassy.

October 24, 1975   Turkey's Ambassador to France Ismail Erez and his driver, Talip Yener, are murdered by Armenian terrorists near the Turkish Embassy in Paris. This attack, and the one on the ambassador to Austria, are thought to have been perpetrated by both the Armenian Secret Army for the Liberation of Armenia (ASALA) and the Armenian Genocide Justice Commandos (JCAG).

December 19, 1975   Five people are killed in two attacks carried out by the UVF affiliated Red Hand Commandos in bars in County Armagh, Northern Ireland, and Dundalk, County Louth, Republic of Ireland. Although it is widely accepted that the Red Hand Commandos is responsible for both attacks, no one is ever charged.

1976	In this year, 307 lives are lost in the Northern Ireland conflict, including 220 civilians, 13 soldiers, 16 UDR members, and 24 Royal Ulster Constabulary (RUC) officers. Republican deaths reach 17, while 13 Loyalists are killed.
January 4, 1976	Three Catholics are killed, including a 17-year-old boy, in a UVF gun attack on their home in County Armagh. Three Catholic civilian political activists, including two men and one teenager, are killed by UVF gunfire at their home in County Down.
January 5, 1976	Ten Protestants are killed in an IRA massacre in south Armagh. The victims are on a minibus traveling home from work when they are stopped at a bogus checkpoint. A number of terrorists from a group calling itself the Republican Action Force order the men off the bus and line them up along the road. They ask each one what his religion is and the one Catholic among them is ordered away from the scene. Then the gang begins spraying bullets at the remaining workers, killing all but one, who is shot 18 times but manages to survive. The event is remembered as the Kingsmills or Whitecross Massacre and the IRA claims the attack is a retaliation for the murders of the members of two Catholic families the previous day. No one is ever charged for the attacks.
January 13, 1976	Four Catholic men and women, including a 19-year-old girl, are killed and 20 more are injured when an IRA bomb explodes prematurely at a shop in central Belfast.
January 17, 1976	The body of a Catholic, alleged to have been a Loyalist informer and shot dead by the IRA, is found in a ditch in west Belfast. A Catholic man and woman are killed in a UVF bombing on the Sheridan Bar in north Belfast.
January 22, 1976	A Catholic man is killed in a UDA shooting attack at his home in north Belfast. A Protestant man is shot dead by the UVF as he is driving with his five Catholic co-workers in his company's van in north Belfast.
February 7, 1976	Two Protestants, a woman and her teenage brother, are killed when an IRA bomb explodes in an abandoned car in Tyrone. A 14-year-old Catholic boy is killed as the result of a hidden Irish National Liberation Army (INLA) bomb meant to target security forces in Armagh. A 55-year-old Catholic man is dead in north Belfast after an attack by the UVF.
February 15, 1976	In a UDA/UFF shooting at a home in north Belfast, three women are killed, including a Catholic woman, her daughter, and their Protestant neighbor, who is visiting.
February 16, 1976	Turkey's First Secretary in Beirut, Oktar Cīrīt, is killed by ASALA terrorists.
February 27, 1976	A Protestant electric meter-reader is killed by an IRA booby-trapped bomb at an abandoned east Belfast home.
March 15, 1976	One is killed and another seriously injured in London by an IRA terrorist at the West Ham Underground station.
March 17, 1976	Four Catholics, including two 13-year-old boys, are killed and 11 are injured when a UVF car bomb explodes outside a bar in a predominantly Catholic sec-

tion of Tyrone. A man is convicted in connection with this attack and another double murder and is given six life sentences, but is later released.

April 7, 1976   Three Protestant civilians—mother, father, and daughter—are killed in a fire in their apartment resulting from a firebomb thrown into the drapery shop below. A man is convicted of the murders in 1980 and sentenced to three 20-year terms in prison. The following year, two sisters are convicted of this manslaughter and of IRA membership; however, they are released from prison in 1985.

April 8, 1976   A Catholic off-duty prison officer is murdered in a drive-by shooting outside his home in Tyrone. This murder is the first act in an IRA campaign against a government decision to get rid of the "special category" status that had been given to Republicans and Loyalists serving time in jail. The issue later leads to the 1981 Republican prison hunger strikes in which ten inmates die.

May 1, 1976   A Catholic man's body is found near Dundalk in County Louth, Republic of Ireland. He is believed to have been shot by members of the Red Hand Commando because of his resemblance to a leading IRA member.

May 13, 1976   The Protestant man suspected of being involved in the 1973 assassination of UDA vice chairman Tommy Herron is shot dead by the UDA/UFF while walking in east Belfast.

May 15, 1976   Five Catholics are killed in two UVF bombings at bars in central Belfast and Charlemont, County Armagh. The first explosion occurs at Clancy's Bar, Belfast, and kills three people. As the perpetrators drive away from the scene they fire at another bar, seriously wounding another man who later dies of his injuries. In September 1977, a man is convicted of the attacks and given three life sentences. Another man is convicted of the murders and receives four life sentences. A third man involved receives four life sentences in February 1979. In a second attack, a bomb goes off in Avenue Bar in central Belfast, killing two Catholic men and injuring 27. In September 1978, a man from Ballysillan is convicted for these and other sectarian murders and receives eight life sentences.

May 21, 1976   Javier de Ybarra y Bergé, a wealthy Basque industrialist, is kidnapped from his home near Bilbao by ETA members who demand a ransom of $15 million. Bergé's body is found on June 22.

May 21, 1976   A Protestant woman dies and many others are injured as the result of an IRA explosion on a train from Lisburn to Moira in Down. Shortly after, a teenage boy is detained for having carried out the attack.

June 4, 1976   A Protestant man is killed by a group of teenagers linked to the UDA. In September 1977, a teenage boy is ordered detained indefinitely for his involvement in the killing.

June 5, 1976   A Catholic man who is also a Sinn Féin political activist is shot and killed in a UDA attack at his home in north Belfast. Two Protestant men are killed when IRA terrorists bomb the Times Bar in north Belfast. Three Catholics and two Protestants are killed in a UVF shooting spree at the Chlorane Bar in west

Belfast. A Catholic man is killed at a bar in County Down as the result of a UVF bombing.

June 25, 1976

At Walker's Bar in Antrim, IRA terrorists assassinate three Protestants, including a woman, her teenage brother, and their cousin, who had been working as a security guard at the pub. The body of a young Catholic man, stabbed to death by UVF members, is discovered at a waste site in north Belfast.

July 2, 1976

A Catholic man and five Protestants are killed in a UVF gun attack at the Ramble Inn bar in Antrim.

July 21, 1976

Christopher Ewart-Biggs, the newly appointed British ambassador to Ireland, and a civil servant are assassinated and two others are wounded when a land mine goes off just outside the ambassador's home in Dublin, destroying the car in which they are driving. Three IRA members responsible for the attack are seen escaping but are never caught. The attack is also claimed by some to be in retaliation for the death of Peter Cleary, an IRA member who was gunned down by the British Army's SAS (special forces) on April 15, 1976.

July 29, 1976

In what is presumed a UVF bombing, three Catholic men are killed at the White Fort Inn in west Belfast.

July 30, 1976

Four Protestant men are killed when IRA members begin spraying bullets at the customers and workers of the Stag Inn in south Belfast.

August 1, 1976

A Protestant convert to Catholicism is shot dead by UDA members as they invade his girlfriend's home. This leads to a "retaliation" killing later that day. A Catholic man is attacked with an ax and badly beaten by an UVF gang known as the Shankill Butchers.

August 10, 1976

Three members of a Catholic family are killed in a freak incident when a soldier in pursuit shoots a fleeing IRA member, Danny Lennon, during a high-speed chase. Lennon loses control of his getaway car, which crashes into the family as they are walking along the sidewalk in west Belfast. Anne Maguire, the mother of the family, recovers from her physical injuries, but commits suicide four years later. The tragedy leads to the formation of the Peace People movement by Maguire's sister, Mairead Corrigan, and another Belfast woman, Betty Williams. Peace People becomes an international movement and Corrigan and Williams win the Nobel Peace Prize for 1976.

August 27, 1976

A Catholic family, including the husband, wife, and their ten-month-old baby, are killed when an UDA/UFF firebomb is thrown into their north Belfast residence.

September 24, 1976

A 17-year-old Catholic girl is shot at her home in north Belfast by the UDA. In an apparent retaliation for the killing, the same day the IRA shoots and kills two Protestant customers at the Cavehill Inn also located in north Belfast. Another Catholic teenager is shot to death by UDA/UFF members at the north Belfast store where she works.

September 25, 1976

A Catholic man is killed in a drive-by shooting in north Belfast while on his way to the Wolfe Tone Club, likely by UDA terrorists. A Protestant man and his daughter are shot in their home in west Belfast by Irish National Liberation Army members. The father, a bank manager, is the likely target as he is believed to be a police officer.

October 4, 1976   Juan Maria de Araluce y Villar, a member of Spain's Council of the Realm and of the Cortes General (the Spanish legislature), is assassinated by several ETA gunmen in San Sebastian. His driver and three bodyguards are also killed in the attack and ten passersby are wounded. While Araluce is a firm opponent of Basque autonomy under Franco's dictatorship, he had recently advocated limited autonomy for the four Spanish Basque provinces.

October 9, 1976   A Protestant prison officer at the Magilligan prison is murdered by IRA gunmen outside his Derry city residence. A Protestant woman is killed as the result of a series of IRA firebomb attacks at a boutique in Antrim. In what seems to be in retaliation for her death, a Catholic man is killed nearby, most likely by Ulster Volunteer Force (UVF) members, who beat him and finally set him on fire.

October 13, 1976   A Scottish man, a former army member, attempting to the join the UDA, sets out for their headquarters but is led to the Windsor Bar instead. There, UVF members interrogate him, torture him, and shoot him dead. A teenage boy and his father, who is an UVF member, are killed as the result of an IRA attack on their Armagh residence.

October 28, 1976   Maire Drumm, among the most prominent public figures of the Republican movement, and former vice president of Sinn Féin, is shot dead by Ulster Defense Association/Ulster Freedom Fighters (UDA/UFF) members at a hospital in north Belfast where she has been admitted for a minor operation. At least four men are taken into custody in relation to the murder, though not all are convicted.

October 30, 1976   A university student who is a well-known Catholic peace activist is abducted and murdered by the UVF Shankill Butchers gang in west Belfast. Two delivery drivers, both Catholic, are killed by the UVF in north Belfast.

November 28, 1976   As the result of an IRA booby-trap bomb in an unoccupied house in Armagh, a Catholic teenage girl is killed and her friend is injured. In another IRA booby-trap explosion the same day in Derry city, a Catholic man is killed and two men are injured by a bomb that had been intended for security forces.

December 6, 1976   A 14-year-old Catholic girl standing outside her home is killed by UVF gunmen.

December 18, 1976   In a joint IRA-INLA attempt to plant a bomb in the Tavern Bar in Armagh, a Protestant security guard is shot as he tries to stop the attackers.

1977   Deaths reach 113 from political violence in Northern Ireland, among them 55 civilians, 14 Ulster police, 15 soldiers, 14 Ulster Defense Regiment (UDR) members, eight Republicans, and seven Loyalists.

January 1, 1977   A Protestant baby is killed by an IRA bomb placed near his parents' residence in north Belfast.

January 23, 1977	The bodies of a Protestant man and a Catholic man who had been stabbed and shot are discovered in a burning car in west Belfast. UDA members are believed to be responsible.
February 7, 1977	The body of a Protestant man is discovered in a stream in west Belfast, likely killed by UDA terrorists.
February 26, 1977	A Protestant justice of the peace is shot and killed by the IRA in Armagh.
February 27, 1977	A Catholic man is murdered by the IRA after leaving a club in north Belfast.
March 1, 1977	A Protestant man is shot by Irish National Liberation Army (INLA) terrorists in Portadown.
March 2, 1977	A Catholic English businessman is shot and killed at his south Belfast office by the IRA.
March 4, 1977	A Catholic assistant public prosecutor for County Down is murdered by IRA gunmen at a bar in Tyrone.
March 16, 1977	A Protestant man is shot to death while riding his bike in Derry. It is not known who was responsible.
March 17, 1977	A Catholic man is murdered by UDA gunfire while driving his car in west Belfast.
April 10, 1977	A ten-year-old Catholic boy is killed by a UVF Shankill Butchers bomb in west Belfast. A Catholic man is shot and killed by the IRA in west Belfast.
April 23, 1977	A 72-year-old security guard is shot dead in a UVF attack at the Legahorey Inn in Armagh.
July 27, 1977	A Catholic man is shot in west Belfast by the Official IRA as he is getting out of a car. In a separate incident, a Catholic man is killed by OIRA gunmen at his west Belfast residence.
October 7, 1977	A Protestant man, the chief principal officer at Maze prison and secretary of the Prison Officers' Association, is killed by IRA gunmen as he is leaving a conference in south Belfast.
December 18, 1977	Bombs placed by four ETA members at the Lemóniz nuclear plant in Spain, which is under construction, kill two workers. The ETA later claims it planned to blow up the reactors.
1978	The party Herri Batasuna (People's Unity) is founded as a coalition of leftist nationalist political groups following the Basque region's rejection of the new Spanish constitution. The party denies any links to the ETA, but many believe Herri Batasuna to be the ETA's political wing.
1978	In the Northern Ireland conflict, some 88 individuals die during the year. Among the fatalities are 46 civilians, ten Ulster Constabulary members, and 16 soldiers. Seven members of the UDR and seven Republicans activists are also killed.

Kurdish Terrorism against Turkey

In Turkey, where both nationhood and nationalism were a far newer phenomenon, Kemal Atatürk had created a unified, secular state in the 1920s. Turkey was thus at the stage reached much earlier in Western Europe. Despite the successful integration of Turks into a nation-state, a situation that had never previously existed in their history, the Kurds remained a potentially dissatisfied sector. In the 1920s, there had been a major Kurdish revolt against Atatürk, albeit on traditionalist grounds opposing his modernization program.

The Kurds are a non-Turkish, non-Arab people spread among modern Iran, Iraq, and Syria, as well as Turkey. They have produced serial and separate nationalist movements which have never succeeded in establishing a Kurdish state. Aside from the possible national grievances, the Kurds lived in the poorest section of Turkey. The Kurdistan Workers' Party (PKK) was a left-wing movement combining Marxism and nationalism. Its use of terrorism, as with many such groups, was partly designed to wipe out the ethnic Turkish presence in the areas it claims. The movement had much in common with Middle East terrorist groups, especially given its sponsorship as a political cat's-paw by Greece, Iran, Iraq, and Syria.

The Turkish state did not hesitate to fight back with the toughest of means, using a variety of counter-terrorist and counterinsurgency techniques. Clearly, the PKK was increasingly facing military defeat in the 1990s. With the loss of Syrian safe haven due to Turkish military pressure and the capture of PKK leader Abdullah Öcalan in February 1998, the PKK gave up its terrorist war, though it revived on a smaller scale thereafter.

1978	The Kurdistan Workers' Party (PKK) becomes officially operational, having been formed in 1974 by a group of students in Turkey. Led by Abdullah "Apo" Öcalan, it is a leftist Kurdish nationalist organization. It wages a vicious campaign of terror against Turkey with the aim of inciting a revolution that would free the Kurdish people and establish an independent Kurdish state.
February 12, 1978	A 70-year-old Catholic woman and her 10-year-old grandson are killed by a UVF firebomb thrown at her house in north Belfast.
February 17, 1978	Twelve Protestants are killed, and over 30 are injured in an IRA firebomb attack at the La Mon House hotel in east Belfast during the annual dinner-dance of the Irish Collie Club. The IRA claims responsibility. In west Belfast, 25 people are arrested in relation to the attack. In September 1981, a man receives 12 life sentences for the murders.
March 3, 1978	A Protestant woman and soldier are murdered by the IRA in north Belfast during Rag Day, an event in which Queen's University students conduct a parade and a fair to raise money for charity. During her funeral, 2,000 Queen's University students march to Belfast city hall.
March 17, 1978	A nuclear power station outside Bilbao, Spain, is bombed by members of Euskadi Ta Askatasuna (ETA), killing two workers and wounding 14 others.
April 8, 1978	A group of masked terrorists invade a west Belfast residence and abduct and murder a man. In March 1999, more than 20 years later, the IRA will issue a statement admitting they killed him.
October 8, 1978	Two members of MHP, a Turkish right-wing extremist party, kill seven university students who are members of the pro-Communist Turkish Labor Party in Ankara. In 1999, two men are found guilty of the attack and sentenced to death.

October 25, 1978   A Catholic man is killed near his home in north Belfast, presumably by the UDA.

November 20, 1978   Two policemen are killed and 11 wounded outside the Basauri police barracks near Bilbao by a group of terrorists, likely from the ETA.

November 26, 1978   A Protestant man, the deputy governor of Maze prison, is shot dead by IRA members at his north Belfast residence.

1979   The Northern Ireland troubles result in 125 fatalities in this year. Among the fatalities, 44 are civilians, 14 are Ulster police officers, 37 are soldiers, and ten are in the UDR. Nine Republicans and two Loyalists are also among the dead.

January 2, 1979   Major José Maria Herrera, adjutant to the military governor of Guipúzcoa Province, is gunned down by ETA terrorists outside his home in San Sebastian. A few hours later, police Corporal Francisco Berlanga Robles is killed while trying to deactivate a bomb planted at the entrance of the home of the Pamplona leader of New Force, an extreme right-wing party.

January 3, 1979   General Constantino Ortin Gil, the military governor of Madrid, is murdered outside his apartment building by two gunmen. He is the sixth-high-ranking military officer killed by the ETA in Spain since November 1977.

January 28, 1979   The body of an Englishman who had been beaten to death by the Irish National Liberation Army (INLA) is discovered outside of Dublin. They claim he was in the British SAS (special forces).

March 22, 1979   Sir Richard Sykes, the British Ambassador to the Netherlands, is killed along with his valet at his official residence in Holland by IRA terrorists.

March 30, 1979   Conservative Member of Parliament and shadow Northern Ireland Secretary Airey Neave is killed in London as the result of an INLA booby-trap bomb placed under his car. In July, INLA announces that it murdered Neave because he was a "militarist."

April 22, 1979   The body of a Catholic man is discovered in a river in Armagh, likely killed by UDA/UFF terrorists.

May 25, 1979   Lieutenant Luis Gomez Hortiguela, Colonels Agustin Laso and Juan Avalos Gomariz and their driver are assassinated in the center of Madrid by ETA members.

June 13, 1979   One worker is killed by a bomb detonated by ETA terrorists in the turbine room of the Lemóniz nuclear reactor.

June 19, 1979   A retired Protestant businessman is killed and four people are injured after an IRA bomb attack on the Marine Hotel in Ballycastle, Antrim.

July 28, 1979   A Catholic man is gunned down by a UVF member in a drive-by shooting in Armagh.

July 29, 1979 Five persons are killed and 113 wounded by three synchronized bombs in Barajas Airport in Madrid and two main railway stations in the Spanish capital. The ETA claims responsibility.

August 22, 1979 Lord Louis Mountbatten, cousin of Britain's Queen Elizabeth II and a retired senior naval officer and diplomat, is killed along with his 14-year-old grandson, his daughter's 82-year-old mother-in-law, and a 15-year-old boat-boy, when an IRA bomb explodes on his boat while the family is vacationing at its home in Sligo, Ireland. On November 23, 1979, Thomas McMahon, an IRA terrorist, is sentenced to life in prison for the assassination, but he is released in August 1998 in accordance with the Good Friday Agreement.

September 19, 1979 A Protestant assistant prison governor is shot dead by the IRA while at a traffic light in north Belfast.

September 23, 1979 Brigadier General Lorenzo Gonzáles Vallés is assassinated by ETA members while strolling with his wife along the seaside esplanade in San Sebastian.

October 12, 1979 Ahmet Benler, son of Turkey's ambassador in The Hague, is killed in an armed attack. Both the Armenian Secret Army for the Liberation of Armenia (ASALA) and the Armenian Genocide Justice Commandos (JCAG) take responsibility.

October 24, 1979 A Protestant restaurant owner is shot dead by the IRA at his west Belfast residence.

October 27, 1979 A Socialist Party worker is assassinated by two ETA terrorists in Spain. The killing spurs protest among Basque workers and labor unions, which organize a 24-hour general strike on October 29.

November 7, 1979 A Protestant prison officer is shot dead by an INLA member at a bus stop in north Belfast.

November 8, 1979 Two Catholic men are killed by the UDA/UFF as they are leaving a bar in east Belfast. In an act of revenge, a Protestant security guard is shot and killed by Republicans outside the factory where he works.

1980 Eighty-six individuals die in the Northern Ireland conflict in 1980, including nine Ulster police officers, 11 soldiers, nine UDR members, five Republican terrorists, and two Loyalist paramilitaries. The remaining dead are civilians.

1980 Following a military coup in Turkey and the declaration of general martial law in the Kurdish provinces, the PKK's activities are brought to a halt. The party moves many of its activities into the Kurdish communities in Western and Northern Europe. Abdullah Öcalan, PKK leader, moves to Syria and uses Syrian facilities to train terrorist groups for cross-border attacks against targets in Turkey. The group will return to Turkey in the summer of 1983.

January 2, 1980 A Protestant truck driver who is a former UDR member is killed when three IRA gunmen shoot him outside his home in Armagh.

January 3, 1980	The body of a Catholic man who had been killed by UDA terrorists is discovered in west Belfast.
January 17, 1980	Three individuals are killed on a train in south Belfast when an IRA bomb goes off prematurely.
April 8, 1980	The relationship between the PKK and ASALA is officially formalized in a joint press conference at Sidon, Lebanon.
July 29, 1980	Spanish General Arturo Criado Amunategui and his bodyguard are killed by three gunmen who fire at his car in Madrid. Police believe ETA is responsible.
July 31, 1980	ASALA gunmen assassinate the Turkish Embassy Administrative Attaché in Athens, Galip Özmen, and his daughter while the family is in their car. His wife and son are seriously wounded.
August 5, 1980	Two ASALA gunmen storm the Turkish Consulate General in Lyon, France, and demand the location of the consul general. When the Turkish doorman does not answer, the gunmen kill him then open fire in the waiting area, killing one visitor and wounding 11.
August 29, 1980	A Catholic man is killed when an INLA road bomb intended for soldiers explodes at an intersection near his home in south Armagh.
September 12, 1980	Following the military coup in Turkey, the MHP, together with other parties, are banned from participating in the government. Alparslan Türkeş, leader of the MHP, is arrested and put on trial. He is released from prison for health reasons in April 1985. In 1987, he is sentenced again to an 11-year prison term, but is soon freed as part of a government amnesty.
1981	One hundred and eighteen people are killed as the result of the Northern Irish conflicts in 1981. Fifty-four of the dead are civilians, 21 from the Ulster Constabulary, 11 soldiers, 13 Ulster Defense Regiment (UDR) members, 16 Republicans, and three Loyalists.
January 21, 1981	Former Speaker of the Stormont Parliament, 86-year-old Sir Norman Stronge, and his son, 48, are murdered when IRA men wearing military-like clothing invade the Stronge mansion in Armagh.
February 6, 1981	José Maria Ryan, the chief engineer of a nuclear plant in Lemóniz, is killed eight days after being kidnapped by three ETA members.
March 27, 1981	In a UDA/UFF drive-by shooting, a Catholic man is killed as he is walking along a road in north Belfast.
May 13, 1981	Mehmet Ali Ağca, a former member of the Grey Wolves (the militant arm of the right-wing Turkish party MHP), attempts to assassinate Pope John Paul II at St. Peter's Square in Rome. The Pope is wounded in the arm and abdomen, but not fatally. In July, Ağca is sentenced to life imprisonment. In June 2000, Italian President Carlo Ciampi pardons Ağca at the request of the Pope. Ağca is returned to Turkey where he is prosecuted for other crimes there and imprisoned again.

June 9, 1981   An ASALA gunman assassinates the Turkish Consulate Secretary, Mehmet Savas Yergüz, as he is leaving his office in Geneva, Switzerland. Swiss authorities apprehend Mardiros Jamgotchian, who is convicted of the murder.

September 19, 1981   A Catholic man is shot dead by Ulster Volunteer Force (UVF) members while walking home in south Belfast.

September 24, 1981   Four ASALA gunmen seize the Turkish Consulate in Paris, taking 56 people hostage for 16 hours. During the siege, one gunman shoots and seriously wounds Consul Kaya İnal and a Turkish security officer who later dies. The terrorists demand the release of certain Armenian political prisoners. The gunmen eventually surrender.

October 11, 1981   Two people are killed as the result of an IRA bombing in London near the Chelsea barracks.

November 14, 1981   Unionist Reverend Robert Bradford becomes the first assassination victim among the serving members in the Northern Ireland parliament. He is shot dead along with another Protestant man by IRA members while attending a meeting at a community center in south Belfast.

1982   Following Israel's invasion of Lebanon and the subsequent expulsion of the Palestine Liberation Organization (PLO) and most ASALA operatives from the country, ASALA transfers many of its activities to Syria.

1982   In the troubles in Northern Ireland, 112 people die this year. Among the victims are 47 civilians, 12 Ulster police officers, 32 soldiers, and seven UDR members. Twelve terrorists also die—seven Republicans and five Loyalists.

January 28, 1982   In Los Angeles, California, two Armenian gunmen assassinate Turkish Consul General to the U.S. Kemal Arikan, in his automobile while he is waiting at an intersection. Armenian Genocide Justice Commandos (JCAG) claims responsibility. One of the assassins, Hampig Sassounian, a 19-year-old Armenian-American member, is arrested soon afterwards. He is convicted of first-degree murder and sentenced to 25 years to life in prison.

March 15, 1982   An 11-year-old Protestant boy is killed and 34 individuals are injured when an IRA car bomb explodes in Down.

April 17, 1982   One policeman is killed and seven are injured in three bazooka attacks staged by members of the ETA. Two of the attacks target Civil Guard installations, while the third attack involves firing at an armored car. The ETA apparently commits these killings to protest against the government's failure to remove all governmental forces from the Basque region within 30 days.

April 17, 1982   In an IRA shooting attack a Protestant man is killed while working on his farm in Armagh. The night before the attack, four masked and armed IRA members hold two older men hostage at the neighboring farm, using the property as the base from which to launch the attack. Later, they escape in their hostages' car.

May 4, 1982   An assassin murders Orhan Gunduz, honorary Turkish Consul General to New England, in Somerville, Massachusetts. The Armenian Genocide Justice Commandos (JCAG) claim credit for the attack.

May 5, 1982	Ángel Pascual Múgica, the director of the Lemóniz nuclear power plant, is assassinated by ETA militants who shoot him in the head from a passing car. Múgica's 16-year-old son, who also is in the car, is wounded in the hand.
May 14, 1982	A Catholic man is shot dead by the UVF at his brother-in-law's store in north Belfast, while two other shop workers are injured.
May 14, 1982	A civil guard in Vitoria is gunned down and a taxi driver is shot and killed in San Sebastian. The police believe the ETA is responsible.
June 6, 1982	ETA gunmen shoot and kill a wine merchant.
July 22, 1982	Domingo Iturbe Abásolo, a senior ETA member, is sentenced to a three-month prison term for illegal possession of arms by a court in Pau in the southwest of France.
August 7, 1982	The Armenian terrorist group ASALA attacks the Esenboga Airport in Ankara, Turkey's capital, killing nine people and injuring 78.
August 26, 1982	A Catholic man is shot and killed by the UDA/UFF in north Belfast while walking to work with his friend.
September 14, 1982	Members of the ETA's military wing fatally machine-gun four policemen on patrol near San Sebastian.
September 16, 1982	Two Catholic boys, one 14 years old and the other 11, are killed along with a soldier after a bomb detonates near an army foot patrol in west Belfast.
November 4, 1982	General Victor Lago Román is murdered in Madrid by members of the ETA's military wing. General Román is the most senior Spanish general commanding an operational unit and the commander of the Brunete Division, which guards Madrid. The next day, Spanish police capture three leading members of the ETA's hard-line military wing.
December 7, 1982	Seventeen people are murdered, among them four Protestants, one Catholic, 11 off-duty soldiers, and a woman visiting from England, in an INLA bombing on a disco in Derry. An additional 30 people are injured in the attack. Most of the victims are killed when the roof collapses on top of them after the explosion. Four Derry residents, two men and two women, are sentenced to life imprisonment for the act. A fifth person receives a ten-year prison sentence.

Basque Nationalist Terrorism against Spain

The Basques are reputedly the oldest people in Europe but organized Basque nationalism is a modern phenomenon. Perhaps this is because the Spanish monarchy never launched a campaign to assimilate forcibly a group which caused no trouble and lived in a relatively remote region of the country. The Basques, however, were strong supporters of the Republican side in the Spanish civil war of the late 1930s and the victorious General Francisco Franco's Fascist government adopted a strong centralizing policy. Most of the Basques' political energy went into a moderate nationalist party but militants turned to violence.

The Euskadi Ta Askatasuna (ETA) waged war on the Spanish government, attacking security forces and officials rather than adapting the anti-civilian, ethnic war strategy that often characterized the Irish Republican Army (IRA) and Kurdish Workers' Party (PKK), as well as Arab radical groups. Civilians, however, were inevitably killed in attacks that took place in public places. In addition, the ETA also tried to intimidate more moderate Basques, who held nationalist views while opposing violent revolution, or those adhering to other political parties. Like terrorist counterparts elsewhere, ETA's goal was to destroy forcibly any political rivals, even those with whom it shared certain aims.

During the post-Franco era, Spain adapted a more decentralized political system, devolving some powers on the country's region and vastly expanding Basque communal and cultural rights. This might have undercut the ETA's base of support but did not discourage extremists from continuing their efforts, despite periodic self-proclaimed cease-fires.

1983	The Anti-Terrorist Liberation Groups, or Grupos Antiterroristas de Liberación (GAL) is formed in the Basque region of southwestern France with the aim of destabilizing the ETA. Many speculate that the Spanish government itself provides support for GAL through links with the Spanish police's Anti-Terrorist Unit and the Spanish Civil Guard. A judicial inquiry and Supreme Court trial in 1994 finally provides a financial link between the Spanish Interior Ministry and GAL.
1983	During the year, 87 die in the Northern Ireland conflict. Among the dead 28 are civilians, 18 are Ulster police offices, five are soldiers, and ten are in the Ulster Defense Regiment (UDR). Eight Republicans and two Loyalists are also among the dead.
January 16, 1983	William Doyle, a prominent Catholic judge, is shot and killed by IRA gunmen as he is leaving a church in south Belfast.
February 2, 1983	A civil guard is killed and two others are wounded by ETA members in the town of Ordizia.
February 5, 1983	Three bank employees are killed and several others are wounded in an explosion at the Bilbao Bank in Spain's Basque region. The ETA's military branch claims credit for the attack
February 28, 1983	An explosion occurs at a Turkish tourism agency in France, and credit is claimed by the Armenian Secret Army for the Liberation of Armenia. One person is killed and four others are wounded.
March 9, 1983	In Belgrade, Yugoslavia, two Armenian gunmen assassinate the Turkish Ambassador to Yugoslavia Galip Balkar and seriously wound his chauffeur, Necati Kayar. JCAG claims responsibility for the assassination.
June 16, 1983	Five bombs explode in front of the Grand Bazaar in Istanbul and two men shoot into a crowd killing two people and wounding 27. One of the attackers is also killed. ASALA claims credit for the incident, which coincides with the anniversary of a 1970 workers' revolt in Turkey.
July 14, 1983	Terrorists assassinate the Turkish administrative attaché in Brussels, Dursun Aksoy, while he is in his automobile. ASALA and the Armenian Revolutionary Army (ARA), an offshoot of the JCAG, claim responsibility.
July 15, 1983	ASALA terrorists bomb the Turkish Airlines ticket counter at Orly Airport in Paris killing seven and wounding 56. Varadjian Garbidjian, claiming to be the head of the ASALA's French branch, takes responsibility.

July 27, 1983   A band of Armenian terrorists shoot their way into the Turkish ambassador's residence in Lisbon, Portugal, then blow themselves up, killing a top diplomat's wife and a Portuguese policeman. The woman's 17-year-old son is seriously wounded and her husband is slightly wounded. The Armenian Revolutionary Army (ARA), takes responsibility for the attack.

October 29, 1983   A Catholic man is killed and his teenage daughter is injured in an Ulster Volunteer Force (UVF) shooting attack on a store in north Belfast.

November 3, 1983   Spanish Prime Minister Felipe Gonzalez announces that anti-terrorist measures in Spain will be tightened. Prison terms will be longer for terrorists and political groups that support terrorism, such as Herri Batasuna (*see* 1978), may be banned.

November 20, 1983   Three Protestant men are killed in a Irish National Liberation Army (INLA) shooting attack at a church service in Armagh.

December 18, 1983   A car bomb placed by the IRA outside Harrods department store in London explodes and kills six individuals, including two police officers.

1984   In 1984, 72 individuals die as a result of the troubles in Northern Ireland, among them 38 civilian bystanders, nine police officers, nine British soldiers, and ten UDR members. The rest are mostly Republican activists.

January 29, 1984   A Catholic man's body is found in Armagh after he was shot by the UVF.

January 29, 1984   Lieutenant General Guillermo Quintana Lacaci, a former military commander, is gunned down by two ETA terrorists as he is walking home from mass in Madrid. His wife and a friend, a retired colonel, are injured.

February 23, 1984   Enrique Casas Vila, a Socialist senator in the Spanish parliament who publicly criticized the ETA, is slain in San Sebastian by two hooded gunmen.

February 25, 1984   A Spanish Basque refugee, likely an ETA member, is killed in the south of France by the Anti-Terrorist Liberation Groups (GAL).

March 6, 1984   A Protestant prison officer is shot dead by the IRA just outside his east Belfast residence while checking his car for a bomb.

April 29, 1984   A Catholic man is killed near Armagh city when a car bomb planted on his vehicle explodes. A group calling itself the Irish Freedom Fighters claims responsibility.

June 20, 1984   A bomb explodes in the car of a Turkish Embassy employee in Vienna, Austria, killing him and wounding five others. The Armenian Revolutionary Army claims responsibility.

July 14, 1984   Two alleged ETA terrorists are arrested in Antwerp, Belgium, and then extradited to Madrid to face charges. This is the first time that Spain succeeds in having ETA terrorists extradited.

October 12, 1984   Five individuals are killed by an IRA bomb that goes off at a hotel in Brighton, England, during the Conservative Party's annual conference with Prime Minister Margaret Thatcher in attendance. Conservative Member of Parliament for Enfield Southgate, Sir Anthony Berry, is among the victims along with the chairman of the North West Area England Conservative Association, the wives of the Tory chief whip, the chairman of the Western Area Conservative Association, and the wife of the chairman of the Scottish Conservative Association. In 1986, the IRA man who plants the bomb receives eight life sentences, with minimum jail time of 35 years.

November 23, 1984   A French policeman is killed and two others wounded by ETA members who attack a tollbooth on the Spanish-French border.

1985   The People's Liberation Army of Kurdistan (ARGK) is established as the military wing of the Kurdistan Workers' Party (PKK).

1985   In the Northern Ireland troubles, 58 people die this year, among them are 23 civilians, 23 Ulster Constabulary officers, six Ulster Defense Regiment (UDR) members, and five Republicans.

January 1985   Lasa Michelena, ETA chief of staff and one of the terrorists most wanted by Spain, is arrested along with ten other ETA suspects by Spanish security forces near Bayonne, France.

February 17, 1985   The body of a Protestant man is discovered in a garbage mound in northwest Belfast, killed by UVF terrorists.

March 7, 1985   Colonel Juan Carlos Arkotxa, the commanding officer of the local Basque police forces, is killed by a booby-trap explosive placed under his car on the outskirts of Vitoria. ETA is responsible.

April 3, 1985   A Catholic man and an Ulster police officer are killed and ten people are injured when an IRA car bomb explodes outside the Newry courthouse in Down.

May 1, 1985   A Catholic man, once a member of the INLA's political section, is murdered in France by INLA members who accuse him of arms smuggling.

June 12, 1985   Colonel Vicente Romero and his military driver are assassinated by ETA terrorists in Madrid. When the police discover the guerrillas' getaway car near a department store in the center of the city, a bomb placed under the car explodes, killing one police officer and injuring several others. The same day, a plainclothes naval officer is killed in Portugalete, near Bilbao. The shootings occur in spite of the high security measures taken for ceremonies celebrating the accession of Spain and Portugal to the European Community.

July 2, 1985   The Spanish authorities arrest 18 members of the ETA group, one of whom, Feliz Zabarte, a leader, is suspected of 16 murders.

July 29, 1985   Vice Admiral Fausto Escrigas Estrada, Spain's director general of defense policy, is killed by two ETA terrorists. He is driving his car to work in Madrid when two men jump from a nearby car and fire into the admiral's vehicle.

August 2, 1985   The owner of a French restaurant, said to be a key member of GAL, is slain in the Spanish resort of Castellón by two ETA gunmen.

September 9, 1985   An American businessman is killed and 18 people, including 16 civil guards, are wounded in a car bomb attack staged by ETA members in central Madrid.

1986   In this year, 68 people die in the Northern Ireland dispute, among them 34 civilians, 12 Ulster police officers, four soldiers, and eight members of the UDR. Six Republicans and two Loyalists were also killed.

January 31, 1986   A Catholic man is killed when a UVF member invades his home in Antrim.

February 6, 1986   Cristóbal Colón de Carvajal y Maroto, a vice admiral in the Spanish navy and a direct descendant of Christopher Columbus, is murdered along with his chauffeur while driving in an elite Madrid neighborhood. The ETA claims the attack.

April 25, 1986   Civil Guards are being transported through central Madrid when a bomb is set off remotely, killing five Civil Guards and injuring eight other people. ETA is responsible.

July 14, 1986   Twelve Civil Guards are killed and 50 people injured when a van loaded with explosives blows up next to their bus at República Dominicana Square in Madrid. The police attribute the bombing to the ETA.

July 26, 1986   Two Civil Guards are killed in a bomb blast detonated by ETA terrorists near Arechavaleta.

September 25, 1986   Four alleged ETA members exiled in France are shot to death in a bar in Bayonne. The Anti-Terrorist Liberation Groups (GAL) claims responsibility for the shootings, but ETA members accuse the governments of France and Spain of engineering the slayings.

October 25, 1986   General Rafael Garrido Gil, the military governor of the Spanish Basque country, is slain in San Sebastian with his wife, Isabel Velasco, and their 21-year-old son, Daniel. Two ETA terrorists on a motorcycle place a bomb under the back of the car while it is stopped at traffic lights.

December 12, 1986   An IRA booby-trap bomb kills a Protestant dairy worker in Tyrone.

December 23, 1986   Juan Atares Pena, a retired Civil Guard, is fatally shot in the head and the back by two armed people in Pamplona, Spain. ETA is likely responsible.

1987   One hundred and six lives are lost in the Northern Ireland troubles this year. Forty-five of the dead are civilians, 16 are Ulster constabulary members, three are soldiers, and eight are UDR members. Twenty-six Republicans and three Loyalists also die.

January 30, 1987   Two people are killed and 40 others are wounded by the explosion of a remote-controlled bomb, which the ETA places in a military bus in Zaragoza, Spain. More than 35,000 people gather in the streets to mourn the victims and to protest against ETA terrorism.

January 21, 1987   In Down, a Protestant man is murdered by an IRA member.

April 25, 1987   Lord Gibson, a prominent judge in Northern Ireland, is killed together with his wife when a bomb explodes in Armagh. The IRA says the attack is in retaliation for the acquittal of three Ulster Constabulary officers who had shot and killed three IRA members.

June 19, 1987   Seventeen people are killed and 40 others wounded when a car bomb explodes in the parking garage of a supermarket in Barcelona. On October 23, 1989, two ETA militants, Domingo Troitiño and Josefina Mercedes Ernaga, are tried and sentenced to a total of 1,588 years in prison for their involvement in the bombing. On July 26, 2003, two top members of the ETA, Rafael Caride Simón and Santiago Arróspide, are sentenced to 790 years in prison for their responsibility.

August 23, 1987   A Catholic man is shot and killed by the UDA/UFF while driving with his family to church in south Belfast. The UFF issues a statement claiming the attack is in retaliation for the killing of an Ulster Defense Regiment (UDR) member by the IRA.

November 8, 1987   Twelve Protestants are killed and over 60 people injured, 19 of them seriously, by the IRA at a Remembrance Sunday ceremony in Fermanagh in what becomes known as the Poppy Day Bombing. The IRA announces it attempted to target security forces and regretted the incident. In retaliation for the attack, the UDA kills a Protestant boy shortly afterwards in the mistaken belief that he is Catholic.

December 11, 1987   Eleven people, including five children, are killed when a car bomb explodes at a Civil Guard barracks in the Zaragoza, in northeastern Spain. At least 34 people are wounded in the attack. The blast occurs as 50 families of the paramilitary Civil Guard corps are sleeping in the barracks. ETA members, including Henri Parot, are suspected and will later be brought to justice.

1988   One hundred and five die in the troubles in Northern Ireland that year. Among the dead, 40 are civilians, six are Ulster police officers, 22 are soldiers, and 12 are in the UDR. Of the paramilitaries who die, 16 are Republican and four are Loyalists.

March 16, 1988   Three are killed after a UFF gunman opens fire and throws grenades at a group of thousands of Catholic mourners gathered at a cemetery in west Belfast for the funeral of three IRA men who had been killed by the SAS (British special forces) in Gibraltar. The gunman, Michael Stone, becomes a well-known symbol for Loyalist violence. Stone is later sentenced to life imprisonment for six murders and many other offenses.

April 25, 1988   Hagop Hagopian, leader of the Armenian terrorist organization Armenian Secret Army for the Liberation of Armenia (ASALA), is assassinated in his Athens home by rival Armenian terrorists.

May 15, 1988   Three Catholic men are shot dead when UVF gunmen attack a bar in central Belfast.

July 23, 1988   An IRA land mine explodes on a road in Armagh, killing three Protestants, a husband and wife and their seven-year-old son. The IRA claims the victims were mistakenly targeted and that the intended victim was a high court judge and the Ulster police officers serving as his bodyguards.

August 21, 1988   Two Civil Guards are killed when a bomb explodes and sets their car ablaze in the northern town of Estella. The ETA claims responsibility for the bombing.

August 31, 1988   Three Catholics go to a Derry apartment in search of details regarding the disappearance of a friend they feared had been kidnapped. They are killed when they set off a booby-trap bomb left by the kidnappers.

September 23, 1988   A Catholic man is shot and killed at his west Belfast residence by the UDA/UFF which believes he had been involved in the murder of a UDA/UFF member a few days earlier.

November 23, 1988   A senior Spanish television executive and a three-year-old boy are killed in an ETA bomb explosion outside the headquarters of Spain's Civil Guard in Madrid. Forty-five other people, including the child's parents, are wounded in the blast.

November 23, 1988   An IRA car bomb kills a Catholic man and his 13-year-old granddaughter and wounds another woman when a parked van explodes next to them in Tyrone.

1989   Eighty-one individuals die in the Northern Ireland conflict that year. Thirty-eight of the dead are civilians, nine are Ulster police officers, 24 are soldiers, and two are in the UDR. Three Republican and three Loyalist terrorists are killed.

February 12, 1989   A well-known Catholic defense attorney is killed by UDA/UFF terrorists at his north Belfast residence.

March 7, 1989   Three Protestant men are murdered by IRA members in a drive-by shooting at a garage in Tyrone. The IRA claims the garage served as a base for Loyalists to plan murders.

April 12, 1989   José Calvo de la Hoz, a 51-year-old Civil Guard, is shot to death near the Basque town of Bilbao by ETA terrorists.

May 25, 1989   Three policemen of a bomb disposal squad are killed and nine others are wounded when ETA terrorists detonate a car bomb in a Bilbao suburb.

July 19, 1989   A Spanish army colonel and a major are slain in Madrid when alleged ETA gunmen fire at their car with automatic gunfire on the southern outskirts of Madrid.

August 25, 1989   A Catholic man, Loughlin Maginn, is shot dead by UDA/UFF gunmen who invade his home in Down. After the killing, UDA/UFF members claim that it had received intelligence information about Maginn from British security forces. This creates a storm of accusations that British security forces are collaborating with Loyalist terrorists. Inquiries by the Ulster Constabulary and later by Amnesty International agreed that there had been some collusion, but disagreed about its extent. Two full-time lower ranking members of the Ulster Defense Regiment (UDR), a special regiment of the British army staffed by residents of Northern Ireland, and another man are eventually found to be connected to the murder.

September 13, 1989

Two ETA terrorists assassinate Carmen Tagle, a senior Spanish magistrate, as she walks home from court in Bilbao. The murder happens a few hours after she sentences two suspected members of the ETA to 21-year prison terms. Once again, Henri Parot is one of the assailants but he escapes.

October 26, 1989

A Royal Air Force (RAF) corporal is killed along with his six-month-old daughter in an IRA shooting in West Germany near the Dutch border.

November 15, 1989

A Protestant man is killed in Tyrone by an IRA car bomb.

1990

Eighty-four people die as a result of the Northern Ireland conflict this year, of whom 47 are civilians. Twelve Ulster police officers, ten soldiers, and eight UDR members are killed. Among the deaths of paramilitary group members are six Republicans and one Loyalist.

January 7, 1990

The body of a Catholic taxi driver is discovered on the side of a road in a taxi in Armagh, the victim of UVF terrorists. The UVF claims to be acting in retaliation for the killings of two Protestant men, one a taxi driver, caused by an IRA bomb a few months earlier.

March 20, 1990

The Irish People's Liberation Organisation (IPLO) kills a Protestant man in his north Belfast home.

April 2, 1990

Henri Parot is arrested by the Spanish police near Seville for his involvement in the ETA. Among other attacks, Parot masterminded the December 1987 bombing of the Civil Guard barracks in Zaragoza and the September 1989 assassination of prosecutor Carmen Tagle. In March 1994, Parot will be sentenced to more than 1,800 years' imprisonment for these attacks.

May 27, 1990

Two Australian men are shot dead while vacationing in Roermand, Holland, when the IRA mistakes them for off-duty British soldiers.

July 30, 1990

Conservative Member of the British Parliament, Ian Gow, a good friend of Margaret Thatcher, is assassinated when an IRA bomb explodes underneath his car just outside his residence in Sussex, England.

September 7, 1990

A Catholic man is shot while sleeping in his south Belfast residence. The UDA/UFF is responsible; the UFF claims he was working for the IRA.

October 24, 1990

A civil worker at a military base is forced by the IRA to drive a bomb to an army checkpoint in Derry and detonate it in the first "human bomb" incident of the Northern Ireland troubles. He is killed along with five soldiers, and 17 civilians are injured.

November 10, 1990

Four Protestant men, two civilians and two Ulster police officers, are killed in an IRA shooting at Castor Bay in Armagh while out duck hunting.

November 18, 1990	A car explodes just as two police vans pass one another in the northern city of Santurce, Spain, killing two policemen and wounding three others. ETA is responsible.
December 8, 1990	A car bomb explodes in Madrid, killing six policemen and two civilians and injuring 15 other people. Police suspect the ETA.
1991	One hundred and two lives are lost in the Northern Ireland conflict in this year. The dead includes 63 civilians, six Ulster Constabulary officers, five soldiers, including eight from the UDR, and 20 paramilitary fighters—13 Republicans and seven Loyalists.
January 27, 1991	A Catholic man is killed by UDA/UFF members at his home in north Belfast.
March 28, 1991	Three Catholics, two teenage girls and a man, are killed in a UVF shooting at a store in Armagh. The owner has reportedly refused to serve customers who are UDR members.
May 21, 1991	The IRA shoot dead a Protestant store owner at his south Belfast fruit and vegetable market. They claim he was supplying food to the security forces.
May 29, 1991	Ten people, all but one of them civilians, are killed and 50 wounded in a car bombing that destroys the Civil Guard barracks in the town of Vich near Barcelona. On May 30, 1991, Spanish policemen near the French border shoot down the two ETA members responsible for this bombing.
August 18, 1991	Three ETA gunmen are killed and two Civil Guards wounded in a shoot-out in San Sebastian. Ten suspected terrorists, believed to be part of the Donosti Commando, which has been blamed for staging over 60 attacks, causing 15 deaths and 60 injuries since 1989, surrender to police.
November 14, 1991	Two Catholic men and one Protestant are shot dead by UVF members as they are driving home from the Armagh factory where they are employed.
December 21, 1991	A 19-year-old Protestant man is shot dead by the IRA while working at his father's store in Tyrone. His father, once a reservist on the Ulster Constabulary, had been the intended target. Two Protestant men are murdered by IPLO members who open fire at a bar in south Belfast. UDA/UFF gunmen kill a Catholic man when they invade his Protestant girlfriend's west Belfast residence.
December 26, 1991	With the fall of the Soviet Union, Armenia is established as an independent country, fulfilling a major objective of most Armenian terrorist groups. Former terrorists now find themselves involved in the government or the military.
1992	Ninety-one people die this year in the Northern Ireland troubles. Sixty-seven are civilians, four are Ulster Constabulary officers, another four are soldiers, and three are in the UDR. Ten Republicans and two Loyalists die as well.
January 16, 1992	Two Spanish military bandsmen are gunned down in Barcelona, likely by ETA terrorists.

January 17, 1992   Eight construction workers, all Protestants, are killed when an IRA land mine explodes at Teebane Crossroads in Tyrone as their van passes on its way home from the Lisanelly military base, their place of employment.

February 5, 1992   Five Catholics are killed, including three teenage boys, and seven are injured in a UFF shooting at a betting shop in south Belfast. Before the gunmen flee the scene they shout, "Remember Teebane," referring to the Teebane attack in January.

February 19, 1992   Two people are killed and 21 others are wounded when a remote-controlled car bomb goes off in the northern Spanish town of Santander. ETA says the intended target was a passing police van.

March 20, 1992   Two people are killed in car bombs in villages near Barcelona.

March 30, 1992   French security forces arrest ten suspected ETA members, including the alleged architect of the wave of bombings and assassinations in Bidart. The most significant captures for Spain's counter-terrorism campaign are Francisco Múgica Garmendia, the ETA's top military commander; José Maria Arregui Erostarbe, the chief bomb-maker; and Luis Alvarez Santa Cristina, who is thought to be the ETA's political and propaganda chief. On June 18, 1993, Garmendia is sentenced to a ten-year prison term by a court in Paris for conspiracy and firearms possession.

April 10, 1992   An IRA bomb explodes in St. Mary Axe, London, a day after general elections for the British Parliament. Three individuals are killed—two men and a 15-year-old girl.

May 5, 1992   A Protestant man is killed when an IPLO member opens fire with a machine gun at a bar in north Belfast.

June 24, 1992   In the Seki village of Batman Province of eastern Turkey, PKK terrorists kill ten, including seven children and a 70-year-old woman.

June 29, 1992   PKK forces stop a minibus and execute ten individuals near the Yolbasti village of Bitlis Province.

September 6, 1992   A Catholic married couple are killed by UVF gunman at their home in Tyrone.

September 11, 1992   The PKK attack a joint U.S./Turkish Shell Oil facility, separate the managers from their employees and then open fire on the former, killing three and wounding one.

October 11, 1992   In the Uludere District of Sirnak Province, Turkey, PKK forces kill 11 individuals in a rocket attack against the homes of village guards.

October 20, 1992   Near the Hazarsah village of Bingöl, Turkey, PKK forces stop a minibus and machine-gun its occupants, killing 19 and wounding six.

November 30, 1992   A Civil Guard is killed and another Civil Guard and a female passerby are wounded when a bomb is set off by remote control in Madrid, likely by ETA terrorists.

1993	The 1993 death toll for the troubles in Northern Ireland stands at 90. Among the dead are 68 civilians, six Ulster police officers, six soldiers, and two from the UDR. Four Republican and three Loyalist paramilitaries are killed that year.
January 3, 1993	A Catholic store owner and his son are shot dead by the UVF in an attack on their grocery store in Tyrone. The killers claim that the father had been a Sinn Féin member.
March 20, 1993	Two children are killed as the result of IRA bombs left in garbage cans in a shopping center in Warrington, Lancashire, England.
March 25, 1993	Four Catholic laborers are killed in a UDA/UFF shooting attack at a construction site in Derry. A 17-year-old boy is shot dead by UDA/UFF members while working at a store in a shopping center in west Belfast.
April 24, 1993	A photographer sent to cover an IRA car bomb alert is himself killed by the attack in Putney in south London.
May 24, 1993	PKK forces stop a bus carrying unarmed Turkish army recruits and machine-gun them all, murdering 36 individuals.
June 21, 1993	Six Spanish soldiers and their driver die and 25 others are injured in central Madrid in a car bomb attack. Police think the ETA engineered this attack as a response to the sentencing of Francisco Múgica Garmendia to ten years in jail.
July 5, 1993	In a raid against the Basbaglar village in Erzincan Province, Turkey, PKK forces execute 30 people and burn 57 houses.
August 4, 1993	In the Mutki District of Bitlis, Turkey, PKK forces stop six minibuses and execute 19 individuals and wound an additional 13. In a raid against the Konakbasi settlement of Bingöl Province, PKK forces kill 11 individuals, including eight children.
September 16, 1993	A retired Civil Guardsman is killed when a car explodes in the Basque town of Andoain.
September 17, 1993	PKK terrorists execute six civil servants in a teachers' club in the Egin District of Diyarbalir, Turkey.
October 12, 1993	PKK forces murder 22 individuals, 14 of whom are children and eight women, in a neighborhood in the city of Siirt, Turkey.
October 23, 1993	Nine Protestants are killed and 57 injured in an IRA bomb attack on a fish shop in west Belfast. One of the two IRA men who commits the attack is also killed and the second perpetrator of the attack receives nine life sentences.
October 25, 1993	PKK forces murder 22 individuals, 14 children and eight women, in Derince village of Siirt, Turkey.
October 25, 1993	Spanish Air Force General Dionisio Herrero is shot and killed and his chauffeur seriously wounded by two hooded ETA operatives who shoot at their car in a

central Madrid shopping district. One of the gunmen, Juan Luis Aguirre Lete, a leader of ETA, is arrested and extradited to Spain on June 5, 1998.

October 30, 1993　　Eight Catholics are killed and 11 are injured as the result of a UDA/UFF shooting attack at a Derry restaurant, in retaliation for the fish shop bombing a week earlier.

November 23, 1993　　A 42-year-old policeman is shot to death in his car as he is driving with his three-year-old son in Bilbao.

December 12, 1993　　In a raid against the Agackonak village in Adiyaman Province, Turkey, PKK forces kill 13 people.

1994　　Sixty-nine lives are lost this year in clashes in Northern Ireland. Among the dead are 52 civilians, six security force members, eight Loyalists, and three Republicans.

January 1, 1994　　PKK forces stop a minibus on the Diyarbakir-Elazig road in Turkey and murder eight individuals.

January 22, 1994　　In the Akyurek and Ormancik villages of Mardin Province, PKK forces kill 20 individuals, including six children and nine women.

January 27, 1994　　A Catholic man is shot dead by a UDA/UFF member while staying at a house in south Belfast. The UFF claims its target had been an IRA member. Two UVF gunmen invade a home in Antrim and kill a Catholic man and wound his wife.

April 2, 1994　　The PKK claims responsibility for bombing Bedesten, the old bazaar in Istanbul, killing a Spanish and a Belgian tourist and wounding 17.

April 4, 1994　　A 29-year-old police officer is killed when a car blows up near his home in Bilbao. The ETA is suspected of having masterminded the bombing.

April 6, 1994　　A Protestant woman at an illegal drinking hall is mistakenly identified as Catholic and beaten and shot dead, most likely by Red Hand Commandos, an elite group within the Ulster Volunteer Force (UVF).

April 18, 1994　　A 35-year-old man is killed and ten other passersby are injured by the explosion of two grenades in a car parked in front of the local military headquarters in Barcelona. The ETA is accused of having engineered the attack.

May 3, 1994　　A Protestant man is gunned down in south Belfast as he and his wife walk to work. The Irish National Liberation Army (INLA) is responsible for his death, claiming he had been a leading Loyalist, though this is unlikely.

May 15, 1994　　PKK forces raid the Edebuk village in Erzincan Province, Turkey, and murder nine individuals.

May 23, 1994　　A Spanish army officer, Lieutenant Miguel Peralta, is slain when a bomb placed under his car blows up in Madrid. ETA is likely responsible.

June 18, 1994	Six Catholic men are killed, and five others receive serious injuries, in a UVF shooting at a bar in a predominantly Catholic area of Down. The UVF claims the attack is revenge for the murder of a UVF man by the INLA two days earlier.
July 1, 1994	A Spanish army general is shot dead on a busy street in Madrid by two alleged ETA terrorists. Juan Luis Aguirre Lete is sentenced to 66 years in prison for his involvement in several crimes including the murder of Dionisio Herrero (*see* October 25, 1993).
July 29, 1994	An army general, his driver, and a civilian are killed and 14 people are injured in a car explosion credited to the ETA.
August 1994	The IRA, along with various other paramilitaries, announces a cease-fire in what is the beginning of a peace process. However, certain IRA members oppose the cease-fire and go on to form splinter groups. Other dissident groups continue to form in the next four years and continue with the violence. UDA splinter groups, such as the Orange Volunteers and Red Hand Defenders, also continue with the violence after the 1994 cease-fire. The UVF refrains from terrorist activity following the 1994 cease-fire and the Belfast Agreement in 1998.
August 21, 1994	A 37-year-old Spanish policeman is shot in the head by two armed members of the ETA in the village of Berango near Bilbao.
November 16, 1994	Two ETA leaders are detained under Spanish custody. The first one, Luis Martin Carmona, alias "Koldo," is suspected to be a key member of the Vizcaya cell which is responsible for 11 murders. The second man, Feliz Alberto López de la Calle, is captured near the southeastern French city of Toulon during a raid co-organized by Spanish and French security forces.
December 15, 1994	Sergeant Alfonso Morcillo is shot to death as he is setting out for work in San Sebastian, where he served as chief investigator for the municipal police.
1995	There are only nine fatalities this year in the Northern Ireland conflict. Eight civilians and one Loyalist paramilitary are killed.
January 1, 1995	In a raid against the Hamzali village in Diyarbakir Province, Turkey, PKK forces kill 19 individuals, including seven children and eight women.
January 12, 1995	In Narlica village, Diyarbakir Province, Turkey, PKK forces kill eight individuals.
January 23, 1995	Gregorio Ordoñez, a deputy of the center-right People's Party (Partido Popular) in the Basque regional parliament and a candidate for the seat of mayor of San Sebastian, is shot and killed in the old part of San Sebastian. Ordoñez was a fearless critic of the ETA and was expected to win the elections against the candidacy of Herri Batasuna. On March 25, 1996, ETA member Valetin Lasarte is captured in Oyarkun. He is charged with leading a cell that carried out several crimes, including Ordoñez's slaying. He is sentenced to 82 years in prison for the crime.
April 29, 1995	In the first organized IRA murder since the 1994 cease-fire, a Catholic man is killed, shot by two IRA members while at a bar in central Belfast. The man

was among several drug dealers targeted by the IRA under their cover name organization, Direct Action Against Drugs (DAAD).

June 19, 1995   A policeman is killed and five persons are wounded in central Madrid in an ETA car bomb explosion.

July 23, 1995   In a raid against the Akdogu village of Van Province, PKK terrorists kill 12 individuals.

August 4, 1995   In a raid against the Gazelusagi village of Hatay Province, Turkey, PKK terrorists kill eight individuals.

August 9, 1995   Spanish police break into an apartment near the royal residence in Majorca and arrest three Basque commandos who confess to planning the assassination of King Juan Carlos.

September 3, 1995   Kurdish activist Seyfettin Kalan is murdered in Neumunster, Germany, by the Grey Wolves, the militant wing of the political party MHP. Two other Kurds are shot and wounded.

September 5, 1995   PKK terrorists attack a mine in Hatay Province, Turkey, and kill eight workers.

November 27, 1995   The body of a Catholic man is discovered in north Belfast. The victim had been beaten to death with an iron bar in an apparent Loyalist sectarian killing not linked to any paramilitary organization.

December, 1995   The PKK activities diminish due to a unilateral cease-fire, which is in effect until the fall of 1996. In total, 48 civilians from rural villages are killed in PKK terrorist acts during the year.

December 11, 1995   Six people are killed and 20 injured when a bomb wrecks a van of the Spanish navy in southeast Madrid. The blast kills four civilian employees of the Spanish armed forces, a passerby, and another unidentified person.

December 16, 1995   A bomb blows up in the Corte Inglés department store in Valencia, killing a 43-year-old woman and injuring eight people. On August 1, 2002, two ETA members, Marcos Sagarza Oyarzabal and Francisco Javier Irastorza Dorronsoro, are arrested in the French town of Saint-Jean-de-Luz and accused of being involved in the bombing.

December 22, 1995   Major Luciano Cortizo Alonso is killed and three people, including his 18-year-old daughter, are injured when a bomb explodes under his car in the northwestern city of León. ETA is responsible.

1996   Twenty-two lives are taken in the conflict in Northern Ireland this year. The deaths include ten civilians, one solider, seven Republicans, and three Loyalists.

February 6, 1996   Fernando Múgica Herzog, a regional leader of the Socialist Party, is gunned down by four ETA gunmen in San Sebastian as he is leaving the city court with his son. On June 5, 1998, Juan Luis Aguirre Lete is extradited to Spain after being arrested by French police. He is later sentenced to 66 years in prison for his involvement in several crimes, including Múgica's murder.

February 9, 1996   The IRA renews its violence after a 17-month cease-fire and bombs the Canary Wharf area in London's Docklands, causing two fatalities.

February 14, 1996   Francisco Tomás y Valiente, former president of Spain's constitutional court, is slain on his way to give a lecture at the University of Madrid. His murderer, ETA member Juan Antonio Olarra Guridi, is arrested in September 2002.

March 15, 1996   A nine-year-old Catholic girl is shot dead and a 19-year-old boy injured in an Irish National Liberation Army (INLA) shooting attack on the girl's home in central Belfast.

June 30, 1996   Despite the PKK cease-fire, sporadic terrorist attacks continue, most notably a suicide bombing against a Turkish military parade in Tunceli. The attack kills nine security forces personnel and wounds another 35. This is the first time the PKK uses a suicide bombing.

July 6, 1996   The Grey Wolves are accused of assassinating the prominent Turkish Cypriot journalist Kutlu Adali, who is shot and killed in front of his house in Nicosia. He is targeted because of his criticism of Turkey's policies in Cyprus.

July 8, 1996   The body of a Catholic taxi driver, who had been shot by the UVF, is discovered in Armagh inside his taxi.

July 12, 1996   On the day of the annual Protestant parade in honor of the 1690 victory of Protestants over the Catholics, the UVF tells its members not to march, as the parade passes through Catholic areas and the UVF wants to avoid jeopardizing the ongoing peace process. The Loyalist Volunteer Force (LVF) is formed after this event by those UVF members not interested in the peace process. The LVF resumes the violence against Catholic targets. The organization falls apart after leader Billy Wright is murdered in prison on December 27, 1997. Following his death, many LVF members join the Ulster Freedom Fighters (UFF).

July 23, 1996   French police capture Julian Achurra Egurrola, who is believed to be one of the three main ETA leaders. Security forces arrest him along with his female companion during a raid in Lasseube on the French side near the border with Spain. On July 9, 2002, Egurrola is sentenced to 46 years in prison for two attempted attacks against a Civil Guard barracks and a Civil Guard officer in July and August 1986.

October 1996   After ending its cease-fire, the PKK steps up its attacks against military and civilian targets in southeastern Turkey. The most noteworthy incidents include two more suicide bombings—one in Adana and one in Sivas—which kill two civilians in addition to eight security forces personnel. The suicide bombing in Sivas is of note because the city, well outside of the southeast, is in an area that the Turkish government previously considered to be relatively secure. In addition, four schoolteachers are murdered outside of Diyarbakir.

November 3, 1996   Abdullah Çatli, leader of the Grey Wolves, is killed in a car crash on a remote highway near the village of Susurluk, 100 miles southwest of Istanbul. In the car with him are his girlfriend, a former beauty queen also turned Grey Wolves member, and a top police official. The investigation uncovers Çatli's links with the Turkish police.

November 29, 1996 Two suspected members of the ETA are captured by the Spanish security forces in the northern Spanish city of Pamplona. Igor Angulo and Kepa Zubizarreta are accused of having engineered several bombings against police barracks.

1997 There are 22 fatalities that year in the troubles in Northern Ireland. Among the dead are 13 civilians, two RUCs, a soldier, a Republican, and three Loyalists.

January 8, 1997 Lieutenant Colonel Jesús Cuesta Abril is gunned down near his home in Madrid by ETA terrorists.

January 13, 1997 Juan Manuel Soares Gamboa is sentenced to 200 years and six months in prison for his role in the April 1986 bomb attack that cost the lives of five Civil Guards and injured four others in Madrid.

February 10, 1997 Rafael Martínez Emperador, a Supreme Court judge, is gunned down in front of his house in central Madrid by two presumed members of the ETA. A civilian employee of the Spanish Air Force is killed and eight others are injured by the explosion of a car bomb in the southern city of Granada, likely by ETA members.

February 11, 1997 Businessman Francisco Arratibel, who had acted as a mediator in an earlier ETA kidnapping, is shot to death by ETA terrorists as he is participating in a carnival in Tolosa, near San Sebastian. According to media report, the ETA accuses him of stealing a part of the ransom paid by the kidnapped man's family.

February 17, 1997 Modesto Rico Pasarin, a policeman, is driving out of the garage of his house, when a bomb placed under his car explodes in the Spanish town of Bilbao. ETA is responsible.

March 11, 1997 A 37-year-old prison psychologist is slain by three ETA armed militants in San Sebastian. One of the terrorists, Fernando Alejalde Tapia, is caught by two plainclothes policemen who happen to witness the murder.

March 24, 1997 A Protestant minister dies from a heart attack resulting from injuries suffered from a severe "punishment beating" by the UVF in his north Belfast residence six weeks earlier. It is the first fatality of a Protestant clergyman.

July 9, 1997 Miguel Ángel Blanco, a local council member for the People's Party, is abducted on his way to work in the Basque town of Ermua and the ETA demands that the government transfer 600 ETA members to prisons in the Basque region. The terrorists kill Blanco the next day.

July 15, 1997 An 18-year-old Catholic girl is shot dead by the Loyalist Volunteer Force (LVF), a UVF breakaway organization, while sleeping at the home of her Protestant boyfriend in Antrim.

July 24, 1997   Spanish police arrest three members of one of ETA's most experienced units as they are planning an attack to take place during the celebration of the festival of Santiago the next day.

September 5, 1997   Daniel Villar Encisco, a police officer, is fatally wounded in Basauri when he switches on the engine of his car and a bomb placed underneath it explodes. ETA is responsible.

October 13, 1997   Two Bulgarian engineers and one Turkish engineer are kidnapped by the PKK in Turkey. The Turkish engineer is killed, while the Bulgarian hostages are released.

December 11, 1997   A 64-year-old member of the People's Party is having a drink in a bar in Irun on the border with France when a hooded ETA member fatally shoots him in the head. Police presume the shooting was organized in reaction to the incarceration of 23 leading members of Herri Batasuna, the political wing of ETA.

1998   Fifty-seven deaths result this year from the Northern Ireland conflict. Fifty of the victims are civilians. One RUC officer, three Loyalists, and one Republican are also killed. Twenty-nine of the deaths are the result of a single bomb attack by the Real IRA.

January 9, 1998   José Ignacio Iruretagoyena, a member of the conservative People's Party and former conservative councilor in the Basque town of Zarauz, near San Sebastian, is killed when a bomb detonates in his car in the Basque region.

March 1998   In northern Iraq, Turkish military commandos capture Semdin Sakik, the PKK's second in command, and bring him to Turkey. Turkish security forces launch a series of successful military campaigns in late spring and early fall which hamper PKK activity in southeast Turkey.

March 1998   As a peace agreement seems imminent for Northern Ireland, the Real IRA is established as a radical splinter group of the IRA, which has observed a cease-fire since 1994. The Continuity IRA, another splinter group established earlier, vows to continue the violence.

April 10, 1998   The British and Irish governments sign the Belfast Agreement, also known as the Good Friday Agreement. The agreement states that the future of Northern Ireland will be decided by its citizens according to a majority vote. In addition, all parties commit to a peaceful and democratic resolution of the conflict. The Ulster Defense Association (UDA) officially adheres to the cease-fire following the Good Friday Agreement, even though the British government claims that it still secretly supports violent acts.

May 27, 1998   In Turkey, the PKK carries out an attack against a police station in Van, killing 20 soldiers and destroying all the military positions around the police station.

June 3, 1998   One person is killed and 14 injured when a bomb explodes on the Sirkeci-Halkali train in Istanbul. The PKK terrorist who places the bomb is captured.

June 25, 1998   A councilor in the Basque town of Renteria is killed and his bodyguard is wounded by the explosion of a bomb. Manuel Zamarreno has been town councilor of Renteria since ETA terrorists killed the previous councilor, José Luis Caso, four weeks earlier.

July 10, 1998   Seven people are killed and 118 injured as a result of a bomb explosion planted in the covered bazaar, Misiar Çarşisi, in Istanbul. PKK claims responsibility.

July 12, 1998   Three young brothers are killed in a UVF firebombing of their home in Antrim. The man who had driven the three attackers to the Antrim residence is sentenced to life in prison.

August 15, 1998   Twenty-nine people are killed, among them 18-month-old and 20-month-old babies, four children, and six teenagers, in a car bombing in Omagh, Tyrone, perpetrated by the Real IRA. The victims included Catholics, Protestants, a Mormon, and two Spanish tourists. The town is crowded, as a carnival is to take place later that day.

September 18, 1998   In Spain, the Basque terrorist group ETA announces an indefinite cease-fire.

October 1998   Turkey informs Syria that it will take action unless the government halts its support for Öcalan and the PKK. The government also formally requests Öcalan's extradition to Turkey. As a result, Öcalan flees to Russia.

December 1, 1998   A female guerrilla from PKK blows herself up outside a grocery store in Lice, Turkey, killing 15 officers and village guards and injuring eight.

1999   The death toll reaches seven for this year in the Northern Ireland conflict, the fatalities including five civilians, one former IRA member, and a Loyalist.

February 16, 1999   Turkish authorities capture Abdullah Öcalan, founder of the PKK, in Kenya following his stay of 12 days under the protection of the Greek Embassy in Nairobi. Öcalan has been a fugitive for four months since being expelled from Syria and seeking asylum in various countries. Immediately after Öcalan's arrest, the PKK conducts a number of attacks in southeastern Turkey in response. In August 1999, Öcalan announces a "peace initiative," ordering members to refrain from violence and requesting dialogue with Ankara on Kurdish issues. The Turkish State Security Court subsequently sentences him to death, but he escapes this punishment when Turkey abolishes the death penalty in 2002. He remains the sole prisoner on the Island of Imrali in the Sea of Marmara.

March 15, 1999   A prominent human rights attorney, a Catholic woman, is killed in Armagh by a Loyalist bomb planted under her car by the Red Hand Defenders.

April 4, 1999   The PKK claims responsibility for a suicide attack on the governor of Turkey's Bingöl Province, Süleyman Kamçi, that also kills a 12-year-old girl and injures 20 in Turkey.

June 5, 1999   A Protestant woman whose husband is Catholic dies as the result of a Loyalist pipe bomb thrown into her home in Armagh.

July 1, 1999

Four civilians and two terrorists are killed and five are injured during a PKK attack in Elazig Province, Turkey, against members of the right-wing political party, the Idealist Club.

July 20, 1999

One man is killed and seven people injured when a group of PKK gunmen opens fire at an outdoor restaurant in Caglayan, in Erzincan Province.

July 22, 1999

Three people are killed and one injured when PKK gunmen open fire at a gas station on the Bingöl-Solhan motorway in Bingöl Province, Turkey.

November 1999

The ETA announces the end of its cease-fire and blames the Spanish government for the lack of progress in talks on Basque demands.

2000

Nineteen fatalities result this year from the Northern Ireland troubles. Among the dead, ten are civilians, five are Ulster Volunteer Force (UVF) members, one is a member of the Real IRA, and three are in the Ulster Defense Association (UDA). Most of the deaths are the result of internal clashes involving the Loyalist groups—the UVF, UDA, and Loyalist Volunteer Force (LVF).

January 2000

Members at a PKK Congress support Öcalan's "peace initiative" of August 1999, which orders them to refrain from violence and request dialogue with Ankara on Kurdish issues.

January 21, 2000

Breaking a cease-fire, ETA terrorists kill a soldier and injure four others in a car explosion in Madrid.

February 19, 2000

In an apparent retaliation for the murder of a UVF member several weeks earlier by the LVF, two men, both Protestants, are killed after being beaten and stabbed and their throats slit. The UVF denies involvement though it is likely they were involved. One of the victims is thought to be linked to the LVF, but the LVF and his family deny this.

February 22, 2000

A Basque Socialist politician and his bodyguard are killed in a car bomb in the Basque capital, Vitoria, as they are walking on the university campus, near the regional Parliament building. On June 26, 2002, ETA members Asier Carrera and Luis Mariñelarena are jailed for more than 100 years for organizing the car bomb attack.

May 5, 2000

A 62-year-old political journalist for a daily Spanish newspaper who had criticized the ETA is gunned down in front of his home in Andoain, a suburb of the Basque port of San Sebastian. His assassination is followed by a series of silent vigils in Madrid, Barcelona, Bilbao, San Sebastian, Seville, and several other small towns.

June 4, 2000

A 57-year-old member of the People's Party in Spain is gunned down by an ETA gunman who shoots a bullet into his back in Durango, near Bilbao.

July 15, 2000

A 49-year-old Spanish conservative politician is murdered by ETA terrorists in Málaga where he is serving as city councilor. On December 17, 2001, the National Court in Madrid sentences his murderers, Igor Solana and Harriet Iragi, to 30 years' imprisonment.

July 29, 2000   The former Socialist governor of the Basque province of Guipúzcoa is assassinated by two ETA gunmen in a cafe on the outskirts of San Sebastian.

August 8, 2000   A 52-year-old business leader is killed in a car explosion attributed to the ETA in the Basque town of Zumaya. José Maria Korta, a well-known entrepreneur and the chairman of the local employers' association, is fatally hit by the blast after he parks his car in front of his office in an industrial area of the city. Korta has criticized the ETA for preventing the region's economic development, and his family reports he received several death threats before his assassination.

August 20, 2000   Two police officers are killed in a car bomb in the town of Sallent de Gallego, Spain, on the border with France. ETA is responsible.

August 29, 2000   A former People's Party councilor is shot to death in his shop in Zumarraga, Spain, near the port of San Sebastian, by two ETA terrorists.

September 2000   The Loyalist paramilitary organization, the Orange Volunteers, calls a cease-fire.

September 16, 2000   Police arrest Ignacio Gracia Arregui, 47, in Bidart in southwestern France. He is considered to have been the leader of the ETA's military wing since 1992. Among other crimes, he is believed to have ordered the failed assassination of King Juan Carlos. On February 13, 2003, a French court convicts him and he is sentenced to 16 years in prison.

September 21, 2000   A 42-year-old member of the People's Party in Spain and councilor for the town of San Adria del Besos is shot to death on his way to his office.

October 9, 2000   A 50-year-old prosecutor of the Superior Justice Tribunal in Spain is gunned down by three ETA terrorists as he enters his apartment building in the southern city of Grenada.

October 22, 2000   A 44-year-old prison official is killed in a car bomb attack planned by ETA in the Basque capital of Vitoria.

October 30, 2000   A car bomb detonates in downtown Madrid, killing three people including José Francisco de Querol y Lombardero, a Supreme Court judge, and injuring at least 66 others. ETA is responsible.

November 21, 2000   A 63-year-old former Socialist health minister of Spain is assassinated by two ETA members in the garage of his house in Barcelona.

December 5, 2000   A Protestant taxi driver is lured to north Belfast expecting to pick up passengers and is shot dead, likely by the IRA.

December 6, 2000   In retaliation for the killing of a Protestant taxi driver, the UDA shoots and kills a Catholic builder as he is working at a house in Antrim.

December 14, 2000   A 45-year-old plumber driving through the town of Terrassa near Barcelona, Spain, is killed when a bomb attached to his car blows up his vehicle. Francisco Cano is also a councilor in the town of Viladecavalls and a member of the People's Party. The ETA is responsible for this attack.

2001   Twenty people are among the dead in the Northern Ireland conflict this year. Sixteen of the dead are civilians and the remaining four are Loyalists.

February 22, 2001   Two people are killed and four others seriously wounded in an ETA car bomb attack in San Sebastian, Spain. Shortly after the attack, the French security forces arrest Francisco Javier Garcia Gaztelu, known as "Txapote," in south-western France. The 35-year-old man is believed to have served as chief of ETA's military wing since the arrest of Ignacio Gracia Arregui in September 2000. Beginning in 2003, Txapote will be convicted of a long string of terrorist attacks from 1994 to his capture.

March 9, 2001   One policeman, Iñaki Totorika Vega, is killed and another is injured in a car bomb attack in the Basque town of Hernani. On May 9, 2003, one of Vega's murderers is captured in France.

March 17, 2001   A policeman is killed in an ETA car bomb explosion in Roses, Spain.

March 31, 2001   A Protestant man is killed by Loyalists who believe he is Catholic as he is walking home from a bar in Antrim.

May 6, 2001   The president of the People's Party in the Aragon region, Manuel Giménez Abad, is shot and killed in Zaragoza. ETA is likely responsible.

May 24, 2001   Santiago Oleaga Elejabarrieta, a newspaper executive whose publication had been critical of the ETA, is shot to death in San Sebastian, Spain. The ETA claims responsibility.

July 10, 2001   A police officer is killed in an ETA car bomb explosion outside the Justice Ministry's information technology department in Madrid.

July 14, 2001   A 44-year-old police offer is killed by ETA terrorists while driving to have dinner with friends in San Sebastian.

July 15, 2001   A town councilor for the city of Leiza, near Pamplona, is killed when a bomb attached to the underside of a car explodes. The councilor, José Javier Múgica, is a member of the Union of the People of Navarra, a small center-right party that opposes Basque autonomy.

July 28, 2001   A 62-year-old general working for Spain's Ministry of Defense is killed in a bomb attack in Madrid. ETA is likely responsible.

August 20, 2001   A woman is killed and her 16-month-old grandson wounded in San Sebastian when a bomb hidden in a gasoline-powered toy car by ETA terrorists explodes.

September 28, 2001   A Catholic reporter from Northern Ireland becomes the first journalist to be killed in the conflict after he is shot dead by the LVF as he is returning home with his wife from a bar in Armagh.

November 7, 2001   A judge who had sentenced six ETA terrorists to jail is murdered outside his home in Bilbao by ETA gunmen.

November 23, 2001	Two police officers are machine-gunned in Beasain, Spain, by two ETA terrorists.
2002	Eleven individuals are killed this year in the troubles in Northern Ireland. Among the dead, nine are Loyalists and two are Republicans. At least four of the deaths result from internal Loyalist disputes.
January 12, 2002	A Catholic postal worker is shot by UFF gunmen as he arrives at work in north Belfast.
April 2002	At its Eighth Party Congress, the Kurdish nationalist PKK changes its name to the Kurdistan Freedom and Democracy Congress and proclaims a commitment to nonviolent activities in support of Kurdish rights.
July 21, 2002	A Catholic 19-year-old is shot dead by the UFF as he is walking home from his friend's house in north Belfast.
August 1, 2002	A Protestant construction worker is killed after a bomb explodes on an army base in Derry city. The Real IRA is responsible.
August 4, 2002	A six-year-old girl and a 57-year-old man are killed and 30 injured when a bomb detonates near a Civil Guard barracks in Santa Pola in southeast Spain.
September 16, 2002	Top ETA terrorist operational leaders, Juan Antonio Olarra Guridi and Ainhoa Múgica Goñi, are arrested.
December 19, 2002	Top leaders of the ETA's military apparatus are captured along with seven other suspected ETA members. Ibon Fernández Iradi and Ainhoa Garcia Montero are arrested at a routine checkpoint in France, on a road in the Pyrenees-Atlantiques Department.
August 17, 2003	A Catholic man who had spoken out against local paramilitaries is shot and killed by the Real IRA in his west Belfast home.
November 8, 2003	A Protestant man is shot dead by the UVF at his brother's Antrim apartment.
November 21, 2003	A Catholic man is killed when he is beaten with baseball bats, most likely by the UDA.
2003	The death toll in the Northern Ireland conflict reaches ten this year.
March 17, 2003	Spain's Supreme Court outlaws the Batasuna party, a Basque nationalist party suspected of links to the ETA. The party leaders deny any connection with the terrorist group, although it has almost always refused to condemn attacks claimed by or blamed on the ETA.
May 31, 2003	Two policemen are killed and one injured after an ETA bomb attack in the northern town of Sanguesa, Spain.

October 2003	KADEK—formerly known as the Kurdistan Workers' Party (PKK)—makes yet another name change, calling itself the Kurdistan People's Congress (KHK or Kongra-Gel) in an effort to masquerade as a political party. KHK launches several attacks, which it claims are in retaliation for losses the group suffered from Turkish counterinsurgency operations.
December 9, 2003	Police arrest Gorka Palacios, the ETA's alleged military commander, during a raid on a house in the village of Lons in southwest France.
2004	The Kurdistan Freedom Falcons, known as TAK because of its acronym in Turkish, is formed. The Freedom Falcons are widely thought to be the urban guerrilla arm of the outlawed separatist Kurdistan Workers' Party (PKK) that has fought Turkish security forces since 1984. Unlike the PKK, the Falcons has concentrated on civilian targets.
February 18, 2004	ETA announces on the Basque regional radio station that a cease-fire in the Catalonia region started on January 1.
April 2, 2004	French police arrest Felix Ignacio Esparza Luri, a member of the ETA's executive council and a senior leader of its logistic apparatus, in the suburb of Dax in southwest France.
April 4, 2004	French police arrest two of the most wanted ETA members during a raid in the French village of Saint-Michel. The first one, Felix Alberto Lopez de la Calle, 43, is thought to be the ETA's military mastermind and is charged with involvement in six murders from 1978 through 1980. The second person is Maria Mercedes Chivite Berango, believed to be the ETA's supply chief.
August 10, 2004	Two hotels in Istanbul are hit simultaneously by bombs, killing two people, including an Iranian, and wounding 11 others. The Kurdistan Freedom Falcons (TAK) and the Abu Hafs al-Masri Brigades both claim responsibility. Turkish officials believe the Kurdish group is responsible.
April 30, 2005	A bomb detonates near a statue of Turkish leader Mustafa Kemal Atatürk in Kusadasi, Turkey, killing a policeman and wounding four other people. The Kurdistan Freedom Falcons (TAK) claims responsibility.
July 16, 2005	An explosive device detonates on a tourist bus in the city of Kusadasi, killing five and wounding 14 others. TAK claims responsibility for this attack.
November 18, 2005	PKK terrorists plant a bomb by a bus stop near an amusement park in Istanbul, killing two and injuring 11.
August 28, 2006	Three are killed and 18 injured after a bomb, set by TAK, detonates at a business center in Antalya, Turkey.
September 3, 2006	A bomb detonates at a cafe in Çatak, Van Province, Turkey, killing two. The PKK is likely responsible.

September 12, 2006 A bomb detonates in Diyarbakir, a Kurdish city in southeastern Turkey, killing ten and wounding 14. TAK claims responsibility.

December 30, 2006 ETA terrorists are likely responsible for a bomb at a parking lot at Madrid's airport that kills two and injures 26.

Social Revolutionary Terrorism in Latin America

Political violence has long been a regular feature of Latin American life, including the frequent appearances of coups, dictatorships, and of repression both in rural (landlord-peasant) and urban (management-labor) social relationships. Yet terrorism has had a very specific role in the region's history as a revolutionary strategy during a specific era.

In contrast to other parts of the world, terrorism has been almost totally a social rather than national revolutionary doctrine. In Puerto Rico, a commonwealth associated with the United States, some nationalist terrorism did develop, but this was a rare exception. Otherwise, though, Latin American states have long had full independence. Consequently, the revolutionary movements there in modern times have sought to transform the existing society, usually in the framework of a Marxist orientation.

For a long time, however, such movements focused on means to gain power. The pro-Moscow Communist parties put the priority on mass organizing, trade unions, and electoral involvement. In some cases, the left took power in elections, as with Argentina's Juan Perón in 1946, Chile's Socialists in 1970, and Perón again in 1973. Sometimes those seeking social transformation engaged in coups—as with the National Revolutionary Movement in Bolivia (1952) and left-leaning officers in Peru (1968). As for nongovernmental right-wing groups, they had no need for systematic terrorism most of the time when they had widespread support from the regime and controlled the law enforcement systems.

The Cuban Revolution of 1959 introduced a new tactic to the revolutionary arsenal. Not only did Fidel Castro's revolution seize power, but it was also the hemisphere's first Communist regime and the first movement of social transformation which seemed to have made a permanent change. The Cuban model swept the continent's imagination, encouraging its advocates and frightening its conservative enemies, who would use the strongest means to prevent a Cuba-like revolution in their own countries. Moreover, the Cuban Revolution was dedicated to spreading revolution throughout the continent. Militant members of Communist parties, idealistic students, and fervent Catholic reformers saw Cuba's aims and methods as alternative means to realize the massive change and utopian goals they sought.

There was a problem in duplicating Castro's success, however. The favored strategy of the Cuban Revolution was rural-based guerrilla warfare. The fighters went into the countryside, struck quickly at the regime's forces when they chose to do so and returned to hiding. According to their theory, they would win over the peasantry by good treatment and the message that liberation was at hand. In turn, the peasants would support, feed, hide, and eventually join the revolutionaries. The promise of victory in guerrilla warfare failed early in practice, however, when Castro's lieutenant, Che Guevara, was killed in Bolivia in 1967 and his guerrilla forces were wiped out. After that, the appeal of rural guerrilla warfare faded except in some countries where there were big areas of largely uninhabited jungle—notably Colombia and Venezuela.

The switch from rural guerrilla warfare to urban guerrilla warfare intensified the importance of terrorism. Instead of marching down jungle paths to ambush an army patrol or capture an isolated police station, urban revolutionaries struck at foreign embassies, corporations, business executives, and other institutions full of civilians. It became a war not only against capitalism and repressive government but against the national infrastructure. In many cases these tactics only damaged countries that were already poor and economically unstable, used up their resources, reduced foreign investment, and thus injured common citizens. Revolutionaries could argue that weakening the society and the regime would advance their cause, but they were also making themselves the enemies of the people's immediate interests and reducing the possibility of gaining mass support for their revolutionary movements.

The other key aspect of the new revolutionary viewpoint was a heightened importance given to foreign factors and especially to the role of the United States. America's involvement in counterinsurgency was an important element in the defeat and death of Che Guevara and its involvement expanded in step with the Cuban-backed revolutionary movements. But the Cubans and their supporters had already concluded that the United States was a critical force in preventing revolution and it remained one of their main targets.

The main policy statement of Cuban foreign strategy, the February 1962 Second Declaration of Havana, constituted a declaration of war on the United States. Latin American states had failed to develop and were even becoming poorer, it charged, because they were in thrall to American imperialism. According to the declaration, only the United States was preventing the solution of such Latin American problems as unemployment, inadequate housing, shaky economies, and a sagging infrastructure.

The Declaration stated: "Even though the Yankee imperialists are preparing a bloodbath for America they will not succeed in drowning the people's struggle. They will evoke universal hatred against themselves." This meant that kidnappings, assassinations, bombings, and murders of foreigners would become important tactics for achieving revolution. In a sense, this innovation subtly changed Cuba's social revolutionary movement into a partly

nationalist one. The enemy included not only the local elites, but also foreign imperialists and their collaborators within the country. This shift never went as far as nationalist terrorist movements in other parts of the world—and was usually not even explicitly made by the terrorists themselves—but it was probably a critical element in making terrorism acceptable as a major tactic and sometimes even as a central strategy.

A combination of these factors thus led to a growth in terrorism by Latin American revolutionary movements. The main points included a belief that rapid revolution was possible; that it must be conducted through armed struggle; and that foreigners and foreign interests were legitimate targets and should be hit to drive them out and stir up the local people's hatred against them.

Ironically, though, Latin American terrorist groups showed little interest in public opinion. Perhaps this was due to their members' elite origins, romantic orientation, and abstruse ideological pursuits. In the history of Latin American terrorism, there is not a single example of a group winning mass support through terrorism. Equally, there were few signs that terrorist operations against foreigners or assassination of members of the local elite won the people's favor.

Terrorist methods not only failed to gain power for the revolutionaries, they also helped undermine democracy where it existed and encouraged the conservative nationalists in the military to seize power. Leaders of the armed forces believed they were the only ones who could defeat the revolutionary threat. To do so, they vastly increased the level of repression, sometimes killing hundreds or even thousands of people who were not even involved in radical movements. The terrorists might argue that such mass terror would bring recruits to their ranks and support for their cause, but this did not in fact happen.

Instead, the result was an expansion in right-wing terrorism, including the creation of death squads which targeted revolutionaries and their supporters as well as whole groups who might be suspected of radical sympathies—students, intellectuals, peasant and trade union activists, foreigners (for example, missionaries), and others. Right-wing terrorist groups often operated with the support of their government and with assistance from its military forces, essentially providing these groups with immunity from prosecution.

In Colombia and Venezuela, the rural revolutionary guerrilla tradition never died out. In those countries, radical movements created virtual empires in which they became the de facto government, far from the main cities. To keep this territory, push out the central government, and finance their operations, they engaged in kidnappings, robberies, and assassinations. Sometimes they even made truce agreements with the ruling regimes, moving toward becoming a permanent fixture on the political scene.

Another unique feature of Latin American terrorism was its involvement—most obviously in Colombia—with narcotics production and trafficking. The drug lords went into politics to preserve their vast enterprises and created their own heavily armed militias. They killed politicians who threatened them or journalists who investigated them too closely. At times, drug lords formed alliances with radical groups; in other cases the terrorist groups themselves went into the drug business.

With the failure of all the strategies aimed at bringing revolution—including urban guerrilla warfare and terrorism—there arose an organization that might be called the highest stage of Latin American terrorism, the Peruvian Shining Path group. Founded by university teachers and students, it developed a unique blend of Maoism, mysticism, Native American romanticism, and terrorism. In direct contrast to the old rural guerrilla concept, Shining Path deliberately terrorized the peasantry and reveled in the maximum amount of killing and destruction. Yet while the Shining Path may have come closer to achieving power than any

other terrorist group in the region, even its desperate effort to murder or intimidate everyone failed by the mid-1990s.

Terrorism as a tactic in Latin America, then, was a massive failure. To some extent, this was recognized by the radicals themselves, who abandoned it in most countries by the mid-1980s. Yet the money, publicity, and revenge such actions brought were too attractive to give up altogether.

The conditions, movements, and issues that produced terrorism in Latin America are highlighted in the following chronology. Groups like the followers of Juan Perón in Argentina, the Puerto Rican nationalist movement, and the Cuban Revolution of the 1950s were to give rise to terrorist offshoots in the 1960s and 1970s. The cycle of military dictatorships alternating with elected governments led to one revolutionary response when military governments repressed desired reforms and another when elected governments proved largely ineffectual at bringing economic change and development.

The selection of events in the chronology is designed to give a sense of the main areas where terrorism was taking place and the types of actions most used, including kidnappings and assassinations. The emphasis on attacking foreigners—both corporate executives and diplomats—reflects the terrorists' attempt to highlight external influences as the cause of the region's problems. Also included are the biggest and most spectacular operations and the counterterrorist efforts which led to the ultimate defeats of those insurgencies.

February 24, 1946   Juan Perón, a populist, wins election in Argentina and makes himself into a reformist dictator. The movement he creates dominates Argentinian politics over the next 30 years.

September 1950   U.S. President Harry Truman signs Public Law 600, the Puerto Rican Commonwealth Bill, which establishes Puerto Rico as a commonwealth under the protection of the United States and authorizes Puerto Rican authorities to write a constitution. Puerto Rican nationalists advocating independence oppose the Commonwealth Bill and demonstrate in Puerto Rican cities. Twenty-seven people are killed and about 100 are injured in the clashes.

October 31, 1950   Two Puerto Rican nationalists attempt to assassinate President Harry Truman. One Secret Service agent is killed and two are wounded in a shoot-out in front of Blair House (where the Truman family is living while the nearby White House is renovated). One of the assassins, Griselio Torresola is killed; the other,

Oscar Collazo, is wounded and captured. He is sentenced to death, but Truman commutes the sentence to life imprisonment. Collazo is released after serving 30 years.

July 4, 1951   Puerto Ricans vote 3-to-1 in favor of the Commonwealth Bill; in 1952, they approve a new constitution and elect their first governor.

1952   The Nationalist Revolutionary Movement (MNR) of Bolivia emerges as a broad-based party. Denied a victory in the 1951 presidential elections, the MNR leads the successful 1952 revolution. Under President Víctor Paz Estenssoro, the MNR introduces universal adult suffrage, carries out a sweeping land reform, promotes rural education, and nationalizes the country's largest tin mines. It also commits many serious violations of human rights.

July 26, 1953   Fidel and Raúl Castro lead 160 poorly armed guerrillas in an unsuccessful attack on the Moncada Barracks, the second-largest military fortress in Cuba, beginning what will become known as the Cuban Revolution. The attack is a total disaster. Sixty-one rebels are killed in the fighting, and one-third of the guerillas, including Fidel Castro, are captured. Half of the men captured are tortured to death. Although Castro is sentenced to death, at the urging of Catholic priests, dictator Fulgencio Batista abolishes the death penalty just before Castro's execution, and he receives a 15-year prison term.

March 1, 1954   In Washington, D.C., four Puerto Rican nationalists shouting "Viva Puerto Rico Libre" fire into the U.S. House of Representatives from the visitors' gallery, wounding five congressmen.

May 1954   General Alfredo Stroessner takes power in Paraguay after being elected to complete the unexpired term of his predecessor. He will be re-elected president seven times, ruling almost continuously under the state-of-siege provision of the constitution with support from the military and the Colorado Party. During Stroessner's 34-year reign, political freedoms will be severely limited, and opponents of the regime will be systematically harassed and persecuted under the banner of national security and anti-communism.

May 1955   A group of prisoners' mothers launch a campaign to free Fidel Castro and the other guerrillas imprisoned with him. The government approves an amnesty bill the same year which frees the prisoners. Castro goes into exile in Mexico.

December 1956   Castro returns to Cuba to start an armed struggle against the ruling dictatorship there. Although they are defeated at first, Castro's forces, the 26th of July movement, retreat to the mountains from where they launch an ultimately successful guerrilla war. His victory will be the inspiration for many Latin American revolutionary movements in ensuing decades, some of which will engage in terrorism.

January 21, 1958   General Marcos Pérez Jiménez of Venezuela is overthrown by a popular uprising. A new government of miltiary officers and civilians takes control led by Rear Admiral Wolfgang Larrazábal.

February 10, 1958   General Ydigoras Fuentes takes power in Guatemala following the murder of President Carlos Castillo Armas. Two years later, in response to his increasingly autocratic rule, a group of junior military officers revolt against the government. They fail and several go into hiding, establishing close ties with Cuba. This group becomes the nucleus of the forces that will be in armed insurrection against the government for the next 36 years.

January 1, 1959   The July 26 revolutionary movement, named after the original attack on the Moncada Barracks in 1953, takes power in Cuba. Batista flees the country, and Castro takes Havana and Santiago de Cuba while his lieutenant, Che Guevara, captures Santa Clara. The term "Cuban Revolution" is used to refer to the overthrow of Batista and to the Marxist economic and social revolution carried out by Castro in the following years.

Late 1950s   Uruguay begins having economic problems that lead to student militancy and labor unrest.

August 6, 1960   Castro nationalizes all U.S. and other foreign-owned property. The United States responds by placing an embargo on Cuba.

April 15, 1961   After Cuba turns toward an alliance with the USSR, the United States sponsors an unsuccessful attack on Cuba, using conservative Cuban exiles as the main source of support. Flying planes provided by the United States, these exiles bomb several Cuban air force bases. Castro declares Cuba a Socialist state. On April 17, 1961, a force of about 1,500 exiles, financed and trained by the U.S. Central Intelligence Agency, lands at the Bay of Pigs, hoping to spark a popular rising against Castro. This does not happen and the invaders are quickly defeated.

1963   In Uruguay, a revolutionary group called the Movement for National Liberation (MLN) is founded by Raúl Sendic, a university student in Montevideo. The group becomes better known as the Tupamaros, named for an Inca chief, Tupac Amaru, who was killed by the Spanish in 1571. In its early years, the group carries out robberies designed to amass funds and supplies and to make the government seem powerless.

1964   The Revolutionary Armed Forces of Colombia (Fuerzas Armadas Revolucionarias de Colombia, known as FARC) is established as the military wing of the Colombian Communist Party. This Marxist group is governed by a secretariat led by septuagenarian Manuel Marulanda (codename "Tirofijo") and six others, including senior military commander Jorge Briceño (codename "Mono Jojoy").

November 4, 1964   A military junta overthrows Bolivian President Paz Estenssoro at the outset of his third term.

1965   The National Liberation Army (ELN) is established in Colombia by urban intellectuals inspired by Fidel Castro and Che Guevara. Like FARC, it seeks a Marxist revolution.

1965   The U.S. Office of Public Safety (OPS) begins operating in Uruguay, training Uruguayan police and intelligence in policing and interrogation techniques.

October 3, 1965   Fidel Castro reads a "Farewell" letter written by Che Guevara in April, in which he resigns from all his official positions in the Cuban government to take up revolutionary activities abroad.

July 1, 1966   President Julio César Méndez Montenegro of Guatemala takes office. The army then undertakes a campaign to break up the guerrilla movement.

Fall 1966   Che Guevara arrives in Bolivia sometime between the second week of September and the first of November, according to different sources. He enters the country with forged Uruguayan passports with plans to organize and lead a Communist guerrilla movement. He begins operations in the spring of 1967.

August 31, 1967   The Bolivian army scores its first victory against the guerrillas, wiping out one-third of Che's men and forcing them to retreat.

September 18, 1967   In Bolivia, the government arrests 15 members of a Communist group who were providing supplies to the guerrillas in the southeastern jungles.

September 26, 1967   A gun battle between the army and Guevara's guerillas in the village of La Higuera, Bolivia, leaves three rebels dead. Four days later, Che and his group are trapped by the army in a jungle canyon in Valle Serrano, south of the Grande River.

October 8, 1967   In Bolivia, troops in a counterinsurgency effort aided by U.S. Army Green Berets and CIA operatives receive information about a band of 17 guerrillas in the Churro Ravine. They enter the area and, encountering a group of six to eight guerrillas, open fire, killing two Cubans and wounding Guevara, who surrenders.

October 9, 1967   Che Guevara is put to death by Bolivian soldiers. Cuba's effort to instigate guerrilla warfare throughout the western hemisphere ends in disaster.

The Era of Urban Guerrilla Terrorism

With the defeat of Guevara in Bolivia and the failure of other rural guerrilla revolutionary efforts, the scene shifted to the cities and to a much more terrorism-oriented strategy. Carlos Marighella, a former Communist Party militant who organized such a group in Brazil, became Guevara's successor as a model for revolution. Marighella's death only a year after starting operations suggested the failure of his approach, but the seeds of continuing urban terrorism had been planted. Within 15 years, other notable urban terrorist groups had been established in Argentina and Uruguay, with imitators set up in a dozen other countries. The kidnapping or assassination of officials, foreign diplomats,

and businessmen became commonplace, prompting conservative forces to support military coups, which in turn brought organized death squads and massive campaigns of repression to oppose the threats of revolution and terror. Yet all this violence brought surprisingly little change. The major developments in the region came about due to more traditional methods, including electoral processes (as in Bolivia and Chile), and rural guerrilla and mass organizing techniques (as in El Salvador and Nicaragua). Governments found it difficult to eliminate terrorism but easier to destroy specific groups which caused fear and suffering for many but had little lasting political or social impact.

1968	Two urban guerrilla groups form in Brazil: The Action for National Liberation (ALN), a splinter group from the Communist party led by Carlos Marighella; and the Popular Revolutionary Vanguard (VPR), created by radical students.
1968	In Uruguay, the Tupamaros kidnap Ulises Pereyra, the unpopular director of the national telephone company. A massive police search succeeds only in setting off a student riot in Montevideo. Pereyra is later released.
August 28, 1968	In Guatemala, two gunmen, most likely with the Rebel Armed Forces (FAR), a terrorist group sympathetic to Cuban leader Fidel Castro, assassinate U.S. Ambassador John Gordon Mein, ambushing his car in Guatemala City. The following day, the FAR issues a communiqué stating that it had planned to kidnap Mein and hold him hostage for the release of Camilo Sanchez, one of the FAR commanders who had been captured earlier by government forces.
September 1968	After months of political unrest in the Mexican capital and echoing worldwide student demonstrations and riots that year, Mexican students decide to exploit the attention focused on Mexico City by the 1968 Olympic Games with mass rioting. Mexican President Gustavo Díaz Ordaz orders the army to occupy the campus of the National Autonomous University of Mexico, and students are beaten and arrested indiscriminately. Rector Javier Barros Sierra resigns in protest on September 23.
October 2, 1968	After growing student demonstrations and strikes, 15,000 students from various universities march through the streets of Mexico City, carrying red carnations to protest the army's occupation of the university campus. By nightfall, 5,000 students and workers, many of them with spouses and children, congregate in the Plaza de las Tres Culturas, site of the ancient Aztec city Tlatelolco, where they are surrounded by army and police forces equipped with armored cars and tanks, who fire into the crowd. The killing continues through the night, with soldiers going through nearby apartment buildings. Most sources report 200–300 deaths with many injured and thousands arrested. The Tlatelolco Massacre galvanizes many political activists in Mexico and the rest of Latin America.
October 3, 1968	Juan Francisco Velasco Alvarado, a leftist army colonel, takes power in Peru in a military coup. His efforts to modernize the Peruvian economy are only partly successful and he will be overthrown in a coup on August 30, 1975.
October 12, 1968	Members of Brazil's VPR machine-gun U.S. Army Captain Charles R. Chandler, in front of his home in São Paulo.
March 11, 1969	A man tries to hijack a Colombian airliner en route from Medellín to Cartagena, but is stopped by passengers and crew. One crewman is shot and killed by police, who mistake him for the hijacker.
September 6, 1969	Twelve men and one woman armed with machine guns hijack two Ecuadorean Air Force transport planes to Cuba. During a refueling stop in Colombia, shooting breaks out; one co-pilot is killed and one crewmember wounded. One of the planes is abandoned in Colombia, while the other continues to Panama and on to Cuba. Passengers on the abandoned plane said the hijackers had explained

their mission as a retaliatory act to protest the deaths of several students in anti-government rioting in Guayaquil, Ecuador, in May.

November 1969   Brazilian terrorist leader Carlos Marighella is killed in a police ambush.

1970   The Shining Path (Sendero Luminoso, or SL) is founded in Peru by Abimael Guzmán, a former university professor. It espouses a Maoist-style doctrine combined with an emphasis on rural guerrilla warfare and the Native American roots of Peruvian identity.

January 20, 1970   Unidentified gunmen enter the British Consulate in Guatemala City, where they shoot and kill the consul's bodyguard.

March 31, 1970   Members of Guatemala's Rebel Armed Forces (FAR) kidnap Count Karl von Spreti, West German ambassador to Guatemala, and take him to a hideout near Guatemala City. The kidnappers demand release of 17 prisoners, later increased to 25 prisoners, and the payment of $700,000 ransom. The Guatemalan government rejects the demands and on April 5 the ambassador's body is found.

April 1970   In El Salvador, the People's Liberation Forces (FPL) is established. FPL is a Marxist group that is anti-foreign investment and anti-American, and is committed to overthrowing the Salvadoran government through a people's war.

April 19, 1970   Supposed fraud in the election for president of Colombia results in victory for conservative Misael Pastrana Borrero and defeat for the more progressive candidate, Gustavo Rojas Pinilla. The M-19 guerrilla movement (19th of April Movement) will eventually be founded in part as a response to this event.

June 18, 1970   Three workers of the Parke-Davis pharmaceutical plant on the outskirts of Buenos Aires, Argentina, are killed by a bomb. It is not known which group is responsible.

July 31, 1970   In Montevideo, the Tupamaros kidnap Daniel A. Mitrione, U.S. public safety advisor in Uruguay, and Aloysio Mares Dias Gomide, Brazilian consul in Uruguay. One week later, they kidnap Claude Fly, a U.S. agricultural advisor. The kidnappers demand release of 150 jailed Tupamaros in exchange for the three hostages. The president of Uruguay refuses to negotiate. During another massive police search for the kidnappers, the Tupamaros kill Mitrione and his body will be found on August 10. Dias Gomide is released after six months when ransom is paid by his family, and Fly is released on March 2, 1971. In March 1973, four terrorists involved in the kidnapping will be arrested by Uruguayan security forces. One of them, Antonio Mas, identified as Mitrione's actual murderer, is later convicted of the crime and sentenced to 42–45 years in prison.

September 4, 1970   After a bruising election campaign revealing polarized political views in Chile, Salvador Allende, the Socialist Party candidate, is elected president with 36.2 percent of the vote.

October 22, 1970   A Costa Rican airliner is hijacked to Cuba. The hijackers are members of a Nicaraguan organization, the Sandinista Front for National Liberation, founded in the early 1960s by university students in Managua and named for Augusto

César Sandino, a national hero who fought against occupation of Nicaragua by the United States in the 1920s and early 1930s. The Sandinistas demand the release of four of their members, who are being held in Costa Rica. The four prisoners are released and flown to Cuba.

December 2, 1970

In Rio de Janeiro, Brazil, members of the Action for National Liberation (ALN) and Popular Revolutionary Vanguard (VPR) kidnap Giovanni Enrico Bucher, the Swiss ambassador to Brazil, and kill his bodyguard. The kidnappers demand the release of 70 prisoners, safe passage out of the country, publication of the prisoners' pictures in the press, the broadcast of a revolutionary manifesto, and the immediate publication by the press of any other rebel communiqués. The Brazilian government agrees to release the prisoners on January 14, 1971, and two days later Bucher is released unharmed. In August 1972, three persons are sentenced to life imprisonment for involvement in this episode.

1971

In Bolivia, the military, the Nationalist Revolutionary Movement (MNR) (*see* 1952), and others install Colonel Hugo Banzer Suárez as president of Bolivia. Banzer rules with MNR support until 1974, when he replaces civilians with members of the armed forces and suspends political activities. The economy will grow impressively during Banzer's presidency, but demands for greater political freedom will undercut his support.

January 20, 1971

Four terrorists enter the British Consulate in Guatemala City, kill a guard, and spray the consulate with machine-gun fire. It is not clear which group is responsible.

March 21, 1972

In Argentina, members of ERP (Ejército Revolucionaria del Pueblo, in English, People's Revolutionary Army), a Marxist, pro-Castro group seeking to overthrow Argentina's dictatorship, kidnap Oberdan Sallustro, president of the Italian-owned company Fiat in Argentina and demand that 50 guerrillas be released, that $1 million in ransom be paid in the form of school supplies and shoes for school children in poor areas of the country, and for Fiat to reinstate 250 workers who had been fired in a labor dispute. Fiat accepts the ransom demand, but the Argentinian government refuses to release the prisoners, warning that Fiat executives will be prosecuted for "illicit associations" unless they break off contact with the kidnappers. When police discover the kidnappers' hideout on April 10, the kidnappers kill Sallustro, then are captured.

October 16, 1972

Members of a leftist political party that supports former Argentinian dictator Juan Perón plant a bomb that explodes in the Sheraton Hotel in Buenos Aires, killing a Canadian tourist.

March 11, 1973

Héctor Cámpora, a stand-in for former dictator Juan Perón, is elected president of Argentina because Perón himself is barred from running. Months later, Cámpora resigns and Perón is elected in his own right.

May 21, 1973

ERP gunmen wound an executive and an employee of Ford Motor Argentina, one of whom, Luis Giovanelli, later dies. On May 23, the ERP issues a communiqué stating that Giovanelli had been shot resisting a kidnapping attempt, and that the kidnapping of Ford executives will continue unless the company pays $1 million in ransom. On the same day, a bomb is defused at the Ford offices in Buenos Aires, and Ford agrees to pay the ransom. In accord with the ERP's instructions, the ransom is paid in the form of ambulances and medical supplies for provincial hospitals and other goods for the poor.

June 27, 1973   The Uruguayan military seizes control of the government in response to growing conflict with the Tupamaros guerrillas. Uruguay soon has the highest per capita percentage of political prisoners in the world. The Uruguayan government is charged with torture and other human rights violations.

June 29, 1973   A tank regiment under the command of Colonel Roberto Souper surrounds the presidential palace (La Moneda) in Chile in a violent but unsuccessful coup attempt against Socialist president Salvador Allende.

September 11, 1973   Chilean armed forces overthrow Salvador Allende, the elected president of Chile. Allende dies during the coup, and a junta led by General Augusto Pinochet assumes power. On September 13, Pinochet dissolves the Congress. The National Stadium is temporarily converted into an immense prison. About 130,000 individuals are arrested in a three-year period, with the number of "disappeared" reaching into the thousands within the first few months.

November 22, 1973   An American executive of Ford Motor Argentina, John A. Swint, and three bodyguards are killed in Córdoba, Argentina, by the Peronist Armed Forces (FAP) terrorists.

March 25, 1974   Jorge Oscar Wahelich, a Brazilian industrialist, is killed in Buenos Aires while resisting a kidnapping attempt by ERP terrorists.

July 1, 1974   Juan Perón dies and is replaced as president of Argentina by his wife, Isabel.

August 27, 1974   Ricardo Goya, labor relations manager of the French-owned IKA-Renault Motor Company in Córdoba, is gunned down while driving to work. FAP claims the assassination.

September 20, 1974   John G. Little, Argentinian executive of Schering Pharmaceutical Company, a subsidiary of the German company, is assassinated on a street corner. The Montoneros, a leftist splinter group of the Peronist Party, is suspected.

September 29, 1974   General Carlos Prats Gonzalez, former commander of the Chilean army under the late President Allende, and his wife are killed in a bomb blast as they drive toward their Buenos Aires home. The general had gone into voluntary exile in Argentina after the 1973 coup in Santiago. A right-wing terrorist group called the Argentine Anti-Communist Alliance, also called the "Triple A" is suspected, though Chileans may have been behind the bombing.

November 1974   The Armed Forces for National Liberation (FALN), a Puerto Rican nationalist group, announces that it has been responsible for five recent bombings, most in New York City and Chicago. In the coming years, they will claim many more terrorist acts against police officers and against property, mostly in the United States but also in Puerto Rico.

February 26, 1975   John Patrick Egan, a U.S. consular agent in Córdoba, Argentina, is kidnapped by Montoneros guerrillas who demand that four leftist Peronists who had disappeared in past months be shown alive on television or Egan will be executed. The government says it will not cooperate, and that night Egan's body is found at the side of the road outside Córdoba.

April 25, 1975

A bomb placed in a car parked in front of the British Embassy residence in Buenos Aires, Argentina, explodes, killing a police guard and injuring two others. The ambassador and his family are not injured.

August 30, 1975

Peruvian leader Juan Francisco Velasco Alvarado is overthrown in a coup and General Francisco Morales Bermúdez takes power. He presides over a return to civilian government, the drawing up of a new constitution in 1979, and democratically held elections in May 1980.

October 29, 1975

Four Montoneros gunmen assassinate a personnel manager with Fiat-Concord, Argentina's largest auto firm. Earlier, the group had threatened to kill company executives if certain demands were not met. In response, the company closed its plant on October 20, but then was compelled to re-open by the government.

January 29, 1976

In Buenos Aires, Argentina, Montoneros terrorists kill two officials of the Bendix Corporation and a policeman attempting to thwart the attack.

January 30, 1976

A guard at the the Spanish Embassy in Bogotá, Colombia, is killed when a bomb detonates. It is not clear which group is responsible.

March 24, 1976

President Isabel Perón of Argentina is overthrown by a military coup.

March 26, 1976

Two security guards of an Argentinian Ford executive are killed by machine-gun fire from a speeding car.

April 7, 1976

Left-wing guerrillas attack the home of Hugo Carlos Sardan, an Argentinian executive of Pfizer, a pharmaceutical firm headquarted in the United States, killing one guard and wounding another.

April 14, 1976

Gunmen in Buenos Aires kill an Argentinian executive of the U.S. Chrysler Corporation.

May 4, 1976

An Italian executive of the Fiat automobile company in Buenos Aires is assassinated by unknown terrorists.

August 9, 1976

Members of CORU, an organization of Anti-Castro Cubans, kidnap and murder two officials at the Cuban Embassy in Buenos Aires. The assistance of the Chilean intelligence agency in this operation is suspected.

August 14, 1976

In San Salvador, El Salvador, a policeman guarding the residence of Nicaragua's ambassador is gunned down by unknown assassins.

August 19, 1976

Leftist gunmen assassinate the deputy manager of Fiat's Materfer subsidiary as he leaves his home in Córdoba, Argentina.

September 9, 1976

An Argentinian executive of the Chrysler factory in Buenos Aires is assassinated in front of his home. The Montoneros claim responsibility. This assassination follows the firing of 121 workers accused by Chrysler and Ford of promoting work stoppages and slowdowns.

September 21, 1976   In Washington, D.C., former Chilean Foreign Minister Orlando Letelier is killed by a bomb placed in his car. A passenger, Letelier's American assistant, is also killed. Letelier served during the Allende administration and was living in exile while supporting opposition to Chile's military regime; Chilean government agents are responsible.

October 10, 1976   Domingo Lozano, Argentinian manager of the French-owned Renault plant in Córdoba, is shot and killed by Montoneros terrorists after leaving church services.

October 18, 1976   In Argentina, five unknown assassins gun down Enrique Aroza Garay, the executive of the German-owned Borgward automobile factory.

November 6, 1976   An executive of the Chrysler Corporation is shot to death in Argentina by two unknown assailants as he leaves his home.

1977   Media in Guatemala receive anonymous announcements of the creation of the Guatemalan Anti-Salvadoran Liberation Action Group, which pledges to kill Salvadorans who take the jobs of Guatemalans.

February 14, 1977   In the village of La Macarena, Colombia, 50 FARC terrorists kill a policeman and kidnap a U.S. citizen, biologist and Peace Corps member Richard C. Starr. FARC offers to release Starr in return for the release of imprisoned terrorist Jaime Guaracas. The U.S. government refuses, and Starr is only released three years later, on February 12, 1980, after a $250,000 ransom has been paid, its amount raised by American newspaper columnist Jack Anderson.

April 11, 1977   In Argentina, an executive of the Surrey Company, which operates under an agreement with General Motors Corporation, is assassinated in Buenos Aires. The Montoneros claim responsibility.

October 1977   Terrorists posing as public works employees detonate an explosive-filled car outside the home of Eduardo Beach, an Argentinian executive of Chrysler Corporation, killing a company bodyguard and a woman neighbor. Montoneros members are thought to be responsible.

October 13, 1977   A car bomb, likely set by Montoneros terrorists, explodes outside the home of an Argentinian executive of the Chrysler subsidiary, killing two and injuring two others.

December 2, 1977   In Buenos Aires, two are killed and one wounded when Montoneros terrorists fire submachine guns at a car carrying three bodyguards of a Chrysler executive.

December 8, 1977   Thirteen people, including two French nuns, are kidnapped in Buenos Aires by Montoneros guerrillas who demand that the Roman Catholic Church repudiate the military government and that the government free 21 prisoners and provide information on prisoners and missing persons, and offer asylum to all persons persecuted for political reasons. The bodies of the 13 hostages are found along with the bodies of other Montoneros prisoners on beaches near Bahia Blanca, 500 miles south of Buenos Aires.

December 16, 1977   Montoneros terrorists kill Andre Gasparoux, the technical director of the subsidiary of the French Peugeot Motor Company, in Argentina.

1978   Bolivian elections this year, and in 1979 and 1980, are inconclusive and marked by fraud, coups, counter-coups, and caretaker governments.

May 17, 1978   In El Salvador, Japanese textile magnate Fujio Matsumoto is kidnapped by the Armed Forces of National Resistance (FARN), a splinter group from earlier Salvadoran leftist groups. FARN claims that Matsumoto is a representative of Japanese imperialism, which exploits the world's underdeveloped peoples. The group demands the release of 33 political prisoners, general amnesty for the prisoners on trial under the law for the defense and guarantee of public order, abolition of this hated law, and a ransom of $4 million. The government rejects the demands. It is later revealed that Matsumoto was accidentally shot and killed the night he was kidnapped.

May 29, 1978   The Colombian general manager of Texas Petroleum Company, a subsidiary of Texaco, is kidnapped in Bogotá. Nicolas Escobar Soto is killed by his kidnappers on January 3, 1979, when police stumble upon their hideout while searching for stolen weapons. At least two kidnappers commit suicide upon being discovered.

August 24, 1978   A new Puetro Rican nationalist terrorist group is formed. The Popular Boricua Army, also known as the Macheteros, is inaugurated with the murder of a police officer. The murder is in retaliation for an attack in which police killed two Puerto Rican nationalist activists.

October 25, 1978   A powerful bomb explodes at the Guatemalan Consulate in the city of Chalchuapa, El Salvador, killing Manuel de Jesus Lopez, a watchman. The People's Liberation Forces (FPL) claims responsibility, saying that the bombing was staged in solidarity with the people

November 7, 1978   Ten Salvadorans are found dead in Guatemala City, believed to be the victims of the Guatemalan Anti-Salvadoran Liberation Action Group.

January 17, 1979   Members of FARN in El Salvador kidnap Ernesto Liebes, a millionaire coffee exporter who also serves as Israel's consul-general, demanding the release of several political prisoners by March 21. Liebes's body is found March 22.

May 3, 1979   Terrorists shoot and kill Switzerland's chargé d'affaires in El Salvador, Hugo Wey, in an apparently botched attempt to kidnap him. The People's Liberation Forces (FPL) are suspected.

September 21, 1979   Gunmen in El Salvador kidnap Dennis McDonald and Fausto Bucheli, two U.S. executives of the Beckman Electronics Company, killing Jose Luis Paz Tartara, their Salvadoran driver. The terrorists also kill a soldier at a checkpoint during the attack. The Revolutionary Party of Central American Workers claims responsibility and demands that the company run worldwide ads calling for an overthrow of the Salvadoran government. The two Americans are released on

November 7, after a reported $10 million ransom is paid and ads appear in the *Los Angeles Times* and *New York Times* calling for a "popular insurrection and liberation war" against the government of El Salvador.

November 9, 1979

The People's Liberation Forces (FPL) bomb the McDonald's restaurant in San Salvador, killing one person.

November 28, 1979

About 20 gunmen from the Popular Liberation Front (PLF) in El Salvador abduct the South African ambassador, Archibald Gardner Dunn, as he leaves his embassy in downtown San Salvador. The kidnapping occurs hours after PLF gunmen kill Lino Guzmán, the former mayor of San Martín, a town 12 miles east of the capital. The kidnappers demand that the government cut relations with South Africa, Israel, and Chile. They threaten to execute Dunn within six days unless $20 million ransom is paid and their communiqués are published widely in the foreign media. On October 10, 1980, it becomes known that the guerillas killed the ambassador when his government refused to comply with their demands.

December 12, 1979

In El Salvador, a bomb planted by People's Revolutionary Army (ERP) guerrillas explodes on the grounds of the Israeli Embassy, killing three policemen and an embassy security guard. The ERP claims that the attack is in solidarity with the FPL.

1980

The Shining Path in Peru turns to terrorist methods to intimidate peasants, destroy the governmental structure, strike at foreign targets, and destroy opposition to its increasing power.

1980

Bolivian General Luis García Meza carries out a violent coup. His government will be notorious for human rights abuses, narcotics trafficking, and economic mismanagement. Later he will be convicted in absentia for crimes including murder and extradited from Brazil in 1995 to begin serving a 30-year sentence.

February 27, 1980

Heavily armed April 19 Movement (M-19) terrorists shoot their way into the Dominican Republic Embassy in Bogotá during a reception for that embassy's Independence Day and take 80 hostages, including 14 ambassadors from various countries, including the United States. A gunfight with security forces leaves one attacker dead and one wounded; four soldiers and the Paraguayan consul and his bodyguard are also wounded. The kidnappers demand ransom of $50 million, publication of a guerrilla manifesto by all the countries the hostages represent, release of over 300 political prisoners, and safe passage from the country. Sixty days later, a deal is negotiated, and the terrorists are allowed to go to Havana, Cuba, along with the 12 remaining hostages, who are freed on their arrival there.

July 11, 1980

In El Salvador, about 15 members of the 28 February People's League shoot their way into the Costa Rican Embassy, killing a policeman and leading about 115 peasants, mostly women and children, inside to stage a protest occupation. Police rush to the scene but pull back at the demand of the Costa Rican ambassador. The peasants claim they are seeking political refuge and wish to speak with foreign ambassadors about their demands for an end to government repression in the countryside: They say the army is killing and torturing peasants. The Costa Rican ambassador begins negotiations with his government for political asylum for the peasants. On July 17, the FPL leads another 115 peasants into the already packed eight-room embassy and conditions become unbearable. On July 18 Costa Rica announces a deadlock in negotiations and that it is moving its embassy. On July 19, the embassy loses its diplomatic status, and the International Red Cross takes custody of the peasants. Costa Rica ultimately provides asylum to about 230 Salvadoran peasants.

September 17, 1980   Exiled former Nicaraguan dictator Anastasio Somoza Debayle is assassinated in Paraguay when a band of men blow up his car and spray it with sub-machine gun fire. His driver and financial advisor are also killed in the attack. Following this event, Paraguay breaks off relations with Nicaragua, claiming it has proof that the Sandinistas (now in power in Nicaragua) worked with Argentinian terrorist groups to accomplish the assassination. Fifteen years later, in October 1995, the leader of Argentina's People's Revolutionary Army (ERP), Enrique Gorriarán Merlo, is arrested and stands trial for several offenses. He claims responsibility for the assassination of Somoza.

September 17, 1980   In El Salvador, 18 leftist guerrillas from the Revolutionary Democratic Front shoot their way into the Organization of American States' (OAS) local offices. They kill a guard, take over the building, and capture 11 hostages. They demand an end to Salvadoran government persecution of leftist sympathizers. The hostages include the OAS delegate from Nicaragua and other diplomats and employees. After five days, negotiations start with an OAS representative from Washington, D.C., and on day ten an OAS assistant director is released because of poor health. On September 28, the leftists free the remaining hostages, having become convinced that the government of El Salvador will investigate the disappearances of hundreds of leftists and the status of alleged political prisoners.

December 2, 1980   Three American Roman Catholic nuns—Ita Ford, Maura Clarke, and Dorothy Kazel—and a social worker, Jean Donovan, are found shot to death and buried in a common grave along a dirt road in El Salvador. Three of the women had been raped before being shot. Shortly after, a justice of the peace who had examined the murdered women is kidnapped and then found dead. U.S. President Jimmy Carter suspends all military and economic aid to El Salvador and sends a mission to investigate. Six members of the Salvadoran National Guard are eventually charged with the murders; five of them stand trial and are convicted. In 1987, they are granted amnesty and released from prison.

December 7, 1980   In Guatemala, an American, Clifford Bevens, who manages a subsidiary of Goodyear, is kidnapped by 15 terrorists. The abductors seek $10 million ransom for the Guerrilla Army of the Poor (EGP). On August 13, Bevens and five of the terrorists are killed during a raid by Guatemalan security forces.

January 19, 1981   In Colombia, the April 19 Movement (M-19) kidnaps Chester Bitterman, an American linguist at the Summer Institute of Linguistics, agreeing to free him when the Colombian government agrees to close down the institute, which M-19 believes is a CIA front. An official for the institute claims that the charges are false. After negotiations fail and the deadline passes, Chester Bitterman's body, shot through the heart, is left on an abandoned bus. In March, the M-19 names three of its dissident members as responsible for the kidnapping and slaying of Bitterman. Leaders of the movement send a communiqué to Bogotá newspapers professing innocence in the murder.

February 3, 1981   Unidentified terrorists firebomb a section of the U.S.-owned Esso Standard Oil compound in San Salvador, killing two people.

July 1, 1981   A baggage handler in the airport in Guatemala City is killed when a bomb hidden in a suitcase, intended for an Eastern Airlines flight bound for Miami, explodes. The Guerrilla Army of the Poor says the bomb was intended to explode during the flight to discourage tourism to Guatemala.

September 17, 1981   John David Troyer, an American Mennonite missionary, is shot in his home in Talama, Guatemala, by unknown terrorists yelling anti-American slogans. Another American missionary is seriously wounded.

October 10, 1981   Gunmen from the Guerrilla Army of the Poor (EGP) kill a Guatemalan police officer guarding the U.S. Embassy in Guatemala City.

November 26, 1981   At an oil exploration camp near Orito, Colombia, M-19 terrorists gun down Nelson Rodriquez Pinillas, a geologist employed by the U.S.-owned Western Petroleum Corporation, who they accuse of being an "army informer."

1982   The four principal left-wing guerrilla groups in Guatemala—the Guerrilla Army of the Poor (EGP), the Revolutionary Organization of Armed People (ORPA), the Rebel Armed Forces (FAR), and the Guatemalan Labor Party (PGT), which all conduct economic sabotage and attack government installations—and members of government security forces combine to form the Guatemalan National Revolutionary Unity (URNG). At the same time, extreme right-wing groups of self-appointed vigilantes, including the Secret Anti-Communist Army (ESA) and the White Hand, torture and murder students, professionals, and peasants suspected of involvement in leftist activities.

January 7, 1982   Unknown gunmen kidnap a Belgian Roman Catholic priest and a Guatemalan priest in the town of Nuevo Concepción, Guatemala, and kill a church caretaker, Eludio Aguilar, because he tried to prevent the abduction. In another incident, in Escuintla Province, gunmen abduct a nun, Victoria de la Roca, after setting a convent on fire. Church sources blame right-wing extremists for the incidents as such extremists have claimed that priests and nuns are often linked to leftist guerrillas fighting to topple Guatemala's military government.

February 13, 1982   Four terrorists, likely from right-wing groups, gun down a 37-year-old American missionary, Christian Brother James Arnold Miller, of Custer, Wisconsin, as he fixes a window outside of a school in Huehuetenango, Guatemala, where he teaches.

March 20, 1982   Members of the Guerrilla Army of the Poor shoot and kill a U.S. citizen, J. Pitts Jarvis, at his plantation in northern Guatemala.

March 23, 1982   Guatemalan army troops commanded by junior officers stage a coup to prevent the assumption of power by General Ángel Anibal Guevara, the handpicked candidate of outgoing President and General Romeo Lucas Garcia. They denounce Guevara's electoral victory as fraudulent and ask retired General

Efraín Ríos Montt to negotiate the departure of Lucas and Guevara. Ríos Montt had been the candidate of the Christian Democracy Party in the 1974 presidential elections and was widely regarded as having been denied his own victory through fraud. Montt takes office, forms a three-member military junta that annuls the 1965 constitution, dissolves Congress, suspends political parties, and cancels the electoral law. After a few months, Montt dismisses his junta colleagues and assumes the title of "President of the Republic." He embarks upon a scorched-earth counterinsurgency campaign in the highlands against URNG, the recently formed umbrella organization for radical organizations. His brief presidency is probably the most violent period of the 36-year internal conflict, which results in the deaths of about 200,000 mostly unarmed civilians.

April 15, 1982   An executive with the Coca-Cola Company is assassinated by unknown assailants in Guatemala.

July 31, 1982   In Santiago Texacuangos, El Salvador, Bernard Dewerchin, a Belgian architect overseeing construction of a hospital for the San Salvador archdiocese, is killed by unidentified gunmen.

September 20, 1982   A policeman is killed by three terrorists, probably from Shining Path, who attack him as he is guarding the East German Embassy in Lima, Peru, and steal his submachine gun.

October 2, 1982   In Guatemala, unidentified gunmen shoot and kill an American businessman, Richard Kehagy, and dump his body in Villanueva, a town 18 miles outside the capital.

The Era of Shining Path

Peru's Shining Path (Sendero Luminoso, or SL) was not the only terrorist group that showed power and the ability to survive during the 1980s and into the 1990s, but it was the most important organization espousing terrorism as a central strategy.

After all, while the title of most durable Latin American revolutionary group should be given to the two Colombian groups, the Revolutionary Armed Forces of Colombia (FARC) and National Liberation Army (ELN), terrorism for them was a sideline to protect their turf and fund their operations. Moreover, neither of them posed any threat to seize control of the central government. Only the Shining Path seemed actually capable of taking over a country. If it had succeeded, those imitating its pathway to power would have brought a firestorm of terrorism across the continent.

The Shining Path, which styled itself as the legitimate Peruvian Communist Party, combined elements of cultism, Maoist rural guerrilla warfare, urban guerrilla warfare, romantic Native American revivalism, and criminality. In contrast to previous terrorist groups that focused their murderous attentions on powerful and wealthy individuals or foreign representatives, the Shining Path was quite willing to murder large groups of civilians.

The horrifying nature and scope of its terrorism actually did intimidate large sectors of the population into passivity. Its spectacular, large-scale, carefully coordinated operations were bolder than those of any previous grouping. So powerful did the organization become that it did provide a serious challenge to the Peruvian government.

Yet it was not long after the peak of its power in the mid-1990s that the Shining Path began a steep decline as the government managed to round up its main leaders and foil many of its key operations. If it had not been defeated, the Shining Path would have set the pace for Western Hemisphere terrorism in a manner unequaled since the Cuban Revolution.

October 26, 1982   Shining Path (SL) is believed responsible for the killing of a Civil Guard posted outside the Indian Embassy in Lima.

1983   In Peru, a new terrorist organization is formed. The Tupac Amaru Revolutionary Movement (MRTA) is a Marxist-Leninist revolutionary movement formed from remnants of the Movement of the Revolutionary Left, an insurgent group active in the 1960s. It aims to establish a Marxist regime and to rid Peru of all imperialist elements, especially U.S. and Japanese influence.

1983   The Manuel Rodriguez Patriotic Front (FPMR) is founded as the armed wing of the Chilean Communist Party and is named for the hero of Chile's war of independence against Spain.

March 7, 1983   In Colombia, Kenneth Bishop, a 57-year-old executive with Texaco, is kidnapped by three terrorists from the People's Revolutionary Organization (ORP), who kill his two bodyguards. Texaco refuses to negotiate, and on April 14, 1983, Bishop is released supposedly after his family paid a ransom. Three Colombians, including a former municipal judge and his wife, are arrested and charged with the kidnapping.

May 25, 1983   In El Salvador, Lieutenant Commander Albert Schaufelberger, a Navy officer, becomes the first American U.S. military advisor to die at the hands of terrorists. He is killed by a two-man assassination team from the Farabundo Marti National Liberation Front (FMLN), an umbrella group representing several earlier revolutionary organizations.

May 27, 1983   In Peru, Shining Path terrorists launch an incursion into Lima, the nation's capital. At 6:20 p.m., during rush hour, the entire city is blacked out for one hour by coordinated bombings which knock down ten electrical pylons. In the ensuing darkness and confusion, Shining Path units detonate 40 bombs targeting, among other things, offices near the U.S. Embassy, the Sheraton Hotel, and the Bayer Chemical Corporation's main industrial plant. An estimated $300 million in damage results to Bayer alone.

August 8, 1983   Montt of Guatemala is deposed by his own Minister of Defense, General Óscar Humberto Mejía Victores, who succeeds him as de facto president. Seven people are killed in the coup, but Montt survives to found a political party (the Guatemalan Republic Front) and to be elected president of Congress in 1995 and 2000. General Mejía allows a managed return to democracy, starting with a July 1, 1984, election for a Constituent Assembly to draft a democratic constitution.

1984   The president of Colombia, Belisario Betancur, a conservative who won 47 percent of the popular vote, negotiates a cease-fire with terrorist groups in return for the release of many imprisoned guerrillas. The cease-fire ends when Democratic Alliance/April 19 Movement (AD/M-19) guerrillas resume fighting in 1985, claiming that the cease-fire was incomplete and questioning the government's real willingness to implement any accords. The government in turn questions the guerrillas' commitment to the process.

1984   Massive protests against the Uruguayan dictatorship break out. After a 24-hour general strike, talks begin and the armed forces announce a plan for return to civilian rule. National elections are held this year, and Colorado Party leader Julio María Sanguinetti wins the presidency, implementing economic reforms and democratization following the country's years under military rule.

October 28, 1984

A U.S. Peace Corps volunteer is shot to death as he is walking in Guatemala City. No group claims responsibility.

November 27, 1984

In Colombia, a bomb explodes under a car parked near the U.S. Embassy in Bogotá, killing a Colombian woman and wounding eight others. The blast comes 12 days after embassy officials receive a threat from cocaine smugglers because President Betancur has agreed to allow extradition of six major drug operators to the U.S. to stand trial.

February 7, 1985

In the northern Colombian city of Medellín, four bombs are detonated in front of four American businesses, killing a private guard. In a joint communiqué, the National Liberation Army (ELN) and the Ricardo Franco Front faction of the Revolutionary Armed Forces of Colombia (FARC) claim responsibility.

March 25, 1985

A right-wing death squad assassinates University of San Carlos professor Flavio Jose Quesada Saldaña, a Nicaraguan national, in Guatemala City.

March 29, 1985

A U.S. journalist, Nicholas Blake, and his American guide, Griffith Davis, disappear in Quiche, Guatemala, while seeking contact with members of the Guerrilla Army of the Poor (EGP). They are held by the EGP for one month and then executed.

May 5, 1985

In Peru, gunmen shoot and kill an American missionary at his home in the Lima suburb of Puente Piedra. It is believed that the gunmen intended to kidnap the missionary's daughter.

May 30, 1985

After nine months of debate, the Constituent Assembly of Guatemala finishes drafting a new constitution, which takes effect immediately. Vinicio Cerezo, a civilian politician and the presidential candidate of the Christian Democracy Party, wins the first election held under the new constitution with almost 70 percent of the vote, and takes office on January 14, 1986.

June 20, 1985

In El Salvador, the Central American Workers' Revolutionary Party, a group under the FMLN umbrella, machine-guns a sidewalk cafe in San Salvador, killing 13, including four U.S. off-duty Marine embassy guards and two American businessmen. A communiqué indicates that their primary target was the Marines. In May 1991, a Salvadoran military court sentences three alleged leftist rebels to prison terms ranging from four to 25 years for the killings.

July 20, 1985

A sixty-pound car bomb explodes in front of the U.S. Consulate in Santiago, Chile, killing one and injuring four others. The Manuel Rodriguez Patriotic Front (FPMR), the armed branch of the Communist Party, is likely responsible.

August 4, 1985

In Guatemala, a makeshift grenade is tossed into the garden of the Mexican Embassy, killing two Guatemalan employees.

August 7, 1985   One of Ecuador's leading bankers, Nahim Isaias, is kidnapped by members of the Alfaro Vive Carajo (AVC) and the Colombian April 19 Movement (M-19) from his weekend home in Guayaquil, Ecuador. The kidnappers' hideout is discovered on August 31, and Isaias is killed by his kidnappers during the raid by army commandos, who kill four of the five kidnappers.

September 5, 1985   Three heavily armed members of the Colombian terrorist group ELN fail in their attempt to kidnap a wealthy Venezuelan cattleman at his home in El Amparo, Venezuela, near the Colombian border, when a maid spots them and screams. The maid is stabbed in the neck and dies en route to the hospital, but neighbors notify the National Guard, which kills two of the attackers as the third escapes.

November 6–7, 1985   Some 35 members of the April 19 Movement (M-19), take 300 lawyers, judges, and Supreme Court magistrates hostage at the Palace of Justice in Bogotá. They want Colombian President Belisario Betancur to be tried in the courts. An attempt by the Colombian military to end the crisis results in a fierce battle in which more than 100 people are killed, including 11 Supreme Court justices and many top M-19 commanders.

November 13, 1985   In Peru, Tupac Amaru members shoot and kill a guard on duty at the Colombian Embassy.

December 10, 1985   Colombian guerrillas claiming to belong to the Popular Liberation Army (EPL) ransack a jungle oil camp in Tibu, taking seven hostages. Most of the hostages are released and instructed to advise authorities that a $6 million ransom will be required to secure the release of two remaining hostages, Edward Sohl and John Geddes, American supervisors of the joint American-Colombian petroleum exploration project. On June 3, 1986, the guerrillas release Geddes, who reports that Sohl had died on May 17 of a heart attack.

1986   A civilian government returns to office in Guatemala. By this time, the Guatamalan National Revolutionary Unity (URNG) recognizes that coming to power through armed struggle is out of the question, and it takes initiatives to negotiate a political solution.

February 16, 1986   Farabundo Marti National Liberation Front (FMLN) guerrillas in El Salvador claim responsibility for the execution of U.S. military advisor Peter Striker Hascall, gunned down in a suburb southeast of the capital.

March 1, 1986   In Guatemala, unidentified terrorists kill Salvadoran businessman Ricardo Boet Rodriguez and injure his companion as Rodriguez's Cessna planet is taxiing on an airstrip near El Naranjo, north of Guatemala City.

April 4, 1986   Tupac Amaru guerrillas bomb the Colombian Consulate in Peru, killing one person and wounding another.

June 15, 1986   In Guatemala City, Norma Jane Wagon, a Jehovah's Witness from the United States, is taken by unknown terrorists to an undisclosed location and locked inside her car. She is killed after an explosive device placed under the car is detonated.

June 18–19, 1986   In Peru, Shining Path inmates at three Lima prisons take prison guards and three journalists hostage as they demand the release of 500 imprisoned for terrorism. During the raid by security officials to end the mutiny some 224 prisoners are killed.

June 26, 1986   In Peru, Shining Path bombs a tourist train en route to Cuzco from Lima, killing seven people including one American, and injuring 40.

September 7, 1986   A failed assassination attempt on Chilean President Augusto Pinochet leaves five of his bodyguards dead when his motorcade is ambushed between El Melocotón and Santiago. Terrorists with the Manuel Rodriguez Patriotic Front (FPMR) are responsible. Three terrorists are arrested for the attack on April 14, 1989, and sentenced to life in prison, but are pardoned in March 1994.

October 22, 1986   In Ayacucho, Peru, Shining Path terrorists spray congregants at a church of the Jehovah's Witnesses with automatic weapons fire, killing five and wounding eight.

December 1986   A Shining Path hit squad guns down the naval attaché Captain Juan Vega Llona, outside the Peruvian Embassy in La Paz, Bolivia. Llona commanded the Peruvian Marine unit which suppressed the prison mutiny on El Frontón Island in June 1986. Shining Path members track him down in La Paz and assign about 22 people to the attack against him. The hit squad comes out of the University of San Andres campus, shoots and kills Vega on his way to the embassy, then returns coolly to the campus.

1987   In Bolivia, the Tupac Katari movement has spent a frustrating decade trying to make headway in the legitimate political system. Now this nativist movement with strong Trotskyite influence goes underground, looking towards Peru for role models on how to begin a revolt. One band splits off from Tupac Katari, calling itself the National Liberation Army Reborn (ELN-R) and copies kidnapping and other techniques of the Guevarist guerrilla Tupac Amaru Revolutionary Movement (MRTA) in Peru. They are quickly swept up by police. The other Katarista splinter group, the Tupac Katari Guerrilla Army (EGTK), studies the methods of Shining Path and makes contacts with them. It has a tightly knit, six-person cell network, uses bombings against public infrastructure as a means of training and propaganda, and develops contacts with coca-growers associations (and, perhaps, traffickers) in the Chapare region.

January 26, 1987   Three police are killed when Shining Path terrorists assault the Indian Embassy in Lima, Peru, with machine-gun fire and dynamite. The location is picked because Peru's President Alan Garcia is visiting India. On the same day, in a related attack, Shining Path guerillas take over a Reuters office in Lima and force correspondents to broadcast statements denouncing the Peruvian and Indian governments.

November 18, 1987   Peruvian gunmen attack a Nissan auto plant in Lima and four people are killed.

December 5, 1987   About 40 members of Shining Path take control of Haquira, an isolated village in the Peruvian Andes. They arrest villagers whose names appear on a list of "lackeys of imperialism and enemies of the revolution," among them two French nationals working for the International Committee for the Development of Agriculture. After haranguing the villagers and denouncing the Lima government and "foreign interference," the invaders cut the throats of five people, including the French workers.

January 14, 1988   A bomb in a Toyota explodes at 5:20 a.m. in front of the entrance of the Medellín building owned by drug kingpin Pablo Escobar, killing two guards, injuring five other people and damaging 40 nearby buildings. Several groups claim credit for the bombing: Death to Drug Traffickers; Communist Working Youths of Colombia; and War on the Mafia (GAMA). GAMA releases a communiqué declaring its aims to eradicate Colombian Mafia members, authorities who collaborate with the Mafia, and the lawyers who defend them.

January 20, 1988   In Chile, a bomb goes off in the waiting room of a doctor in Valparaiso who treats patients of the National Defense Employees Pension Fund, killing one person and injuring 20 others.

May 1988   A coup attempt by dissatisfied military personnel in Guatemala fails.

May 3, 1988   In Colombia, members of the pro-Cuban and Maoist National Liberation Army (ELN) and the People's Liberation Army engage in coordinated attacks on diplomats and Colombian government officials. They kidnap Sigfried Marketkurt, the West Germany honorary consul in Bucaramanga; Hellmuth Lücker, the West German honorary consul in Medellín; Jean Christopher Rampal, a public information officer at the French Embassy; Sigilfred Marquez, Dutch honorary consul in Bucaramanga; two Swiss trade officials; and several Colombian journalists. Other government officials escape kidnap attempts and one policeman is shot dead while pursuing the culprits. The 15 hostages are released on May 12.

June 15, 1988   An American and his Peruvian companion, who both worked for the U.S. Agency for International Development, are shot and killed by members of Shining Path near Huancayo, 125 miles east of Lima.

July 3, 1988   In Colombia, Fidel Lillo Shifihno, an executive of General American Pipe Company, an oil-related company, is kidnapped and his body is discovered near the town of Sabana de Torres on July 27. The People's Liberation Army is suspected.

December 1, 1988   Suspected Shining Path forces damage a special tourist train, filled with foreign and local dignataries en route from Cuzco to Machu Picchu, killing two women, one the wife of a New Jersey mayor, and wounding nine others.

December 6, 1988   In La Paz, Bolivia, a woman guns down the Peruvian naval attaché in front of the Peruvian Embassy. The Workers Revolutionary Party claims responsibility for the attack.

1989   Jaime Paz Zamora, the new president of Bolivia, takes a hard line against domestic terrorists. He orders a government attack on the Néstor Paz Zamora Committee (CNPZ—named after the president's brother, who died in the

Teoponte uprising against the Bolivian government in 1970) and in early 1992, a crackdown against the Tupac Katari Guerrilla Army (EGTK).

February 1989   Police arrest the leader of the Tupac Amaru Revolutionary Movement (MRTA), Victor Polay, and imprison him in Canto Grande prison in Lima.

February 3, 1989   General Stroessner, ruler of Paraguay, is overthrown in a military coup headed by General Andrés Rodríguez. Rodríguez, the Colorado Party candidate, easily wins the presidency in elections held that May. As president, Rodríguez institutes political, legal, and economic reforms and initiates a rapprochement with the international community.

March 2, 1989   Shining Path terrorists kill a French tourist in Cuzco Department.

April 18, 1989   In Peru, Austrian journalist Joseph Piescher is tortured and killed by alleged members of Shining Path.

May 1989   In Guatemala, dissatisfied military officers attempt the second coup in a year, but fail again.

May 12, 1989   Two West German tourists in Peru are forced off a bus by members of Shining Path and murdered in front of the other passengers.

May 24, 1989   An attack on a tourist convoy by Shining Path in the Department of Ancash, north of Lima, leaves one British tourist dead and six other tourists injured.

May 24, 1989   In Bolivia, Zarate Willka Armed Forces of Liberation members kill two Mormon missionaries. The terrorist group is aimed at criticizing what the group terms as "Yankee invaders and their lackeys." The attack comes as a group of U.S. military engineers, technicians, and troops arrive in the country to build an airport in the city of Potosi.

June 1989   A Lithuanian citizen, Barbara Dachille, who had been working as the chief of the ecology section of the Peruvian newspaper *El Comercio,* and a companion are shot and killed by Shining Path members in Peru. They had been traveling in a UN Food and Agriculture Organization station wagon.

August 9, 1989   In El Salvador, a U.S. businessman is killed during a kidnapping attempt at his home in San Salvador.

October 31, 1989   In El Salvador, ten are killed, including two Americans, and 35 wounded when a bomb detonates at the offices of the leftist National Trade Union Federation of Salvadoran Workers. Some have charged that the organization, which calls itself an umbrella group for more than 250 unions, is in fact part of the FMLN.

November 21, 1989   Shining Path terrorists kill Todd Smith, a reporter for the *Tampa Tribune,* in the Upper Huallaga River Valley of Peru. Smith was working on an article about drug trade and guerrilla violence.

November 27, 1989   The Extraditables, a group formed by the Medellín drug cartel, claims immediate responsibility for an explosion aboard an Avianca airliner, en route from

Bogotá to Cali, which kills 110 people. The Extraditables say it targeted the flight because six alleged police informers were on board, one of whom had reportedly told police the location of the jungle hideout of Medellín cocaine leader Pablo Escobar, whose home was raided by Colombian police on November 22. The group's name comes from threats by the Colombian government that leaders of the drug trade could be extradited to the United States and tried under U.S. law.

December 21, 1989   Unknown terrorists gun down a Nicaraguan diplomat in Guatemala City.

Late 1980s   The AD/M-19 and several smaller guerrilla groups in Colombia are successfully incorporated into a peace process which culminates in a national assembly to write a new constitution, which will take effect in 1991. The FARC has declared a unilateral cease-fire under Betancur, which leads to the establishment of the Unión Patriótica (UP), a legal and nonclandestine political organization. Many of the FARC's armed guerrillas and militiamen do not demobilize, however, as this is not a requirement of the process. After growing violence against its UP members (including several presidential candidates) from private paramilitary organizations, increasingly powerful drug dealers, and a number of paramilitary sympathizers within the armed forces, the truce with the FARC will end in 1990.

January 1990   In Chile, more than 40 suspected members of the Manuel Rodriguez Patriotic Front (FPMR) and Manuel Rodriguez Patriotic Front–Dissidents (FPMR/D) stage a mass jailbreak. Several of the escapees had been involved in the 1986 attempt against Pinochet.

January 9, 1990   In Peru, a Tupac Amaru movement (MRTA) commando shoots former Defense Minister E. López Albújar, who had ordered the execution of MRTA prisoners on April 28, 1989.

January 12, 1990   In Guatemala, a Salvadoran leftist and the Guatemalan woman driving him to the airport are abducted near Guatemala City. Their bodies are discovered the next day.

February 9, 1990   An American is found murdered in the city of Cuzco, Peru. It is not known which group is responsible.

February 11, 1990   Two murdered Coca-Cola union representatives are discovered in San Cristóbal, Guatemala.

February 28, 1990   In Guatemala City, a security guard is discovered murdered at the Swedish Embassy. It is not clear which group is responsible.

March and April 1990   Suspected narco-terrorists assassinate the two leading leftist presidential candidates in Colombia.

March 2, 1990   In Panama City, an American serviceman is killed and 27 wounded, 15 of them Americans, after a grenade attack on an American-owned disco. The terrorist who threw the grenade was a supporter of a group calling itself the Movement of December 20, which later claims responsibility for the bombing. This date comes from the day in 1989 that U.S. forces invaded Panama and captured its leader, General Manuel Noriega, who was then brought to the United States and tried for extensive drug dealing.

March 22, 1990

Bernardo Jaramillo Ossa, a presidential candidate of the Colombian Communist Party, is assassinated as he is on the campaign trail in Bogotá. His death remains an unsolved crime. After his assassination other members in or related to his party are also killed.

April 11, 1990

José Dionisio Suárez y Esquivel, implicated in the assassination of former Chilean Ambassador Orlando Letelier and his aide Ronni Moffitt in Washington, D.C., (*see* September 1976) is arrested in St. Petersburg, Florida. On April 18, he pleads not guilty, but on September 10, 1990, he changes his plea to guilty in exchange for a sentence of no more than 12 years for conspiracy to murder Letelier. On September 12, 1991, Virgilio Paz Romero is sentenced to 12 years in prison after pleading guilty to the same charge. The assassination was planned by the Chilean intelligence services during the regime of General Pinochet, and two high-ranking members will be convicted of their part in the crime in Chile in 1993.

April 11, 1990

In Peru, the main leader of the Tupac Amaru Revolutionary Movement (MRTA), Victor Polay, and 46 MRTA inmates stage an escape from the Canto Grande prison through a 315-meter-long tunnel. Polay is captured in 1992.

June 5, 1990

An American businessman is kidnapped and decapitated in the northern department of Petén, Guatemala. Nine Guatemalan soldiers are accused of the act and five are later convicted. The murder leads the U.S. Congress to suspend military aid to Guatemala on December 27, 1990. In August 1991, an appeals court orders army captain Hugo Roberto Contreras Alvarado, also charged with the kidnapping and murder, jailed.

June 11, 1990

The leftist Néstor Paz Zamora Commission (CNPZ) in Bolivia kidnaps the owner of a Coca-Cola bottling plant near his office in La Paz and demands a $2 million ransom for the executive's release. His family agrees to pay $500,000, but the victim is killed on December 5, when police surround the La Paz residence where he is being held. The CNPZ claims to represent oppressed ethnic groups from the Amazon and Andean regions.

July 28, 1990

On Peru's Independence Day and the inauguration day of President Alberto Fujimori, 300 people seize a small piece of privately owned but idle land in Ate-Vitarte. The action is organized by Shining Path, who charges 100 families $10 each for the right to a plot. This is part of the group's larger strategy to set up residential areas with means and ways to live and then indoctrinate the residents into their beliefs. Police try to dislodge the squatters, and two people die in the fray. The settlement, a walled compound, takes on the name of one of the martyrs, Félix Raucana. In August 1991, after a year-long trial, the judge issues an eviction order. An estimated 2,000 protesters, many of whom probably think they are supporting the neighbors' claims to shelter, not backing a Shining Path initiative, march to the Ate-Vitarte business district and confront police until the army is called in. The same evening, Shining Path sets off a car bomb outside a textile plant belonging to the landowner whose property had been taken. He asks the judge to withdraw the eviction order the following day. In late April

1992, two Raucana community leaders are arrested and the residents confront the army garrison set up in September 1991. Two people die and another 14 are wounded.

August 22, 1990   Shining Path members kill two Mormon missionaries in Huancayo, Peru.

August 30, 1990   In Colombia, six journalists are kidnapped by Medellín cocaine leaders who call themselves "the Extraditables" while on their way to interview leftist guerrillas. Most of the journalists, including Diana Turbay, daughter of a former Colombian president, have family ties to Colombia's political elite. One hostage is released in November 1990 because of heart pains and at least two others are released in December. During a police raid in January 1991, one hostage escapes and Turbay is killed.

October 19, 1990   In Peru, a private guard is killed in an attack against the U.S.-owned Bata shoe factory in Lima.

1991   In Bolivia, President Paz Zamora's government, having broken up a number of drug-trafficking networks, issues a decree giving lenient sentences to the biggest narcotics kingpins. Three years later, the Bolivian Congress will investigate the president's personal ties to accused major trafficker Isaac Chavarria.

1991   Pablo Escobar, head of the Medellín drug cartel in Colombia, turns himself into Colombian authorities to escape extradition to the United States or assassination by his enemies. He becomes confined in a luxury prison that he has designed. His arrest results in a sharp decrease in narcotics-related violence in Colombia. As a result, several paramilitary groups publicly demobilize, claiming that with Escobar behind bars the battle they had been fighting was over.

1991   In Chile, the National Truth and National Reconciliation Commission Report (Rettig Report) is released, detailing human rights violations during the Pinochet regime.

January 1991   In Ecuador, gunmen from Alfaro Vive Carajo (AVC), a small Marxist-Leninist extremist group, occupy the French Consulate in Guayaquil, but the Ecuadorian government chooses not to prosecute.

January 2, 1991   In El Salvador, terrorists from the Farabundo Marti National Liberation Front (FMLN) shoot down a U.S. helicopter carrying three U.S. military advisors en route from El Salvador to Honduras. Two of them, Lieutenant Colonel David Pickett and crew chief Private First Class Earnest Dawson, are killed by their attackers after surviving the crash. The third, Chief Warrant Officer Daniel Scott, dies of his injuries.

February 1991   In Ecuador, a handful of AVC members turns in 65 guns in a ceremony after negotiations with the government in which they agree to participate in the legitimate political process. In October, some of the members publicly announce their desire to join President Borja's Democratic Left Party, while a dissident faction denounces the move to abandon clandestine terrorist activities.

February 13, 1991 An American who had been tortured is found dead in the Escuintla Department in Guatemala. The assassins are unknown.

March 15, 1991   In Chile, the Lautaro Youth Movement (MJL), an offshoot of earlier leftist groups organized against the Pinochet regime, continues terrorist acts even after Pinochet is removed from power in 1990. On this day it claims responsibility for the murder of investigations police chief Hector Sarmiento Hidalgo in Concepción.

April 1, 1991   In Chile, Jaime Guzmán, a senator and founding member of a Fascist movement in Chile, is assassinated by Manuel Rodriguez Patriotic Front (FPMR) gunmen as he leaves his office at Catholic University in Santiago.

April 1, 1991   FARC terrorists kidnap an American living in Colombia and kill him two months later during an attempted rescue.

May 10, 1991   Unknown terrorists kill the Peruvian vice president of a U.S. firm near Lima.

May 17, 1991   In Peru, a Canadian evangelical aid worker and a Colombian working with him are killed by Shining Path terrorists. The killings come as Shining Path has its eleventh anniversary.

May 22, 1991   In Peru's Junín Department, 80 Shining Path terrorists seize an Australian nun and four town officials. The group is taken by truck to the town's main square and after subjecting their victims to a "people's trial," they are killed when explosives are hurled at them.

June 5, 1991   In Peru, a Soviet national who supervises a textile factory whose workers have been on strike is gunned down by Shining Path members while driving outside Lima.

July 12, 1991   Three Japanese engineers are killed at the Technical Center of Vegetable Cultivation in Huaral, Peru. Shining Path terrorists are responsible. Nine of the 15 terrorists responsible are captured on May 10, 1994.

July 16, 1991   In Huaral, Peru, Tupac Amaru Revolutionary Movement (MRTA) terrorists kidnap and then kill a businessman of Japanese background.

July 25, 1991   In Puno, Peru, one is killed and two injured after Shining Path terrorists detonate a bomb at the Land Recovery Program office, supported by the European Community.

August 9, 1991   In attacks on three towns north of Lima, Shining Path terrorists kill two Polish Franciscan priests and four municipal officials. An Italian nun is later released.

August 26, 1991   Shining Path terrorists assassinate an Italian Catholic priest who had been running social programs in the country as he is driving about 200 miles north of Lima.

September 1991   In El Salvador, two military officers are convicted for the 1989 murder of six Jesuit priests, marking the first time a military officer has been convicted for right-wing terrorism.

November 1991   The administration in Peru issues a series of legislative decrees designed to strengthen the government's counter-terrorism capabilities. Among these decrees are measures to reduce sentences in exchange for information, to increase the powers of military commanders in areas outside emergency zones, and to reorganize the police and intelligence services.

November 3, 1991   In Peru, 17 persons are killed in the Barrios Altos neighborhood of Lima by a group of armed men. Those responsible will later be found to be a death squad composed of members of the Peruvian military.

December 19, 1991   A nine-crewmember Honduran military helicopter infiltrates the airspace of El Salvador because of bad weather and is shot down by FMLN terrorists.

December 31, 1991   In El Salvador, FMLN signs a cease-fire agreement with the government.

1992   Peruvian intelligence sources claim that Shining Path is working with Bolivia's Marxists. They maintain that at least three Shining Path cadres are serving with the radical organization EGTK (Tupac Katari Guerrilla Army, *see* 1989), and that the Peruvian Army has found several Bolivians in Shining Path columns in Cuzco, indicating an active exchange of personnel. In July, Shining Path forces launch an offensive in Lima and bomb the Bolivian Embassy. Bolivia responds by ordering tightened controls at its Peruvian border and closer investigation of Bolivian radical groups.

January 12, 1992   Three U.S. nationals are killed when Shining Path members shoot down a helicopter in the Upper Huallaga Valley.

February 15, 1992   In the midst of a crowded rally in Peru's Villa El Salvador, a respected community leader, Maria Elena Moyano, is assassinated by Shining Path terrorists. Moyano had been outspoken in opposing the Shining Path.

May 2, 1992   A mounted Shining Path column attacks the U.S.-owned Northern Peru Mining Company, killing the mine's superintendent and chief engineer.

May 9, 1992   In Peru, Shining Path inmates at Canto Grande maximum security prison take over the prison. Finally, 80 hours later, police SWAT teams backed by the army retake control. The inmates had connected men's and women's cell blocks, built defensive positions, and collected weapons for 660 prisoners. They were protesting an imminent transfer of inmates to other penitentiaries. In the end, 47 inmates and two policemen die.

June 10, 1992   Peruvian terrorist leader Victor Polay, who had escaped from Canto Grande prison, is recaptured in Lima. His imprisonment results in period of internal feuding in the Tupac Amaru Revolutionary Movement (MRTA) and on July 8, MRTA stages a brief seizure of a northern jungle town in order to show that Polay's capture has not hurt the organization.

July 5, 1992   In Lima, Peruvian police capture Oscar Ramirez Durand, allegedly the number-three man in the Shining Path organization in Lima.

July 16, 1992   Two car bombs detonate in a crowded shopping district of Miraflores, Peru, killing 24 and wounding nearly 200. Shining Path is responsible.

July 20, 1992   In Peru, a powerful explosive goes off in front of the Miraflores office of the Institution of Liberty and Democracy (ILD), killing three people and injuring 16. It is an attempt by Shining Path to silence Hernando de Soto, the ILD founder and an advocate of free markets and reduced state interference in the economy.

July 22–23, 1992   Shining Path calls for a citywide "armed strike" in Lima designed to bring productive activity to a halt. Few of the 7,000 privately owned buses dare to venture onto the streets; only state-owned buses make their routes. In one incident, Shining Path demonstrators stop a taxi driver and order him out of his vehicle. When the driver refuses, he is shot, doused with gasoline, and burnt alive in his car. During the two days, 17 people lose their lives and another 40 are injured.

July 25, 1992   Peru's President Alberto Fujimori makes a nationally telecast speech about government countermeasures to the violence in Lima.

August 1992   Thirty students at the National University of the Center in Huancayo are reported missing this month. Seventeen of them will be found dead, each shot in the head and showing signs of torture. According to military sources, the killings are a result of feuds between the Shining Path and the Tupac Amaru Revolutionary Movement (MRTA). Others say that the students were picked up by security forces in vehicles typically used by the army and are innocent victims of the government's war against terrorism.

August 26, 1992   Security forces capture the head of the Shining Path metropolitan committee's hit squad, Gilberto Iparraguirre, the first major capture in months.

September 12, 1992   An elite unit of Peru's National Directorate Against Terrorism (DINCOTE), raids a residence in the middle-class neighborhood of Surco in Lima and captures Abimael Guzmán, 57, Shining Path's supreme leader and the most wanted man in Peru for more than a decade. DINCOTE captures nine other people at the safe house, including two well-known activists: Laura Zambrano, a prominent metropolitan Lima leader, and Elena Iparraguire, Guzmán's companion. DINCOTE units raid two other safe houses, arresting 30 more people. The raids also obtain a cache of documents, notes, and computer disks. In the following days, police units capture the national coordinator responsible for liaison with the regional committees and the coordinator of the northern Lima zone.

September 27, 1992   Shining Path leader Abimael Guzmán is imprisoned at a submarine base on San Lorenzo Island near Callao under the custody of the Peruvian navy. President Fujimori has placed 42 percent of national territory and 47 percent of Peru's 22.6 million citizens under emergency military control.

October 1992   Peru's DINCOTE captures Marta Huatay, a prominent Shining Path leader, in Lima. A Guzmán protégée, Huatay played a high-profile role in the late 1980s as president of the Association of Democratic Lawyers (Asociación de Abogados Democráticos—AAD), a Shining Path front organization that provided legal defense to militants and sympathizers. She had been underground since 1989 because of death threats.

October 2, 1992   Shining Path terrorists kill a lay Italian missionary worker, Giuglio Rocca, in Huaraz, 190 miles northeast of Lima.

October 10, 1992   A band of about 100 Shining Path members sweeps down on the community of Huayllao in La Mar province, Ayacucho, 200 miles southeast of Lima. Some 47 people are killed, including 19 women and seven children. The action against Huayllao is revenge for the community's support of the government's strategy of setting up a civil militia. The community had been a militia stronghold and had given refuge to civil defense members fleeing from a militia stronghold in the Apurimac Valley that the Shining Path had attacked in July.

October 4, 1992   A court convicts Abimael Guzmán of terrorism and high treason and sentences him to life imprisonment and payment of damages totaling $25 billion. The tribunal also convicts Shining Path national coordinator Zenon Vargas and Elena Iparraguire. Two other military courts simultaneously sentence eight other Shining Path leaders to life prison terms and $20 million fines each. Judges and prosecutors wear ski masks and signs with numbers instead of names to protect their identities.

October 23, 1992   In Colombia, a British employee affiliated with the American banana company Standard Fruit is kidnapped by FARC. Three days later, he is killed during a raid by police.

December 4, 1992   In Colombia, National Liberation Army (ELN) terrorists detonate a bomb at Medellín International Airport, killing a night watchman, and attack several other airfields.

January 22, 1993   Shining Path terrorists kill a guard at the Coca-Cola bottling plant in Lima and then abandon a van packed with explosives. The bomb detonates, killing a guard from Lima Electric Power Enterprise, and injuring four others.

May 1, 1993   In Peru, two foreign tourists—one Swiss, the other Austrian—are reported missing. They are found dead and tortured in the nation's Andean highlands on July 7, 1993. Shining Path members, who may have mistaken them for spies, are responsible.

May 25, 1993   Guatemalan President Jorge Serrano illegally dissolves Congress and the Supreme Court and tries to restrict civil freedoms, allegedly to fight corruption. This measure fails due to unified protests by most elements of Guatemalan society, international pressure, and the army's enforcement of the decisions of the Court of Constitutionality, which rules against the president's acts. In the face of this pressure, Serrano flees the country.

June 5, 1993   The Congress of Guatemala elects ombudsman Ramiro de León Carpio to complete President Serrano's term. De León, not a member of any political party, launches an anti-corruption campaign and demands the resignations of all members of Congress and the Supreme Court. In August 1994, a new Congress is elected to complete the unexpired term. Controlled by the anti-corruption parties—the populist Guatemalan Republican Front (FRG) headed by Efraín Ríos Montt, and the center-right National Advancement Party (PAN)—the new Congress will begin to move away from the corruption that characterized its predecessors.

October 21, 1993

Three are killed and 50 wounded after a bomb explodes at a hotel in Peru. Shining Path is responsible.

October 25, 1993

Near Lima, Peru, terrorists explode a bomb under a minibus in the parking lot near the departure terminal of the international airport, killing a driver and injuring 20.

December 2, 1993

Pablo Escobar is found by Colombian security officials 18 months after the government had sought to move him from his own luxury prison to more secure facilities. Escobar engages in a shoot-out with police and is killed.

January 16, 1994

In Colombia, two U.S. missionaries are kidnapped and a ransom demanded for their release by FARC terrorists in San Jose, near Villavicencio, to protest against the stationing of members of the U.S. Army Corps of Engineers in the country. The bodies of the Americans are found on June 19, 1995, in Cundinamarca Province.

February 1994

Two are killed when a 175-pound car bomb detonates outside the Air Force headquarters building in central Lima. Shining Path is likely responsible.

March 1994

The government of Guatemala and the terrorist group Guatemalan National Revolutionary Unity (URNG) (*see* 1982) sign agreements on human rights. This is followed three months later by agreements on resettlement of displaced persons and historical clarification (June 1994), and one year later by agreements on the rights of indigenous peoples (March 1995).

June 1994

The Chilean government captures Lautaro Youth Movement (MJL, *see* March 15, 1991) founder and leader, Guillermo Ossandón. Those lower down in the organization's hierarchy are arrested in August. Two prominent members of the Manuel Rodriguez Patriotic Front (FPMR) voluntarily return from exile to Chile and are arrested by police. One of them, Sergio Buschman—wanted for his role in directing a shipment of Cuban-supplied weapons into Chile in 1986—had escaped from a Chilean prison in 1987 and lived for several years in Nicaragua.

September 22, 1994

A boy is killed and two are injured—a U.S. Embassy worker and his wife—after a bomb goes off at a fast-food restaurant in Guatemala City.

January 26, 1995

In Venezuela, seven members of of the National Liberation Army (ELN) kidnap three Venezuelan Corpoven engineers and kill a fourth near La Victoria.

April 1995

Counter-terrorist police in Peru arrest approximately 20 members of Shining Path in the cities of Lima, Callao, Huancayo, and Arequipa, disrupting the group's terrorist plans for the national elections this month. Among those captured are Central Committee member and the organization's number-two leader, Margi Clavo Peralta. Clavo later publicly announces her support for peace talks with the government, which jailed Shining Path leader and founder Abimael Guzmán first advocated in 1993.

May 24, 1995   Presumed members of the Shining Path detonate a 100-pound car bomb in front of the Maria Angola Hotel in a suburb of Lima, killing three hotel employees and a passerby. About 30 others are injured.

June 1, 1995   Members of the ELN kidnap four engineers of different nationalities from a Canadian-owned gold mine in the Zaragoza municipality of the Antioquia Department. A rescue mission by the Colombian army results in three men being released, including an American, and a Colombian engineer getting killed.

June 11, 1995   A Peruvian geologist working for a U.S. company in Huamachuco is shot and killed by Shining Path rebels.

June 24, 1995   In Colombia, a British university student, son of an Exxon employee, is kidnapped from Formeque by FARC terrorists and a ransom demanded for his release. The victim's bullet-ridden body is found on August 12, 1995, near the town of Caqueza.

November 27, 1995   In Guatemala, a Mexican United Nations worker with the International Labor Organization that develops local handicrafts is kidnapped and then killed.

November 30, 1995   In Peru, 30 Tupac Amaristas (members of MRTA) are arrested after their plot to occupy the Peruvian Congress and hold its members hostage is foiled. They planned to demand the release of imprisoned colleagues in exchange for releasing Congress members.

December 1, 1995   The number-two leader of MRTA still at large, Miguel Rincón, surrenders to police after a raid of an MRTA safe house that also results in the arrest of more than a dozen other MRTA members.

1996   The UN brokers a peace process in which the Guatemalan National Revolutionary Unity lays down its arms, later to become a legitimate political party.

January 11, 1996   A Peruvian military tribunal convicts an American, Lori Berenson, of helping the MRTA and sentences her to life in prison. After changes in the nation's anti-terrorism laws, Peru retries Berenson in a civilian court in 2001, where her sentence is reduced to 20 years.

February 16, 1996   In Mexico's Chiapas Province, Zapatista (EZLN) representatives sign an agreement with the Mexican government on the rights of indigenous peoples and make a commitment to negotiate a political settlement.

February 17, 1996   Two alleged members of the ELN kill two Venezuelan guards at a gasoline station near the Colombian-Venezuelan border in La Victoria and abscond with their weapons.

March 23, 1996   In La Victoria, Venezuela, members of the ELN kill a policeman, and injure another officer and a civilian.

April 1996   In Paraguay, government leaders and people take an important step to strengthen democracy, rejecting an attempt by Army Chief General Lino Oviedo to oust President Wasmosy.

June 8, 1996

In Apure State, Venezuela, near the Colombian border, ten ELN gunmen kill a local man who they believe is a National Guard informant.

June 28, 1996

In Mexico, the self-proclaimed Popular Revolutionary Army (EPR), the military wing of Partido Democrático Popular Revolucionario (PDPR), announces itself in the southwestern state of Guerrero during a ceremony marking the anniversary of a state police massacre of local peasants.

October 10, 1996

At the Venezuela-Colombia border, suspected ELN guerrillas kidnap and then kill a Venezuelan cattleman.

December 11, 1996

In Colombia, an American geologist, Frank Pescatore, is kidnapped from a gas exploration site in Hato Nuevo, La Guajira Department. Another American escapes capture. Pescatore's body is recovered in February 1997. FARC is suspected.

December 17, 1996

In Lima, Peru, a party given by the Japanese ambassador in the Japanese Embassy compound is interrupted by 23 MRTA members who want terrorist group members released from Peruvian jails. They take several hundred party-goers hostage, including some U.S. officials, foreign ambassadors, and Peruvian government officials. Although some hostages are released, 81 Peruvians and Japanese citizens continue to be held for several months. On April 22, 1997, Peruvian special forces launch a raid on the embassy compound, liberate all but one of the remaining 72 hostages, and kill all 14 MRTA militants, including the group's leader, Néstor Cerpa.

December 30, 1996

In Chile, four FPMR members stage an escape from prison in Santiago, Chile, using a helicopter.

February 7, 1997

Several Revolutionary Armed Forces of Colombia (FARC) guerrillas kidnap two German and two Austrian tourists in Los Katios National Park and demand a $15 million ransom. On March 4, Colombia soldiers patrolling an area in Chocó Department spot the kidnappers and their captors. The rebels kill two of the hostages, and the ensuing gun battle leaves four guerrillas dead and two hostages freed.

April 1997

In Colombia, the United Self-Defense Forces (AUC), commonly referred to as the paramilitaries, is formed this month as an umbrella organization for many local and regional paramilitary groups with the mission to protect economic interests and combat FARC and ELN insurgents.

April 22, 1997

In Chile, the Manuel Rodriguez Patriotic Front (FPMR) holds a clandestine press conference in Santiago to announce that it is leaving the armed struggle and seeking to become a legal political organization.

May 16, 1997

In Ureña, Venezuela, four armed men kidnap a Venezuelan politician and take him across the border to Colombia, where he is shot and killed while attempting to escape. ELN and FARC both operate in the area where the politician was abducted.

July 30, 1997   ELN guerrillas bomb the Caño Limòn–Coveñas oil pipeline in Norte de Santander, Colombia, wrapping sticks of dynamite around the pipes of the pump, causing a major oil spill and suspending pumping operations for more than a week, which results in millions of dollars in lost revenue.

September 4, 1997   Bombs explode within minutes of each other at three hotels in Cuba, killing an Italian tourist and causing minor damage. On September 10, the Interior Ministry announces the arrest of a Salvadoran citizen who confesses to the bombings of September 4 and to the bombings of two other hotels on July 12 in which three are injured. Cuban authorities say that anti-Castro Cubans supported the attacks.

1998   In Paraguay, General Lino Oviedo becomes the candidate of the Colorado Party for president, but in April the Supreme Court upholds his conviction on charges related to a 1996 coup attempt, and he is not allowed to run. His former running mate, Raúl Cubas, becomes the Colorado Party's candidate instead and is elected in May, but the Cubas presidency will be dominated by conflict over the status of Oviedo, who retains influence over the Cubas government. Cubas attempts to commute Oviedo's sentence and release him from confinement, but in December 1998, the Supreme Court declares this unconstitutional. Cubas refuses to return Oviedo to jail. Then on March 23, 1999, longtime Oviedo rival Luis María Argaña is murdered, and the Cubas regime is suspected of involvement. This leads the Chamber of Deputies to impeach Cubas the next day. Two days later, eight student anti-government demonstrators are killed, most likely by Oviedo supporters. The Senate schedules a vote to remove Cubas on March 29, and Cubas resigns on March 28. Senate President Luis Ángel González Macchi, a Cubas opponent, is peacefully sworn in as president the same day. Cubas flees to Brazil, receiving asylum, and Oviedo flees first to Argentina, then to Brazil.

January 3, 1998   In Peru, three Shining Path gunmen open fire on a car transporting the family members of Mario Paredes Cueva, a former congressman of the ruling party who died of cancer. Paredes Cueva's wife and daughter are killed along with their bodyguard.

January 7, 1998   In Guatemala, Danita Gonzalez Plank de Orellana, a U.S. citizen and daughter of the Progressive Liberator Party candidate for vice president, is kidnapped along with her infant daughter. The baby, seriously injured, is discovered in a cardboard box soon after the kidnapping. The mother's body is discovered eight days later.

March 21, 1998   A union leader and his daughter are shot and killed by four Shining Path terrorists in the Ate-Vitarte District of Lima, Peru.

April 20–24, 1998   Police capture Pedro Domingo Quintero, the second-highest ranking Shining Path rebel, and the right-hand man of the organization's leader. On April 24, in a dawn raid on shantytowns, police capture Shining Path's local field leader, Alberto Ramirez, together with the organization's head of operations,

Maximo Anosa. Also captured is Rodolfo Condori, the organization's explosives expert.

April 26, 1998

In Guatemala City, Bishop Juan Gerardi, coordinator of the archbishop's Office of Human Rights, is beaten to death two days after presenting a report on human rights violations and civil crimes in the country from 1960 to 1996.

August 8, 1998

Thirty militants attack the main square of Saposoa, Peru, during a political rally and assassinate Celso Rodriguez Vargas, mayor of the town. They also attack the local National Police post, killing two civilians.

October 18, 1998

In the Antioquia Department of Colombia, a bomb placed by ELN terrorists explodes on the Ocensa pipeline, killing about 70 persons and injuring at least 100 others. The pipeline is jointly owned by the Colombia State Oil Company Ecopetrol, and a consortium including U.S., French, British, and Canadian companies.

December 13, 1998

In a referendum, Puerto Ricans vote for continued commonwealth status by a wide margin. Only 2.5 percent support full independence, the aim of nationalist terrorist groups.

1999

ELN begins a dialogue with Colombian officials following a campaign of mass kidnappings, but peace talks eventually break down.

February 25, 1999

The FARC in Colombia kidnaps three U.S. citizens who work for the Hawaii-based Pacific Cultural Conservancy International. On March 4, their bodies are found in Venezuela. FARC leaders claim that rogue elements within the organization are responsible.

March 1999

FARC executes three U.S. Indian rights activists on Venezuelan territory after kidnapping them in Colombia.

July 14, 1999

The last remaining commander of the Shining Path, Oscar Ramirez Durand, alias "Feliciano," is captured by the Peruvian military.

Decline of Terrorism in the Mid-1990s

The defeat of the Shining Path left Latin America without a single terrorist group that seemed capable of posing a major threat, much less staging a revolution. There were many reasons for this outcome, including the prevalence of electoral democracy in the region during this era, the collapse of Marxism as an ideology, and the experience of learning from so many failed revolutionary movements. Even anti-Americanism declined relative to past levels.

International trends contributed to the situation. Social revolutionary terrorism was down in Europe, while radical Arab and Islamist revolution, then active and energetic in other parts of the world, had no appeal in South and Central America. The heady days of the 1970s and 1980s were gone, and few could seriously believe that revolution was imminent.

This did not mean that terrorism disappeared altogether, but it was increasingly sporadic in many countries and linked to criminal activities in others. Actually, the number of terrorist incidents in Latin America remained high, but almost all of these events were small scale, short lived, and localized. Colombia and Peru remained the main centers of violence.

August 11, 1999   U.S. President Bill Clinton offers freedom or reduced prison terms to 16 Puerto Rican nationalist terrorists in federal prisons on the condition that they renounce terrorism and do not become involved in pro-independence movements again. Fourteen of them accept the offer.

October 5, 2000   Leading Shining Path fugitive Eloy Carlos Garcia, alias "Comrade Cirilo," said to be a 20-year member of the group and one of its leading figures, is reportedly arrested in the rural town of Yurinaqui, where he is working as a teacher. Cirilo, 46, was caught in 1981, but escaped from prison when fellow Shining Path rebels stormed the prison.

October 12, 2000   In Sucumbíos Province, Ecuador, a group of armed kidnappers led by former members of the defunct Colombian terrorist organization the Popular Liberation Army (EPL) take ten employees of Spanish energy consortium REPSOL hostage. Two victims escape four days later. On January 30, 2001, the kidnappers murder the American hostage, Ronald Sander, and the remaining hostages are released on February 23 following the payment of $13 million in ransom by the oil companies.

November 2000   In Colombia, the FARC suspends peace talks with the government to protest what it calls "paramilitary terrorism," but returns to the negotiating table in February 2001, following two days of meetings between President Pastrana and FARC leader Manuel Marulanda. The Colombian government and ELN continue discussions aimed at opening a formal peace process.

June 1, 2001   Unknown terrorists kidnap a German pharmaceutical executive, demand $1 million for his release and then kill him after 20 days when the ransom is unpaid.

September 27, 2001   The U.S. Embassy in Chile receives a letter bomb which local police destroy safely. In September 2002, a Chilean judge sentences two individuals—Lenin Guardia and Humberto López—to ten years and 300 days in prison for sending the letter bomb. The motivation of Guardia, the professed ringleader, was to use the false terrorist incident to encourage fear among the local population in order to generate business for his security-consulting firm.

2002   Argentina, Brazil, and Paraguay invite the United States to join a new "Three Plus One" counter-terrorism group to analyze and combat any terrorist-related threats in the Triborder area, the region where the three nations' territories meet.

2002   Some elements of the paramilitary AUC (United Self-Defense Forces of Colombia) disband and reconstitute themselves in an effort to seek political legitimacy, but their ties to narco-trafficking and human rights abuses persist.

February 2002   The Colombian government, under former President Pastrana, cuts off long-running peace talks with the Revolutionary Armed Forces of Colombia (FARC) after a series of provocative actions, including a plane hijacking and the kidnapping of a Colombian senator on the plane.

March 17, 2002	In Cali, Colombia, FARC terrorists gun down Archbishop Isaias Duarte Cancino who had sharply criticized terrorist groups. In January 2005, a FARC commander, John Fredy Jiménez, is sentenced to 37 years in prison for the killing.
March 20, 2002	Ten Peruvians are killed after Shining Path terrorists detonate a car bombing at a shopping center across from the U.S. Embassy in Lima two days before a state visit by President Bush. A second bomb fails to explode. Eight Shining Path members are later arrested for this crime.
April 12, 2002	President of Venezuela, Hugo Chávez, is briefly deposed and arrested in a coup d'état which installs a businessman, Pedro Carmona, as interim president. This event generates a widespread uprising in support of Chávez that is repressed by the Metropolitan Police. The coup attempt collapses only after Chávez's Presidential Guard retakes the presidential palace. Chávez remains held in a secret location and the presidency is assumed by vice president Diosdado Cabello until Chávez can return. The coup is publicly condemned by Latin American nations and international organizations.
May 2, 2002	In Colombia, during a clash between FARC terrorists and paramilitary forces in Boyajá, Chocó, FARC guerrillas fire a homemade mortar that strikes a church where women and children are hiding from the fighting, killing 119, including at least 48 children. In July 2005, Gilberto de Jesus Torres, a suspected FARC member, is indicted for the church deaths.
August 7, 2002	During the inauguration of Colombian President Álvaro Uribe, FARC terrorists fire a mortar, aimed at the presidential palace, that instead kills 21 residents in a Bogotá slum.
August and September 2002	Chilean authorities discover several small arms caches in Santiago and other cities as well as the remnants of explosive material at two communications transmission towers outside Santiago. The weapons and explosives are believed to belong to the largely defunct terrorist group Manuel Rodriguez Patriotic Front (FPMR). Law enforcement agents believe the weapons were smuggled into Chile in the 1980s at the height of FPMR's activity, but some view the caches as evidence of an FPMR comeback.
November 16, 2002	One Peruvian police officer dies and four others are injured in a clash with Shining Path members. The police unit was sent to the area to search for terrorists who had called for an armed strike on the days that Peru was to hold elections. At least 15 other incidents involving Shining Path members are reported in neighborhoods where residents have been warned to boycott Sunday's election.
December 2002	In Colombia, the paramilitary group United Self-Defense Forces of Colombia (AUC) declares a unilateral cease-fire and seeks peace negotiations with the government.
February 8, 2003	In Bogotá, Colombia, FARC terrorists are responsible for a car bomb that detonates in a garage underneath a social club, killing 36. In September 2005, Fernando Arellán, one of the masterminds of the attack, is captured.

April 7, 2003   In Peru, Gaudencio Victor Torres Malvecida, a councilman of Ponto in Huari and an active member of the militant party Peru Possible, is killed by five assailants. Two local merchants riding inside the truck are seriously injured. Shining Path is responsible.

April 8, 2003   Juan Valle, a 45-year-old governor of Lacabamba village and active Peru Possible member, is gunned down by Shining Path terrorists outside his house.

November 9, 2003   Peruvian soldiers capture a leader of the Shining Path rebel group after a clash in the Andes in which four guerrillas are killed and an officer wounded.

January 2005   In Colombia, FARC terrorists kidnap and kill Efrén Pascal Nastacuas, governor of the Kuambi Yalasbi indigenous reserve of Ricaurte, Nariño Department.

February 15, 2005   FARC terrorists kill the mayor of Genova, Colombia, as he is inspecting a construction site.

February 16, 2005   In Colombia, AUC terrorists kill a human rights activist who led a resistance movement against its activities.

February 16, 2005   The body of Cecilia Cubas, the daughter of former Paraguayan President Raúl Cubas, is found in house near Asunción, the nation's capital. Cubas was abducted in September 2004 by gunmen near her home, and her father had paid a ransom for her release. Paraguayan authorities aggressively prosecute members of the leftist Free Fatherland Party (Partido Patria Libre, or PPL) and reveal that the perpetrators had sought and received advice on the kidnapping from a member of the FARC. In October, a Paraguayan judge indicts 25 individuals for the crime.

April 14, 2005   Hundreds of FARC terrorists simultaneously attack the town of Toribío, Colombia. The town is home to the Nasa indigenous people, who have rejected armed groups. This is the beginning of an offensive by FARC, which comes into direct combat with Colombian security forces. In the first attack on Toribío, a nine-year-old child is killed along with three policemen, five soldiers, and eight terrorists. Three days later, FARC launches another offensive on the town.

April 28, 2005   FARC terrorists abduct Douglas Hernan Bautista, a municipal councilor and former mayor of Hobo, Colombia, as he is taking his children to schools. During a shoot-out with police, Bautista is killed along with two policemen.

May 24, 2005   Several FARC members enter a town hall meeting in the village of Puerto Rico in Colombia's Caquetá Department and kill four councilors and the council secretary.

August 5, 2005   The president of El Paujil Municipality Council in Colombia is killed by FARC terrorists.

August 19, 2005   Father Jesus Adrian Sanchez is shot and killed by members of FARC.

August 24, 2005	FARC terrorists kill a schoolteacher in Puerto Nuevo on the school's soccer field, in front of students and parents.
August 24, 2005	Fourteen coca leaf pickers are killed by FARC terrorists in Taraza, Colombia.
September 10, 2005	In Colombia, a leader in the National Union for Workers of the Food Industry disappears after returning home from Spain, where he was placed in an international protection program at the end of 2004 because he received death threats by paramilitary groups. His body is found on September 12.
October 21, 2005	A bus is set on fire by FARC terrorists on the Caracoli-Medellín route, killing the driver and his assistant.
November 26, 2005	FARC terrorists bomb a hospital in Florencia, Colombia, during a meeting between municipal councilors and regional hospital labor leaders, killing one person and injuring 39.
December 1, 2005	The president of the El Paujil Municipality Council in Colombia is killed by FARC terrorists. His predecessor was also assassinated.
December 3, 2005	Jaime Lozada Perdomo, a former senator and former governor of Huila Department, is killed along with his son when FARC terrorists ambush the car in which he is driving in the department of Huila. Lozada paid ransom in 2004 to the FARC to release his two kidnapped sons, who had been held for three years, but his wife, a legislator, who was kidnapped at the same time remains in captivity.
January 7, 2006	In Colombia, unknown perpetrators assassinate a senatorial candidate, a son of the ex-governor of La Guajira, as he is sitting in a barbershop in Riohacha.
January 19, 2006	Two are killed when FARC terrorists detonate a bomb on a bus in Cauca, Colombia.
February 9, 2006	FARC terrorists kill the principal of a school in Ovejas, Colombia.
February 25, 2006	FARC terrorists gun down a public bus in El Diamonte, Colombia, killing nine civilian passengers and injuring 14.
March 8, 2006	In the town of Arauca, Colombia, FARC terrorists kill an indigenous leader after he disobeys the terrorists' call for an armed strike and a traffic strike. His wife is killed when she comes to take his body.
March 18, 2006	FARC members, continuing a shutdown and traffic strike, ambush a civilian caravan in Caquetá, Colombia, kill one driver, wound two men, and burn three cars.
April 4, 2006	ELN terrorists kill a Coromoro Municipality councilman and his neighbor in the town of La Mina, Colombia.
April 8, 2006	A Carmen Municipality councilman is killed by FARC terrorists in Colombia.
April 25, 2006	A councilman is murdered in Huila, Colombia, by FARC terrorists.

April 27, 2006   In a botched kidnapping attempt, FARC terrorists kill Liliana Gaviria Trujillo, sister of former Colombian president and former secretary general of the Organization of American States (OAS), César Gaviria. Her body is found in the town of Pereira.

May 10, 2006   A mayoral candidate in the Funza Municipality of Colombia is killed by two men on a motorcycle in Facatativa. FARC is likely responsible.

October 12, 2006   In Colombia, FARC terrorists ambush an ambulance and murder its driver in the Florencia Municipality of Cauca. The terrorists were likely targeting the mayor of San Pablo, known to travel in a similar-looking vehicle on the same road.

October 13, 2006   The municipal councilor of Yumbo is shot and killed by two men on a motorcycle in downtown Cali, Colombia.

December 7, 2006   FARC terrorists detonate a bomb on the street that hits a bus in Buenaventura, Colombia, killing one and injuring three others.

Revolutionaries of Asia and Africa

The ethnic and religious diversity of Asia and Africa has led frequently to conflicts based on competing nationalisms. This has been the largest source of terrorism on these two vast continents. When militant groups reject the idea that other communities have rights and when other political strategies have failed, such groups turn to extremist nationalist ideologies and terrorism becomes the tactic of first choice or last resort.

Some of the important characteristics of non-Islamist terrorist groups in Asia and Africa include their local nature, their relative lack of connection to or support from international radical groups, and their persistent failure. Yet in many cases, these movements have been able to survive and function over long periods of time. Since the collapse of the Soviet Union and the end of the Cold War in 1991, Communist or leftist movements in Nepal, India, the Philippines, and elsewhere have not enjoyed support from Moscow or from the Chinese regime in Beijing. Asian and African movements using terrorism often focus on goals short of achieving total political victory. Only among the Tamils of Sri Lanka has any terrorist movement reached a considerable size and influence. Some engage in semi-criminal activities, for which terrorism can be a useful tool.

In some cases, maintaining a state of disorder may in itself be an objective. The uncertainty and fear engendered by terrorist acts can drive out a target ethnic group or discourage it from immigrating in the first place. Terrorism can also reduce investment from abroad and deter members of the terrorists' own ethnic-religious group from modifying their customs. In such cases, the real goal of the terrorist movement may be to block change rather than force it. At the same time, the terrorist group may be able to maintain a large element of control in the region where it operates, even though it falls far short of taking over the government. These movements may be patterned on the age-old practices of warlords and bandits, who used terror tactics to enforce their orders. Whatever modern rhetoric is employed, many Asian and African terrorist movements pursue traditional agendas, with terrorism playing the role filled in the past by lower levels of political violence.

In other cases, terrorism has been used by groups seeking to revolutionize society. Just as communism sparked terrorism in the West among some radicals, so Maoism from nearby China became the ideology of groups in Asia. A number of Maoist-type groups in India have carried out terrorist attacks there on local political leaders and ordinary civilians. One of the groups' allies is the Communist Party of Nepal-Maoist, which has targeted Nepalese officials and placed bombs in public places. The same pattern has applied in the Philippines where the New People's Army has also used terrorist methods.

More often, however, terrorism has been a tool of ethnic nationalists who want to carve independent states from larger nation-states. They target both government institutions and other ethnic or

religious communities which they want to terrorize or drive out. Since the 1970s, such nationalist
terrorism has been practiced by groups seeking
independence in India, Sri Lanka, the Philippines,
Indonesia, Myanmar (Burma), Uganda, and
Rwanda.

Two of the most persistent terrorist campaigns
in Asia were those of radical Sikhs in India and
Tamils in Sri Lanka. These two cases have significant parallels and also reveal some important
points about political terrorism. The Sikhs are
adherents to a religion, but like so many such
groups in the Middle East and Asia they also form a
distinct community that may be considered an ethnic group. The Tamils are a minority ethnic group
in Sri Lanka that is also distinguished by its Hindu
religion; the majority Sinhalese are predominantly
Buddhist. In both cases, then, religion and ethnicity come together to reinforce identity.

In both cases, the terrorist groups are concentrated in specific regions of the country where
they form the majority (or an influential minority) of the population. Nation-states can address
this situation by offering limited autonomy in a
federal government, but nationalist extremists
may reject such a compromise and demand full
independence. Their efforts to gain extreme goals
have proved futile, however, because they do not
have the ability to overturn the rulers. Both in Sri
Lanka and India, terrorists even assassinated the
leader of the target government yet failed to gain
their objectives.

The Tamil and Sikh terrorist campaigns also
illustrate the point that terrorist organizations
represent only a small fraction of their ethnic or
religious group. Most Tamils in Sri Lanka and
Sikhs in India favor cooperation with the existing
state in exchange for fair treatment and certain
special rights. In order to maintain their authority,
the radical groups often intimidate the moderates
among their own compatriots, forcing them to
remain silent for fear of retribution.

The main targets of the radical nationalist movements are government officials and ordinary members of other groups living in their claimed territory. Killing officials is designed to show the weakness of the government and the success of terrorist
methods. At the same time, the radicals hope to
frighten the regime into surrender. Killing members of "enemy" ethnic groups is meant to sow fear
and confusion among them and to drive them out

of regions controlled by the radical groups. Similar
patterns of nationalist terrorism occur in many
other conflicts in the rest of the world.

Among the nation-states fighting terrorists, no
Asian country has been subject to more terrorist
groups and incidents than India. Conflicts between
the predominantly Hindu India and predominantly
Muslim Pakistan over the disputed areas of Jammu
and Kashmir brought terrorist activities on both
sides beginning in the 1980s. In addition, India
still faced the task of maintaining a national
state that contains many diverse communities.
Ethnic conflict erupted repeatedly when separatist
groups demanded independence. At the same time,
social and economic discontent in other provinces
brought the growth of Communist groups, many
with a strong ethnic-communal flavor, which carried out terrorist attacks in the hope of gaining
political power.

The conflict between India and Pakistan over
Jammu and Kashmir is mainly covered in chapter
7 because in recent years Islamist radicals have
been the main source of terrorist attacks. They
demand bringing parts of the region under the
control of Pakistan. The earlier struggle, however, was conducted by nationalist-oriented terrorist groups like the Jammu Kashmir Liberation
Front (JKLF), which used violence both in its
region and in other parts of India to seek its
goal of independence. By the early twenty-first
century, Kashmiri terrorist groups were making numerous attacks on elected Indian and
Kashmiri politicians, targeting civilians in public
areas, and attacking security forces. Hundreds
of noncombatants were killed, most of whom
were Kashmiri Muslims. The Jaish-e-Mohammed
(JEM) claimed responsibility for many of these
later attacks.

Finally, India was vexed by nationalist-inspired
terrorism in its northeast region. These seven
small states, largely cut off from India by the territory of Bangladesh (formerly East Pakistan),
were immersed in nationalist-inspired violence.
Nationalist groups demanded independence from
India or for increased rights for tribal people.

In addition, mass immigration of people from
Bangladesh sparked violent opposition aimed at
terrorizing them into fleeing, notably during the
1980s in the state of Assam where terrorist groups
pressured the government to deport the newcom-
ers. The agitation ended with an accord between

the radical group and the government, but the accord was never implemented, helping to spark a growing independence movement. One of the largest such groups was the United Liberation Front of Assam (ULFA), which sought to establish a sovereign Assam through armed struggle. Its assassinations included that of a Soviet mining expert, a social activist and relative of a high-ranking Indian diplomat, and an Assam government minister. Later, the ULFA leadership moved its base of operation to Bangladesh, converted to Islam, and began to pursue a new goal—establishment of an Islamic Bengali homeland in Assam.

The Bodos, a tribal group within Assam, carried out their own ethnic movement, which spawned several terrorist groups, the largest being the National Democratic Front of Bodoland (NDFB). This group has killed migrant workers in the area and detonated a bomb on a passenger train that killed 14. Assam was also plagued by inter-ethnic killings by other tribal groups including the Hmar and Dimasa.

Similar problems faced the state of Tripura, a state carved out of Assam in the 1970s. Here the massive influx of Bengali refugees from Bangladesh radically changed the demographics of the state. Indigenous people, who once made up 95 percent of the population, became a minority representing only 31 percent. The National Liberation Front of Tripura (NLFT) was founded to establish an independent Christian state there.

Meanwhile, in the northwest region of India, in Punjab state, radical Sikhs also sought their own state, which they call Khalistan. A major confrontation in June 1984 between the Indian army and Sikhs occupying the Golden Temple in Amritsar, the holiest Sikh shrine, paved the way for several confrontations with India. In October 1984, Indian Prime Minister Indira Gandhi was assassinated by two of her Sikh bodyguards. Seven months after that, Sikh terrorists placed a bomb on an Air India plane en route from Toronto to Bombay. It exploded over the west coast of Ireland, killing all 329 people aboard—the bloodiest airline-related terrorist act prior to September 11, 2001.

In Sri Lanka, ethnic tensions are key to terrorism. About 75 percent of the population belongs to the Sinhalese majority, which is predominantly Buddhist. Almost 20 percent of the population are Tamils, immigrants from southern India who are predominantly Hindu. Terrorism in Sri Lanka

began in 1970 with the formation of a militant student body called the Tamil Students Movement. This movement quickly went underground and turned to overt terrorist activities with the formation of the Liberation Tigers of Tamil Eelam (LTTE).

The LTTE was one of the first terrorist organizations to use suicide bombers. It succeeded in high-profile political assassinations; suicide bomber attacks killed both Indian Prime Minister Rajiv Gandhi in 1991 and Sri Lankan President Ranasinghe Premadasa in 1993. The LTTE detonated two massive truck bombs directed against the Sri Lankan economy, one at the Central Bank in January 1996 and another at the Colombo World Trade Center in October 1997. Other targets included several ships in Sri Lankan waters, including foreign commercial vessels, and infrastructure targets such as commuter trains, buses, oil tanks, and power stations.

In Africa, a unique instance of genocidal terrorism took place in 1994 in Rwanda, when a radical faction of the Hutu tribe seized power and urged its tribal members to massacre members of the opposing Tutsi tribe. Thousands of Hutus murdered Tutsis and moderate Hutus until the death toll reached 900,000 people. It was a shocking example of how ethnic hatreds can produce what might be called a participatory populist terrorism. Such horrific acts can only take place when terrorist acts by a few are applauded and encouraged by a much larger group. The events in Rwanda illustrate the kind of backing many terrorist groups seek but rarely receive.

Finally, terrorism has also been used by messianic cult-style religious groups ranging from the Lord's Resistance Army in Uganda, which once ordered its potential victims to perform cannibalism, to God's Army, a group that believed that the 12-year-old Htoo twins of Myanmar (Burma) were imbued with magical powers, and a would-be messiah in Japan who perpetrated the only major terrorist attack in Asia using chemical weapons. The Lord's Resistance Army (LRA) was formed in 1989 and promotes a radical form of Christianity which it wants to make the foundation of a new Ugandan government. They bombed popular nightspots; attacked a bus full of people, killing 22; and murdered an Italian priest. Other victims included World Food Program volunteers and a former president of Uganda.

August 15, 1947   After many years of rule by the British, India is partioned into two separate independent countries—India, with a majority Hindu population, and Pakistan, which is largely Muslim.

February 4, 1948   The island republic of Ceylon, off the southeastern shore of India, becomes an independent country. It will later be renamed Sri Lanka.

October 15, 1949   Several new areas that will later become regions of terrorism become part of India. Among them are Tripura, whose population includes 19 tribes, and Manipur, both of which will become full-fledged states in India in the 1970s. The delay in gaining full statehood will encourage nationalist movements among tribal groups in the region.

December 1963   The Free Papua Movement (OPM) is established as a political organization that seeks independence and autonomy for the indigenous people of West Papua from Indonesia, of which it is a part. It has an armed wing, the Liberation Army of the Free Papua Movement (TPN).

November 24, 1964   In northeast India's Manipur State, the United National Liberation Front (UNLF) is founded to achieve independence and establish a Socialist society in Manipur.

December 1968   A breakaway group of the UNLF, led by Oinam Sudhir Kumar, establishes a government-in-exile called the Revolutionary Government of Manipur (RGM) with headquarters in Shylhet, in East Pakistan (present-day Bangladesh). Its goal is to "liberate" Manipur through an armed struggle.

1969   The Maoist Communist Center (MCC) is formed in India, committed to establishing a Communist government based on the ideology of Mao Zedong. It is active in West Bengal in northeast India. The group's formation is inspired by the May 25, 1967, peasant uprising at Naxalbari in the Darjeeling District of West Bengal. For this reason, Communists in the region are known as "Naxalites."

December 1969   In the Philippines, the New People's Army (NPA) is created as the armed wing of the banned Communist Party of the Philippines. The goal of the NPA is to overthrow the Filipino government and replace it with a Communist state.

August 31, 1970   Thirty-three terrorists representing the South Moluccan Islands kill a Dutch policeman in The Hague during their effort to break into the residence of the Indonesian ambassador to the Netherlands. They are protesting the scheduled visit of the Indonesian leader and are seeking independence for the South Moluccan Islands, a Pacific archipelago seized by Indonesian troops shortly after Indonesia declared its independence from the Netherlands in April 1950.

January 22, 1971   In the Philippines, NPA terrorists bomb the Manila headquarters of the U.S. oil companies Esso and Caltex, killing a Filipino employee.

July 27, 1975   In Sri Lanka, Alfred Duraiappah, mayor of Jaffna, is assassinated in his car during a visit to the Krishnan Temple in Ponnalai, Sri Lanka. The attack is committed by Velupillai Prabhakaran, who would become head of the Liberation

Tigers of Tamil Eelam (LTTE), which seeks a separate state in Sri Lanka for the Tamil people.

December 2, 1975   Terrorists seeking independence for the South Moluccan Islands from Indonesia seize a train in Wiister, Holland, taking 50 passengers hostage, killing the engineer and then killing two of the passengers in front of television cameras. Finally, they are persuaded to turn themselves in.

May 5, 1976   The LTTE is established by Velupillai Prabhakaran (*see* July 27, 1975). The group, also known as the Tamil Tigers, seeks an independent Tamil state in Sri Lanka. It is a radical splinter group from the Tamil United Liberation Front, which was created four years earlier as an advocacy group for the Tamil people in Sri Lanka. LTTE will become one of the world's most successful terrorist groups, combining a strategy of terror with mass support and control over territory.

May 1977   The Jammu Kashmir Liberation Front (JKLF), committed to self-determination for the people of Jammu and Kashmir, is founded in the United Kingdom by Amanullah Khan, a co-founder of an earlier group called the Jammu and Kashmir National Liberation Front, after most of his original organization is either killed or captured by Indian security forces.

May 23, 1977   South Moluccan Suicide Commando terrorists, seeking Dutch support for their struggle for independence of the South Moluccan Islands in Indonesia, take over a school in Bovensmilde, in the northern Netherlands, taking 110 hostages, and hijack a passenger train on the nearby Bovensmilde-Assan route, taking 45 hostages. They demand the release of 21 political prisoners. On July 11, the Dutch army stages a rescue attempt in which two hostages from the train and six hostage-takers are killed, but all the rest of the hostages are saved.

March 12, 1978   Terrorists from the South Moluccan Suicide Commando storm a government complex in Assen, Netherlands, killing one man and injuring four others. They take 70 hostages and threaten to kill them if the government does not meet their demands for the release of 21 jailed comrades, a plane out of the country with some of the hostages, and a $13 million ransom. The incident ends when Dutch Marines storm the government complex. Three terrorists will be convicted on charges related to the incident and sentenced to 15 years in prison.

April 13, 1978   As the Nirankari sect, a splinter group of Sikhism, holds its annual convention at Amritsar, it is attacked by a gang of radical Sikhs led by Jarnail Singh Bhindranwale and Fauja Singh in which 13 Sikhs are killed, including Fauja Singh, along with three Nirankaris. The incident is the first in a spate of Sikh violence. Sixty-two Nirankaris, including the head of the sect, Baba Gurbachan Singh, are charged and tried. In April 1980, they will be acquitted on the grounds that they acted in self-defense.

September 25, 1978   N. Bisheswar Singh forms the People's Liberation Army (PLA) to achieve independence for Manipur from India through armed struggle.

April 7, 1979   The United Liberation Front of Assam (ULFA) is formed in the Indian state of Assam with the goal of establishing a "sovereign socialist Assam" through armed struggle.

July 8, 1979

The All-Assam Students Union and the All-Assam *Gana Sangram Parishad* launch a mass movement for the detection of illegal immigrants (mainly from neighboring Bangladesh), their deletion from the voters' list, and their deportation. The agitators demanded that the process of detection should cover all migrants who entered India since 1951. In December 1979, the central government of India takes direct control of Assam's government. The anti-foreigner agitation soon takes a violent turn and begins to display secessionist tendencies.

1980

In India, the People's War Group is established. This Maoist terrorist organization seeks a Communist state in India. The group is primarily active in the eastern Indian states of Andhra Pradesh, Orissa, and Bihar.

April 24, 1980

Baba Gurbachan Singh, head of the Nirankari sect of Sikhism, is shot dead in New Delhi. Radical Sikhs are likely responsible in revenge for the events of April 1978.

1983

Tensions between the Sinhalese majority and the Tamil minority erupt in violence following the killing of 13 soldiers of the Sri Lankan army in Jaffna, a Tamil stronghold. Riots break out throughout the country and hundreds of Tamils are killed over a three-day period. Many more became refugees.

February 3, 1984

Jammu Kashmir Liberation Front (JKLF) members kidnap the Indian Deputy High Commissioner Ravindra Mhatre in Birmingham, England, and demand the release of JKLF terrorists imprisoned in India, including co-founder Maqbool Bhat. JKLF members kill Mhatre. Eight days later, Bhat is hanged by the British government.

June 4–6, 1984

The Indian army stages a military assault against radical Sikhs in the Golden Temple in Amritsar, India, which the radicals had occupied and made into a military stronghold several months earlier. The Indian army had surrounded the temple in March. On June 4, the temple is filled with worshippers celebrating one of the holiest Sikh holidays. The Indian army orders those inside the temple to come out. When they refuse, a fierce battle begins. Nearly 500 Sikhs are killed, including their leader Sant Jarnail Singh. The army reports 83 deaths and many more injured. The radical Sikhs are seeking an independent homeland in the Punjab region of India they want to call Khalistan.

August 3, 1984

A powerful bomb kills at least 31 persons and injures 19 in the airport in the southern Indian city of Madras. The Sri Lankan terrorist group LTTE is responsible. The bomb is placed in two suitcases left in a departure lounge.

October 31, 1984

Indian Prime Minister Indira Gandhi is assassinated by her two Sikh bodyguards, Beant Singh and Satwant Singh, in the garden of her home in New Delhi. The assassination is followed by several days of confrontation between the Indian government and Sikhs.

May 10, 1985

Sikh terrorists bomb buses, a train, and neighborhoods in New Delhi and other cities of northern India, killing 80 and wounding over 150.

May 14, 1985	LTTE terrorists in Anuradhapura, Sri Lanka, massacre about 120 Sinhalese and injure 85 others, many of them pilgrims who were inside the Sacred Bo Tree temple.
June 23, 1985	Two baggage handlers at Tokyo Narita Airport are killed when a bomb detonates in a suitcase they are transferring to an Air India flight bound for Bangkok. Less than an hour later, a bomb explodes on another Air India plane en route from Toronto to Bombay while it is above the western coast of Ireland, killing all 329 people aboard. The sabotage is claimed by the Sikh group, Dashmesh Regiment. Three Canadian Sikhs are suspected in the attack. One of them, Talwinder Singh Parmar, will be killed in a struggle with police in 1992, while the other two will be acquitted of charges against them. In 2003, Canadian-British Inderjit Singh Reyat pleaded will plead guilty of making the bomb and be sentenced to five years' imprisonment in return for his promise to testify against the other two suspects, a commitment on which he later reneged.
August 15, 1985	The Assam Accord is signed, ending the six-year-long Assam agitation led by the All-Assam Students Union (AASU) and an alliance of small regional political parties. Their central demand is the expulsion of foreign nationals illegally staying in Assam. According to the terms of the accord, all foreigners who entered Assam on or after March 25, 1971, are to be deported.
April 13, 1986	A group of Sikhs meeting in the Golden Temple approve a declaration calling for an independent state called Khalistan. They unsuccessfully seek support from western governments and the UN.
May 3, 1986	A bomb detonates on a Sri Lankan jet on the ground at Colombo International Airport killing 21—including citizens from Japan, France, Ceylon, West Germany, and the Maldives—and injuring 40. LTTE terrorists are responsible.
August 15, 1986	In Sri Lanka, a Danish woman, who had been working on a government-sponsored project opposed by Tamils, is murdered along with her husband by the LTTE. They are killed while driving along a country road.
September 25, 1986	In Sri Lanka, LTTE terrorists murder a German engineer employed by a German radio relay station. The engineer had gotten involved in a dispute between rival terrorist groups in Sri Lanka.
1987	Aum Shinrikyo is established in Japan by Shoko Asahara, initially as a religious cult. By 1990, it will even run candidates in the Japanese parliamentary elections. The cult will begin to emphasize the imminence of the end of the world and the belief that the United States would initiate "Armageddon" by starting World War III with Japan.
March 15, 1987	A bomb at a railway station in Madras, India, kills 25 people and wounds about 150 others. LTTE terrorists are responsible.
April 1987	The Hmar People's Convention-Democracy (HPC-D) begins an armed struggle seeking self-government for all Hmars in Mizoram, Assam, and Manipur, India.

April 21, 1987   LTTE terrorists bomb the central bus station in Colombo, Sri Lanka, killing 106 people and wounding 295 others.

June 2, 1987   Twenty LTTE terrorists ambush a bus filled with Buddhist monks south of Batticaloa, Sri Lanka, massacring 33.

October 10, 1987   In the Philippines, terrorists from the New People's Army (NPA) assassinate a reporter for Japan's Kyodo News Service, claiming he was responsible for a broadcast critical of their group.

1988   The National Army for the Liberation of Uganda is formed, committed to overthrowing the government of President Yoweri Museveni. The terrorist group is also opposed to the presence of foreigners in the country, especially Rwandan refugees.

1988   The National Democratic Front of Bodoland (NDFB) is formed, committed to creating a separate homeland for the Bodo people in India's Assam region.

March 29, 1988   A Japanese tourist is assassinated as he drives down a street in Manila. The New People's Army is suspected.

May 10, 1988   A bomb explodes at a Citibank branch in New Delhi, India, killing one and wounding 14. Radical Sikhs are suspected.

August 4, 1988   An Australian sawmill operator is murdered at his home on Negros Island, Philippines, likely by NPA terrorists.

August 4, 1988   Tamil terrorists kill a Red Cross official and his driver in Jaffna, Sri Lanka.

1989   The Lord's Resistance Army (LRA) is formed. It is committed to destabilizing and overthrowing the government of Uganda and establishing a radical form of Christianity as the state religion.

March 12, 1989   The National Liberation Front of Tripura (NLFT) is formed, becoming one of several terrorist organizations operating in India's northeastern states. The goal of NLFT is independence for a Tripura state under a Christian government.

September 26, 1989   In the Philippines, two U.S. employees of the Ford Aerospace Corporation are killed by NPA terrorists on a U.S. Air Force training range north of Manila.

November 4, 1989   Anti-cult lawyer Tsutsumi Sakamoto, his wife, and their one-year-old child are murdered in Japan. Aum Shinrikyo members are suspected.

February 21, 1990   In the Philippines, NPA terrorists assassinate three in Bohol Province—an American geologist, his wife, and his father-in-law.

March 1, 1990   An American citizen who owns a cattle ranch in the Philippines is assassinated by NPA members for refusing to pay money to the organization.

March 26, 1990   The NPA is likely responsible for the assassination of the Filipino vice president of Nestlé Philippines, as he is attending a company tennis match.

July 11, 1990	The All-Tripura Tiger Force (ATTF) is formed. It seeks independence for all tribal areas within Tripura and the deportation of Bengalis who moved to Tripura after 1956.
July 27, 1990	NPA terrorists in Manila assassinate a businessman from Singapore, his driver, and a bodyguard.
March 2, 1991	Liberation Tigers of Tamil Eelam (LTTE) terrorists kill Sri Lankan Defense Minister Ranjan Wijeratne and 19 others in Colombo.
May 21, 1991	Former Indian Premier Rajiv Gandhi and 17 others are killed by an LTTE suicide bomber during a campaign stop in the southern Indian state of Tamil Nadu. The Indian government convicts 26 LTTE supporters for the assassination. The terrorist organization wanted to prevent Gandhi from getting elected because he had sent Indian troops into Sri Lanka in 1987 after he survived an assassination attempt there.
June 27, 1991	LTTE terrorists detonate a bomb under a tourist bus in Sri Lanka, then open fire on the passengers, killing 14 and injuring nine others.
July 1, 1991	In Guwahati, Assam (India), Soviet coal mining expert Sergei Gritchenko is kidnapped by the United Liberation Front of Assam (ULFA). He is killed while attempting an escape on July 9.
September 6, 1991	A so-called Goodwill Train between India and Pakistan is attacked by Sikh extremists, who kill a Pakistani woman.
1992	A large number of United Liberation Front of Assam (ULFA) members surrender to government authorities and form a group known as SULFA. They are allowed to retain their weapons to defend themselves against former colleagues and are offered bank loans to establish new lives.
July 16, 1992	A Filipino-Chinese businessman is killed by NPA terrorists while driving through Manila.
October 15, 1992	Talwinder Singh Parmar, the alleged mastermind of the mid-air explosion of Air India Flight 182 off the Irish coast in 1985, is killed in a firefight with police in Bombay.
November 16, 1992	A LTTE suicide bomber assassinates Sri Lanka's naval commander and three aides in Colombo.
February 20, 1993	An accord is signed between the government of India, the state government of Assam, and the All Bodo Student's Union, creating the Bodoland Autonomous Council (BAC) within Assam. The agreement is opposed by both the National Democratic Front of Bodoland (NDFB) and the future Bodo Liberation Tiger Force (BLTF), which continue using terrorism against other ethnic groups within "Bodo areas."
May 1, 1993	Sri Lankan President Ranasinghe Premadasa is assassinated by an LTTE suicide bomber as he watches the May Day parade in Colombo.

June 29, 1993   In northeast India, eight civilians and 26 security forces are killed by terrorists in an ambush on the national highway in Manipur. The terrorists are from the National Socialist Council of Nagaland-Isak-Muivah (NSCN-IM), an insurgency group opposing a compromise agreement with the Indian government signed by the NNC (Naga National Council). The group aims to establish a "Greater Nagaland" based on Mao Zedong's ideology.

September 2, 1993   In Manipur, NSCN-IM terrorists kill Naga political leader Ankim Khumto Anal.

April 6, 1994   President Juvénal Habyarimana of Rwanda and President Cyprien Ntaryamira of Burundi, are killed when their plane is shot down as it prepares to land in Kigali, Rwanda. Radical Hutu nationalists in the Presidential Guard are likely responsible. The assassination serves as a trigger for military and militia groups in Rwanda to begin a widespread massacre. The prime minister and her 10 Belgian bodyguards are killed. A massacre of the Tutsi population follows that results in the deaths of more than 900,000. The killings finally end in July 1994, when the radical junta is defeated by regular army units. Some Tutsis are killed by militia groups known as the Interahamwe, while average Hutus are prompted to kill by inflammatory radio broadcasts and helped to do so by activists in the radical Hutu Party.

June 27, 1994   Members of Aum Shinrikyo release the potent nerve gas sarin in several neighborhoods in the central Japanese city of Matsumoto, killing seven people. It is aimed at judges expected to rule against the cult in a court dispute.

March 20, 1995   The deadly gas sarin is released into the Tokyo subway system, killing 12 and injuring over 5,000, including several foreigners. Aum Shinrikyo is held responsible. In February 2004, after an eight-year trial, cult head Shoko Asahara is sentenced to death for this and several other attacks. Asahara is the twelfth Aum Shinrikyo defendant to be sentenced to death by the Tokyo District Court. However, the executions will be delayed for years while the cases are appealed.

April–May 1995   Armed forces from India and Myanmar launch Operation Golden Bird along their border in an effort to trap a large group of Manipuri and Assamese terrorists. Fifty militants are killed during this operation and huge quantities of arms and ammunition are recovered.

December 28, 1995   The Kamtapur Liberation Organization (KLO) is formed. The group seeks an independent Kamtapur state in India comprising six districts—Cooch Behar, Darjeeling, Jalpaiguri, Malda, and North and South Dinajpur—in West Bengal and four districts—Kokrajhar, Bongaigaon, Dhubri, and Goalpara—in Assam.

1996   The Allied Democratic Forces (ADF) is formed, committed to overthrowing the Ugandan government. Based in the Ruwenzori Mountains of western Uganda, the ADF is a combination of fundamentalist Tabliq Muslim rebels and remnants of another rebel group, the National Army for the Liberation of Uganda (NALU).

1996   In India's Assam region, the Dima Halam Daoga (DHD) is formed, committed to independence for the Dimasa tribe.

January 7, 1996   Fourteen people on a scientific expedition organized by the World Wide Fund for Nature (known in the United States and Canada as the World Wildlife Fund) are kidnapped by Free Papua Movement terrorists in the Jayawijaya region of the Indonesian province of Papua, on the western half of the island of New Guinea. During a rescue mission in May by Indonesian security officials, two of the Indonesian hostages and six terrorists are killed.

January 31, 1996   In Sri Lanka, Liberation Tigers of Tamil Eelam (LTTE) terrorists drive a truck bomb into the Central Bank building in Colombo, killing 96 people and injuring over 1,400, including two U.S. citizens.

February 6, 1996   On the day of a a visit by Prince Charles of the United Kingdom for the celebration of Sri Lanka's fiftieth anniversary of independence, a female suicide bomber from the LTTE detonates an explosion at a military checkpoint that kills nine, including two civilians, and wounds at least seven others.

February 13, 1996   Members of the People's War Group of the Communist Party of Nepal-Maoist (CPN-M) emerge in Nepal, committed to Maoist revolution. The group is a radical splinter group of the Communist United People's Front of Nepal.

June 4, 1996   In the Philippines, a Canadian geologist employed by a mining corporation is killed near the town of Didipio when New People's Army terrorists fire on the helicopter in which he is flying.

June 24, 1996   In northern Uganda, terrorists from the West Nile Bank Front attack Sudanese refugee camps in Koboko, killing ten, including a Red Cross worker, and injuring 23. The group was started in the early 1990s by former members of the government of Ugandan dictator Idi Amin, seeking his return.

July 18, 1996   The Bodo Liberation Tigers, also known as the Bodo Liberation Tiger Force (BLTF), is formed with the goal of seeking a separate state of Bodoland in Assam in northeast India.

January 18, 1997   In Rwanda, Hutu militants assassinate three Spanish aid workers from Doctors of the World and wound one U.S. citizen.

February 4, 1997   Hutu terrorists kill five members of the Human Rights Field Operation in Rwanda.

June 1997   The Zomi Revolutionary Army is formed to promote the reunification of Zomi peoples in northeast India, Bangladesh, and Myanmar, and establishment of a Zomi state.

July 4, 1997   Social activist Sanjay Ghose is abducted by the United Liberation Front of Assam (ULFA) in Majuli, India, and killed soon after.

July 7, 1997   Members of the LTTE board and take command of a North Korean cargo ship anchored off the Jaffna Peninsula, Sri Lanka. One crew member is killed trying to escape. The others are freed five days later.

September 9, 1997   Off the coast of Sri Lanka, a merchant ship owned by the China Ocean Shipping Company of Hong Kong and carrying ilmenite, a metal ore mined in Sri Lanka, is hit by rocket-propelled grenades, killing about 20. The LTTE claims responsibility.

October 15, 1997   A truck bomb explodes at the Colombo World Trade Center in Sri Lanka, killing 18 people and injuring 110. LTTE terrorists are responsible.

January 23, 1998   Days prior to local elections to be held in Jaffna, Sri Lanka, LTTE terrorists attack an Eelam People's Democratic Party office in Pungudutivu, an island in Jaffna, killing eight party members.

January 25, 1998   Three LTTE suicide terrorists detonate a truck bomb in front of Sri Lanka's holiest temple in the ancient capital of Kandy, killing eight and injuring 25 others.

February 22, 1998   Zomi Revolutionary Army extremists kill seven Kuki tribesmen in Toining, India.

March 5, 1998   Thirty-two people are killed and another 252 wounded when LTTE terrorists detonate a bomb in a private bus in Colombo, Sri Lanka.

April 4, 1998   Bombs explode at two restaurants in Kampala, Uganda, killing five persons—including one Swedish and one Rwandan national—and wounding at least six others. The Allied Democratic Forces, an anti-government group supported by Sudan, may be responsible.

April 25, 1998   A bomb explodes on a passenger bus bound from Uganda for Rwanda which then rams into a minibus. Thirty people are killed and six are wounded. The attack is claimed by the National Army for the Liberation of Uganda (NALU).

May 1, 1998   Twenty terrorists of the National Democratic Front of Bodoland (NDFB) kill five young Adivasi tribal people in Anjora, India.

May 2, 1998   Ten NDFB terrorists murder four Santhals (the largest tribal group in India) from a private bus near Deoshree within Kokrajhar District, India.

May 3, 1998   NDFB terrorists kill 14 Adivasis and injure four others after dragging them out of a bus in Kokrajhar, India.

May 9, 1998   NDFB terrorists massacre 16 Santhal Adivasis and injure 12 others at Borbil near Gosaingon town.

May 17, 1998   The Mayor of Jaffna, Sri Lanka, Sarojini Yogeswaran, is assassinated at her home by LTTE terrorists.

June 8, 1998   In western Uganda, the Allied Democratic Forces (ADF) attack the Kichwamba Technical College in Kabarole District, and at least 80 students are gunned down as they are trying to escape or their locked dormitories are set on fire. An additional 80 students are abducted in the raid and taken to the Congo, where their whereabouts are unknown.

June 17, 1998	Four Adivasis are killed by NDFB terrorists in Kokrajhar District, India.
June 26, 1998	In Uganda, the ADF attacks Banyangule village in Bundibugyo District, resulting in the death or injury of about 11 victims.
August 1, 1998	ADF terrorists attack Kasese town, Uganda, burning shops and houses and killing three people.
August 2, 1998	National Liberation Front of Tripura (NLFT) terrorists kill three people and abduct one other from Amarpur, South Tripura District, India.
August 6, 1998	ADF terrorists attack the town of Kyarumba near Kasese, Uganda, killing 33 people.
August 16, 1998	In Andhra Pradesh State, India, an activist in the regional Telugu Desam Party is killed by terrorists from the People's War Group, a Maoist group (*see* 1980).
August 24, 1998	Two people are killed and 20 injured after a bomb detonates at the main railway station in Guwahati, Assam, India. The United Liberation Front of Assam (ULFA) claims responsibility for the attack.
September 11, 1998	In Sri Lanka, a bomb set by LTTE terrorists explodes in the city offices of Jaffna, Sri Lanka, killing 12 people, including the city's new mayor, and wounding 12 others.
September 15, 1998	NDFB terrorists kill 14 Santhal Adivasis in Gosaigon, Assam, India.
October 11, 1998	NDFB terrorists kill 13 Assamese and Bengali-speaking people in Darrang, Assam, India.
November 27, 1998	Thirty Lord's Resistance Army terrorists (*see* 1989) attack a convoy in Kololo, including a bus and van belonging to the World Food Program, killing 16.
December 26, 1998	In Sri Lanka, the secretary of the Jaffna district branch of the Tamil United Liberation Front (TULF) is assassinated by Liberation Tigers of Tamil Eelam (LTTE) terrorists at a public event in the Nallur area.
February 14, 1999	In Kampala, Uganda, a pipe bomb explodes inside a bar, killing five persons and injuring 35 others. Ugandan authorities believe that Allied Democratic Forces are responsible.
March 1999	The United People's Democratic Solidarity (UPDS) in India is formed by the merger of two other terrorist groups—Karbi National Volunteers and Karbi People's Front. The group wants a separate Karbi Anglong nation in Assam, India.
March 1, 1999	Some 150 Hutu Interahamwe terrorists infiltrate three tourist camps in southwestern Uganda and take 14 hostages, killing eight and releasing the rest.

March 27, 1999   Hutu terrorists attack a village in Kisoro, Uganda, killing three persons.

June 1, 1999   In Sri Lanka, LTTE terrorists kill 11 civilians and injure six in Kiri Ibanwewa, a remote settlement in Welioya area.

June 22, 1999   Ten people are killed and 59 wounded—most of them soldiers—when a suitcase bomb explodes at the Jalpaiguri railway station in eastern India. The United Liberation Front of Assam (ULFA) claims responsibility for the blast.

July 25, 1999   In Sri Lanka, LTTE terrorists bomb a ferry docked in the Trincomalee harbor only hours before it is to take on passengers. One crew member is killed. Most of the passengers are Tamil refugees returning to homes they had fled during fighting between the Tamil Tiger rebels and government forces.

July 29, 1999   A member of parliament in Sri Lanka, Neelan Thiruchelvam, is killed along with two others when a suicide bomber detonates a bomb as he is traveling from his house to his office in Colombo. The LTTE is responsible.

September 18, 1999 LTTE terrorists killed 46 Sinhalese with machetes and knives in an attack on a Gonegalle village in Amapara District, Sri Lanka, and murder four others in two nearby villages. Two days earlier, Sri Lankan security officials had killed 21 Tamil refugees.

September 20, 1999 ULFA terrorists kidnap and kill Pannalal Oswal, a candidate for a seat in the Dhubri Lok Sabha (Parliament), along with three other party leaders as he is returning from an election meeting in Dhubri to Bilasipara. The party leaders are released, but Oswal's dead body is found four days later.

November 12, 1999   A bomb explodes on the Punjab Express bound for New Delhi, killing 13 persons and injuring some 50 others. The Khalistan Zindabad Force, a Sikh separatist group, is responsible.

November 17, 1999   Seventeen people are killed and 11 injured when All-Tripura Tiger Force (ATTF) terrorists fire upon crowds at Panchavati Bazaar in West Tripura District, India.

November 21, 1999   In Sri Lanka, 35 are killed and some 60 wounded when LTTE terrorists fire shells at a Catholic shrine in the northern Wanni region.

December 1999   The Kuki Revolutionary Army is formed to seek an autonomous administrative council for the Christian Kuki tribe, a minority tribe in the Karbi Anglong District of Assam, India. The group is formed by the National Socialist Council of Nagaland-Isak-Muivah (NSCN-IM), which wants the group to help dilute power of the Kuki National Army (KNA); the latter is fighting for an independent country for the Kuki tribe on land the NSCN-IM claims for the Naga tribe.

December 18, 1999   LTTE terrorists detonate a bomb at an election rally outside of Colombo, Sri Lanka, killing two, including a former army general.

January 5, 2000   A woman LTTE suicide bomber detonates a bomb outside of the Sri Lankan prime minister's residence in Colombo killing herself and six security personnel.

January 7, 2000	A senior Sri Lankan cabinet minister and 20 others are killed and 60 injured when an LTTE suicide bomber detonates himself during a march to commemorate Heroes Day in Ratmalana, Sri Lanka.
February 7, 2000	LTTE terrorists detonate bombs on two public buses in Monaragala, Sri Lanka, killing one person and injuring at least 41.
February 9, 2000	At least three people are killed and 33 injured when bombs explode on two buses in Sri Lanka.
February 27, 2000	Assam Forest Minister Nagen Sharma and three others are killed when United Liberation Front of Assam (ULFA) terrorists detonate a bomb in his motorcade in the Nijbahjani area of Nalbari.
March 10, 2000	LTTE suicide bombers waiting near the parliament in Colombo, Sri Lanka, detonate a bomb but miss their target, Deputy Defense Minister Anirudh Rattawate. Some 30 other people are killed in the attack.
March 22, 2000	Fourteen Kenyans are killed when their truck runs over a land mine while crossing the Kenyan-Ethiopian border near Moyale. This is the first attack by the Oromo Liberation Front (OLF), whose members want a separate state within Ethiopia as a homeland for the Oromo people, estimated to make up some 40 percent of Ethiopia's population.
April 9, 2000	In Karbi Anglong District, India, terrorists of the United People's Democratic Solidarity (UPDS) massacre 11 persons.
April 19, 2000	UPDS terrorists kill 11 persons in two separate attacks in Karbi Anglong District, India.
May 18, 2000	In Batticaloa, Sri Lanka, LTTE terrorists kill 22 in a bomb attack near a Buddhist temple where worshippers are celebrating Vesak, a Buddhist festival.
May 25, 2000	In Freetown, Sierra Leone, terrorists ambush two military vehicles carrying four journalists, killing a Spaniard and a U.S. citizen. The Revolutionary United Front (RUF), seeking to overthrow the government of Sierra Leone and to retain control of the lucrative diamond-producing regions of the country, is responsible.
June 7, 2000	An LTTE suicide bomber kills C.V. Goonaratne, Sri Lankan minister for industrial development, his wife, and 20 others during a rally in Colombo.
July 9, 2000	Near the Rwandan border, Interahamwe terrorists in Congo attack a refugee camp, killing 30 persons and kidnapping four others.
July 15, 2000	Terrorists of the UPDS massacre 10 persons, including two women and four children, in Langparpang, Karbi Anglong District, India.
July 31, 2000	National Democratic Front of Bodoland (NDFB) terrorists detonate a bomb on a passenger train bound for Rangiya at Soonmari, about 40 miles from Guwahati, killing 14 passengers.

August 7, 2000   Kamtapur Liberation Organization (KLO) terrorists (*see* December 28, 1995) kill a local leader of the Communist Party of India in Jalpaiguri.

August 21, 2000   In northeast India, NDFB terrorists kill five Muslim civilians in Dhubri. At Garagaon, another group kills the Bodo legislator Mohini Basumatary.

September 2000   In northeast India, the Borok National Council of Tripura (BNCT) is formed as a splinter organization of the larger Tripuran separatist group, the National Liberation Front of Tripura (NLFT). It is also committed to the establishment of an independent state of Tripura, but is Christian fundamentalist.

September 10, 2000   In Sri Lanka, Liberation Tigers of Tamil Eelam (LTTE) terrorists kill a Batticaloa District candidate and another man in Kalmunai.

September 14, 2000   National Socialist Council of Nagaland-Isak-Muivah (NSCN-IM) (*see* June 29, 1993) and UPDS terrorists kill ten policemen and one civilian, in an ambush near Diphu, India.

October 1, 2000   In the Philippines, nine people are killed and 15 injured when New People's Army terrorists ambush a medical mission in Santo Ramos, Davao del Norte, Philippines.

October 1, 2000   An Italian priest is killed by Lord's Resistance Army terrorists in northern Uganda.

October 3, 2000   In eastern Sri Lanka, 24 are killed, including a parliamentary candidate, and 50 injured in an attack by an LTTE suicide bomber at an election rally.

October 5, 2000   Sri Lankan Deputy Minister for Health and Indigenous Medicine Tissa Karaliyaddea survives an LTTE suicide bomb attack at an election rally in Nagarkovil, although 12 others are killed.

October 6, 2000   In Medawachchiya, Sri Lanka, an LTTE suicide bomber walks into a People's Alliance meeting and detonates a bomb, killing ten and injuring 25.

October 8, 2000   Lord's Resistance Army terrorists in Gulu, Uganda, attack two discotheques in grenade attacks, killing nine and wounding 60 others.

October 19, 2000   In Colombo, Sri Lanka, three people are killed when an LTTE suicide bomber detonates a bomb near the town hall.

October 23, 2000   Terrorists from the United Liberation Front of Assam (ULFA) kill 15 people in two separate incidents in Tinsukia and Dibrugarh districts, India.

October 27, 2000   ULFA terrorists massacre nine persons and injure 12 others in the Nalbari District, India.

November 8, 2000   Eight civilians, including seven of a non-Assamese community, are killed by suspected National Democratic Front of Bodoland (NDFB) terrorists in Barpeta District.

November 25, 2000   Eight woodcutters are killed by NDFB terrorists in the Lung Sung forest reserve.

November 28, 2000 — Three members of the Bihari ethnic group in India are killed by ULFA terrorists in Tinsukia District, Assam, India.

December 1, 2000 — Five laborers at the Birjur tea estate in India are killed by United Liberation Front of Assam (ULFA) terrorists.

December 6, 2000 — Near Batticaloa, Sri Lanka, LTTE terrorists detonate a bomb aimed at a bus, killing four and injuring 21.

December 28, 2000 — Eight persons from the Hindi-speaking community are killed by United People's Democratic Solidarity (UPDS) terrorists at Ranganagar village in Karbi Anglong District.

December 29, 2000 — In Assam, eight Hindi-speaking Biharis are gunned down by UPDS terrorists.

December 31, 2000 — Terrorists from a group calling itself God's Army attack a grocery store in Suan Phung, Myanmar (Burma), during New Year celebrations, killing six persons. God's Army is a breakaway group of the Keren National Union, established in 1959, which is committed to an independent homeland for the predominantly Christian Keren people of Myanmar. The army is headed by adolescent twin brothers Johnny and Luther Htoo, who are believed to have magical powers that make them invincible in battle. The group claims to have several hundred fighters.

December 31, 2000 — Four Hindi-speaking persons are killed by UPDS terrorists at Disobai forest in the Karbi Anglong District of northeast India.

January 13, 2001 — Four are killed by NDFB terrorists in the Nalbari District of India.

January 17, 2001 — Johnny and Luther Htoo, twin boy leaders of God's Army in Myanmar (Burma), surrender with 14 of their followers to authorities in Thailand.

February 3, 2001 — In Surkhet, Nepal, six people are killed in an attack on Chief Justice Keshav Prasad Upadhyaya. The Communist Party of Nepal-Maoist (CPN-M) is responsible.

February 12, 2001 — In Mangalsen, Nepal, at least two are killed and nine others injured when a bomb detonates outside a home. The CPN-M is likely responsible.

March 18, 2001 — In northeast India, six persons, including two children, are killed and five others injured by NDFB terrorists at Ramgaon village in Kamrup District.

April 9, 2001 — National Liberation Front of Tripura (NLFT) terrorists shoot and kill a Marxist tribal leader in Tripura. He is the seventh leader to have been shot that week.

April 14, 2001 — Maoist Communist Center (MCC) terrorists (*see* 1969) massacre 14 village security guards at Belpu village, Hazaribagh District, in the state of Jharkhand, India.

April 20, 2001	In the Bicol region of the Philippines, a mayoral candidate is assassinated by the New People's Army (NPA).
April 26, 2001	In the province of Ituri, Congo, tribesmen abduct International Committee of the Red Cross (ICRC) workers, killing six persons—one Colombian, one Swiss, and four Congolese. No one claims responsibility.
May 12, 2001	Two days before elections in the Philippines, a congressman and his bodyguard are killed by NPA terrorists as they are attending a campaign rally in Tiaong.
May 19, 2001	Maoist Communist Center (MCC) members shoot five girls after the terrorists are not able to locate the father in Ranchi, the capital of Jharkhand State, India, killing two and injuring three.
June 3, 2001	In Assam, India, terrorists in the National Democratic Front of Bodoland (NDFB), who had ordered an end to logging in Bodo areas, assassinate ten woodcutters.
June 12, 2001	In Tueguecarao, Philippines, New People's Army terrorists kill a congressman and his bodyguard.
July 24, 2001	In Colombo, Sri Lanka, Liberation Tigers of Tamil Eelam (LTTE) terrorists attack the international and military airports, killing six persons—four military and two civilians—and injuring nine others.
July 31, 2001	People's War Group terrorists in India attack a passenger train, killing a train guard and injuring a policeman. On the same day, terrorists from the Maoist Communist Center kill the son of a mayor in nearby Dumari village.
July 31, 2001	Bodo terrorists in the National Democractic Front of Bodoland (NDFB) detonate a bomb on a passenger train bound for Rangiya, India, as it passes through Soonmari, killing 14.
August 1, 2001	Six Bhutanese are killed when a bomb detonates in their truck in Assam Province. Police blame the NDFB.
August 1, 2001	A Socialist leader is shot dead and his son wounded in Manirtat, West Bengal State, India. The Communist Party of India is suspected.
August 9, 2001	National Liberation Front of Tripura (NLFT) members assassinate a Marxist tribal leader in Tripura, northeast India.
August 25, 2001	UPDS terrorists kill four persons by blowing up a truck at Bhuligaon, near Bokajan in Karbi Anglong District, India.
September 1, 2001	In Nimule, Uganda, five are killed and two wounded when terrorists ambush a vehicle belonging to Catholic Relief Services. The Lord's Resistance Army is likely responsible.
October 12, 2001	In Bellankadawala, Sri Lanka, two government officials are killed by a bomb planted by LTTE terrorists.

October 25, 2001	National Democratic Front of Bodoland (NDFB) terrorists detonate an explosive at a Hindu celebration in Gauripur, India, killing three people and wounding a dozen more.
October 29, 2001	In Colombo, Sri Lanka, a half hour after the prime minister of Sri Lanka passes by in a motorcade, a suicide bomb explodes, killing at least three people and wounding 16. The LTTE is responsible.
November 17, 2001	LTTE terrorists assassinate a candidate of the opposition United National Party in Batticaloa, Sri Lanka.
December 3, 2001	United People's Democractic Solidarity (UPDS) terrorists detonate a bomb that kills nine persons, including six polling officials at Lamelangshu in Karbi Anglong District, India. Five others are injured in the attack.
December 7, 2001	National Democratic Front of Bodoland (NDFB) terrorists kill four woodcutters in two separate incidents in Assam. The NDFB opposes continued logging in the region.
December 26, 2001	In Paya Sikameh, Indonesia, a religious education teacher in a primary school is shot and killed. The Free Aceh Movement is suspected of the attack.
January 15, 2002	NDFB terrorists massacre 13 civilians at Dailongjhar in Bongaigaon District, India.
January 21, 2002	Some 30 NDFB terrorists attack a village on India's border with Bhutan, killing 16 people, including women and children.
January 30, 2002	Two European tourists hiking on Mount Macapiyan in Pampanga are killed in the Philippines by New People's Army terrorists.
January 31, 2002	An American tourist hiking on the slopes of the Pinatubo volcano in the Philippines is killed and his German companion is injured by New People's Army terrorists.
February 5, 2002	National Liberation Front of Tripura (NLFT) terrorists kill six members of the local ruling left-wing party in the Dhalai District of Tripura, India.
February 10, 2002	In Maharashtra State, India, the vehicle of a local political leader is ambushed by People's War Group terrorists, and the leader is shot to death.
February 20, 2002	Maoist Communist Center (MCC) terrorists kill three people at a roadblock in Hazaribagh, Jharkhand State, India, and injure six others.
March 22, 2002	In Kalosaric, Uganda, gunmen stop a vehicle on the Moroto-Kotido road, killing three persons—an Irish Catholic priest, his driver, and his cook. Gunmen from the Karamojong, a nomadic tribe with a strong warrior tradition, are probably responsible.
March 26, 2002	In Kafountine, Casamance Province, Senegal, terrorists attack a resort, killing five persons and wounding four others including a French citizen. The

Casamance Movement of Democratic Forces, seeking autonomy of the province from Senegal, is probably responsible.

April 19, 2002   Communist Party of Nepal-Maoist (CPN-M) terrorists assassinate a ruling Nepali Congress Party activist in Baskarkha, Nepal.

April 21, 2002   In Tripura State, India, four tribal members of the ruling Communist Party of India-Marxist (CPI-M) are murdered by National Liberation Front of Tripura members.

April 22, 2002   In Jonestown in the northern Philippines, New People's Army terrorists assassinate the mayor.

April 24, 2002   CPN-M terrorists kidnap and kill a ruling Nepali Congress Party activist in Sunsari.

April 26, 2002   In Tripura State, India, National Liberation Front of Tripura (NLFT) terrorists kill four Communist Party of India members, all of whom are village council members.

May 6, 2002   People's War Group terrorists kill six low-caste people in Bhojpur, Bihar State, India.

May 20, 2002   United People's Democractic Solidarity (UPDS) terrorists kill four members of a non-Assamese family at Matikhola village, Karbi Anglong District, India.

May 23, 2002   UPDS signs a cease-fire agreement with the Union government. The group splits between those who are pro-agreement, and those who want to continue terrorist activities.

June 2, 2002   National Democratic Front of Bodoland (NDFB) terrorists kill three members of a family at Bongshijhora village in Dhubri District.

June 14, 2002   In Guinayangan, Philippines, New People's Army terrorists kill three people.

June 18, 2002   In two separate incidents, NDFB terrorists kill three civilians and injure another in Runikhata, Kokrajhar District, India.

June 19, 2002   In the Indonesian province of Aceh, terrorists from the Free Aceh Movement murder a village chief in the Bireuen District.

June 21, 2002   NDFB terrorists kill three businessmen at Yogibeel, near the Assam–Arunachal Pradesh border.

June 23, 2002   In Aceh Province, Indonesia, five workers at a state-run plantation are killed by Free Aceh Movement terrorists.

June 25, 2002   In Assam State, India, eight employees of an oil and gas company are killed in an ambush by terrorists with the Dima Halam Daoga (DHD), who are seeking independence for the Dimasa tribe.

July 5, 2002	CPN-M terrorists murder the vice chairman of a forest users' committee in Manahari, Nepal.
July 5, 2002	In northeast India, suspected NDFB terrorists kill a businessman in Madhya-santipur area, Dhubri District.
July 14, 2002	NDFB terrorists attack a relief camp in Kokrajhar, Assam, killing nine people.
August 17, 2002	Terrorists of the Kamtapur Liberation Organization (KLO) kill five activists of the Communist Party of India-Marxist (CPI-M) and injure 14 others at its local office in Dhupguri town, Jalpaiguri District, West Bengal State, India.
August 22, 2002	The head of the UPDS, Long Kumar Kiling, dies after being attacked by a wild animal in the forests of Karbi Anglong District.
September 11, 2002	In Addis Ababa, Ethiopia, a bomb detonated by the Oromo Liberation Front (OLF) kills three and injures 38 at the Tigray Hotel.
September 28, 2002	In Aceh Province, Indonesia, a female student at the Al-Muslim Teachers College is assassinated, likely by Free Aceh Movement terrorists.
October 5, 2002	Maoist Communist Center (MCC) terrorists kill a local leader of the Bharatiya Janata Party (BJP), a Hindu nationalist party, in Bokaro District, Jharkhand State, India.
October 21, 2002	A village chairman in Ormoc City, Philippines, is assassinated by three terror-ists, likely from the New People's Army.
October 23, 2002	Eight NDFB terrorists kill two among a group of woodcutters in the Deosankar Reserve Forest, Assam, India.
October 27, 2002	Terrorists from the NDFB massacre 22 from the Datgiri village in Assam, India.
November 1, 2002	The president of the Kathmandu chapter of the Nepali Congress Party is assas-sinated by CPN-M terrorists at his home in Panga, Nepal.
November 4, 2002	CPN-M terrorists burn a passenger bus in east Nepal, killing two and injuring at least eight.
November 9, 2002	Deepak Prasad Pokharel, the security supervisor for the U.S. Embassy in Nepal, is shot dead at his home in Kathmandu by three CPN-M gunmen.
November 23, 2002	CPN-M terrorists kidnap an activist of the Communist Party of Nepal-United Marxist-Leninist in Dolakha District, Nepal. He is found dead on December 2, 2002.
November 26, 2002	In Orissa State, India, Maoist terrorists in the People's War Group kill Jajati Sahu, an official with the ruling Biju Janata Dal (BJD) Party.
December 4, 2002	A civilian is killed and another hurt after a grenade attack by NDFB terrorists in Kokrajhar District, Assam, India.

December 6, 2002	Shital Chaudhai, the chairman of Puhalmampur village and an activist in the Communist Party of Nepal, is abducted from his home and found beheaded near his village two days later. The CPN-M is blamed for the attack.
December 11, 2002	Two residents of the Nayapara village, Kokrajhar District, Assam, India, are killed by members of the National Democratic Front of Bodoland (NDFB).
December 20, 2002	In Jammu and Kashmir, a legislator of the ruling People's Democratic Party (PDP), Abdul Aziz Mir, is assassinated in Pampore while he is walking home from prayers at a mosque. The Save Kashmir Movement, a nationalist/separatist movement opposed to Indian rule of Kashmir, claims responsibility.
December 22, 2002	People's War Group terrorists destroy a railroad track, causing the Kacheguda-Bangalore Express from Hyderabad to derail, leaving two people dead and 87 injured.
December 25, 2002	In Assam, India, two are dead and some 20 injured after members of the United Liberation Front of Assam (ULFA) detonates a mortar in the Ambari and Kalibari areas of Guwahati.
December 31, 2002	In West Bengal State, India, members of the Maoist Communist Center (MCC) slit the throat of Lakshmi Bag, the leader of the Democratic Youth Federation of India (DYFI), the ruling Communist party, at his home in Jangipara, Hooghly District.
January 15, 2003	In Tripura State, India, in one of a series of attacks on supporters of the CPI-M, National Liberation Front of Tripura members kill a schoolteacher at his home in Karbook.
January 24, 2003	In Andhra Pradesh State, India, People's War Group terrorists kill the leader of the ruling Telugu Desam Party in Warangal.
January 25, 2003	Four villagers from a migrant family near Diphu, Assam, India, are gunned down by Karbi nationalists from the United People's Democratic Solidarity (UPDS).
January 26, 2003	Terrorists from the National Liberation Front of Tripura (NLFT) acting independently attack a CPI-M election rally in Mandai village (West Tripura District), killing 11 people and injuring 12. A wave of violence occurs in Tripura as factions compete for elections to be held on February 26.
January 26, 2003	National Democratic Front of Bodoland (NDFB) terrorists kill a schoolteacher in Nadihira village, Assam.
February 2, 2003	In Chhattisgarh State, India, People's War Group terrorists bomb a bus near Basagura in Bijapur District killing eight, including three children.
February 4, 2003	In Tripura, India, an Indigenous Nationalist Party of Tripura (INPT) activist is killed in the Khowai subdivision of West Tripura District by gunmen from the All-Tripura Tiger Force (ATTF).

February 4, 2003	In Tripura, India, a Communist Party of India-Marxist (CPI-M) activist is killed by National Liberation Front of Tripura (NLFT) terrorists in New Dalapatipara, Dhalai District.
February 4, 2003	A CPI-M supporter and his granddaughter are killed by gunmen from the NLFT at his home in Laksmansardarpara, in the West Tripura District.
February 7, 2003	The Bangladesh Nationalist Party's (BNP) district vice president, Abdul Wahed Mondol is killed by terrorists in Taherpur. It is the first attack by the Purbo Banglar Communist Party (PBCP), which seeks a Maoist revolution in Bangladesh.
February 11, 2003	In Karnataka State, India, a senior Telugu Desam Party (TDP) activist and village party president is beaten to death in Kambalapalli.
February 15, 2003	In Tripura State, India, All-Tripura Tiger Force (ATTF) terrorists raid Karnasinghpara, a tribal hamlet, and abduct and later kill two members of the Indigenous Nationalist Party of Tripura (INPT).
February 16, 2003	In Bangladesh, five people are killed in the Kutidurgapur village of Jhenidah District. The Purbo Banglar Communist Party (PBCP) claims responsibility.
February 17, 2003	In Tripura, India, a CPI-M activist is killed by gunmen from the NLFT in Kakraicherra village.
February 19, 2003	In Tripura, India, a CPI-M activist is assassinated after being taken from his home in Radhanagara village by NLFT terrorists.
February 26, 2003	ATTF terrorists opposed to elections being held today in Tripura attack a vehicle transporting election workers killing six, five security officers and a civilian driver, and wounding four election workers.
March 1, 2003	Two women members of the CPI-M are killed in Asharmbari village, West Tripura, by Borok National Council of Tripura (BNCT) members.
March 15, 2003	Two CPI-M supporters from Karnasinghpara village, Dhalai District, are killed by the NLFT.
March 16, 2003	In Andhra Pradesh State, India, V. Jaggaiah, president of the state's ruling Telugu Desam Party (TDP), is assassinated by terrorists with the People's War Group in the Gundala village of Khammam District.
March 16, 2003	In Assam, India, six civilians are killed and 55 more injured after terrorists from the United Liberation Front of Assam (ULFA) bomb a passenger bus in Bamunghopha, Goalpara district.

March 20, 2003	In Sri Lanka, Liberation Tigers of Tamil Eelam (LTTE) members kill 16 fishermen after sinking a fishing boat from China, northwest of Mullaithivu.
March 24, 2003	A group of Bodo Liberation Tiger Force (BLTF) terrorists kill a newspaper journalist in Banyatari, Assam, India.
March 31, 2003	In Assam, India, 26 Dimasa villagers are killed by Hmar People's Convention-Democracy (HPC-D) terrorists in Chekerchand village of Cachar District.
March 31, 2003	Maoist Communist Center (MCC) terrorists kill the leader of Samatha village in West Singhbum District, Jharkhand State, India.
April 8, 2003	In Tripura, India, five people are killed and eight injured when a group of National Liberation Front of Tripura (NLFT) terrorists attack a group meeting of friends in Jagabandhpura, Dhalai District.
May 31, 2003	Hmar nationalists from the Hmar People's Convention-Democracy (HPC-D) kill two in a village of the Dimasa tribes in Assam's North Cachar Hills District.
June 6, 2003	Hmar nationalists from the HPC-D attack Lodi Basti, a Dimasa village in Assam, and kill three tribe members.
June 8, 2003	In Assam, India, two women are killed and a dozen others injured in an attack by HPC-D militants in the Kalinagar village of Cachar District.
June 8, 2003	In Khulna, Bangladesh, three people are gunned down by Purbo Banglar Communist Party (PBCP) members.
June 11, 2003	In Andhra Pradesh State, India, People's War Group terrorists kill a former president of the Telugu Desam Party (TDP).
June 13, 2003	In Andhra Pradesh, India, People's War Group terrorists kill a former Bharatiya Janata Party (BJP) leader in Karimnagar.
June 14, 2003	United People's Democratic Solidarity (UPDS) terrorists kill four persons and injure three more in a village in Karbi Anglong District, Assam, India.
June 14, 2003	In Jaffna, Sri Lanka, LTTE terrorists kill a top leader of the Eelam People's Revolutionary Liberation Front (EPRLF).
June 26, 2003	ULFA terrorists assassinate a member of the Assam Legislative Assembly (MLA) in the Barpeta District of Assam, India.
July 4, 2003	A girl is killed by HPC-D terrorists in Berelang village, North Cachar Hills District, Assam, India.
July 14, 2003	Bodo nationalists in the National Democratic Front of Bodoland (NDFB) kill three persons in separate incidents in Kokrajhar District, Assam, India.
August 3, 2003	United Liberation Front of Assam (ULFA) terrorists kill a tea estate owner and his two sons at Diasajan in Tinsukia District, Assam, India.

August 13, 2003	All-Tripura Tiger Force (ATTF) terrorists kill two and injure four after shooting at a crowd in a market near Agartala, the capital of Tripura State, India.
August 14, 2003	ATTF terrorists kill 30 Bengali villagers in Assam.
August 14, 2003	At least five people are killed and 15 injured in a bomb blast on a bus in Manipur, northeast India. The Revolutionary People's Front, the political wing of the People's Liberation Army, claims responsibility.
August 21, 2003	A family of five is gunned down in the Karbi Anglong District of Assam, India, by UPDS terrorists. The family was likely targeted because they had come to live in Assam from another part of India.
August 24, 2003	ULFA terrorists kill a woman and her son at Basugaon in Kokrajhar District, Assam, India.
August 25, 2003	In Khulna, Bangladesh, the Purbo Banglar Communist Party (PBCP) assassinates senior Bangladeshi opposition leader Monjurul Imam and the rickshaw puller who is carrying him.
September 1, 2003	In Atiriri, Uganda, terrorists from the Lord's Revolutionary Army ambush a bus, killing 22 passengers.
September 7, 2003	A reporter for Nepal's state-run news agency is killed by Communist Party of Nepal-Maoists (CPN-M) terrorists in Sindhupalchowk.
September 8, 2003	CPN-M terrorists kill an eight-year-old boy during an attack on a bank in Balwata, Nepal.
September 18, 2003	CPN-M members shoot and kill a Nepali Congress activist in Dhanusha.
September 19, 2003	CPN-M terrorists assassinate a member of the central committee of the National Democratic Party (NDP) in Arghakhanchi, Nepal. In another incident, two other NDP village activists who had served on village development committees are killed in the southeastern Saptari and Dhanusha districts.
September 20, 2003	People's War Group terrorists kill a Samata Party leader at Lodhki village, Jharkhand State, India.
October 1, 2003	In Pokhara, Nepal, at least one person is killed and two injured when a bomb explodes at the building of Employees' Provident Fund. CPN-M terrorists are responsible.
October 2, 2003	ULFA terrorists kill a village chief at Kailash in the Tinsukia District of Assam, India.
October 11, 2003	In Assam, India, five persons are killed and another is injured in an attack by the ULFA near a tea estate in the Tinsukia District.
October 13, 2003	In Apalalyec, Uganda, Lord's Resistance Army (LRA) terrorists attack a bar, killing 22 customers and injuring 20 others.

October 28, 2003   In Pokhara, Nepal, CPN-M terrorists kill a policewoman after bombing the Gandaki Cooperative Transport office building.

November 4, 2003   United People's Democratic Solidarity (UPDS) terrorists and the Karbi National Volunteers (KNV) kill a Khasi man in Psiar, a village along the border between Assam and Meghalaya in northeast India.

November 4, 2003   In Manipur State, India, the eight-year-old daughter of Education Minister Francis Ngajokpa is kidnapped for ransom, and her body is found tucked inside a sack eight days later. Nationalists from the United National Liberation Front (UNLF) are responsible.

November 9, 2003   Karbi nationalists from the UPDS and KNV kill a Khasi civilian at Deinler village along the Meghalaya-Assam boundary in northeast India.

November 11, 2003   UPDS terrorists abduct and kill four Kuki students from Hidim Teron village near Manja in the Karbi Anglong District, Assam, India.

November 11, 2003   UPDS terrorists in Assam kill six Kuki civilians in Gangjam village in Karbi Anglong District.

November 12, 2003   UPDS terrorists in Assam set fire to five Kuki houses, killing three children at Lenmol village in the Diphu District.

November 14, 2003   Terrorists with the anti-talks faction of the UPDS kill nine Kuki civilians in Gangjam village in Singhasan hills area of Karbi Anglong District, Assam, India.

November 15, 2003   United Liberation Front of Assam (ULFA) terrorists kill two businessmen at a market in Dhubri District, Assam, India.

November 16, 2003   ULFA terrorists kill two members of Nakerbari village in the Nalbari District, Assam, India.

November 18, 2003   In Lira, Uganda, Lord's Resistance Army terrorists kill 12 youths.

November 18, 2003   Five truck drivers are killed and seven others are injured as ULFA terrorists open fire at Basirhat in Dhubri District of Assam, India.

November 19, 2003   ULFA terrorists kill four Hindi-speakers in Nalbari town, Assam, India.

November 19, 2003   Four women are killed and seven others injured as ULFA terrorists open fire at a village in the Bongaigaon District, Assam, India.

November 22, 2003   ULFA terrorists kill 11 migrant laborers and injure seven others who they accuse of taking away their jobs in the Bordubi area of Tinsukia District, Assam, India.

November 23, 2003   In Nepal, CPN-M terrorists kidnap and kill two Nepali Congress workers in Dailekh.

November 24, 2003 National Democratic Front of Bodoland (NDFB) terrorists kill three Biharis and injure nine others at Khanglabari in Darrang District, Assam, India.

December 6, 2003 More than 2,500 members of the Bodo Liberation Tiger Force (BLTF) renounce violence and surrender at Kokrajhar, marking an end to seven years of insurgency. On the following day, an interim 12-member executive council of the Bodoland Territorial Council (BTC) is formed in Kokrajhar, Assam State, India.

December 8, 2003 Three persons are killed and six others wounded when a bomb planted by ULFA terrorists explodes in a market in the Tinsukia District, Assam, India.

December 26, 2003 ULFA's founder member Bhimakanta Buragohain turns himself in along with three other ULFA leaders to the Indian army at Tezpur in Sonitpur District, Assam, India.

February 1, 2004 In Lira, northern Uganda, Lord's Resistance Army terrorists kill eight women as they are on their way to collect food.

February 5, 2004 The Lord's Resistance Army attacks the Abia refugee camp in Lira, northern Uganda, resulting in 47 deaths and 50 injuries.

February 12, 2004 Terrorists from the Communist Party of Nepal-Maoists (CPN-M) bomb a passenger bus in Kathmandu, Nepal, killing six.

February 21, 2004 Lord's Resistance Army terrorists kill more than 200 in an attack on a refugee camp in Lira, northern Uganda.

March 2, 2004 CPN-M members attack a telephone tower in Bhojpur, Nepal, killing some 21 security personnel.

March 9, 2004 UPDS terrorists kill four Kukis at Thengbong village in the Karbi Anglong District, Assam, India.

April 8, 2004 In Baramulla, Kashmir, terrorists detonate a bomb during a People's Democratic Party election rally, killing nine and injuring about 50 others. The Save Kashmir Movement claims responsibility for the blast.

April 11, 2004 One person is killed when NDFB terrorists throw a grenade at a gasoline pump in Bokajan, in the Karbi Anglong District, Assam, India.

April 14, 2004 Lord's Resistance Army terrorists ambush a civilian convoy in Gulu, northern Uganda, killing 13 and wounding eight.

April 21, 2004 In an effort to disrupt voting in Kashmir, Maoist Communist Center (MCC) members kill magistrate Ajay Kumar, who was overseeing a poll in Dhanbad, and injure four policemen.

April 26, 2004 Two persons are killed and seven others sustain injuries when suspected Bodo and Dimasa terrorists detonate a grenade at Khatkhati in the Karbi Anglong District.

May 2, 2004   In Bishoftu, Ethiopia, one is killed and three injured by a hand-grenade attack. The Oromo Liberation Front is suspected.

May 10, 2004   A schoolteacher of Kukurmara village is killed by two ULFA terrorists in the Kamrup District, Assam, India.

May 16, 2004   A faction of the UPDS opposed to a cease-fire splits off to become the Karbi Longri North Cachar Hills Liberation Front (KLNLF) and its armed wing is known as the Karbi Longri North Cachar Hills Resistance Force (KNPR).

May 17, 2004   Members of the Lord's Resistance Army attack two vehicles carrying students in Kitgum, northern Uganda, killing seven and injuring another ten.

June 24, 2004   Seven bus passengers are killed and 15 others sustain injuries as suspected ULFA terrorists detonate a bomb inside a bus at Majgaon in the Sibsagar District, Assam, India.

July 9, 2004   United Liberation Front of Assam (ULFA) terrorists assassinate dead two local Congress Party leaders in the Nalbari District, Assam, India.

July 17, 2004   A trader at a Kabaitari market in the Bongaigaon District, Assam, India, is killed by ULFA terrorists for refusing to pay extortion money.

July 19, 2004   A tea garden employee and his security guard are killed by NDFB terrorists near Sootea in Sonitpur District, Assam, India.

August 4, 2004   At least 12 people are killed when ULFA terrorists explode a bomb during Independence Day celebrations in Dhemaji town.

August 14, 2004   One civilian is killed and 18 others are injured when ULFA terrorists trigger a grenade blast inside a movie theater in Gauripur, Dhubri District, Assam, India.

August 15, 2004   An explosion in Assam by ULFA terrorists kills ten to 15 people.

August 16, 2004   In Colombo, Sri Lanka, LTTE members assassinate a pro-government politician.

August 25, 2004   One person is killed and ten others, including two police personnel, are injured in a grenade attack by ULFA terrorists in front of a movie theater at Dibrugarh town, Assam, India.

August 26, 2004   Six people are killed and 80 wounded when ULFA terrorists detonate six bomb blasts in different areas of Assam.

September 21, 2004   The Communist Party of India-Maoist (CPI-Maoist) is formed, representing a merger of the Maoist Communist Center (MCC) and People's War Group. The group is committed to a Maoist revolution in India.

September 21, 2004   ULFA terrorists kill a civilian at Rashigaon in Bongaigaon District, Assam, India.

October 2, 2004	A group of National Democratic Front of Bodoland (NDFB) terrorists open fire in a busy market, killing 16 people and injuring 20 others near Makrijhora in Dhubri District, Assam, India.
October 4, 2004	NDFB terrorists open fire in Gelapukhuri village in Sonitpur District, Assam, India, killing six and injuring seven others.
October 5, 2004	NDFB terrorists shoot dead at least ten and wound seven others in the Jalabila village of Dhubri District, Assam, India.
November 11, 2004	One person is killed and four others injured in a grenade attack by Karbi terrorists in the KLNLF (*see* May 16, 2004) in Umrangsho in North Cachar Hills District, Assam, India.
December 1, 2004	Three family members and two others are killed by NDFB terrorists in Lutubari near Amguri in the West Garo Hills in Meghalaya State, northeast India.
December 10, 2004	Near Juba, Sudan, Lord's Resistance Army terrorists murder seven and wound eight.
December 11, 2004	In Colombo, Sri Lanka, a Liberation Tigers of Tamil Eelam (LTTE) bomb kills two and injures 15 at the end of a concert by Shahrukh Khan, an Indian film actor.
December 13, 2004	Two explosions near the Assam Assembly building kill two and injure eight. The attacks are carried out by the United Liberation Front of Assam (ULFA).
December 14, 2004	Several bombs are detonated in Assam by members of the ULFA, killing two and injuring 26 at the Maya Bazaar in Morigaon town.
December 16, 2004	One person is killed and 12 others injured by a grenade detonated by ULFA terrorists in the Paltan Bazaar area of Guwahati city, Assam.
December 20, 2004	In Lagile, northern Uganda, Lord's Resistance Army (LRA) terrorists kill a councilman and a woman after ambushing a vehicle.
January 19, 2005	About 12 Lord's Resistance Army terrorists in Tekulu break into the home of a member of Uganda's parliament and end up killing his brother.
March 9, 2005	Lord's Resistance Army terrorists kill six and injure 16 in three villages in Adjumani, northwestern Uganda.
March 15, 2005	Two are killed and seven kidnapped by LRA terrorists in Gulu, northern Uganda.
April 3, 2005	Communist Party of Nepal-Maoist (CPN-M) terrorists detonate a bomb in a hotel in Pokhara, killing one and injuring three.
April 22, 2005	In Myanmar (Burma), eight are killed and 15 wounded when Keren National Union terrorists attack a convoy of trucks and buses filled with university students and teachers near Dawei.
April 24, 2005	CPN-M terrorists kill five people, including two from the Nepali Congress Party, in Bhairahawa, Nepal.

April 27, 2005   In Chhatisgarh, India, Communist Party of India-Maoist (CPI-Maoist) terrorists kill five, including a leader of the Bharatiya Janata Party and the head of the village of Venkateswarlu.

May 5, 2005   Ten are killed and 15 injured by Lord's Resistance Army terrorists during an attack on a displaced persons' camp in Koch Goma, Uganda.

May 5, 2005   Lord's Resistance Army terrorists ambush a vehicle used by students and kill four and injure several others in Kalongo, Uganda.

May 7, 2005   Three bombs detonate in Yangon, Myanmar, killing 11 and injuring 162. The Keren National Union (KNU), the Shan State Army (SSN), the Karenni National Progressive Party (KNPP), or the National Coalition Government of the Union of Burma (NCGUB), all nationalist and separatist groups, are believed responsible.

May 10, 2005   New People's Army terrorists in the Philippines assassinate the mayor of Santa Rosa along with one of his security guards at a town hall where he was presiding over a wedding.

May 22, 2005   A Sikh terrorist group kills one and injures 60 by detonating simultaneous bombs in two movie theaters in Delhi. Two Sikh suspects are arrested.

June 10, 2005   A teacher is kidnapped and two weeks later found dead in Gaonkharka, Nepal, killed by CPN-M terrorists.

June 12, 2005   CPN-M terrorists kill three in Pokhara, Nepal.

June 13, 2005   CPN-M terrorists kill three near Bade village in Nepal's Bastar region.

June 19, 2005   In Andhra Pradesh State, India, CPI-Maoist terrorists kill three Telugu Desam Party (TDP) activists and injure two others in the Prakasam District. In a separate incident, CPI-Maoist terrorists kill eight and injure 100 others in the Dantewara District, Chhattisgarh State, India.

June 20, 2005   In the Batticaloa District of Sri Lanka, LTTE terrorists kill an activist of the Eelam People's Democratic Party.

June 21, 2005   A Nepali Congress-Democratic activist is killed in the Siraha District of Nepal by CPN-M terrorists.

June 25, 2005   In Andhra Pradesh State, India, the leader of the Congress Party is shot dead by CPI-Maoist terrorists in a village in the Cuddapah District.

July 2, 2005   CPI-Maoist terrorists detonate a bomb at a hospital in Warangal, India, killing one and injuring ten.

July 5, 2005   CPI-Maoist terrorists kill three members of an anti-Communist group in Gumla, India.

July 9, 2005   CPI-Maoist terrorists kill a member of the Communist Party of India-Marxist (CPI-M) in Purulia, India.

July 10, 2005	A village headman of the Congress Party is killed by CPI-Maoist terrorists in the Cuddapah District of Andhra Pradesh, India.
July 10, 2005	In Uganda, LRA terrorists kill some 14 people as they are going from Kitgum town to the the Palamek market.
July 19, 2005	CPI-Maoist terrorists kill two from a village in the Dantewara District, Dantewara, India.
July 19, 2005	CPI-Maoist terrorists kill a schoolteacher in the Prakasam District of Andhra Pradesh, India.
July 20, 2005	In the Batticaloa District of Sri Lanka, a village officer is assassinated by LTTE terrorists.
July 26, 2005	An Eelam People's Democratic Party member is assassinated by LTTE terrorists in Sri Lanka's Batticaloa District.
July 28, 2005	Seven are killed by CPI-Maoist terrorists in the Bastar region of Chhattisgarh, India.
July 31, 2005	In Bangladesh, terrorists from the United People's Democratic Front (UPDF) kill three activists of the Parbatya Chattagram Jana Sanghati Samity in the Logang Amtali area of Khagrachhari. This is the first attack by the UPDF, a group seeking independence for the Chittagong Hill Tracts of Bangladesh.
August 1, 2005	LTTE terrorists throw a grenade at a market in the Batticaloa District, Sri Lanka, killing one.
August 7, 2005	ULFA terrorists detonate a bomb at a bus stand at Boko in the Kamrup District, Assam, India, killing four and injuring 12.
August 9, 2005	KLNLF terrorists kill one after ambushing a convoy of trucks in Karbi Anglong District, Assam, India.
August 9, 2005	CPI-Maoist terrorists kill two relatives of the leader of the opposition in Chhattisgarh's State Legislative Assembly in Dantewara, India.
August 10, 2005	ULFA terrorists assassinate a civilian in the Tinsukia District, Assam, India.
August 12, 2005	Sri Lanka's Foreign Affairs Minister, Lakshman Kadirgamar, is assassinated by LTTE terrorists near his home in Colombo. Sixteen suspects are arrested.
August 12, 2005	LTTE terrorists kill a husband and wife inside an office in Wellawatta, Sri Lanka.
August 13, 2005	CPI-Maoist terrorists kill a tribal leader in Cherupuru village, Andhra Pradesh, India.
August 14, 2005	In Nepal, CPN-M terrorists assassinate the chairperson of Bouddha Community Service and a policeman in Kathmandu.

August 20, 2005   In Sri Lanka, LTTE terrorists kill an Eelam People's Democratic Party (EPDP) member in the Vavuniya District.

August 24, 2005   CPN-M terrorists kill the coordinator of the District Monitoring Committee inside his office in Banke, Nepal.

August 27, 2005   In Nepal, a bomb kills seven on a passenger bus traveling from Kathmandu to Dang, killing seven and injuring three. CPN-M terrorists are responsible.

August 28, 2005   In Manipur, India, the United Kuki Liberation Front (UKLF) kills a civilian in Pallel. The UKLF seeks a state for the Kuki tribes as part of the Indian state of Manipur.

September 14, 2005   Karbi Revolutionary Army terrorists kill eight members of the Thekerajan village, in Karbi Anglong District, Assam, India.

September 25, 2005   National Liberation Front of Tripura (NLFT) terrorists kill eight villagers and wound three in India's West Tripura area.

October 24, 2005   A prominent senior tribal leader who was a member of the ruling Communist Party of India (Marxist-Leninist) disappears from his home in Dhalai and is found dead four days later. He was killed by NLFT terrorists.

November 2, 2005   CPI-Maoist terrorists break into the house of a former Bharatiya Janata Party Minister in Malkangiri, India, and kill one person, but the minister is unharmed.

November 2, 2005   Two are killed when Karbi Longri North Cachar Hills Resistance Force (KNPR) attacks a passenger bus traveling near Sorsori, Karbi Anglong District, Assam, India.

November 7, 2005   A leader in the Bharatiya Janata Party, Yuva Morcha, is shot and killed by CPI-Maoist terrorists in the Rajnandgaon District, Chhattisgarh State, India.

November 11, 2005   CPI-Maoist terrorists fire on a group of government officials in Kanker, India, killing one and injuring five.

November 15, 2005   Suspected Tripura nationalists in the NLFT kill three women and injure two other villagers at Bambpur in the South Tripura District, India.

December 11, 2005   The head of a local village is killed by CPI-Maoist terrorists in Betauna, India.

December 14, 2005   More than 30 CPI-Maoist terrorists kill a deputy village head and Communist Party of India (Marxist-Leninist) activist in Kurnapalli village, India.

December 15, 2005   A village headman is killed by CPI-Maoist terrorists in Dantewara, India.

December 22, 2005   CPI-Maoist terrorists kill a shopkeeper in Pangidi Madharam village in India.

December 29, 2005   CPI-Maoist terrorists kill a Telugu Desam Party activist in the Mangapet area of Warangal District, Andhra Pradesh, India.

December 30, 2005   Two are killed in Dantewara District, India, by CPI-Maoist terrorists.

May 22, 2006   In Nepal, CPN-M terrorists bomb the house of the Nepal Congress Rautahat District leader in Inarwa, killing him and two of his sons.

June 15, 2006   A land mine detonates by a bus in Anurah-Bura, Sri Lanka, killing 68 and wounding 60. LTTE terrorists are likely responsible.

September 6, 2006   Three members of the Salwa Judum tribe who were kidnapped a week ago by CPI-Maoist terrorists are found dead in Dantewara, Chhattisgarh, India.

September 6, 2006   In Sri Lanka, a member of the Eelam People's Democratic Party is assassinated by LTTE terrorists in Valaichchenai.

September 24, 2006 CPI-Maoist terrorists kill a Congress Party activist in Dantewara, India.

October 8, 2006   In Ampara, Sri Lanka, an official with the Poverty Alleviation Program is assassinated by LTTE terrorists.

November 5, 2006   The ULFA is likely responsible for a bomb that detonates in a shopping area in Guwahati, Assam, India, which kills 13 and injures 25.

November 20, 2006   A bomb rips through a passenger train in West Bengal killing ten and injuring 60. No groups claims responsibility, but the Kamtapur Liberation Organization (KLO), which has ties to the ULFA, is believed to have planted the bomb.

November 26, 2006   LTTE terrorists assassinate a man who had been village leader, in Point Pedro, Sri Lanka.

Terrorism in the Middle East

The Arab-Israeli conflict formally began in 1948 but terrorism had appeared earlier during the battles under the British mandatory government. The Arab belief that the Jews could be driven out by violence was periodically implemented during riots in the 1920s and 1930s. As a decision on the country's future approached in the late 1940s, attacks intensified. In addition, two right-wing Jewish groups—the Lehi and the Irgun—carried out attacks on British soldiers and on Arabs. This era was ended with the 1948 war which divided the land into the state of Israel, the West Bank annexed by Jordan, and the Gaza Strip governed by Egypt.

During the mid-1960s, the Palestinian movement consciously adopted terrorism as the centerpiece of its strategy. Although in later years it would use other means to pursue its aims, including diplomacy, this essential choice remained in place for the next half century. It was a central factor in the length and apparent insolubility of the conflict.

There were clear reasons for the decision to adopt and keep terrorism as well as important factors which made it hard to relinquish. Four in particular should be mentioned: First, in Palestinian perceptions—and largely in those of other Arabs—terrorism was justified. Israelis, and often Jews in general, were so evil, criminal, and threatening that killing them was considered justifiable. This was the same basic concept that had underpinned genocide elsewhere.

Second, there was an expectation that terrorism would be a successful strategy. Israel was believed to be a weak and artificial country which, if hit hard enough, would collapse. The Jews would surrender, flee, or make massive concessions if faced with such consistent anti-civilian violence. Israel would cease to function, its society paralyzed and economy decisively subverted. In the earlier period, many engaged in or supporting terrorism thought that outrages would trigger a war between Israel and Arab states that would result in Israel's destruction.

In some more radical (originally leftist but in later years Islamist) circles, it was also argued that terrorism against Western targets would sever support for Israel in those countries, without which—given the argument of vulnerability and artificiality—Israel would collapse. More realistically, terrorism was thought to be a marvelous way to obtain publicity. In later decades, it was also used—paradoxically—to generate Western sympathy, since Palestinians could claim to be the victim of warfare even if it was initiated and continued due to their own terrorist attacks.

Moreover, terrorism could be used to promote the power of individual groups—including the Palestine Liberation Organization (PLO) itself, member organizations, and Islamist ones—which by the frequency and effectiveness of their attacks could prove their superiority to rivals. Finally, and most effectively of all, terrorism was a very useful way to sabotage any possibility of a negotiated compromise agreement to end the conflict. In this way, it was at times used against moderate Arabs and even PLO officials considered too willing to make such a deal.

Third, terrorism was the product of extremist goals. Precisely because the general objective of the movement was to eliminate Israel and replace it with a Palestinian state—among the Islamists, even further reaching it would be an Islamist state—more temperate measures did not suffice. The use of terrorism became linked with this goal and thus the abandonment of terrorism was equated with a treasonous intention to abandon this objective.

Fourth, terrorism was a preferred policy because of the lack—in part due to choice, in part to circumstances—of any preferred strategy. The Palestinian movement never put a priority on mass organizing. The Arab states' militaries failed to bring victory and the short-lived attempt to launch a guerrilla war against Israel ended in disaster. Realizing that confrontation with Israel's army would not bring him a triumph, Yasir Arafat chose to make war on a society.

Many of these same factors made it very hard for the movement to dispense with terrorism in later years. This would have required a thoroughgoing examination of past mistakes and major changes in the national political culture. Individuals who had risen to power and prominence through the use of terrorism—including Arafat himself—saw it as a pillar of their position. Strong interest groups, ranging from semi-criminal elements who combined revolution with extortion to radical Islamists who used terrorism in their competition with Fatah, championed the continued use of the tactic. Opposition, and hence moderation, was equated with treason. Any attempt to suppress the terrorist groups or stop them could lead to civil war. The movement was thus caught in a paradox, one from which it found great difficulty from escaping even if—arguably—it would be more pragmatic and serve material self-interest to do so.

For the Arab world's states, the second half of the twentieth century was one of crushing military defeats. The wars instigated against Israel in 1949, 1967, and 1973 resulted only in massive casualties and losses of Arab territory. The only way to battle the Jewish state was through terrorism.

For the Palestinians in particular, for whom such defeats mattered most, terrorism was attractive as the only violent tactic they could execute solo. So significant to Palestinian leader Yasir Arafat and his supporters was terrorism that the date of their first attack against Israel, a bomb planted in that nation's water system on January 1, 1965, is also the date that his organization, Fatah, chose as its official founding, even though the organization had begun six years earlier. The vast majority of the 61 attacks attempted against Israel from 1965 to 1967, including the first one, were unsuccessful thanks to Israeli counter-terrorism and faulty planning.

But terrorism remained Arafat's major tactic because it was easy, appropriate, and, eventually, successful. Terrorism mobilized Palestinian and Arab support for the PLO, raised the Palestinian issue's international priority, prevented other Palestinians and Arab states from negotiating peace with Israel, and made many Western leaders eager to appease Arafat. Although attacks on Israel never came near to destroying that country, terrorism gave the appearance that the struggle was advancing and revenge being taken in contrast to the vague promises and posturing made by Arab leaders.

The Palestinian targets were always civilian, part of Arafat's strategy to undermine the morale of the Jewish state. He believed that like France in Algeria during the 1960s, Israel would eventually abandon the country they ruled—a grave misunderstanding of the Jewish state. In 1971, Arafat created Black September, a covert international terrorist group within Fatah headed by one of his most trusted deputies, Abu Iyad. Black September was responsible for many successful terrorist attacks during the 1970s, the most notorious attack being the assault upon Israeli athletes at the 1972 Olympic Games in Munich. Many other terrorist attacks during this period, in particular a spate of plane hijackings and airport attacks, came from smaller groups that had sprung from the PLO such as the Popular Front for the Liberation of Palestinian (PFLP), Democratic Front for the Liberation of Palestine and Abu Nidal—all of which saw themselves as more extreme than Fatah.

Neither Arafat personally nor the Palestinians as a whole ever paid an international price for terrorism. Even while Black September was at the height of its success and just 18 months after the Munich Olympics, Arafat was invited in 1974 to speak at the United Nations and pose as a man of peace carrying an olive branch. Arafat was a master at ensuring he could always personally disassociate himself from terrorism as much as possible. Terrorism was being committed by other groups and some Westerners saw a need to cultivate Arafat so he could help deter them.

Not only did terrorism not tarnish the Palestinian image irreparably, it helped to enhance it. A later terrorist of note, Abu Ubied al-Qurashi, a top aide to Osama bin Ladin, said that he saw PLO attacks such as at the Olympics as a model for al-Qaeda. He pointed out that after that attack, millions became familiar with the Palestinian cause, thousands of young Palestinians joined the PLO, and many new groups arose in the Middle East using terrorism as a strategy.

Nor did Arafat pay the price when terrorism moved beyond Israel and was used to attack the West. There is ample evidence that Arafat played a personal role in the 1974 murder of the American ambassador in Sudan, which, albeit suspected by many American officials, didn't deter the U.S. government from seeking ties with Arafat. More problematic for Arafat was the targeting of Arab victims. A major target was Jordan, upon which Arafat was extracting blood revenge for the September 1970 war and his deportation from that country for instigating violence. Later, when Egypt signed a peace agreement with Israel, that country would be added as were moderates within the PLO. Arafat's contribution to the violence that suffused Lebanon in the 1980s also resulted in his being deported out of there.

The 1980s with the overthrow of the Iranian government by an Islamic ideology and the Soviet invasion of Afghanistan saw the rise of Islamist violence in the Middle East aimed at the United States. (See chapter 8 for a full description.) It was also the decade in which non-Islamic Arab terrorism against the United States started. Libya was a major sponsor of the attacks with the worst attack against Americans to date, the December 1988 bombing of a Pan Am plane.

But Libyan and non-Islamic attacks against the United States remained limited. Not so Palestinian terrorism whose parameters shifted in 1987. The Palestinians in the West Bank and Gaza became the ones igniting the violent struggle against Israel as the Arab word, the "intifada," entered the international lexicon. For the first time ever, Arafat and the PLO, then in Tunisia, were forced to react, not leading the way. More potentially dangerous for terrorism in the region was the founding at this time of Hamas, a radical Islamist group justifying all forms of violence in its goal to create an Islamic Palestinian state in place of Israel. As a social welfare group, Hamas began recruiting scores of young

Palestinian men and molding them into potential religious martyrs. But several years of the first intifada produced more Palestinian casualities than Israeli ones. Among them was Abu Jihad, Arafat's deputy and in charge of running the intifada from Tunis, who was assassinated in his Tunis home in a spectacular Israeli raid.

Increasingly, it became clear that Israel would not follow France's model and withdraw due to violence alone from the West Bank and Gaza. Indeed, during the late 1980s, the country was revitalized with a massive emigration of Soviet Jews. Meanwhile, the Palestinians were in complete disarray. The final disaster was Arafat's decision to back his old friend, Iraqi leader Saddam Hussein, after his invasion of Kuwait in the belief that Hussein might finally be the Arab leader that would help him gain Palestine. When Hussein was defeated, retribution against the Palestinians from the wealthy Gulf states who had been their financial patrons, notably Saudi Arabia, brought the PLO to the brink of disaster. A new strategy had to be adopted.

Faced with few other options, Arafat the terrorist transformed himself into Arafat the peacemaker. In 1992, he and Israeli Prime Minister Yitzhak Rabin signed the Oslo Agreement on the White House lawn in which Arafat agreed to renounce violence and accept the existence of Israel and a Palestinian governing entity that, at its largest, would be restricted to the West Bank, Gaza, and East Jerusalem. Arafat did so amidst opposition from other Palestinian groups such as the Islamic fundamentalists that were growing in strength.

The Palestinian Authority (PA) was established in 1994 as Israeli forces departed from Gaza and initially Jericho and later other major towns in the West Bank. Now hundreds of former PLO men from across the Arab world committed to terrorism formed the ranks of the new armed PA security forces, charged with cracking down on terrorists. For a few short years, there was a relative calm as the Palestinian Authority had a mixed record of tracking down and prosecuting terrorists. But even as Fatah kept to its promise of not perpetrating terrorism, Hamas and another Islamic fundamentalist group, Islamic Jihad, were increasingly using the new technique of suicide bombings against civilian targets within Israel. When Arafat lowered his pressure against these groups, the results were especially devastating. In March 1996, there were a spate of deadly attacks inside Israel which resulted in the downfall of Labor Prime Minister Shimon Peres, who had replaced the slain Yitzhak Rabin—another victim of the peace process—and the election of Benjamin Netanyahu who wanted to take a harder stand against Arafat. A vicious cycle occurred in which Israel could not move ahead on the peace process because of increasing terrorism, and Palestinian frustration with the slow pace of the peace process helped to increase support for terrorism.

But there is also ample evidence that Arafat all along intended to use the Oslo Agreement to gain a foothold in the area and had not given up on his dream of attaining all of Israel. That became clear in July 2000 during talks with Prime Minister Ehud Barak, overseen by President Bill Clinton at the presidential retreat of Camp David. Arafat turned down the offer of a Palestinian state on all of the Gaza Strip and most of the West Bank, and financial compensation for thousands of refugees. With diplomatic solutions at a standstill, the Palestinians returned to violence. They now had an armed Palestinian police force turned deadly, the creation of a new Fatah militia known as the Tanzim, the new technique of suicide bombings and calls for violence throughout the media and leadership—a vicious brew which made this intifada far deadlier for Israel.

Throughout 2001–2003, Israel suffered the worst terrorist attacks of its history with several deaths a week reaching within the core of daily life—in buses, restaurants, and stores. One of the most devastating attacks was the October 2001 assassination by PFLP terrorists of the Israeli minister of tourism in a Jerusalem hotel. Israel responded to the terrorism by targeted assassinations of terrorists, preventing Arafat from leaving the region, and even redeploying in parts of the West Bank and Gaza. But the attacks continued as even women, for the first time, joined the ranks of suicide bombers.

A breaking point came in March 2002 when a terrorist walked into a hotel in Netanya during Passover and detonated his bomb as a Seder was being conducted. Israel sent forces into Ramallah and created a siege around Arafat's compound that lasted several weeks until a U.S.-brokered deal.

The deadly attacks of the new intifada only diminished when Israel killed such top terrorist leaders as Sheikh Yassin, founder of Hamas, and his successor, and began building a security fence to prevent Palestinians from illegally slipping into Israel. The death of Yasir Arafat in November 2004 and other factors brought to an end this wave of violence. But the number of attempted attacks remained high and terrorism was still very much a part of a long-term, continuing conflict. This was especially made likely by the Israel-Hezbollah war of 2006 and the Hamas takeover of the Gaza Strip in 2007.

April 20, 1920	Thousands of Arab pilgrims in Jerusalem who have arrived for the Muslim festival of Nebi Musa are roused to join in an anti-British political demonstration. The march turns into an outburst of anti-Jewish frenzy. The Arab police under British control make no attempt to end the violence; some even join their fellow Arabs in the rioting, which lasts several days. Five Jews are killed and 211 injured.
May 4–7, 1921	Arabs attack Jewish shops and homes in Palestine. These attacks leave 47 Jews and 48 Arabs dead and 146 Jews and 73 Arabs wounded.
November 2, 1921	Arab riots break out in the Jewish Quarter of Jerusalem. Five Jewish residents and three Arab attackers are killed.
August 24, 1929	Rumors that Jews are planning to seize the al-Aqsa mosque in Jerusalem set off Arab rioting. In Hebron, more than 70 Jews are killed and over 50 wounded.
August 28, 1929	In Safed, Arab rioters attack Jewish homes and institutions, killing 45 people.
April 15, 1936	A Palestinian Arab group stops ten cars on the Tel Aviv–Haifa highway, singles out three Jews, and kills them.

April 19, 1936   An Arab attack in Jaffa results in three Jewish fatalities.

April 25, 1936   The Arab High Committee organizes a general strike in Palestine until its demands for a fundamental change in British policy in Palestine are met. The strike is accompanied by violence; Jews are assaulted and stoned in various cities. In rural areas Arab farmers attack Jewish settlements and the British police. These activities are supplemented by guerrilla warfare carried out by organized Arab units from the hills.

1937   The Peel Commission, a British government body empowered to recommend the future of Palestine, criticizes the Arab use of violence and calls for partition of the country into a Jewish and an Arab state. Palestinian Arabs and Arab states reject the proposal. The supporters of Amin al-Husseini, the grand mufti and political leader, embark on a revolt that will last two years. Many Jews, Arab supporters of the rival Nashashibi faction, and British civilians are murdered.

1937   The Irgun Tsvai-Leumi (Irgun) splits away from the Jewish communal self-defense force, the Haganah, demanding a more militant policy.

September 26, 1937   Yelland Andrews, the British district commissioner for Galilee, is assassinated by Palestinian Arab nationalists. The British arrest the members of the Arab High Committee, holding them responsible for the killing, and deport them to the Seychelles Islands.

October 4, 1938   Two large Arab fighting units attack Tiberias for several hours before British troops drive them away. Nineteen Jews are killed and three wounded.

1939   Yair Stern leads an even more militant right-wing Zionist splinter group out of the Irgun called Lehi (or the Stern Gang).

February 27, 1939   The Irgun attacks Arabs in a half-dozen cities of Palestine with bombs, grenades, and rifles, killing or wounding many.

November 6, 1944   Lord Moyne, British minister of state for the Middle East, and his driver are shot and killed in Cairo by Eliahu Hakim and Eliah Bet-Zouri of the Stern Gang, apparently because he opposes Jewish immigration to Palestine. An Egyptian court sentences them both to death and they are hanged on March 22, 1945.

December 1944   Zionist leaders in Palestine, putting top priority on fighting alongside Britain in the war against Germany and critical of the murder of Lord Moyne, order the Haganah to hunt down Lehi and Irgun members and turn them over to the British authorities. About 1,000 activists are captured and transferred to British custody.

July 22, 1946   Ninety-one people, mostly civilians and 17 of them Jews, are killed, and 45 injured in a bomb attack by the Irgun on the King David Hotel in Jerusalem, which serves as British military headquarters. The attack is in response to massive raids and arrests of Jewish activists and officials by the British.

October 31, 1946   In its first international attack, the Irgun bombs the British Embassy in Rome. The building is completely demolished in the blast, but there are no fatalities.

March 30, 1947	Tel Aviv Lehi members kill a British soldier's wife in Tel Aviv.
August 10, 1947	Four Jews are murdered by Arabs at a cafe in Tel Aviv. Among the dead is the famous actor Meir Te'omi. Arabs claim that the murders are a retaliation for the killing of two Arabs by the Haganah in Fega two months prior. In a separate incident, the Haganah bombs an Arab home near Tel Aviv. Eleven are left dead, among them a woman and four children.
August 23, 1947	Five Arabs are killed probably by Jewish paramilitaries in a revenge attack for the British arrest of two leading Irgun members.
November 22, 1947	Lehi members kill an Arab in Haifa after the British kill five of their members on November 12.
November 29, 1947	United Nations Resolution 181 is passed, calling for a Jewish and an Arab state to be established and for Jerusalem to become an international city. The Zionist leadership accepts the plan. The Palestinian Arab leadership and all Arab states reject it. Violence breaks out in December 1947.
December 2–5, 1947	During a three-day Arab general strike, 20 Jews and 15 Arabs are killed in intercommunal fighting. Arabs pillage and set fire to a Jewish business area in Jerusalem. Max Pinn, a Jewish Agency trade official, is murdered in his car by Arabs.
December 12, 1947	Seven Jews are murdered in an Arab attack at Mishmar Hanegev. The same day, three Jewish workers are killed by Arabs in Lod.
December 13, 1947	Two weeks of violence bring 220 deaths in Palestine. The rioting spreads to Aden (later South Yemen); 111 Jews are murdered in Arab rioting. Arab attacks in Jaffa and Tel Aviv leave 30 Jews and Arabs dead.
December 13, 1947	Arabs gun down and kill a Jew in Haifa. Three Jews are murdered by Arabs in Gevulot. In Jerusalem, Arab attackers murder a Jewish child.
December 13, 1947	A series of Irgun bomb attacks in Jerusalem and Jaffa cause at least 16 Arab deaths and injuries to 67. In addition, there are arson attacks on Arab homes in Jaffa.
December 14, 1947	Fourteen Jews are killed in an Arab ambush on a civilian bus convoy near Lydda. Arabs open fire on a Jewish convoy on its way to a children's village in Bet Shemesh to deliver supplies. Fourteen Jews are shot dead. In Jaffa, a Jew is murdered by Arab gunmen.
December 16, 1947	Arab terrorists kill a Jew in Halutza.
December 18, 1947	A Jew is slain by Arabs in Silwan.
December 18, 1947	In a Haganah attack on Khisas in the north, ten Arabs, among them five children, are killed.
December 19, 1947	In an Arab attack on a convoy making its way to Jerusalem, one Jew is killed. In a separate incident the same day, a Jew accidentally enters Haifa's Arab Quarter and is attacked and murdered by Arabs.

December 22, 1947   A Jew is attacked and killed by Arabs in Jerusalem.

December 23, 1947   Arabs attack two Jews in Jerusalem, killing them both.

December 24, 1947   Arabs open fire on a group of Jews in Haifa, killing four.

December 29, 1947   Irgun members carry out two bombings. One attack at the Nablus Gate of Jerusalem's Old City results in 44 people being killed or injured, and one at the Damascus Gate in Jerusalem leaves 11 Arabs and two British dead.

December 30, 1947   An Irgun bomb attack just outside the Haifa oil refineries leaves six Arabs dead and 42 wounded. Immediately after the attack, Arab refinery workers begin rioting and go on a killing rampage, invading the factory facilities and murdering 41 Jewish workers and injuring another 49.

December 31, 1947   Since the approval of the UN partition plan on November 29, the death toll reaches 489.

January 1, 1948   A Jew is murdered by Arabs in Ginnosaur, Israel.

January 3, 1948   Three Jews are killed after they are attacked by Arabs in Jerusalem.

January 4, 1948   In Tel Aviv, a Jewish woman is murdered by Arabs. Fourteen die and 100 are wounded when Lehi attacks the Arab National Committee headquarters in Jaffa.

January 5, 1948   Fifteen Arabs die as the result of a Haganah bomb attack on the Semiramis Hotel in Jerusalem.

January 6, 1948   A Jew is murdered by Arabs in Jerusalem.

January 7, 1948   In an Irgun bombing at the Jaffa Gate in Jerusalem, 14 Arabs are killed.

January 8, 1948   Two Jews are slain by Arabs in Jerusalem.

January 9, 1948   Arabs attack Kfar Etzion and murder 35 Jews.

January 11, 1948   Two Jews are murdered by Arabs in Kfar Uriya.

January 13, 1948   In Kfar Etzion, two Jews are killed by Arabs. A Jew is murdered by Arabs in Har Tuv.

January 14, 1948   Two Jews are slain by Arabs in Kfar Etzion.

January 15, 1948   Arabs murder two Jews in Jerusalem.

January 18, 1948   A Jew is killed by Arabs in Afula.

January 20, 1948   A Jew is murdered by Arabs in Kastel. A Jew is killed in Jerusalem in an Arab attack.

January 22, 1948   Seven Jews are shot by Arabs in Yazur.

January 25, 1948   Ten Jews are killed by Arab assailants in Kastel.

January 25, 1948   According to British authorities, the death toll for the eight weeks since the Partition Agreement of violence has reached 1,160. Among the dead are 721 Arabs, 408 Jews, 19 others, and 12 British police officers. During this period an additional 1,171 Arabs, 749 Jews, 13 others, and 37 British officers are injured.

January 27, 1948   In an Arab attack on a convoy, a British soldier and one Jew are murdered.

February 1, 1948   A car bomb planted by Arabs kills nine in the center of Jerusalem.

February 5, 1948   A Jew is murdered by Arabs in Tel Aviv.

February 7, 1948   A Jew is murdered by Arabs in Gaza. In Tsfat the same day, two Jews are murdered and mutilated by Arabs.

February 8, 1948   Arabs murder three Jews in Tel Aviv. The same day in Jerusalem, six Jews are killed by Arab assailants. In yet another incident that day, Arabs murder a Jew in Tsfat.

February 12, 1948   Four Jews are slain by Arabs in Jerusalem.

February 23, 1948   In an Arab bomb attack in Jerusalem, 55 Jews are killed.

February 25, 1948   Arabs murder three Jews as they are traveling on the road to Tel Aviv. In a separate incident, three Jews are killed on the road to Jerusalem. In an additional road attack, Arabs murder two Jews on the road from Haifa to Jenin.

February 28, 1948   In an attack on Kfar Saba, a Jew is killed by Arabs.

March 1, 1948   As the Arab road attacks continue, eight Jews are murdered in three separate terror incidents on the Tel Aviv-to-Jerusalem Road.

March 4, 1948   In an Arab shell attack on Tel Aviv, a child is killed. The same day, a Jew is killed by an Arab mine. In yet another attack that day, 16 Jews are murdered in an Arab ambush on the road near Atarot.

March 14, 1948   In an Arab ambush near Fallujah, seven Jews are slain.

March 17, 1948   In an Arab sniper attack in Tel Aviv, a Jewish woman is killed.

March 18, 1948   Arabs attack a convoy in Acre, killing four Jews and five British soldiers.

March 20, 1948   Seven Jews are slain by Arabs in Ein Harud.

March 28, 1948   On the road to Kibbutz Yehiam, Arabs attack a convoy and murder 47 Jews. The same day, in an Arab attack on a convoy in Gaza, two Jews are killed.

March 29, 1948   Arabs murder two Jewish civilians in Tel Aviv.

May 15, 1948   Pursuant to the UN resolution of November 1947 calling for partition, the British leave Palestine, ending their rule over the country. Israel declares independence. The Arab states and Palestinian leadership reject partition and attack Israel.

September 17, 1948   In Jerusalem, Lehi members murder UN mediator Count Folke Bernadotte, a Swede, whom they accuse of planning to support an unfavorable negotiated settlement for Israel. The organization is banned, its newspaper closed, and the group's two leaders, Natan Yellin-Mor and Mattityahu Shmuelevitz, are imprisoned by Israel.

April 3, 1949   Israel and Arab states agree to an armistice. The armistice lines leave the Gaza Strip under Egyptian control and the West Bank ruled by Jordan, which annexes that territory.

October 10, 1959   Yasir Arafat, a Palestinian nationalist working in Kuwait, and other Palestinians there found Fatah, a movement committed to using armed struggle to destroy Israel and establish a Palestinian Arab state in its place. The movement is intended to be a broad front that will include Palestinians of all ideological and political views. It quickly obtains Syrian sponsorship.

May 29, 1964   The Palestine Liberation Organization (PLO) is founded in Jordanian-ruled East Jerusalem, committed to "liberating all of Palestine" and destroying Israel. Its leader is Ahmad Shukeiri, a Palestinian who had worked for Arab states and is handpicked by Egyptian President Gamal Abdel Nasser, whose country controls the organization. The PLO establishes its own parliament, the Palestine National Council, and the Palestine Liberation Army (PLA), but carries out no military actions in its own name.

January 1, 1965   A bomb is placed in Israel's national water carrier system in the Bet Netofa Valley in northern Israel but fails to explode. It is the first attack against Israel by Fatah, which officially dates its founding from this event.

May 1967   The Popular Struggle Front (PSF) is founded by Samir Ghosheh and Bahjat Abu Gharbiah as a splinter group from Fatah, and begins attacks against Israel. While always remaining a small group, it enjoys the sponsorship of various Arab states over its complex history. After a brief reunification with Fatah in 1971–1974, it breaks away again and comes at various times under the influence of Iraq, Syria, and Libya. In 1993, Ghosheh returns to supporting Arafat.

June 5–11, 1967   In a war lasting six days, Israel destroys the Egyptian and Syrian air forces, captures the Sinai Peninsula and Gaza Strip from Egypt, and then captures the West Bank from Jordan, and the Golan Heights from Syria.

December 11, 1967   George Habash, a Palestinian Greek Orthodox Christian, founds the Popular Front for the Liberation of Palestine (PFLP). The PFLP espouses a neo-Marxist philosophy, uses terrorism (including international attacks) as a strategy, takes an anti-Western stance, and advocates revolution in all Arab states.

March 18, 1968   A school bus in Israel's Negev desert hits a land mine placed by Fatah terrorists, killing two adults and injuring 28 children. Israel retaliates by attacking the main Fatah base in Karameh, Jordan. Even though Israel captures the base, killing 150 terrorists and capturing 150 more, Fatah claims victory. The battle inspires a big upsurge in Palestinian and Arab support for Fatah, marking a turning point in its rise.

June 5, 1968   U.S. Senator Robert F. Kennedy, brother of assassinated president John F. Kennedy and a leading presidential candidate, is murdered by a Palestinian, Sirhan Sirhan, in Los Angeles. Sirhan is sentenced to life imprisonment. Demands to free him are featured in several terrorist attacks by Fatah and other Palestinian groups.

September 4, 1968   Three bombs placed by Palestinian terrorists detonate near a bus station in Tel Aviv, killing one and injuring three people.

October 1968   The Popular Front for the Liberation of Palestine-General Command (PFLP-GC), a Syrian-backed group led by Ahmad Jibril, breaks away from the PFLP, ostensibly because it wants to focus completely on attacks against Israel.

November 22, 1968   A bomb placed by Palestinian terrorists in Jerusalem's Mahane Yehuda market kills 12 and injures 62.

December 26, 1968   An El Al plane at the Athens airport about to depart for Paris is attacked by two PFLP terrorists, who use grenades and machine guns on the passengers and crew, killing one and injuring two others. The terrorists are caught and eventually convicted in Greece.

February 1969   With Egyptian support, Arafat becomes chairman of the PLO, marking the takeover of that group by Fatah. Arafat directs the PLO toward a terrorist strategy, though actual attacks are always carried out by member groups.

February 18, 1969   Three PFLP terrorists fire on an El Al jet about to take off from Zurich to Tel Aviv, killing the pilot. In the exchange of gunfire between the terrorists and an Israeli airline security guard, one attacker is killed and three Israeli crew members and three passengers wounded. The terrorists surrender and are sentenced to 12 years in jail.

February 21, 1969   A bomb placed by Palestinian terrorists kills two and wounds eight people in a Jerusalem supermarket.

February 22, 1969   The Democratic Front for the Liberation of Palestine (DFLP) splits from the PFLP in order to put more emphasis on Marxist-Leninist ideology along with continuing terror attacks on Israel and Western targets.

June 17, 1969   Shirley Louise Anderson, a tourist from Rochester, New York, is killed when PLO terrorists shell an Israeli resort town.

August 7, 1969   PFLP members blow up a bomb in Israel, killing two people and wounding 12.

October 22, 1969 Two apartments in Haifa are bombed by PFLP terrorists, killing two people and wounding 20.

November 27, 1969 Two Popular Struggle Front terrorists throw a hand grenade into the El Al office in Athens, killing a Greek child and injuring 13 other people. They are sentenced to 11- and eight-year jail terms, but are freed after others hijack an Olympic Airways plane to Cairo on July 22, 1970, and demand their release, along with five other Palestinian terrorists imprisoned in Greece.

December 27, 1969 Leon Holtz, 48, a tourist from Brooklyn, New York, is killed when terrorists fire at a tourist bus near Hebron.

February 10, 1970 Palestinian terrorists attack El Al Israel Airlines passengers at the Munich airport, killing one and injuring 11. The Action Organization for the Liberation of Palestine and the Popular Democratic Front for the Liberation of Palestine claim responsibility for the attack.

February 21, 1970 Popular Front for the Liberation of Palestine-General Command (PFLP-GC) terrorists plant a bomb that detonates on a Swissair plane bound for Tel Aviv, which explodes, causing the death of all 47 passengers and crew. That same day, Barbara Ertle of Grandville, Michigan, is killed during a PLO shooting attack on a busload of pilgrims in the West Bank town of Halhoul.

May 4, 1970 Two armed Palestinians break into the office of the Israeli Consulate in Asunción, Paraguay, and shoot at the employees, killing an Israeli secretary.

May 22, 1970 PFLP terrorists fire on a school bus in Avivim, an agricultural community in northern Israel, killing nine children and three adults.

June 10, 1970 Major Bob Perry, an assistant U.S. Army attaché in Jordan, is murdered by PFLP gunmen in Amman, Jordan's capital.

September 6, 1970 PFLP terrorists hijack four passenger airliners—TWA, Pan American, Swissair and El Al—in an attempt to win the release of Palestinian terrorists imprisoned in Europe. They fly two of the hijacked planes to Dawson's Field in Jordan and blow up one in Cairo after releasing the crew. On the fourth plane, an El Al Airlines flight from Amsterdam to New York, the crew and passengers attack the terrorists, killing one of them, a San Francisco-born Nicaraguan, and overpowering the other, Leila Khaled. Khaled is taken into custody in Britain, where the plane lands. The next day, a British plane is hijacked and joins the other two at Dawson's Field, where they are surrounded by Jordanian tanks. The terrorists negotiate for the release of Khaled and other terrorist prisoners held in the countries of the three hijacked airliners—Britain, Germany, and Switzerland. The terrorists release all but 56 out of the 255 hostages and blow up the three planes. Great Britain eventually releases Khaled and six other Palestinian terrorists in exchange for the remaining hostages. The incident adds to Jordanian King Hussein's mounting frustration with Yasir Arafat and the PLO. The Jordanian army attacks the PLO forces and expels them from Jordan.

The Era of Black September

The PLO's defeat and expulsion from Jordan forced it to reassemble in Lebanon. It was only one more in a long series of tactical frustrations. The PLO's original goal of inspiring Arab states to fight Israel had ended in disaster. The same was true for the attempts in the 1967–1969 period of organizing a guerrilla war within the West Bank and Gaza Strip. Similarly, while the PLO grew greatly during the period, the cross-border terrorism and attacks from Jordan had neither defeated Israel nor found a stable base among Palestinians in Jordan—largely through Arafat's own miscalculations.

After the PLO's expulsion from Jordan in September 1970, it created a new secret organization, Black September, whose purpose was to carry out international terrorist attacks—against both Western and Arab targets—for which the PLO could deny responsibility. Indeed, the PLO incurred no major costs because of such activities, even when its forces dared attack the Olympic games to kidnap and murder Israeli athletes. By the end of 1973, however, this era came to a close in large part because Saudi Arabia threatened to withdraw financial support to the PLO.

By this time, the PLO was already successfully using Lebanon as a base for cross-border terrorist attacks in which the goal was usually to kill the maximum number of Israeli civilians. The Lebanese civil war, caused in part by PLO activities, complicated but did not essentially interfere with these operations, since for all practical purposes the PLO ruled southern Lebanon. Again, though, the casualties the PLO inflicted on Israel had little material effect. At the same time, however, another Arab military defeat in the 1973 war even further discredited the strategy of direct military assault.

November 6, 1970	Two bombs explode in the Tel Aviv bus station, killing two people and wounding 34.
1971	During this year, Arafat creates a covert international terrorist group within Fatah called Black September, a reference to the PLO forces' expulsion from Jordan in September 1970. Black September is headed by Abu Iyad and staffed by Fatah's intelligence personnel. It uses Fatah facilities and funds for its terrorist operations. It carries out operations against Arab and Western targets as well as Israeli targets. Arafat also forms Force-17 as an elite bodyguard and operations group. In later years, it engages in terrorist attacks against Israelis and rival Palestinians in Europe and the Middle East.
January 1, 1971	Palestinian terrorists throw a grenade into a crowded Jerusalem marketplace, killing one Arab and injuring five other people.
January 2, 1971	Palestinian terrorists attack an Israeli family in the Gaza Strip, killing two children and wounding their mother.
May 17, 1971	Three terrorists with the Turkish Liberation Army, a small group linked to the PFLP, kidnap the Israeli consul general in Istanbul, Efraim Elrom, and demand the release of all terrorists held by the Turkish government. After the government rejects the demand, Elrom's body is found.
July 7, 1971	Palestinian terrorists launch Katyusha rockets on Petah Tiqva, near Tel Aviv, killing four people and wounding 30.
November 28, 1971	Six Black September terrorists assassinate Jordanian Prime Minister Wasfi al-Tal as he is returns from lunch with the Arab League's secretary-general

in Cairo. This is the first of a series of high-profile attacks against Jordanian officials in retaliation for the expulsion of the PLO from Jordan in September 1970.

May 30, 1972

Three terrorists from the Red Army, a Japanese terrorist group allied with the PFLP, open fire at Israel's Lod airport, killing 26 people and wounding 78 others. One of the terrorists runs out of ammunition and is killed by his companions, another commits suicide, and the third, Kozo Okamoto, is captured. Okamoto, whose older brother, Takedia Okamoto, is one of the Red Army terrorists who hijacked a Japan Airlines flight to North Korea in 1970, is freed in May 1983 in a prisoner exchange between Israeli and Palestinian forces. He is granted asylum in Lebanon where he reportedly rejoins the Red Army.

June 20, 1972

Members of the PFLP-GC fire rockets at an Israeli bus in the Golan Heights, killing two and injuring several others.

July 8, 1972

Ghassan Kanafani, a PFLP official, is killed in Lebanon when his booby-trapped car explodes. His 17-year-old niece, traveling unexpectedly with him, also dies. Israeli security is likely responsible.

September 5, 1972

During the Olympic games in Munich, Germany, eight Black September terrorists penetrate the Olympic Village and enter the Israeli team's quarters, where they kill two Israeli athletes and take nine others hostage. The terrorists demand the release of over 200 Arabs jailed in Israel, two jailed in Germany, and safe passage out of the country for themselves. Israel rejects the demands, but the West German government says it will fly the terrorists out of the country. As the terrorists land in helicopters at an airfield where a plane awaits to take them to Cairo, German police snipers open fire. In the gunfight all nine Israeli athletes, a German policeman, and five terrorists are killed. The three Palestinian gunmen who are captured are released on October 29, 1972, after a Lufthansa plane en route from Beirut to Ankara is hijacked by Fatah terrorists and held hostage for their release. Abu Daoud, a Black September leader who organized the Olympics attack, later writes that the PLO is directly responsible for the assault and that Arafat himself had wished him success with it.

September 19, 1972

The agricultural counselor at the Israeli Embassy in England, Ami Shechori, is murdered by a letter bomb. Black September claims responsibility.

December 8, 1972

The chief representative of the PLO and Fatah in Paris, Mahmoud Hamshari, who is also a Black September operative and a planner of the Olympics massacre, is killed in his Paris home after he answers his telephone, to which a bomb has been attached. Israeli intelligence is suspected.

March 2, 1973

About a half-dozen Black September terrorists break into a reception at the Embassy of Saudi Arabia in Khartoum, Sudan, and take the guests, including the U.S. ambassador, hostage. They demand the release of prisoners in several countries including Sirhan Sirhan, the Palestinian assassin of Senator Robert Kennedy in 1968. While the captured Arab and Eastern European ambassadors are quickly released, the terrorists accuse U.S Ambassador Cleo Noel and Deputy Chief of Staff George Curtis Moore of being behind efforts to stop the "Black September revolution" and of aiding Israel. The Sudanese government offers the terrorists safe passage out of the country, but they refuse, making clear that they are planning to kill the hostages. The government accepts Arafat's offer of help, but intercepted conversations between Arafat and PLO leader Abu Iyad later reveal Arafat's instructions to kill Moore, Noel and Guy Eid, a Belgian diplomat the terrorists mistakenly think is Jewish. The instructions are carried out. After surrendering, two of the gunmen are released by the Sudanese authorities; six others are quickly tried, convicted of murder, then handed over to the PLO and flown out of the country.

July 1, 1973   Black September terrorists fatally shoot Yosef Ayalon, an Israeli air force attaché in Washington, D.C.

July 21, 1973   Israeli Mossad agents visit Lillehammer, Norway, on a mission to assassinate Ali Hassan Salameh, a Black September leader responsible for many terrorist attacks including the one on Israeli athletes at the Munich Olympics. The agents mistake a Moroccan waiter, Ahmed Boushiki, for Salameh and kill him. The six agents are captured by the Norwegian authorities, convicted of the killing, and imprisoned, but are soon released and return to Israel.

August 5, 1973   Black September terrorists attack a passenger lounge at the Athens airport killing three Americans and wounding over 55 people waiting to board a TWA flight to New York. The two terrorists, one Lebanese, the other Palestinian, are sentenced to jail but are deported to Libya on February 2, 1974, after Palestinians hijack a Greek freighter in Karachi and hold it hostage for their release.

October 6, 1973   Egypt and Syria attack Israel. At first they advance into the territory they lost in the 1967 war, but Israel pushes them back during the next three weeks. By the time a cease-fire ends the fighting, Israel has captured additional land from which it withdraws in post-war agreements.

December 17, 1973   Five Palestinian terrorists shoot at passengers waiting in an El Al Israel Airlines lounge at a Rome airport, killing two people. They then hurl grenades at an American Airlines plane preparing to take off, killing all 29 people aboard. Next, they take six Italian hostages into a Lufthansa jetliner, kill an Italian customs officer as he tries to escape, and orders the pilot to fly to Beirut. When Lebanese officials refuse to allow the plane to land, the hijackers order the plane crew to fly on to Athens. The terrorists demand the release of two Arab terrorists held since August 1973 for an attack on the Athens airport. The terrorists kill one hostage and throw his body onto the tarmac in Athens before flying on to Damascus, then to their final stop, Kuwait. The terrorists release their hostages in return for free passage to an unknown destination. On March 2, 1974, the five are flown to Cairo "under the responsibility" of the PLO.

1974   The Fatah Revolutionary Council is founded by Sabri al-Bana, known as "Abu Nidal," as a splinter group from Fatah. It soon becomes known as the Abu Nidal Organization (ANO). It opposes any political activity or strategy other than constant armed struggle until Israel is destroyed. At various times it becomes a client of Syria, Iraq, and Libya. Usually under contract with its patrons, it also targets PLO officials and Arab regimes viewed as too moderate.

March 5, 1974   Eight PLO terrorists land on the Tel Aviv shore in a boat, take over a hotel and hostages, and kill three Israeli soldiers before being killed or captured themselves.

April 11, 1974   Three PFLP-GC terrorists attack an apartment building in Kiryat Shemona, northern Israel, killing 18. One of the terrorists' communiqués demands that Israel release 100 prisoners including Kozo Okamoto, a Japanese terrorist serving a life sentence for the attack on Lod Airport.

May 15, 1974   Three Democratic Front for the Liberation of Palestine (DFLP) terrorists cross the border from Lebanon into Israel, where they kill 24 people in a series of attacks. They start by firing on a van bringing Israeli Arab women home from work, killing two and wounding one. The terrorists then enter the Israeli town of Ma'alot, where they kill three more people and seize about 90 teenagers in a school building. They demand the release of 23 jailed terrorists. Israel says it will agree, but minutes before the deadline Israeli security forces rush the school. The three terrorists are killed along with 20 children and one Israeli soldier.

June 24, 1974   Three Arab terrorists seize hostages in an apartment building in Nahariya, northern Israel, where they kill four persons and wound eight before they themselves are killed in a gun battle.

September 7, 1974 A TWA jet with 88 passengers en route from Tel Aviv to Athens to Rome crashes into the Ionian Sea off Greece, killing all on board after a bomb hidden in the baggage compartment explodes. The bomb was planted by the PFLP-GC.

November 18, 1974 Three DFLP terrorists infiltrate an apartment house in Beit She'an and kill four civilians before they are overtaken by an Israeli assault team. The terrorists are seeking hostages that could be traded for 20 being held in Israeli jails, including the Greek Orthodox archbishop of Jerusalem, Hilarion Capucci, who has been accused of smuggling arms to terrorists.

November 20, 1974 PLO terrorists enter from Syria into Israel's Ramat Magshimim settlement, killing three students and wounding two.

November 30, 1974 Two Fatah terrorists enter the Israeli Arab town of Rihaniya, which they mistakenly believe to be a Jewish town, shoot an Israeli Muslim to death, and wound his wife. The attackers then surrender to Israeli forces.

December 11, 1974 A PFLP terrorist throws a bomb into a Tel Aviv movie theater, killing two. The terrorist was born in Ghana, lives in Turkey, and holds a British passport.

April 1975   Civil war begins in Lebanon as Muslim and Druze forces combine with the PLO to fight the Christian-led government.

May 4, 1975   Terrorists from the Popular Struggle Front explode a bomb in a Jerusalem apartment building killing one and injuring three.

June 15, 1975   Four Arab Liberation Front terrorists take a family hostage in Kfar Yuval, Israel, killing one member and demanding the release of 12, including the Greek Orthodox archbishop of Jerusalem, Hilarion Capucci. Israeli soldiers storm the house and during a battle two men in the family and four terrorists are killed.

July 4, 1975

A Palestinian terrorist bomb explodes among a crowd of Israeli shoppers in Jerusalem, killing 13 persons and wounding 72.

November 13, 1975

A terrorist bomb explodes among shoppers and pedestrians in Zion Square, Jerusalem's main shopping street, killing six people and injuring 40 others. Both Fatah and the DFLP claim responsibility.

November 21, 1975

Michael Nadler, an American-Israeli student from Miami Beach, Florida, is killed with an axe by DFLP terrorists in Ramat Hamagshimim in the Golan Heights.

May 3, 1976

A bomb set by DFLP terrorists on a motor scooter in Jerusalem kills one and injures 29.

May 25, 1976

Two people are killed and nine injured as a result of an explosion at the Tel Aviv airport. The PFLP claims responsibility for the bombing.

June 27, 1976

Four terrorists—two from the PFLP and two from Germany's Red Army Faction (also known as the Baader-Meinhof Gang)—hijack an Air France plane en route from Tel Aviv to Paris via Athens, and divert it to Entebbe, Uganda, where they are protected by Ugandan dictator Idi Amin. The hijackers demand the release of 53 terrorists imprisoned in Israel and four other countries. On July 1, the hijackers release all non-Israeli hostages and offer to release the crew, who opt to stay with the plane. As the deadline for the terrorist threat to blow up the plane approaches, an elite Israeli commando unit storms the plane and kills all the terrorists and 20 Ugandan soldiers. Also killed in the rescue mission are the leader of the Israeli assault force, Yonatan Netanyahu, and one of the Israeli hostages.

August 11, 1976

The PFLP launches an attack on the El Al offices at the Istanbul airport in Turkey, killing four, including Harold Rosenthal of Philadelphia, and injuring 20. The terrorists also take a Turkish policewoman hostage before finally surrendering. The two terrorists are sentenced to life imprisonment by a Turkish criminal court.

September 26, 1976

Four terrorists seize a hotel in Damascus, Syria, and hold 90 people hostage until Syrian troops storm the hotel. In a three-hour battle, four hostages and one terrorist are killed. The three remaining terrorists are captured and publicly hanged. The terrorists say they are part of a radical Palestinian group called Black June and claim to be members of Fatah whose goal is to bargain for the release of Palestinians held in Syrian prisons and to protest Syrian interference in Lebanon.

November 17, 1976

Four Palestinians take hostage several guests staying at the InterContinental Hotel in Amman, Jordan. Jordanian army commandos respond, and during the shoot-out three gunmen, two hotel employees, and two soldiers are killed. The gunmen call themselves members of the radical Palestinian group Black June.

April 24, 1977 The Palestine Liberation Front (PLF) is established after splitting from the PFLP-General Command (PFLP-GC). The new organization is headed by the man who takes the name Abu al-Abbas and by Tal'at Ya'akub and is based in Lebanon. Like other PLO groups, the PLF launches terrorist attacks against Israel across the Lebanese border.

July 6, 1977 A pipe bomb planted by the DFLP under a vegetable stand in Petah Tiqva, a Tel Aviv suburb, kills one and injures 22.

October 13, 1977 Four Palestinian terrorists hijack a Lufthansa flight en route from Mallorca to Frankfurt. They order the pilot to land at several Middle East destinations over four days and demand the release of 11 Palestinians from West German prisons, two from Turkish prisons, and $15 million. After the plane's pilot is killed by the terrorists in Mogadishu, Somalia, it is stormed by German counter-terrorist troops assisted by two British Army Special Air Service (SAS) soldiers. All the 90 hostages are rescued and three terrorists are killed. A Palestinian group headed by Waddi Haddad, the Popular Front for the Liberation of Palestine-Special Operations, claims responsibility for the hijacking. The fourth terrorist, Suhaila al-Sayeh, a woman, is wounded. She is sentenced to 20 years in prison, but in January 1978, Palestinian terrorists force her release and she goes to Baghdad.

November 13, 1977 A DFLP bomb explodes near an Arab school in the Christian section of Jerusalem's Old City, killing a student and wounding four other persons. A second bomb explodes three hours later in the Jewish district of Talpiot, across the street from a nursery school, killing an Arab teenager and injuring a man.

December 8, 1977 PLO terrorists launch a Katyusha rocket at Nahariya, Israel, killing one woman.

January 4, 1978 Abu Nidal terrorists assassinate Said Hammami, the PLO representative in London, who had met with Israeli peace activists.

February 14, 1978 Two people are killed and 48 injured by a bombing on a bus in Jerusalem. Palestinian terrorists and responsible.

February 17, 1978 In Jerusalem, a PLO time bomb hidden in a trash can near a bench in the main square of Hebrew University explodes, killing an Arab passerby and seriously wounding another.

February 18, 1978 Youssef al-Seba'i, editor of *al-Ahram*, Egypt's leading newspaper, and president of the Conference of the Organization for the Solidarity with the Peoples of Africa, Asia and Latin America, is killed by Abu Nidal terrorists during an attack on a hotel in Cyprus. After the killing, the terrorists take 16 hostages and escape in a Cyprus Airways plane. But after being refused a place to land, the plane returns to Cyprus. On February 19, the Egyptian government sends commandos to Cyprus to attack the plane. Unaware of the identity of the armed men, Cypriot forces open fire on them, resulting in the deaths of 15 Egyptians from the rescue team. All the hostages remain unharmed, and the two Palestinian terrorists surrender to the authorities.

March 11, 1978 Eleven Fatah terrorists from Lebanon land on the beach of Kibbutz Ma'agan

Michael in dinghies. First, they hijack a bus and force the driver to travel to Tel Aviv. While on the coastal highway, the terrorists fire on passing cars from the bus. When the bus approaches a blockade set up by the police at an entrance to Tel Aviv, a shoot-out takes place. The terrorists leave the bus and fire on it, causing the vehicle to burst into flames. Passengers are either burned alive or killed by terrorist gunfire. In the carnage, 43 Israeli civilians are killed and 72 are wounded. Nine of the terrorists are also killed. The two captured terrorists are sentenced to life terms by an Israeli military court in October 1979.

March 17, 1978 PLO terrorists fire Katyusha rockets at northern Israel, killing two and wounding two.

April 26, 1978 Two West German tourists returning to Jerusalem on a bus from an outing in the Galilee region are killed and several others injured when a grenade is thrown through an open bus window and explodes.

May 20, 1978 Three PFLP terrorists attack passengers waiting at the El Al terminal at Orly Airport in Paris, killing two and wounding two others. The terrorists are also killed in the shoot-out with police.

June 2, 1978 A PLO bomb blows up in a bus in Jerusalem killing six, including Richard Fishman, a medical student from Maryland.

June 15, 1978 Abu Nidal terrorists assassinate Ali Yassin, the PLO representative in Kuwait.

June 30, 1978 A planted bomb detonates in a crowded marketplace in Jerusalem, killing two persons and wounding 47.

August 3, 1978 Abu Nidal terrorists assassinate Izz al-Din al-Kalak, the PLO representative in Paris, and one of his assistants before being captured by police. Two Arabs are found guilty of the crime on March 8, 1980, and sentenced to 15 years' imprisonment.

August 3, 1978 A bomb blows up in the Carmel Market in Tel Aviv, killing one and wounding nearly 50.

August 20, 1978 PFLP terrorists attack an El Al Airlines crew bus in London, killing a flight attendant and wounding eight airline employees.

November 19, 1978 Four are killed and 37 injured in the bombing of an intercity bus in the West Bank. Fatah and the DFLP both claim responsibility for the incident, which occurs on the first anniversary of Egyptian President Sadat's visit to Jerusalem.

December 21, 1978 PLO terrorists launch a rocket into northern Israel from Lebanon, which kills one and wounds ten in Kiryat Shemona.

1979 The Palestinian Islamic Jihad (PIJ), inspired by the Iranian Revolution, is formed by a group of Palestinian students. The founders—Fathi Shaqaqi, Abd al-Aziz Odah, and Bashir Musa—are disappointed by what they perceive as the moderation of the Egyptian Muslim Brotherhood and its ignoring of the

Palestinian problem. Shqaqi and Musa claim that Islamist movements are the key to unifying the Arab and Islamic world.

January 29, 1979   Two persons are killed and 34 wounded when a time bomb planted by PLO terrorists explodes in a crowded business section of Netanya, Israel.

March 26, 1979   A peace treaty is signed between Egypt and Israel in Washington, D.C., calling for mutual recognition and the withdrawal of Israeli troops from the Sinai. The presence of Egyptian forces in Sinai is limited. The agreement provides also for Palestinian autonomy in the West Bank and Gaza Strip if their leadership decides to negotiate an agreement.

March 27, 1979   PLO terrorists detonate a bomb in downtown Jerusalem, killing one and wounding 14.

April 10, 1979   PLO terrorists detonate a bomb in the open-air Carmel Market in Tel Aviv, killing one Israeli and wounding 36.

April 19, 1979   A box of cigars explodes at Cairo's main post office, killing a female customs inspector and injuring four persons. A group called the Eagles of the Palestinian Revolution, a Fatah front group, claims the attack as retribution for Egypt's peace treaty with Israel.

April 22, 1979   A squad of Palestine Liberation Front terrorists sails from Lebanon to Nahariya in Israel, using a rubber boat. They murder three Israelis—a father, his daughter, and a police officer—and injure four others.

May 4, 1979   A bomb planted by the PLO in Tiberias detonates, killing two teenagers and injuring 32, including two Americans. In August, Ziad Abu Ein, a Palestinian, is arrested in Chicago, Illinois, and charged with the bombing. Losing a legal fight to avoid extradition, Ein is sent to Israel on December 12, 1981, to stand trial. On June 17, 1982, he is sentenced to life imprisonment.

May 23, 1979   Three are killed and 13 injured in a bombing by PLO terrorists at a bus stop in Petah Tiqva, near Tel Aviv.

July 13, 1979   Four terrorists claiming to be affiliated with the Eagles of the Palestinian Revolution kill two Turkish guards at the Egyptian Embassy in Ankara, Turkey. They take the embassy employees, including the ambassador, hostage and demand that Turkey recognize a Palestinian state, end diplomatic relations with Israel, and obtain the release of two terrorists from Egyptian jails. A hostage dies after jumping from a window on the third floor. After surrendering, the four Palestinians are sentenced to death.

September 19, 1979   One person is killed and at least 38 injured when a PLO bomb planted on a bicycle explodes at a crowded pedestrian mall in Jerusalem.

January 2, 1980   Abraham Elazar, the manager of the El Al office in Ankara, Turkey, is shot and killed by two men. The Marxist Leninist Armed Propaganda Union, the Anti-Camp David Front, and the Sons of the Land later claim responsibility.

January 17, 1980   In Paris, France, Abu Nidal terrorists assassinate Yusef Mubarak, director of the Palestinian library shop there.

March 3, 1980   A lawyer in Madrid, Adolfo Cotello, is murdered by Abu Nidal Organization terrorists who believe him to be a Spanish Jewish leader.

April 7, 1980   Five PLO terrorists attack Kibbutz Misgav Am near Israel's northern border, seize a children's dormitory, and take nine infants as hostages. During an Israeli rescue mission, three Israelis, including one child, are killed and 16 are injured, four of them children. All the terrorists are killed. The terrorists are members of the Arab Liberation Front.

May 2, 1980   PLO terrorists attack worshippers walking home from a synagogue in the West Bank town of Hebron, killing six, including Eli Haze'ev, an American-Israeli from Alexandria, Virginia.

July 25, 1980   The Israel Commercial Attaché in Brussels, Yosef Halachi, is assassinated by members of the Abu Nidal Organization.

July 27, 1980   Abu Nidal terrorists hurl hand grenades into a group of teenage Jews in Antwerp, Belgium, killing one and injuring 17. Two of the attackers, Sa'id Abdel Wahib and Nihad Declas, are subsequently tried and convicted by the Belgian authorities.

October 3, 1980   Four are killed and 12 others injured in a bomb attack on a synagogue in Paris. PLO terrorists are believed responsible.

October 5, 1980   A bomb planted by PLO terrorists in a package explodes in a post office in Givatayim, Israel, killing three and wounding seven.

November 25, 1980   Jewish owners of a travel agency in Paris specializing in trips to Israel are shot and killed. The terrorists are unknown.

December 31, 1980   A bomb blast at the Norfolk Hotel in Nairobi, Kenya, kills 16 people and injures 87. The hotel is owned by a prominent member of the local Jewish community who has close ties to Israel. Kenya may have been targeted because it aided the Israeli commando team that rescued the hostages hijacked by Palestinians in neighboring Uganda in July 1976. The suspected terrorist is a member of the PFLP.

May 1, 1981   Heinz Nittel, president of the Austrian-Israeli Friendship League, is killed in Vienna by ANO terrorists. Bahij Muhammad Younis is convicted of the assassination and sentenced to life imprisonment.

June 1, 1981   Naim Khader, the PLO representative in Brussels, Belgium, is assassinated by Abu Nidal terrorists.

July 22, 1981   PFLP terrorists bomb a tour agency in Athens, killing two Greeks—the company's owner and her employee, whom the terrorists claim was an Israeli intelligence agent.

August 29, 1981   Two Abu Nidal terrorists assassinate congregants at a synagogue in Vienna, killing two and wounding 17 others. In October 1981, a Jordanian, Husham

Rajih confesses to this attack and the Heinz Nittel murder on May 1. He and an accomplice are sentenced to life imprisonment for the incident.

September 12, 1981   A hand grenade is thrown into a group of 47 Italian pilgrims outside the old walled city of Jerusalem, killing one and wounding 28 others.

October 20, 1981   Just before a ceremony at a synagogue in Antwerp, Belgium, a bomb explodes, killing four people and injuring 95. Black September claims the attack.

December 20, 1981   A bomb explodes on the Greek ship the *Orion* shortly before it enters Haifa port, killing two and wounding two others. The Abu Ibrahim group claims responsibility.

January 15, 1982   Terrorists bomb a Jewish restaurant in Berlin, killing one child and injuring 46 adults. The Arab Organization of 15 May and the People's League for Free Palestine both claim responsibility.

April 5, 1982   Arsonists start a fire which destroys a Lebanese restaurant in Brooklyn, New York, killing a woman who lives upstairs. The attack is claimed by a caller representing the Jewish Defense League (JDL), who maintains that the restaurant is used as a headquarters for the PLO, although the JDL officially denies any involvement in the incident.

Displaced from Lebanon

In 1981, a cease-fire was reached between the PLO and Israel regarding the Lebanon-Israel border. Terrorist attacks diminished, but still took place periodically. At the same time, PLO forces were being built up in southern Lebanon. Israel conducted secret negotiations with Lebanese Christian leaders to plan for the PLO's removal and a Christian-led government. The attempted assassination of Israeli Ambassador to England Shlomo Argov on June 3, 1982—later revealed to be an Iraqi operation aimed at creating an Arab-Israeli crisis to mobilize support for Iraq in its war with Iran—set off a new war in Lebanon.

Israeli forces crossed the border on June 6 and defeated the PLO and Syrian military forces. Lebanese leaders asked Arafat to remove the PLO from the country, and he sailed off to a new headquarters in Tunisia. Arafat returned to Lebanon the following year only to be expelled again by Syrian forces during the Lebanese civil war. While the expulsion of the PLO office weakened Palestinian assets in attacking Israel, terrorist attacks continued both across Israel's borders and internationally throughout the 1980s and into the early 1990s.

June 3, 1982   The Israeli Ambassador in London, England, Shlomo Argov, is shot and seriously injured by Abu Nidal terrorists working for Iraq as he is getting into his car after a banquet at a hotel in London. The attack is a catalyst for the Israeli military operation into Lebanon seeking to remove PLO forces from southern Lebanon, which begins three days later. Israel has concluded an agreement with Lebanese Christian leader Bashir Gemayel, who promises secret support in return for the help to gain election as president of Lebanon and to expel the PLO. PLO forces retreat in disarray as the Israeli army advances to Beirut, also defeating Syrian army units.

July 1982

Hezbollah (Party of God) forms as an umbrella organization of various radical Shiite groups in Lebanon. The group is subsidized and sponsored by Iran to launch a *jihad* (holy war) to destroy Israel as well as to take over Lebanon and turn it into a Shia Muslim Islamist state.

August 9, 1982

Abu Nidal terrorists kill six and wound 22 during an attack on a Jewish restaurant in Paris.

August 30, 1982

With Beirut besieged by Israeli forces, Lebanese leaders angrily demand that Arafat and PLO military units leave the country. Under a U.S. and French safe passage agreement, Arafat and several thousand PLO fighters leave Beirut, Lebanon. When no Arab country will take them in, the United States urges Tunisia to do so, and that country becomes the PLO's new headquarters.

September 14, 1982

Nine days before he is to be inaugurated president of Lebanon, Bashir Gemayel, the Lebanese Christian leader who has allied himself with Israel, is assassinated along with 26 of his followers by a car bomb parked outside his party's Beirut headquarters. Members of the Syrian-sponsored Syrian Socialist Nationalist Party are responsible.

September 16, 1982

The Israeli army, having received reports of armed terrorists in the Palestinian refugee camps of Sabra and Shatila in southern Lebanon, let some 300 Christian militiamen enter the camps. In revenge for Palestinian attacks against their people and the assassination of Bashir Gemayel, the Christians massacre about 700 to 800 residents of the camps, most of them Palestinian.

September 16, 1982

Abu Nidal terrorists assassinate a Kuwaiti diplomat in Madrid, Spain.

September 24, 1982

Some 1,200 U.S. Marines and British and French forces are deployed to serve in a temporary multinational force to facilitate the restoration of Lebanese government sovereignty.

September 27, 1982

Three bombs explode in Frankfurt offices dealing with Israel, killing one and wounding two. No one claims responsibility.

October 9, 1982

Abu Nidal terrorists attack the main Rome synagogue, killing one child and injuring 37 adults.

April 10, 1983

PLO official Issam Sartawi, who favors a peace agreement with Israel, is assassinated by Abu Nidal terrorists at the Socialist International conference in Lisbon, Portugal.

July 1, 1983

Aharon Gross, 19, an Israeli-American from New York, is stabbed to death by PLO terrorists in the Hebron marketplace.

October 25, 1983

The Jordanian ambassador to India is assassinated in New Delhi by Abu Nidal terrorists.

October 26, 1983

The Jordanian ambassador to Italy is assassinated in Rome by Abu Nidal terrorists.

November 7, 1983

A security guard is killed during an Abu Nidal attack on the Jordanian Embassy in Athens, Greece.

December 6, 1983

PLO terrorists attack a bus in Jerusalem, killing six Israeli citizens and wounding 50. Both the PLO and anti-Arafat PLO rebels claim responsibility.

December 19, 1983

Serena Sussman, a 60-year-old tourist from Anderson, South Carolina, is killed when the PLO bombs a bus in Jerusalem.

December 29, 1983

The Jordanian ambassador to Spain is assassinated in Madrid by Abu Nidal terrorists.

February 8, 1984

Abu Nidal terrorists assassinate the ambassador of the United Arab Emirates to France in Paris.

March 7, 1984

A bomb on a bus in Ashdod, Israel, kills three and wounds nine. Abu Nidal claims responsibility.

March 28, 1984

The director of the British Council in Athens, Kenneth Whitty, is assassinated, probably by Abu Nidal terrorists. Whitty may have been mistaken for a British intelligence officer from whom Whitty had bought his car.

April 2, 1984

A Palestinian opens fire in West Jerusalem killing one and injuring 60 people.

April 12, 1984

Four PFLP terrorists hijack an Israeli bus en route from Tel Aviv to Ashkelon with 41 passengers and force the driver to travel to the Deir el-Balah refugee camp in the Gaza Strip. As the bus is surrounded at the border by Israeli security officials, the terrorists demand the release of some 500 PLO terrorists in Israeli jails. Just before dawn, an elite unit of the Israeli Defense Forces storms the bus. In the rescue, one female passenger and two terrorists are killed, and seven passengers wounded. Two terrorists are captured alive and later beaten to death by Israeli General Security Service agents.

October 28, 1984

An Israeli soldier fires at a bus carrying 25 Arabs from East Jerusalem to Hebron, killing one man and injuring ten others.

November 27, 1984

The British Deputy High Commissioner for Western India, Percy Norris, is shot to death as he is being driven to work in Bombay (Mumbai). The Revolutionary Organization of Socialist Muslims, an Abu Nidal front, claims responsibility for the attack.

February 23, 1985

A bomb kills one man and injures 18 others at a Paris branch of the British store Marks & Spencer. Three members of the Arab Organization of 15 May are subsequently arrested and tried for the attack. The Arab Organization of 15 May, led by Abu Ibrahim, was formed in 1979 as a splinter group from the PFLP and later merged into Fatah.

June 27, 1985	An Israeli man and woman are shot to death near Beit Shemesh by Fatah terrorists.

July 11, 1985 Bombs detonate in two popular cafes in Kuwait City, leaving 11 people dead and 89 wounded. The dead include a top Kuwaiti security official in charge of criminal investigations who, according to a communiqué put out by the "Arab Revolutionary Brigades," is the intended target of the attacks. This group is believed to be affiliated with Abu Nidal. In January 1987, two men are sentenced to death after being convicted of planting the bombs in the cafes. A third defendant is sentenced to life imprisonment and a fourth accessory receives a three-year term.

July 22, 1985 A bomb explodes in Scandinavia's oldest synagogue in Copenhagen, killing one and wounding 27. Islamic Jihad claims responsibility.

August 20, 1985 An Israeli attaché in Cairo, Albert Atrakchi, is shot and killed while driving in his car. His wife and an embassy secretary are wounded. Egyptian Islamic Jihad claims responsibility.

September 5, 1985 An airliner operated by Pan American Airlines in Karachi, Pakistan, is seized by four Arabs disguised as airport security guards as it prepares to depart. The hijackers demand the release of three terrorists who are currently in prison in Cyprus for the recent murder of three Israelis. During the hijacking, a lack of power plunges the plane into darkness, causing the terrorists to open fire on the passengers, killing 19 and wounding 127. After the incident is over, the terrorists are taken into custody to stand trial in Pakistani courts. In July 1988, five Palestinians, believed to be members of the Abu Nidal organization, are sentenced to death by hanging for their involvement in the hijacking.

September 25, 1985 A Force-17 terrorist squad kills three Israeli tourists aboard a yacht in the marina of Larnaca, Cyprus. The three terrorists, including Briton Ian Davidson, are convicted and imprisoned by the Cypriot authorities.

October 5, 1985 An Egyptian soldier opens fire on a group of Israeli tourists in the Sinai Peninsula, killing seven, including four children.

October 7, 1985 Four terrorists from the Palestine Liberation Front, a faction of the Palestine Liberation Organization (PLO), take over the Italian cruise liner *Achille Lauro* as it leaves Egypt on a Mediterranean cruise whose planned stops include Israel. The terrorists take the 400 passengers hostage, demanding the release of Palestinian terrorists in Israeli jails. The terrorists kill Leon Klinghoffer, a wheelchair-bound American tourist, and throw him overboard. They agree to surrender in exchange for safe passage after a high-ranking PLO official orders them to do so in order to forestall an American rescue attempt. As an Egyptian plane is flying the terrorists to Tunis, U.S. Navy fighter planes force it to land at a NATO base in Italy. Insisting that it has legal jurisdiction, the Italian government immediately releases Abu al-Abbas, the mastermind of the hijacking, and another terrorist, allowing them to leave the country. In 1986, al-Abbas is convicted in absentia to life imprisonment by an Italian court. Finally, in 2004, he is captured by U.S. forces in Iraq. The other Palestinian hijackers are tried and sent to Italian prisons from which two escape in 1996. One is recaptured in Italy; the other, Magied al-Molqi, the man who shot Klinghoffer, is caught in Spain.

October 8, 1985

A policeman hired to guard the Ghriba synagogue in Djerba, Tunisia, opens fire on members of the congregation, killing four and wounding 13.

November 23, 1985

Five Abu Nidal terrorists hijack an Egyptian airliner en route from Athens to Cairo. As the terrorists begin interrogating passengers, a fight ensues when an Egyptian security guard kills a terrorist. The gun battle forces the plane to land in Malta, where the terrorists begin shooting passengers, killing three, including two Israelis and an American. As Maltese authorities storm the plane, 60 people are killed, including four hijackers. The surviving hijacker, Omar Muhammad Ali Rezaq, a Palestinian from Lebanon, is convicted and sentenced to 25 years in prison in Malta. He is released after seven years because of pressure from Libya and sent to Ghana, where he is held in custody. With the cooperation of Ghana and Nigeria, the FBI arrests him in Nigeria in July 1993.

December 4, 1985

Abu Nidal terrorists assassinate a Jordanian diplomat in Bucharest, Romania.

December 25, 1985

PLO terrorists are responsible for an explosion in the central power station in Hadera, Israel, in which three employees are killed.

December 27, 1985

Abu Nidal terrorists attack the check-in counters for Israel's El Al airlines in Rome and Vienna. A total of 20 people die in the two attacks, including three of the four terrorists in Rome and one of the three in Vienna.

December 29, 1985

Fahd Qawasma, a PLO member and mayor of Hebron, is assassinated in Amman, Jordan, by PFLP terrorists, who believe he is a collaborator with Israel.

March 19, 1986

Eti Telor, wife of an employee in the Israeli Embassy in Cairo, is killed and three embassy employees injured in an attack on their car near the Israeli pavilion at the Cairo Trade Fair. The Egyptian Revolution, believed to be part of the Abu Nidal Organization, claims responsibility.

March 19, 1986

A car bomb in Jerusalem kills one and injures three. Fatah's Force-17 claims responsibility.

March 28, 1986

Leigh Douglas, a British political science professor at the American University in Beirut, and Philip Padfield, director of the international language center there, are abducted in West Beirut, and are killed the following month. The Arab Revolutionary Cells, linked to Abu Nidal, claims responsibility.

April 2, 1986

A bomb goes off on a TWA jetliner en route from Rome to Greece, killing four American passengers and injuring nine other passengers. In Beirut, the Arab Revolutionary Cells claims responsibility for the bomb. Authorities suspect that a woman, known to be a Syrian Socialist Nationalist Party member, may have planted the bomb.

April 5, 1986

Three people—two U.S. soldiers and a Turkish woman—are killed and 197 injured when a bomb goes off at La Belle discotheque in West Berlin. The bombing is aimed at the many U.S. servicemen who frequent the place. When Libya is implicated as sponsor of the attack, the United States stages retaliatory air strikes against two cities in that country. Four people—a Libyan, a Palestinian, and a Lebanese married couple—are found guilty of the attack in a Berlin court. The Berlin court upholds claims that Libyan secret service agents and embassy staff planned the attack. After enduring international sanctions for years, in 2003 Libya admits responsibility for the attack and agrees the next year to pay compensation to the victims.

September 6, 1986

Two members of the Abu Nidal Organization attack the Neve Shalom synagogue in Istanbul, Turkey, with grenades and machine guns, killing 22 members of the congregation and injuring four others during morning prayers. The attackers then detonate belts containing explosives and are killed.

October 15, 1986

A terrorist throws a grenade at the Western Wall of the Temple in Jerusalem, killing a U.S. citizen and injuring 69 people.

July 22, 1987

Palestinian cartoonist Nagy El-Ali is shot to death in London, where he lives. El-Ali is known for his political cartoons against the Palestinian leadership, including Arafat. The investigation by Britain's Scotland Yard eventually leads to the arrest of members of Force-17, and there is evidence that Arafat himself approved this attack.

October 21, 1987

Palestinian terrorists murder an eight-year-old girl from the Jewish settlement of Elon Moreh in the West Bank.

December 9, 1987

Four residents of the Jabalya Palestinian refugee camp in Gaza are killed in a traffic accident, leading to rumors that they have been killed by Israelis. Riots follow and this event marks the beginning of the intifada, or uprising, which eventually spreads throughout the Gaza Strip and then throughout the West Bank. The Palestinians use demonstrations, rock-throwing, strikes, a boycott of Israeli goods, and general unrest in an attempt to force Israel to leave these areas.

December 14, 1987

Palestinian Sheikh Ahmad Yassin creates Hamas, an Arabic acronym for Islamic Resistance Movement and also an Arabic word meaning "zeal." It is a radical Islamist group justifying all forms of violence in its goal to create an Islamic Palestinian state in place of Israel. Also a social welfare group, Hamas gains broad support by assisting the needy. Terrorist attacks are carried out by its military wing, the Izz al-Din el-Kassam squads. Hamas hopes to supplant the PLO, but it is committed to avoiding direct confrontation with the Palestinian nationalist forces.

March 7, 1988

Fatah terrorists cross from Egypt into Israel, where they hijack a bus and demand the release of all Palestinian prisoners from Israeli jails. After the terrorists kill a passenger, an anti-terrorist police squad storms the bus. In the rescue attempt, two female passengers and three terrorists are killed.

April 8, 1988

Palestinian gunmen attack a group of hikers in Israel, killing one girl and wounding 15.

April 16, 1988   An Israeli commando force assassinates PLO leader Khalil al-Wazir (Abu Jihad), Arafat's second-ranking associate, in an attack on his home in Tunis. Al-Wazir is targeted because he is directing the intifada.

May 11, 1988   Abu Nidal terrorists detonate a car bomb at the Israeli Embassy in Nicosia, Cyprus, killing three people and wounding 19 others.

May 15, 1988   Abu Nidal terrorists carry out machine-gun and grenade attacks on Westerners in the Acropolis Hotel and the nearby Sudan Club in Khartoum, Sudan, killing a total of seven people and wounding 21, including three Americans. In October 1988, five terrorists belonging to a front group for Abu Nidal are sentenced to death for these attacks.

July 11, 1988   Abu Nidal gunmen attack passengers on a Greek cruise liner, killing nine, including an American, and wounding 98, then escaping. In October 1989, two Abu Nidal group members are convicted of murder in connection with this case.

October 30, 1988   Palestinians firebomb an Israeli bus in Jericho, killing a mother and her three children. One of the terrorists involved is sentenced to life imprisonment in March 1989.

December 21, 1988   Pan Am Flight 103, en route from London to New York, explodes and crashes into the Scottish village of Lockerbie. The bomb was planted in a radio inside a suitcase, which was transferred to the plane from an earlier connecting flight in Frankfurt, West Germany. All 259 people on board are killed. In addition, 11 people on the ground are killed and 12 others are seriously injured. Of the passengers, 189 are U.S. citizens, making the attack the worst against Americans to this date.

After three years of investigation by the Scottish Police and the FBI, the suspects are identified as Abdel Basset Ali al-Megrahi, a Libyan intelligence officer and head of security for Libyan Arab Airlines, and Lamin Khalifah Fhimah, the airline's manager in Malta. Libyan leader Colonel Muammar Qaddafi's refusal to surrender the men results in stringent economic sanctions against his country by UN mandate. In April 1999, the two suspects are handed over to Scottish police in the Netherlands, which had been chosen as a neutral venue. On January 31, 2001, al-Megrahi is convicted of murder by a panel of three Scottish judges at The Hague and sentenced to 27 years in prison. Fhimah is acquitted. On October 2002, the Libyan government agrees to a compensation offer of $2.7 billion, about $10 million per victim, for the attack. On August 15, 2003, Libya formally accepts responsibility for the bombing of Flight 103 and for the earlier bombing of a discotheque in West Berlin (*see* April 5, 1986). As a result, economic sanctions against the country are lifted.

February 16, 1989   An Israeli soldier, Sergeant Avi Sasportas, is kidnapped and shot to death while hitchhiking from his base to his home in Ashdod. The kidnapper, Abed Rabbo Abu Husa, is a senior Hamas militant later hired by Palestinian security forces. In November 2001, an Israeli commando unit captures Abu Husa.

May 3, 1989   Two elderly Israelis are stabbed in central Jerusalem by a West Bank Palestinian, his affiliation unknown.

June 18, 1989   A Palestinian stabs an American-born Israeli settler to death near the West Bank settlement of Ariel.

July 6, 1989   A bus traveling between Tel Aviv and Jerusalem is attacked by Islamic Jihad and 16 passengers are killed, including one American, Rita Levine from Philadelphia; another 27 are injured.

August 8, 1989   A Jordanian soldier infiltrates southern Israel, where he enters a kibbutz and kills an American visitor. The assailant then takes another person hostage before he is killed by security forces.

October 3, 1989   Joseph Wybran, the leader of the Belgian Jewish community, is assassinated by a gunman in the parking lot of the hospital in Brussels where he works. Abu Nidal terrorists working with Iran are believed responsible.

February 4, 1990   Palestinian Islamic Jihad terrorists attack an Israeli tourist bus near Cairo, killing 11, including nine Israeli tourists.

May 28, 1990   A bomb hidden in a food vendor's cart explodes at the Mahane Yehuda market in Jerusalem, killing one person and injuring 12 others.

June 7, 1990   Islamic Jihad claims responsibility for a bomb blast in a Jerusalem shopping center that results in the death of one and injury of nine others.

July 28, 1990   A Canadian tourist is killed by a bomb planted on a Tel Aviv beach by Palestinian terrorists.

August 2, 1990   Iraqi forces invade Kuwait, and Yasir Arafat throws his support behind Iraqi dictator Saddam Hussein.

August 4, 1990   Palestinians kidnap and murder two Israeli teenagers from Jerusalem.

October 21, 1990   A Palestinian laborer from the West Bank stabs three Israelis to death in the Baka neighborhood in Jerusalem.

November 5, 1990   Rabbi Meir Kahane, founder of the Jewish Defense League, is assassinated at a New York City hotel by El Sayyid Nosair, a naturalized American of Egyptian origin. Nosair is convicted and sentenced to life for the killing and a subsequent conviction of conspiring to bomb the World Trade Center and other New York landmarks in 1993.

November 25, 1990 An Egyptian terrorist dressed as a border policeman crosses the border into Israel and fires at military and civilian vehicles near Eilat, killing four Israelis and injuring 26. He escapes back into Egypt, but is arrested by authorities there.

December 2, 1990   Three Hamas terrorists stab and kill an Israeli and wound three others on a bus between Petah Tiqva and Tel Aviv.

December 14, 1990 Two Hamas terrorists kill three employees of a metalworks factory in Jaffa.

January 14, 1991   PLO deputy chief Abu Iyad, a top Fatah official who co-founded the group with Arafat, and Abu el-Hol (a nom de guerre meaning "Father of Terror"), who is commander of Fatah's Western Sector forces, are assassinated by an Abu Nidal terrorist in Tunis. They are targeted because of Abu Iyad's role in combating the Abu Nidal group and his outspoken opposition to PLO support for Abu Nidal's sponsor, Iraq, and its invasion of Kuwait.

January–March 1991   A U.S.-led coalition drives Iraq out of Kuwait and back towards Baghdad. During the fighting, Iraq fires about three dozen missiles at Israeli targets. At the end of the war, Kuwait, Saudi Arabia, and other Arab Gulf states expel Palestinians to protest Arafat's support of Iraq. In addition, they cut off financial support to the PLO, leading to a financial crisis for the organization and increased diplomatic isolation.

March 18, 1991   An unknown Palestinian murders four Israeli women in Jerusalem.

April 17, 1991   Palestinian terrorists from Jordan infiltrate Kibbutz Neve Ur, where they shoot and kill a farmer, and wound three others.

April 19, 1991   A bomb, intended for the British Consulate in Patras, Greece, instead detonates prematurely at a courier's office nearby, killing six Greek citizens and the terrorist. Six other Palestinians are arrested in connection with the incident. The Islamic Holy War Movement claims responsibility.

October 16, 1991   Sheikh Ahmad Yassin is sentenced by an Israeli court to life in prison after pleading guilty to planning the killing of four Palestinians suspected of collaborating with Israel. Yassin is arrested in May 1989 after the abduction and murder of Israeli soldier Ilan Sa'adon, and the discovery of the body of another soldier, Avi Sasportas, who was also abducted and murdered. Yassin admits that he ordered Hamas to kidnap Israeli soldiers inside Israel, murder them, and bury their bodies in a manner that would allow Hamas to negotiate the exchange of bodies for Hamas prisoners from jails in Israel.

October 28, 1991   Terrorists fire on a bus carrying Israeli settlers, killing two Israelis and wounding several others. Islamic Jihad and the PFLP claim responsibility.

November 1991   An international peace conference meets in Madrid, marking the first time that Arab states—including Syria and Saudi Arabia—have negotiated with Israel. The outcome includes separate bilateral talks between Syria and Israel and between a Jordanian-Palestinian delegation and Israel, along with multinational talks involving both Middle Eastern and other countries on such issues as water, refugees, economic development, and the environment.

March 17, 1992   A car bomb explodes at the Israeli Embassy in Buenos Aires, Argentina, killing 29 and injuring 252 people. Among the dead are four Israeli Embassy personnel, four Argentinean Embassy employees, several residents of a nearby nursing home, and schoolchildren on a passing bus. Hezbollah is believed responsible for the attack.

May 17, 1992   An Israeli is shot and killed by Hamas terrorists in Bet LeHiyeh, Gaza.

May 24, 1992	A 15-year-old girl is stabbed to death by a Hamas terrorist as she waits at a bus stop in Bat Yam.
May 27, 1992	An Israeli rabbi from Gush Katif settlement in Gaza is stabbed to death by a Hamas activist.
May 30, 1992	Two Palestinians swim across from Jordan to Eilat, Israel, and kill a security guard before being stopped by a soldier, who kills one and captures the other.
June 25, 1992	Hamas terrorists stab to death two Israelis in a Gaza packing house.
December 13, 1992	Border policeman Nissim Toledano is kidnapped in Lod by Hamas terrorists. They demand the release of Sheikh Ahmad Yassin. Toledano's body is found on December 15.
February 24, 1993	An 11-year-old Israeli girl is killed when Fatah terrorists throw rocks at the car she is riding in near the Jewish settlement of Karmei Tzur in the West Bank.
March 29, 1993	An Israeli man is killed by two Palestinian men wielding an axe in Petah Tiqva. The terrorists' affiliation is unknown.
April 16, 1993	In the first Hamas suicide bombing, a Hamas terrorist detonates a bomb in the parking lot of a restaurant near the West Bank settlement of Mekholah, killing one.
May 28, 1993	A yeshiva student is murdered in Hebron while walking to synagogue.
July 1, 1993	Three Palestinians take over a bus in Jerusalem, killing one passenger and injuring two others, but are finally overpowered by the bus driver. Two of the hijackers escape by kidnapping a female motorist and forcing her to drive them away. The hijackers shoot the woman when they approach a roadblock, but then lose their own lives.
August 5, 1993	A hitchhiking Israeli soldier is kidnapped and murdered after accepting a ride from men who turn out to be Hamas terrorists.

The Oslo Peace Process

During secret negotiations in Oslo, Norway, Israel and the PLO agreed in August 1993 on a plan to bring about peace. The plan would begin with the agreement of Arafat and thousands of other PLO officials and soldiers to return to the Gaza Strip and the West Bank from their long exile to establish a Palestinian government. Beginning with control over the Gaza Strip and the West Bank town of Jericho, the new Palestinian Authority would gradually extend its control further. Within five years, comprehensive negotiations would be held and an

agreement reached. One of the most important PLO pledges was to stop terrorism, punish those responsible for attacks, and disarm those who were determined to continue carrying out terrorism.

Despite Israel's release of prisoners involved in past attacks and essentially pardoning PLO members responsible for pre-1993 terrorist attacks, Arafat did not effectively stop new terrorism. He generally kept Fatah members from participating in attacks, except on certain occasions when he wanted to use terrorist violence as leverage, most notably in early 1996. Ironically, the institution of PLO control over all of Gaza and much of the West Bank—ruling over virtually all Palestinians in those places—actually made it easier to carry out terrorism.

PLO forces, given arms with Israel's agreement and trained by foreign states, were now just across from a virtually open "border." Although they were supposed to stop terrorist attacks, they often acted to incite them, and did nothing to prevent them or to punish the perpetrators afterwards. Since Israeli intelligence sources were executed by the Palestinian Authority if caught, Israel's ability to gain useful intelligence about terrorism in the territories was weakened. The daily crossing by thousands of Palestinians to work in Israel also increased access to the country. The growing use of suicide bombers was particularly devastating in terms of Israeli civilian casualties.

While the political course of negotiations was quite complex, and issues of implementation by both sides often provoked controversies, the continued permissiveness and even use of terrorism by the Palestinian movement was a prime factor in slowing the process and subverting its progress.

September 13, 1993	Israeli Prime Minister Yitzhak Rabin and PLO Chairman Yasir Arafat, together with U.S. President Bill Clinton, sign of the Oslo Accords, during a ceremony at the White House. The PLO promises to disavow violence and recognize Israel, and Israel agrees to a phased withdrawal of Israeli forces from the West Bank and Gaza and the creation of a Palestinian self-governing entity. The agreement mandates a series of negotiations leading to a comprehensive resolution of all issues within five years of the start of implementation.
September 24, 1993	Hamas terrorists stab an Israeli outside his home near the West Bank village of Basra.
October 9, 1993	The PFLP and Islamic Jihad each claim responsibility for murdering two Israelis in Wadi Kelt in the Judean desert.
October 24, 1993	Outside a Jewish settlement in Gaza, two Israeli Defense Forces (IDF) soldiers are shot to death when they hitch a ride in a car with Israeli license plates being driven by Hamas terrorists.
October 29, 1993	An Israeli from the West Bank settlement of Beit El is kidnapped from a poultry farm near the West Bank town of Ramallah by three terrorists. He is murdered and his body burned. Three Fatah members are convicted of the murder on July 27, 1994.
November 7, 1993	Hamas terrorists shoot an Israeli near Hebron.
November 9, 1993	A Bedouin motorist is mistaken for a Jew and killed when a truck driven by three Palestinians from Gaza deliberately hits him.
November 17, 1993	An Islamic Jihad terrorist stabs an Israeli in a cafeteria at the Gaza Strip entrance.
December 1, 1993	After parking their car near the side of the road in Ramallah because of engine trouble, two Israelis are shot to death by Hamas terrorists.
December 5, 1993	An Islamic Jihad terrorist fires on a bus in Holon, killing one passenger.

December 6, 1993   An Israeli and his son are shot to death by Hamas terrorists near Hebron.

December 22, 1993   Two Israelis traveling in a car are killed by shots fired by Hamas terrorists in the West Bank near Ramallah.

December 23, 1993   A Fatah terrorist stabs to death a security guard on duty at a construction site in Ashdod, Israel.

December 31, 1993   PFLP terrorists murder two Israelis in an apartment in Ramle, near Tel Aviv.

January 12, 1994   An Israeli man working in his orchard in Rishon LeZion is stabbed to death by his three Palestinian employees. The PFLP claims responsibility.

January 14, 1994   A Hamas terrorist stabs to death an Israeli in the industrial zone at the Erez Junction, the border between Gaza and Israel.

February 9, 1994   Islamic Jihad terrorists kidnap and then murder an Israeli taxi driver from Jerusalem.

February 10, 1994   An Israeli farmer is murdered at Kibbutz Na'an, near Rehovot, likely by Islamic Jihad terrorists.

February 19, 1994   Hamas terrorists ambush and kill a pregnant woman from Ariel, a West Bank settlement, while she is driving on the Trans-Samaria Highway.

February 25, 1994   An Israeli dies after being assaulted with an axe by an unknown Palestinian in Kfar Saba, Israel.

February 25, 1994   Baruch Goldstein, an American immigrant living in a West Bank settlement, fires upon a crowd of Muslim worshippers at the Tomb of the Patriarchs in Hebron with a machine gun, killing 29 and wounding 170. Worshippers end his rampage by spraying him with a fire extinguisher, then the crowd beats him to death. News of the attack leads to rioting which kills 26 more Palestinians and two Israelis.

March 1, 1994   Rashad Baz, a naturalized U.S. citizen from Lebanon, fires on a minibus containing Jewish students from a Lubavitcher yeshiva near the Brooklyn Bridge in New York City, killing one and injuring three others. He is later convicted of murder.

March 23, 1994   PFLP terrorists shoot and kill an Israeli guard at the income tax offices in East Jerusalem.

March 29, 1994   Two Palestinians in Petah Tiqva bludgeon to death a 70-year-old man on a construction site. After being caught, the terrorists, who are from Gaza, state that they carried out the attack in order to clear themselves of suspected collaboration with the Israeli authorities.

March 31, 1994   An Israeli is discovered dead in his apartment near Gedera with a leaflet of the DFLP "Red Star," explaining that the murder is carried out in revenge for the shooting of one of its members by an Israeli citizen.

April 6, 1994   Seven people are killed after a Hamas suicide bomber blows up a bus in Afula in northern Israel. The bomber crashes a car packed with explosives and nails into the bus as it is pulling into a bus stop.

April 7, 1994   A Hamas terrorist shoots and kills an Israeli at a hitchhiking post near Ashdod.

April 13, 1994   A Hamas suicide bombing on a bus in the central bus station of Hadera results in the death of five people.

May 4, 1994   An agreement is signed in Cairo calling for Israel to withdraw from much of the Gaza Strip and from the West Bank town of Jericho, which will be turned over to Arafat to rule under the Palestinian Authority. After the withdrawal of Israeli troops, the authority will have its own police force, which will be charged with preventing terrorist acts against Israel that originated in Palestinian territory.

May 17, 1994   Two Israelis are killed when their car is fired upon by unknown terrorists in a passing car near the West Bank settlement of Beit Haggai, south of Hebron.

July 1, 1994   Arafat enters the Gaza Strip for the first time in 27 years to set up the new Palestinian Authority there. The Palestinian Authority, which at this stage includes the entire Gaza Strip and the West Bank town of Jericho, will administer the areas turned over to Arafat's rule. A primary responsibility will be to prevent terrorism against Israelis.

July 1, 1994   An Israeli is stabbed to death when an unidentified terrorist breaks into his home in the West Bank settlement of Kiryat Netafim.

July 7, 1994   An Israeli is shot to death when unidentified terrorists open fire from a car passing near the entrance to the West Bank settlement of Kiryat Arba.

July 18, 1994   A car bomb outside a Jewish community center building in Buenos Aires, Argentina, causes the building to collapse, killing 100 and injuring 200 others. It is later revealed that the attack has been organized by the Iranian government, using Hezbollah operatives and working with neo-Nazi sympathizers associated with the local police.

July 19, 1994   A small passenger plane explodes in mid-air while en route from Colón to Panama City, Panama, killing all 18 passengers and three crew. Among the victims are Israeli nationals, dual Israeli-Panamanian citizens, and U.S. citizens. Twelve of the victims are Jews. The Partisans of God (Ansar al-Allah), a Hezbollah-linked group, claims responsibility.

August 26, 1994   Two Israeli construction workers are murdered at their building site in Ramle by Hamas terrorists.

September 5, 1994 An Israeli woman from Ashdod is strangled to death. In March 2001, a Palestinian, arrested for being in Israel illegally, pleads guilty to the murder, which he carried out to gain acceptance into a terrorist organization.

October 9, 1994	Two Hamas terrorists run down a busy street in Jerusalem firing AK-47 rifles and hurling hand grenades, killing two people—an Israeli and a Palestinian. Among the 13 persons injured is an American diplomat. The two terrorists—one from the Gaza Strip and the other from Egypt—are shot to death by police and armed civilians.
October 11, 1994	Corporal Nahshon Wachsman, an Israeli soldier with dual Israeli-U.S. citizenship, is abducted by Hamas terrorists after he accepts a ride in central Israel. His captors demand the release of Sheikh Ahmad Yassin and 200 Palestinian prisoners from Israeli jails. His kidnapping sets off a nationwide search for his whereabouts with the help of Palestinian security officials, and he is eventually found in a West Bank town. During a rescue effort by Israeli Defense Forces, Wachsman is murdered. One Israeli soldier and three kidnappers are also killed.
October 19, 1994	A Hamas suicide bomb on a bus in downtown Tel Aviv kills 22 Israelis and one Dutch national.
October 26, 1994	Israel and Jordan sign a peace treaty near their border, ending the historic conflict between them and establishing full diplomatic relations.
November 2, 1994	Hani Abed, leader of Islamic Jihad, is killed in Gaza when a bomb attached to the trunk of his car explodes as he opens it.
November 27, 1994	An Israeli rabbi is killed near Hebron by Hamas gunmen, who spray his car with bullets.
1995	Arafat establishes the Tanzim, a Fatah militia whose leaders are former activists in the first intifada. It is intended as a counterweight to attract Palestinian extremists who might otherwise be drawn to Islamist groups. With Arafat's support, it will launch terrorist attacks starting in 2000.
January 6, 1995	An Israeli is killed when terrorists open fire on her car north of the West Bank settlement of Beit El.
January 22, 1995	Two bombs explode at a bus stop at the Beit Lid Junction near Netanya, where many soldiers meet to hitch rides. Nineteen soldiers and one civilian are killed. Islamic Jihad and Hamas worked together to carry out the attack.
February 6, 1995	A security guard escorting a gasoline truck to a Gaza Strip filling station is killed when terrorists open fire from a passing car on a road between Jabalya and Gaza City.
February 13, 1995	A taxi driver is fatally stabbed on the road between Jerusalem and the nearby West Bank settlement of Ma'aleh Adumim.
March 19, 1995	Two Israelis are killed when terrorists fire on a bus near the entrance to Hebron.
April 9, 1995	A van loaded with explosives detonates alongside a bus near the Kfar Darom settlement in the Gaza Strip, killing seven Israelis and one U.S. citizen, Alisa

Flatow, 20. Over 50 other persons, including two U.S. citizens, are injured. Islamic Jihad claims responsibility for the attack.

July 18, 1995   Two Israelis are killed by PFLP terrorists while hiking in the Wadi Kelt.

July 24, 1995   A suicide bomb attack on a bus in Ramat Gan, outside Tel Aviv, kills six people. Hamas claims responsibility.

August 21, 1995   A bomb explodes on a bus in Jerusalem, killing six persons, including one U.S. citizen, and wounding two other U.S. citizens and over 100 others. Hamas claims responsibility.

September 5, 1995   PFLP terrorists stab to death an Israeli settler of British origin and wound his U.S.-born wife in the West Bank settlement of Michmash near Ramallah.

September 28, 1995   The Oslo II Agreement is signed, providing for Israel to withdraw from all West Bank towns except Hebron in favor of governance by the Palestinian Authority.

October 26, 1995   Fathi Shqaqi, founder and leader of the Palestinian Islamic Jihad, is killed in Malta while traveling from Libya to Syria. Israeli agents likely carried out the attack.

November 4, 1995   Israeli Prime Minister Yitzhak Rabin attends a large demonstration in front of Tel Aviv's city hall in support of the peace process. As he is leaving, Rabin is shot to death by Yigal Amir, an extreme right-wing law school student, who believes that killing Rabin will stop the peace process. Amir is sentenced to life in prison. Shimon Peres becomes prime minister.

January 5, 1996   Yahya Ayyash, a Hamas terrorist nicknamed "the Engineer" for his bomb-making abilities, which had resulted in the deaths of about 70 Israelis, is killed in Gaza. His cell phone, which has been packed with 50 grams of explosive, detonates when he answers it. Israeli intelligence is responsible.

January 20, 1996   Palestinian elections are held for the first time ever. Voters throughout the West Bank, Gaza, and East Jerusalem overwhelmingly elect Arafat as leader of the Palestinian Authority and most of his slate of candidates for the Palestinian Legislative Council.

February 25, 1996   A suicide bomber explodes a bomb on a bus in Jerusalem, killing 23 people, including three Americans, and injuring 50 others. Hamas claims responsibility in retaliation for the killing of Yahya Ayyash and also to mark the second anniversary of the attack by Jewish settler Baruch Goldstein on Muslim worshippers in Hebron. Some minutes after the Jerusalem bombing, a Hamas suicide bomber, disguised as an Israeli soldier, approaches a hitchhiking post outside Ashkelon and detonates a bomb, killing three people and injuring 25.

February 26, 1996   An Israeli is killed when a terrorist drives a car into a bus stop at the French Hill Junction in Jerusalem.

March 3, 1996   A suicide bomber detonates a bomb on a bus in Jerusalem, killing 19 people and injuring six others. Hamas and Islamic Jihad both claim responsibility for the bombing.

March 4, 1996   In the oil-rich Persian Gulf kingdom of Bahrain, DFLP terrorists pour gasoline at the entrance to a restaurant in Sitrah, then ignite it with Molotov cocktails, killing seven Bangladeshi employees and destroying the restaurant.

March 4, 1996   A suicide bomber from Islamic Jihad tries to enter a major shopping center in downtown Tel Aviv. Deterred by security inside, he detonates his 45-pound nail bomb while crossing a street, killing 13 people.

March 30, 1996   Hezbollah terrorists fire a number of rockets into northern Israel, killing two Israeli civilians.

April 18, 1996   Members of al-Gama'a al-Islamiyya kill 18 Greek tourists and wound 21 others, of whom 12 are Greek, in an assault on the Europa Hotel in Cairo. The terrorists mistakenly believe they are targeting Israeli tourists.

April 22, 1996   Arafat leads a Palestinian National Council meeting in Gaza that votes to revoke clauses in the PLO Charter calling for the liquidation of Israel.

May 13, 1996   Gunmen open fire on a bus and a group of yeshiva students near the Beth El settlement, killing a dual U.S.-Israeli citizen, David Boim, and wounding three Israelis.

May 31, 1996   After a wave of terrorism hits Israel, Shimon Peres is defeated in his bid to remain prime minister, and Benjamin Netanyahu, the leader of the Likud Party who has run on a platform of opposition to the Oslo Accords, is elected.

June 9, 1996   Two Israelis, one also a U.S. citizen, are killed when PFLP terrorists fire on their car near Beit Shemesh, Israel.

June 16, 1996   An off-duty Israeli policeman is shot and killed by terrorists while shopping in a toy store in the West Bank village of Bidiya.

June 26, 1996   Three Israelis are killed in an ambush along the Jordan River north of Jericho by terrorists who infiltrate from Jordan. In a separate incident, three Israelis are killed by terrorists in a drive-by shooting attack near Beit Shemesh.

September 27, 1996 Prime Minister Netanyahu announces his decision to open a tunnel allowing visitors access to the buried portions of the Western Wall of the Jewish Temple in East Jerusalem. The wall also serves as a retaining wall for the al-Aqsa mosque, an important shrine for Muslims. The news results in rioting by Palestinians who believe false rumors that the tunnel is a plot to destroy the mosque. In the ensuing gun battles between Palestinian Authority and Israeli troops, 86 Palestinians and 15 Israelis are killed and many more wounded.

December 11, 1996   Three PFLP terrorists attack a car carrying Israeli settlers near the West Bank settlement of Bet El, killing a woman and her 12-year-old son.

January 14, 1997   Israelis and Palestinians sign a long-delayed agreement outlining the steps for Israeli troop redeployment from Hebron and other parts of the West Bank. Soon after, 80 percent of Hebron becomes part of the Palestinian Authority. The Palestinian Authority now controls all West Bank towns and has political rule over all villages, though Israel retains the right of security control in the villages. Israel also maintains control of all Jewish settlements in the West Bank and in most of its unincorporated area.

January 31, 1997   Musa Abu Marzuk, a high-ranking Hamas official, is expelled from the United States to Jordan because of his leadership role in a terrorist organization.

February 23, 1997   On the observation deck of New York's Empire State Building, a Palestinian, Ali Hassan Abu Kamal, begins shooting at other visitors, killing one and wounding five others before killing himself. In a suicide note he says the United States is using Israel as an instrument against Palestinians.

March 13, 1997   Ahmed Daqamseh, a Jordanian soldier, fires on seven Israeli schoolgirls who are touring a peace park in Jordan near the border with Israel. The soldier is sentenced in July to life in prison. King Hussein of Jordan comes to Israel to pay condolences to the families personally. In August 1999, the government refuses to grant a request by a Jordanian parliamentary committee to pardon Daqamseh.

March 21, 1997   Three Israelis are killed and 48 wounded when a Hamas suicide bomber detonates a bomb on the terrace of a Tel Aviv cafe.

July 20, 1997   An Israeli is beaten to death after being attacked by two Arabs at a Rishon LeZion construction site.

July 30, 1997   Two Hamas suicide bombings strike the Mahane Yehuda market in Jerusalem, killing 16 and wounding 178.

September 4, 1997   Five people, including a dual U.S.-Israeli citizen, are killed and 181 wounded in three Hamas suicide bombings on the Ben Yehuda pedestrian mall in Jerusalem.

September 22, 1997   In Amman, Jordan, two Israeli Embassy security guards are killed in a drive-by shooting. The Jordanian Islamic Resistance claims responsibility.

September 25, 1997   Israeli security agents attempt to assassinate Hamas official Khalid Mishal outside his office in Amman, Jordan, by injecting him with a lethal substance, but are thwarted by Mishal's chauffeur and security guard. The Israeli agents are captured by Jordanian security officials and returned to Israel only after the Israeli government releases Hamas founder Sheikh Ahmad Yassin. After Yassin's release from jail in October, he calls for further violence against Israelis.

November 20, 1997   Unknown terrorists assassinate a Hungarian yeshiva student and wound an Israeli student in the Old City of Jerusalem.

December 31, 1997   An Israeli woman is killed after terrorists fire upon her car between the Jewish settlements of Ariel and Alei Zahav.

January 14, 1998   A videocassette rigged with a bomb explodes at the Fatima border crossing near Metulla in northern Israel, killing one Lebanese citizen and injuring five civilians—two Lebanese and three Israelis. The Lebanese Shia Muslim Amal movement claims responsibility.

April 19, 1998   An American-Israeli farmer is killed by Fatah terrorists on the Ma'on farm near Hebron.

May 6, 1998   A yeshiva student is stabbed to death on his way to pray at the Western Wall in Jerusalem.

August 5, 1998   Two Israelis patrolling the West Bank settlement of Yitzhar are shot and killed.

August 20, 1998   A Hamas terrorist murders a prominent rabbi while he is asleep in his home in Hebron. The terrorist is caught and sentenced to three life sentences in July 1999.

September 10, 1998   Israeli security officials raid a farmhouse near Hebron and kill two leading Hamas terrorists—Adil and Imad Awadallah.

October 13, 1998   One man is killed and another critically wounded in a Hamas terrorist attack as they swim in a spring in the Jerusalem Hills.

October 23, 1998   After nine days of negotiations, Arafat and Netanyahu sign the Wye Agreement in Washington, D.C. The agreement is an effort to make progress on implementing the peace process outlined in the Oslo II Agreement. Arafat agrees to take measures to prevent acts of terrorism against Israel, to apprehend individuals suspected of perpetrating acts of violence and terror, and to punish all persons involved in acts of violence and terror.

October 26, 1998   An Israeli from Kiryat Arba is shot to death in Hebron by terrorists.

October 29, 1998   In the Gaza Strip, a Hamas suicide bomber driving a vehicle filled with explosives detonates alongside a school bus carrying children from the Jewish settlement of Kfar Darom to a regional school, killing one and wounding six.

December 2, 1998   An Arab man who works in the Jerusalem municipality is stabbed to death not far from his home in Jerusalem by a Jewish extremist associated with Kach, the radical Jewish group established by U.S. Rabbi Meir Kahane.

May 17, 1999   Labor Party leader Ehud Barak is elected prime minister of Israel on a campaign of promising to make a successful peace agreement with the Palestinians and Syrians.

August 7, 1999   The body of an Israeli, shot in the head by Hamas terrorists, is found in a burned vehicle near Jenin.

August 30, 1999   Two Israeli hikers are killed close to Jenin. Two Israeli Arabs affiliated with Islamist groups are later arrested for the murders.

September 15, 1999 Israel grants permission for the return to the West Bank of Mustafa al-Zibri (also known as Abu Ali Mustafa). The decision is made under condition that the Palestinian Authority guarantees he will not revert to terrorism. He bases himself in Ramallah (also Arafat's headquarters), and becomes head of the PFLP in July 2000. After the start of the second intifada in September 2000, he and the PFLP carry out a number of terrorist attacks.

May 22, 2000   Israeli troops re-deploy from the security zone in southern Lebanon, ending 18 years of Israeli military presence there. Its client militia, the South Lebanon Army, disintegrates and Hezbollah militia forces take up positions along the border. Although the UN certifies that Israel has withdrawn, Hezbollah maintains that Israel still occupies a portion of Lebanon and continues sporadic attacks, including the firing of rockets across the border.

June 10, 2000   President Hafez al-Assad, the dictator of Syria who has long resisted peace with Israel, dies from an illness. His son Bashar succeeds him, raising hope that a new Syrian policy might emerge, though this is soon doomed to disappointment.

July 11–25, 2000   Peace negotiations are held between Chairman Arafat and Prime Minister Barak with the mediation of U.S. President Bill Clinton at Camp David, the U.S. presidential retreat in Maryland. Negotiations collapse when Arafat rejects the American-mediated Israeli offer of an independent Palestinian state in all of the Gaza Strip and in most of the West Bank and East Jerusalem in addition to financial compensation for Palestinian refugees.

Arafat Rejects Peace

The culmination of the peace process came in 2000. Both at the Camp David meeting and in response to Clinton's peace plan at the end of the year, Arafat rejected a proposed framework for negotiations that would have given the Palestinians an independent state with its capital in East Jerusalem. Instead, Arafat began planning for renewed violence, which began in late September. What followed was a four-year-long war waged by the Palestinians using terrorist violence. In contrast to the previous period, Palestinian Authority security forces openly participated in such attacks, no one was arrested or detained for terrorist operations, and they were praised and encouraged in the official Palestinian media.

As always, the purpose of the terrorism was threefold. First, it was to demoralize Israelis and press them into making unilateral concessions beyond anything Arafat could achieve at the negotiating table. Ideally, the attacks would bring about the total collapse of the country. Second, terrorism's goal was to mobilize Palestinians, who applauded terrorist successes and ignored their leadership's inability to obtain for them a state, peace, or higher living standards. Third, terrorism was to create a crisis so great as to bring the intervention of wealthy and powerful countries on the Palestinian side, which could make possible major gains for which they would not have to reciprocate.

This war generally failed to bring the desired results, however. By the time of Arafat's death, in November 2004, it was clear that Israel was able to protect its security and to recapture any part of the territories at any time it desired. In contrast, the Palestinian infrastructure was destroyed. Arafat's policy of deliberately fostering anarchy also weakened Fatah and led to the strengthening of Hamas, the Islamist group which was a strong proponent of a long-term terrorist campaign to destroy Israel. The Palestinians made some gains regarding Western public opinion—at least until the Islamist attacks on the United States on September 11, 2001—but these gains brought no material advantage to them.

In early 2005, after succeeding Arafat, the new Palestinian leadership declared a cease-fire. Yet it did not develop an alternative worldview and set of goals for the movement nor did it defeat or disarm the most extreme groups. While a comprehensive peace might be expected to halt the problem of terrorism, the paradox was that the power of the terrorists—and the appeal of that tactic in the

Palestinian movement—also made it almost impossible to reach such an agreement.

The movement had still not really confronted the question of whether its goal was a Palestinian state living peacefully alongside Israel or a Palestinian state that included a conquered Israel. Thus, aside from the difficulty of obtaining peace, the question remained open as to whether such an agreement would bring terrorism to an end or merely open a new round of cross-border terrorism in which Palestinians might operate from a stronger position. Given its failures, shortcomings, and the strategic cleverness of its Islamist adversaries, Fatah was defeated and thrown out of the Gaza Strip in 2007 by Hamas, a group for whom terrorism was even more rationalized and central.

September 28, 2000 — Ariel Sharon, leader of the Israeli opposition, visits the Temple Mount/al-Aqsa mosque area. Saying this visit is a desecration of Muslim holy land with nefarious intentions, Palestinians launch a new intifada. There is ample evidence that the uprising was planned earlier, following failed negotiations at Camp David.

September 29, 2000 — Palestinians begin rioting in what escalates into a war of attacks on Israeli soldiers and civilians in Israel, the West Bank, and Gaza, using a wide range of methods, including suicide bombing, roadside bombing, shooting, lynching, stabbing, and rock-throwing. Attacks are carried out by a new group, the al-Aqsa Martyrs Brigades, organized by the Tanzim, Fatah's grassroots organization, and financed by Arafat. In response, the Israeli army shoots armed Palestinians and civilians during violent demonstrations and gun battles, assassinates terrorist leaders, and arrests militants. Palestinian civilians are frequently killed in the fighting. At times, Israel places Palestinian towns under curfew and later begins construction of an anti-terrorist security fence.

October 2, 2000 — An Israeli man is killed in the village of Masha on the Trans-Samaria Highway by unidentified terrorists.

October 8, 2000 — The bullet-riddled body of a resident of the West Bank Jewish settlement of Elon Moreh is found at the southern entrance to Nablus. It is not known which terrorists are responsible.

October 12, 2000 — Two Israeli soldiers serving on reserve army duty as drivers take a wrong turn and end up in downtown Ramallah. Palestinians drag them out of their car and beat them. Palestinian police bring them to a police station, but a mob bursts in, murders the two reservists, and mutilates their bodies. The body of one is fastened to the back of a car and driven through the streets of Ramallah.

October 19, 2000 — An Israeli is killed when Fatah members and Palestinian security forces open fire on a group of Israeli families on a trip to Mount Ebal near Nablus.

October 28, 2000 — The body of an Israeli is found inside his burned-out car between the village of Bitunia and Ramallah in the West Bank. He had been killed by Fatah terrorists.

October 30, 2000   An Israeli is killed by Force-17 terrorists while on duty as a security guard at the National Insurance Institute's East Jerusalem branch.

November 2, 2000   Two Israelis are killed and ten wounded in an Islamic Jihad car bomb explosion near the Mahane Yehuda market in Jerusalem.

November 8, 2000   Three Fatah Tanzim gunmen ambush the car of an Israeli woman working as a customs employee at the Rafah border crossing and then kill her.

November 13, 2000   An Israeli schoolteacher is killed by gunfire from a passing car while traveling near Ofra, north of Ramallah. On March 16, 2001, the Israeli General Security Service apprehends three members of a terror cell organized by Force-17, which is responsible for this attack and others. Also on this day, Fatah Tanzim gunmen kill an Israeli truck driver traveling near the Kissufim Junction in the Gaza Strip.

November 18, 2000   An Israeli is shot and killed by a senior Palestinian Preventive Security Service officer who infiltrates the Kfar Darom greenhouses in the Gaza Strip.

November 20, 2000   A roadside bomb explodes alongside a bus carrying children from the Gaza Jewish settlement area of Kfar Darom to school in Gush Katif, killing two Israelis and wounding nine. Two groups—one affiliated with the Fatah and other with Hamas—claim responsibility.

November 21, 2000   Fatah Tanzim gunmen kill an 18-year-old Israeli at the Gush Katif Junction.

November 22, 2000   A car bomb detonates alongside a passing bus on the main street of Hadera in northern Israel, killing two and wounding 60. Islamic Jihad is responsible.

November 24, 2000   An Israeli man is killed after being shot at by Force-17 terrorists while driving on the Otzarin-Nablus road in the West Bank.

December 8, 2000   Fatah Tanzim gunmen open fire on a passing public bus traveling from Tiberias to Jerusalem on the Jericho bypass road, killing an Israeli soldier. Also on this day, two Israelis are killed when gunmen in a car open fire on a van carrying schoolteachers on their way to work near the West Bank Jewish settlement of Kiryat Arba. On March 7, 2001, a Hamas terrorist, Marwan Mahtasav, who had been arrested by Israeli security forces three days after the attack, is formally charged with the attack.

December 13, 2000   A Hamas terrorist, Abbas Othman Ewaywi, is assassinated by Israeli security forces in front of a shop in Hebron.

December 21, 2000   An Israeli motorist from Mod'in in central Israel is killed by Force-17 terrorists waiting in ambush on the road between Givat Ze'ev and Beit Horon in the West Bank.

December 23, 2000   Clinton presents a peace plan, approved by Barak, which would create an independent Palestinian state in all of the Gaza Strip, almost all the West Bank, and much of East Jerusalem. Israel would swap some of its own territory equivalent to any places it retained. Arafat rejects the plan.

December 31, 2000   Binyamin Zeev Kahane, son of the late extreme right-wing leader Meir Kahane, and his wife, Talia, are killed when Force-17 terrorists open fire while they are driving near the West Bank settlement of Beit El. Five of their children, aged two months to 10 years, are injured. On March 16, 2001, three members of a terror cell organized by Force-17, who are responsible for this attack, are arrested.

January 5, 2001   The body of an Israeli man from Hadera is discovered in nearby Caesarea, killed by unknown terrorists.

January 14, 2001   The body of an Israeli is found in one of the agricultural hothouses in the Gaza Strip. Both a Fatah and a Hamas organization claim responsibility for the murder.

January 17, 2001   Under direction from Fatah Tanzim, a Palestinian woman poses as an American as she corresponds romantically over the Internet with a 16-year-old Israeli boy from Ashkelon. When he travels to Jerusalem to meet her, the woman drives him towards a location in Ramallah, where he is murdered by three Fatah Tanzim gunmen.

January 23, 2001   Two Israeli cousins and co-owners of a restaurant in Tel Aviv are killed in the West Bank town of Tulkarem. The two had traveled there with an Israeli Arab friend to shop for flowerpots. As they are leaving a local restaurant after having lunch, Hamas gunmen arrive and kidnap the two Israelis. They drive them a few meters over the line into an Israeli-administered zone of the West Bank and shoot them both dead.

January 25, 2001   Fatah Tanzim terrorists assassinate an Israeli man near the Atarot industrial zone north of Jerusalem.

January 29, 2001   Force-17 gunmen shoot dead an Israeli man who is traveling near Ramallah.

February 1, 2001   Fatah Tanzim gunmen fire at an Israeli car near the Aroub refugee camp on the Jerusalem-Hebron highway killing the driver. Also on this day, Palestinian terrorists of unknown affiliation gun down an Israeli when he arrives at an Arab village near Jenin to pick up his car at a repair shop.

February 6, 2001   Likud leader Ariel Sharon defeats incumbent Prime Minister Ehud Barak by an overwhelming majority, reflecting public disillusionment with the peace process.

February 11, 2001   An Israeli is shot and killed by Fatah Tanzim gunmen as he drives from Jerusalem to his home in Gush Katif.

February 14, 2001   Halil Abu Olba, a resident of Gaza employed to transport Palestinians to work in Israel, deliberately plows a bus into a group of Israelis waiting at a bus stop outside Holon, near Tel Aviv, killing eight and wounding 25. On June 12, 2001, Abu Olba, whose attack was organized by Hamas, is sentenced to life in prison in Israel.

February 26, 2001   The body of an Israeli from Kfar Saba is found shot to death in an olive grove near Moshav Hagor, likely murdered by Fatah Tanzim members.

March 1, 2001   One Israeli is killed and nine injured when a terrorist detonates a bomb in a Tel Aviv-to-Tiberias taxi as it is stopping near Um el-Fahem, Israel's largest Arab city. It is not clear which Palestinian group perpetrated this attack.

March 4, 2001   A Hamas suicide bomber detonates his explosives opposite the central bus station in Netanya, killing three and wounding 60.

March 19, 2001   An Israeli is killed by shots fired at his car by PFLP terrorists while driving to work in Jerusalem from his home in the Gush Etzion area.

March 26, 2001   A ten-month-old baby girl is killed by sniper fire from Fatah Tanzim terrorists at the entrance to a Jewish settlement in Hebron.

March 27, 2001   The explosion from a Hamas suicide bomber kills one person on a bus in Jerusalem's French Hill.

March 28, 2001   Two children are killed and four people injured, including a U.S. citizen, after a Hamas suicide bombing at a bus stop in Kfar Saba, near Tel Aviv.

April 1, 2001   An Israeli woman is stabbed to death on the street in Haifa. Six members of a Hezbollah-linked Palestinian terrorist cell responsible for the murder, thought to be a terrorist group initiation rite, are arrested in July.

April 5, 2001   Iyyad Hardan, a senior leader of Islamic Jihad, dies in an explosion set by Israeli security forces at a public telephone booth in Jenin.

April 21, 2001   An Israeli man from Beit Shemesh is murdered by Palestinian terrorists and stuffed into the trunk of his car parked near a village north of Ramallah. It is not known which Palestinian group is responsible.

April 22, 2001   A Hamas terrorist detonates a bomb at a crowded bus stop in Kfar Saba, killing an Israeli.

April 28, 2001   Al-Aqsa Martyrs Brigades terrorists shoot at an Israeli car on the Wadi Arava highway in Galilee, killing an Israeli soldier and wounding four other passengers.

April 28, 2001   An Israeli woman is stabbed to death near Karmiel in Galilee. Six members of a Hezbollah-linked Palestinian terrorist cell, for one of whom it is an initiation rite into the organization, are arrested in July.

May 1, 2001   An Israeli is killed when his vehicle is fired upon by Fatah Tanzim terrorists and overturned at a junction between the West Bank settlements of Ofra and Beit El.

May 7, 2001   Israeli naval forces capture the *Santorini,* a ship on its way from Lebanon to the Gaza Strip, which is carrying a wide variety of weaponry, including land-to-air missiles, rocket-propelled grenades, mortar bombs, mines, guns, and ammunition. The PFLP is responsible for the shipment.

May 8, 2001   An Israeli security guard at Binyamin Farm, a small, isolated Jewish settlement near the larger West Bank settlement of Itamar in Samaria, is murdered in an attack claimed by the Hassan Kadi Brigade, affiliated with Fatah.

May 9, 2001	Two 14-year-old boys—one of them, a dual Israeli-American citizen—are stoned to death in a cave just outside the West Bank settlement of Tekoa where they live. Islamic Jihad terrorists are responsible.
May 10, 2001	Two Romanian workers are killed in a Hamas bomb attack while repairing a vandalized fence at the Kissufim crossing into the Gaza Strip.
May 15, 2001	Fatah Tanzim terrorists assassinate three family members inside a car on the Alon highway.
May 18, 2001	A Hamas suicide bombing at a mall in Netanya results in the death of five and injuring of over 100. Also on this day, on a road north of Jerusalem, an off-duty Israeli soldier is killed and his mother seriously wounded in a Fatah Tanzim ambush.
May 23, 2001	An Israeli motorist is killed by Fatah Tanzim terrorists outside the Jewish settlement of Ariel.
May 25, 2001	The burned body of an Israeli is discovered near the West Bank city of Tulkarem, the victim of Fatah terrorists.
May 29, 2001	An Israeli from the West Bank settlement of Itamar is shot dead in a Fatah Tanzim ambush while driving between the settlements of Kedumim and Yizhar. Also on this day, Fatah Tanzim terrorists ambush a car near the settlement of Neve Daniel in the Gush Etzion bloc on the West Bank, killing two Israeli women, one a U.S. citizen.
May 31, 2001	An Israeli is killed in a drive-by shooting attack by Fatah Tanzim terrorists north of Tulkarem on the West Bank.
June 1, 2001	A Hamas suicide terrorist mingles with a crowd waiting to get inside a seaside discotheque in Tel Aviv late on a Friday night and then detonates his bomb, killing 21 persons and wounding 120. Most of the casualties are teenagers who had emigrated from the former Soviet Union. Arafat condemns the violence to the Western media, but writes a letter praising the act to the terrorist's family.
June 5, 2001	A five-month-old baby is killed after a rock is thrown at the family's car near the West Bank settlement of Shilo. Those responsible are affiliated with the Fatah Tanzim.
June 12, 2001	A Greek Orthodox monk from St. George's Monastery in Wadi Kelt in the Judean desert is shot and killed while driving on the Jerusalem-to-Ma'ale Adumim road. Tanzim leader, Marwan Barghouti, is later convicted of direct responsibility for this murder, among others.
June 13, 2001	Jewish extremists in Hebron assassinate a Palestinian civilian.
June 18, 2001	An Israeli is killed in a drive-by shooting attack between the West Bank settlements of Homesh and Shavei Shomron, near Nablus. Terrorists from the al-Aqsa Martyrs Brigades are responsible. In another incident, a Fatah assassin fires at a car near the entrance to Einav, near Tulkarem, killing an Israeli motorist.

June 20, 2001   A Fatah Tanzim terrorist fatally shoots an Israeli who has gone to visit a Palestinian business partner in the Palestinian town of Silat a-Dahar.

June 28, 2001   An Israeli is killed and another woman injured by shots fired at a two-car convoy on the Jenin bypass road. The al-Aqsa Martyrs Brigades claims responsibility for the attack.

July 2, 2001   An Israeli is shot and killed near the West Bank city of Tulkarem after shopping at a local market. The assailants are from the al-Aqsa Martyrs Brigades.

July 12, 2001   Four Fatah Tanzim terrorists shoot at a van outside the West Bank settlement of Kiryat Arba, killing the driver.

July 13, 2001   As a group of Kiryat Arba officials are investigating the site of a fatal shooting the previous day, Fatah Tanzim terrorists fire upon them, killing one.

July 16, 2001   An Islamic Jihad suicide bomber explodes his bomb at a bus stop near the train station in Binyamina, halfway between Netanya and Haifa, killing two and wounding 11.

July 19, 2001   Three members of a Palestinian family, one a three-month-old infant, are killed after their car is fired upon at the entrance of the West Bank town of Kafr Idna. An extremist Jewish group calling itself "The Committee for Security on the Roads" claims responsibility for the attack.

July 24, 2001   An Israeli teenager is found murdered in Ramallah, where he had been lured by a Palestinian acquaintance on the pretext of hiring him to renovate an apartment there. Al-Aqsa Martyrs Brigades claims responsibility.

July 26, 2001   Fatah Tanzim terrorists fatally shoot an Israeli motorist near the main entrance to the West Bank settlement of Givat Ze'ev.

August 5, 2001   An Israeli is killed and three wounded when Palestinian gunmen open fire on a car between the West Bank settlements of Alfei Menashe and Karnei Shomron near Kalkilya on the West Bank.

August 6, 2001   In Amman, Jordan, an Israeli diamond merchant is shot dead outside his apartment. Two new groups—Nobles of Jordan and Holy Warriors for Ahmed Daqamseh—say they are responsible. Daqamseh is the Jordanian soldier serving a life sentence for killing seven Israeli schoolgirls in 1997.

August 7, 2001   An Israeli is shot and killed by terrorists while driving home at night on the Trans-Samaria Highway. The al-Aqsa Martyrs Brigades claims responsibility.

August 9, 2001   A Hamas suicide bomber detonates himself in a crowded Sbarro pizzeria in the center of Jerusalem, killing 15 persons, including two U.S. citizens, and wounding 130 others, including four U.S. citizens. Also on this day, an Israeli is killed and three injured by Tanzim terrorists in a drive-by shooting at the entrance to a kibbutz in the Gilboa region, west of Beit She'an.

August 16, 2001   A Palestinian taxi driver, Kamal Sa'id Musallam, is killed and several passengers in his taxi wounded after it is hit by a rock between Rehalim and Tapuah, possibly by Israelis in a passing car.

August 19, 2001   Abu Nidal (Sabri al-Banna) dies in Baghdad. The Iraqi Intelligence chief claims that the terrorist chief committed suicide in order to avoid being taken into custody for allegedly plotting with Kuwait to overthrow Saddam Hussein's regime. However, there are reports that his body had four gunshot wounds, and some speculate that Saddam Hussein ordered him assassinated because he refused to train groups of al-Qaeda fighters who had arrived in northern Iraq after fleeing Afghanistan or that his presence was an embarrassment for the regime at a time when it was facing international sanctions.

August 25, 2001   Three Israelis are killed when al-Aqsa gunmen open fire on their car as they are returning home on the road linking Jerusalem to Modi'in.

August 26, 2001   An Israeli is killed in a shooting attack near the entrance to the Palestinian village of Zaita, north of Tulkarem. The al-Aqsa Martyrs Brigades claims responsibility for the attack.

August 27, 2001   Abu Ali Mustafa, general secretary of the PFLP who is believed to have planned several terrorist attacks, is killed when an Israeli helicopter fires rockets at his office in Ramallah. Ahmed Sadat is elected PFLP general secretary on October 3, 2001.

August 27, 2001   PFLP terrorists ambush and kill an Israeli driving between the West Bank settlements of Har Bracha and Itamar.

August 29, 2001   A truck driver working for an Israeli energy company is killed in a terrorist shooting attack outside the Palestinian village of Kutchin, west of Nablus. The al-Aqsa Martyrs Brigades claims responsibility. On the same day, a Palestinian man is shot to death by assailants in a passing vehicle between the villages of Hizme and Anatot, north of Jerusalem. Jewish extremists are likely responsible.

August 30, 2001   An Israeli is shot to death by a masked gunman in the Arab village of Na'alin, while dining at a restaurant owned by close friends. The affiliation of the culprits is unknown.

September 5, 2001   FBI and Customs Service agents raid the Dallas offices of InfoCom and freeze its assets. This Internet services company is suspected of links to Hamas.

September 6, 2001   An off-duty Israeli officer is killed and his passenger wounded in an ambush shooting near Kibbutz Bahan, east of Hadera, while they are traveling to a wedding.

September 9, 2001   Islamic Jihad terrorists attack a minibus transporting teachers to the regional school south of the Adam Junction in the Jordan Valley, killing two Israelis. In a separate incident, three Israelis are killed and some 90 injured in a suicide bombing near the Nahariya train station in northern Israel. The attack is carried out by an Israeli Arab from Galilee who is operating for Hamas.

September 12, 2001   An Israeli is killed after being shot at from a passing vehicle near the village of Habla near Kalkilya.

September 15, 2001   Al-Aqsa Martyrs Brigades terrorists fatally shoot an Israeli driving on the Ramot-French Hill road in northern Jerusalem.

September 20, 2001   An Israeli is killed and her husband seriously wounded in a drive-by shooting attack by Fatah terrorists near the West Bank settlement of Tekoa.

September 24, 2001   Islamic Jihad terrorists kill an Israeli with gunfire near the West Bank settlement of Shadmot Mehola.

October 2, 2001   Two Hamas terrorists infiltrate the Jewish settlement of Alei Sinai in Gaza, opening fire on residents and hurling grenades into homes, killing two and wounding 14.

October 4, 2001   An al-Aqsa Martyrs Brigades terrorist, dressed as an Israeli paratrooper, opens fire on a group of Israelis waiting at the central bus station in Afula, killing three and wounding 13.

October 5, 2001   An Israeli is killed by Tanzim terrorists in a drive-by shooting near Avnei Hefetz in central Israel.

October 7, 2001   An Israeli is killed when an Islamic Jihad suicide terrorist detonates a bomb near the entrance of Kibbutz Sheluhot in the Beit She'an Valley.

October 17, 2001   Israeli Tourism Minister Rechavam Zeevi is assassinated outside his room at the Hyatt Hotel in Jerusalem. The PFLP claims responsibility for the attack as a response to the killing of its leader, Abu Ali Mustafa, by Israeli security officials. Four Palestinians, including PFLP head Ahmed Sadat, are convicted of the killing in a Palestinian Authority court, but Arafat refuses to jail them. In March 2002, they move into his Ramallah compound. The harboring of these convicted terrorist leaders becomes a major reason for Israel's decision to create a siege of the compound that month.

October 18, 2001   Fatah Tanzim terrorists kill an Israeli and wound another after firing at their jeep in the Judean desert, near the Mar Saba monastery.

October 28, 2001   Two Islamic Jihad terrorists, who are also members of the Palestinian police, open fire with assault weapons on Israeli pedestrians at a bus stop in downtown Hadera, killing four and wounding 40. The terrorists are killed by police.

November 4, 2001   In East Jerusalem, two Israeli teenagers are killed and more than 40 Israelis wounded after an Islamic Jihad gunman opens fire on a bus.

November 9, 2001   An al-Aqsa Martyrs Brigades terrorist kills an Israeli as she drives from work in the West Bank settlement of Shaked.

November 11, 2001   The head of security at Kfar Hess, a Jewish agricultural cooperative near Netanya, is shot and killed at the entrance after being summoned to investigate a suspicious person. The terrorist, likely a Fatah member, escapes.

November 27, 2001   Two terrorists, who are also members of the Palestinian security forces, open fire with Kalashnikov assault rifles on a crowd of people near the central bus station in Afula, killing two and wounding 50. Islamic Jihad and the al-Aqsa Martyrs Brigades claim joint responsibility. Also on this day, an Israeli is killed and three others injured when a Hamas terrorist throws grenades and opens fire at vehicles on the road between the Kissufim crossing and Gush Katif in the Gaza Strip.

November 29, 2001   An Islamic Jihad suicide bomber detonates explosives near Hadera on a bus en route from Nazareth to Tel Aviv, killing three and wounding nine.

December 1, 2001   Two Hamas suicide bombers detonate their bombs on Ben Yehuda street, a crowded pedestrian mall in downtown Jerusalem, killing 11 and wounding about 180. As rescue workers arrive on the scene, a third bomb explodes nearby, causing no serious injuries, but creating further havoc.

December 2, 2001   An Israeli is killed when a Hamas gunman opens fire on his car near the Gaza settlement of Elei Sinai. Also on this day, a Hamas suicide bombing on a bus in Haifa kills 15 and wounds 40.

December 4, 2001   Israeli missiles destroy Arafat's three helicopters and landing strip at Gaza International Airport to prevent him from leaving Gaza.

December 12, 2001   Three terrorists attack a bus and several passenger cars with a roadside bomb, anti-tank grenades, and light arms fire near the entrance to the West Bank settlement of Emmanuel, killing 11 and wounding about 30 others. Both Fatah and Hamas claim responsibility for the attack.

January 3, 2002   Israeli commandos capture the *Karine A,* a freighter in the Red Sea that is bound for Gaza. The vessel is carrying 50 tons of weapons, including Katyusha rockets, anti-tank missiles, mortars, mines, explosives, sniper rifles, and bullets from Iran. It is determined that Arafat had ordered the shipment, although he denies it. The U.S. government's conclusion that Arafat lied on this issue is a major factor leading to an American policy that Arafat should be replaced by a democratic Palestinian regime.

January 15, 2002   Israel security forces assassinate Raed al-Karmi, an al-Aqsa Martyrs Brigades commander, whom it accuses of involvement in the murder of ten Israelis.

January 15, 2002   A 45-year-old Israeli woman is shot and killed by Fatah Tanzim terrorists near a gas station at the entrance to the West Bank settlement of Givat Ze'ev. Also on this day, a resident of the West Bank settlement of Ma'ale Adumim just outside Jerusalem is kidnapped at a Palestinian Authority security checkpoint in Beit Jala. His bullet-riddled body is found in a car in Beit Sahur, in the Bethlehem area. The al-Aqsa Martyrs Brigades claims responsibility for the murder.

January 16, 2002   An Arab resident of Beit Hanina in East Jerusalem, mistaken for an Israeli, is killed in a drive-by Fatah terrorist shooting near Jenin in the West Bank.

January 17, 2002   An Al-Aqsa Martyrs Brigades terrorist burst into a bat mitzvah reception in a banquet hall in Hadera and detonates his explosives, killing six.

January 21, 2002   Israeli troops temporarily seize the West Bank town of Tulkarem, which has become a major launching point for cross-border attacks, imposing a curfew and conducting house-to-house searches for Palestinian fugitives. It is the first time since the uprising began that the Israelis have occupied an entire town.

January 22, 2002   A terrorist from the al-Aqsa Martyrs Brigades opens fire with an M-16 assault rifle near a bus stop in downtown Jerusalem, killing two and injuring 40.

January 24, 2002   Members of the Israeli army kill a senior Hamas commander, Bakr Hamdan, and two of his associates, by firing a missile at his car in Gaza.

January 27, 2002   In the first Palestinian suicide attack carried out by a woman, a Fatah terrorist detonates a bomb on a busy street corner in Jerusalem, killing one and wounding over 150 people.

February 6, 2002   A woman and her 11-year-old daughter are murdered in their home when an armed terrorist dressed as an Israeli soldier infiltrates Moshav Hamra, halfway between Jericho and Beit She'an. Both Hamas and Fatah claim responsibility for the attack.

February 8, 2002   An Israeli is stabbed to death by four unidentified Palestinian teenagers at Jerusalem's Sherover Promenade, a scenic walkway in southern Jerusalem.

February 9, 2002   Fatah Tanzim terrorists murder an Israeli woman and injure her son in a shooting on the Trans-Samaria Highway, as they are returning to their home in the West Bank settlement of Ma'aleh Ephraim.

February 16, 2002   A PFLP suicide bomber blows himself up at a pizzeria in the shopping mall in the West Bank settlement of Karnei Shomron, killing three and wounding 30.

February 18, 2002   A woman and two Israeli soldiers trying to assist her are killed when a Palestinian terrorist opens fire on her car in Gaza. The al-Aqsa Martyrs Brigades claims responsibility for the attack.

February 22, 2002   An Israeli is killed by terrorists in a drive-by shooting on the Atarot-to-Givat Ze'ev road north of Jerusalem. The al-Aqsa Martyrs Brigades claims responsibility for the attack.

February 25, 2002   Two are killed in a terrorist shooting attack between the West Bank settlements of Tekoa and Nokdim, south of Bethlehem. In another incident, an Israeli is killed and eight others wounded when a terrorist opens fire at a bus stop in northern Jerusalem. The al-Aqsa Martyrs Brigades claims responsibility for both attacks.

February 27, 2002   An Israeli is shot and killed by one of his Palestinian employees in a factory in the Atarot industrial area, north of Jerusalem. Two Fatah groups issue a joint statement taking responsibility for the murder.

March 2, 2002   Eleven people are killed and over 50 injured in a suicide bombing in Jerusalem near a synagogue during bar mitzvah celebrations. An al-Aqsa Martyrs Brigades terrorist detonates the bomb next to a group of women and babies waiting outside the synagogue for their husbands.

March 5, 2002   An al-Aqsa Martyrs Brigades terrorist opens fires on two adjacent restaurants in Tel Aviv, killing three and wounding over 30. In a second incident, a woman is killed and her husband injured in a shooting attack on the Bethlehem bypass road south of Jerusalem. The al-Aqsa Martyrs Brigades claims responsibility for the attack. In a third incident on this day, an Islamic Jihad suicide bomber detonates explosives in a bus as it enters the Afula central bus station, killing one.

March 7, 2002   Five Israeli teens are killed and 23 others wounded when a Hamas terrorist infiltrates the Gaza settlement of Atzmona, opens fires in all directions, and throws grenades before being shot dead by soldiers.

March 9, 2002   Two al-Aqsa Martyrs Brigades terrorists open fire and throw grenades at cars and pedestrians outside and then inside the lobby of a hotel in Netanya, killing two and injuring 50. They are killed by a border policeman. Also on this day, a Hamas suicide bomber explodes in a crowded cafe in downtown Jerusalem, near the prime minister's home, killing 11 and injuring 54.

March 12, 2002   Two Hezbollah terrorists, disguised in Israeli army uniforms, open fire after ambushing Israeli vehicles traveling between Shlomi and Kibbutz Metzuba near the northern border with Lebanon, killing six and wounding seven. In another incident, an Israeli building contractor is killed and another Israeli injured in a shooting attack by Tanzim terrorists near Kiryat Sefer in Samaria.

March 17, 2002   An al-Aqsa Martyrs Brigades terrorist opens fire on passersby in the center of the Israeli town of Kfar Saba, killing an 18-year-old girl and injuring 16.

March 20, 2002   An Islamic Jihad suicide bomb on a public bus on the Wadi Arava road near Afula kills seven and wounds 30.

March 21, 2002   An al-Aqsa Martyrs Brigades terrorist and former Palestinian Authority police officer detonates a suicide bomb outside a cafe in the center of a crowd of shoppers in Jerusalem, killing three and injuring 86.

March 24, 2002   A woman is killed in a drive-by shooting northwest of Ramallah. In another incident, an Israeli man is killed in a terrorist shooting south of Hebron. Both attacks are carried out by al-Aqsa Martyrs Brigades terrorists.

March 27, 2002   A Hamas suicide bomber enters the Park Hotel in Netanya while the security guard is on a break and detonates himself in the dining room as guests are in the midst of a Passover service, killing 29 people and injuring 140.

March 28, 2002   Reacting to the Passover attack and other provocations, the Israeli army advances into Ramallah and seizes the compound of Arafat, who is inside it at the time. Israel demands that Arafat turn over the PFLP terrorists responsible for the October 2001 murder of Israeli cabinet minister Rechavam Zeevi, who are in the compound under his protection. The army seizes weapons and arrests other suspected terrorists in Ramallah and then does the same in other towns under Arafat's jurisdiction—Bethlehem, Tulkarem, Nablus, and Jenin. The confinement of Arafat lasts until May 1, when he is released as the result of a compromise proposed by the U.S. The PFLP terrorists are placed in a Palestinian Authority jail in Jericho under the inspection of U.S. and British wardens.

March 28, 2002   Four members of a family—a couple, son, and grandfather—are shot to death by a Hamas terrorist who enters their home in the West Bank settlement of Elon Moreh.

March 29, 2002   Two Israelis are killed when an Islamic Jihad terrorist infiltrates the Netzarim Jewish settlement in the Gaza Strip by cutting through the fence. The terrorist hides in the synagogue and stabs to death the first two worshippers who enter the next morning. The terrorist is eventually shot dead by an Israeli security man. In a second incident, in Jerusalem, two Israelis are killed and 28 people injured when a female suicide bomber blows herself up in a supermarket. The al-Aqsa Martyrs Brigades claims responsibility for the attack.

March 30, 2002   One Israeli is killed and about 24 injured when a suicide bomber detonates an explosive device in a cafe in downtown Tel Aviv. The al-Aqsa Martyrs Brigades claims responsibility.

March 31, 2002   Fourteen people are killed and over 40 injured in a suicide bombing by Hamas in a Haifa restaurant.

April 2, 2002   In a further response to the attack on a group celebrating Passover, tanks move into the West Bank city of Bethlehem. Palestinian terrorists, including 13 on Israel's most wanted list, and a number of civilians seek refuge in the Church of the Nativity, the Christian shrine in Bethlehem. The Israeli army surrounds the compound, demanding that those inside give themselves up, but the Palestinians refuse. After negotiations lasting five weeks, the remaining Palestinians leave on May 10 and those who are wanted fugitives are allowed safe passage to other countries.

April 10, 2002   Eight Israelis are killed and 22 people injured in a suicide bombing on a bus en route from Haifa to Jerusalem, which explodes near Kibbutz Yagur, east of Haifa. The Hamas suicide bomber, from the Jenin refugee camp, boarded the bus disguised as an Israeli soldier.

April 12, 2002   A border policeman is killed and three Palestinian workers are injured when a Palestinian Islamic Jihad gunman, posing as a worker en route to Israel, opens fire near the Erez crossing in the Gaza Strip. Meanwhile in Jerusalem, a female al-Aqsa Martyrs Brigades suicide bomber detonates her explosives near the entrance to the Mahane Yehuda market, killing six and wounding 104.

April 15, 2002   Marwan Barghouti, Fatah's leader of the West Bank, commander of Tanzim, and founder of the al-Aqsa Martyrs Brigades, is captured by an elite Israeli army unit in Ramallah, near Arafat's presidential compound. He is tried and convicted in June 2004 for causing the deaths of five people and sentenced to life imprisonment.

April 27, 2002   Two Hamas terrorists disguised as Israeli soldiers infiltrate the settlement of Adora, near Hebron, and begin shooting residents, killing four and injuring seven before being killed themselves by soldiers.

May 7, 2002 A Hamas suicide bomber detonates a powerful bomb in a crowded billiards hall in Rishon LeZion, Israel, killing 15 and wounding more than 50.

May 19, 2002 Three people are killed and 59 injured when a suicide bomber, disguised as a soldier, blows himself up in a market in Netanya. Both Hamas and the PFLP take responsibility for the attack.

May 19, 2002 The second-in-command of the PFLP-GC, Jihad Jibril, chief of operations and son of the organization's leader, Ahmed Jibril, is killed by a car bomb in Beirut. An unknown group calling itself the Movement of Lebanese Nationalists takes responsibility for the bombing.

May 22, 2002 Two people are killed and about 40 wounded when a suicide bomber detonates his explosives in a downtown pedestrian mall in Rishon LeZion.

May 27, 2002 A grandmother and her infant granddaughter are killed and 37 people injured when a suicide bomber sets off his explosives near an ice cream parlor in Petah Tiqva near Tel Aviv. The al-Aqsa Martyrs Brigades claims responsibility for the attack.

May 28, 2002 An al-Aqsa Martyrs Brigades terrorist kills a man by firing at the car in which he is traveling on the Ramallah bypass road. That same day, another al-Aqsa Martyrs Brigades gunman infiltrates the Jewish settlement of Itamar near Nablus and opens fire on a group of teenagers playing basketball, killing three and wounding two. The terrorist is shot dead by a security guard.

June 5, 2002 Seventeen people are killed and 38 injured when a car packed with explosives hits a bus traveling from Tel Aviv to Tiberias at the Megiddo Junction near Afula. Islamic Jihad claims responsibility for the attack.

June 6, 2002 An Israeli high school student dies of gunshot wounds after an al-Aqsa Martyrs Brigades terrorist opens fire near the Jewish settlement of Ofra.

June 8, 2002 Three Israelis are killed by Hamas terrorists who infiltrate the Karmei Tzur settlement in the West Bank. One terrorist is killed and the other is wounded, but still manages to escape.

June 11, 2002 A 14-year-old girl is killed and 15 others are wounded when an al-Aqsa Martyrs Brigades suicide bomber sets off a pipe bomb at a fast-food restaurant in Herzliya, near Tel Aviv.

June 16, 2002 Israel begins work on a security fence designed to block Palestinian terrorists from entering Israel. The first phase of the fence separates the towns of Jenin, Tulkarem, and Kalkilya from Israeli cities. The route is controversial, as it walls off sections of the West Bank from Palestinians. A number of changes are made to reduce the size of the area incorporated by the wall based on court cases filed by Israelis and Palestinians as well as by U.S. suggestions. Construction proceeds slowly, but in areas where the fence is completed the number of terrorist attacks declines sharply.

June 18, 2002	A Hamas suicide bomber kills 19 and injures 74 in south Jerusalem when he detonates a nail-studded bomb on a packed bus.
June 19, 2002	In Jerusalem, an al-Aqsa Martyrs Brigades suicide bomber jumps out of a car, runs into the concrete shelter of a bus stop, and detonates the explosive device he is wearing, killing six persons and wounding 43 others, including two U.S. citizens.
June 20, 2002	A PFLP terrorist infiltrates the West Bank settlement of Itamar and shoots dead five people, including a mother and three of her children. Two other children are wounded.
June 21, 2002	A Palestinian is killed when armed Jewish settlers from Itamar, returning from funerals after the June 20 attack on their community, go on a violent rampage in the streets of Hawara village near Nablus.
July 4, 2002	An Egyptian residing in the United States opens fire at the El Al Airlines ticket counter in Los Angeles International Airport, killing two people and wounding four before being shot dead by an airlines security guard. The terrorist, Hesham Mohamed Hadayet, appears to have acted alone.
July 16, 2002	A bus traveling from Jerusalem to the West Bank settlement of Emmanuel is hit by an explosive charge and gunfire from Hamas terrorists waiting in ambush, killing nine passengers and wounding 20.
July 17, 2002	Five people are killed—two Israeli and three foreign workers—and about 40 injured in a double suicide bombing in a central Tel Aviv neighborhood. The terrorists detonate their explosives in an outdoor area mostly frequented by foreign workers. Islamic Jihad claims responsibility for the attack, but Fatah may also have been responsible.
July 23, 2002	The head of the Hamas military wing Izz a-Din el-Kassam, Salah Shehadeh, is killed along with his wife, daughter, and a bodyguard when an Israeli missile is fired into his Gaza City home.
July 25, 2002	Al-Aqsa Martyrs Brigades terrorists kill an Israeli rabbi after firing at a car driving on the road between the West Bank settlements of Alei Zahav and Peduel, near Kalkilya.
July 26, 2002	Four Israelis are killed in an ambush on two Israeli cars near the Palestinian village of Yatta, south of Hebron. Al-Aqsa Martyrs Brigades is responsible.
July 30, 2002	Two Israeli brothers, who sell diesel fuel to residents of Palestinian villages, are shot to death in a Palestinian village near Ariel. Al-Aqsa Martyrs Brigades terrorists are responsible.
July 31, 2002	A bomb hidden in a handbag that is placed on a table at an international student center in Hebrew University in Jerusalem detonates, killing nine persons, including five U.S. citizens, and wounding approximately 87 others. Hamas claims responsibility.

August 1, 2002   An Israeli man, his hands and feet bound, is found shot to death in an industrial zone near Tulkarem.

August 4, 2002   An al-Aqsa Martyrs Brigades terrorist opens fire on a phone company car near Jerusalem's Old City, killing an Israeli and a Palestinian before being shot to death by Israeli security officials. Also on this day, nine people are killed and 50 wounded in a Hamas suicide bombing of a bus traveling from Haifa to Safed at the Meron Junction in northern Israel.

August 5, 2002   Al-Aqsa Martyrs Brigades terrorists open fire on a car on the main road between Ramallah and Nablus, killing an Israeli couple and wounding two of their children.

August 10, 2002   An al-Aqsa Martyrs Brigades terrorist infiltrates Moshav Mechora in the Jordan Valley where he fatally shoots a mother of two and wounds her husband before being shot dead himself.

September 18, 2002   An elderly Israeli man is murdered near el-Azzariya, a Palestinian village close to the West Bank settlement of Ma'ale Adumim, after having gone with Palestinian workers to buy housing materials. Three al-Aqsa Martyrs Brigades terrorists are found responsible. Also in the West Bank, an al-Aqsa Martyrs Brigades terrorist ambushes a vehicle on the Mevo Dotan-to-Hermesh Road, killing an Israeli and wounding a Romanian worker. In a third incident, at a bus stop at the Um el Fahem Junction, a police sergeant is killed and three people are wounded in an Islamic Jihad suicide bombing.

September 19, 2002   Islamic Jihad and Hamas both claim responsibility for a bomb on a bus in downtown Tel Aviv that kills six and wounds about 70.

September 19, 2002   In response to the spate of terrorist attacks, the Israeli military surrounds and besieges Arafat's compound in Ramallah. The siege is lifted on September 30.

September 23, 2002   A Palestinian gunman opens fire on a crowd celebrating the Jewish holiday of Sukkot in Hebron, killing an Israeli man and wounding three of his children.

October 6, 2002   A Palestinian man is shot dead and another man wounded by Jewish settlers near the West Bank village of Akraba, next to Nablus.

October 8, 2002   Hamas terrorists kill an Israeli motorist near the Zif Junction south of Hebron.

October 10, 2002   One Israeli is killed and about 30 people are wounded when a Hamas suicide bomber blows himself up while trying to board a bus near Bar-Ilan University outside Tel Aviv.

October 21, 2002   An Islamic Jihad suicide bomber driving a jeep explodes his vehicle as a bus en route from Kiryat Shemona to Tel Aviv stops along the Wadi Arava road near Hadera, killing 14 people and wounding 50.

October 27, 2002   Three Israeli soldiers are killed and about 20 people wounded as they try to prevent a Hamas suicide bombing at a gas station in the West Bank settlement of Ariel.

October 29, 2002   A Palestinian terrorist infiltrates the West Bank settlement of Hermesh, near Jenin, killing a woman and two 14-year-old girls and wounding three.

November 4, 2002   Two people are killed and about 70 wounded in an Islamic Jihad suicide bombing at a shopping mall in Kfar Sava in central Israel.

November 6, 2002   Two Israelis are killed and at least one wounded when a Hamas gunman opens fire on agriculture workers in the Gush Katif settlement in Gaza, before being shot by a settlement security officer.

November 10, 2002   Al-Aqsa Martyrs Brigades terrorists infiltrate Kibbutz Metzer in northern Israel and gun down five people, including two children, and then escape. Ironically, the kibbutz is known for its emphasis on peaceful coexistence with its Arab neighbors.

November 15, 2002   Islamic Jihad terrorists in Hebron open fire and throw grenades at a group of Jewish worshippers and their guards as they are walking home from prayers at the Cave of the Patriarchs, killing 12 people—nine soldiers and three civilians—and wounding 15. The three terrorists are also killed in a shoot-out.

November 18, 2002   An Israeli mother of seven is killed by an al-Aqsa Martyrs Brigades terrorist near Rimonim, a Jewish settlement in the West Bank.

November 21, 2002   A Hamas suicide bomber detonates explosives on a Jerusalem bus, killing 11 persons and wounding 50.

November 28, 2002   Al-Aqsa Martyrs Brigades terrorists attack the Likud Party headquarters in Beit She'an as members are voting in party primaries, killing six and wounding 43.

November 28, 2002   Near Mombasa, Kenya, 13—three Israelis and ten Kenyans—are killed and about 80 people injured when a car bomb explodes in the lobby of the Israeli-owned Paradise Hotel. Also on that day, two missiles are fired at an Israeli Arkia airplane taking off from Mombasa airport en route to Israel, but they cause no damage or injuries. Al-Qaeda is responsible for both attacks.

December 2, 2002   A Palestinian is killed and nine others are injured when Islamic Jihad terrorists fire two mortars at the Erez industrial zone in the Gaza Strip.

December 20, 2002   A rabbi is killed in the Gaza Strip after his car is ambushed by Islamic Jihad terrorists.

December 27, 2002   An Islamic Jihad terrorist infiltrates the Otniel yeshiva in the West Bank and kills four Israelis before being shot to death by soldiers.

January 2, 2003   The body of an Israeli from the Lower Galilee is found in the northern Jordan Valley in his burned-out car. Al-Aqsa Martyrs Brigades claims responsibility for the murder.

January 5, 2003   Twenty-two people are killed and about 120 wounded in a double suicide bombing near the old central bus station in Tel Aviv. The attack was likely committed jointly by Islamic Jihad and Hamas and also possibly included the al-Aqsa Martyrs Brigades.

January 12, 2003   Two Islamic Jihad terrorists infiltrate Moshav Gadish, near Afula, and fatally shoot one resident before being shot dead by two border policemen.

January 18, 2003   Hamas gunmen infiltrate an outpost near the Jewish settlement of Kiryat Arba and kill one Israeli and injure three others, before being killed themselves in a gun battle with residents and security forces.

February 20, 2003   U.S. officials arrest University of Southern Florida computer engineering professor Sami Al-Arian at his home in Tampa and charge him with being a financial planner and a chief U.S. fund-raiser for Palestinian Islamic Jihad.

March 5, 2003   Seventeen people are killed and 53 wounded in a Hamas suicide bombing of a bus in Haifa.

March 7, 2003   Hamas gunmen, disguised as religious Jews, infiltrate the West Bank settlement of Kiryat Arba and murder a couple in their home.

March 19, 2003   An Israeli is shot and killed while driving in his car between Mevo Dotan and Shaked in northern Samaria. Al-Aqsa Martyrs Brigades claims responsibility for the attack.

April 15, 2003   A Hamas gunman opens fire and throws grenades at the Karni border crossing between Israel and the Gaza Strip, killing two Palestinians and wounding four Israelis before soldiers shoot the assailant.

April 16, 2003   Abu al-Abbas, the mastermind of the *Achille Lauro* hijacking, is arrested on the outskirts of Baghdad by U.S. Special Forces. U.S. troops are invading Iraq as a part of the country's war on terror.

April 24, 2003   A security guard from Bat Yam is killed as he tries to prevent a suicide attack outside a train station in Kfar Sava in which 13 are wounded. The Fatah al-Aqsa Martyrs Brigades and PFLP claim joint responsibility for the attack.

April 30, 2003   Three people are killed and about 60 people are wounded when a suicide bomber blows himself up at a beachfront pub near the U.S. Embassy in Tel Aviv. The Fatah Tanzim and Hamas claim responsibility for the attack, carried out as a joint operation, which also involved two British Muslims.

May 4, 2003   The body of an Israeli woman is discovered in a garage in Rosh Ha'ayin with numerous stab wounds. The victim's boyfriend, an Arab resident of Kfar Qasem, is believed to have carried out the murder as part of a "loyalty test" administered by Palestinian terrorist organizations.

May 5, 2003   Al-Aqsa Martyrs Brigades terrorists open fire on an Israeli vehicle near Shvut Rachel, in Samaria, killing one Israeli and wounding his six-year-old and a soldier.

May 11, 2003   An Israeli motorist is killed by Palestinians in a roadside ambush near the Jewish settlement of Ofra. Both Fatah and the PFLP claim responsibility for the attack.

May 16, 2003   Five suicide bomb attacks against a series of Jewish targets in Casablanca, Morocco, kill 40 people and wound 65. Those targets include a hotel, Jewish community center, Jewish-owned Italian restaurant, and a Spanish club. Al-Qaeda is believed to be behind the attacks.

May 17, 2003   An Israeli couple strolling in Hebron is killed by a Hamas suicide bomber.

May 18, 2003   A Hamas suicide bomber, disguised as a Jewish religious student, kills seven and wounds 20 on a Jerusalem bus.

May 19, 2003   Three people are killed and about 70 wounded in a suicide bombing at the entrance to a mall in Afula. The Islamic Jihad and the al-Aqsa Martyrs Brigades both claim responsibility for the attack in which the bomber is a woman.

June 8, 2003   Four Israelis are killed and four other are wounded when three gunmen from the al-Aqsa Martyrs Brigades, disguised as Israeli solders, open fire near the Erez checkpoint in the northern Gaza Strip.

June 11, 2003   A Hamas suicide bomber enters a bus in downtown Jerusalem, then detonates explosives, killing 17 and wounding over 100.

June 12, 2003   Al-Aqsa Martyrs Brigades terrorists fatally shoot an Israeli motorist in a northern West Bank town.

June 17, 2003   A seven-year-old Israeli girl is killed and her five-year-old sister seriously wounded in a shooting attack near the Kibbutz Eyal junction on the Trans-Israel Highway near Kalkilya. The al-Aqsa Martyrs Brigades and PFLP claim responsibility.

June 19, 2003   An Islamic Jihad suicide bomber blows up in a grocery at Moshav Sde Trumot, south of Beit She'an, killing one.

June 20, 2003   A Hamas ambush of an Israeli car near the West Bank settlement of Ofra results in the death of one and wounding of three.

June 26, 2003   An Israeli is killed in a shooting attack in the Israeli Arab town of Baka al-Garbiyeh by an al-Aqsa Martyrs Brigades terrorist.

June 30, 2003   Al-Aqsa Martyrs Brigades terrorists shoot at a truck in the West Bank village of Yabed, killing a Bulgarian construction worker.

July 7, 2003   An Islamic Jihad terrorist kills a 65-year-old woman in Moshav Kfar Yavetz near Netanya by setting off his explosives in her kitchen.

July 15, 2003   An Israeli man is killed and two others wounded when an al-Aqsa Martyrs Brigades terrorist armed with a knife stabs passersby on Tel Aviv's beachfront promenade, close to Jaffa. He is finally apprehended by a civilian who grabs a security guard's gun and chases him.

August 10, 2003	An Israeli teenager is killed and five Israelis are injured when Hezbollah terrorists in southern Lebanon fire shells into the northern Israeli border town of Shlomi.
August 12, 2003	An al-Aqsa Martyrs Brigades suicide bomber detonates in a supermarket in Rosh Ha'ayin, a suburb of Tel Aviv, killing one and wounding ten. Also on this day, a Hamas bomber detonates his explosives at a bus stop in the West Bank settlement of Ariel, killing one and wounding two.
August 19, 2003	Twenty-three people are killed and over 130 wounded when a suicide bomber detonates himself on a bus in Jerusalem. Islamic Jihad claims responsibility for the attack, but Israeli security sources says the bomber is a member of Hamas.
August 29, 2003	An Israeli motorist is killed in a shooting attack northeast of Ramallah by al-Aqsa Martyrs Brigades terrorists.
September 9, 2003	A Hamas suicide bomber kills nine soldiers and wounds 30 people after blowing himself up at a hitchhiking post for soldiers outside a main entrance to the Tzrifin army base and Assaf Harofeh hospital near Rishon LeZion. On the same day in Jerusalem, 15 people, including a dual U.S.-Israeli citizen, are killed and 50 injured by a Hamas suicide bomber at a cafe. Several customers become suspicious of the young man as he tries to enter the restaurant. When they try to shove him out, he blows himself up.
September 11, 2003	A Moroccan Jew is shot dead near his shop in Casablanca, Morocco, by two terrorists. On November 24, 2003, a former policeman is sentenced to 20 years in jail for the murder, while eight co-defendants receive sentences ranging from two to 15 years.
September 26, 2003	An Islamic Jihad terrorist infiltrates the West Bank Jewish settlement of Negohot and kills two residents before being killed.
October 4, 2003	A female suicide bomber from Islamic Jihad detonates a bomb in the middle of a busy restaurant in Haifa, killing 22 people, including four children, and wounding over 60. The bomber is identified as an apprentice lawyer from the West Bank city of Jenin whose brother and a cousin, both Islamic Jihad militants, were killed in June in a gunfight with Israeli troops. The Haifa restaurant, jointly owned by an Israeli Arab family and a Jewish family, had been a model of peaceful coexistence.
October 15, 2003	Terrorists in the Gaza Strip ambush and then detonate a bomb near a U.S. diplomatic convoy, killing three Americans who are providing security. The convoy is transporting U.S. officials to interview Palestinian candidates for Fulbright scholarships. Four Palestinians are arrested and charged, but a Palestinian Authority court orders their release due to insufficient evidence.
November 15, 2003	In Istanbul, Turkey, 23 people are killed and 300 injured in consecutive suicide car bomb attacks on the Neve Shalom and Beth Israel synagogues during Shabbat services. The two bombers are Turkish nationals with links to al-Qaeda. One suspect, believed to have been one of the leaders, is arrested in

Turkey in November 2003 as he is trying to flee to Iran, and is subsequently charged with treason.

November 19, 2003

A Jordanian gunman opens fire on a group of Ecuadorian tourists as they cross the border from Jordan into Eilat, Israel, killing one and wounding five. Israeli security guards kill the gunman.

November 22, 2003

Palestinian gunmen kill two private security guards at a construction site in East Jerusalem. The Jenin Martyrs Brigades, affiliated with Fatah, claims responsibility for the attack.

December 25, 2003

Four Israelis are killed and over 20 people wounded in a suicide bombing at a bus stop at the Geha Junction, east of Tel Aviv. The PFLP claims responsibility for the attack.

January 13, 2004

An Israeli motorist is shot dead and three of his passengers are wounded when their car is fired upon by terrorists near Talmon, west of Ramallah. The al-Aqsa Martyrs Brigades claims responsibility for the attack.

January 14, 2004

A female suicide bomber detonates a bomb at the Erez crossing in the Gaza Strip killing four—three soldiers and one civilian—and wounding ten. Hamas and the al-Aqsa Martyrs Brigades claim joint responsibility for the attack.

January 29, 2004

Eleven people are killed and over 50 wounded in a suicide bombing of a bus in Jerusalem. The bomber, Ali Yusuf Jaara, a Palestinian policeman from Bethlehem, is a member of the al-Aqsa Martyrs Brigades.

February 22, 2004

A suicide bomber blows himself up on a bus in the center of Jerusalem, killing eight people and wounding 70. The al-Aqsa Martyrs Brigades claims responsibility.

March 14, 2004

Two Palestinian suicide bombers blow themselves up in the Israeli seaport of Ashdod, killing ten Israelis and wounding 18. The al-Aqsa Martyrs Brigades and Hamas claim joint responsibility.

March 22, 2004

After leaving a mosque in Gaza following morning prayers, Hamas leader Sheikh Ahmad Yassin is killed by missiles fired at his car by Israeli air force helicopters. Seven bodyguards, reportedly including Yassin's son, are also killed.

April 17, 2004

After just 25 days as the new leader of Hamas, Abdel Aziz Rantissi is assassinated by Israeli helicopter gunships in Gaza along with one of his sons and a bodyguard. He is being driven through a central thoroughfare near his home when the car in which he is traveling is struck by rockets.

April 17, 2004

A suicide attack at the Erez crossing in Gaza results in the death of one border guard and injury of three others. The attack is jointly claimed by Hamas and Fatah.

May 2, 2004

An Israeli woman and her four daughters are killed when two Palestinian terrorists fire on her car at the entrance to the Gaza Strip settlement bloc of Gush Katif. Fatah and Islamic Jihad claim joint responsibility for the attack.

May 30, 2004	An Israeli Apache helicopter fires two rockets at a motorcycle in Gaza City, killing Wael Nassar, head of Izz al-Din el-Kassam, Hamas' military wing, his assistant, and a bystander.
June 21, 2004	A Thai worker is killed after being hit by shrapnel from a mortar fired into greenhouses in Kfar Darom in the Gaza Strip. Hamas claims responsibility for the attack.
June 28, 2004	A Kassam rocket fired by Hamas terrorists in the Gaza Strip strikes a nursery school in the northern Negev town of Sderot, killing two Israelis.
July 11, 2004	A bomb explodes next to a Tel Aviv bus stop, killing one woman and injuring 32. The al-Aqsa Martyrs Brigades claims responsibility for the attack.
August 12, 2004	A Fatah Tanzim terrorist detonates an explosive device amidst a crowd of Palestinians waiting at a checkpoint in Kalandiyah, located between Jerusalem and Ramallah, killing two Palestinian civilians and injuring 12 Palestinians and six Israeli border guards.
August 13, 2004	An al-Aqsa Martyrs Brigades terrorist kills one Israeli after firing outside the Jewish settlement of Itamar in Samaria.
August 31, 2004	In two separate incidents, Hamas suicide bombers detonate explosives on two commuter buses in Beersheba in southern Israel, killing at least 16 people and injuring more than 80.
September 22, 2004	Two Israeli policemen are killed and 17 Israelis wounded in a suicide bombing carried out by a female terrorist at a hitchhiking post in northern Jerusalem. The al-Aqsa Martyrs Brigades claims responsibility for the attack.
September 24, 2004	A mortar strike by Hamas on the Gush Katif Jewish settlements in Gaza kills one.
September 29, 2004	Two Israeli infants are killed and 20 injured when a Kassam rocket fired by Hamas in Gaza hits the Israeli town of Sderot.
September 30, 2004	Hamas terrorists kill an Israeli jogger and a soldier who tries to help her in the Jewish settlement of Nissanit in the Gaza Strip. The terrorists are killed by soldiers.
October 6, 2004	A greenhouse worker from Thailand is killed when Hamas terrorists infiltrate the hothouse area of Kfar Darom in the Gaza Strip.
October 7, 2004	Two car bombs detonate at the Hilton Hotel in Taba, Egypt, killing 29 people. Soon after, two more bombs detonate at Ras al-Shaitan, a camping area south of Taba, killing three. Both sites are popular with Israeli tourists, many of whom were visiting over a Jewish holiday period. Israeli security officials believe al-Qaeda is responsible for the attack.
October 21, 2004	A mission strike launch by the Israeli army in Gaza kills a top Hamas military wing terrorist, Adnan al-Ghoul, and his deputy.

October 29, 2004   Having fallen seriously ill, Yasir Arafat is airlifted out of Ramallah to Paris to receive medical treatment.

November 1, 2004   An explosion goes off in the open-air market of Tel Aviv, killing four people. The PFLP claims responsibility.

November 11, 2004   Arafat dies in Paris.

November 12, 2004   A memorial service is held for Arafat in Cairo followed by his burial in Ramallah.

January 11, 2005   Hamas fires three mortar shells at the Jewish settlement of Nissanit and also at the Erez crossing, injuring two, one of whom later dies of his wounds.

January 13, 2005   Two suicide bombers—one from Hamas, the other from the al-Aqsa Martyrs Brigades—kill six Israelis and wound five others at the Karni crossing between Israel and the Gaza Strip.

January 15, 2005   Two Kassam rockets are fired by Hamas terrorists at the Israeli town of Sderot, killing one and wounding three others. The same day, at the Kissufim crossing in Gaza, the PFLP and Islamic Jihad are responsible for killing two after attacking cars belonging to Jewish settlers.

February 25, 2005   An Islamic Jihad suicide bomber kills five Israelis and wounds 50 others after detonating explosives outside a Tel Aviv nightclub.

June 7, 2005   Islamic Jihad terrorists fire mortars at the Jewish settlement of Ganey Tal in Gaza, killing three laborers working on the greenhouse—one Chinese and two Palestinians—and wounding five Palestinian workers.

June 20, 2005   Islamic Jihad terrorists ambush a vehicle in the West Bank, killing one settler and wounding the other.

June 24, 2005   Both Fatah and Islamic Jihad terrorists fire on Israelis at a hitchhiking post near Hebron, killing two Israelis and wounding three others.

July 12, 2005   An Islamic Jihad suicide bomber detonates explosives outside a shopping mall in Netanya, killing two and wounding 30 others, three of whom later die of their wounds.

July 14, 2005   A woman is killed after al-Aqsa Martyrs Brigades terrorists fire four rockets at a kibbutz near the Gaza Strip.

July 23, 2005   Gunmen fire on a convoy of Israeli vehicles on a main road connecting the Gaza Strip with Israel, killing two Israelis and wounding five others. The attack is jointly claimed by Islamic Jihad and the al-Aqsa Martyrs Brigades.

August 4, 2005   A 19-year-old Israeli soldier, Eden Natan-Zada, opens fire on Arab-Israeli passengers of a bus as it is entering the Arab town of Shfaram, killing four and wounding 13 others. Natan-Zada is beaten to death by an angry mob.

September 7, 2005	Palestinian presidential security advisor Moussa Arafat is shot to death and run over by a car after some 80 gunmen storm his home in Gaza City. The Popular Resistance Committee, a terrorist group comprised of former Fatah, Hamas, and Islamic Jihad members and security officials, claims responsibility, saying that Arafat was targeted because of personal corruption.
September 12, 2005	Israel completes its military withdrawal from the Gaza Strip, ending 38 years of rule there.
September 21, 2005	An Israeli candy manufacturer is kidnapped in East Jerusalem by two Hamas terrorists who had once worked for him. Five days later his dead body is found in Bitunya, West Bank.
October 16, 2005	Al-Aqsa Martyrs Brigades terrorists kill three Israelis and wound five others in two different shootings of motorists in the West Bank.
October 26, 2005	An Islamic Jihad suicide bomber detonates himself near a food stand in Hadera, Israel, killing six and wounding 26.
December 5, 2005	A suicide bomber from Islamic Jihad kills at least five people outside a shopping center in Netanya, Israel.
January 26, 2006	Hamas claims a majority in the Palestinian Legislative Council, defeating the longtime ruler, Fatah. They will go on to appoint a Hamas prime minister.
March 30, 2006	A suicide bomber from the al-Aqsa Martyrs Brigades kills himself and four others at the Kedumim Junction in the West Bank.
April 17, 2006	A Palestinian suicide bomber detonates an explosive device in Tel Aviv, killing nine and injuring 40. The Islamic Jihad and al-Aqsa Martyrs Brigades both claim responsibility for the attack.
June 25, 2006	An 18-year-old Israeli student is kidnapped by members of the Popular Resistance Committee while he is hitchhiking in the West Bank. His dead body is found four days later.
July 12, 2006	Two Israeli soldiers are kidnapped by Hezbollah terrorists who cross into Israel from Lebanon. Israel calls the kidnapping an act of war and launches a military operation in Lebanon with bombings. Hezbollah in turn fires thousands of rockets into Israel. On August 14, 2006, a cease-fire begins.

7

Radical Islamist Terrorism

Islam has existed for almost 1,400 years, but it is only in the last 70 that a radical Islamist political philosophy has arisen. While supporters of this ideology maintain that they provide the correct interpretation of their religion, such groups have remained a minority that uses an arguably selective reading of Islamic texts and a set of goals and tactics never before practiced in their religion. While using elements of traditional Islamic thought, radical Islamism and the terrorism it espouses is a reaction to the dislocations of modern times, the impact of Western ideas, and the perceived failure of other political philosophies in places where Muslims live.

The father of this radical philosophy is Hasan al-Banna, an Egyptian political leader and founder of the Muslim Brotherhood in 1929, whose writings continue to inspire Islamists. Al-Banna was assassinated 20 years later by political enemies and President Gamal Abdel Nasser suppressed the Muslim Brotherhood after it tried to assassinate him.

Al-Banna's work was carried on by Sayyid Qutb, who developed the concept that contemporary society, even in Muslim countries, is comparable to the pre-Islamic era of *jahiliyya* and thus requires a revolution to make it properly Islamic. The definition of *jihad* is interpreted as requiring all Muslims to wage holy war against non-Muslims and against states with Muslim populations deemed to be in a state of *jahiliyya*. Qutb was executed by the Egyptian government in 1966.

During the 1950s and 1960s, and well into the 1970s, incipient Islamist movements were eclipsed politically and largely suppressed altogether by Arab nationalist regimes. The turning point came in 1979, when Iranian Islamists took the leading role in overthrowing the shah and established what they called an Islamist state. The Iranian Revolution had the same effect on radical Islamists that the Russian Revolution had on leftist revolutionaries in the West and Nasser's 1952 revolution in Egypt had on Arab nationalists. It galvanized their cause, seeming to provide a set of ideas and tactics, and to offer backing for Islamist movements elsewhere.

Ayatollah Ruhollah Khomeini, the leader of Iran's revolution and the new state that emerged, conceived of Islam as a revolutionary religion, in contrast to mainstream Islam, which was politically passive and usually supported rulers if they were Muslims. Khomeini insisted that Islam must be in direct political power and must set the norms for all aspects of society. He also advocated the idea, hitherto considered literally heretical, that many people who professed to be Muslim are in fact traitors who deserve to be killed.

In addition to developing an Islamist political philosophy, set of tactics, and a new type of regime, Khomeini also had a major impact in Islamic thinking on international affairs. He preached that everyone must take part in the worldwide struggle between the forces of Islam and those of corrupt materialism, not only in the West but also in the Arab world. Iran's revolution also convinced many that an otherwise all-powerful America could be defeated by a revolutionary Islamist movement. In 1979, Khomeini's followers seized the U.S. Embassy in Tehran and held employees there hostage for 444 days. This event seemed to show the weakness of a U.S. government powerless to win the confrontation or rescue its kidnapped officials.

Even so, it still took another 20 years for direct terrorism against the United States to become the basis of a new Jihadist Islamism. In the 1980s and 1990s, the main Islamist effort was to wage revolutions against Arab governments and overthrow them. During the 1980s, Iran emerged as the main state sponsor of Islamist terrorism, though its immediate clients were responsible for only a small proportion of the overall attacks. Still, Tehran's agents gunned down Iranian dissidents across the globe, its clients kidnapped or murdered Westerners in Lebanon, assassinated both Arab and Western diplomats, and waged many attacks. The Iranian regime even engaged openly in promoting terrorism by calling publicly for the murder of British author Salman Rushdie, who had written a book which they alleged defamed Islam's founder. The book also contained a devastatingly critical portrait of Khomeini himself

A second pivotal event shaping the radical Islamist movement occurred soon after the Iranian Revolution. In December 1979, Soviet armies invaded Afghanistan to keep a Communist regime in power there. That event triggered the mobilization of Muslim opposition worldwide to force a Soviet withdrawal. The Taliban group seized power and created a radical Islamist regime in Afghanistan. These events were interpreted by Islamists elsewhere as another proof that their worldview and methods could defeat even a great superpower.

Moreover, in the fighting in Afghanistan, Islamists developed military experience and a set of networks. Many of the volunteer Arab fighters returned home to foment revolutionary movements there. One of the Muslim organizers active in Afghanistan was a young man from a wealthy Saudi family, Osama bin Laden. Radical Islamist violence continued to grow in the 1990s; it spread to other countries and reached new heights.

In December 1991, the government in Algeria decided to cancel parliamentary elections when it became apparent that an Islamist party would win. This act triggered a wave of terrorism by Islamist forces. In the ensuing conflict, tens of thousands of people were killed. One of the main terrorist forces

that emerged was the Armed Islamic Group (GIA). In Egypt, Islamist terrorists started a revolutionary bid that included attacks on Westerners designed to undermine the nation's tourist industry. Their most spectacular attack was in November 1997, when al-Gama'a al-Islamiyya terrorists gunned down 58 tourists and four Egyptians at a popular Egyptian tourist site near Luxor. Later, however, government crackdowns in Algeria and Egypt defeated both Islamist insurgencies.

In the Philippines, a long battle to create a Muslim state in the south heated up in the 1990s, particularly with the 1991 founding of the Abu Sayyaf Group, which used terrorism to intimidate its opponents. In another part of Asia, Islamist terrorists in the disputed Jammu and Kashmir area under Indian control used terrorism to make life impossible for non-Muslims in the region. The creation of several new terrorist organizations, such as the Lashkar-e-Tayyiba (also known as Lashkar-e-Taiba, Lashkar-e-Toiba or LeT) in 1993, led to many attacks, as did the later founding of the Jaish-e-Mohammed (JEM) there.

Meanwhile, in Russia, separatists in the Russian republic of Chechnya adapted Islamist ideology and terrorist methods in the late 1990s. They also extended their attacks to other parts of Russia, believing that killing civilians might persuade Moscow to give up and grant them independence. In December 2001, a group of Chechen terrorists, including widows who had lost their husbands in the struggle with Russia, kidnapped the entire audience in a Moscow theater. A botched rescue attempt by Russian commandos led to the death of hundreds of hostages. In another wave of attacks beginning in August 2004, Chechen terrorists carried out the simultaneous bombing of two Russian airliners and a Moscow subway station and the seizure of a school in Beslan, North Ossetia, which borders Chechnya, where 100 hostages, many of them children, were killed.

By the end of the 1990s it had become clear that terrorist tactics had failed in every country to overthrow the existing regimes and bring Islamist governments to power. A new version of radical Islamist strategy, generally called Jihadist, was developed by bin Laden, who had organized al-Qaeda as an international terrorist group in 1988, though his network functioned mainly as a loose association of separate organizations. He argued for a priority on international terrorism against

Western targets rather than revolutionary activity within Muslim-majority states. These external enemies, he argued, were keeping the regimes of many Muslim countries in power. Besides, bin Laden and his colleagues claimed, putting the priority on killing non-Muslims would be more popular among their target audience than killing fellow Muslims.

Al-Qaeda came to worldwide attention after the attack on the United States on September 11, 2001. These spectacular actions—flying hijacked passenger airliners into prominent symbols of American wealth and strength, killing thousands—first made bin Laden's approach seem attractive to many radical Islamists. In the following years, however, countermeasures by the United States and its Western allies reduced the effectiveness of the Jihadist approach and may also have undermined its appeal. The United States overthrew the Taliban regime in Afghanistan and then attacked Iraq and overthrew the radical Arab nationalist government there. Afterwards, hybrid terrorist campaigns developed in both countries, led by the Taliban in Afghanistan and by al-Qaeda—in conjunction with Sunni communal movements against the Shia majority government—in Iraq.

At the same time, though, more "traditional" terrorist strategies continued and even increased in the Middle East, especially against Israel, Lebanon, and Saudi Arabia. This chapter presents Islamist attacks seeking to overthrow governments or by separatist movements in Kashmir, Chechnya, and the Philippines. Attacks on Israel are covered in Chapter 6, while the events of September 11, 2001, and Jihadist attacks directly on American and other Western targets are included in chapter 8.

1929	Hasan al-Banna creates the Muslim Brotherhood in Egypt, with branches in other countries, advocating that the entire Arab world be governed by a strict interpretation of Islam. In Egypt, the Brotherhood seeks to overthrow that country's government through a combination of organizing and violent means. A secret terrorist group is later established to carry out assassinations.
October 1947	The new countries of India and Pakistan go to war over Jammu and Kashmir, a largely Muslim-populated area whose ruler decides to join India.
May 15, 1948	A UN decision of November 1947 is implemented as Israel declares independence. Arab armies, including Muslim Brotherhood volunteers, cross the border to destroy that country. In the war, Arab forces are largely defeated but, at the end, Egypt holds the Gaza Strip and Jordan rules over the West Bank and East Jerusalem. (For a fuller account of the Arab-Israeli conflict, see chapter 6.)
December 28, 1948	In retaliation for government harassment of the movement, a Muslim Brotherhood member kills Egyptian Prime Minister Mahmoud Fahmi Nuqrashi.
January 1, 1949	A cease-fire agreement on Kashmir calls for a referendum to determine the area's future, but the vote is never held. Pakistan controls one-third and India two-thirds, but Pakistan claims the whole area.
February 12, 1949	Muslim Brotherhood founder Hasan al-Banna is gunned down in the streets of Cairo, probably by agents of King Farouk's government, which worries about the growing strength of the group.
October 16, 1951	The first prime minister of Pakistan, Liaquat Ali Khan, is shot by an assassin in Rawalpindi, Pakistan, just before giving a speech. His assassin, Saad Akbar, is captured, but his motive is never discovered.

The Era of Arab Nationalism

The 1952 coup that overthrew the monarchy in Egypt and brought Gamal Abdel Nasser to power was a big defeat for Islamist movements. Nasser's radical Arab nationalism became the dominant political philosophy in the Arab world, taking power eventually in Syria, Iraq, Algeria, and other countries. Arab nationalists and Islamists saw each other as enemies and the nationalists suppressed the Islamists with great success. In Egypt, Muslim Brotherhood leaders were executed or sent to concentration camps. Within the region and especially in Saudi Arabia, "Islam" became the political banner of conservative forces which were eager to combat and discredit Arab nationalism.

By the 1970s, however, Arab nationalist regimes had become discredited. They had failed to unite the Arab world, counter Western influence, destroy Israel, or bring rapid economic progress. Such trends as urbanization, modernization, and the influx of Western culture put tremendous strains on Arab and Iranian societies, bringing a form of culture shock. In this vacuum, Islamism arose in a more coherent and stronger form. Worship was the one activity that could not be completely controlled or closed down by the secular-oriented nationalist regimes, while conservative monarchies often fostered religious piety.

July 23, 1952 — Egyptian officers overthrow the government of King Farouk. Gamal Abdel Nasser emerges as the leader and becomes president.

October 26, 1954 — After a Muslim Brotherhood member unsuccessfully attempts to assassinate him, Egypt's President Nasser moves to destroy the organization. The group is outlawed, six Muslim Brotherhood members are executed, and hundreds of leaders and activists are imprisoned.

November 11, 1964 — Ayatollah Ruhollah Khomeini is deported from Iran a few months after making a speech condemning the dependence of the shah's regime on foreign powers. He eventually settles in France.

August 1965 — War begins when Pakistan's government launches a covert offensive across the cease-fire line into the Indian-administered Jammu and Kashmir. In early September, India invades Pakistan. After three weeks of fighting, the two sides accept an UN-sponsored cease-fire.

January 1966 — India and Pakistan sign a declaration affirming their commitment to solve their disputes through peaceful means and agree to withdraw to their pre-war positions.

August 29, 1966 — After he proclaims that Egypt under Nasser is not a true Islamic state and should be overthrown, Sayyid Qutb, the most important theorist of revolutionary Islamism, is executed along with two other top Muslim Brotherhood leaders. Many other members are imprisoned. Nasser states that his offensive against the Brotherhood is connected to another failed assassination plot against him. The group denies the charge.

June 1967 — After Nasser forces the removal of UN peacekeeping forces from the Sinai Peninsula, blocks Israeli shipping, and threatens to destroy Israel, Israeli forces launch an attack and defeat Egyptian, Syrian, and Jordanian armies. In six days of fighting, Israel captures the Sinai, the Gaza Strip, West Bank, East Jerusalem, and the Golan Heights. The failure of Arab nationalist regimes to fulfill their promises of victory is apparent.

March 22, 1968   In Thailand, the Pattani United Liberation Organization is founded. It is a nationalist-Islamic resistance movement fighting for the separation of Muslim enclaves in the south from Thailand's overwhelmingly Buddhist majority.

1971   Egyptian President Anwar Sadat begins releasing Muslim Brotherhood members from prison camps and allows a resumption of publication of its journal *al-Dawa*. He believes a growth in conservative Islam will help him against leftist rivals contesting his succession to Nasser.

1972   In the Philippines, Nur Misuari, who had formed a Muslim advocacy group in the late 1960s called the Mindanao Independence Movement, now transforms it into an armed terrorist rebel organization called the Moro National Liberation Front (MNLF). Its goal is the creation of a Muslim state in the southern Philippines. Followers of Islam make up a sizable population of the region, including the islands of Mindanao, Sulu, Basilan, Tawi-Tawi, and Palawan.

September 1973   Egyptian and Syrian forces attack Israeli forces in the Sinai and Golan Heights. At first they make gains but are then forced back by Israeli counterattacks. The war ends in three weeks with a cease-fire and Israel controlling additional territory. U.S. diplomatic efforts lead to partial Israeli withdrawals during the next two years.

April 1975   Civil war begins in Lebanon as Muslim and Druze forces combine with the Palestine Liberation Organization (PLO) to fight the Christian-led government.

June 16, 1976   Francis E. Meloy, U.S. ambassador in Lebanon, Robert O. Waring, U.S. economic counselor, and their Lebanese driver disappear at a militia checkpoint on the border between Beirut's Christian and Muslim sectors. Their bullet-riddled bodies are found in Muslim West Beirut. Two Lebanese men are convicted for this attack but are later released in a 1990 amnesty for crimes committed during Lebanon's civil war.

August 28, 1976   Three U.S. employees of Rockwell International are assassinated as they are being driven to work at an Iranian Air Force installation in Tehran. The People's Strugglers (Mujahideen-e Khalq), seeking to overthrow the shah's government, is responsible.

1977   In the Philippines, the Moro Islamic Liberation Front (MILF) is formed by the second-in-command of the Moro National Liberation Front (MNLF) after the MNLF leader signs an accord with the Filipino government giving up violence. The MILF seeks an independent Muslim state in the southern Philippines and is willing to use terrorism in its campaigns.

1977   In Egypt, an extreme Islamist splinter group from the Muslim Brotherhood, called al-Takfir Wa al-Hijra, kidnaps a moderate Islamic preacher, Sheikh Muhammad al-Dhahabi, and subsequently murders him. The group's leader, Shukri Mustafa, and 400 other members are arrested. Mustafa is tried for the crime, found guilty, and executed.

April 1977   The Student's Islamic Movement of India (SIMI) is founded in Uttar Pradesh State. The group is committed to using terrorism to make India a religious Muslim state.

November 17, 1977   A rocket attack on the Egyptian Embassy in Beirut kills a security guard and wounds two guards and six Saudi Arabian soldiers.

The Iranian Revolution and the War in Afghanistan

The revolution against Iran's shah was carried out by a widely diverse group of political forces including Islamists, liberals, and Marxists. But the charismatic role of Khomeini and the better organization of Islamist forces steered the uprising in their direction. As a successful Islamist revolution and later as a regime that openly challenged the United States, Iran had both a direct appeal as a new regional force and an indirect attraction as an example of victorious Islamism.

Still, the fact that this revolution and regime was Persian, not Arab, and Shia Muslim, not Sunni Muslim, limited its direct influence on the Arab world. Iran had its strongest links with Shia Muslim terrorist groups in Lebanon and the Persian Gulf, supplying training, money, and even direction. Islamist terrorist groups developed more independently in Algeria, Egypt, and among the Palestinians, often drawing on more militant members of the Muslim Brotherhood.

In Afghanistan, the war against the Soviets was fought largely by Islamists from a large variety of local groupings and viewpoints often operating along ethnic lines. Terrorism was also used by the Communist government in Afghanistan against opposition groups across the border in Pakistan.

In Afghanistan, the Islamist Arab volunteers had their first experiences in a revolutionary war and, after the victory, in an Islamist regime. They would return home determined to transform their own countries in a similar manner using similar methods.

Yet the Islamists were not adept at mass organizing and were handicapped in this respect by the actions of dictatorial regimes. Moreover, the majority of the population did not support them, being loyal to Arab nationalism or a more conservative, traditional brand of Islam. The doctrines of the Islamists often seemed theologically heretical—demanding that Islam be the country's directing force politically and declaring that some practicing Muslims are infidels because of their political beliefs or practices.

The radical Islamists were thus frustrated three times over. The masses did not support them, the governments repressed them, and their efforts failed. Like their European predecessors in this respect, the anarchists, radical Islamists turned to terrorism. It was simultaneously a means of revenge, a way to intimidate the rulers into surrender, and "propaganda of the deed" intended to mobilize the masses.

February 1978   Iranian Revolution begins under the charismatic leadership of the Ayatollah Ruholla Khomeini. It gathers momentum over the year, with the government gradually being taken over, especially after September, by radical Islamist forces.

January 16, 1979   The embattled shah of Iran departs his country for Egypt. He leaves a moderate nationalist opposition leader, Shapour Bakhtiar, as prime minister.

February 1979   Ayatollah Khomeini returns to Tehran from exile in Paris to a joyous and massive welcome.

February 14, 1979   U.S. Ambassador to Afghanistan Adolph Dubs is driving to work when he is abducted by a group of Afghans dressed as policeman. He is held in a hotel room in downtown Kabul as his captors demand the release of Muslim religious leaders. Afghan police, acting against U.S. requests, storm the room and engage in a shoot-out, later discovering Dubs' dead body.

March 26, 1979   A peace treaty is signed between Egypt and Israel in Washington, D.C., calling for mutual recognition and the withdrawal of Israeli troops from the Sinai. The presence of Egyptian forces in Sinai is limited. The agreement provides also for Palestinian autonomy in the West Bank and Gaza Strip if their leadership decides to negotiate an agreement.

May 6, 1979   Khomeini consolidates power and the revolution is declared to be an Islamic one. He announces formation of a special force to help movements in other countries and spread Iran's Islamic revolution throughout the world. This is the beginning of Iran's policy of sponsoring Islamist terrorism for revolutionary purposes.

May 13, 1979   Ayatollah Sadegh Khalkhali, head of Iran's Central Revolutionary Court, announces that the shah and key supporters in exile are sentenced to death and urges that they be killed. The death list includes the former shah's wife, members of the royal family, and former prime ministers including Bakhtiar. Several of these people will face assassination attempts, sometimes successful, by Iranian agents in later years.

September 9, 1979   Afghan Islamist rebels seize a British tour bus crossing Afghanistan en route from Istanbul to New Delhi, resulting in the deaths of two—a Canadian and a Swiss citizen—and wounding of several others.

November 4, 1979   Some 30,000 Iranian students supporting the new Islamist government in Iran demonstrate at the U.S. Embassy in Tehran. They are protesting past U.S. support of the government of the now-deposed Shah Muhammad Pahlevi, and, more immediately, for allowing him to receive medical care in New York. As the demonstrators march by the embassy, several hundred militants scale the compound walls and take 66 embassy workers and visitors hostage. The hostage-taking is supported by Khomeini and Iran's government. Some hostages later escape, women and African-Americans are soon released, and one hostage is freed for medical reasons, leaving 52 in captivity.

November 6, 1979   Iranian Prime Minister Mehdi Bazargan, a moderate, resigns as Khomeini announces that control over the government now belongs to the militant Islamic Revolutionary Council.

November 20, 1979   In Saudi Arabia, 200 Islamists of a radical sect, seeking to topple the Saudi royal family, seize the Grand Mosque in Mecca, Islam's holiest place, and take hundreds of pilgrims hostage. Saudi and French security forces help retake the shrine after an intense battle in which 250 are killed and 600 wounded. In January 1980, 63 of the attackers are executed and 107 are jailed in Saudi Arabia for the attack.

November 21, 1979   In Islamabad, Pakistan, two American guards are killed as they protect the U.S. Embassy, which is being attacked and set on fire by an angry mob. The protestors are acting on false rumors repeated on radio broadcasts asserting that Americans are responsible for the seizure of the Grand Mosque in Mecca.

December 24, 1979   Soviet troops seize control of airfields and telecommunications in Kabul, Afghanistan, beginning the Soviet invasion of the country. The goal is to ensure the survival of a pro-Moscow Communist regime there. The resulting war, which would last nearly ten years, draws thousands of Muslim fighters to Afghanistan. The United States gives covert support to the Afghans. Osama bin Laden and Palestinian Muslim Brotherhood leader Abdallah Azzam, among others, recruit young Muslims worldwide to join the fight in Afghanistan. Hundreds of thousands of Afghans flee to Pakistan.

1980
Harakat ul-Jihad-I-Islami (HUJI), a Sunni extremist group that follows the Deobandi tradition of Islam, is founded in Afghanistan. Its original purpose is to fight Soviet control. After that conflict ends, the group begins attacking targets in India as part of a campaign to make Kashmir a part of Pakistan.

1980s
The Harakat ul-Mujahideen is founded in Pakistan by Islamic religious elements. The organization begins by recruiting and training volunteers to Afghanistan.

April 25, 1980
Operation Eagle Claw, a U.S. military mission to rescue the American hostages in Iran, ends in disaster after several military helicopters are grounded inside Iran because of mechanical failure and another collides with a cargo plane, killing five Air Force personnel and three Marines and injuring dozens of others.

April 30, 1980
Six Iraqi-backed Iranians storm the Iranian Embassy in London, taking 20 hostages. The gunmen want the release of 91 political prisoners held in Iran as well as an aircraft to take them and the hostages out of England. Six days later, after the terrorists kill the Iranian press attaché and dump his body out the window, British Special Air Service (SAS) anti-terrorist troops storm the embassy, killing five of the terrorists and freeing the remaining hostages.

June 4, 1980
Two terrorists shouting "Viva Khomeini" unsuccessfully attempt to enter the Iraqi Embassy in Rome with a time bomb. They kill an embassy employee. An Islamic group committed to overthrowing the Iraqi government claims responsibility.

July 18, 1980
Former Iranian Prime Minister Shapour Bakhtiar escapes an assassination attempt in Paris by Iranian intelligence agents, but a French policeman and a passerby are killed.

July 23, 1980
Ali-Akbar Tabataba'I, a diplomat under the shah of Iran and an outspoken critic of the Islamist Iranian government, is shot and killed at his home outside Washington, D.C., by a man disguised as a postal worker. The terrorist is an African-American Muslim sponsored by the Iranian government; he flees to Iran after the murder.

September 22, 1980
Iraq launches an invasion of Iran, marking the beginning of the Iran-Iraq War.

January 20, 1981
After 444 days of captivity, the remaining 52 U.S. hostages in Iran are released. The release comes after the death of the shah, the start of the Iran-Iraq War, and the defeat of Jimmy Carter by Ronald Reagan in the 1980 U.S. presidential election. The United States also agrees to release Iranian assets in the United States that Carter had frozen. In a final snub to Carter, the captors wait until a few hours after Reagan's inauguration to release the hostages.

June 28, 1981   In Tehran, Iran, a bomb set by the Mujahideen-e Khalq (MEK), a leftist group with a philosophy combining Marxism and Islam, explodes at the headquarters of the ruling Islamic Republican Party, killing 73 people, including the party's founder, chief justice Ayatollah Mohammad Beheshti, four cabinet ministers, and 23 parliament members. Formed in the 1960s, the MEK staged terrorist attacks in the 1970s against the shah's government and U.S. targets. But when it is left out of the new Islamist government, the MEK remains an opposition group, using terrorism against it.

August 29, 1981   One person is killed and two seriously wounded in an explosion at the Iranian radio and television bureau in Beirut. No one claims responsibility for the attack.

August 30, 1981   MEK terrorists detonate a bomb during a meeting in the Iranian prime minister's office, killing newly elected Prime Minister Muhammad-Javad Bahonar, President Mohammad-Ali Rajaei, and the police chief.

September 4, 1981   The French Ambassador to Lebanon, Louis Delamare, is shot to death by assassins as he drives to his home in West Beirut. No one claims responsibility for the incident, which may have been perpetrated by pro-Iranian elements because France has granted asylum to Iran's former president, Abolhassan Bani-Sadr.

October 6, 1981   Egyptian President Anwar Sadat, attending a military parade in Cairo to commemorate the 1973 war, is shot to death by al-Jihad terrorists, one of them a lieutenant colonel in Egypt's army. In March 1982, a military court condemns four assassins and al-Jihad's leader, Mohammed Abd al-Salam Faraj, to death. Many other militants and conspirators are arrested.

December 8, 1981   A bomb explodes near the Beirut residence of the new French ambassador fails to hit its target, but kills a man and wounds four others.

January 18, 1982   Lieutenant Colonel Charles R. Ray, an assistant military attaché at the U.S. Embassy in Paris, is shot dead by members of the Lebanese Armed Revolutionary Faction.

February 8, 1982   Mousa Khiabani, the MEK commander inside Iran, is killed in a gun battle with Khomeini's forces.

March 6, 1982   The manager of Air France's office in Beirut is killed in a bombing blamed on Iran.

April 18, 1982   A terrorist drives a van loaded with 400 pounds of explosives into the U.S. Embassy in Beirut, killing 63 and wounding 120. Seventeen of the victims are Americans, including a number of Central Intelligence Agency analysts. Radical Lebanese Shia groups, which will soon be forming the Hezbollah organization, claim responsibility, but Iranian and Syrian intelligence services are also implicated in the attack.

May 24, 1982   An automobile packed with 77 pounds of explosives blows up inside the gates of the French Embassy in West Beirut, killing 14 people and injuring 22 others. The dead are Lebanese nationals lining up outside the embassy's visa section and four embassy staff workers. The Front for the Liberation of Lebanon from Foreigners claims responsibility for the attack.

June 6, 1982

Following the attempted assassination of Shlomo Argov, the Israeli ambassador to Britain, Israel launches an invasion of Lebanon, Operation Peace for Galilee. Forces of the Palestine Liberation Organization (PLO), which had exercised considerable control in south Lebanon, eventually retreat, and the Syrian army suffers defeat.

July 1982

Hezbollah (Party of God) forms as an umbrella organization for various radical Shiite groups in Lebanon. The group is subsidized and sponsored by Iran to launch a *jihad* to destroy Israel as well as to take over Lebanon and turn it into a Shia Muslim Islamist state.

July 19, 1982

David Dodge, acting president of the American University of Beirut, is seized by terrorists and taken to jail in Tehran, the first of many Westerners to be kidnapped in Lebanon during this period. He is released on July 21, 1983.

October 1, 1982

MEK terrorists detonate a truck bomb at Iman Square in Tehran killing 60 and injuring over 700.

October 22, 1982

Daniel Jordan, an academic from California who is a leader in the Bahá'i faith, is assassinated in Stamford, Connecticut, probably by terrorists sponsored by the Iranian government. Many followers of the Bahá'i faith, which the Islamist regime considers a heretical religion, are persecuted in Iran.

December 2, 1982

A bomb left in a briefcase destroys the former Iraqi Consulate in Bangkok, Thailand, killing the police department's top bomb disposal expert and injuring six policemen and 11 civilians. The attack is claimed by a pro-Iranian Shiite Muslim force calling itself the April 20 Group.

April 18, 1983

A bomb shatters the U.S. Embassy in Beirut, killing at least 57 people, 17 of them Americans, and wounding at least 100. The Islamic Jihad Organization (Islamic Holy War), an Iran-sponsored group, claims responsibility.

October 23, 1983

Two simultaneous bomb attacks on military headquarters in Beirut kill 242 American Marines and 58 French servicemen. Suicide terrorists in two trucks, each carrying 400 pounds of dynamite wrapped around glass cylinders, crash through the security perimeter of the U.S. Battalion Landing Team headquarters and the French paratroopers' base situated just four miles away. The bombers are identified as members of a previously unknown group called the Free Islamic Revolutionary Movement, composed of Lebanese Shia Muslims and an extremist faction of the Amal militia based in Syrian-occupied eastern Lebanon. Others, including Iran, Syria, and PLO members, may also be involved. In response, President Ronald Reagan orders the battleship *USS New Jersey* to shell the hills near Beirut while France launches an air strike in the Bekáa Valley against Iranian Revolutionary Guard positions.

December 12, 1983

Terrorists with the Hizb al-Da'wa al-Islamiyya (The Party of the Islamic Call), kill seven and wound 80 in Kuwait. They set off bombs at the U.S. and French embassies, the airport control tower, a main oil refinery, and a residential area for employees of the American corporation Raytheon. Kuwaiti officials imprison 17 for their involvement in the attacks, including Mustafa Youssef Badreddin, a brother-in-law of one of Hezbollah's senior officers, Imad Mughniyah. Later, several kidnappers of Western hostages and plane hijackers demand the release of the so-called al-Da'wa 17. Hizb al-Da'wa al-Islamiyya is a Shia Muslim Islamist party based in Iraq that seeks to overthrow the secular Baathist regime there in order to create an Iranian-style Islamic republic.

December 12, 1983   An Islamic Jihad terrorist claims credit for a remote-controlled car bomb at the Kuwaiti International Airport that kills an Egyptian technician.

January 18, 1984   Malcolm Kerr, president of the American University of Beirut (AUB), is assassinated by two Hezbollah gunmen outside his office.

March 16, 1984   Terrorists with the Islamic Jihad faction of Hezbollah kidnap William F. Buckley, the CIA Station chief, in Beirut. Buckley is taken to Iran where he is brutally tortured and held captive for 15 months before dying from his mistreatment. In 1991, his corpse is found dumped on a road near the Beirut airport.

March 28, 1984   A gunman kills a British cultural attaché, Kenneth Whitty, and another British employee in Athens. A group calling itself the Revolutionary Organization of Socialist Muslims claims responsibility, saying that Whitty's killing is in response to "British attempts to resume former colonial rule in the world by spreading colonialist culture under a new guise."

July 28, 1984   A booby-trapped car explodes outside the headquarters of a major Afghan rebel group in the Pakistan frontier town of Peshawar, killing four people and wounding 12. The Soviet KGB (secret police) is suspected of having planted the bomb.

September 20, 1984   A suicide bomb planted by Hezbollah at the U.S. Embassy annex in Beirut kills 23 people, including two Americans, and injures 71, including the U.S. and British ambassadors.

October 5, 1984   Islamic terrorists are believed responsible for bombing the Bank of Central Asia in Indonesia, leaving two dead and 16 injured.

December 3, 1984   Peter Kilburn, a librarian at American University and an U.S. citizen, is taken hostage by Hezbollah terrorists. Libya's act is revenge for the U.S. bombing of Tripoli that month, which was in retaliation for the death of a U.S. serviceman in a Libyan-backed bombing. Libyan agents purchase Kilburn from his Lebanese kidnappers and kill him along with two British citizens. He is found dead in April 1986.

December 4, 1984   Five Islamic Jihad terrorists hijack a Kuwaiti flight en route from Dubai, United Arab Emirates, to Karachi, Pakistan, and divert it to Tehran. The hijackers demand the release from Kuwaiti jails of the 17 imprisoned members of al-Da'wa. When the demand is not met, the hijackers kill two American passengers who are officials from the U.S. Agency for International Development. On the sixth day, Iranian security forces storm the plane and free the remaining hostages. Iran arrests the hijackers and says they will be brought to trial. But the trial never takes place and the hijackers are allowed to leave the country. U.S. officials believe Iran aided the terrorists; Hezbollah's Imad Mughniyah is also found to be linked to the hijackings.

1985	The Great East Islamic Raiders Front is founded in Turkey as a breakaway radical faction of the Islamist party the National Salvation Party. Its goal is the establishment of an Islamic state in Turkey through violent means.
1985	Harakat ul-Mujahideen (HUM) is formed as a breakaway from an earlier group to help Afghan guerrillas. At the end of that conflict, the group becomes involved in waging *jihad* in Jammu and Kashmir.
March 8, 1985	A massive car bomb explodes in front of the Beirut residence of Hezbollah spiritual guide and Shia Muslim cleric, Muhammad Hussein Fadlallah. Fadlallah, believed to be responsible for many terrorist attacks against the United States, escapes unharmed, but more than 80 people are killed and 200 injured in the attack. It is later speculated that CIA Director William Casey, frustrated by his agency's bureaucracy and opposition to a pre-emptive strike against Fadlallah, paid $3 million for Saudi intelligence to mount the attack.
March 14, 1985	A Dutch Roman Catholic priest, Nicolas Kluiters, disappears while traveling in the Syrian-controlled Bekáa Valley in eastern Lebanon, and his corpse is later found in a pit.
April 12, 1985	A bomb placed in a restaurant in Torrejon, Spain, near a U.S. Air Force base, kills 18 U.S. servicemen and injures 83 people. Hezbollah is seen as being responsible.
May 5, 1985	Egypt's parliament defeats an effort sponsored by the Muslim Brotherhood to make Sharia (Islamic law) the law of the land.
May 19, 1985	Two explosions within minutes of each other in Riyadh, Saudi Arabia, leave one person dead and three injured. A local group called Islamic Jihad, committed to overthrowing the Saudi monarchy, claims responsibility.
May 25, 1985	An al-Da'wa suicide driver drives a car wired with explosives into the motorcade of the emir of Kuwait. The emir suffers only minor injuries, but four people traveling with him are killed.
May 26, 1985	Michel Seurat, a researcher from Paris, is kidnapped in Beirut. In March 1986, pictures showing Seurat's dead body are released by Islamic Jihad. His remains are never found.
June 6, 1985	Most Israeli troops withdraw from Lebanon, but some remain to support the mainly Christian South Lebanon Army (SLA) led by Major General Antoine Lahd, which operates in a "security zone" in southern Lebanon.
June 14, 1985	A TWA flight en route to Rome from Athens is hijacked by two Hezbollah terrorists who force the pilot to fly to Beirut. There the Hezbollah hijackers torture and shoot one of the hostages, a U.S. Navy sailor, Robert Stethem, and dump his body out on the runway. After flying to Algiers where some passengers are released, the airplane returns to Beirut. Some of the hostages' demands are then met, including that Israel releases 435 Lebanese and Palestinian

prisoners. It takes until June 30 for all the hostages to be freed. In 1989, one of the hijackers, Mohammed Ali Hamadei, is sentenced to life in prison in Frankfurt, Germany. But on December 15, 2005, German authorities release him on parole.

August 20, 1985 Colonel Behrouz Shahverdilou, a leader of the Iranian National Movement of Resistance, is killed in Istanbul, Turkey. Iranian government agents are likely responsible.

September 1985 The Sipah-e-Sahaba Pakistan (SSP), a terrorist organization committed to making Pakistan a Sunni Islamist state, is founded. The group sponsors attacks in Pakistan against Shia Muslims.

September 30, 1985 In Beirut, terrorists kidnap four Soviet diplomats and kill one, then release the other three. The Soviets reportedly obtain the release by threatening to kill relatives of those responsible. A Sunni group called the Islamic Liberation Organization claims responsibility.

March 25, 1986 British writer Alec Collett, on assignment in Lebanon for the United Nations Relief and Works Agency for Palestine Refugees in the Near East, is kidnapped in Beirut by a pro-Libyan group called the Revolutionary Organization of Socialist Muslims, which is demanding the release of Muslim prisoners in Kuwait. He is never seen again and is likely killed in 1986.

March 27, 1986 A bomb explodes at an Afghan refugee hostel in Peshawar, Pakistan, killing four people and injuring 17. Pakistani police believe Afghan secret police placed the device. Pakistan is the base for Afghan fighters battling the Soviet presence in Afghanistan.

June 6, 1986 A car bomb explodes in front of the building occupied by the Afghan Consulate in Peshawar, killing five people and wounding at least 30.

June 23, 1986 Islamic Jihad terrorists detonate a car bomb about 30 kilometers south of Cairo, Egypt, killing ten people and injuring 15 others.

July 13, 1986 A bomb explodes in a rest home at the Pakistani border settlement of Teri Mengal, killing ten Afghans and injuring 15. Pakistan blames bombings in these areas on the Afghani government.

September 7, 1986 In Salvador, in the southern Philippines, five Moro Islamic Liberation Front terrorists throw a grenade into a wedding party inside a Catholic church, killing ten people and wounding 90.

September 8, 1986 The post office in the Paris City Hall is bombed, killing four. The attack is claimed by the Committee of Solidarity with the Arab and Middle East Political Prisoners (CSPPA), known to be sponsored by the Iranian government.

September 14, 1986 In the fourth bomb placed in Paris over the last ten days, one policeman is killed and two others are seriously injured in an explosion at a busy Champs Elysées restaurant. The CSPPA claims responsibility.

September 15, 1986   A bomb detonates in the Paris police headquarters, killing one and wounding 51 others. The CSPPA claims responsibility.

September 17, 1986   A bomb detonates in a crowded discount clothing and textile store in Paris, killing five and injuring 60. The CSPPA is likely responsible.

October 1, 1986   Afghan rebels attack the Soviet Embassy in Kabul, killing two Soviet children and a guard.

October 24, 1986   Ahmad Hamed Monfared, a former bodyguard to the shah, is shot by two people while waiting for a bus in Istanbul, Turkey. The police arrest Iranian government agents.

December 23, 1986   Hadi Aziz-Moradi, an Iranian commando colonel under the shah, is assassinated at his home in Istanbul. Iranian government agents are believed responsible.

December 25, 1986   Shia terrorists assassinate Libyan diplomat Musbah Gharibeh in a Syrian-controlled area of Beirut.

December 25, 1986   An Iraqi Airways jetliner en route from Baghdad to Saudi Arabia with 67 people on board crashes in the Saudi Arabian desert after being hijacked by a gunmen shortly after takeoff. Islamic Jihad and a group called the Revolutionary Work Organization claim responsibility for the hijacking.

January 15, 1987   Ali-Akbar Mohammadi, a former pilot for Iranian President Akbar Hashemi Rafsanjani, is assassinated in the street in Hamburg, Germany, by Iranian government agents.

February 1, 1987   A car bomb explodes in front of the Indian Embassy in Kabul killing four. Afghan officials blame Islamists for the attack, but no one claims responsibility.

February 19, 1987   Ten people are killed and 62 others injured when a truck bomb explodes outside an Afghan guerrilla office in Peshawar. Afghan guerrillas blame Soviet and Afghan agents for the attack.

July 14, 1987   Four bombs explode within a half hour of each other in a busy shopping area of Karachi, Pakistan, killing 72 and wounding over 300. Pakistan blames Afghan intelligence operatives for the blasts.

July 24, 1987   A member of Hezbollah, Hussein Hariri, hijacks an Air Afrique plane en route from Brazzaville, Congo, to Paris after it stops in Italy. He demands that the plane be flown to Beirut and that Lebanese and Tunisian prisoners in France, Germany, and Israel be released, including Mohammed Ali Hamadei, one of the hijackers of an U.S. passenger flight in June 1985. During a refueling in Geneva, Hariri murders a French passenger. A Swiss security team captures the hijacker while passengers open emergency doors and slide down chutes to escape. In 1989, Hariri is sentenced to life in prison. He escapes from a Swiss jail, and is arrested in Morocco and extradited back to Switzerland.

August 5, 1987
Two bombs detonate in Peshawar, killing two and injuring one. Afghan intelligence agents are suspected.

August 10, 1987
Two bombs explode at a bus station in Mardan, Pakistan, resulting in seven dead and 45 injured. Afghan agents are suspected.

August 10, 1987
Ahmad Moradi-Talebi, a former Iranian military pilot under the shah awaiting asylum in Switzerland, is assassinated by two gunmen in Geneva.

September 10, 1987
A bomb goes off at a fruit stand in Peshawar, killing two and injuring 25. Afghan agents are suspected.

October 23, 1987
A bomb hidden under a fruit stand near an Afghan refugee camp explodes, killing four persons and wounding 17 others. Afghan agents are suspected.

December 22, 1987
In Afghanistan, Andy Skrypkowiak, a British cameraman, is captured and killed by members of the Hezb-e Eslami (Gulbuddin Hikmatyar) Party, which is fighting both the Soviets and other Afghan guerrilla groups.

December 26, 1987
Three car bombs explode in downtown shopping areas in Islamabad, Pakistan, killing one person and injuring 40 others. The incident occurs on the eighth anniversary of the Soviet troop intervention in Afghanistan.

January 22, 1988
A funeral for Pathan leader Khan Abdul Ghaffar Khan in Jalalabad, Afghanistan, is rocked by bombs that kill eight people and wound many others. It is not clear which group is responsible.

January 23, 1988
A bomb goes off in a black-market bazaar in Quetta, Afghanistan, killing two, and injuring eight others. Quetta is a center for Afghani anti-Communist guerrillas and Afghani agents are believed responsible.

January 24, 1988
A bomb goes off in a government-owned bus in Pakistan, killing ten and wounding 19 others. Afghani agents are being blamed.

January 31, 1988
Three Afghani refugees and two Pakistanis are killed when a bomb hidden inside a tomato crate explodes in Peshawar.

February 17, 1988
U.S. Marine Corps Lieutenant Colonel Williams Higgins, who had been serving with the United Nations Truce Supervision Organization (UNTSO) in southern Lebanon, is kidnapped by Hezbollah while driving from Tyre to Nakura. Hostage-takers demand the withdrawal of Israeli forces from Lebanon and release of all Palestinians and Lebanese held prisoner in Israel. When demands are not met, Higgins is killed.

February 22, 1988
A man is killed when a bomb detonates in a hotel bathroom in Peshawar. Afghani agents are blamed.

February 27, 1988
An explosion at a bazaar in Thal, district of Kohat, in Afghanistan, kills five people and wounds 11. Afghani agents are blamed.

March 1, 1988   One person is killed and three others injured in a bomb blast in Peshawar. Afghani agents are suspected.

March 31, 1988   A bomb kills seven people and injures 15 others at a bazaar in Sadda, Afghanistan. Afghani agents are suspected.

April 5, 1988   A Kuwaiti Airlines flight en route from Bangkok to Kuwait is hijacked by members of Hezbollah, who demand the release of members of the al-Da'wa 17. The plane, whose passengers include three members of the Kuwaiti royal family, makes a three-day stopover in Mashad, Iran, where some sources believe additional hijackers and weapons are loaded with the help of Iranian officials. Next, they fly to Cyprus, where two Kuwaiti passengers are murdered and dumped onto the runway. The plane's last stop is Algiers, where negotiators from the Iranian and Algerian governments, as well the Palestine Liberation Organization, arrange safe passage for all the hijackers on the sixteenth day.

April 11, 1988   A bomb explodes in a train near Peshawar, killing two railway workers and injuring three.

April 16, 1988   A bomb detonates at a bus station in Charsadda, Pakistan, killing four and injuring 11. Afghani agents are suspected.

June 25, 1988   A bomb explodes at the Prince Hotel in Peshawar, killing 13. Afghani agents are suspected.

July 1988   Iran, suffering defeats to Iraqi forces on the battlefield and rising international opposition, accepts a UN cease-fire, ending the Iran-Iraq War.

August 8, 1988   Two children are killed when a bomb wrapped in a sack is exploded by a group of children playing near Peshawar. Afghani agents are suspected.

August 11, 1988   Osama bin Laden splits from his mentor, Palestinian Muslim Brotherhood leader Abdallah Azzam, to form a new organization called al-Qaeda that will expand beyond Azzam's focus on the anti-Soviet struggle in Afghanistan. The new organization is committed to the overthrow of what it sees as the corrupt and heretical governments of Muslim states, and their replacement with the rule of Islamic law. Al-Qaeda is intensely anti-Western, and views the United States in particular as the prime enemy of Islam.

September 3, 1988   A bomb goes off on a train traveling between Islamabad and Peshawar, killing three and wounding 13 others. Afghani agents are suspected.

September 11, 1988   Ten people are killed and 22 injured when a bomb explodes near the Pakistani Embassy in Kabul.

October 18, 1988   Three people are killed and 18 others injured when a bomb goes off at a market in Charsadda, Pakistan. Afghani agents are suspected.

October 25, 1988   The Islamic Jihad-Hijaz, an Iranian-backed Shia opposition group in Saudi Arabia, claims responsibility for assassinating a Saudi Arabian diplomat in Ankara, Turkey.

October 25, 1988

Abdul Ghani Bedawi, the second secretary at the Embassy of Saudi Arabia in Turkey and believed to be an intelligence agent, is gunned down by an assailant in Ankara, Turkey. A professional killer, arrested in March 1996 for the crime, says he was hired by agents from Iran.

December 12, 1988

An armed man opens fire on Iranian refugees waiting in line in front of the headquarters of the United Nations High Commissioner for Refugees in Karachi, killing one and wounding five others.

January 4, 1989

Saleh Abdullah al-Maliki, the third secretary at the Saudi Embassy in Bangkok, Thailand, is murdered by Islamic Jihad.

February 5, 1989

A bomb at a bus station in Quetta, Afghanistan, kills three and injures five others. Afghani agents are blamed.

February 14, 1989

Iranian leader Ayatollah Khomeini issues a *fatwa,* an Islamic religious decree, condemning British author Salman Rushdie to death. Rushdie's novel, *The Satanic Verses,* is deemed to be slanderous to the Prophet Muhammad. Rushdie goes into hiding. The *fatwa* is renewed 12 years later but later abandoned by the Iranian government.

February 15, 1989

Worn down by Afghani resistance and beset by internal problems, the Soviet Union removes its last troops from Afghanistan. The Communist government in Kabul remains in power.

February 15, 1989

An American citizen married to a local Muslim is killed by gunmen as she drives through a small town in Lebanon. Islamists are suspected.

February 26, 1989

A bomb at the British Council library in Karachi results in the death of a security guard. The attack is believed to have been carried out by Islamists protesting British government protection for the author Salman Rushdie.

March 29, 1989

Abdallah Ahdal, the Saudi imam of a Brussels mosque, who has taken a moderate stand toward *The Satanic Verses,* and his deputy are shot to death. Iranian agents are likely responsible.

June 4, 1989

Terrorists sponsored by the Iranian government assassinate a former military intelligence colonel under the shah and anti-government activist, Atellah Bayahmadi, in his hotel room in Dubai, United Arab Emirates.

July 4, 1989

Ten people are killed and another 29 injured by a bus bombing in Peshawar, Pakistan. Afghani agents are likely responsible.

July 10, 1989

Terrorists plant two bombs during the Muslim pilgrimage in Mecca, killing a Pakistani. On September 16, 1989, 16 pro-Iranian Kuwaitis, who say they were trained by Iranian officials, are executed for their role in these incidents.

July 13, 1989

The leader of the Iranian Democratic Party of Kurdistan and two of his deputies are assassinated in a Vienna apartment by three Iranian officials with whom they are meeting. The Austrian government is unable to arrest those responsible; two of them left the country and the other hid in the Iranian Embassy in Vienna.

August 5, 1989	Four people are killed and another 30 injured when a bomb, likely placed by Afghani agents, explodes at a Peshawar vegetable market.
August 26, 1989	An Iranian opposition figure who is a high-ranking member of the underground Iranian Communist Party and its Komala Kurdish guerrilla forces is assassinated by two gunmen, likely sponsored by the Iranian government, after he arrives in Cyprus from Sweden.
September 1989	The Hizbul Mujahideen (HM) is formed in the Kashmir Valley, committed to using violence to make Jammu and Kashmir Islamic and part of Pakistan. It is one of the largest terrorist groups operating there. Most of its early members are Jammu and Kashmir Liberation Front members. Its head, Master Ahsan Dar, is arrested by security forces in December 1993.
September 18, 1989	Three people are killed and two others are injured by a bomb explosion on a bus in Peshawar. The Afghan government is blamed.
October 9, 1989	Members of Islamic Jihad plant a bomb on a French airline, Union des Transports, en route from Brazzaville, Republic of Congo, to Paris, killing 171, seven of them American citizens.
November 1, 1989	Terrorists assassinate Ali al-Marzuq, a Saudi Arabian diplomat in Beirut. The killing is claimed by Hezbollah.
November 24, 1989	Sheikh Abdullah Azzam is killed along with two of his sons by three bombs planted along a road in Afghanistan. The identity and sponsors of the assailants is never discovered. Azzam, a radical Palestinian university professor, is one of the first to urge Muslims worldwide to join him in waging *jihad* in Afghanistan. Among his protégés is Osama bin Laden.
November 24, 1989	A remote-control bomb in Pakistan kills three people, including the Saudi official responsible for coordinating aid in Pakistan to the Afghani resistance movement. Iranian agents are believed responsible.
December 1989	Mushtaq Ahmed Zargar breaks from the Jammu and Kashmir Liberation Front (JKLF) and forms the al-Umar Mujahideen (AuM) organization, committed to using armed struggle to liberate the Indian state of Jammu and Kashmir and make it part of Pakistan.
1990	The al-Ittihad al-Islami (Islamic Union) forms as the largest militant Islamic group in Somalia following the collapse of the Siad Barre regime. It seeks to establish an Islamic regime in Somalia and force the secession of the Ogaden region of Ethiopia, and has ties to al-Qaeda.
February 1, 1990	Three Saudi diplomats in Bangkok, Thailand, are assassinated, probably by pro-Iranian radical Shia terrorists.
February 23, 1990	Maulana Haq Nawaz Jhangvi, one of the founding members of Sipah-e-Sahaba Pakistan, committed to making Pakistan a Sunni Islamist state, is assassinated, likely by Shia terrorists.

March 7, 1990	In Istanbul, an Islamist group claims responsibility for the assassination of a leading Turkish journalist critical of Islamists and his driver.
April 15, 1990	After a false rumor that a five-year-old Muslim girl had been raped by a Coptic Christian, Muslims attack a church in Egypt's Fayyum Province, killing a guard and wounding 12 others.
April 24, 1990	Kazem Radjavij, a prominent anti-Iranian government dissident, is assassinated outside his home near Geneva, Switzerland. Iranian agents are suspected.
May 6, 1990	Afghan agents bomb a train near Lahore, Pakistan, killing 11 and wounding 35.
May 21, 1990	A prominent Muslim cleric, Mirwaiz Mohammad Farooq, is assassinated by the Hizbul Mujahideen because he calls for moderation towards India.
July 31, 1990	An attack on the residence of the ambassador of Bahrain in Egypt by Islamists opposing the Bahrain government results in the death of a policeman.
August 2, 1990	Iraqi forces invade Kuwait and quickly annex it. The United States bans trade with Iraq and freezes Iraqi and Kuwaiti assets. The UN Security Council passes Resolution 660, which condemns the Iraqi invasion and calls for immediate and unconditional withdrawal from Kuwait.
September 2, 1990	Egyptian security officers kill Dr. Ala Mohy al-Din Ashour, the spokesman of the terrorist group al-Gama'a al-Islamiyya (also known as Islamic Group) on a Cairo street. This group and Islamic Jihad wage a violent revolutionary struggle to overthrow the Egyptian government during most of the 1990s, assassinating officials, attacking Christians, and murdering foreign tourists.
September 6, 1990	Efat Ghazi, the wife of an Iranian Kurdish leader, is killed in Sweden by a bomb intended for her husband. Iranian agents are suspected.
October 6, 1990	Bahriye Ucok, an associate professor at Ankara University's faculty of divinity known for her strong secularist views, is killed by a letter bomb. Her murder remains unsolved, but Islamists are likely involved.
October 12, 1990	Al-Gama'a al-Islamiyya terrorists kill Egypt's Assembly speaker, Rif'at al-Mahgoub, and five guards during an assault on his motorcade in Cairo.
October 23, 1990	Cyrus Elahi, a high-ranking member of the pro-democracy Iranian opposition movement, the Flag of Freedom Organization, is assassinated in the lobby of his residence in Paris. Iranian government agents are suspected.
November 7, 1990	Rockets are fired into the Kabul International Airport by mujahideen rebels, killing three.
December 19, 1990	Sadeq Ganji, an Iranian diplomat in Lahore, Pakistan, is killed by Sunni terrorists in retaliation for the murder of Maulana Haq Nawaz Jhangvi on February 23.
1991	In the Philippines, the new terrorist group Abu Sayyaf, "bearer of the sword," is formed as a splinter group from the Moro National Liberation Front in pro-

test against that organization's negotiations with the government. Abu Sayyaf is committed to establishing an Islamist government in the western Mindanao and Sulu Archipelago areas in the southern Philippines, which are heavily populated by Muslims. It becomes the most violent of all the separatist groups in the southern Philippines, with ties to al-Qaeda.

January 17, 1991   The United States and its coalition partners launch massive air and missile attacks at Iraqi forces in Kuwait and Iraq. After an aerial attack, allied ground troops advance, destroying Iraqi forces in Kuwait. During the buildup to the war and the fighting, the United States establishes a large military presence in the region, including Saudi Arabia.

February 28, 1991   A cease-fire ends the war with Iraq over Kuwait, with the complete defeat of Baghdad's forces.

April 1991   Bin Laden flees Saudi Arabia after being confined to Jeddah for his opposition to the Saudi alliance with the United States. He moves first to Afghanistan and then, by 1992, to Khartoum, Sudan.

April 18, 1991   Abdol-Rahman Boroumand, an active member of the Iranian National Resistance Movement, is stabbed to death outside his home in Paris. The terrorists are likely Iranian government agents.

June 17, 1991   Eight people, mostly Afghan refugees, are killed and another 18 injured when a powerful bomb detonates at a restaurant in Landay Kowtal, a Pakistani town bordering Afghanistan.

June 27, 1991   Twelve armed terrorists with the Guardians of the Islamic Revolution, a small Iranian-influenced group of Islamists seeking the union of Kashmir with Pakistan, abduct seven Israelis and one Dutch woman from a houseboat on Dal Lake in Srinagar, a popular resort area in Kashmir. The terrorists release the two women. The men attempt an escape, which results in the death of one Israeli and two terrorists. The hostages eventually escape and one is rescued by a rival separatist group, the Jammu and Kashmir Liberation Front.

July 12, 1991   Hitoshi Igarashi, the Japanese translator of *The Satanic Verses,* is stabbed to death at Tsukuba University, northeast of Tokyo, where he is a professor of Islamic studies.

August 6, 1991   The Iranian shah's last prime minister, Shapour Bakhtiar, and his secretary are stabbed to death near Bakhtiar's home in Paris. In 1994, two Iranians, who admit they are government agents, are sentenced to jail terms for the attack.

October 28, 1991   When a bomb goes off in his car in Ankara, U.S. Air Force Staff Sergeant Victor Marvick is killed and his wife injured. The Turkish Islamic Jihad claims responsibility.

November 1991   Chechen nationalist leader Dzhokar Dudayev unilaterally declares independence from Russia, the new country that is emerging from the dissolution of the Soviet Union. Although many former Soviet republics are becoming independent states, Chechnya is firmly within Russia's declared boundaries.

In response, Russian President Boris Yeltsin announces a state of emergency and dispatchs troops to the region. The Chechens mobilize 60,000 volunteers to defend against a probable Russian invasion.

November 8, 1991 A car bomb destroys the administration building of American University in Beirut, killing one and wounding at least a dozen. No group claims responsibility.

December 26, 1991 An Islamist party in Algeria, the Islamic Salvation Front (FIS), wins the first round of parliamentary elections and is poised to obtain a majority in the second round. The Algerian military nullifies the victory, forces the president to resign, and establishes a Higher State Council, headed by Mohamed Boudiaf, which bans the FIS. A radical splinter group, the Armed Islamic Group (GIA), breaks from the FIS to wage an armed struggle seeking an Islamist state, including terrorist acts aimed at the civilian population. In the fighting, as many as 100,000 Algerians are killed from 1992 to 1998.

1992 Following the final collapse of the Soviet Union and the overthrow of its own Communist government, Chechnya adopts a constitution defining itself as an independent secular state governed by a president and parliament.

April 18, 1992 The Communist government in Afghanistan is overthrown by Islamic Afghan guerrilla leaders who take control of Kabul and declare the Islamic State of Afghanistan. Within the country, Islamist groups struggle for power.

April 22, 1992 An Icelandic male nurse with the International Committee of the Red Cross (ICRC) is murdered outside Kabul, Afghanistan, by an assailant who says he is directed by his mullah to kill non-Muslims.

June 10, 1992 Members of al-Gama'a al-Islamiyya assassinate Faraj Foda, a prominent Egyptian writer known for his criticism of Islamist extremism, outside his Cairo office. At the trial of Foda's killers, Sheikh Muhammad al-Ghazali, a cleric at al-Azhar, the prestigious institution of Islamic teaching, declares that anyone who resists Islamic law is an apostate and may be killed.

June 14, 1992 A Japanese UN employee involved in providing humanitarian and economic aid to Afghani refugees is assassinated outside his home in Peshawar, Pakistan. Authorities suspect Afghani Islamists.

June 29, 1992 Algeria's head of state Mohamed Boudiaf is assassinated during a public speech at the opening of a cultural center in Annaba by one of his bodyguards with suspected Islamist ties.

August 8, 1992 Feridoun Farokhzad, an Iranian entertainer, is stabbed in Bonn, Germany, by Iranian intelligence agents.

August 18, 1992 A German journalist in Beirut is killed by a car bomb. It is not clear which group is responsible.

August 28, 1992 Nine people are killed and over 100 injured when a bomb detonates at the Air France counter at the main airport in Algeria. The Armed Islamic Group (GIA) agents convicted of this crime are executed on August 31, 1993.

September 17, 1992   The leader of the Kurdistan Democratic Party of Iran and three colleagues are shot dead while eating at the Mykonos Restaurant in Berlin, Germany. In April 1997, a German court sentences an Iranian and three Lebanese for the crime. The judge further states that the Mykonos murders had been approved at the most senior levels of the Iranian government, including the minister of intelligence and security, the foreign minister, the president, and the supreme spiritual leader. In March 1996, the German federal prosecutor issues an international arrest warrant for Iranian Intelligence Minister Ali Fallahian for having ordered the killings.

October 21, 1992   A bus carrying foreign tourists is attacked by two gunmen in Dayrut, Egypt. They kill one British tourist and wound two others. Al-Gama'a al-Islamiyya claims responsibility.

November 1992   Egyptian President Hosni Mubarak announces that some 40,000 private mosques, some of which are believed to be the breeding ground for terrorists, will be taken under government control. The edict is announced only days after a mosque in Assiut calls on its members to join an armed struggle against the central government and condemns Christians and Jews as a "common enemy."

November 1992   Two Jordanian legislators are convicted for involvement with a subversive Muslim group, Shabab al-Nafeer al-Islami (Vanguard of the Islamic Youth), which is alleged to have attacked the U.S., British, and French embassies in Amman and conducted cross-border raids into the West Bank. The men are sentenced to 20 years at hard labor but are released a few days later when King Hussein grants a general pardon to prisoners convicted of political crimes in Jordan.

November 7, 1992   Italian National Police officers arrest more than two dozen suspected members of the Algerian GIA.

December 1992   Egyptian president Husni Mubarak initiates a weeklong large-scale military operation in Cairo's Imbaba district involving 14,000 soldiers. It results in 700 arrests along with the seizure of weapons.

December 26, 1992   Major Abbas Gholizadeh, a member of the Iranian opposition group the Flag of Freedom, is abducted near his home in Istanbul and later murdered by members of Islamic Action, a Turkish Islamist group financed by Iran.

December 29, 1992   An explosion at two hotels in Aden Yemen, housing U.S. Marines results in the death of an Austrian tourist and a hotel employee. This is believed to be Osama bin Laden's first terrorist attack.

1993   Lashkar-e-Tayyiba emerges as the terrorist arm of the Markaz Dawa-Wal-Irshad, a Wahhabi-influenced Islamist sect in Pakistan. It is committed not only to establishing an Islamic state in Jammu and Kashmir but also to spreading Islamic rule over India and is one of the largest groups operating there.

1993   Indian security officials capture Mushtaq Ahmed Zargar, the head of al-Umar Mujahideen (*see* December 1989), during a raid on a hideout in the old town of

Srinagar. He is later released in return for hostages taken on a hijacked Indian airlines plane.

1993 — Jemaah Islamiyah is founded in Johor, Malaysia, committed to the creation of an Islamic state across Southeast Asia to include Singapore, Indonesia, Malaysia, Brunei, southern Thailand, and southern Philippines.

January 24, 1993 — Turkish journalist Ugur Mumcu, known for his critical views of Islamist extremism and Iranian subversion in Turkey, is killed when a bomb explodes under his car in Ankara. Prime suspects are members of Islamic Action, an Iranian-backed group in Turkey, and three Iranian diplomats.

January 25, 1993 — Mir Aimal Kansi, a Pakistani, shoots an AK-47 assault rifle into cars waiting at a stoplight in front of the Central Intelligence Agency headquarters in McLean, Virginia, killing two employees. Following the killings, Kansi flees the United States and is a fugitive for over four years in an area of Pakistan along the Afghan border that is outside government control. After a $2 million reward for his return is posted, he is finally handed over by some of those who had been hiding him. In November 10, 1997, Kansi is convicted by a jury in Fairfax, Virginia, for murder and five years later he is executed.

February 1, 1993 — Gunmen ambush an UN convoy on its way from Peshawar to Jalalabad, Pakistan, killing four people—a British worker for the UN Center for Human Settlements, a Dutch water resources expert, and two Afghan drivers.

February 26, 1993 — Al-Gama'a al-Islamiyya terrorists plant a bomb in a jacket left on a chair at a crowded Cairo cafe. It explodes, killing four—a Swede, a Turk, a Somali, and an Egyptian—and injuring 20 including several foreign tourists. Five members of the terrorist group are arrested for the crime.

February 26, 1993 — A bomb weighing more than 1,000 pounds explodes inside a car parked in the garage of New York's World Trade Center. Six people are killed, and smoke fills much of the 107-story structure, injuring more than 1,000. Ramzi Ahmed Yousef, the operation's alleged mastermind, is arrested in Pakistan and extradited to the United States in February 1995. Two months later, Abd al-Hakim Murad, another suspected conspirator in the bombing, is arrested by local authorities in the Philippines and handed over to the United States. The two, along with two other terrorists, are tried in the United States and sentenced to 240 years' imprisonment in January 1998. They are followers of Sheik Omar Abdel Rahman, a radical Egyptian cleric who preaches in the New York City area.

March 12, 1993 — Some 13 bombs detonate within 90 minutes of each other in Mumbai, India, killing about 317 and injuring 1,200. The car bombs target the Air India headquarters, government offices, the Stock Exchange, luxury hotels, and movie theaters. On August 5, 1994, the Indian government arrests a key suspect in the case, Yaqub Memon, an Islamist with links to the government of Pakistan.

March 16, 1993 — Mohammad Hossein Naghdi, a representative of the Mujahideen-e Khalq (MEK)-led National Council of Resistance of Iran, is shot dead in Rome by two terrorists linked to the Iranian government.

June 8, 1993

Al-Gama'a al-Islamiyya terrorists detonate a bomb planted in a highway underpass in Cairo as a tour bus passes on its way to the pyramids, killing two Egyptians.

July 2, 1993

Thirty-seven people die in a hotel fire in Sivas, Turkey, while participating in a cultural conference commemorating Pir Sultan Abdal, a sixteenth-century poet sometimes called "Turkey's first socialist." The fire is set by members of the Islamic Great Eastern Raiders' Front, a Sunni Jihadist group that advocates Islamist rule in Turkey. They target the conference participants because they are Alevis, a Shia sect widely seen by Sunni Muslims as apostates, and because the group has recently sponsored a Turkish translation of Salman Rushdie's book *The Satanic Verses*.

August 18, 1993

A bomb kills five persons and wounds some 150 others on a road in Cairo. The bomb is directed at Egyptian Interior Minister Hassen al-Alfi, who is slightly injured. The Islamist extremist group, New Jihad, claims responsibility.

September 20, 1993

One Moroccan and two French surveyors are kidnapped by Islamist terrorists as they drive between Oran and Sidi Bel Abbes in Algeria. The Moroccan citizen is released unharmed but the two Frenchmen are later found murdered.

October 1993

Two groups—Harakat ul-Jihad al-Islami and Harakat ul-Mujahideen—merge to become Harakat ul-Ansar (HUA), an Islamist militant group based in Pakistan. The group is committed to waging *jihad* worldwide but operating primarily in Kashmir.

October 16, 1993

Terrorists kill two Russian military officers and wound a third outside an apartment building near an Algerian military academy where the Russians are instructors.

October 19, 1993

In Tiaret, Algeria, Armed Islamic Group (GIA) terrorists kidnap and then kill a Peruvian, a Filipino, and a Colombian from the cafeteria of an Italian construction firm. The three are technicians employed by the firm.

October 24, 1993

GIA terrorists kidnap three French diplomats as they leave their apartment in Algiers and kill a police officer who attempts to prevent the abduction. A week later, the three diplomats are released unharmed.

November 25, 1993

A car bomb explodes near the motorcade of Egyptian Prime Minister Atif Sedki, missing its target but killing a teenage girl and wounding at least 18 people. Al-Jihad later claims responsibility.

November 30, 1993

The GIA orders foreigners to leave Algeria immediately or be killed.

December 2, 1993

A Spanish businessman is killed near Algiers by the GIA. He is the first casualty after the demand for all foreigners to leave the country.

December 5, 1993

The GIA kills the Russian wife of an Algerian in Algiers.

December 7, 1993

The GIA kills a Frenchman in Blida, Algeria. In a separate incident in Algeria, GIA terrorists shoot and kill a British citizen at a gas station in Arzew.

December 14, 1993   A large group of GIA terrorists attack a work camp of a hydroelectric project in Tamezguida, Algeria, and murder 12 Croatian citizens, while two other Croatians escape with injuries. The group says the attack is part of an ongoing campaign to rid Algeria of all foreigners and to avenge Muslim deaths in Bosnia.

December 29, 1993   A couple, one Algerian and the other Belgian, is murdered by GIA terrorists in their home in Bouira near Algiers.

1994   The Islamic Army of Aden (IAA) is formed with the goal of overthrowing the Yemeni government and conducting operations against U.S. and other Western interests in Yemen.

January 29, 1994   Naeb Umran Maaitah, the number-two diplomat at Jordan's embassy in Beirut, is assassinated in Syrian-controlled West Beirut. The attack is likely committed by Iranian intelligence using Hezbollah members. Jordan deports 21 Iranian diplomats for their involvement in the attack.

February 1, 1994   Two journalists, one French and the other Australian, are killed by Islamist extremists in the Casbah of Algiers.

February 26, 1994   Mourad Sid Ahmed (Djafaar al-Afghani), the first leader of the GIA, is killed in Algiers along with nine other GIA members by Algerian security forces.

March 4, 1994   Members of al-Gama'a al-Islamiyya open fire on a Nile tourist cruise ship, killing one German tourist.

March 28, 1994   Islamist extremists murder a Russian Embassy employee in Algiers.

April 3, 1994   Assailants fire on a car near Sulaymaniyah, Iraq, killing a German journalist and her bodyguard.

April 12, 1994   An Iraqi opposition figure is assassinated near his West Beirut home. Two Iraqi diplomats arrested confess that they are acting on orders from Baghdad.

May 8, 1994   Two French priests are killed by GIA terrorists in Algiers.

May 19, 1994   A bus filled with Russian citizens is attacked near Ziam, Algeria, resulting in the deaths of three Russians and 11 Algerian guards. The attackers are also all killed.

May 29, 1994   An Iranian dissident, Seyyed Ahmad Sadr Lahijani, is killed as he drives his car through Ghalebieh, Iraq. Iranian agents are responsible.

June 20, 1994   A bomb explosion at the Shia Muslim shrine of the Eighth Imam in Mashad, Iran, kills 12. Iran blames the blast on the Mujahideen-e Khalq (MEK).

July 11, 1994   Islamists kill four men—two Serbians and two Algerians—in a restaurant at the Algiers Zoological Gardens.

July 12, 1994   Three GIA gunmen attack a police car at the gates of the Italian Embassy in Algiers, killing two policemen. Two of the attackers are also killed in the shoot-out.

August 3, 1994   GIA terrorists kill five French Embassy employees and injure one at a French residential compound in Algiers.

August 24, 1994   Three gunmen open fire in the lobby of a hotel in Marrakech, Morocco, killing two Spanish tourists and injuring two others. In January 1997, several members of "de Fes," an Islamist group which organized the series of attacks, are given sentences of between one and eight years' imprisonment.

September 1, 1994   Five people are killed when a police car escorting UN staff is fired upon between Luxor and Dandara in Egypt.

September 26, 1994 Algerian security forces kill Ahmed Abu Abdallah, also known as Sherif Ghousmi, head of the GIA. On the same day, GIA terrorists kill a Bosnian national in Algiers.

September 27, 1994 A terrorist with al-Gama'a al-Islamiyya kills two Egyptians and one German and wounds two after firing on a downtown tourist area in Hurghada, Egypt.

October 2, 1994   A French engineer is kidnapped from Meftah, Algeria, and his body is found six days later. The GIA claims responsibility.

October 13, 1994   Islamic extremists shoot and kill a South Korean businessman, employed by Daewoo Corporation, near his home in Algiers.

October 18, 1994   Some 30 members of the GIA attack an oil field in Algeria, killing two workers—one French and the other Italian.

October 23, 1994   GIA terrorists shoot and kill a British tourist and wound three others in an attack on a bus near Luxor, Egypt.

November 5, 1994   A Frenchman is killed in Bouira, near Algiers, by GIA terrorists.

December 11, 1994   Russian troops enter Chechnya to quash the independence movement. It is estimated that up to 100,000 people—many of them civilians—are killed in the 20-month war that follows.

December 11, 1994   Abu Sayyaf Group members plant a bomb on a Philippine airliner en route from Manila to Tokyo, killing one Japanese citizen and injuring ten others. Masterminding the plot is Ramzi Yousef, a Pakistani-born terrorist with links to al-Qaeda who had been sent to the Philippines by bin Laden to organize attacks against the United States. The explosion is believed to be a dry run for a plan known as Project Bojinka, a grandiose plan to blow up 12 U.S. jumbo jets over the Pacific.

December 21, 1994   A car bomb explodes in a Shia Muslim suburb of Beirut killing three people and injuring 16 others. Among the dead is the brother of terrorist Imad Mughniyah.

December 24, 1994   GIA members hijack an Air France plane at the airport in Algiers. During a rescue operation by a counter-terrorist unit, terrorists kill three hostages before all four of them are killed.

December 28, 1994 GIA terrorists murder four Catholic priests, three of them French and the fourth Belgian, in Tizi-Ouzou, Algeria. In June 1995, Algerian security forces kill five men who are believed to be the attackers.

1995 The Gerakan Mujahideen Islam Pattani (or Pattani Islamic Mujahideen Movement) is formed in southern Thailand by Afghanistan veterans with the aim of creating an independent Islamic state.

January 22, 1995 GIA gunmen shoot and kill a Frenchman as he drives through a park in Algiers, Algeria.

February 8, 1995 Pakistan arrests and extradites to the United States Ramzi Ahmed Yousef for his involvement in the bombing of the World Trade Center in 1993 and a plot against U.S. airlines in East Asia.

February 14, 1995 Three gunmen shoot and kill a former Afghan brigadier affiliated with the moderate, pro-Afghanistan Council for Understanding and National Unity at his residence in Pakistan. No group claims responsibility.

March 3, 1995 An Algerian-Palestinian student from the Algerian Arab College is murdered by GIA members.

March 8, 1995 Two gunmen armed with AK-47 assault rifles open fire on a U.S. Consulate van in Karachi, Pakistan, killing two U.S. diplomats and wounding a third.

April 4, 1995 Abu Sayyaf terrorists attack the Christian town of Ipil in Mindanao, killing 53 civilians and soldiers.

April 12, 1995 Abdul Hakim Murad is extradited to the United States by the Philippines for suspected involvement with Ramzi Yousef in the plot known as Project Bojinka, a plan to blow up 12 U.S. jumbo jets over the Pacific.

April 25, 1995 A New Zealand businessman is kidnapped and then killed near Chisimayu, Somalia, by Islamists.

May 5, 1995 Members of the GIA attack employees of a pipeline company in Algeria killing eight, including two Frenchmen, a Briton, a Canadian, and a Tunisian.

May 7, 1995 Armed assailants ambush a two-vehicle advance for a convoy of foreigners in Algeria, including Britons and Canadians, being escorted from a work site to their housing, killing three of their security force personnel.

May 17, 1995 Effat Haddad and Fereshteh Esfandiari, two MEK leaders, are murdered in Baghdad. It is the first operation mounted by the new office in charge of Iraq at the headquarters of the Iranian Revolutionary Guard.

June 5, 1995 Two members of the Iranian Kurdish "Toilers" Party (Komelah) in Sulaymaniyah are murdered by Iranian intelligence agents.

June 7, 1995 GIA terrorists shoot and kill a French couple in Algiers.

June 12, 1995   A Vietnamese lecturer at Tiaret University in Algeria is killed by GIA terrorists.

June 14, 1995   Chechen terrorists led by Shamil Basayev seize 2,000 hostages at a hospital in Budennovsk, southern Russia, and some 150 in a Russian commando operation are sent to free them. The terrorists demand an end to the war in Chechnya, withdrawal of Russian troops, and free passage out of Russia for themselves. The government finally agrees on free passage, allowing Basayev and his confederates to escape after a week. During this period, 129 of the hostages were killed and more than 400 injured.

June 26, 1995   Al-Gama'a al-Islamiyya unsuccessfully attempts to assassinate Egyptian President Hosni Mubarak in Addis Ababa, Ethiopia, but succeeds only in killing two Ethiopian military guards. Mubarak is in a motorcade headed from the airport to a meeting of the Organization of Africa Unity when two vehicles try to block the road and several gunmen fire at his armored limousine.

July 4, 1995   Six tourists—two U.S. citizens, two Britons, a Norwegian, and a German—are taken hostage in Kashmir by terrorists with al-Faran, a front group for the Pakistan-based Harakat ul-Ansar. One of the U.S. citizens escapes on July 8, but on August 13, the terrorists murder the Norwegian national and the other four are reportedly killed in December.

July 11, 1995   Abdelbaki Sahraoui, an imam known for his moderate calls for reconciliation and one of the founders of the Algerian Islamic Salvation Front (FIS), is assassinated by GIA terrorists in a Paris mosque. Another person is killed trying to protect him.

July 25, 1995   GIA terrorists bomb a Paris Metro station, killing seven. The bombing is the beginning of a spate of eight bombings or attempted bombings of French public transportation. On August 21, 1995, an Algerian, Abdeldrim Deneche, is arrested and held in Sweden under an anti-terrorism law as a suspect in this bombing. In October 1995, Sweden decides not to extradite him to France, but deports him instead.

August 1, 1995   A French Roman Catholic Bishop, Pierre Claverie, and his chauffeur are killed when a bomb the GIA plants explodes at his home in Oran, Algeria. In October 1997, Algerian security services shoot dead the terrorists suspected of killing him.

August 31, 1995   In Beirut, members of Asbat al-Ansar assassinate Sheikh Nizar al-Halabi, the head of a Sunni charitable organization opposing Islamist movements in Lebanon. The head of Asbat al-Ansar is sentenced to death in absentia in 1996 for this attack.

September 2, 1995   GIA militants shoot and kill an Italian in Oran, Algeria.

September 3, 1995   GIA assailants shoot and kill two nuns—one French, the other Maltese—in Algiers.

September 6, 1995   A crowd of 5,000 opposed to Taliban rule in Afghanistan set fire to the Pakistani Embassy in Kabul, killing two people and injuring the Pakistani ambassador. The group believes that Pakistan is supporting the Taliban.

September 7, 1995   A package bomb delivered by a woman explodes in the BBC/Reuters offices in Kashmir, killing a photographer and injuring two others. The likely perpetrators are the Dukhtaran-e-Millat group, a woman's organization committed to making Jammu and Kashmir a part of Islamic Pakistan.

September 17, 1995   Hashem Abdollahi, the son of the chief witness in the trial of those accused of murdering former Iranian prime minister Shapour Bakhtiar, is assassinated when terrorists, apparently Iranian government agents, break into his father's apartment.

October 1, 1995   Sheik Omar Abdel Rahman and nine codefendants are convicted in a Manhattan federal court for involvement in the 1993 bombing of the World Trade Center and for conspiring to bomb the UN, the FBI building in New York, the Lincoln and Holland tunnels, and other New York landmarks. Abdel Rahman is also found guilty of plotting to murder Egyptian President Husni Mubarak, and defendant El Sayyid Nosair is also convicted of "murder in aid of racketeering" in relation to the death of Rabbi Meir Kahane, the American founder of an arch-conservative Jewish group, in 1990. Abdel Rahman and Nosair receive life in prison; the others receive prison terms ranging from 25 to 57 years.

October 20, 1995   A car bomb detonates outside the local police headquarters building in Rijeka, Croatia, killing the driver and injuring 29 bystanders. Al-Gama'a al-Islamiyya claims responsibility. Croatia is targeted to pressure authorities there into releasing the group's spokesman, Tala'at Fuad Kassem, who had been detained by Croatian police in Zagreb earlier in the year. After the bombing, Croatian authorities say that Kassem is no longer in the country.

November 13, 1995   A van packed with 100 pounds of the plastic explosive Semtex explodes outside the Office of the Program Manager of the Saudi Arabian National Guard in Riyadh, killing seven people, including five Americans and a Filipino, and wounding 60. The attack is claimed by several terrorist groups with links to Iran, Libya, Syria, and Saudi Arabia. On April 22, 1996, Saudi authorities televise the confessions of four Sunni Saudi nationals opposed to the government; the men are executed on May 31.

November 13, 1995   An Egyptian diplomat known to be active in tracking down Egyptian Islamist activists is shot to death in the underground garage of his apartment building in Geneva, Switzerland.

November 18, 1995   Al-Gama'a al-Islamiyya members open fire on a train filled with tourists en route from Aswan to Cairo about 250 miles south of Cairo, killing an Egyptian train worker and injuring another.

November 19, 1995   A suicide bomber drives a vehicle loaded with a bomb into the Egyptian Embassy in Islamabad, killing at least 16 persons and injuring some 60 others. Al-Gama'a al-Islamiyya, the Jihad Group, and the International Justice Group all claim responsibility for the bombing. In February 1996, the Pakistani government arrests three Sudanese in connection with the attack. In August 1996, Egypt's security services announce that Jihad is responsible for the bombing and that 41 members have been arrested and have made confessions.

November 30, 1995   Four suspected GIA terrorists shoot and kill two Latvian seamen and wound a third in Algeria.

December 21, 1995   A car bomb explodes in a market in Peshawar, killing 45 people and injuring 100, probably by Afghan terrorists.

1996   The Islamic Movement of Uzbekistan (IMU), an Islamist coalition, is formed to turn their country into an Islamist state. IMU fighters train in camps in Afghanistan, some controlled by Osama bin Laden.

1996   The Salafist Group for Preaching and Combat (GSPC) forms as a splinter group from the GIA. It is committed to toppling Algeria's secular government and waging high-profile attacks against Western interests. By 2000, the GSPC takes over the GIA's external networks across Europe and North Africa and moves to establish an Islamic International under the aegis of Osama bin Laden.

1996   Lashkar-e-Jhangvi (LIJ), also known as Lashkar-e-Jhangvi, a Sunni-Deobandi group, is established to create a Sunni Islamist state in Pakistan. The group's original targets are the Shia minority in Pakistan.

1996   The Moro National Liberation Front signs a peace treaty with the Philippines government, and the organization's leader, Nur Misuari, becomes governor of a four-province Muslim semi-autonomous area on Mindanao. Many members defect to the Abu Sayyaf Group and the Moro Islamic Liberation Front. Terrorists continue to claim attacks in the name of the "Moro National Liberation Front" even after the peace accord is signed in 1996.

January 18, 1996   A bomb planted by the Somalian al-Ittihad al-Islami explodes at a hotel in Addis Ababa, Ethiopia, killing at least four persons and injuring 20 others.

February 20, 1996   Two members of the Iranian MEK are found dead in their Istanbul apartment. In April 1996, authorities apprehend several suspects, who claim they received their orders for the attack from Iranian diplomats stationed in Turkey.

March 4, 1996   Molavi Abdul-Malek, the son of a prominent Sunni cleric in Iraq and a well-known opponent of Iran's radical Shiite regime, is murdered along with an associate by two gunmen as he is leaving his house in Karachi, Pakistan.

March 14, 1996   Assailants set fire to a restaurant in Sitrah, Bahrain, and throw Molotov cocktails inside, killing seven Bangladeshi employees. Three Shia Muslims are sentenced to death in July 1996 for the attack.

March 21, 1996   A car bomb is detonated in a crowded New Delhi marketplace, killing 25 people and injuring more than 50. The Jammu and Kashmir Islamic Front claims responsibility.

March 27, 1996   GIA terrorists kidnap seven French monks from their monastery in Algeria's Medea region. On April 26, the terrorists offer to free the monks in exchange for the release of GIA members held in France, but the French government refuses and the monks are killed.

April 1996	The U.S. Department of State expels a Sudanese diplomat at the UN who has ties to conspirators planning to bomb the UN building and other targets in New York in 1993.
April 18, 1996	Four al-Gama'a al-Islamiyya militants open fire on a group of Greek tourists in front of the Europa Hotel in Cairo, killing 18 Greeks and injuring 12 Greeks and two Egyptians. The group claims it intended to attack a group of Israeli tourists they believed were staying at the hotel.
April 21, 1996	A bomb explodes at a guesthouse popular with foreign backpackers in New Delhi, killing 12. Three groups claim joint responsibility: the Jammu and Kashmir Islamic Front; Harkat-ul-Momineen, another group seeking Jammu's inclusion in Pakistan; and the Khalistan Liberation Force, a pro-Sikh organization.
April 23, 1996	Dzhokar Dudayev, the first president elected in the self-proclaimed Chechen Republic, is killed by a Russian missile attack in southwestern Chechnya.
May 1996	In response to U.S. pressure and the threat of UN sanctions, Sudan expels Osama bin Laden. Within a month, bin Laden takes refuge in Afghanistan.
May 5, 1996	Unknown Islamist separatists kill eight Hindu Nepalese migrant workers near Srinagar, Kashmir.
May 27, 1996	Reza Mazlouman, a government official under the shah and a dissident activist, is murdered in Paris by an Iranian resident of Germany with alleged ties to Iran's Ministry of Intelligence and Security (MOIS). German authorities arrest and then extradite to France an Iranian national in Bonn on suspicion of participating in the assassination.
June 4, 1996	Two Russian servicemen's wives are shot while visiting a cemetery in Dushanbe, Tajikstan. Members of "Muzlokandov's Gang," an Islamic extremist group, are suspected.
June 25, 1996	A fuel truck carrying a bomb explodes outside the U.S. military's Khobar Towers housing facility in Dhahran, Saudi Arabia, killing 19 U.S. military personnel and wounding 515 persons, including 240 U.S. personnel. In June 2001, a U.S. district court in Alexandria, Virginia, identifies Saudi Hezbollah as the culprit.
July 1996	Djamel Zitouni, head of the Armed Islamic Group (GIA), is killed in factional fighting in Algeria.
July 8, 1996	Two al-Ittihad al-Islami terrorists open fire on the Ethiopian minister of transport and communications as he arrives at his office in Addis Ababa, killing two guards and two passersby, and wounding their target.
July 25, 1996	A bomb goes off in a commuter train in Paris, killing four and injuring 62 people. No group claims responsibility.
August 1, 1996	A bomb planted by the GIA explodes at the home of the French archbishop of Oran, Algeria, killing him and his chauffeur. Algerian security services kill three terrorists for involvement in the attack.

August 5, 1996	The chief representatives of the Kurdistan Democratic Party and a delegate of the "Iraqi Kurdish Autonomous Government" are murdered in Paris. Local Kurdish leaders blame Iraqi or Iranian state agents for the crime.
August 11, 1996	Suspected gunmen from al-Ittihad al-Islami gunmen (*see* 1990) kill two Ethiopian businessmen in Beledweyne, Somalia, to avenge Ethiopia's two-day military incursion into Somalia earlier that month.

The Era of Global Jihadist War

The Islamist successes in Iran and Afghanistan proved hard to repeat elsewhere. In Algeria and Egypt, Islamist insurgencies that depended heavily on terrorism against civilians and the assassination of officials had failed. As for Saudi Arabia, bin Laden's personal top priority, the rebellion had barely carried out a few attacks.

Not only was government repression defeating them militarily, but the radicals did not win mass support. On the contrary, their extremist ideology and use of terrorism against fellow Muslims alienated the great majority of the population. In southern Lebanon, Hezbollah attacks had brought an Israeli withdrawal but that group is no closer to its goal of taking over the country or destroying Israel. The same point applied to the Palestinian Islamist groups Hamas and Islamic Jihad, whose terrorism helped sabotage the peace process but did not threaten Israel's existence.

Rather than admit flaws in their ideology, strat-egy, tactics, and overall goal, it was easier for bin Laden and others to pin the blame on the United States, the West, and Israel—often put in terms of the Christians and Jews. These enemies were said to be responsible for all the problems of the Muslims and also for the failure of the previous revolutionary efforts. Thus, the main targets should be these foreign forces rather than Arab governments.

Not all Islamist movements, or even Islamist terrorist groups, accepted this new orientation. For one thing, bin Laden's activities increased Western security measures, which included expelling Islamists who were not Jihadists but had been operating, for example, against Egypt. Moreover, some charged that bin Laden's doctrine took the heat off Arab regimes, in effect helping them to survive. Others, notably in Egypt, simply decided to give up—at least in terms of using violence—concluding that they had been following the wrong path.

August 23, 1996	Osama bin Laden issues a "declaration of war" against Christians and Jews throughout the world.
September 23, 1996	Four gunmen open fire indiscriminately at a Sunni mosque in Multan, Pakistan, killing 23 worshippers and wounding 50 others. In 2001, ten men were sentenced to life imprisonment for the crime.
September 26, 1996	The Taliban militia, which has been fighting a civil war in Afghanistan, captures the capital city, Kabul. It establishes the Islamic Emirate of Afghanistan and hosts Islamist radicals from around the world for military training.
November 15, 1996	In Hammamet, Algeria, GIA terrorists behead a Bulgarian businessman who is the former Bulgarian defense attaché to Algeria.
November 17, 1996	A fire at a hotel in Istanbul kills 17 Ukrainians and injures 40 other people. Turkish Islamic Jihad claims responsibility for the incident.
November 19, 1996	In Islamabad, Pakistan, a suicide bomber drives a vehicle into the Egyptian Embassy compound, killing at least 16 and injuring 60 persons.

December 3, 1996   A bomb set by GIA terrorists explodes aboard a Paris subway train, killing four—two French nationals, a Moroccan, and a Canadian—and injuring 86 persons.

December 17, 1996   Gunmen break into a residential area for workers with the International Committee of the Red Cross in Novyye Atagi, Chechnya, fatally shooting six staff employees and wounding a seventh. The victims include two Norwegians, a Dutch national, a Canadian, a New Zealander, a Spaniard, and a Swiss national.

December 31, 1996   Terrorists bomb a bus en route from Damascus to Aleppo, Syria, killing 11 and wounding 42 passengers. The Saudi group Islamic Movement for Change claims responsibility for the attack.

January 4, 1997   A car bomb explodes near a major marketplace in Dushanbe, Tajikistan, killing a Russian soldier and wounding four other persons. Islamist opposition fighters are suspected.

January 18, 1997   A bomb blast at the Lahore Sessions Court in Pakistan results in the deaths of 30, including Maulana Zia-ur-Rehman Farooqi, head of the Sipah-e-Sahaba Pakistan.

February 12, 1997   Al-Gama'a al-Islamiyya terrorists enter a church near Minya in Upper Egypt and open fire on those attending a weekly religious gathering, killing nine Coptic Christians.

February 20, 1997   Two members of the militant Muslim group Lashkar-e-Jhangvi detonate a bomb at the Iranian Cultural Centre in Multan, Pakistan, killing its director, Agha Syed Muhammad Ali Rahimi, and seven others. The two gunmen want revenge against Iran, which they blame for the bomb blast in the Lahore court on January 18, 1997.

February 21, 1997   Terrorists assassinate a prominent member of Azerbaijan's parliament in the lobby of his Baku apartment building.

March 14, 1997   Islamist militants enter a Christian town 300 miles south of Cairo and begin shooting, killing a total of 13 men.

June 13, 1997   Shia extremists set fire to an upholstery shop in Manama, Bahrain, killing four Indian expatriates who are trapped in their home above the shop.

June 22, 1997   GIA assailants kill a French woman in Bouzeguene, Algeria, and dump her body in a well.

July 6, 1997   Shia extremists set fire to a store in Sitra, India, killing a Bangladeshi and injuring another.

September 18, 1997   Gunmen attack a tourist bus in front of the Egyptian National Antiquities Museum in Cairo, killing nine German tourists and their Egyptian bus driver, and wounding eight others.

October 1, 1997   Three bombs explode on a passenger train as it approaches Ghaziabad, in Uttar Pradesh, India, killing two persons and injuring 38 others, including one Japanese and four Australian passengers.

November 12, 1997   Two gunmen assassinate four U.S. auditors from Union Texas Petroleum Corporation and their Pakistani driver after they drive away from the Sheraton Hotel in Karachi, Pakistan. Two groups claim responsibility for the attack—the Aimal Khufia Action Committee (previously unheard of) and the Islami Inqilabi Mahaz, a Lahore-based group of Afghan veterans.

November 17, 1997   In a popular Egyptian tourist site, the Hatshepsut Temple in the Valley of the Kings near Luxor, al-Gama'a al-Islamiyya (IG) gunmen shoot and kill 58 tourists and four Egyptians and wound 26 others. The six gunmen are killed in a two-hour battle with police. The attack comes as 65 alleged members of the IG go on trial in Cairo accused of conspiracy to murder. Following the massacre, the IG says that its armed attacks will continue until the group's demands are met, including the introduction of Sharia law, severing diplomatic relations with Israel, the return to Egypt of Sheik Omar Abdel Rahman (imprisoned in the U.S.), the release of Islamist detainees, and an end to trials by military courts.

November 22, 1997   GIA terrorists kill a German-born convert to Islam who is married to an Algerian woman in their home in Ain el Hajar, Saida Province, Algeria.

December 31, 1997   In one of the worst attacks in Algeria, GIA terrorists kill more than 400 civilians in Relizane Province, some 150 miles southwest of Algiers. The terrorists cut their victims' throats and chop them to death using knives and hatchets.

January 1, 1998   Rebel leader Shamil Basayev is appointed prime minister of Chechnya for six months. He then resigns to form a network of armed groups to fight the Russians and recruits fighters from other countries.

January 11, 1998   Some 100 GIA terrorists open fire in a movie theater in Sidi Ahmed, Algeria, and explode a bomb in a mosque in nearby Haouche Sahraoui, killing between 120 to 400 civilians. The attacks occur on the sixth anniversary of the army's decision to cancel national elections apparently won by the FIS.

January 11, 1998   In Lahore, terrorists massacre 25 Shia Muslims, mostly women and children, as they gather for a Koranic recital at a cemetery. Lashkar-e-Jhangvi claims responsibility for the attack.

January 14, 1998   A bomb attack on a mosque kills one person and injures ten others in Baraki, Algeria.

January 21, 1998   A bomb detonates at the campus of Algiers University killing two and injuring many. In a separate incident, a bomb detonates on a bus in Algeria and kills three people. In a third bombing, this one in a market in Zeralda, Algeria, three are killed and 30 wounded. The GIA is responsible for all these bombings.

January 25, 1998   Lashkar-e-Tayyiba and Hizbul Mujahideen terrorists murder 23 Hindus in Wandhama, a village near Srinagar, Kashmir.

February 14, 1998   Seventeen bombs explode in Coimbatore, India, during a political rally for the Hindu nationalist BJP Party, killing 50 and wounding over 200. The al-Umma group, an Indian Islamist group, is responsible.

February 17, 1998   Four boys are killed and three children wounded when a bomb detonates at a playground in Coimbatore, India. It is not clear which group is responsible.

February 21, 1998   A gunmen on a motorbike fatally shoots two Iranian engineers in Karachi, Pakistan. It is not clear which group is responsible.

February 23, 1998   Bin Laden announces the creation of a new alliance of terrorist organizations, the International Islamic Front for Jihad Against the Jews and Crusaders. The Front includes al-Gama'a al-Islamiyya, the Egyptian Islamic Jihad, the Harakat ul-Ansar, Jamiat-ul-Ulema-e-Pakistan, and Jihad Movement in Bangladesh. It issues the following *fatwa* to all Muslims: "The ruling to kill the Americans and their allies—civilians and military—is an individual duty for every Muslim who can do it in any country in which it is possible to do it, in order to liberate the al-Aqsa Mosque and the holy mosque [Mecca] from their grip, and in order for their armies to move out of all the lands of Islam, defeated and unable to threaten any Muslim."

February 23, 1998   Eighteen people are killed and 25 wounded in an explosion aboard a train in Tirat, Algeria. GIA is responsible.

March 7, 1998   Belgian police arrest ten suspected GIA terrorists in Brussels. The arrests are part of a joint security operation with France, Britain, Sweden, and Italy before the World Cup soccer match in Paris.

March 30, 1998   A radio broadcaster is gunned down while at work in Zamboanga City, Philippines. The Abu Sayyaf Group claims responsibility, saying the journalist is killed because of his strong criticisms of its organization.

March 31, 1998   A bomb explodes at a road near Hasbayya, Lebanon, killing five civilians who are in a van and wounding one. Hezbollah is responsible.

April 1998   GIA terrorists kill ten Moroccans near the border town of Oujda, Morocco.

April 10, 1998   MEK terrorists assassinate Brigadier General Ali Sayyad Shirazi, the Iranian armed forces deputy chief of the joint staff, outside his home in Tehran.

April 18, 1998   Lashkar-e-Tayyiba terrorists attack Barankot village in Udhampur District, Kashmir, killing 29 persons.

April 22, 1998   A gunman shoots and kills an Iranian clergyman and injures his two companions in Najaf, Iraq. No one claims responsibility for the attack.

April 24, 1998   A bomb at a mosque in Sanaa, Yemen, kills six people and injures 27 others. It is not clear which group is responsible.

May 4, 1998	Muslim militants kill nine—four members of a village defense committee, four other villagers, and one police officer near Jammu City, Kashmir.
May 5, 1998	Four people are killed in a home at Surankote, north of Jammu City, by Islamic militants.
May 6, 1998	Suspected Muslim militants kill five Hindu family members during a funeral procession outside the town of Poonch, Kashmir.
May 16, 1998	Two people are killed and seven others injured in blasts at two hotels in Karachi, Pakistan. It is not clear which group is responsible.
June 1998	Al Badr, another Islamic group advocating that Kashmir become part of Pakistan, is formed.
June 1, 1998	A bomb explodes at a busy market in the heart of Jammu City, Kashmir, killing one child and injuring 19 other persons. It is not clear which group is responsible.
June 2, 1998	Two people are killed and two injured in an explosion at the Islamic Revolution Court in Tehran. The Mujahideen-e Khalq (MEK) claims responsibility for the attack, stating that the attack is carried out in retaliation for the slaying of eight members of their group in a clash with Iranian security forces last November.
June 5, 1998	Three people are killed and one seriously injured by a bomb blast at a movie theater in Lahore, Pakistan. It is not clear which group is responsible.
June 7, 1998	A bomb detonates on an 18-car passenger train en route from Karachi to Peshawar, killing 23 persons and wounding at least 32 others. Pakistan blames India for the bombing. Indian officials deny the accusation.
June 18, 1998	Ayatollah Gharavi-Tabrizi, a Shia cleric from Najaf, Iraq, is killed along with his son, son-in-law, and driver. Iraqi agents are suspected.
June 19, 1998	Five Lashkar-e-Tayyiba terrorists attack the Hindu village of Champnari in Jammu, killing at least 25 members of a wedding party, and injuring seven others.
June 25, 1998	A popular Berber singer in Algeria, Lounes Matoub, is killed by GIA terrorists after they stop him at a roadblock. He is targeted because his songs criticize Islamist militants as well as the military-backed government.
June 28, 1998	A bomb hidden in a lunch box detonates in a popular picnic spot in Anantnag, Kashmir, killing two and injuring 15. It is not clear which group is responsible.
July 11, 1998	Muslim terrorists in Ain Defla, Algeria, kill two people at a fake roadblock. The same day, a bomb explodes at an Algiers flea market, killing 17 people and injuring 42.

July 23, 1998   A car bomb explodes while Chechnya's President Aslan Maskhadov is traveling through the streets of Grozny, killing two of his bodyguards and wounding others. No organization claims responsibility.

July 24, 1998   A bomb explodes near railroad tracks in Jammu and Kashmir as a train passes by, killing one soldier and injuring two civilians.

July 26, 1998   In separate incidents in western Algeria, 15 are killed in the village of Khelil and eight killed in Sidi Athmane. Muslim militants are likely responsible.

July 28, 1998   In Doda, Kashmir, Muslim terrorists kill at least eight members of two Hindu families and wound three others.

July 28, 1998   Muslim militants kill ten villagers northwest of Doda, Kashmir.

August 3, 1998   Lashkar-e-Tayyiba militants massacre 19 in Jammu's Poonch District, including women and children of three families.

August 4, 1998   Terrorists fire upon on a group of workers sleeping at a construction site in Himachal Pradesh, India, which borders Kashmir, killing 26 persons and wounding eight others. En route back to Kashmir, the terrorists target a second group of workers, killing eight persons and wounding three others. Islamic terrorists are responsible.

August 7, 1998   A suicide bomber drives a truck packed with explosives to the rear entrance of the U.S. Embassy in Nairobi, Kenya, and detonates his charge, killing 292 people, including 12 U.S. citizens, and injuring over 5,000. About nine minutes later, another terrorist detonates a truck fitted with an explosive device at the gate of the U.S. Embassy in Dar es Salaam, Tanzania, killing 11 and wounding 86, none of them Americans. Al-Qaeda is responsible for both blasts. On October 18, 2001, four al-Qaeda members—Wadih el-Hage, Khalfan Khamis Mohamed, Mohamed Sadeek Odeh, and Mohamed Rashed Daoud al-'Owhali—are convicted by a federal judge in New York of planning both embassy bombings and sentenced to life in prison without the possibility of parole.

August 10, 1998   Islamists throw a grenade and fire automatic weapons into a crowded bus in Anantnag, Kashmir, killing four persons and injuring seven others.

August 20, 1998   In retaliation for the bombing of the U.S. embassies in Kenya and Tanzania, the U.S. military strikes a number of facilities associated with bin Laden's network, including six terrorist training camps and a pharmaceuticals factory in Sudan, which intelligence sources believe produced components of chemical weapons. The U.S. administration later admits that the attack on the factory was a mistake.

August 23, 1998   In Iran, the Mujahideen-e Khalq (MEK) claims responsibility for the killing of Asadollah Lajevardi, former director of Tehran's Evin Prison, gunning him down in Tehran's Grand Bazaar. One of his bodyguards is also killed and several others wounded.

August 25, 1998   A Planet Hollywood restaurant in Cape Town, South Africa, is hit by a bomb that kills two people and injures 25. A group calling itself Muslims Against Global Oppression says the blast is in retaliation for the U.S. strike on Sudan.

August 31, 1998	An explosion set by the GIA rips through a crowded square in Algiers, killing at least 17 people and wounding 60.
August 31, 1998	Muhammad Ismail Memon, chairman of the Board of Secondary Education in Karachi, and his driver are killed by unknown assailants while he is returning home from his office.
September 1, 1998	Twenty-five people are killed in a bomb explosion in central Algeria. The GIA is likely responsible.
September 5, 1998	Seventeen people are killed and at least 68 others are injured in a powerful car bomb blast in Makhachkala, the capital of the Russian Republic of Dagestan. Two men are arrested and serving sentences for the attack.
October 3, 1998	Four telecommunication engineers (three Britons and one New Zealander) are kidnapped by Chechen terrorists in Grozny where they are working on installing a mobile phone system. Badrudi Murtazayev, a Chechen terrorist who is accused of ordering their deaths, is arrested in Azerbaijan in March 7, 2001, and handed over to the Russians with another wanted rebel leader.
October 9, 1998	Terrorists fire upon the Iranian Cultural Center in Multan, Pakistan, killing one Pakistani security guard and wounding another. It is not clear which group is responsible.
November 1998	France prosecutes eight suspected members of Algeria's FIS on charges of smuggling arms to terrorists. The suspects allegedly belong to a network headed by FIS leader Djamel Lounici, who is under house arrest in Italy pending trial. A French court sentences Lounici in absentia to five years in prison for arms smuggling in another case concerning Morocco.
November 17, 1998	A bomb explodes near the Madana bridge in Surankote, Kashmir, killing four persons and injuring several others. It is not clear which group is responsible.
November 24, 1998	A car bomb explodes near the German Embassy in Sanaa, Yemen, killing two Yemenis and injuring several others. It is not clear which group is responsible, but the target may have been the home of a sheikh from the Waela tribe.
December 9, 1998	In Bandipura, Kashmir, unknown Muslim terrorists throw a grenade at a group near a bus station, killing three persons and injuring 20 others.
December 10, 1998	GIA terrorists attack three villages near Tadjana, southwest of Algiers, killing 81 people. They target families, including children, with relatives in the civil defense forces.
December 18, 1998	The leader of the Abu Sayyaf Group, Abdurajak Abubakar Janjalani, is killed in a clash with Filipino police in the village of Lamitan on Basilan Island. His younger brother, Khadaffy Janjalani, replaces him as leader of the group.
December 28, 1998	Sixteen tourists—12 Britons, two Americans, and two Australians—are taken hostage by the Islamic Army in Abyan Province, Yemen. The terrorists demand the release from jail of several members of their group, including their leader,

Saleh Haidara al-Atwi, and the lifting of sanctions imposed on Iraq, Libya, and Sudan. One Briton and a Yemeni guide escape. The rest are held for six days until Yemeni security forces stage a rescue attempt that results in four hostages being killed by their captors. On October 18, 1999, Yemeni authorities execute Zein al-Abidin Abu Bakr al-Mehdar, known as Abu al-Hassan, the leader of the Aden-Abyan Islamic Army, a Sunni extremist group seeking the overthrown of the Yeminite government, for the attack.

December 31, 1998   Salih Izzet Erdis, head of the Great East Islamic Raiders Front, is captured in Turkey. He is sentenced to death in April 2001 for "attempting to overthrow Turkey's secular state by force." But his death sentence is later commuted when Ankara abolishes the death penalty in August 2002.

January 3, 1999   In Jolo, southern Philippines, Abu Sayyaf terrorists throw a grenade into a crowd that has gathered to watch firemen fight a blaze in a supermarket, killing ten people.

February 9, 1999   Lashkar-e-Tayyiba terrorists in Kashmir attack a village, killing a family of four—relatives of a member of the local village defense committee—and injuring one other person.

February 15, 1999   Muslim terrorists assassinate the owner of a video shop in Srinagar, Kashmir.

February 15, 1999   A bomb explodes in a crowded marketplace in Srinagar, Kashmir, injuring six persons. It is not clear which group is responsible.

February 16, 1999   Islamic Movement in Uzbekistan terrorists detonate five car bombs near government buildings in the capital, Tashkent, killing 16 and injuring over a 100. The terrorists are targeting President Islam Karimov, who says he narrowly escaped. Twenty-two are convicted of the bombings, and six are sentenced to death while the rest receive lengthy prison sentences.

February 20, 1999   Members of Lashkar-e-Tayyiba massacre 20 persons in two districts in Jammu.

February 22, 1999   In Kashmir, Lashkar-e-Tayyiba militants kill three persons.

February 22, 1999   Muslim militants kill a politician from the dominant National Conference Party in Kashmir.

March 1999   Al-Gama'a al-Islamiyya leaders in Egypt issue a cease-fire, although it is rejected by the organization's spiritual leader Sheik Omar Abdel Rahman, who is imprisoned in the United States.

March 1999   Moscow's top envoy to Chechnya, General Gennadiy Shpigun, is kidnapped from the airport in Grozny, and his corpse is found in Chechnya in March 2000.

March 11, 1999   Terrorists fatally shoot three—a man and his two daughters—and wound four, including his wife, in Srinagar, Kashmir. It is not clear which group is responsible.

March 19, 1999   Chechen terrorists kill 60 people in an explosion in a market in Vladikavkaz, the capital of the Republic of North Ossetia in Russia.

March 21, 1999   In the fourth recent attempt to assassinate Chechen President Aslan Maskhadov, a bomb explodes along the path of his motorcade only moments after his car has passed, killing one person and injuring eight others. The president once again escapes death.

April 1999   The Egyptian government convicts more than 100 Egyptian extremists, including many Islamic Jihad members responsible for planning an attack against the U.S. Embassy in Albania in August 1998.

April 1999   The Jordanian State Security Court sentences members of the outlawed Reform and Defiance Movement—a radical Islamist group—for conducting small bombings in Amman between mid-March and early May 1998 targeting Jordanian security forces, the Modern American School, and a major hotel. Three are convicted in absentia and sentenced to life imprisonment with hard labor, while another receives a 15-year prison sentence. Three others are acquitted.

April 1, 1999   Islamic militants shoot and kill three family members in their home in Kashmir.

April 10, 1999   General Ali Sayyad Shirazi, deputy chief of the joint staff of the Iranian armed forces and advisor to Iran's supreme leader, Ayatollah Ali Khamenei, is assassinated in Tehran. The MEK claims responsibility, saying it targeted Shirazi as revenge for his role as commander of Iranian ground forces during the 1980–1988 Iran-Iraq War.

April 20, 1999   In Rajauri, Kashmir, a bomb explodes in a goldsmith shop, killing five persons, injuring 47 others, and causing major damage. It is not clear which group is responsible.

May 11, 1999   Muslim militants kill four members of a family in Kupwara District, Kashmir.

May 19, 1999   An explosion on a bus in Jammu kills one person and injures eight others. Kashmiri militants are suspected.

May 24, 1999   A bomb explodes on the route in Grozny taken by vehicles carrying Chechen Mufti Akhmad-Khadzhi Kadyrov, killing five of his bodyguards. This is the fourth attempt on the life of the mufti who is sympathetic to Moscow.

June 5, 1999   Algeria's AIS announces that it is calling a halt to its fight against the Algerian government in return for amnesty for its fighters. A reported 6,000 terrorists turn themselves and receive amnesty under President Abdelaziz Bouteflika's "civil concord" plan.

June 9, 1999   In Baghdad, a car bomb explodes next to a bus carrying members of the MEK, killing seven members and injuring 23 others, including 15 Iraqi civilians. The Iranian government is likely responsible.

August–September 1999   Chechen terrorists Shamil Basayev and Ibn-ul-Khattab lead a small army of Islamists in an unsuccessful attempt to take over the neighboring Republic of Dagestan and establish a Chechen-Dagestan Islamic republic.

September 4, 1999   An apartment building for soldiers' families in Buinaksk, Dagestan, in south Russia, explodes, killing 62 people and injuring at least 200. A previously unknown group, the Dagestan Liberation Army, claims responsibility in retaliation for Russian attacks on Islamists in neighboring Chechnya.

September 7, 1999   Police in Egypt kill four members of al-Gama'a al-Islamiyya, including Farid Kidwani, the group's operational leader in Egypt. The terrorists are killed after opening fire on police who had come to arrest them in an apartment in the suburb of Giza.

September 8, 1999   A bomb explodes in a nine-story apartment building in Moscow, killing 95 and injuring over 200. The Dagestan Liberation Army claims responsibility.

September 13, 1999   As residents of Moscow prepare to mark a day of mourning for victims of the September 8 explosion, a second apartment block is hit four miles away, killing 120 people. The Dagestan Liberation Army claims responsibility.

September 16, 1999   In the fourth attack on Russian apartment buildings in ten days, a car bomb explodes next to apartments in Volgodonsk in the Rostov region of south Russia, killing 18 people. The Dagestan Liberation Army claims responsibility.

October 1999   A Belgian court sentences Farid Melouk, a French citizen of Algerian origin who is head of the Brussels network of the GIA, to imprisonment for nine years. He was previously convicted in absentia by a French court as an accessory in the Paris Metro bombings in 1995.

October 1999   After abandoning its fragile peace treaty with Chechen terrorists, Russia redeploys in Chechnya following a string of terrorist attacks and creates its own government there called the State Council of the Republic of Chechnya.

October 4, 1999   A land mine explodes near a polling station in Pampore, Kashmir, killing one election officer, wounding another, and injuring three police officers. Authorities suspect Muslim militants.

October 15, 1999   Siddig Ibrahim Siddig Ali is sentenced to 11 years in prison by an U.S. court for his role in a plot to bomb New York City landmarks and to assassinate Egyptian President Husni Mubarak in 1993.

October 21, 1999   Ahmet Taner Kislali, a prominent Turkish academic and former minister of culture known for his secular views, is killed by a bomb outside his home in Ankara. The Islamic Great East Front is responsible.

November 4, 1999   Terrorists detonate three separate bombs in Lahore, Pakistan, killing two, one at a restaurant and another at a bus stop. The attacks, blamed on India, come as the Lashkar-e-Tayyiba militant group holds a convention.

November 23, 1999   A senior official of the FIS in Algeria, Abdelkader Hachani, a government opponent and peace activist, is assassinated while he is at a dental clinic in Algiers.

November 29, 1999   A group supporting deposed Pakistani premier Nawaz Sharif claims responsibility for a bus bomb in Hyderabad, Pakistan, that kills two and injures nine others.

December 1999   Jordanian authorities arrest a group (which includes Jordanians, an Iraqi, and an Algerian) with ties to al-Qaeda who are planning to carry out terrorist operations against U.S. and Israeli tourists visiting Jordan.

December 24, 1999   Harakat ul-Mujahideen members hijack an Indian Airlines plane en route from Kathmandu, Nepal, to New Delhi. The plane is diverted to Dubai, United Arab Emirates, where an Indian passenger is killed on board and 27 hostages are freed. The hijackers order the plane to Kandahar, Afghanistan, where they demand the release of a number of Islamic militants imprisoned in India. On December 31, the Indian government agrees to the demand, releasing in exchange for the hostages' safe return Masood Azhar, a Muslim cleric and general secretary of the Harakat ul-Mujahideen in jail since February 1994, Mushtaq Ahmed Zargar, head of al-Umar Mujahideen, and Ahmed Omar Saeed Sheikh, who becomes an al-Qaeda activist.

December 30, 1999   The Lashkar-e-Tayyiba leader in Jammu and Kashmir, Abu Muwaih Shankarpora, is killed in Jammu.

January 2000   Just days after he is released from an Indian jail, Masood Azhar forms the Jaish-e-Mohammed (JEM), an Islamic extremist group committed to uniting Kashmir with Pakistan and to establishing an Islamic state in India.

January 1–3, 2000   After a dispute between a Christian store owner and a Muslim patron, Muslim villagers of al-Kosheh in upper Egypt go on a three-day rampage in several villages, killing 21 Coptic Christians.

January 4, 2000   Rocket-propelled grenades are fired at the Russian Embassy in Beirut, killing a policeman and wounding six others before one attacker is shot dead by security forces. The terrorists are members of Asbat al-Ansar, a Lebanon-based Sunni Islamic group, which targets Russia because of its actions in Chechnya.

January 17, 2000   Turkish security forces kill Huseyin Velioglu, the leader of Turkish Hezbollah. The attack is the impetus for a yearlong series of operations against the group throughout Turkey that results in the detention of some 2,000 individuals and the discovery of 70 bodies of Turkish and Kurdish businessmen and journalists that Turkish Hezbollah murdered during the mid- to late-1990s. Turkish Hezbollah is a Kurdish group that arose in the late 1980s in the Diyarbakir area, seeking to create an independent Kurdish Islamist state.

January 17, 2000   Eight persons are killed and 31 others injured in a bomb explosion at a bus stop in Karachi. Supporters of the deposed government of Mohammad Nawaz Sharif claimed responsibility.

January 22, 2000   The corpse of Konca Kuris, a feminist writer and student of Islam, is discovered in Turkey. Kuris is the only woman among many bodies showing signs of torture found in the hideout of the Hizbollahi Ilim, a pro-Iranian radical group that advocates turning Turkey into an Islamist state. A 39-year-old mother of five, Kuris is targeted because of her outspoken views on women and Islam.

February 5, 2000   A mortar attack by the MEK on Iran's Presidential Palace results in the death of one person and injuries to five others.

February 5, 2000   Eight persons are killed and 40 others injured in a bomb explosion in a train at Hyderabad, Pakistan.

March 3, 2000   A bomb detonates on a crowded bus parked on a ferry traveling across Pangil Bay to Ozamis in the southern Philippines, killing 26 people and wounding dozens more. The Moro Islamic Liberation Front is likely responsible.

March 3, 2000   A bomb explodes on a bus in Sirhind, Punjab, India, killing eight persons and injuring seven others. The Indian government believes either Kashmiri militants or Sikh radicals are responsible.

March 4, 2000   A restaurant is bombed by Islamist terrorists in Basilan, Philippines, killing one person and injuring 17.

March 20, 2000   Thirty-five Sikhs are massacred in Chattisinghpora, a Jammu and Kashmir village. The attack is timed to coincide with President Bill Clinton's arrival in India for a state visit. Lashkar-e-Tayyiba and the Hizbul Mujahideen are both involved in the attack.

March 28, 2000   Seven persons are killed and 16 others injured in a bomb blast at a crowded market in the town of Torkham, Afghanistan, on the border of Pakistan.

April 12, 2000   Assailants, whose affiliation is unknown, attack a crowded Shia mosque in Mulawali, Pakistan, with rifles and grenades, killing 15 and injuring more that 20.

April 23, 2000   In their first attack on foreign soil, Abu Sayyaf terrorists raid a divers' resort on Sipadan Island, Malaysia, on the coast of Borneo, and kidnap 21 foreign tourists and Malaysian hotel workers, taking them to their terrorist hideout on Jolo Island in the Philippines. The kidnappers demand the establishment of a separate Muslim state in Mindanao and multimillion-dollar ransoms in cash. The terrorists then kidnap a German and three French journalists who have come to cover the crisis and 13 Filipino Christian evangelists who have come to offer spiritual guidance. All but one of the hostages is released on August 29 after Libyan leader Muammar Qaddafi reportedly pays $1 million ransom for each hostage. Libya has long-standing ties with Muslim rebels in the Philippines and has helped negotiate in previous kidnappings. The release also wins Qaddafi favorable international publicity at a time when he has been working to end years of international isolation. The last remaining hostage, Roland Ulla, a Filipino who worked at the dive resort, remains with his captors until June 4, 2003, when he escapes.

May 12, 2000   A bus carrying local inhabitants is blown up by a remote-controlled mine near the village of Dzhaglargi in Chechnya, killing three people and wounding 18. Chechen terrorist groups are responsible.

May 18, 2000   Five people are killed and at least 58 wounded in grenade and bomb blasts in a busy market and a bakery in Zamboanga, southern Philippines, by Abu Sayyaf terrorists.

May 21, 2000   A bomb explodes at a movie theater in Manila's largest shopping mall, killing one person and injuring 11 others. Islamist terrorists are likely responsible.

May 30, 2000	In Grozny, the capital of Chechnya, a car carrying the deputy of the Russian envoy to Chechnya, Grozny Mayor Supyan Makhchayev, and the mayor's aide is blown up by two remote-controlled mines as it enters the city, killing the envoy's deputy and the mayoral aide. Chechen terrorists are responsible.
July 9, 2000	Five people are killed and 17 wounded in a blast at the central market in Vladikavkaz, in the Russian Republic of North Ossetia, also site of a March 1999 explosion. Chechen terrorists are responsible.
July 16, 2000	A powerful bomb explodes at a market in a Christian town in the southern Philippines, killing two people and wounding 33 others. Authorities believe the Moro Islamic Liberation Front is responsible, although it denies involvement.
July 17, 2000	Ten persons are killed in a train blast in Hyderabad, Pakistan. It is not clear which group is responsible.
August 1, 2000	A bomb detonates at the home of the Filipino ambassador in Jakarta, Indonesia, killing two people and injuring dozens including the ambassador. In June 2003, murder charges for this and other terrorist attacks are filed against Muslim extremist Fathur al-Ghozi, who is said to have acted as the main liaison officer between Jemaah Islamiyah and the Moro Islamic Liberation Front (MILF).
August 1–2, 2000	The Lashkar-e-Tayibba engages in a 24-hour terrorist spree spread over three districts of Jammu and Kashmir, killing more than 100 persons.
August 12, 2000	Four American mountain climbers in the Kara-Su Valley of Kyrgyzstan are taken hostage by the Islamic Movement of Uzbekistan rebels along with one Kyrgyzstani soldier. The rebels kill the soldier, but the four Americans manage to escape six days later.
September 13, 2000	A bomb explodes in the Jakarta, Indonesia, Stock Exchange basement parking garage, killing six and injuring dozens. The Free Aceh Movement (GAM) is likely responsible. The group seeks an independent Islamic country in Aceh Province on the Indonesian island of Sumatra.
September 18, 2000	The Jordanian State Security Court convicts several Sunni extremists, some in absentia, for plotting terrorist attacks against U.S. and Israeli targets during the millennium celebrations in late 1999. Eight defendants receive life imprisonment, while 14 receive prison sentences ranging from seven-and-a-half to 15 years.
September 19, 2000	Twelve persons are killed in a bomb explosion in Islamabad. It is not clear which group is responsible.
October 1, 2000	Terrorists in Tajikistan detonate two bombs in a Christian church in Dushanbe, killing seven persons and injuring 70 others. The church was founded by a Korean-born U.S. citizen, and most of those killed and wounded are Korean.
October 12, 2000	In Aden, Yemen, a small dinghy carrying explosives rams the U.S. destroyer *USS Cole,* killing 17 U.S. sailors and injuring 39 others. Al-Qaeda is responsible for the attack. The mastermind of the bombing is identified as Yemeni Abdul

Rahman Hussein Mohammed al-Saafani (real name: Abd al-Rahim al-Nashiri), who flees abroad. Eight individuals, including civil servants, implicated in the attack stand trial in Yemen.

November 3, 2000 In Kashmir, a prominent Shia politician, Agha Syed Mehdi, his driver, and four bodyguards are killed by the explosion of a land mine beneath his car. Sipah-e-Sahaba Pakistan terrorists are responsible.

December 9, 2000 A car bomb explosion in the Chechen village of Alkhan-Yurt kills 21 people and injures 30. The bomb is likely planted by Chechen Islamists.

December 23, 2000 Terrorists storm the Red Fort, a seventeenth-century landmark, tourist attraction, and symbol of Indian independence in New Delhi, killing three people with firearms. The Lashkar-e-Tayyiba is responsible.

December 30, 2000 A series of bombs explodes in Manila, killing 22 and injuring 100. The most devastating explosion is in the front car of a crowded elevated train as it is pulling into a station. Another bomb detonates on a park bench near the U.S. Embassy. In May 2003, MILF terrorist Saifulla Unos admits to organizing the attacks.

January 8, 2001 In Annaba, Algeria, GIA militants kill six Russian citizens.

January 24, 2001 About 20 Turkish Hezbollah terrorists ambush the motorcade of police chief in Diyarbakir, a largely Kurdish-populated city, and assassinate him and five other officers.

January 28, 2001 Gunmen attack a van carrying Sunni Muslims from a religious school in Karachi, Pakistan, killing five and wounding three. Sipah-e-Sahaba Pakistan is responsible.

February 11, 2001 GIA terrorists fire on a shantytown in northern Algeria, killing at least 27 people, half of whom are children.

March 3, 2001 An explosive device placed under a seat in a cinema in Muzaffarabad, in Pakistani-controlled Kashmir, detonates during a movie, killing four. No group claims responsibility, but Pakistani officials blame Indian intelligence.

March 14, 2001 As the Filipino president is visiting Mindanao, there is a rocket attack on a residential area in Maguindanao that kills three people. It is not clear which group is responsible.

March 15, 2001 Three Chechens hijack a Russian charter jet carrying 175 passengers, en route from Istanbul to Moscow. Fuel limitations force the plane to land in Medina, Saudi Arabia. There Saudi special forces storm the plane. One crew member, one passenger, and one hijacker are killed.

April 6, 2001 Algerian national Ahmed Ressam is convicted in Los Angeles for a plot to bomb Los Angeles International Airport at the peak of travel around January 1, 2000.

April 12, 2001   The deputy head of the Chechnya administration, Shamalu Deniyev, is killed when a bomb explodes during a news interview he is giving near Grozny. Chechen Islamists are likely responsible.

April 13, 2001   The National Conference Party bloc president for Beerwah, Kashmir, Haji Ghulam Mohammad, is assassinated and his son injured by Islamic terrorists.

April 16, 2001   Muhammad Suban, a newly elected official, is shot and killed by militants at the Challar village in the Arnas area of Udhampur District, Kashmir.

May 11, 2001   Six Hindu villagers are decapitated and three injured by terrorists in the Doda District of Kashmir. Muslim militants are likely responsible.

May 18, 2001   Maulana Salim Qadri, chairman of the Sunni Tehrik (Sunni Movement), is killed in Karachi, Pakistan, along with four others—his nephew, brother-in-law, driver, and a policeman—while driving to the mosque for Friday prayers. Sipah-e-Sahaba Pakistan is responsible. In April 2003, a member of the group is sentenced to death in a Karachi court for the attack.

May 22, 2001   Moro National Liberation Front guerrillas raid the luxurious Pearl Farm beach resort on Samal Island in the southern Philippines, killing two resort workers and wounding three others.

May 27, 2001   The Abu Sayyaf Group kidnaps 20 individuals, including three U.S. citizens—Martin and Gracia Burnham and Guillermo Sobero—from the Dos Palmas Island Resort, a diving resort located on the island of Palawan in the Philippines. The hostages are taken to Basilan Island in the Sulu Archipelago, and the terrorists demand the release of convicted prisoners in the United States and $10 million in ransom. On June 11, 2001, the Abu Sayyaf members behead American hostage Guillermo Sobero. On June 7, 2002, Martin Burnham and a Filipina nurse, Ediborah Yap, die in a firefight when Philippine military forces try to free the hostages.

June 3, 2001   An explosive device in a Catholic church in Baniarchar, Bangladesh, results in nine deaths and 25 injuries. Radical Islamists are the likely perpetrators.

June 6, 2001   Unknown terrorists gun down the leader of the Gekhi-Chu village administration in Chechnya.

June 11, 2001   Three gunmen, likely radical Muslims, kill a trader near the Andro Kaharam village in Imphal, India.

June 14, 2001   Free Aceh Movement (GAM) terrorists kill a civil servant and his wife in Peukan Bilue, Indonesia.

June 15, 2001   A grenade detonates, killing two and injuring 31 in Iligan, a predominantly Christian city in the southern Philippines.

June 16, 2001   Arbi Barayev, a Chechen warlord, murders three in Gekhi, Chechnya—the Moscow-appointed mayor, his wife, and a Russian officer in the mayor's house.

June 16, 2001   An explosive device detonates in Narayanganj, Bangladesh, at a meeting of the ruling Awami League Party, leaving 21 people dead and at least 110 injured. Female suicide bombers from the Islami Chhatra Shibir, a student group committed to establishing a strict Islamist regime in Bangladesh, are likely responsible.

June 17, 2001   Three car bombs explode in Gudermes, Chechnya's second-largest city, targeting a police department, a court, and a prosecutor's office. Two are killed and 37 are injured.

June 20, 2001   In North Cotabato, Philippines, the Pentagon Gang abducts a Chinese engineer working for a Japanese-funded irrigation project. On August 12, three Chinese nationals and a local Philippine businessman are kidnapped when they try to deliver the ransom payment for the engineer. On August 19, Philippine military forces attempt a rescue, which results in the deaths of two Chinese. On October 19, the one remaining Chinese hostage is released, reportedly after a ransom is paid. The Pentagon Gang is an Islamist group composed of former MNLF and MILF terrorists.

June 25, 2001   Chechen warlord Arbi Barayev is killed in a Russian military operation against rebels in Chechnya.

July 8, 2001   Police in the Philippines arrest Nadjmi Sabdula (known as "Commander Global"), one of the chief leaders of the Abu Sayyaf organization, in General Santos, southern Philippines. Sabdula is believed to have planned the kidnapping of 20 people from an island resort six weeks earlier.

July 12, 2001   The brother of an Indian member of parliament is shot and killed by Muslim militants in Kashmir.

July 17, 2001   Karin Yuldashev, an advisor to the president of Tajikistan, is assassinated in Dushanbe by members of the United Tajik Opposition (UTO), an Islamist organization.

July 21, 2001   Terrorists kill 14 Hindu pilgrims after detonating two grenades in Sheshnag in Jammu and Kashmir. Lashkar-e-Tayyiba is suspected.

July 22, 2001   Islamic terrorists abduct 15 Hindus from their houses in Kashmir and then shoot and kill them.

July 26, 2001   The managing director of Pakistan State Oil and his chauffeur are shot and killed by two gunmen in Karachi. Lashkar-e-Tayyiba claims responsibility.

July 28, 2001   A French-Algerian, Djamel Beghal, is arrested in the Dubai airport while traveling to Europe from Pakistan and confesses to plotting to destroy the U.S. Embassy in Paris on the orders of Abu Zubaydah, a top al-Qaeda operative. Beghal is extradited to France, and his capture leads to the arrests of 20 network operatives in Belgium, the Netherlands, Spain, and France.

August 1, 2001   Abu Sayyaf Group terrorists kidnap more than 30 hostages from a Christian village on Basilan Island in the Philippines, later killing nine of them and releasing the rest.

August 2, 2001	In Kashmir, two women in the Udhampur District are killed by terrorists while a man in Doda District is shot and killed in his home by two terrorists. The terrorists' affiliation is unknown.
August 7, 2001	Unknown Islamic terrorists shoot at a railroad station as a train arrives in Jammu City, Kashmir, killing 11 and wounding 23.
August 9, 2001	Thirty-one workers at a palm plantation in Aceh are assassinated, likely by Free Aceh Movement members.
August 14, 2001	A bomb on a train in Muradnagar, India, kills three and injures 18 on the eve of India's Independence Day. It is not clear who perpetrated the attack.
August 14, 2001	Unknown terrorists, likely Islamists, shoot and kill five Hindus in the village of Sarar Bagga in Kashmir.
August 27, 2001	Two Hindu priests are killed by terrorists in India-controlled Kashmir.
August 27, 2001	In Cotabato, Philippines, terrorists kill an Irish parish priest in a botched kidnapping attempt. Moro National Liberation Front terrorists are suspected.
August 28, 2001	Militants kill a Muslim family of five in Kashmir, apparently for refusing to give them food.
September 9, 2001	Ahmed Shah Masood, the leader of Afghanistan's Northern Alliance, is killed along with the Afghan opposition's ambassador to India by a Taliban suicide squad posing as journalists. The attack may have been timed to remove the most effective opponent of the Taliban and al-Qaeda in Pakistan prior to the attacks on the United States two days later.
September 11, 2001	Al-Qaeda terrorists hijack four airliners in the northeast United States. Two of them are flown into the World Trade Center Towers in New York City, causing their collapse. A third plane is crashed into the Pentagon, the headquarters of the U.S. Defense Department near Washington, D.C. The fourth plane crashes prematurely in rural Pennsylvania when the passengers and crew attack the hijackers. In all, nearly 3,000 people are killed. The attack focuses intense scrutiny on international terrorist organizations in the United States, Europe, and beyond, and will cause the U.S. to invade Afghanistan in a matter of weeks. For further details, see chapter 8.
September 19, 2001	Six people are killed and some 55 injured after a bomb detonates at a marketplace in Sialkot, Pakistan, near the border with India. It is not clear which group is responsible.
September 26, 2001	A bomb detonates during a religious ceremony in Kashmir, killing four and wounding 25. It is not clear which group is responsible.

October 1, 2001   Two Jaish-e-Mohammed (JEM) terrorists begin shooting in the Jammu and Kashmir legislative assembly building in Srinagar, killing at least 31 persons. After several hours, they are killed by Indian security forces.

October 2, 2001   A bomb planted by GIA terrorists at a pizza parlor in Laghouat, Algeria, kills one and wounds eight.

October 4, 2001   Unidentified terrorists open fire on a Shiite mosque in Karachi, Pakistan, killing five and wounding nine.

October 13, 2001   Abu Sayyaf terrorists kidnap four farmers on Basilan Island, Philippines. Two are killed when they try to escape, and two successfully escape.

October 28, 2001   A bomb blast at a food court in Zamboanga, Philippines, kills 11 people. Abu Sayyaf terrorists are likely responsible.

October 29, 2001   Members of the Free Aceh Movement kill three migrants from Java and injure three others in Jambi Baru, Indonesia.

November 19, 2001   Five years after signing a peace treaty with the Philippine government, Nur Misuari, founder of the MNLF and now governor of a semi-autonomous Muslim region in the Philippines, leads an armed struggle in Jolo during his campaign for re-election, apparently because he seems likely be defeated. More than 100 are killed at an army base.

November 22, 2001   Terrorists from the Uighur Holy War Organization in Xinjiang, China, raid a police station, killing the chief.

November 23, 2001   Nur Misuari, who has fled to Malaysia, is arrested there for illegal entry. A few months later, he is extradited to the Philippines.

December 4, 2001   In Chechnya, an important political figure, Rizvan Lorsanov, is killed near his home in Novyye Atagi. No group claims responsibility.

December 13, 2001   After gaining entrance by car to the grounds of the Indian Parliament building in New Delhi, five terrorists set off explosives and begin shooting, killing six policemen and a gardener. All the terrorists, citizens of Pakistan, are killed in by police. In December 2002, four members of Jaish-e-Mohammed, including Mohammad Afral, are convicted of involvement in the attack and sentenced to death.

December 13, 2001   A top terrorist of the Hizbul Mujahideen, Nazir Ahmed Yatoo, is killed by government security forces in Kashmir.

December 29, 2001   Gunmen, likely from the Moro Islamic Liberation Front, attack the village of Naga on Mindanao Island, Philippines, and take ten hostages whom they later kill.

January 1, 2002   Terrorists massacre six members of a Hindu family in Poonch, Jammu and Kashmir. It is not clear which group is responsible.

January 11, 2002   Abu Sayyaf terrorists attack a passenger car on Basilan, southern Philippines, killing three people, including a mother and her child.

January 15, 2002   Philippine authorities arrest an Indonesian citizen, Fathur Rahman Al-Ghozi, the leader of the Jemaah Islamiya who also has close connections to the Moro Islamic Liberation Front (MILF). He later receives a jail term of ten to 12 years.

January 18, 2002   A Russian worker in the Federal Communications office is shot to death in Nazran, Ingushetia, a Russian republic which borders Chechnya.

January 21, 2002   Terrorists kill 12 members of a family, including eight children, in a village in Poonch District, Jammu and Kashmir. Islamic terrorists from Pakistan are likely responsible.

January 22, 2002   A bomb explodes in Jammu and Kashmir, killing one and injuring nine others.

February 8, 2002   Anter Zowabri, head of the GIA's Green Battalion and considered the most dangerous terrorist in Algeria, is killed by Algerian security forces during a gun battle at Boufarik, near Algiers. On April 15, the GIA names its new leader, Rachid Oukali.

February 13, 2002   Lashkar-e-Tayyiba terrorists, in search of a police officer to kill, instead kill an officer's father in Bachay, India.

February 26, 2002   Ten worshippers are killed and at least 21 injured in a shooting attack on a Shia mosque in Rawalpindi, Pakistan. Sipah-e-Sahaba Pakistan (SSP) and Lashkar-e-Jhangvi are suspected.

March 11, 2002   Two leaders of a Pakistani Shia group are killed by terrorists in a home in Karachi. No group claims responsibility.

March 19, 2002   A Muslim scholar of the arch-conservative Wahhabi school and his driver are shot dead by two terrorists in Lahore.

March 19, 2002   Elite Russian troops kill Amir Khattab, an Arab terrorist with alleged al-Qaeda links who lived in Chechnya and engaged in terrorist attacks. It is rumored that he is killed when a Chechen messenger bribed by the Russians delivers a poisoned letter.

March 30, 2002   Lashkar-e-Tayyiba terrorists attack the Raghunath Temple in Jammu, killing ten and injuring 19.

March 30, 2002   Terrorists assassinate a caretaker of a Shiite institution and his son in Bahawalpur, Pakistan.

April 2002   The Turkish government sentences six members of Hizb ut-Tahrir, an extremist political movement that wants to establish an Islamist state throughout the entire Muslim world, to up to seven years in prison for attempted terrorist activities.

April 20, 2002   Six Jehovah's Witnesses are kidnapped by Abu Sayyaf terrorists on the Philippine island of Jolo. Two of the hostages are murdered, while the four remaining hostages escape.

April 21, 2002   Some 18 bombs set by Abu Sayyaf terrorists detonate in public places, including a department store and a radio station office in General Santos City in the southern Philippines, killing 15 and injuring more than 70.

April 25, 2002   In Pakistan, 13 people are killed and 25 injured when a bomb detonates in the women's area of a Shiite mosque in Bhakkar City. The attack is a sectarian targeted killing, most of which take place against Shias in Pakistan's southern city of Karachi.

April 26, 2002   In Gharat, Kashmir, a bomb detonates under a bus, killing one person and injuring 21 others. No one claims responsibility.

April 27, 2002   A bomb detonates at a Shiite mosque in eastern Pakistan, killing 12.

April 28, 2002   A bomb kills seven and injures 36 at a marketplace in Vladikavkaz in southern Russia, likely by Chechen terrorists.

May 2002   A court in Azerbaijan convicts seven men who received military and other training in Georgia and who had intended to fight in Chechnya. Four receive suspended sentences, and the others are sentenced to four to five years in prison.

May 3, 2002   Terrorists, likely from the Hizbul Mujahideen, assassinate five people in three different villages in the Marmat area of Doda District in Kashmir.

May 5, 2002   A member of a Sunni religious party is shot dead in central Karachi, Pakistan.

May 6, 2002   A Shia principal of a technical college in Karachi, his driver, and a friend are shot and killed as they come to work.

May 7, 2002   A prominent Sunni religious scholar and his driver are assassinated by two terrorists on a motorcycle in Karachi.

May 9, 2002   Thirty persons are killed and close to 140 wounded when a bomb explodes during Victory Day celebrations in the town of Kaspiisk in Dagestan, southern Russia.

May 10, 2002   Indian police shoot and kill two Lashkar-e-Tayyiba terrorists, arrest three, and seize guns and explosives in New Delhi, India.

May 14, 2002   In Kaluchak, Jammu, terrorists fire on a passenger bus, killing seven people, then enter a military housing complex and kill three soldiers, four soldiers' wives, and three children. Al-Mansoorian, likely a front for the Lashkar-e-Tayyiba, and another terrorist group, Jamiat ul-Mujahideen, claim responsibility.

May 21, 2002   Abdul Gani Lone, senior leader of the All-Parties Hurriyat Conference, a coalition of separatist parties, is assassinated by terrorists in Srinagar.

May 29, 2002   A journalist of local English daily *Kashmir Images* is assassinated by three terrorists at his office in Srinagar.

June 2002   A conference held by the Egyptian government at a prison is attended by 500 prisoners, primarily members of al-Gama'a al-Islamiyya, who are serving sentences for past armed attacks. They discuss ending their involvement in violence. Many of them, in light of their failed revolutionary efforts, decide to follow a reformist path in exchange for being released from prison. This government offer has already been accepted by 1,500 members of the organization.

June 1, 2002   In Jolo, The Philippines, Abu Sayyaf terrorists abduct four Indonesian sailors on a coal barge. One sailor dies in captivity, and the rest escape.

June 20, 2002   Armed militants in Kashmir fire on a passenger bus, which plunges over a cliff, killing ten and injuring 12 others. No one claims responsibility.

June 30, 2002   In Bishtek, Kyrgyzstan, two terrorists kill the first secretary of the Chinese Embassy and his Kyrgyz companion. The terrorists are members of the East Turkestan Liberation Organization, committed to separating Xinjiang from China.

June 30, 2002   In Quetta, Pakistan, a leader of the minority Baloch people, Noor Mohammed, is gunned down by six men in his house.

July 5, 2002   GIA terrorists detonate a bomb in a market in Algeria, killing 30 persons and wounding 36 others.

July 8, 2002   In Indh, Kashmir, a bomb explodes near a water tank, killing three persons. No one claims responsibility.

July 13, 2002   In Jammu, Lashkar-e-Tayyiba terrorists attack a village, killing 27 persons.

July 20, 2002   Mir Ghulam Qadir Baloch, an important leader of the Balochistan National Movement, is assassinated as he gets out of his car in the largest bazaar in Quetta, Pakistan.

August 1, 2002   In Jolo, The Philippines, six Filipino Christian preachers are abducted by Abu Sayyaf terrorists. Two men are beheaded, two (both women) manage to escape, and two remain as hostages, their fate unknown.

August 6, 2002   Terrorists in Pahalgam, Kashmir, throw grenades at and then fire on a group of Hindu pilgrims, killing nine persons and injuring 32 others. Al-Mansoorian, a front for the Lashkar-e-Tayyiba, is likely responsible.

August 9, 2002   A bomb explodes at a coastal resort near Skikda, Algeria, killing five and injuring six. GIA terrorists are responsible.

August 20, 2002   Six Jehovah's Witnesses are abducted by Abu Sayyaf terrorists on Jolo Island, Philippines, and two of them are killed the following day. The fate of the others is unknown.

August 25, 2002   Security forces in Magallanes, Philippines, kill Faisal Marohombsar, leader of the Pentagon Gang (*see* June 20, 2001).

September 3, 2002 In Langet, Kashmir, terrorists of unknown affiliation attack a political rally, killing three persons and injuring four others.

September 8, 2002 In Dodasanpal, Kashmir, unidentified terrorists kill five persons and injure one other.

September 8, 2002 In Tikipora, Kashmir, terrorists kill the law minister and his six security guards. Three different groups claim responsibility: Lashkar-e-Tayyiba, Jamiat ul-Mujahideen, and Hizbul Mujahideen.

September 9, 2002 An Egyptian military court convicts 51 Muslim terrorists and sentences them to two to 15 years in prison. The group is called al-Wa'ad (the Promise).

September 9, 2002 The leader of the Chechen district of Nadterechny and his aide are killed. No group claims responsibility.

September 15, 2002 In Kashmir, Lashkar-e-Jhangvi terrorists detonate a bomb by the motorcade of Jammu and Kashmir Tourism Minister Sakina Itoo in Dhamhal Hanjipora, killing a civilian and a policeman and wounding two.

September 17, 2002 In Bandgam, Kashmir, terrorists assassinate the president of the ruling government bloc, which is dominated by the National Conference. No group claims responsibility for the attack.

September 18, 2002 Terrorists assassinate a National Conference bloc secretary outside his house in Srinagar, Kashmir. Al-Arifeen, likely a Lashkar-e-Tayyiba front, claims the killing.

September 21, 2002 Another bomb detonates on the motorcade of Jammu and Kashmir Tourism Minister Itoo, killing her bodyguard and a bystander and injuring four near Shemhal Bernjupora in Anantnag. Hizbul Mujahideen claims responsibility. It is the fourth attack on Itoo, the only female minister in the ruling National Conference government.

September 24, 2002 Terrorists attack the Akshardham Tempel in Gujarat, India, killing 32. The attack is a joint operation of Jaish-e-Mohammed and Lashkar-e-Tayyiba. On July 1, 2006, a court gives death sentences to three involved in the plot.

September 28, 2002 A bomb detonates in a movie theater in Satkhira, Bangladesh, killing one and wounding 90. Five minutes later, a second bomb explodes at the Satkhira stadium, resulting in two deaths and 35 injuries. Officials suspect the Islamic Shashantantra Andolon, a group known to oppose what they perceive as "indecent shows" in both attacks.

September 28, 2002 In a village in Anantnag District, Kashmir, a National Congress Party candidate is targeted in a bomb blast that kills four people, including her father. The candidate survives.

September 30, 2002 In Manda Chowk, Kashmir, a bomb detonates on a bus filled with Hindu pilgrims, killing one person and injuring 18 others. No one claims responsibility.

October 1, 2002	In Kathu, Kashmir, terrorists fire grenades at a minivan, killing nine passengers. Al-Arifeen, a front for Lashkar-e-Tayyiba, claims responsibility.
October 2, 2002	Ali-Arifeen terrorists kill three National Conference Party workers in the town of Haihama, Kashmir.
October 10, 2002	A bomb detonates at a bus station in North Cotabato Province, Philippines, killing eight and injuring 19. Abu Sayyaf Group and the New People's Army are likely both responsible.
October 15, 2002	GIA terrorists shoot two Koranic students in the Chlef region of Algeria.
October 16, 2002	GIA terrorists attack a Koranic school in Algiers, killing 13 students and wounding another.
October 17, 2002	In the Philippines, a bomb detonates at a mall in Zamboanga, killing six and injuring some 144. Abu Sayyaf is likely responsible.
October 19, 2002	A bomb rips through a bus in Manila, killing at least three people and injuring 23 others. Abu Sayyaf is responsible.
October 20, 2002	The Egyptian government tries 26 members of the Islamic Liberation Party in the Supreme State Security Court. They are accused of joining a banned group, attempting to recruit members for that group, and spreading extremist ideology.
October 20, 2002	In Onagam, India, unknown terrorists kill three persons and injure two others by a mosque.
October 20, 2002	A bomb placed near a Catholic site in Zamboanga detonates, killing a soldier and injuring some 13 others. Abu Sayyaf Group is likely responsible.
October 23, 2002	Forty-one male and female Chechen terrorists from three major terrorist groups in Chechnya—the Islamic International Brigade, the Special Purpose Islamic Regiment (SPIR), and the Riyad us-Saliheyn—seize the Dubrovka Theater in Moscow in the middle of a performance of the musical *Nord-Ost*. The terrorists take more than 800 people hostage and threaten to detonate explosive strapped to their waists if the Russian government does not meet their demands, including the withdrawal of Russian forces from Chechnya. Four days later, a Russian commando squad sprays anesthetic gas into the theater. They then kill all the terrorists, including SPIR leader Movzar Barayev. However, the gas also causes the deaths of 129 hostages. The terrorist attack is the most serious carried out by Chechen separatist groups outside of south Russia. The separatists are Sunni Islamic radicals who seek both Chechen independence and establishment of an Islamic caliphate throughout Chechnya and the North Caucasus region.
October 25, 2002	In Moscow, a bomb explodes in a car parked in a McDonald's parking lot, killing one person and injuring eight others. Chechen terrorists are responsible.

November 8, 2002   Moro Islamic Liberation Front terrorists attack a village in Mindanao in the southern Philippines with automatic rifle fire, killing seven people.

November 19, 2002   In Chechnya, Islamist terrorists kill Sayid-Pasha Salikhov, a respected leader of traditional Islam, and his son at their home in Stariye Atagi village.

November 24, 2002   In Jammu and Kashmir, terrorists from Lashkar-e-Tayyiba attack the Raghunath and Shiv temples, killing 13 persons and wounding 50 others.

December 18, 2002   Necip Hablemitoglu, a prominent Turkish historian and writer who is an outspoken opponent of radical Islam, is murdered in front of his home in Ankara. It is not clear which group is responsible.

December 19, 2002   Imran Khusiyev, administrative chief of Tsotsan-Yurt village in Chechnya, is assassinated in a neighbor's home along with three others. No group claims responsibility.

December 20, 2002   Terrorists assassinated a People's Democratic Party member of the Kashmiri legislative assembly, Abdul Aziz Mir, in Pampore. It is the first attack by the Save Kashmir Movement, a terrorist organization opposed to Indian rule in Kashmir.

December 24, 2002   A bomb set by the Moro Islamic Liberation Front explodes outside the home of the mayor in Maguindanao, Philippines, killing him and 12 other people.

December 26, 2002   In Zamboanga del Norte, Philippines, Moro Islamic Liberation Front terrorists attack a bus carrying Filipino workers from a Canadian mining company, killing 13 persons and injuring 10 others.

December 27, 2002   In Grozny, Chechnya, suicide bombers detonate two bombs outside the headquarters of the pro-Moscow government, killing 72 persons and wounding 210 others. The Riyad us-Saliheyn Martyr's Brigade is responsible.

December 28, 2002   In Sanaa, Yemen, Jarallah Omar, deputy secretary general of the Yemeni Socialist Party and a pro-democracy activist, is assassinated after delivering a speech at the Yemeni Congregation for Reform. The man arrested is a radical Islamist.

December 31, 2002   A Moro Islamic Liberation Front terrorist detonates a grenade at a group of New Year's Eve celebrants in Tacurong, Philippines, killing nine and injuring 35.

February 15, 2003   Two groups of adventure travelers from European countries (Holland, Austria, Switzerland, and Germany) are taken hostage in a remote region of the Sahara Desert in southern Algeria, by the Salafist Group for Preaching and Combat (GSPC). On May 14, the Algerian army rescues 17 of the captives. All but one of the remaining hostages are freed by their captors on August 18 and handed over to the government in Mali. A ransom may have been paid. The remaining hostage, a 46-year-old German woman, dies of heatstroke on June 28 while in captivity.

| February 16, 2003 | After a week of fighting, soldiers in the Philippines overrun a large camp belonging to the Moro Islamic Liberation Front in Mindanao, killing 177, including seven civilians. |

February 16, 2003 — In Karachi, Pakistan, Khalid bin Waleed, a former member of the Sindh assembly and a leader of the Muttahida Quami Movement, the party of Muslims immigrants from India, is gunned down by terrorists.

February 20, 2003 — A van filled with explosives detonates outside the Cotabato airport in the southern Philippines, killing one person and injuring five others. The Moro Islamic Liberation Front is likely responsible.

February 22, 2003 — Terrorists attack a Shia Mehdi mosque in Karachi, Pakistan, killing nine and wounding nine more. Sunni extremist groups Sipah-e-Sahaba Pakistan and Lashkar-e-Jhangvi are suspected.

March 4, 2003 — A bomb placed in a backpack detonates at an airport in Davao, southern Philippines, killing 19 people, including an American, and wounding more than 100. The Moro Islamic Liberation Front is likely responsible.

March 11, 2003 — In Rajouri, Kashmir, a bomb explodes in a candy store, killing two persons and injuring four others. No group claims responsibility.

March 11, 2003 — Nine Shia Muslims in Karachi are killed by Lashkar-e-Jhangvi terrorists.

March 12, 2003 — A bomb explodes in Mumbai, India, killing ten and injuring 70. The Students Islamic Movement of India (*see* April 1977) and the Jaish-e-Mohammed (*see* January 2000) are jointly responsible.

March 13, 2003 — Four are killed when a bomb explodes on a bus in Rajouri, Kashmir. No one claims responsibility.

March 16, 2003 — Terrorists intercept a passenger bus en route from Bishkek, Kyrgyzstan, to China, eventually killing all 20 passengers. The East Turkestan Liberation Organization is likely responsible.

March 18, 2003 — Members of the Moro Islamic Liberation Front attack a minibus between the cities of Cotabato and General Santos, southern Philippines, killing nine people.

March 20, 2003 — A bomb placed by an unknown terrorist detonates in a housing complex outside Sidon, Lebanon, killing two and wounding nine. The Dutch wife of a Lebanese man residing there is believed to be the target.

March 23, 2003 — Majid Dar, a former chief commander of Hizbul Mujahideen, is killed by gunmen at his brother's home in Sopore, Kashmir. Members of al-Nasirin and the Save Kashmir Movement are possibly responsible.

March 24, 2003   In Kashmir, terrorists clad in military uniforms kill 24 Hindu residents in Nadimag village. Either Lashkar-e-Tayyiba or Jaish-e-Mohammed terrorists are responsible.

March 30, 2003   In Poonch, Kashmir, a bomb explodes in a field where a cricket match is being played, killing one person and injuring two others. No one claims responsibility.

April 2, 2003   In Davao City, a bomb planted near the entrance gate of a passenger terminal at the Sasa Wharf in the southern Philippines explodes, killing 16 people and injuring 55 others. The Moro Islamic Liberation Front (MILF) is likely responsible.

April 21, 2003   In the Philippines, a bomb blast kills 14 people and wounds 55 others in General Santos. Either Abu Sayyaf or Moro Islamic Liberation Front members are responsible.

April 22, 2003   In Gulshanpora Batagund, Kashmir, a bomb detonates in a dairy yard, killing six persons and injuring 12 others. No group claims responsibility.

April 24, 2003   In the Philippines, MILF terrorists attack the town of Maigo, killing 13 people.

April 25, 2003   In Patan, Kashmir, a bomb explodes outside a courthouse, killing three persons and injuring 34 others. No one claims responsibility.

May 4, 2003   Some 100 rebels of the MILF terrorists stage attacks in Siocon, southern Philippines, resulting in the death of 22.

May 5, 2003   In Doda, Kashmir, a bomb explodes at a bus stand, killing one person and injuring 25 others. No one claims responsibility.

May 6, 2003   A bomb planted outside the home of a Dutch missionary in Tripoli, Lebanon, kills a neighbor instead. No one claims responsibility for the attack.

May 10, 2003   Terrorists bomb a market place in South Cotabato, Philippines, killing 15 and wounding 31. MILF or Abu Sayyaf terrorists are responsible.

May 12, 2003   A truck bomb detonates outside a government building in Znamenskoye, Chechnya, killing 52 and injuring over 110. Chechen terrorists are responsible.

May 24, 2003   A woman and her two children are killed by terrorists near Chlef, Algeria. The GIA and the Salafist Group for Preaching and Combat are jointly responsible.

May 30, 2003   In Chechnya, a bomb detonates on a street in Grozny, as a minibus passes, killing three people and injuring at least nine others.

June 4, 2003   GIA terrorists kill 12 people and wound two at a fake checkpoint at Boumedefaa, Algeria.

June 11, 2003   Unknown gunmen in Karachi assassinate a former speaker of the Sindh provincial assembly and member of the ruling Pakistan Muslim League as he is driving in his car.

June 17, 2003   In Kashmir, terrorists kill the son of a Muslim politician in his home. No one claims responsibility.

June 20, 2003   A truck bomb detonates near Russia's Justice Ministry and government headquarters in Grozny, killing two people and injuring 18.

June 23, 2003   In Pulwama, Kashmir, a hand grenade aimed at a military vehicle misses its intended target, killing two civilians and wounding 48 other passersby.

July 4, 2003   In Quetta, Pakistan, terrorists attack a crowded Shiite Hazara mosque, killing 53 people and injuring 60.

July 4, 2003   In Kashmir, terrorists attack a meeting between the Jammu-Kashmir minister for rural development and health officials in Larnu, killing four and wounding 19 others including the minister. Jamiat ul-Mujahideen and Tehreek-e-Jehad-e-Islami (TJI), another group seeking Islamist rule in Kashmir, jointly claim responsibility for the attack.

July 5, 2003   Two female Chechen suicide bombers detonate their bombs at a crowded rock concert near Moscow killing 16 and injuring more than 60.

July 5, 2003   In Quetta, Pakistan, two suicide bombers blew themselves up in a Shiite mosque, killing 48 people.

July 10, 2003   At least two people are killed when a bomb explodes in a crowded market in Koronadal, southern Philippines. The Moro Islamic Liberation Front (MILF) is believed responsible.

July 21, 2003   In Jammua and Kashmir, two grenades detonate at a community kitchen, killing seven persons and injuring 42 others. No one claims responsibility.

July 28, 2003   A bomb rips through a bus in downtown Bombay, killing at least four people and injuring 31. The Lashkar-e-Tayyiba is responsible.

August 1, 2003   In Mozdok, a city near Chechnya, a truck loaded with explosives detonates at a military hospital, killing 50 and wounding 64. Chechen rebel leader Shamil Basayev is behind the attack.

August 4, 2003   Unknown terrorists assassinate an educator in Mahore Tehsil, Kashmir.

August 4, 2003   In two separate attacks, terrorists assassinate seven members of the Islamic missionary group Tablighi Jamaat in Karachi, Pakistan. The attackers are unknown.

August 5, 2003   In Katjidhok, Kashmir, unknown terrorists shoot and kill one person.

August 13, 2003   Several blasts in different parts of Kashmir kill two persons and injure 50. Hizbul Mujahideen is responsible.

August 25, 2003   Two bombs hidden in taxis explode in downtown Mumbai, killing 52 and injuring 150. The Students Islamic Movement, Lashkar-e-Tayyiba and Jaish-e-Mohammed were found to be responsible.

August 26, 2003
In Bouira, a member of the Algerian Republican National Alliance, which withdrew from Algeria's 2002 elections in protest and has since been an outspoken critic of President Bouteflika's amnesty program, is shot to death by terrorists.

September 6, 2003
In Kashmir, a bomb explodes in a busy marketplace in Srinagar, killing six persons and injuring 37 others.

September 15, 2003
Chechen terrorists detonate a truck filled with explosives outside a government security building in Magas, Ingushetia, killing four people and injuring some 40.

October 2, 2003
In Shali, Chechnya, the mayor and his son are assassinated when their car is ambushed. Chechen field commander Rizvan Chitigove is suspected of planning the attack.

October 2, 2003
Abu Sayyaf terrorists kidnap six persons—three Indonesians, two Filipinos, and a Malaysian—from a resort area in Sabah, Philippines, and execute five; the sixth prisoner escapes.

October 3, 2003
In Karachi, Pakistan, six people are gunned down and eight others wounded while going to a Shia mosque for Friday prayers. The 313, an alliance of Lashkar-e-Jhangvi, Harakat ul-Mujahideen al-Alami, and the Harakat ul-Jihad al-Islami, is responsible.

October 3, 2003
In Quetta, a Pakistan railway engineer is killed and two others are wounded when armed men attack the train with rockets. It is not clear which group is responsible.

October 6, 2003
Maulana Azam Tariq, head of the Sunni militant group Sipah-e-Sahaba Pakistan and a member of parliament, is assassinated along with four other persons by three gunmen in Islamabad.

October 26, 2003
In Gagal, Kashmir, unknown terrorists clad in army uniforms hijack a car, killing two of the occupants and injuring four others.

October 27, 2003
In Gagal, Kashmir, terrorists overtake a car, kill two of the occupants and injure four others.

November 28, 2003
Talal bin Abdelaziz Al-Rasheed, a poet from Saudi Arabia, is killed in an ambush on his hunting group near Djelfa, Algeria. Salafist Group for Preaching and Combat terrorists are likely responsible.

December 4, 2003
An ambush on the car of the governor of Shabwa in southeast Yemen results in his brother being killed and the governor wounded. The Islamist group Takfir wal Hijra is likely responsible.

December 5, 2003
A suicide attacker detonates an explosive on a commuter train near Chechnya, killing 42 people and wounding nearly 200. Chechen Black Widows, a group

of female suicide bombers, many of whom lost husbands in the Chechen wars against Russia, claims responsibility.

December 7, 2003 A top Abu Sayyaf rebel leader, Galib Andang ("Commander Robot") is captured after a firefight with Philippine troops in Jolo. He was responsible for the kidnapping of dozens of foreign and local hostages over the past few years, including the raid on Malaysian resorts on Sipadan Island. (*See* April 23, 2000).

December 8, 2003 A member of the district election commission representing the United Russia Party, Yunus Yakubov, is killed in the town of Gudermes, Chechnya.

December 9, 2003 A suicide bomber detonates his explosives outside the Kremlin and parliament building in Moscow, killing at least five people. The Chechen Black Widows claims responsibility for the attack.

January 1, 2004 Ten people are killed and at least 30 others injured when an explosive device detonates at a music concert in Peureulak, Aceh Province, Indonesia. Authorities blame the Free Aceh Movement, but the group denies responsibility, stating that it never targets civilians.

January 4, 2004 A bomb on a motorcycle detonates in Parang on Mindanao Island, Philippines, killing 14 people and injuring at least 87 others, including the target, the city's Christian mayor. No group claims responsibility.

January 6, 2004 Islamic terrorists in Kashmir fire at a police car and kill a civilian.

January 9, 2004 A bomb is thrown into a mosque in Srinagar, Kashmir, killing two people and injuring 18 in a nearby store. The police believe the United Jihad Council, a coalition of groups fighting for the creation of an Islamic state in Jammu and Kashmir, is responsible.

January 10, 2004 United Jihad Council terrorists murder a Muslim couple in Kashmir.

January 10, 2004 A human rights worker is kidnapped from the village of Avtury in Chechnya and eventually murdered.

January 11, 2004 United Jihad Council terrorists throw a grenade into a home in a village in Kashmir, killing one.

February 3, 2004 A bomb explodes near the market in Vladikavkaz, the capital of North Ossetia, southern Russia, killing three and wounding ten. Chechen terrorists are responsible.

February 4, 2004 In a village in Budgam District, Kashmir, India, terrorists infiltrate a home and kill a Muslim couple and their neighbor. No group claims responsibility.

February 6, 2004 In Chechnya, a bomb detonates in a wooded area in the Achkhoy-Martan District, killing six and wounding seven others.

February 6, 2004   A suicide bomber detonates a bomb on a subway car in Moscow, killing 41 people and injuring 230 others. No group claims responsibility, but Chechen terrorists are suspected.

February 7, 2004   In Shopian, Kashmir, Islamic terrorists throw a grenade into a crowd and begin shooting, killing two civilians and wounding 28. No group claims responsibility.

February 13, 2004   In Doha, capital of the Persian Gulf state of Qatar, Zelimkhan Yandarbiyev, a former president of Chechnya, who had been living there, and two of his bodyguards are assassinated in a car bomb explosion. Yandarbiyev had called for government overthrow in Dagestan. On June 30, 2004, Qatari officials arrest two men assigned to the Russian Embassy in Doha. They are convicted of the attack and sentenced to life imprisonment. The assassination results in Qatar's first anti-terrorism law, declaring lethal "terrorist acts" punishable by death or life imprisonment.

February 15, 2004   In Budgam, Kashmir, Islamic militants assassinate two men, one a Kashmir political party worker. No group claims responsibility.

February 16, 2004   In Srinagar, Kashmir, terrorists kill a political leader and a nearby police officer, and wound another officer. The Save Kashmir Movement claims responsibility.

February 17, 2004   Islamic militants assassinate a political leader in Budgam, Kashmir. No group claims responsibility.

February 22, 2004   A political candidate is killed in Bugdam, Kashmir. Al-Mansoorian claims responsibility.

February 23, 2004   A bomb explodes in Tral, Kashmir, killing one Muslim teenager and wounding four others. No group claims responsibility.

February 27, 2004   Terrorists fire grenades at an event presided over by Kashmiri Chief Minister Mufti Mohammed Sayeed in Srinagar, killing a child and injuring three.

February 27, 2004   In the worst terrorist attack in Philippine history to this date, a bomb hidden in a television set detonates on a a large passenger ferry sailing out of Manila, killing 118 people. In October, six Abu Sayyaf terrorists are arrested in connection with the bombing, although the masterminds remain at large. Abu Sayyaf may have bombed the ferry because the company that owned it, WG&A, did not pay extortion money to the organization.

February 29, 2004   In Pulwama District, Kashmir, terrorists shoot and kill two People's Democratic Party's workers. No group claims responsibility.

March 9, 2004   In Budgam, Kashmir, a grenade is thrown into a crowd trying to stop a terrorist from abducting a local person, killing five civilians and injuring 42 others. No group claims responsibility.

March 12, 2004   Two men, one an elected official of the Municipal People's Assembly, are assassinated in Dellys, Algeria, by Salafist Group for Preaching and Combat terrorists.

March 16, 2004   Terrorists attack two ambulances traveling the Medea-Berrouaghia road in Algeria, killing eight and injuring two. The Salafist Group for Preaching and Combat is suspected in the attack.

March 18, 2004   Terrorists shoot a political party activist in Srinagar. No group claims responsibility.

March 21, 2004   The head of a village in Yala Province in Thailand is assassinated by Islamic terrorists.

March 27, 2004   In Doda District, Kashmir, terrorists assassinate a resident in his home.

April 2004   A Philippine military unit kills six Abu Sayyaf members on Basilan Island, including Hamsiraji Sali, a senior leader wanted by the United States for his role in the kidnappings of Americans Guillermo Sobero and Gracia and Martin Burnham and Sobero's and Martin Burnham's subsequent deaths (*see* May 27, 2001).

April 7, 2004   In Anantnag District, Kashmir, terrorists invade a home and shoot and kill a young girl. No group claims responsibility. In Pulwama District, Kashmir, India, armed militants invade a house, and shoot and kill the occupant. In Dadarhama village, Pulwama, Kashmir, terrorists shoot and kill a man. All these incidents occur as India is preparing for national elections.

April 8, 2004   A bomb detonates at an election rally in Kashmir, India, killing nine civilians and wounding 50 others. The Save Kashmir Movement claims responsibility.

April 11, 2004   In the Anantnag District, Kashmir, India, unknown terrorists shoot and kill a member of the ruling People's Democratic Party.

April 11, 2004   On a barge near Lingkian Island, between the Philippines and Malaysia, Abu Sayyaf terrorists kidnap two Malaysians and one Indonesian and take them to islands near Malaysia. In November, Filipino soldiers find skeletal remains, believed to be their bodies.

April 22, 2004   In Srinagar, Kashmir, a truck bomb explodes, killing two people and wounding one other.

April 25, 2004   In the Kulgam District, Kashmir, terrorists attack the motorcade of the People's Democratic Party president, killing four people and wounding 45 others. The politician escapes unharmed. No group claims responsibility.

April 26, 2004   In Kupwara District, Kashmir, terrorists assassinate a civilian outside his home. No group claims responsibility.

April 28, 2004	In Kashmir, a bomb detonates at an election rally in Doda District, killing three and injuring 49 others. The attackers are likely Lashkar-e-Tayyiba.
May 3, 2004	A car bomb explodes in southwestern Pakistan, killing three Chinese engineers working on a seaport and injuring 11. It is not clear which group is responsible.
May 5, 2004	In the Anantnag District, Kashmir, terrorists detonate a grenade at an election polling facility, killing one civilian and wounding three others. No group claims responsibility.
May 9, 2004	Islamic militants, likely from Hizbul Mujahideen, throw a grenade at a motorcade in Kashmir's Doda District, killing one government official and wounding four police officers and 17 civilians.
May 9, 2004	Akhmad Kadyrov, the Kremlin-backed president of Chechnya, is killed along with 30 others as a land mine detonates under a stadium in Grozny during Victory Day, marking the defeat of the Nazis in World War II. Chechen terrorist leader Shamil Basayev claims responsibility for the attack.
May 17, 2004	In Kupwara District, Kashmir, terrorists infiltrate a home, killing two and injuring one. No group claims responsibility.
May 20, 2004	Unknown terrorists in Baramulla, Kashmir, assassinate two people in their homes.
May 21, 2004	A bomb explodes at the Shrine of Saint Hazrat Shahjalal in Dhaka, Bangladesh, killing three people and injuring 100 others, including the British high commissioner to Bangladesh, the likely target. No group claims responsibility.
May 21, 2004	In Budgam District, Kashmir, terrorists detonate a bomb near a security post, killing three, including two children, and wounding 24 others. Authorities believe Hizbul Mujahideen is responsible.
May 23, 2004	Hizbul Mujahideen terrorists detonate a bomb under a bus in Lower Munda, Kashmir, killing nine civilians and 19 police officers, and wounding two civilians and 13 police officers.
May 31, 2004	In Karachi, a bomb explodes inside a Shiite mosque, killing 19 and injuring dozens of others. Sipah-e-Sahaba Pakistan is responsible.
June 2, 2004	In Anantnag, Kashmir, unidentified terrorists shoot and kill a People's Democratic Party member outside his home.
June 4, 2004	A bomb detonates in a market in Samarra, Russia, killing 11 and wounding 76. Chechen separatists from Kazakhstan are arrested for the attack.
June 6, 2004	Philippine authorities arrest suspected Abu Sayyaf commander Ibno Alih Ordonez on charges that he kidnapped dozens of people, some of whom were beheaded or tortured to death.

June 7, 2004	A Buddhist teacher who taught Thai at an Islamic religious school in Pattani, Thailand, is assassinated in the parking lot of the school. It is not known which group is responsible.
June 12, 2004	Al-Nasreen terrorists throw a grenade into a hotel in Kashmir, killing four and wounding 24.
June 14, 2004	Unknown terrorists in Baramulla, Kashmir, throw a grenade at a home, killing two civilians and injuring one other.
June 14, 2004	Kashmiri terrorists kill a government worker near Kunzer village. No group claims responsibility.
June 15, 2004	Unknown terrorists in Dangerpora area, Kashmir, assassinate the brother of a local politician.
June 17, 2004	In Karachi, the leader of the Pakistan People's Party in Sindh Province is attacked and killed by unknown terrorists. He is believed to be targeted because he represents the democratic opposition.
June 25, 2004	Kashmiri terrorists fire wildly in the village of Tiali Kathamara, killing 12 civilians and injuring 12 others. No group claims responsibility.
June 26, 2004	Unknown terrorists in a village in Kashmir's Poonch District break into homes and begin shooting, killing 12 and wounding ten.
June 26, 2004	In Lahore, Pakistan, a politician from the the Muslim League, an opposition party, and two aides are gunned down in front of Punjab University. Two of his associates are also killed.
July 3, 2004	In Srinagar, Kashmir, unknown terrorists detonate a roadside bomb near a tourist attraction, killing two people and wounding 29 others.
July 13, 2004	In Srinagar, unknown Islamic terrorists detonate a bomb near the public gardens, killing one civilian and injuring 12.
July 18, 2004	In Shopian, Kashmir, unknown terrorists toss a grenade into the home of a senior Congress leader, killing him and his wife and seriously injuring their daughter.
July 21, 2004	Terrorists in Anantnag District, Kashmir, assassinate a People's Democratic Party member.
July 27, 2004	In Srinagar, Kashmir, two al-Mansoorian terrorists shoot at a hotel, killing five soldiers and wounding five others.
July 31, 2004	In Kashmir, terrorists invade a home in Doda District, killing two men and injuring two others. No group claims responsibility.

July 31, 2004 A suicide bomber detonates his bomb next to the car of Pakistan's newly appointed prime minister, killing six and injuring 50 in Jaffar, Pakistan. The prime minister, Shaukat Aziz of the Muslim League, survives and is sworn into office in August.

August 1, 2004 An explosion at an electricity company in Jijel Province, Algeria, kills three. Salafist Group for Preaching and Combat are likely perpetrators.

August 3, 2004 In Rajouri, Kashmir, terrorists enter a home and a kill two Muslims. No group claims responsibility.

August 18, 2004 Lashkar-e-Tayyiba terrorists murder four members of a family, a father and his three children, in Udhampur District, Kashmir.

August 24, 2004 Suicide bombs detonate on two Russian airliners flying out from Moscow airport within minutes of each other en route to other destinations in Russia, killing all 90 passengers and crew on the two planes. A group calling itself the Islambouli Brigades claims responsibility for the attack, saying it is in support of the Chechen rebels. The group is named after Khaled Islambouli, the Egyptian army officer who assassinated Egyptian President Anwar Sadat in 1981. But Chechen nationalist leader Shamil Basayev also later claims responsibility for this attack and the others claimed by the Islambouli Brigades.

August 31, 2004 A female suicide bomber detonates her bomb outside a Moscow subway station, killing ten and wounding 50. The Islambouli Brigades, the same group claiming responsibility for the plane crashes, is responsible.

September 1, 2004 A politician is killed in Bagdam District, Kashmir. It is not clear which group is responsible.

September 1, 2004 Terrorists seize a school in Beslan, a city in North Ossetia, Russia, near Chechnya, taking hundreds hostages during a ceremony marking the beginning of the school year. During a rescue attempt by Russian commandos, 100 people are killed and some 400 wounded. Chechen terrorist leader Shamil Basayev claims responsibility for the attack.

September 12, 2004 In Poonch, Kashmir, militants kill three members of a family. Lashkar-e-Tayyiba terrorists are responsible.

September 18, 2004 In Pattani Province, Thailand, Naya Sema, an imam at Ban Bunae Tungoh Mosque, is shot and killed by unknown gunmen.

September 30, 2004 A member of the People's Liberation League is killed in Srinagar, Kashmir.

October 7, 2004 A political party worker is killed in Kashmir by Harakat ul-Mujahideen terrorists.

October 14, 2004 Al-Mansoorian terrorists assassinate a land broker in Jammu.

October 24, 2004 A bomb at a funeral kills one in Kashmir. In another incident in Udampur, terrorists attack a home killing two, while in a third incident, Doda terrorists invade a home and kill a child.

October 28, 2004	A bomb at a tourist bar in Narathiwat, Thailand, kills two and injures 20. Islamic terrorists are responsible.
October 29, 2004	A Congress Party politician and his son are killed in Kashmir and his wife is wounded. It is not clear which group is responsible.
November 2, 2004	A member of the People's Democratic Party is killed in Srinagar. It is not clear which group is responsible.
November 6, 2004	The home of an Indian Congress Party member is attacked in Budgam, Kashmir, and a civilian and guard are killed. No group claims responsibility.
November 8, 2004	Unidentified terrorists attack at the home of an Indian Congress Party member in Kashmir, miss their target, and kill a civilian.
November 9, 2004	Islamic terrorists kill a Buddhist man in Narathiwat Province, Thailand.
November 15, 2004	In Badgam, Kashmir, six people are killed in a private home by Hizbul Mujahideen terrorists.
November 15, 2004	In Krong Pinang, Thailand, Islamic terrorists kill two in a home—a retired policeman and a teenager from Burma.
November 17, 2004	A bomb at a funeral in Doda, Kashmir, kills one and injures four. It is not clear which group is responsible.
December 15, 2004	In Handwara, Kashmir, a civilian and his daughter are killed by Hizbul Mujahideen terrorists.
January 14, 2005	Two are killed and 70 wounded after a bomb detonates during a folk theater performance in Laxikola village, Bangladesh. Shafiqullah, a terrorist with Jamatul Mujahideen, which seeks Islamic rule in Bangladesh, is arrested in connection with this attack.
February 14, 2005	In the Philippines, a bomb rips through a bus in Manila, and simultaneous attacks occur in Davao and General Santos, altogether killing four and injuring 140. In October 2005, two members of Abu Sayyaf and an Indonesian with Jemaah Islamiyah are sentenced to death by a Philippine court for the attack.
February 17, 2005	Seven people are dead and 50 injured by a car bomb outside a hotel in Sungai Kolok, southern Thailand. Islamists are responsible.
March 5, 2005	Russian authorities announce that they have succeeded in killing Chechen terrorist Aslan Maskhadov, a leader of the separatist movement in Chechnya, although they will not reveal the circumstances of his death.
April 1, 2005	Al-Mansoorian terrorists infiltrate the house of a minister in the Kashmir valley, killing a Congress worker and five police officers.
April 3, 2005	Islamic terrorists in southern Thailand kill two and wound 70 after detonat-

ing three bombs in southern Thailand. The bombs detonate at the airport in Songkhla. Islamic separatists are responsible.

April 7, 2005   Terrorists erect a fake roadblock in Tablat, Blida Province, Algeria, where they fire on five vehicles, killing 13 civilians and wounding one. The Salafist Group for Preaching and Combat (GSPC) is believed to be responsible.

May 1, 2005   In Kashmir, al-Nasirin terrorists kill the nephew of the local municipal council head in Pattan.

May 3, 2005   In Pattan, Kashmir, Ramzan Miyan, the recently elected head of the local municipal council, and his two guards are killed by four terrorists while inspecting the main market. Al-Arifeen claims responsibility.

May 17, 2005   Six people are kidnapped and then killed by unknown perpetrators in the Chak Dhara section of Harwan in the state of Jammu and Kashmir. Officials believe Lashkar-e-Tayyiba is responsible.

June 13, 2005   A car bomb explodes outside a high school in Pulwama, Kashmir, killing 16 people and injuring over a 100. The attack is perpetrated jointly by Hizbul Mujahideen (HM) and Harakat ul-Mujahideen (HUM).

June 19, 2005   In Srinagar, Kashmir, the regional president of the People's Democratic Party (PDP), Ghulam Rasool Bhat, is shot by two terrorists. The Harakat ul-Mujahideen (HUM) claims responsibility for the attack.

July 28, 2005   A train en route from Patna to New Delhi is the target of a bomb which detonates in Jaunpur, Uttar Pradesh, killing 13 and wounding 50. It is not clear which group is responsible, although it is highly likely an Islamic terrorist organization.

October 13, 2005   In Nalchik, southern Russia, 12 civilians are killed when 200–300 Chechen terrorists attack federal buildings, police stations, and the aiport. Also killed are 24 law enforcement officials and 91 Chechen gunmen. Thirty-nine other attackers are captured.

October 18, 2005   Ghulam Nabi Lone, Education Minister of Jammu and Kashmir, is killed in Srinagar along with three others when terrorists break into his home. One terrorist is killed in a shoot-out with Lone's security officials. Al-Mansoorian and the Jammu and Kashmir Islamic Front claim responsibility.

October 29, 2005   Three bombs are detonated in New Delhi, India's capital—two in a marketplace and the third on a bus—killing 62 and injuring more than 200 on the eve of Diwali, India's most important Hindu holiday. Lashkar-e-Tayyiba is believed responsible. In November, Indian security authorities arrest Tariq Ahmad Dar in Kashmir and charge him as an organizer of the attacks.

November 2, 2005   A car bomb detonates in Srinagar near the home of the Jammu and Kashmir chief minister just as his successor is being sworn in, killing at least ten people and injuring 18 others. The outgoing chief minister, Mufti Mohammad Sayeed, survives. Jaish-e-Mohammed is responsible.

November 14, 2005 Four people are killed and 17 injured after an attack in a Lalchowk business district in Srinagar, Kashmir. Al-Mansoorian and the Jammu and Kashmir Islamic Front claim responsibility.

November 15, 2005 In Tangmarg, Baramulla District, Kashmir, six persons are killed and 90 others injured when terrorists target a public meeting being held by former Minister and PDP leader Ghulam Hassan Mir with a grenade explosion. Mir is among those wounded.

November 16, 2005 Four are killed and 72 injured in Srinagar, Kashmir, after a car bomb explodes outside the entrance of the Jammu & Kashmir Bank headquarters. Al-Arifeen terrorists are believed to be responsible.

March 7, 2006 Bombs detonate in a railway station and a temple in Varanasi, India, a Hindu holy area, killing 28 and injuring more than 100. No group claims responsibility for the attacks.

April 2, 2006 Terrorists, their affiliation unclear, gun down a municipal legislator in the Baramulla District, Kashmir.

April 9, 2006 Terrorists shoot dead three members of a family, including two brothers, at Challad, a village in the Udhampur District of Kashmir.

April 11, 2006 A suicide bomber explodes himself before Sunni worshippers in Karachi, Pakistan, killing 57.

April 14, 2006 Terrorists trigger seven grenade blasts in Srinagar, Kashmir, killing five civilians and injuring 44 persons. Jamiat ul-Mujahideen, al-Mansoorian, Jaish-e-Mohammed, and Jammu and Kashmir Islamic Front all claim responsibility.

April 29–30, 2006 Terrorists gun down four Hindus from a village in Udhampur, Kashmir, and take nine other hostages who are found dead the next day. Police believe Lashkar-e-Tayyiba is responsible.

May 1, 2006 Lashkar-e-Tayyiba gunmen kill 19 Hindus from a village in Doda, Kashmir.

May 21, 2006 Two terrorists disguised as policemen attack a rally of the Youth Congress at a park in Srinagar, Kashmir, killing three political activists and two police officers and injuring 25. The terrorists are later killed in a shoot-out with police. Lashkar-e-Tayyiba and al-Mansoorian claim responsibility.

June 17, 2006 Chechen separatist rebel leader Abdul-Khalim Sadulayev is killed in a gun battle with Russian security forces in Argun. Sadulayev was appointed in 2005 to replace Aslan Maskhadov after the rebel president died in a Russian attack.

July 8, 2006 Five persons are killed and 42 others are injured in a terrorist attack outside a shrine at Kulgam, Kashmir. Senior National Conference leader and former legislator Ghulam Nabi Dar is among the dead, while former minister Sakina Itoo suffers minor injuries. It is not clear which group is responsible.

July 10, 2006   Shamil Basayev, a Chechen leader responsible for several large-scale terrorist attacks, is accidently killed when a truck loaded with dynamite explodes in his convoy in Ingushetia. Three other terrorists are also killed.

July 11, 2006   Eight persons are killed and 43 others sustain injuries in a series of grenade attacks by suspected Lashkar-e-Tayyiba terrorists in the capital Srinagar.

July 11, 2006   Eight bombs detonate in seven suburban trains and stations in Bombay, killing 208 people and injuring another 663. Police arrest three members of the Students Islamic Movement of India and one from Lashkar-e-Tayyiba.

July 12, 2006   In the Poonch District of Kashmir, two girls and two boys of the Hindu community are killed and two others are injured in a terrorist attack on two families.

July 14, 2006   A suicide bomber in Karachi, Pakistan, kills a Shiite Islamic cleric, Allama Hasan Turabi, and his nephew.

July 24, 2006   Islamic terrorists in Narathiwat, Thailand, assassinate a Buddhist teacher as he is teaching his fourth-grade class. It is not clear which group is responsible.

August 24, 2006   An explosion at a television tower in Grozny, the capital of Chechnya, kills four and wounds one. Chechen Islamic terrorists are responsible.

September 16, 2006 Four people are killed and 82 injured when bombs detonate in department stores in Hat Yai in southern Thailand. The Gerakan Mujahideen Islam Pattani (GMIP), a group seeking a separate Islam state in southern Thailand, is responsible for the attack.

November 10, 2006   Six persons are killed and over 50 others wounded when Hizbul Mujahideen terrorists hurl a grenade outside a mosque at Tahab village in the Pulwama District of Kashmir.

December 31, 2006   Four bombs detonate in different parts of Bangkok during New Year's Eve celebrations leaving three dead and 38 injured. An Islamist terrorist group is likely responsible. Thai officials believe the attack was a joint effort of Jemaah Islamiyah and the Patani United Liberation Organization.

Global Jihad, September 11 and Afterwards

The attacks on the United States on September 11, 2001, planned and carried out by the Islamist group al-Qaeda, changed the face of terrorism around the world in three important respects. First, they showed the potential of such devastating mega-attacks which could do so much damage on modern societies and have such an international impact. The attacks were an implementation of "propaganda of the deed" on a global scale, perhaps the greatest single example in history on how a small group of people could use terrorism to gain a "multiplying effect."

Second, the attacks showed that the main terrorism of the post–Cold War era would be radical Islamist in inspiration. To an extent, this revitalization for terrorism came at a moment when in many places it was on the decline—for example, in Algeria, Egypt, Ireland, and Spain—where it had become politically ineffective and had failed to reach its goals.

Third, the event made counter-terrorism a much higher priority, not only for the United States, but also for most other countries. The tough international reaction to 9/11 made it more difficult for terrorists to stage similar types of attacks, and disrupted their international networks. Ultimately, it brought into question the strategy of al-Qaeda itself. Still, Islamic terrorist groups could take comfort in one respect. After the United States and its allies overthrew terrorism-sponsoring regimes in Afghanistan and Iraq, they faced intense resistance in the form of major terror campaigns.

The question remained as to what constituted "success" for terrorists. If the answer was gaining publicity, exacting revenge, or destroying individual targets, there is no doubt that terrorists had achieved success. But if success meant achieving political goals—to overturn the government or change the world, as almost always had been true—terrorism continued to be a failed political strategy.

In the case of September 11, apparent success was based not only on the sheer number of people killed (nearly 3,000 civilians), but also on the realization that the world's most powerful country could be hit so effectively on its own soil. Al-Qaeda, the radical Islamist organization headed by Osama bin Laden, was a group of a completely different kind. On the one hand, it was a private organization funded by an individual. On the other hand, it presided over a loose terrorist international using the most modern methods. The use of suicide bombers was an important aspect in its tactics as well.

After September 11, prevention of terrorism became a much higher priority for many nations. In the United States, that could be seen across the full scope of American government. President George W. Bush established an Office of Homeland Security to "develop and coordinate the implementation of a comprehensive national strategy to secure the United States from terrorist threats or attacks." Congress passed a law known as the Patriot Act that would make it easier for law enforcement and intelligence officials to coordinate among themselves, intercept communications, block suspected foreign terrorists from entering the United States, and detain or deport those already present.

Local law enforcement officials nationwide stepped up their arrests of suspected terrorists and the judicial system moved to indict them. In September 2002, six U.S. citizens of Yemeni background from Lackawanna, New York, were found guilty on charges of providing material support to al-Qaeda and given sentences ranging from seven to ten years. A year later, a U.S. District Court sentenced three, including a former U.S. Marine Corps instructor, for participating in a local terrorist group known as the "Virginia jihad network."

Less than a month after September 11, the United States, with the aid of Britain, staged air strikes in Afghanistan and soon toppled the ruling Taliban government that had given sanctuary to al-Qaeda members including bin Laden, many of whose forces fled to Arab countries and Iran. With the aid of several countries, notably Pakistan, the United States eliminated several of al-Qaeda's top leaders. They include Mohammed Atef, second-in-command of al-Qaeda, who was killed during a U.S. air strike in Afghanistan; Abu Zubaydah, the third-ranking figure in al-Qaeda, captured in Faisalabad, Afghanistan; Abu Zubair al-Haili, a senior al-Qaeda member, arrested in Morocco along with six other suspects after authorities foiled an apparent plot to use a dinghy packed with explosives to attack U.S. and British warships in the Strait of Gibraltar; and Abd al-Rahim al-Nashiri, Osama bin Laden's second-in-command and a key operations planner believed to have planned the attack on the USS *Cole* in Yemen in October 2000 and to have been involved in the bombings of U.S. embassies in east Africa in 1998.

While there was no major successful attack on American soil in the years after September 11, terrorism against the United States continued abroad. In Saudi Arabia, there were several attacks aimed at the expatriate community, including a May 2003 bombing of a housing compound in Riyadh that killed 20, including seven Americans. A few months later, a bomb struck the U.S.-owned Marriott Hotel in Jakarta, Indonesia, killing 13.

There were many attacks in Pakistan, where a bomb detonated outside the U.S. Consulate in Karachi, killing 11 and injuring 51 others. In early 2002, Daniel Pearl, a *Wall Street Journal* reporter, was kidnapped while researching a story in Karachi about the "shoe bomber" Richard Reid, who a few

weeks earlier had tried to detonate plastic explosives hidden in his sneakers while flying on a commercial airliner from Paris to Miami. Pearl's subsequent execution was videotaped and broadcast, a chilling use of technology that would be copied many times. Another American, Laurence Foley, a senior administrator at the U.S. Agency for International Development, was killed later that year in Amman, Jordan. Responsible for Foley's death was Abu Musab al-Zarqawi, the leader of the terrorist group Jama'at al-Tawhid wa'al-Jihad (Monotheism and Jihad). Al-Zarqawi then moved on to Iraq, where his group conducted terrorist operations in support of the Sunnis and later pledged his support to bin Laden, becoming the top terrorist in that country.

It was not only the United States that was a target of terrorism. About half of the 187 victims of a car bomb attack in October 2002 in Bali, Indonesia, were Australian. In March 2004, several bombs detonated on commuter trains in Madrid killing 191. In November 2004, prominent Dutch film director Theo Van Gogh, outspoken in his criticism of radical Islam, was stabbed to death while walking the streets of Amsterdam. His assassin belonged to the Hofstad Network, an Islamist terrorist cell of Dutch Muslims.

In March 2003, the United States and a coalition —notably including England, Australia, Italy, and Spain—attacked Iraq, capturing the country within three weeks. Saddam Hussein and his colleagues were forced underground or were arrested. Saddam himself was captured in December 2003 in a hiding place on a farm near his hometown of Tikrit.

Then Iraq became the main front of terrorist activity. Most of the terrorists were Sunni Muslims, a combination of Saddam Hussein supporters, radical Islamists, and communal militants. Sunnis, who had controlled Iraq under Saddam Hussein, knew that as a minority they would not be able to rule a democratic Iraq. Many Islamists came from abroad, especially Saudi Arabia, with their arming and free passage facilitated by Syria. Their targets included American troops and foreign workers, Iraqi government officials and police, and ordinary citizens—especially Shia Muslims, who made up the majority of Iraqi citizens.

The biggest attack in the early months of American occupation was a blast at Iraq's holiest Shia shrine in Najaf in August 2003, killing 75 people, among them Mohammed Baqer al-Hakim, one of the country's most important Muslim clerics, who had just returned from long exile in Iran. Also targeted were foreigners involved in the nation's reconstruction efforts, including engineers, contractors, humanitarian aid workers, journalists, and truck drivers. The terrorists often demanded that the hostage's country pull out of Iraq; when the demand was refused, they sent out videotapes of the foreign hostage being killed. Still another target was the international community. Also in August 2003, a bomb detonated in the driveway of the Marriott Hotel, headquarters of the UN High Commission for Refugees, killing 23 persons—including the program's director.

Nick Berg, an American businessman seeking telecommunications work in Iraq, was abducted by militants in 2004. In May, his captors decapitated him, capturing the act on videotape, which was later shown on television and released to the Internet. Berg's death was the first of a series of such killings of foreign hostages in Iraq. At the end of 2004, Margaret Hassan, the Irish woman who directed CARE International operations in Iraq, became a victim.

In November 2006, in the most deadly single attack in Iraq since the American invasion, militants detonated at least five car bombs and launched several mortars on Sadr City, the predominately Shiite area of Baghdad, killing at least 215 people and wounding upwards of 257 others.

September 11, 2001 During a carefully coordinated attack, 19 hijackers seize four U.S. passenger airliners in the eastern United States. Two of them crash into the World Trade Center towers in New York City, and a third crashes into the Pentagon, headquarters of the U.S. Defense Department, near Washington, D.C. The fourth plane, also on its way to Washington, crashes prematurely in a field in Pennsylvania after its crew and passengers attack the hijackers. In all, nearly 3,000 people are killed. The World Trade Center towers, each 107 stories high, collapse completely within a few hours of the attacks, killing or injuring hundreds of firefighters, police officers, and other rescue workers.

On the ground, U.S. investigators determine that Osama bin Laden's al-Qaeda group is responsible. At 8.30 p.m., President George Bush addresses the nation, saying, "Thousands of lives were suddenly ended by evil. The pictures of airplanes flying into buildings, fires burning, huge structures collapsing has filled us with disbelief, terrible sadness and a quiet, unyielding anger." The president says the U.S. government will track down the perpetrators and "make no distinction between the terrorists who committed the acts and those who harbor them."

September 20, 2001 President Bush addresses a joint session of Congress. He says that the September 11 terrorists are members of al-Qaeda, whose members "practice a fringe form of Islamic extremism that has been rejected by Muslim scholars and the vast majority of Muslim clerics . . . whose directive commands them to kill Christians and Jews, to kill all Americans and make no distinction between military and civilians, including women and children." In vowing to go after terrorists, Bush says, "We will pursue nations that provide aid or safe haven to terrorism. Every nation in every region now has a decision to make. Either you are with us or you are with the terrorists. From this day forward any nations that continue to harbor or support terrorism will be regarded by the United States as a hostile regime." Specifically, he calls upon the Taliban regime in Afghanistan, which shelters Osama bin Laden and his al-Qaeda terrorist network, to hand over terrorists and give the United States access to their training camps or share in the terrorists' fate.

September 20, 2001 A bomb explodes by the Sheraton Hotel in Sanaa, Yemen, where a group of FBI agents are staying, killing four people. The terrorists are unknown.

September 24, 2001 President George Bush signs the Executive Order on Blocking Terrorist Financing, aimed at undercutting financing backing for terrorists by authorizing the seizure of property of any individual or organization linked to terrorism.

September 27, 2001 The Federal Bureau of Investigation releases a list of 11 of the hijackers of September 11.

September 28, 2001 The United Nations Security Council passes Resolution 1373 calling on all nations to seize the financial asserts of individuals or companies linked to terrorism, not to provide any support—including safe haven—for terrorists, and to cooperate in prosecuting anyone who provides such support.

September 28, 2001 The U.S. Congress passes a law called Uniting and Strengthening America by Providing Appropriate Tools Required to Intercept and Obstruct Terrorism, known as the Patriot Act. This law makes it easier for law enforcement and intelligence officials to coordinate among themselves, intercept communications, block suspected foreign terrorists from entering the United States, and detain and deport those already present. It also authorizes the collection of information about foreigners who are in the country on student visas.

October 2001 Asbat al-Ansar, (League of the Followers, or Partisans' League) is founded in Lebanon. It is a Sunni extremist group, composed primarily of Palestinians and associated with al-Qaeda, committed to overthrowing the Lebanese government and thwarting perceived anti-Islamic and pro-Western influences in the country.

October 1, 2001 British Prime Minister Tony Blair delivers a major address to the British public providing an assessment of the evils of the al-Qaeda network and the Taliban regime, and a reassurance that retaliatory attacks are fully justified. As a result of September 11, laws are being changed "not to deny basic liberties, but to prevent their abuse and protect the most basic liberty of all: freedom from terror," he says.

October 7, 2001 Osama bin Laden broadcasts his first television message, warning of more attacks to come.

October 7, 2001 U.S. and British forces begin air strikes against Afghanistan, whose Taliban regime is accused of harboring al-Qaeda members. The attacks are "designed to disrupt the use of Afghanistan as a terrorist base of operations, and to attack the military capability of the Taliban regime," as Bush explains in his address to the nation.

October 8, 2001 President George Bush signs an executive order establishing an Office of Homeland Security, whose mission is to develop, coordinate, and oversee the national fight against terrorism.

October 10, 2001 Sulaiman Abu Ghaith, a close aide of bin Laden, releases a statement saying that the U.S. retaliation for the September 11 attacks is merely the latest of many

U.S. assaults against Muslims. He warns: "There are thousands of the Islamic nation's youths who are eager to die just as the Americans are eager to live."

October 28, 2001   Gunmen fire on Catholic worshippers in Bahawalpur, Pakistan, killing 18 and injuring five. A new terrorist group, Lashkar-I-Omar, claims responsibility. This group, which sometimes goes under the name al-Qanoon, is founded as a coalition of Lashkar-e-Jhangvi, Harakat-ul-Jihad-I-Islami and Jaish-e-Mohammed.

November 10, 2001   President Bush addresses the United Nations General Assembly, stressing that the September 11 victims came from all over the world. There is no such thing as a good terrorist, he further asserts, and all nations must maintain the principle that "no national aspiration, no remembered wrong can ever justify the deliberate murder of the innocent."

The Fall of the Taliban

The Taliban regime in Afghanistan had openly provided refuge to Osama bin Laden and his forces, which used their bases in the country to plan the September 11 attacks. In November 2001, U.S. and coalition forces captured Kabul and deposed the Taliban government there. This was the first time in recent history that a terrorism-sponsoring regime had been overthrown by foreign forces from countries it had victimized.

This operation disrupted the al-Qaeda forces, but many of them managed to flee, re-establishing themselves in other countries. On a strategic level, the priority on direct attacks against Western countries was now mixed with the terrorist-based war in Iraq, the attempt to use terrorism to promote revolution in Saudi Arabia, and other types of operations.

November 13, 2001   After weeks of fierce air assaults by U.S. and coalition forces, Taliban fighters abandon Kabul, the Afghan capital. U.S.-backed Northern Alliance fighters take over the city.

November 13, 2001   President George Bush signs the Executive Order on Detention, Treatment, and Trial of Certain Non-Citizens in the War Against Terrorism, which establishes military tribunals to try any non-U.S. citizen believed to be a member of a terrorist group. The tribunals would be conducted under different rules from other courts. Conviction and sentencing requires concurrence of two-thirds of the commission members, not all of them as is the case in regular courts. Defendants are also not permitted to seek appeals in any other U.S. or international court.

November 14–17, 2001   Mohammed Atef (also known as Abu Hafs), a brother-in-law of bin Laden and second-in-command of al-Qaeda, is killed during this three-day period of U.S. air strikes in Afghanistan. Atef had principal responsibility for supervising the training of al-Qaeda members, and was indicted in connection with the 1998 bombings of U.S. embassies in Kenya and Tanzania.

November 19, 2001   Juma Namangoni, an Uzbek nationalist in exile in Afghanistan who had become a field commander of the Taliban and one of bin Laden's assistants, is killed in

Afghanistan following a bomb blast in Mazar-e-Sharif, northern Afghanistan's largest city.

December 2001   Ansar al-Islam, an Islamic fundamentalist organization headquartered in the Kurdish area of northern Iraq, is formed with the goal of establishing an independent Islamic state in Iraq. It closely allies itself with al-Qaeda.

December 2001   The U.S. government accuses the Holy Land Foundation for Relief and Development, based in Richardson, Texas, of being the chief fund-raising group in the United States for Hamas, the radical Palestinian group that has pursued terrorist tactics against Israel. The organization bills itself as the largest Islamic charity in the U.S. The organization's offices in Richardson and three other cities are shut down and its assets are frozen. Following a challenge to the government's decision, in June 2003, the U.S. Circuit Court of Appeals for the District of Columbia upholds the government's decision to freeze the foundation's assets.

December 11, 2001   Zacarias Moussaoui, a French national of Moroccan heritage, is indicted for involvement in the September 11 terror attacks. U.S. officials arrested him a month before the September 11 attacks based on the concerns of flight school staff where he was taking flying lessons and detained him in Minnesota for an immigration violation. Although FBI officials in Minnesota became increasingly suspicious after questioning Moussaoui, they could not convince FBI headquarters to take his veiled threats seriously. Officials conclude he was either supposed to be the twentieth hijacker on September 11 or was part of a hijacking team targeting a fifth plane that day. On April 22, 2005, during a court session, Moussaoui will plead guilty to all the charges against him but insist that he was involved in an independent operation to hijack a plane in an attempt to free Omar Abdel Rahman, the Egyptian Islamist who was convicted and imprisoned for his role in the 1993 World Trade Center bombing. On May 3, 2003, he is sentenced to life in prison without the possibility of parole.

December 24, 2001   While on an American Airlines flight en route from Paris to Miami, Richard Reid, a British national and convert to Islam, strikes a match and applies it to his sneakers in an attempt to detonate plastic explosives hidden there. He is spotted by a flight attendant and subdued by passengers and crew members. The flight is diverted to Boston, where Reid is taken into custody. He will be tried and convicted of attempting to bring down the plane as part of a terrorist plot and sentenced to life in prison.

January 2002   The Pakistan government arrests and transfers to U.S. custody nearly 500 suspected al-Qaeda and Taliban terrorists, detains hundreds of extremists, and bans five extremist organizations: Lashkar-e-Tayyiba, Jaish-e-Mohammed, Sipah-e-Sahaba Pakistan, Tehrik-i-Jafria Pakistan, and Tehrik-i-Nifaz-i-Shariat-i Mohammadi.

January 16, 2002   Mokhtar Haouari, an Algerian, is sentenced to 24 years in prison for conspiring to bomb Los Angeles International Airport during the city's millennial celebrations.

January 22, 2002   Gunmen open fire outside the American Center in Calcutta, killing four Indian guards and injuring 14. The Harakat ul-Jihad-I-Islami, which is fighting Indian rule in Kashmir, and the Asif Raza Commandos, a group named after its leader, a Calcutta criminal with links to radical Islamic groups, is responsible.

January 23, 2002   Daniel Pearl, a reporter for the *Wall Street Journal,* is kidnapped on his way to interview a Muslim fundamentalist leader in Karachi, Pakistan, for a story about Richard Reid, the so-called shoe bomber. Four days later, a group calling itself the National Movement for the Restoration of Pakistani Sovereignty says it has Pearl and wants the release of several Pakistani nationals being held by the U.S. at Guantánamo Bay, Cuba, and in the U.S. as terrorist suspects. On February 21, a videotape obtained by investigators in Pakistan shows Pearl having his throat slit. It was not clear when he was killed, but investigators believed it was several weeks earlier. In July, a Pakistani court sentences Ahmad Omar Saeed Sheikh, a leader of the radical Islamic group Jaish-e-Mohammed, to death for masterminding Pearl's abduction and killing. Three other Pakistanis are imprisoned for life, while other suspects are still at large. Jaish-e-Mohammed's ally, Harakat ul-Mujahideen, is also believed to have been behind the kidnapping.

February 28, 2002   A shooting attack on a Shiite mosque in Rawalpindi, Pakistan, results in the death of ten worshippers and 24 being injured Sipah-e-Sahaba Pakistan and Lashkar-e-Jhangvi are suspected.

February 28, 2002   In Amman, Jordan, a bomb placed in a car is detonated by a timing device, killing an Egyptian and an Iraqi laborer who worked in a nearby food shop. The car belongs to the wife of the head of the Jordanian Anti-Terrorism Unit and was parked near their home. No one claims responsibility.

March 2, 2002   The U.S. military begins Operation Anaconda, a large ground operation to eliminate Taliban and al-Qaeda holdouts in a mountainous area of southeastern Afghanistan.

March 2, 2002   Terrorists assassinate seven Afghan tribal elders in eastern Kunar Province as the men are returning from a meeting near the provincial capital of Asadabad. The terrorists are unknown.

March 6, 2002   In Kandahar, Afghanistan, a new video store which under the Taliban had been banned, is hit by a grenade, killing the owner.

March 7, 2002   Terrorists infiltrate the home of a former Harakat-e Islami (Shia group) commander in Farah City, Afghanistan, and kill him and his mother and injure several of his family members.

March 17, 2002   Five people—including a U.S. Embassy employee and her teenage daughter—are killed and 45 others injured when two unidentified militants throw grenades into Islamabad's main Protestant church during Sunday services. The Lashkar-e-Tayyiba is responsible.

March 28, 2002   Abu Zubaydah, the third-ranking figure in al-Qaeda, is killed during a joint U.S.-Pakistani raid on an al-Qaeda hideout in Faisalabad, Afghanistan.

April 1, 2002   In Pakistan, a grenade attack on a mosque in Chaman near the Pakistan-Afghanistan border results in the death of two and injuring of 35. The assailants are unknown.

April 1, 2002   One person is killed and another 12 injured when a bomb explodes on a bus bound for Karachi from South Waziristan, Pakistan. No group takes responsibility.

April 8, 2002   A bomb detonates near a convoy in Jalalabad carrying Afghan Defense Minister General Mohammed Qasim Fahim, killing four and wounding 16 others. Fahim escapes unharmed. No group takes responsibility.

April 18, 2002   At least three people are killed and two injured when an explosion strikes the main bazaar in Khost, Afghanistan. No group takes responsibility.

April 19, 2002   Four associates of the jailed Egyptian cleric and leader of al-Gama'a al-Islamiyya (IG), Sheikh Omar Abdel Rahman, are indicted in a U.S. court. The four, which includes Rahman's lawyer, a U.S. citizen, are charged with aiding Rahman in continuing to direct the terrorist activities of the IG from his prison cell in the United States.

April 24, 2002   Two unknown gunmen fatally shoot a former senior commander of the Taliban, Hafiz Abdul Majid near the Afghani-Pakistani border town of Chaman.

April 25, 2002   Qari Obaydollah, a supporter of Afghanistan's former king, is killed in southern Afghanistan by unknown terrorists.

April 27, 2002   Two unknown terrorists in Karachi assassinate two former Pakistani government members—one with the National Assembly and the other with the Senate—who belong to a party sympathetic to the government of President Pervez Musharraf.

May 8, 2002   Jose Padilla is arrested after arriving at Chicago's O'Hare airport from Pakistan, for what the U.S. authorities say was a reconnaissance mission. Padilla, a convert to Islam of Puerto Rican origin, has links to al-Qaeda and is said to have traveled to Pakistan for instructions in making a dirty bomb. In May 2007, the trial of Padilla begins in a federal court, and on August 16 he is found guilty.

May 8, 2002   A suicide bomber detonates a van packed with explosives outside a hotel in Karachi, Pakistan, as a group of French naval engineers helping construct a submarine board a bus, killing 14, including 11 Frenchmen. Al-Qaeda is likely responsible.

May 14, 2002   Riaz Basra, the chief of Lashkar-e-Jhangvi, and three other gunmen are killed by Pakistani security officials in Vehari, Pakistan.

May 19, 2002   A candidate for Afghanistan's Loya Jirga (traditional assembly) who is poised for victory is shot dead in Chaghcharan by unknown terrorists.

June 2002   Abu Zubair al-Haili, a senior al-Qaeda member, is arrested in Morocco along with six other suspects after authorities foil an apparent plot to use a dinghy packed with explosives to attack U.S. and British warships in the Strait of Gibraltar. Al-Haili, a Saudi, is one of al-Qaeda's "top 25" leaders, and plays a vital role in bringing potential fighters to training camps in Afghanistan before September 11.

June 14, 2002 A suicide attacker crashes a van packed with explosives into a guard post outside the U.S. Consulate in Karachi, Pakistan, killing 11 and injuring 51 others. Al-Qanoon, an Islamist group seeking to overthrow the government of Pakistan, claims the attack.

June 18, 2002 The Saudi Arabian government announces that it is holding 11 Saudis, an Iraqi, and a Sudanese man suspected of planning terrorist attacks inside the kingdom. At least seven of the suspects are members of al-Qaeda, who are plotting to use missiles and other explosives in attacks on military installations in Saudi Arabia, including an air base used by the U.S.

June 25, 2002 The president of Pakistan's National Democratic Party and former pro-Musharraf federal minister is shot to death while driving in Karachi by unknown terrorists.

July 6, 2002 Haji Abdul Qadir, one of Afghanistan's five vice presidents and a prominent member of the Pashtun ethnic group, and his driver are assassinated outside the gates of a government ministry in Kabul. The terrorists are unknown.

August 2, 2002 A Spanish man, accused of preaching Christianity, and his female Palestinian employee, are murdered in Bumburat, Pakistan. The assailants are unknown.

August 5, 2002 In Murree, Pakistan, gunmen attack a Christian school killing six persons and injuring one. A new Islamist group called al-Intiqmi al-Pakistani claims responsibility.

August 9, 2002 A grenade attack on a Presbyterian Missionary Hospital in Taxila, Pakistan, kills five nurses and wounds another 23 people. Lashkar-e-Tayyiba is likely responsible.

August 29, 2002 James Ujaama, an American Muslim, is indicted by a federal grand jury in Seattle on one charge of conspiracy to provide material support and resources for al-Qaeda. He later pleads guilty to lesser charges and is sentenced to two years in prison.

August 29, 2002 Six men in America are indicted on charges of supporting Islamic terrorist activities, including an alleged five-man "sleeper cell" in Detroit and a former worshipper at a radical mosque in London. The suspected cell—some of whom worked at the Detroit airport—are accused of having surveillance videos of Disneyland in California and the MGM Grand Hotel and Casino in Las Vegas that law enforcement agents believe were to be the targets of their attacks. The government says the suspects were members of the Salafi Group for Preaching and Combat, a Muslim militant group launched in Algeria and supported by bin Laden. They are also accused of trying to recruit terrorists for attacks on a U.S. air base in Turkey and a hospital in Jordan. Two men will be convicted of some charges, but will later be released when courts discover serious misconduct by prosecutors in the first trial.

September 2002 Ramzi bin al-Shibh, a former roommate of Muhammad Atta, the leader of the September 11 hijackers, who authorities say trained to be the "twentieth hijacker," and five other al-Qaeda suspects are arrested in Pakistan.

September 5, 2002 A car bomb detonates in a busy market area of Kabul, killing 30 people and wounding 17. As with other attacks in Afghanistan, it is likely carried out either by remnants of the Taliban or by al-Qaeda. A third possible culprit is warlord Gulbuddin Hekmatyar, head of the Hezb-e-Islami, made up of fundamentalist Sunni Muslim Pashtuns. Hekmatyar has vowed to continue *jihad* until foreign troops are gone from Afghanistan and Afghans have set up an Islamic government, but later he will offer grudging support to the U.S.-supported regime of Hamid Karzai.

September 8, 2002   A U.S. District Court files an indictment against Uzair Paracha, a 22-year-old Pakistani national residing in the United States, for aiding al-Qaeda. He will be convicted in 2005 of using false papers in support of an al-Qaeda operative, but his supporters in the United States and Pakistan will continue to contest guilt.

September 13, 2002   On the first anniversary of September 11, FBI agents arrest five U.S. citizens of Yemeni background who live in Lackawanna, New York, on charges of providing material support to al-Qaeda. A sixth suspect is arrested two days later. The individuals are believed to have participated in weapons training in the early summer of 2001 at a terrorist training camp in Afghanistan known to be used by al-Qaeda. After pleading guilty, the men will be given sentences ranging from seven to ten years.

September 15, 2002   One person is killed and another six are injured when a bomb planted under a seat on a Karachi-to-Hyderabad bus explodes. It is not clear who is responsible.

October 6, 2002   The French supertanker *Limberg,* docked in Yemen, is destroyed by an explosion, killing a Bulgarian crew member. Al-Qaeda is responsible.

October 8, 2002   In Gardez, Afghanistan, unknown terrorists kill four by firing an anti-tank weapon at a vehicle carrying civilians.

October 10, 2002   Unknown gunmen fire on a convoy carrying the governor of Khost Province in eastern Afghanistan, killing two of his bodyguards and wounding four others.

October 12, 2002   In Bali, Indonesia, a car bomb explodes outside a discotheque in a busy tourist area, killing at least 187 international tourists—85 of them Australians—and injuring about 300 others. Al-Qaeda claims responsibility for this attack, which becomes known as the Australian September 11. On August 7, 2003, an Indonesian court sentences Islamic militant Amrozi bin Nurhasyim to death for his role in the bombings.

October 18, 2002   Four people are killed and 40 wounded when a wedding ceremony, which includes music that had been banned under the Taliban regime, is attacked with hand grenades in the Paghman District of Afghanistan. No group takes responsibility.

October 20, 2002   A bomb explodes in the bazaar in Kamra, Pakistan, killing one and wounding 20. It is likely an al-Qaeda operation.

October 28, 2002   Terrorists shoot and kill Laurence Foley, a senior administrator at the U.S. Agency for International Development (USAID) outside his home in Amman, Jordan. A group called the Honest People of Jordan claims responsibility. In December, Jordanian authorities arrest two men, a Libyan and a Jordanian, who later admit to carrying out the assassination after receiving money from Abu Musab al-Zarqawi, a top al-Qaeda leader in Jordan.

November 2002

In an undisclosed foreign country, U.S. officials capture Abd al-Rahim al-Nashiri, bin Laden's second-in-command and a key al-Qaeda operational planner, who is believed to have masterminded the attack on the USS *Cole* in Yemen in October 2000 (*see* chapter 7) and was involved in the bombings of U.S. embassies in east Africa in 1998.

November 3, 2002

A CIA Predator drone fires a missile at a car in rural Yemen carrying several suspected al-Qaeda operatives, killing Qaed Salim Sinan al-Harethi, al-Qaeda's top member in Yemen who was involved in the *Cole* plot. Also killed in that rocket attack is a Yemeni-American suspected of being the ringleader of the "Lackawanna Six" (*see* September 13, 2002).

November 4, 2002

Kuwaiti security officials arrest a reputed senior al-Qaeda figure, known as Mosen, accused of plotting a suicide bomb attack on a Sanaa, Yemen, hotel frequented by Westerners. Mosen is believed to be a regional commander for al-Qaeda responsible for attacks on the *Limberg* and the *Cole*.

November 7, 2002

A car carrying a well-known anti-Taliban commander who is a son of a former provincial governor is attacked between Torkham and Jalalabad, Afghanistan. The commander's bodyguard is killed. No group takes responsibility.

November 15, 2002

A bomb explodes on a passenger bus traveling on a road in Hyderabad, Afghanistan, killing two people and injuring nine. No group takes responsibility.

November 19, 2002

An Italian journalist, Australian television cameraman, Afghan photographer, and Spanish reporter are killed in an ambush on their car by unknown terrorists traveling to Kabul.

November 21, 2002

American missionary Bonnie Weatherall is shot to death at the health clinic where she works in Sidon, Lebanon. Terrorists linked to Asbat al-Ansar are likely responsible.

November 21, 2002

An Afghan woman working for a Japanese aid agency is killed in her house near Mazar-e Sharif, Afghanistan. Afghan women working for foreign nongovernmental organizations (NGOs) are a target of the Taliban.

December 2002

Federal authorities arrest four brothers in Dallas who worked for InfoCom, a company that hosts Internet Web sites, many of them for Middle Eastern organizations. They are charged on 33 counts of money laundering, illegal shipments of computer equipment to designated state sponsors of terror Syria and Libya, and financial dealings with Hamas, the Palestinian organization considered a terrorist group by the U.S. government. InfoCom may also have financial and other ties to al-Qaeda.

December 5, 2002

In Makassar, Indonesia, a bomb explodes in a McDonald's restaurant, killing three persons and injuring 11 others. On the same day, a bomb explodes at an automobile showroom with no injuries. The mastermind of these attacks is believed to be Agung Abdul Hamid, the head of KTL, a local terrorist group.

December 5, 2002   A bomb detonates at the Macedonian Consulate in Karachi. Three Pakistani staffers are found in the rubble, and had apparently been stabbed before the blast. The attack may be related to the killing of six Pakistanis in Macedonia in March. On August 25, 2004, nine Pakistanis who belong to the Harakat ul-Mujahideen are given life sentences for carrying out this attack.

December 16, 2002   A Hindu is killed when unknown gunmen open fire in front of a children's hospital in Gardez, Afghanistan. The attackers leave papers telling non-Muslims to leave.

December 21, 2002   Two workers, with an international health program—one Indian and one Afghan—are killed in Gardez, Afghanistan. A statement is left on the site, warning that all foreign workers in the area will be killed.

December 25, 2002   Two attackers, dressed in *burqas,* the traditional Muslim woman's head-to-toe garment, toss a grenade into a small church during Christmas services in Chianwala, Pakistan, killing three and injuring 16. It is not clear which group is behind the attack.

December 30, 2002   A gunman, determined to "get closer to Allah," bursts into a meeting room in a Baptist mission hospital in Jibla, Yemen, and begins shooting, killing three Americans and wounding another.

January 2003   Egypt authorities arrest 43 members of Gund Allah, an Islamist group, for planning attacks against U.S. and Israeli interests.

January 17, 2003   One person is killed and another injured when a bomb concealed in a radio explodes in the northern city of Balkh, Afghanistan. Al-Qaeda may be involved.

January 21, 2003   A gunman kills a U.S. civilian contractor for the U.S. Army and wounds another one by ambushing a vehicle in Kuwait City, where the U.S. is beginning a military buildup leading to the proposed invasion of Iraq. Two days later, an al-Qaeda supporter is caught while trying to cross the border into Saudi Arabia and confesses to the crime.

January 26, 2003   Shots are fired on a United Nations High Commission for Refugees (UNHCR) convoy traveling near Jalalabad, Afghanistan, killing two Afghan security officers and wounding their driver. The perpetrators are either al-Qaeda, Gulbuddin Hekmatyar's Hezb-e-Islam Party, or Taliban members.

January 27, 2003   A bomb explodes in Kandahar, Afghanistan, killing one person and injuring two others. The terrorists are unknown.

January 31, 2003   A large bomb destroys a bridge outside the southern city of Kandahar, killing 18 people and injuring two on a passing bus. Police blame al-Qaeda, the Taliban, or Gulluddin Hekmatyra.

February 5, 2003   In a speech to the United Nations, U.S. Secretary of State Colin Powell lays out the case for an U.S. invasion of Iraq. Powell says that Iraqi leader Saddam Hussein is hiding chemical and biological weapons, is developing weapons of mass destruction, and has collaborated with terrorists.

February 8, 2003   Ansar al-Islam terrorists assassinate Shawkat Hajji Mushir, a member of the Kurdish parliament and a founder of the Patriotic Union of Kurdistan, and four others at a home in Qamesh Tapa, Iraq.

February 20, 2003   In Riyadh, Saudi Arabia, a gunman ambushes a car at a stoplight, killing a British citizen employed by British Aerospace Engineering. The gunman, a Yemen-born Saudi and al-Qaeda supporter, is arrested by Saudi police.

February 26, 2003   An Ansar al-Islam suicide bomber kills four Kurds at a checkpoint in northern Iraq.

March 1, 2003   Pakistani intelligence agents arrest Khalid Shaykh Muhammad, who is high on the FBI's list of most wanted terrorists, in Islamabad. Muhammad is believed to be the chief operational planner of the September 11, 2001, attacks on New York's World Trade Center and the Pentagon. He is turned over to the United States, where he will remain in custody in various secret locations.

March 10, 2003   A bomb explodes as participants are leaving a tribal meeting in Kandahar, Afghanistan, killing three and wounding five others.

March 17, 2003   President Bush tells Saddam Hussein he must leave Iraq within 48 hours or the United States will invade.

Two Wars in Iraq

The U.S.-led war in Iraq was controversial. A number of reasons were given for the operation, including the alleged development of weapons of mass destruction in Iraq and the regime's role as a state sponsor of terrorism. Attempts were made, with only a limited degree of success, to show links between the Iraqi government and al-Qaeda before September 11. It was also argued that the overthrow of Saddam would reduce the strength of terrorist forces. This assertion may have been true for world terrorism, but post-Saddam Iraq itself became a new focus for terrorism.

Once Saddam was overthrown, a second war began in Iraq in which an insurgency operated mainly through terrorist methods. This provided an especially interesting case study of terrorism

because the conflict brought together the three basic types of terrorism. The Iraqi insurgents simultaneously represented a revolutionary, a nationalist, and a state-sponsored terrorist campaign.

They were revolutionary in the sense that they were trying to overthrow an existing government (the post-Saddam Iraqi government) and to institute a new type of regime and society (Islamist). They were nationalist in two ways. First, terrorist groups claimed they represented Iraqi nationalism against a foreign threat and occupier, the United States and its allies; second, Iraq's Sunni minority pursued a narrower nationalist cause of trying to return itself to power by defeating the other ethnic groups, the Shia Muslims and Kurds. The Sunni insurgency was also state-sponsored in that much of the organizational leadership, infrastructure, and financing was based in Syria. In tactical terms, terrorists in Iraq used a full array of terrorist methods. These included bombing public places, assassinating government officials, targeting foreigners, taking hostages, using suicide bombers, and so on. In doing these things, their goal was to mobilize Sunni/Shia/Kurdish Muslims against ethnic adversaries and foreign enemies (whose deaths they would supposedly celebrate) while trying to terrorize and intimidate the foreigners into leaving the country and discourage local citizens from participating in or supporting their own government. They rarely engaged enemy troops in direct combat, the main activity of conventional warfare. In effect, the insurgency in Iraq—far more than the scattered operations elsewhere—represented the highest stage of terrorism.

March 19, 2003 The United States and its coalition partners—notably Britain—begin their air and ground assault on Iraq. The Iraqi army offers only token resistance, and within three weeks Saddam Hussein and his allies are forced underground. The United States and its allies begin to set up an occupation government.

March 22, 2003 In Sayed Sadiq, Kurdish-controlled northern Iraq, four Kurds and an Australian cameraman are killed and 24 others wounded by a car bomb. The Kurdish terror group Ansar al-Islam is believed to be responsible.

March 28, 2003 In Tirin Kot, Afghanistan, unknown terrorists kill a Salvadoran Red Cross worker.

April 1, 2003 An Afghani who is close to Afghan President Hamid Karzai and his nephew are shot dead outside their home in Uruzgan Province, central Afghanistan. Taliban sympathizers are suspected.

April 10, 2003 Two Shia clerics—including Abdul Majid al-Khoei, who had recently returned to Iraq from exile in London—are hacked to death by a mob outside a mosque in Najaf, Iraq. Moqtada al-Sadr, an extreme Shia cleric, is suspected of being behind the attack.

April 11, 2003 The U.S. Army publishes a pack of 55 playing cards identifying its most wanted suspects in Iraq, top-level Baath officials and supporters.

April 12, 2003 An Italian tourist is shot dead in southern Afghanistan, likely by Taliban supporters.

April 13, 2003 Terrorists kill two and wound one as they target the vehicle of the governor of Kandahar, Afghanistan, as the official is driving to Chaman, Pakistan. The governor survives the attack. The terrorists, likely either members of the Taliban or al-Qaeda, escape.

April 14, 2003 An anti-terrorism court in Karachi convicts four members of Harakat ul-Mujahideen, for the car bombing outside the U.S. Consulate in June 2002. Two of the defendants are sentenced to death by hanging, and the two others to life imprisonment.

April 25, 2003 An Uzbek man working for the World Food Program is killed in Mazar-e-Sharif, Afghanistan, by unknown terrorists.

April 29, 2003 Pakistani police arrest Ali Abd al-Aziz (Ammar al-Baluchi), who provided funds to Muhammad Atta and other 9/11 hijackers to finance their flight lessons and living expenses in the U.S., and Walid Ba'Attash, believed to have organized the October 2000 bombing of the USS *Cole* in Yemen.

May 1, 2003   Ansar al-Sunna, a group committed to establishing a religious Islamic state in Iraq and the withdrawal of foreign forces, is formed. The group includes members from the Kurdish terrorist organization Ansar al-Islam, foreigners from al-Qaeda, and Iraqi Sunnis.

May 7, 2003   A prominent religious scholar with ties to the government is shot dead as he leaves a mosque in Afghanistan's central Uruzgan Province. Al-Qaeda or Taliban sympathizes are likely responsible.

May 12, 2003   Several car bombs detonate in front of three American expatriate housing compounds in Riyadh, Saudi Arabia, killing a total of 20, including seven Americans. Al-Qaeda is considered responsible.

May 29, 2003   A bomb placed by unknown terrorists in a mosque in Teshkan, Afghanistan, kills a cleric.

June 2003   First mention noted of the 1920 Revolution Brigades, a Sunni Islamic extremist terrorist group seeking an end to U.S. military in Iraq and the establishment of an Islamic nation.

June 1, 2003   Terrorists in central Iraq shoot dead a newspaper manager who had been critical of Saddam Hussein. The gunmen leave behind a message calling themselves Saddam's Knights, and threatening those cooperating with the Americans.

June 2, 2003   French authorities at Charles de Gaulle airport arrest Christian Ganczarski, a German convert to Islam with ties to al-Qaeda who was likely involved in an attack on the synagogue in Djerba, Tunisia.

June 5, 2003   French authorities arrest Moroccan national and German resident Karim Mehdi at Charles de Gaulle airport on suspicion of having ties to the al-Qaeda cell in Hamburg and for plotting against tourist places on Reunion Island.

June 11, 2003   Twelve Pashtun Afghans are killed and four others are injured in an attack on a bus by Hazaras in central Afghanistan's Uruzgan Province. The terrorists are unknown.

June 17, 2003   Unknown terrorists kill a Red Crescent society relief worker in Afghanistan's Nangarhar Province.

June 18, 2003   Pakistani officials arrest two suspected al-Qaeda members in Peshawar, including Adil al-Jazeeri of Algeria, a longtime aide to bin Laden.

June 25, 2003   An engineer dealing with electricity is shot dead at her Baghdad home. It is not clear which group is responsible.

July 4, 2003   A bomb explodes in a Shia mosque in Quetta, Pakistan, killing 53 and wounding 60. Lashkar-e-Jhangvi claims responsibility but Pakistani officials, who arrest 14 Sunnis for this attack, believe India and Afghanistan may be involved.

July 5, 2003   A British journalist is shot dead by terrorists as he stands outside the national museum in Baghdad. It is not clear which group is responsible.

July 5, 2003   Six unknown terrorists assassinate a Roman Catholic priest in his home in Okara, Pakistan.

July 16, 2003   The mayor of Haditha, Iraq, and his son are shot to death while driving through the city. Unidentified supporters of Saddam Hussein are suspected.

July 22, 2003   Uday and Qusay, Saddam Hussein's sons and his most feared lieutenants, are killed in a gun battle at their hideout in the northern Iraqi town of Mosul.

July 23, 2003   An Afghan accused of working with American troops is stabbed to death in Khost Province by unknown gunmen.

July 27, 2003   Two Afghans working for a foreign aid agency are shot dead and two others wounded in Kandahar. The Taliban is likely responsible.

July 29, 2003   A member of the Kandahar city council who had opposed the Taliban is assassinated.

August 2, 2003   A bomb in a vehicle explodes in front of the Jordanian Embassy in Baghdad, killing 19 and injuring 50 others. Ansar al-Islam is suspected.

August 5, 2003   In Jakarta, Indonesia, a car bomb explodes in the front of the Marriott Hotel during lunchtime, killing 13 persons and injuring 149 others. Al-Qaeda claims responsibility.

August 5, 2003   In Tikrit, Iraq, a bomb detonates beneath a U.S. vehicle, killing a U.S. citizen working as a contractor. No group claims responsibility.

August 13, 2003   Riduan Issamuddin, alias "Hambali," the former operations chief of Jemaah Islamiyah, is arrested in Thailand and extradited to the United States. Hambali, the only non-Arab to sit on al-Qaeda's ruling Shura Council, helped plan the September 11, 2001, attacks.

August 16, 2003   In the continuation of fighting between Shias and Sunnis in Pakistan, terrorists assassinate two Shias in Karachi.

August 19, 2003   In Baghdad, a truck enters the driveway of the Marriott Hotel, the headquarters of the UN High Commission for Refugees and explodes, killing 23 persons. The most prominent is the High Commissioner of the UNHCR, Sergio Vieira de Mello, a Brazilian who had become special representative of the UN secretary general in Iraq. Three U.S. citizens are also killed, and more than 100 others of many nationalities are injured. The blast badly damages several stories of the Marriott Hotel and causes minor damage up to a mile away. A previously unknown group called the Armed Vanguards of the Second Mohammed Army, a Sunni Islamist group, claims responsibility.

August 21, 2003   U.S. troops in Iraq capture Ali Hasan al-Majid, also known as "Chemical Ali," for his role in chemical weapons attacks against the Kurds. He is number five on the U.S. most wanted list. In June 2007, he is sentenced to death for his crimes.

August 29, 2003	A car bomb explodes at Iraq's holiest Shia shrine in Najaf, the Imam Ali mosque, killing 75 people and wounding some 175. Among the fatalities is Mohammed Baqer al-Hakim, one of the country's most important Muslim clerics who had just returned from exile in Iran. Al-Qaeda in Iraq is the likely instigator. In July 2004, a Libyan national and al-Qaeda member, is arrested along with other members of the organization for their involvement in the attack.
August 30, 2003	A court in Belgium convicts 23 al-Qaeda sympathizers. The group includes Tarek Maaroufi, a Tunisian-born Belgian citizen and al-Qaeda recruiter in Europe, who is sentenced to six years in jail for his involvement in the assassination of Ahmed Shah Masood, a leading Afghan anti-Taliban commander, who was killed on September 9, 2001, two days before the 9/11 attacks in the United States.
September 3, 2003	Two people are killed and 14 injured in a bomb that detonates during a wedding in Chaparhar, Afghanistan. Al-Qaeda may be responsible.
September 8, 2003	Near Moqor, Afghanistan, terrorists, likely Taliban, kill four Danish citizens working for a relief organization helping local Afghanis on an irrigation project.
September 17, 2003	Spain's leading investigating judge, Baltasar Garzón, issues an indictment against bin Laden for the September 11 attacks. He accuses al-Qaeda of using Spain as a base to plot the September 11 attacks and indicts 35 people for terrorist activities connected to bin Laden's al-Qaeda network in Spain.
September 19, 2003	Iraq's former defense minister under Saddam Hussein, General Sultan Hashim Ahmed, surrenders to U.S. forces in Mosul, Iraq. He is number 27 on the Americans' most wanted list.
September 20, 2003	Aqila al-Hashimi, one of three women on Iraq's governing council, is gunned down after her car is ambushed outside her Baghdad home. She dies five days later. Supporters of Saddam Hussein are likely responsible.
September 24, 2003	An explosion detonates at a movie theater in Mosul, Iraq, killing two people and injuring up to 20 others. The theater was showing a pornographic film at the time of the explosion. It is not clear which group is responsible.
September 24, 2003	In Baghdad, a remotely detonated bomb left by indentified terrorists on the road destroys two commuter buses, killing one Iraqi and injuring 22 others.
September 25, 2003	An Afghan aid worker is killed in Helmand, Afghanistan. Taliban is responsible.
September 25, 2003	A bomb explodes at the Baghdad office of the U.S. television network NBC, killing a Somali guard and injuring another. Unknown terrorists are responsible.
September 26, 2003	Taliban terrorists kill a district administrator in Kandahar and eight men traveling with him.
September 31, 2003	A court in Brussels, Belgium, convicts 18 of Islamist terrorist activities. The group includes Nizar Trabelsi, a Tunisian who spent several years as a minor league professional soccer player in Germany, who is sentenced to ten years for plotting a suicide attack on a U.S. military base in Belgium.

October 2003   Pakistani soldiers in western Pakistan kill Hassan Makhsum, leader of the
                            Eastern Turkestan Islamic Movement (ETIM) on the Pakistan-Afghanistan
                            border. This small Islamic extremist group based in China's western Xinjiang
                            Province seeks to turn that area into an independent Islamist state. It is report-
                            ed to have links to al-Qaeda.

October 2003   Egypt completes the release from prison of 1,000 leaders, members and sup-
                            porters of al-Gama'a al-Islamiyya, long the country's most powerful mili-
                            tant group, known as the IG. This release, begun a year earlier, is granted
                            because the government believes the IG leadership has adopted a nonviolent
                            philosophy.

October 3, 2003   Five radical Islamic groups join the al-Qaeda organization—the Egyptian Jihad,
                            the Yemen Jihad, the Aden-Abyan Army, the Saudi Ahfad al-Sahaba, and the
                            Algerian al-Jama'a al-Salafiya al-Daawa.

October 12, 2003   A suicide car bombing outside the Baghdad Hotel kills eight and wounds 32.
                            The hotel is where CIA members, American contractors, and senior Iraqi offi-
                            cials stay. Al-Qaeda claims responsibility.

October 13, 2003   Fathur Rohman al-Ghozi, a key member of Jemaah Islamiyah, is killed by
                            Filipino police in North Cotabato.

October 14, 2003   Unknown terrorists detonate a suicide car bomb outside the Turkish Embassy
                            in Baghdad, killing a bystander and wounding 13 others.

October 26, 2003   Rockets are fired by unknown terrorists at the al-Rashid Hotel in Baghdad,
                            which houses U.S. and coalition forces, killing a U.S. colonel and injuring 15
                            others. Deputy Secretary of Defense Paul Wolfowitz is staying at the hotel when
                            the attack occurs.

October 27, 2003   In Baghdad, a car bomb explodes inside the headquarters of the International
                            Committee of the Red Cross, killing 12 persons and injuring 22 others. It is not
                            established which group is responsible.

October 27, 2003   Terrorists ambush and kill two U.S. government contract workers in Shkin,
                            Afghanistan. Taliban terrorists are likely responsible.

October 28, 2003   An editor of an Iraqi weekly newspaper is fatally shot by unknown terrorists on
                            the roof of his office's building in Mosul.

November 7, 2003   Haji Mohammad Zaker, son of the former governor of Nangarhar Province
                            in eastern Afghanistan and known for his anti-Taliban views, survives an
                            attempt on his life that kills one of his bodyguards and injures another. The
                            attack takes place in the Daka area, on the main road between Torkham and
                            Jalalabad.

November 8, 2003   A gunman infiltrates an upscale residential compound in Riyadh, Saudi Arabia,
                            where he begins firing, eventually killing 17 and wounding about 90 before
                            being captured.

November 16, 2003	Terrorists gun down a French female employee of the UN refugee agency as she is on a motorcycle in Ghazni, Afghanistan. Two Taliban members are arrested in connection with this attack.
November 19, 2003	The director general of the Education Ministry in Iraq's Diwaniyah Province is assassinated by unknown assailants.
November 20, 2003	Two bombs are detonated in downtown Istanbul—one targeting the British and Israeli consulates and the second the HSBC Bank headquarters and the Metro City shopping center—killing 28 and wounding 450. The Abu Hafz al-Masri Brigades, part of al-Qaeda, claims responsibility. On May 31, 2005, suspected members of a Turkish al-Qaeda cell are put on trial for connection with this attack and a second at a synagogue in Istanbul. In 2007, six men were convicted to life in prison for the attacks.
November 20, 2003	A truck bomb explodes near a Kurdish party office in Kirkuk, Iraq, killing five people and wounding 30. Islamic extremists linked to al-Qaeda are likely responsible.
November 29 2003	Separate attacks in Iraq result in ten deaths—seven Spanish intelligence agents, two Japanese diplomats, and a Colombian contractor. The Japanese diplomats are shot and killed in Tikrit by unknown terrorists as they buy a drink from a roadside stall. A Colombian civilian contractor is killed and two colleagues wounded in a firearms attack on their convoy in Balad. The seven Spanish intelligence officers are killed when their convoy is ambushed by a mortar and grenade attack near Suwayrah, 30 miles south of Baghdad. The attacks are claimed by the "al-Faruq Brigades," a radical Islamist group committed to "Cleanse Baghdad, the City of Peace, of the invaders, by the grace of God, on a day when the Believers will rejoice at God's triumph."
November 30, 2003	Two South Koreans helping to build a power transmission line in Iraq are killed by unknown terrorists when their car is fired upon near Tikrit, Iraq.
December 3, 2003	A U.S. District Court judge in Buffalo sentences two Yemeni Americans of the so-called Lackawanna Six group to prison terms of ten and eight years for attending an al-Qaeda training camp in Afghanistan.
December 9, 2003	A rocket attack on a Sunni mosque in Baghdad kills three people and injures two. It is unclear which group is responsible.
December 12, 2003	In Beyci, Iraq, unknown terrorists kill two Turkish truck drivers at a restaurant.
December 13, 2003	Saddam Hussein, Iraq's deposed leader, is found by U.S. forces at the bottom of a hole on a farm near his hometown of Tikrit. Saddam, who is bearded and haggard, surrenders without resistance. After a trial, he is sentenced to death on November 5, 2006.
December 21, 2003	Two workers, one Indian and one Afghani, with an international health program, are killed in Gardez, in Afghanistan's eastern Raktia Province. Taliban terrorists are likely responsible.
December 22, 2003	A Kurdish judge is shot dead while driving in Mosul. The terrorists are likely supporters of Saddam Hussein who have been targeting judges.

December 25, 2003   In an unsuccessful attempt to kill Pakistani President Musharraf, two suicide car bombers detonate their explosives in a public square in Rawalpindi, Pakistan, killing 17 people and wounding 50. An al-Qaeda leader, Abu Farraj al-Libbi, is arrested in May 2005 for masterminding the attack.

December 27, 2003   An Iraqi lawyer working with U.S. forces is gunned down outside his home in Mosul by unidentified assailants.

December 29, 2003   In Mahmudiyah, Iraq, unknown terrorists open fire on a vehicle killing two Iraqi sentries and a British engineer. They had been targeting foreign workers.

December 31, 2003   A bomb detonates in a crowded Baghdad restaurant during New Year's festivities, killing eight and wounding at least 30. The target of the blast, the Nabil Restaurant, is popular with foreigners and upper-middle-class Iraqis. It is not clear which group is responsible.

January 4, 2004   A bomb detonates in a taxi in Mosul, killing two Iraqis and injuring a resident of Jordan. It is not clear which group is responsible.

January 5, 2004   Two French contractors are shot and killed and a third wounded after their car breaks down in Falluja and unidentified gunmen in a passing car open fire.

January 6, 2004   Sixteen people are killed and over 35 are injured in a car bombing attack in Kandahar, Afghanistan. The senior Taliban commander, Mullah Sabir Momin, later apologizes for the attack whose target was supposed to be U.S. troops.

January 9, 2004   A bomb explodes near a Shia mosque in Baquba, central Iraq, killing five people and wounding 39. It is not clear which group is responsible.

January 11, 2004   In Afghanistan, Taliban terrorists kill a man as he is driving on the Gardez-Khost main road.

January 14, 2004   Three contractors working for a U.S. company, one of whom is an American citizen, are killed when their convoy is attacked by unknown terrorists near Tikrit.

January 15, 2004   Sami Mohammed Ali Said al-Ja'af, also known as "Abu Omar al-Kurdi" or "Abu Yusef," is captured by Iraqi security forces. He is the deputy of Abu Musab al-Zarqawi, leader of the Iraqi insurgency and a member of al-Qaeda, and is responsible for building many car bombs.

January 20, 2004   A U.S. contractor working for the U.S. military is killed and another wounded when their vehicle is sprayed with gunfire near the main U.S. army camp, Camp Doha, in Kuwait City.

January 22, 2004   Unknown terrorists detonate a bomb at the offices of Iraq's Communist Party in Baghdad, killing two party members.

January 22, 2004   Hassan Ghul, a high-ranking al-Qaeda member operating in Iraq, is arrested while attempting to cross the Iran-Iraq border. He is held by U.S. authorities at a secret location.

January 25, 2004	Unidentified terrorists kill a Jordanian truck driver, taking a mobile home to a Japanese army officer, on the Ramadi-to-Baghdad road.
January 27, 2004	Two Iraqis employed at CNN-TV are gunned down in their car near Baghdad by an unknown terrorist.
January 28, 2004	A car bomb explodes in front of a hotel in downtown Baghdad, killing three people and injuring 11. It is not known which group is responsible.
February 1, 2004	Two suicide bombers in Irbil, Iraq, simultaneously explode their bombs at the offices of two rival Kurdish political parties packed with hundreds of people celebrating a Muslim holiday, killing about 109 and wounding some 221. Ansar al-Sunna claims responsibility.
February 14, 2004	Between Babil and Baghdad, unidentified gunmen open fire on a taxi, killing a Baptist minister from Rhode Island and wounding three other Baptist ministers from Connecticut, Massachusetts, and New York. No group claims responsibility.
February 16, 2004	An employee of the American Service Center in Baghdad is killed by an unknown gunman.
February 22, 2004	A helicopter belonging to a foreign organization overseeing the building of a health clinic in Kandahar Province, Afghanistan, is hit by a gunman who succeeds in killing the Australian pilot and wounding three others, including one American. The Taliban claims responsibility.
February 23, 2004	A bomb explodes by a car in Iskandariyah in Iraq, killing one U.S. contractor and wounding three others. No group claims responsibility.
March 2, 2004	Two major attacks during the Shia festival of Ashura result in the deaths of about 170 Shias and wounding of about 500. Nine bombs detonate in the center of Karbala packed with Shia pilgrims killing some 100 and wounding 233. Another 70 are killed and about 170 wounded as three bombs go off at a Shia shrine in Baghdad. Al-Qaeda is responsible.
March 3, 2004	In another attack during the Shia festival of Ashura, about 47 people are killed and 120 injured after an attack on a Shia parade in Quetta, Pakistan.
March 4, 2004	Three Muslims are found guilty in a U.S. District Court of being part of the "Virginia *jihad* network" that underwent paramilitary training in 2000 and 2001 in preparation for joining the Taliban. Two receive sentences of 11-1/2 years, and the third, convicted on lesser charges of arms possession, receives four years' imprisonment.
March 5, 2004	In Zabol Province, Afghanistan, Taliban terrorists fire on a car carrying subcontractors working for a U.S. construction firm, killing a Turk and an Afghan. Another two are kidnapped and aren't released until June.
March 7, 2004	Gunmen ambush the car of and kill a Provincial Red Crescent Society worker while he is traveling on the road between Qalat and Naw Khiez in southeast Afghanistan. The Taliban is likely responsible.

March 9, 2004	Unidentified terrorists assassinate a member of the Mosul municipal council as he is driving near the city.
March 9, 2004	Moammar al-Awwami (Ibin al-Shadid) is sentenced to 20 years in jail by a Lebanese military court for a bomb blast on April 2003 that wounded three people in a McDonald's restaurant in Beirut.
March 9, 2004	Two assailants detonate a bomb in a Masonic lodge in Istanbul, killing two and injuring five others. Turkish officials arrest 18 radical Islamist militants.
March 9, 2004	Terrorists disguised as policemen stop two U.S. civilian workers and their Iraqi interpreter in Hilla, Iraq, and gun them down. One of the victims, Fern Holland, was a lawyer who was helping Iraqi women organize politically. It is not clear which group is responsible.
March 11, 2004	Unknown gunmen kill two Iraqi women working as translators for the British army. The two women, sisters, are riding home in a taxi in Basra when gunmen ambush the vehicle and gun down its occupants.

Terrorism as Diplomatic Strategy

A major terrorist attack on Spain in March 2004 represented a particularly sophisticated strategic use of terrorism. The goal was to affect the outcome of imminent national elections and help bring to power a government ready to withdraw Spanish troops from Iraq. The effort succeeded. Thus, in this case, terrorism involved the political equivalent of common crime. While most terrorist incidents are oriented towards ordinary intimidation and extortion, the demonstrated ability to carry out sophisticated attacks such as this may be used as a highly focused form of political blackmail.

The demands of terrorist groups are not always meant to be fulfilled. The true goal may be to show the victim's weakness, culpability, or intransigence. In the case of Spain, however, the terrorists had an immediate and calculated objective. Some terrorist groups characterized the events in Spain as their own version of regime change, hoping to repeat the success elsewhere.

March 11, 2004	Ten bombs detonate on three crowded commuter trains in Madrid, killing 191 and wounding almost 2,000. The bombs, hidden in backpacks, are placed in stations and on trains along a single rail line. The attacks come just days before Spain's general elections when a key issue is Spain's participation in Iraq as a U.S. ally. In the election, the government goes down to defeat, and the newly elected government will withdraw Spanish forces from Iraq the following month. The attack is found to be executed by the Moroccan Islamic Combatant Group (GICM) a previously unknown group of mostly Moroccan immigrants living in Spain who are inspired by, but without direction from, al-Qaeda. Spanish authorities arrest over 20 people in connection with the attacks, but the investigation is weakened when police surround a building where other suspects are hiding, prompting six of them to blow themselves up.
March 13, 2004	A man is killed as two missiles are fired near the home of the governor of Laghman Province, Afghanistan. It is not clear which group is responsible.

March 14, 2004	The director-general of the Iraqi Health Ministry, Mu'tasam abd-al-Rahman, is killed and his driver injured when their vehicle is ambushed in Mosul. The assassins are unknown.
March 15, 2004	Unidentified terrorists assassinate Akkar Nazal al-Someideh, leader of the Arab community in Kirkuk, and one of his bodyguards.
March 15, 2004	Four Americans from the Southern Baptist International Mission Board are killed and one wounded by unknown terrorists in a drive-by shooting in Mosul.
March 16, 2004	Four German hydraulic engineers and two Iraqis are killed and two Germans wounded in an attack on their car in Karbala. No group claims responsibility.
March 16, 2004	Two European engineers and two Iraqis are killed in Hilla by unknown terrorists.
March 17, 2004	A car bomb explodes at the Mount Lebanon Hotel in Baghdad, killing seven, including one Briton, and wounding 35 others. Either Abu Musab al-Zarqawi's Jama'at al-Tawhid wa'al-Jihad, al-Qaeda, or Ansar al-Islam is responsible for the attack. On April 6, a Web site linked to Ansar al-Islam carried audiotape from a speaker who identified himself as al-Zarqawi and claimed responsibility for the bombing.
March 18, 2004	A bomb attack at a hotel in Basra by terrorists kills two and wounds two others. It is not clear which group is responsible for the attack.
March 18, 2004	In Baquba, Iraq, a bus filled with employees of an Iraqi television station is fired upon by an indentified gunmen who kills three and wounds ten.
March 18, 2004	Seven people are killed and 35 wounded when a powerful car bomb destroys the Mount Lebanon Hotel, which houses foreigners in Baghdad, just days ahead of the anniversary of the U.S.-led invasion of Iraq. No group claims responsibility, but authorities believe that either Ansar al-Islam, Al Qaeda, or Abu Musab al-Zarqawi's group, Tawhid and Jihad, are responsible.
March 20, 2004	A mortar attack on the offices of the Patriotic Union of Kurdistan in Mosul kills one and injures four. It is not clear which group is responsible.
March 22, 2004	Two Finnish businessmen are killed when their vehicle is ambushed as they are on their way to a meeting at the Ministry of Electricity in Baghdad. No group claims responsibility.
March 24, 2004	A foreign security guard and an Iraqi child are killed by unknown assassins in a drive-by shooting outside of Falluja.
March 25, 2004	An Egyptian court convicts 26 people, including three Britons, for membership in an illegal Islamic group, Hizb al-Tahrir, and sentences them to between one and five years in prison, far less than the 25 years sought by prosecutors. Hizb al-Tahrir was banned by the Egyptian government after allegedly attempting a coup in 1974.

March 27, 2004   An unidentified terrorist kills two civilians and wounds 19 people after firing Katyusha rockets at the provincial governor's office in Mosul.

March 28, 2004   A female suicide bomber detonates her bomb at an apartment building in Bukhara, Uzbekistan, killing six and injuring four. Uzbekistan is helping the U.S. in the war in Iraq.

March 28, 2004   An assassination attempt in Mosul against the Iraqi Public Works Minister Nesreen Berwari kills two officials and wounds another two, although the minister is unharmed.

March 29, 2004   Two female suicide bombers detonate their blasts at the biggest bazaar and a bus stop in Tashkent, Uzbekistan, killing four and injuring 21. It is not clear which group is responsible.

March 31, 2004   Gunmen kill four U.S. civilian contractors after their convoy is ambushed in Falluja. The terrorists drag the dead bodies through the streets and leave two hanging from a bridge over the Euphrates River. It is the first and so far only attack by a previously unknown group calling itself the Brigades of Martyr Ahmed Yassim.

April 2, 2004   Near Berbera, Somalia, militants attack aid workers from the German Agency for Technical Assistance, killing a Kenyan and injuring a German aid worker. Al-Qaeda is likely responsible.

April 6, 2004   A Bulgarian driver in Nasiriyah, Iraq, is gunned down by unidentified terrorists who attacked a convoy of trucks.

April 7, 2004   A convoy of Iraqi diplomats and a government minister traveling from Amman, Jordan, is hit by a rocket-propelled grenade near Baghdad, killing a South African contractor. No group claims responsibility.

April 7, 2004   A security contractor for South Africa is killed by unknown terrorists who infiltrate his home in Kut, Iraq.

April 9, 2004   Terrorists kidnap U.S. businessman Nicholas Berg in Baghdad. The attack is claimed by Tawhid and Jihad (Jama'at al-Tawhid wa'al-Jihad), the group loyal to Abu Musab al-Zarqawi. Berg is later killed (*see* May 8, 2004).

April 9, 2004   Near Baghdad, unknown assailants attack a civilian vehicle, and kidnap eight U.S. contractors. Six of the men are found dead, one escapes, and one remains missing. No group claims responsibility.

April 9, 2004   A vehicle drives over a land mine in Baghdad, killing two Nepalese occupants. No group claims responsibility.

April 10, 2004   An Iraqi Red Crescent official and his wife are killed as they are driving near Mosul. It is not clear who are the assassins.

April 10, 2004   In Taji, Iraq, unknown assailants kill a Danish citizen. No group claims responsibility.

April 12, 2004   Jordanian security forces announce that they have thwarted a "mega-terror" attack by a group linked to al-Qaeda. The attack would have targeted the headquarters of the Jordanian secret service with a chemical bomb and used "deadly gas against the U.S. Embassy and the office of the Jordanian prime minister in Amman . . . and other public buildings in Jordan."

April 12, 2004   Terrorists from an Islamist group kidnap four Italians working for a U.S. security firm near Baghdad and kill one after the Italian government refuses the demand to remove its troops from Iraq. On June 8, the remaining hostages are rescued, along with a Polish construction worker who had been kidnapped. The kidnappers identify themselves as being from the Green Brigade of the Prophet.

April 16, 2004   Khalil Naimi, the first secretary of the Iranian Embassy in Iraq, is shot in the head by unknown assailants while driving in Baghdad.

April 16, 2004   Two Jordanians are killed when their vehicle is hit by rockets near Ramadi, Iraq.

April 21, 2004   In Riyadh, Saudi Arabia, suicide bombers detonate car bombs outside the headquarters of the Saudi national police, who have been cracking down on militants, killing at least eight people and injuring 125. Al-Haramein Brigade, a group affiliated with al-Qaeda, claims responsibility for the bombing.

April 21, 2004   Five car bombs that target three police stations in Basra include many kindergarten children among the 70 casualties. The children were on a bus traveling to school when it was caught in the blast. It is not clear which group is responsible for the attack.

April 24, 2004   About nine Iraqis are killed when bombs detonate at a market in a Shiite suburb of Baghdad.

April 27, 2004   Terrorists attack the Coordination of Humanitarian Aid agency in Kandahar, Afghanistan, killing four and wounding six.

April 30, 2004   In Falluja, unknown terrorists open fire killing a South African civilian.

April 30, 2004   Terrorists in southern Iraq open fire at a convoy of vans, killing three civilians—one Filipino and three Ukrainians. No group claims responsibility.

May 2, 2004   Five Westerners and a National Guard officer are killed in Yanbu, Saudi Arabia, when four terrorists, likely from al-Qaeda, infiltrate the office of a Saudi contractor.

May 5, 2004   Taliban terrorists in Mandol, Laghman Province, Afghanistan, kill two British election experts and their Afghan translator.

May 7, 2004   Two Polish journalists are killed and a cameraman is injured when their car is fired on outside Baghdad on the road to Najaf. No group claims responsibility.

May 7, 2004   Fifteen people are killed when an unknown suicide bomber blows himself up in a mosque in Pakistan, killing 15 and wounding 100.

May 8, 2004   The body of U.S. citizen, Nick Berg, who was kidnapped on April 9, is found on a highway in Baghdad. On May 11, the website of al-Ansar shows a videotape of Berg's death by beheading. The video suggests that he was beheaded by Abu Musab al-Zarqawi himself.

May 9, 2004   Six people are killed and nine wounded after a bomb detonates in a Baghdad marketplace.

May 9, 2004   Italian police in Florence arrest an Algerian imam and four Tunisians suspected of planning suicide attacks against Western targets in Iraq.

May 10, 2004   A vehicle whose occupants are supporters of former Kandahar Province governor Gol Agha Sherza is ambushed and two of its occupants, including the governor of the province, are killed. The Taliban claims responsibility.

May 10, 2004   In Musayyib, Iraq, Sunni insurgents attack a vehicle, killing one Russian, injuring an Iraqi, and abducting two other Russians who are later released. No group claims responsibility.

May 10, 2004   Terrorists in Kirkuk, their affiliation unknown, kill a New Zealand engineer, a South African engineer, and an Iraqi driver.

May 11, 2004   Four people are killed and 25 wounded after unknown terrorists detonate a bomb in a Kurdish area of Kirkuk.

May 11, 2004   In Mosul, Iraq, terrorists attack two employees of a Turkish construction firm. No group claims responsibility.

May 14, 2004   Unknown terrorists infiltrate the Baghdad home of a British contractor and kill him.

May 15, 2004   In Kandahar Province, Afghanistan, a bomb in the Spin Boldak district kills one. The Taliban and al-Qaeda both claim the attack.

May 17, 2004   The head of the Iraqi Governing Council, Ezzedin Salim, and five other Iraqis are killed when a suicide car bombing detonates near an entrance to the coalition headquarters in Baghdad. In January 2005, Iraqi officials will arrest Sami Mohammed Ali Said al-Ja'af, a lieutenant of Abu Musab al-Zarqawi, for over 32 bombings in Iraq, including this one.

May 18, 2004   In Mosul, Iraq, terrorists ambush two vehicles, killing a British security contractor. No group claims responsibility.

May 22, 2004   Terrorists shoot and kill a German national in Riyadh, Saudi Arabia. No group claims responsibility.

May 22, 2004   A car bomb detonates near the Baghdad home of the Iraqi deputy interior minister, killing four Iraqi policemen and a bystander. Abu Musab al-Zarqawi's group, Tawhid and Jihad, later claims responsibility for this attack.

May 23, 2004   Unidentified gunmen on the road from Baghdad to Baquba kill a police captain and a university student.

May 24, 2004	Unknown terrorists detonate a bomb in Iraq hoping to blow up a U.S. convoy on the road but instead kill three Iraqi civilians who drive by first.
May 26, 2004	Two Russian civilian contractors and at least one Iraqi are killed south of Baghdad. It is not clear who is responsible for the crime.
May 27, 2004	British authorities arrest Abu Hamza al-Masri, a radical Islamic cleric in London who is a professed supporter of Osama bin Laden. He is tried and convicted. On February 7, 2006, he is sentenced to seven years' imprisonment for charges including incitement to murder Jews.
May 27, 2004	Taliban supporters detonate a bomb near the Kabul airport which kills two children.
May 27, 2004	Terrorists in Iraq fire on a civilian vehicle, killing two Japanese journalists and one Iraqi translator, and injuring their Iraqi driver. No group claims responsibility.
May 28, 2004	A car on the road from Samawah to Baghad is ambushed and two Japanese journalists are killed and their driver injured. No one claims responsibility for the attack.
May 29, 2004	Unknown gunmen on a road in Kirkuk target a car and kill four occupants—the head of city's fire department and member of the Patriotic Union of Kurdistan Party and three of his relatives.
May 30, 2004	In Baghdad, an American contractor loses his life after terrorists fire upon on a convoy traveling to the airport. No group claims responsibility.
May 30, 2004	Terrorists infiltrate oil industry offices and employee apartments in Khobar, Saudi Arabia, killing 22 people. Most of the victims are foreign nationals. The terrorists also take 50 hostages, all but nine of whom are released after a gun battle with Saudi security officials. Al-Qaeda claims responsibility for the attack.
May 31, 2004	Pakistan's education minister, Zobaida Jalal, survives after a rocket is fired at her home in Quetta, but one of her servants is killed.
May 31, 2004	The vehicles of four U.S. civilian contractors are ambushed by gunmen and all four men are killed. The attack is claimed by a group known as the Brigades of Martyr Ahmed Yassim, which seeks an end to the U.S. occupation of Iraq. It says the attack is a response to the killing of Sheik Ahmed Yassin, leader of Hamas, the Palestinian militant group, by Israeli military forces several days earlier.
June 1, 2004	Twenty-five people are killed and several others injured after a car bomb detonates in front of the offices of the Patriotic Union of Kurdistan (PUK) in Baghdad. No group claims responsibility.
June 1, 2004	In Baiji, Iraq, a roadside bomb detonated by unknown terrorists kills 11 Iraqis and wounds 23 others.

June 2, 2004	A car explodes in a Baghdad neighborhood killing at least four people and wounding about 20. No group claims responsibility.
June 2, 2004	A vehicle carrying employees of foreign relief organizations, including Doctors Without Borders, is targeted by Taliban terrorists in Khair Khana District, Afghanistan, claiming five lives. Of the victims, one is from Belgium, one from the Netherlands, one from Norway, and two are natives of Afghanistan.
June 2, 2004	A bomb in southern Iraq detonates alongside a passing vehicle, killing an American contractor. No group claims responsibility.
June 3, 2004	An Iraqi is killed and three are injured after mortar shells fired by unknown terrorists are fired at the Italian Embassy in Baghdad.
June 5, 2004	Terrorists kill four foreign security contractors in Baghdad, two of them Americans, and injure one. Abu Musab al-Zarqawi's Tawhid and Jihad (Jama'at al-Tawhid wa'al-Jihad) claims responsibility.
June 5, 2004	In Al Asad, Iraq, a vehicle strikes a land mine, killing an American contractor. No group claims responsibility.
June 6, 2004	A cameraman for the BBC is shot dead and a reporter seriously wounded in Riyadh, Saudi Arabia. Al-Qaeda is likely responsible.
June 7, 2004	Grenades targeting a religious school in Afghanistan kill two. No group claims responsibility.
June 8, 2004	Three suicide bombers, their affiliation unknown, sitting in a taxi set off their explosives near the office of the mayor of Mosul, killing nine and wounding 25.
June 8, 2004	An American working for a defense contractor is killed in Riyadh, Saudi Arabia. Al-Qaeda claims responsibility.
June 10, 2004	Eleven Chinese construction workers are killed and four wounded in Kanduz, Afghanistan, after terrorists infiltrate their housing compound. Also killed are two Afghan security officials at the compound. The Taliban and Hizbul-i-Islami are likely both involved in the attack.
June 12, 2004	Terrorists in Saudi Arabia release a videotape showing the decapitation of Paul Johnson, U.S. a civilian helicopter technician. Johnson had been kidnapped by a group calling themselves al-Qaeda in the Arabian Peninsula, which threatened to murder him if all foreigners did not leave the kingdom.
June 12, 2004	Iraq's Deputy Foreign Minister Bassam Salih Kubba is assassinated in Baghdad as he is traveling to work. Also in Baghdad, a Lebanese man and two Iraqis, all employees of a foreign company who were taken hostage, are killed. No one claims responsibility.
June 12, 2004	In Falluja, Iraq, unknown terrorists kidnap and kill a Lebanese citizen.
June 13, 2004	An Iraqi Education Ministry official is killed outside his Baghdad home. The assassins are unidentified.

June 13, 2004	A religious leader of the Sunni Muslim community who has been openly critical of attacks against the U.S. Army is killed by unknown terrorists in Kirkuk.
June 14, 2004	A car bomb explodes in Baghdad killing 13, five of them foreign contractors, including one American. Abu Musab al-Zarqawi's Tawhid and Jihad claims responsibility.
June 15, 2004	In Afghanistan, the head of the Kandahar Refugees Department is assassinated. The Taliban is likely responsible.
June 16, 2004	Gunmen open fire on a car in Kirkuk, Iraq, killing its occupant—the security chief for Iraq's Northern Oil Company—and wounding the driver. The terrorists are unknown.
June 16, 2004	Unknown terrorists kill nine people, including four foreigners, and wound ten when a vehicle is bombed in Ramadi, Iraqi.
June 16, 2004	Near Kunduz City, Afghanistan, four Afghans are killed and one wounded after a bomb explodes by a vehicle belonging to the German-run Provincial Reconstruction Team. Al-Qaeda is likely responsible.
June 17, 2004	A Red Crescent society worker is killed in Nangarhar Province, Afghanistan.
June 17, 2004	Two Iraqis are killed and five injured by a car bomb attack on an electric utility station south of Baghdad.
June 17, 2004	Terrorists kidnap and later behead a South Korean contractor. Abu Musab al-Zarqawi's Tawhid and Jihad (Jama'at al-Tawhid wa'al-Jihad) claims responsibility.
June 17, 2004	A land mine explodes as a convoy passes in an unspecified part of Iraq, killing a U.S. contractor. No group claims responsibility.
June 18, 2004	The leader of al-Qaeda in Saudi Arabia, Abdel Aziz al-Muqrin, is found disposing of the corpse of Paul Johnson, the American hostage who had been killed earlier in June. Al-Muqrin and three other terrorists are killed in a shoot-out with police.
June 19, 2004	Near Basra, a bomb explodes, killing a Portuguese national, an Iraqi police officer, and an Iraqi oil worker. No group claims responsibility.
June 22, 2004	A South Korean man taken hostage in Falluja is killed by terrorists affiliated with Tawhid and Jihad.
June 22, 2004	Two are killed—a government minister's bodyguard and a boy—when a car bomb explodes in Baghdad. No group claims responsibility.
June 22, 2004	In a western suburb of Baghdad, three Iraqis are killed and several wounded by a car bomb. The terrorists are unknown.
June 24, 2004	Four UN officials helping with pending elections are killed by a roadside bomb in Paktia Province, Afghanistan. A radical Islamist group called Jaish-ul-Muslimin claims responsibility for the attack.

June 25, 2004   Sixteen people trying to register to vote in Afghanistan's upcoming elections are killed in Uruzgan. The Taliban, which is opposed to elections, is suspected.

June 26, 2004   Seventeen lives are lost when a bomb explodes in the center of Hilla, Iraq. The terrorists are unidentified.

June 26, 2004   The headquarters of the Supreme Council of the Islamic Revolution, a Shia political party, in Baquba, Iraq, is hit by a grenade that kills three and injures two.

June 26, 2004   A bomb explodes in Jalalabad inside a bus carrying Afghan election workers, all women, to voter registration sites. Two are killed and 11 are injured. The Taliban is responsible.

June 27, 2004   Taliban terrorists kill ten men in southern Afghanistan after they register for national elections.

June 28, 2004   In Iraq, the U.S.-led Coalition Provisional Authority formally transfers sovereignty to the Iraqi interim government.

July 1, 2004   A bomb in Baghdad targeting an official in the Iraqi Finance Ministry kills three and wounds the official and four others. No group claims responsibility.

July 1, 2004   A U.S. contractor is killed in Balad, Iraq, when a roadside bomb explodes near his vehicle. No group claims responsibility.

July 1, 2004   The head of Iraq's Finance Ministry's audit board, who is looking into allegations that the Saddam Hussein regime stole money from the UN oil-for-food program, is killed by a car bomb in Baghdad along with his driver and bodyguard. No group claims responsibility

July 5, 2004   Terrorists in Iraq fire upon a building belonging to a Khalisa city council official, killing two of his relatives and injuring another two people. Ansar al-Sunna claims responsibility for the attack.

July 6, 2004   A car bomb in Khalisa targets a tent filled with mourners of those killed the previous day. The bomb kills 14 and wounds 37. Ansar al-Sunna claims responsibility for the attack.

July 7, 2004   Gunmen assassinate the son of the head of the al-Dulaimi tribe and chairman of the city council in Ramadi, Iraq. It is not known which group is responsible.

July 8, 2004   A UN employee working on Afghanistan's upcoming elections is killed when her vehicle hits a land mine. The Taliban claims responsibility.

July 8, 2004   Taliban terrorists targeting Turkish construction engineers end up killing six Afghan security guards in Kandahar.

July 8, 2004   Two Bulgarian truck drivers are kidnapped in Iraq by Tawhid and Jihad (Jama'at al-Tawhid wa'al-Jihad). Five days later, a videotape is released showing their decapitation.

July 9, 2004	In Samarra, Iraq, unknown gunmen fire at a tanker truck and kill the Turkish driver and his passenger.
July 9, 2004	Three mortar shells aimed at a Baghdad hotel frequented by foreigners land at a private home, killing a child and injuring three. No group claims responsibility.
July 10, 2004	Bomb blasts aimed at liquor stores in Baquba, Iraq, kill one. No group claims responsibility, but both Shia and Sunni Islamists have attacked such stores which they consider to be against the teachings of Islam, which forbids use of alcohol.
July 10, 2004	Unknown terrorists firing at the offices of the Union of Farming Cooperatives near Kirkuk, Iraq, kill one guard.
July 13, 2004	An auditor for the Iraqi Industry Ministry is assassinated outside his office in Baghdad. No group claims responsibility.
July 13, 2004	Pakistani security officials apprehend Muhammad Naeem Noor Khan, an alleged al-Qaeda computer expert who was plotting attacks against various U.S. financial buildings and Heathrow Airport in England.
July 14, 2004	A car bomb explodes near the Baghdad neighborhood filled with international offices and embassies, killing ten and wounding 40. No group claims responsibility.
July 14, 2004	Unknown attackers kill the governor of Mosul as he is driving in a convoy of vehicles towards Baghdad.
July 15, 2004	A car bomb explodes near police and government buildings in Haditha, Iraq, killing ten people and wounding 27 others. No group claims responsibility.
July 15, 2004	A rocket attack on a house in Kirkuk kills four. No group claims credit.
July 17, 2004	Near Ramadi, Iraq, unknown terrorists gun down a Jordanian truck driver taking material from Amman to Baghdad.
July 17, 2004	After attacking a convoy in Mosul, unknown terrorists kill a Turk and kidnap a Turkish driver, who is later released.
July 17, 2004	Iraq's justice minister escapes a suicide car bomb in Baghdad intended to detonate at his convoy of cars which instead kills five people and injures eight others. Abu Musab al-Zarqawi claims responsibility for the attack.
July 17, 2004	Unknown terrorists in Baghdad assassinate Sheikh Abdul Samad Ismail al-Adhami, a Sunni Muslim cleric and member of the Iraqi Islamic Party who had been critical to Saddam Hussein's government.
July 17, 2004	In Samarra, Iraq, several unknown attackers kill the Iraqi National Party's leader and his father.
July 18, 2004	A leading figure in the Iraqi Defense Ministry and his bodyguard are killed after being fired upon in Baghdad.

July 19, 2004   In Mosul, unknown terrorists gun down Leith Hussein Ali, a television journalist and Turkoman activist, while he is driving in his car.

July 20, 2004   Unknown terrorists in Basra assassinate the city's interim governor as he is pulling out of his driveway.

July 21, 2004   A Baghdad car bomb kills at least four people. Elsewhere, terrorists kill two after firing a rocket at a Baghdad hospital.

July 22, 2004   A bomb detonates in a Baghdad suburb, killing two and injuring another two.

July 23, 2004   Two Pakistani contractors and their Iraqi driver are kidnapped. The Pakistanis are killed and the Iraqi is freed after six days. The Islamic Army in Iraq (IAI), a Baathist and Islamist group, claims responsibility.

July 24, 2004   A roadside bomb aimed at an Islamic seminary in Karachi, Pakistan, kills one and injures six. It is not clear which group is responsible.

July 25, 2004   Ahmed Khalfan Ghailani, an al-Qaeda member involved in the 1998 attacks on the U.S. embassies in Kenya and Tanzania, is captured in Gujrat, Pakistan, after a shoot-out with Pakistani security forces.

July 26, 2004   Unknown terrorists kill two female employees at the Basra airport and injure two others as they are driving in Basra.

July 26, 2004   A senior Iraqi interior minister and his two guards are shot and killed in a drive-by attack in Baghdad.

July 27, 2004   An Iraqi garbage collector is killed and 15 wounded—all but one U.S. soldiers—in a mortar attack on a residential neighborhood in central Baghdad. It is not clear which group is responsible.

July 27, 2004   The deputy director of Mahmudiya hospital, south of Baghdad, is gunned down by unknown terrorists.

July 28, 2004   In Ghazni Province, Afghanistan, a bomb detonates at a mosque during voter registration, killing six people and injuring seven. No group claims credit.

July 28, 2004   A bomb attack in Baquba's downtown area results in the death of some 70 people and injuring of 56. Abu Musab al-Zarqawi is suspected.

July 29, 2004   Two are killed in Tashkent, Uzebekistan, when suicide bombers strike the U.S. and Israeli embassies and prosecutor general's office. The attacks are timed with the trial of 15 Uzbeks accused of taking part in attacks against the government earlier in the year.

July 29, 2004   A member of the Kandahar Council in Afghanistan who had denounced the Taliban is assassinated.

July 29, 2004   In Baghdad, terrorists infiltrate the apartment of a Jordanian businessman, killing one Jordanian and abducting another who is later released.

July 31, 2004	Terrorists kill the head of the Mahmudiya Teachers Institute near Baghdad. No group claims responsibility.
July 31, 2004	The head of Khaneshin District of Helmand Province in Afghanistan and his four bodyguards are killed by terrorists in Afghanistan.
August 1, 2004	Eleven are killed and more than 50 injured after bombs detonated by unknown terrorists strike four churches in Baghdad and one in Mosul.
August 2, 2004	Sunni terrorists in Iraq kidnap three Turkish truck drivers, kill one and release the other two when the transport company promises to stop shipping goods into Iraq for the U.S. military. Abu Musab al-Zarqawi's Tawhid and Jihad (Jama'at al-Tawhid wa'al-Jihad) claims responsibility.
August 3, 2004	Terrorists, likely al-Qaeda members, gun down an Irish civil engineer in Riyadh, Saudi Arabia.
August 4, 2004	Three people are killed and four injured in Logar, Afghanistan. The Taliban claims responsibility.
August 4, 2004	In Paktia, Afghanistan, two German workers in a nongovernmental organization are killed when terrorists attack their vehicle. No group claims responsibility.
August 6, 2004	Taliban terrorists attack a convoy and then kill a UN election worker and a driver as they are traveling from Charchino to Kajran, Afghanistan.
August 9, 2004	A suicide car bomb targeting the Diyala deputy governor's motorcade kills one and wounds six. No group claims responsibility.
August 10, 2004	Terrorists kidnap and then murder an Egyptian man in Iraq. Abu Musab al-Zarqawi's Tawhid and Jihad claims responsibility.
August 11, 2004	Six are killed when a bomb detonates at a market in the village of Khan Bani Saad, Iraq, killing four people and wounding ten. It is not clear which group is responsible.
August 11, 2004	Two Patriot Union of Kurdistan (PUK) members and their driver are gunned down in their car by a gunman in a passing car.
August 12, 2004	An Indian contractor is killed in Baghdad. No group claims responsibility.
August 13, 2004	In their first terrorist attack, the Saraya al-Shuhada, also known as the Jihadist Martyrs Brigades, kidnap U.S. journalist Micah Garen and his translator in Najaf. They demand the withdrawal of foreign forces from Najaf. The group decides to release the two on August 22. The group is likely Shia in background.
August 14, 2004	Terrorists in Mosul, Iraq, kidnap and then kill two Turkish truck drivers. Abu Musab al-Zarqawi's Tawhid and Jihad (Jama'at al-Tawhid wa'al-Jihad) claims responsibility.

August 16, 2004   Unknown terrorists attack a civilian convoy in Mosul, killing a South African security contractor.

August 17, 2004   An explosion in central Baghdad kills seven. It is not clear which group is responsible.

August 18, 2004   Five children are killed by a rocket attack in a marketplace in Mosul, Iraq. It is not clear which group is responsible.

August 20, 2004   Members of the Islamic Army in Iraq ambush the car of Enzo Baldoni, an Italian journalist, kidnapping him and killing his driver as they are en route from Baghdad to Najaf. The captors demand that Italy withdraw its troops from Iraq. Six days later, a videotape showing Baldoni's murder is released.

August 20, 2004   Ansar al-Sunna terrorists kill 12 Nepalese employees of a Jordanian firm.

August 22, 2004   A car bomb detonated by unknown terrorists explodes in the Iraqi city of Baqubah, killing two people and injuring four others.

August 22, 2004   An Indonesian contractor and two Iraqis are killed and a Filipino wounded as they are driving from Mosul. It is not clear which group is responsible.

August 27, 2004   Unknown terrorists kidnap and then kill an Egyptian worker in Baiji, Iraq.

August 28, 2004   Eight children are killed when a bomb detonates outside a school in Paktia, Afghanistan. The Taliban is likely responsible.

August 28, 2004   The head of translation at Mosul University's College of Art is gunned down in her car. It is not clear which group is responsible.

August 29, 2004   Ten people, including three Americans, are killed and 22 injured in a bomb attack on a U.S. security firm in Kabul. The Taliban is responsible.

September 3, 2004   A bomb detonates by a car in Kandahar, Afghanistan, killing one man and wounding four. Taliban terrorists are likely responsible.

September 7, 2004   The son of the governor for Niniveh, the northern Iraqi province, is assassinated in Mosul. It is not clear which group is responsible.

September 9, 2004   Ten people are killed and 180 injured when a car bomb detonates outside the Australian Embassy in Jakarta, Indonesia. Jemaah Islamiyah claims responsibility for the attack.

September 10, 2004   Uknown terrorists break into a Baghdad house and murder three Lebanese working in Baghdad.

September 11, 2004   A bomb outside the U.S. Consulate office in Basra, Iraq, kills one. No group claims responsibility.

September 13, 2004   Members of the Army of the Followers of Sunni Islam kidnap and then kill three Iraqi truck drivers in Basra who were working with U.S. forces. The group is opposed to the U.S. military presence in Iraq.

September 14, 2004   A car bomb outside a Baghdad police station kills at least 47 people and injures 114. Many of the victims had sought to join the police. Tawhid and Jihad claims responsibility for the attack.

September 15, 2004   Two Americans and a British civil engineer are kidnapped from their home in Baghdad by Tawhid and Jihad militants, who demand that female prisoners be released from U.S. detention facilities. When U.S. authorities refuse, all three are killed.

September 18, 2004   A bomb explodes in a small side street in central Baghdad, killing one person and wounding two others. No group claims responsibility.

September 19, 2004   Gunmen murder Sheik Hazem al-Zeidi, a Sunni cleric, as he leaves a mosque in Baghdad. It is not clear which group is responsible.

September 21, 2004   A car packed with explosives blows up in a residential neighborhood in Mosul, killing its driver and two people in a passing vehicle.

September 22, 2004   In Baiji, Iraq, unknown terrorists gun down a Turkish truck driver in his truck.

September 23, 2004   A senior official of Iraq's North Oil Company is killed in Mosul. No group claims responsibility.

September 25, 2004   A French technician at a nearby naval base is shot while driving his car near a supermarket in Jeddah, Saudi Arabia. Al-Qaeda is responsible.

September 26, 2004   Amjad Hussain Farooqi, a senior member of al-Qaeda, is killed in a shoot-out with Pakistani security officials. Farooqi helped abduct and kill *Wall Street Journal* writer Daniel Pearl. He also directed two failed assassination attempts on Pakistani President Pervez Musharraf and the 1999 hijacking of an Indian airliner.

September 27, 2004   A South African engineer and an Iraqi driver are killed and a British man injured in an attack by unknown terrorists outside the Iraqi National Oil Company in Kirkuk.

October 4, 2004   A car bomb explodes near a Baghdad hotel popular with Westerners, killing two and injuring 17. No group claims responsibility.

October 4, 2004   Two employees of the Ministry of Science and Technology are killed in Baghdad. It is not clear which group is responsible.

October 5, 2004   A series of car bombs in Baghdad and Mosul kill at least 21 people.

October 9, 2004   Two Chinese engineers working on a dam project in South Waziristan, Pakistan, are kidnapped. One is killed and the other rescued by Pakistani police. It is not clear which group is responsible.

October 9, 2004   In the first democratic presidential elections ever held in Afghanistan, voters elect Hamid Karzai president.

October 11, 2004	In Baghdad, an Iraqi Kurdish translator and a Turkish construction contractor who had been kidnapped by members of the Army of Ansar al-Sunna are killed. Their beheading is videotaped and shown on the Internet.
October 12, 2004	A Kurdish member of the Nineveh Governorate Council is killed in Mosul.
October 14, 2004	Four U.S. civilians are killed and 18 people wounded when a bomb explodes at an outdoor shopping area in Baghdad. Tawhid and Jihad is responsible.
October 14, 2004	Unknown terrorists in Baghdad gun down Abdulamir Khadem, an investigative judge in the city.
October 14, 2004	In Baghdad, unidentified terrorists kill a female broadcaster employed at a Kurdish television station.
October 17, 2004	A car bomb explodes at a Baghdad cafe, killing seven and injuring 20. No group claims responsibility.
October 19, 2004	Tawhid and Jihad, the Iraqi militant group of Abu Musab al-Zarqawi, announces a name change following its merger with al-Qaeda. It now calls itself Tanzim Qa'idat al-Jihad fi Bilad al-Rafidayn, or al-Qaeda and Jihad in the Land Between Two Rivers. It is often known in English as al-Qaeda in Iraq.
October 19, 2004	Margaret Hassan, an Irish citizen married to an Iraqi and head of CARE International operations in Iraq, is abducted in Baghdad. She is killed four weeks later. In June 2006, an Iraqi court sentences Mustafa Salman al-Jubouri to life imprisonment for his assisistance in the kidnapping, although two other defendants were acquitted. It is not clear what group, if any, was behind the attack.
October 20, 2004	A car bomb in Samarra explodes in front of a U.S. Army convoy, which is near a nursery school, killing four children and injuring 20. No group claims responsibility.
October 23, 2004	The Taliban detonates a bomb in a Kabul shopping area, killing two, including an American, and wounding three Icelandic soldiers.
October 23, 2004	In Balidyat, Iraq, a Turkish and a Croatian truck driver are killed after being fired on by unknown terrorists.
October 24, 2004	A Japanese citizen is killed in Baghdad. Al-Qaeda in Iraq claims responsibility.
October 24, 2004	In Baiji, a Turkish truck driver is killed by unknown terrorists.
October 25, 2004	A car bomb explodes at the regional government building in Mosul, killing the head of the National Assembly of Iraqi Tribes and two of his associates. No group claims responsibility.
October 28, 2004	Gunmen kill Leqaa Abdul Razzaq, an anchorwoman for al-Sharqiyah television, as she is riding in a taxi to her Baghdad home. No group claims responsibility.

October 30, 2004	A bomb detonates outside the al-Arabiya news station, killing seven and wounding 14. The Jihadist Martyrs Brigades in Iraq later takes credit for this attack.
November 2, 2004	Four Jordanian truck drivers are ambushed in Rutba, Iraq. One is killed and the rest are kidnapped and later released. No group claims responsibility.
November 3, 2004	A videotape is released showing the execution of Shosei Koda, a Japanese journalist, who had been kidnapped in October by terrorists demanding the withdrawal of Japanese humanitarian workers from Iraq. Al-Qaeda in Iraq is responsible.
November 10, 2004	Theo Van Gogh, a leading Dutch film director, is stabbed to death while walking in Amsterdam. Van Gogh had been outspoken against Islamist extremists. The assassin is Mohammed Bouyeri, a Moroccan immigrant and member of the Hofstad Network, an Islamist terrorist cell of Dutch Muslims of mainly North African ancestry. In July 2005, a Dutch court sentences Bouyeri to life imprisonment for Van Gogh's murder.
November 14, 2004	A Turkish truck driver is killed by unknown terrorists in Baiji, Iraq.
November 20, 2004	Unknown terrorists assassinate four government employees from the Ministry of Public Works in Baghdad.
November 23, 2004	Sheik Ghalib Ali al-Zuhairi, a member of the Association of Muslim Scholars, a Sunni organization, is assassinated as he leaves a mosque in the town of Muqdadiyah.
November 23, 2004	A U.S. diplomat working with the Iraqi Ministry of Education is shot to death in Baghdad. Al-Qaeda in Iraq claims responsibility.
December 3, 2004	A car bomb kills 18 people outside a Shiite mosque in Baghdad. No group claims responsibility.
December 6, 2004	An al-Qaeda attack on the U.S. Consulate in Jeddah, Saudi Arabia, results in five deaths. No U.S. citizens are killed.
December 8, 2004	A convoy en route from Taji to Baghdad carrying civilian contractors is attacked by unknown terrorists, killing two Americans and an Iraqi.
December 10, 2004	Unknown terrorists kill three election workers from Iraq's Hezbollah Shiite movement in northern Baghdad.
December 13, 2004	A suicide bomb kills 13 Iraqis and wounds 15 at the entrance to the Green Zone on the first anniversary of the capture of Saddam Hussein. Al-Qaeda in Iraq claims responsibility for the attack.
December 14, 2004	A Turkish engineer who had been working on a road project is kidnapped and later killed in Konar, Afghanistan. The Taliban is likely responsible.
December 16, 2004	In Ramadi, Iraq, an Italian aid worker is killed by members of the Islamic Movement of Iraqi Mujahideen.

December 16, 2004	An explosion outside a Shiite shrine in Karbala kills ten Iraqis and wounds four. No group claims responsibility.
December 19, 2004	In Najaf and Karbala, a car bombs kill 67 Iraqis and wound 120 others.
December 19, 2004	Unknown terrorists assassinate three election officials in Baghdad.
December 20, 2004	In Tikrit and Mosul, a total of two Turkish drivers are killed.
December 24, 2004	A truck with explosives detonates in western Baghdad, killing nine Iraqis.
December 27, 2004	Abdul Aziz al-Hakim, leader of the Supreme Council for the Islamic Revolution in Iraq, is the target of a car bomb outside his party's headquarters in Baghdad. He survives, but nine security guards are killed and 67 are wounded.
December 28, 2004	As police are raiding a house in Baghdad used by terrorists, a bomb explodes, killing at least 28 people.
December 29, 2004	In Samarra, unknown terrorists kill a Turkish driver.
December 29, 2004	Fadil Hussain Ahmed al-Kurdi, who helped coordinate activities between the al-Zarqawi group and al-Qaeda, is captured in Baghdad along with two other terrorists.
January 15, 2005	Unknown terrorists in al-Latifiyah, Iraq, gun down 13 civilians.
January 19, 2005	Five suicide bombings take place in Baghdad on a single day, killing a total of 26 people and wounding at least 30. The blasts are aimed at army, police, and civilian targets. They are all claimed by al-Qaeda in Iraq.
January 21, 2005	Twenty-one people are killed and 12 are wounded when a car bomb hidden inside an ambulance detonates at a Shia wedding party in Youssifiyah village, Iraq. No group claims responsibility.
January 21, 2005	Al-Qaeda in Irag detonates a car bomb outside a Baghdad Shia mosque which kills 14 civilians and wounds 40.
January 26, 2005	Fifteen civilians are killed and 30 are wounded when a tanker bomb is detonated outside the offices of the Kurdistan National Party in Sinjar, Iraq. Al-Qaeda in Iraq claims responsibility.
January 27, 2005	Eight Iraqi soldiers and three civilians are killed, and four Iraqi soldiers and three civilians are wounded when two bombs are detonated by unidentified attackers outside a polling station in Samarra, Iraq. No group claims responsibility.
January 30, 2005	In attacks on 13 polling stations around the country on this election day, al-Qaeda kills about 40 people.
February 8, 2005	Twenty truck drivers, two police officers, and two Iraqi soldiers are killed when unidentified assailants attack a convoy of government trucks carrying sugar near al-Suwayrah, Iraq. No group claims responsibility.

February 8, 2005	Unknown terrorists in Baghdad seeking to assassinate Mithal Alusi, a political candidate who had been kicked out of the Iraqi National Congress Party because he visited Israel, end up killing his two sons and his bodyguard.
February 8, 2005	Unknown assassins in Mosul gun down two members of the Kurdistan Demcoratic Party.
February 9, 2005	A Shiite television journalist and political activist is killed along with his four-year-old son when gunmen attack his car in Basra. It is the first attack by the Brigades of Imam al-Hassan al-Basri, a Sunni-Islamist group, which later joins with al-Qaeda in Iraq.
February 9, 2005	Unknown terrorists fire upon a car in Baghdad killing an employee of the Ministry of Culture and Housing.
February 11, 2005	Thirteen civilians are killed and 40 are wounded when a truck bomb explodes outside a Shiite mosque in Balad Ruz, Iraq. It is believed that Sunni Islamic extremists are responsible.
February 11, 2005	Eleven are killed in Baghdad when two unknown gunmen fire upon two different bakeries in a Shiite neighborhood.
February 12, 2005	Three Iraqi police officers and 18 civilians are killed, and three police officers and 18 civilians are wounded when a suicide bomber attacks a hospital in the Iraqi town of Musayyib. No group claims responsibility.
February 14, 2005	Rafik Hariri, a former prime minister of Lebanon who had recently resigned from government, is assassinated when his motorcade in Beirut is blown up by explosives. Twenty-one others are killed, including the former minister of economy. An investigation into the attack sponsored by the United Nations Security Council and headed by a German judge find Lebanese and Syrian guilty, including Syria's military intelligence chief, Asif Shawkat, and President Bashar al-Assad.
February 18, 2005	Sunni terrorists in Iraq, their affiliation unknown, stage attacks against five Shia mosques the day before Ashura, the holiest day in the Shia religious year, killing some 40 and wounding 53. All of the attacks are in Baghad, except one which occurs in Iskandariyah The worst attack kills 17 and wounds 30 outside the al-Kahdimain mosque in Baghdad.
February 19, 2005	Twenty civilians, including one child, are killed and 40 are wounded when a suicide bomber boards a bus carrying Shia pilgrims celebrating the holy day of Ashura in Aden Square, Baghdad, and sets off an explosive device. Four police officers responding to the attack are killed when an improvised explosive device is detonated. No group claims responsibility.
February 28, 2005	One hundred twenty-five people are killed and 133 are wounded when a suicide car bomber attacks a crowd of people outside a hospital in Hilla, Iraq, as they wait in line for physicals. Many of the killed were those seeking the physicals so they could obtain government jobs. Al-Qaeda in Iraq claims responsibility.

March 7, 2005	In Kabul, Afghanistan, the British advisor to the Afghan government is shot and killed by Taliban terrorists who ambush his vehicle.
March 8, 2005	The beheaded corpses of 15 Iraqis are found on an old military base in al-Latifiyah, Iraq. The victims are believed to be Shia pilgrims who disappeared on their way to Karbala and Najaf. No group claims responsibility.
March 10, 2005	Fifty-three people are killed and over 100 are wounded when a suicide bomber attacks the courtyard of the Shahedyein Mosque in Mosul, Iraq, where a Shia funeral is being held for a Mosul University professor. The Soldiers of the Prophet's Companions, a Sunni terrorist group, claims responsibility.
March 17, 2005	Two simultaneous and coordinated attacks in Afghanistan kill five and injure 31. The first is a bomb that detonates in a taxi passing through Kandahar; the other is an attack on an international development truck en route from Panjaw to Herat. The Taliban is responsible.
March 25, 2005	Taliban members kill a senior Education Department official in Uruzgan, Afghanistan.
March 25, 2005	Qazi Abdul Aziz, an Afghan judge, is killed by Taliban members in Uruzgan, Afghanistan.
April 7, 2005	A suicide bomber detonates his bomb in the largest bazaar of Cairo, Egypt, killing three tourists—an American, and two French nationals. A new group, the Islamic Glory Brigades in the Land of the Nile, claims responsibility.
April 9, 2005	Unknown gunmen kill ten truck drivers working for the Multinational Forces in Hit, Iraq.
April 13, 2005	In Kirkuk, Iraq, the director of the Bajwan Oil Company and 11 other employees are killed and three are wounded by a blast under an oil pipeline near Kirkuk, Iraq. Ansar al-Sunna and al-Qaeda in Iraq claim the attack.
April 14, 2005	Fourteen civilians and one police officer are killed, and 27 civilians and three police officers are wounded when two suicide bombs are detonated near the Interior Ministry Building in Baghdad. Al-Qaeda in Iraq claims responsibility.
April 20, 2005	The corpses of 19 fishermen are discovered in Hadithah. In another similar discovery, in al-Suwayrah, Wasit, Iraq, 57 bodies of men, women, and children are found floating in the Tigris River. It is not known who is responsible for either killing but Sunni extremists are suspected.
April 22, 2005	A bomb, likely detonated by Sunni terrorists, kills 11 and injures 26 outside the al-Subayh Shia mosque in Baghdad.
April 24, 2005	Twenty-three people are killed and 41 are wounded when a suicide bomber detonates his explosives near the Shia Ahl al-Bayt mosque in Baghdad, and

another bomb is detonated outside a restaurant. Al-Qaeda in Iraq claims responsibility.

May 1, 2005   Twenty-five mourners are killed and 35 are injured when vehicle-borne improvised explosive devices are detonated at the funeral of a member of the Ninawa Governorate Council and an official of the Kurdish Democratic Party held in Tal Afar, Iraq. No group claims responsibility.

May 6, 2005   Thirty-one civilians are killed and 45 are wounded by a a suicide bomber at a vegetable market in al-Suwayrah, Iraq. Soldiers of the Prophet's Companions claims responsibility.

May 7, 2005   Two al-Qaeda in Iraq suicide bombers target civilian security officials accompanying a school bus, killing 20 and wounding 59.

May 11, 2005   Thirty-eight civilians are killed and 84 are wounded when a vehicle-borne improvised explosive device is detonated in Tikrit, Iraq. Ansar al-Sunna claims responsibility.

May 12, 2005   Fifteen civilians are killed and 84 are injured when a vehicle-borne improvised explosive device is detonated by a suicide bomber at a crowded market square in Baghdad. Fifteen minutes later, a second timed vehicle-borne improvised explosive device explodes close by and an additional three civilians are injured. No group claims responsibility.

May 16, 2005   Nine Iraqi soldiers and one civilian are killed and 28 civilians are injured when two vehicle-borne improvised explosive devices are detonated within minutes of each other at a Shia-populated market in Baghdad. No group claims responsibility.

May 18, 2005   Taliban terrorists attack a group of Afghan employees of a U.S. consulting firm as they are driving from Helmand from Kandahar, killing five.

May 23, 2005   A suicide car bomb detonates outside the Abul-Fadi Abbas Shiite mosque in Baghdad, just before the start of evening prayers, killing at least ten and wounding 30. The terrorists may be Sudanese.

May 23, 2005   Twenty are killed and 20 are injured when two unknown suicide bombers detonate their explosives at the home of a Turkman Shia sheikh and Provincial Council member in Tal Afar, Iraq.

May 30, 2005   Twenty-seven civilians are killed and 100 are wounded when two suicide bombers attack outside a health clinic and at a demonstration of former policemen demanding jobs in Hilla, Iraq. Al-Qaeda in Iraq claims responsibility.

June 1, 2005   An al-Qaeda suicide bomber detonates at the Abdul Rab mosque in Kabul, Afghanistan, during the funeral of an anti-Taliban cleric, killing 21, including Kabul's police chief, and injuring 52.

June 2, 2005   In Beirut, Lebanon, Samir Kassir, an anti-Syrian journalist, is killed by a bomb placed in his car outside his home. The attack is claimed by a previously unknown group calling itself "Strugglers for the Unity and Freedom of Greater Syria," a group believed to be a surrogate for Syria.

June 2, 2005 Twelve are killed and 37 injured when a vehicle-borne improvised explosive device is detonated by a suicide bomber at a restaurant in Tozkhurmato, Iraq. Ansar al-Sunna claims responsibility.

June 2, 2005 Ten civilians are killed and 12 are wounded when unknown suicide bombers attack a meeting of Muslim Sufis in Balad, Iraq. No group claims responsibility.

June 2, 2005 The Deputy Head of Diyala's provincial council, Hussein Alwan al-Tamimi, and three of his bodyguards are killed in Baquba. The attack is claimed by a terrorist group called al-Bara bin Malek Brigades, which is part of Abu Musab al-Zarqawi's al-Qaeda in Iraq.

June 10, 2005 Eleven are killed and 29 are wounded when a vehicle-borne improvised explosive device is detonated near a marketplace, medical center, and ice cream parlor in Baghdad. No group claims responsibility.

June 11, 2005 Ten Shias are killed and three are injured when gunmen attack their vehicle in Mahmudiya, Iraq. No group claims responsibility.

June 12, 2005 Seven Iraqi and four Nepalese construction contractors are killed when assailants attack their convoy with grenades near Ramadi, Iraq. No group claims responsibility.

June 12, 2005 Ten people are killed and over 80 injured when seven bombs explode in Tehran and Ahvaz, Iran. Several groups claim responsibility for the attacks in Ahvaz. On October 30, Iranian officials reported that 30 had confessed to the bombing. Some of those involved may have been separatists or political advocates for Khuzestan, Iran's oil-rich region with a large Sunni Arab minority that has been persecuted by Iran's Shia government.

June 14, 2005 Twenty-three civilians are killed and 100 are wounded when an improvised explosive device is detonated by an Ansar al-Sunna suicide bomber outside of Rafidiyan Bank in Kirkuk, Iraq.

June 15, 2005 In Afghanistan, Taliban terrorists kill a parliamentary candidate, Abdol Wahed, in the Maiwand District, southern Kandahar Province.

June 16, 2005 Taliban attackers gun down tribal leader, Haji Abdul Wahid, at his house in the Maiwand District of Kandahar, Afghanistan.

June 19, 2005 Twenty-three are killed, including seven policemen, and 36 are wounded when an improvised explosive device is detonated by a suicide bomber at a restaurant in Baghdad. Al-Qaeda in Iraq claims responsibility.

June 19, 2005 An intelligence official, a judge, and their guest are killed in the Nad-e District of the Helmand Province, Afghanistan, by Taliban terrorists.

June 19, 2005 The district commander of the Washir District in Afghanistan and a policemen are killed and five people injured by Taliban terrorists in the Helmand Province.

June 21, 2005   A vehicle with election officials and their relatives is attacked by suspected Taliban rebels, killing one and injuring another in Kandahar, Afghanistan.

June 22, 2005   In Chora District, Afghanistan, Taliban terrorists kill three—provincial council candidate Haji Mohammed Wali and his two bodyguards—after ambushing their vehicle.

June 22, 2005   Two car bombs explode in front of a restaurant in a Shiite neighborhood in Baghdad and a third at a nearby bus stop, killing 11 people and wounding 28. The attack is claimed by both al-Qaeda in Iraq and the Ansar al-Sunna Army.

June 23, 2005   Bomb attacks in Baghdad's Shiite Karrada neighborhood kill 17 civilians and wound 16. One attack is a car bomb in front of the Shiite Albu Jumaa mosque that kills six and injures six. A second attack is a car bomb in the central shopping area that kills 11 and injures ten. For both these attacks Ansar al-Sunna claims responsibility as part of a joint operation with the Islamic Army in Iraq (IAI) and the Mujahideen Army.

June 28, 2005   In Sayedan village in the Uruzgan District of Afghanistan, the Taliban kidnap and kill nine civilians.

July 5, 2005   Taliban forces detonate a roadside bomb in Ghazni, Afghanistan, injuring two Turkish engineers and killing their Afghani driver.

July 6, 2005   A total of 13 civilians are killed and 30 are wounded when a suicide bomber detonates explosives at a crowded car market in Jbeila, Iraq. A second vehicle-borne improvised explosive device is detonated after rescue workers take care of those injured in the first attack. No group claims responsibility.

July 7, 2005   Taliban terrorists in Spin Boldak, Afghanistan, kill three after detonating a bomb on a truck carrying cars.

July 7, 2005   Four suicide bombers—all British citizens—blow themselves up on three London subway trains and one bus, killing 56 persons and injuring more than 700. Two weeks later, another group of terrorists tries unsuccessfully to set off bombs in the London Underground. The attacks in London prompt the British government to seek tougher counter-terrorism legislation that will allow for prosecution of groups and individuals that glorify or incite terrorism.

July 8, 2005   Taliban members in Paktika, Afghanistan, kill a Muslim religious leader and government supporter along with his wife at their home.

July 13, 2005   In a second attack on a religious figure who is a government supporter, the head of the Religious Scholars Council in Helmand Province is gunned down by Taliban terrorists as he is en route to his mosque.

July 14, 2005   Taliban forces kidnap the head of the Zabol Province local council and eventually kill him.

July 16, 2005   Ninety-eight civilians are killed and 200 are wounded when a suicide bomber detonates explosives by a fuel tanker that had been stolen, and so creates a conflagration that spreads to a nearby Shiite mosque in Babil, Iraq, jammed with those going to evening prayer. Al-Qaeda in Iraq claims responsibility. On July 23, Iraqi police announce that they have arrested the man who planned the attack.

July 23, 2005   In Sharm al-Sheikh, Egypt, three bombs targeting tourist areas kill 88, all but 20 are Egyptians, and wound 127. The targets are the Ghazala Gardens Hotel, the coffee shop in the Old Market, and a parking area near Naema Bay. Several groups claim responsibility, but al-Qaeda is found responsible.

July 26, 2005   A candidate in the upcoming parliamentary elections in Afghanistan and his mother is wounded in Sharana when the car in which he is driving is blown up by a remote-detonated device.

July 26, 2005   Seventeen workers from a factory that is run by the Industries Ministry in Baghdad are killed and 27 are wounded as gunmen attack two buses on which they are riding. No group claims responsibility.

July 30, 2005   Taliban terrorists leave a bomb on the road that kills three, the head of the Charchino District of Uruzgan Province in Afghanistan and two of his colleagues.

August 1, 2005   Taliban terrorists kill an election worker in the Kajaki District of Helmand Province, Afghanistan.

August 8, 2005   Muhammad Hashem, a Communist parliamentary election candidate in Andar District of Ghazni Province in Afghanistan, is the victim of Taliban terrorists.

August 10, 2005   Ten Iraqi doctors are killed en route to work near Ramadi, Iraq. No group claims responsibility.

August 17, 2005   Over 75 civilians are killed and at least 95 are injured when five coordinated vehicle-borne improvised explosive devices are detonated by suicide bombers across Baghdad, including two at a bus station, one near a police patrol responding to the first two attacks, and two at a hospital. No group claims responsibility.

August 21, 2005   Taliban terrorists assassinate a pro-government Islamic cleric and another man in Kandahar Province, Afghanistan.

August 24, 2005   Fourteen civilians and three police officers are killed and more than 40 civilians and 13 police officers are wounded when they are attacked by militants using a car bomb, small arms fire, and rocket-propelled grenades in Baghdad. No group claims responsibility.

August 25, 2005   Taliban terrorists assassinate two, one a mapmaker and the other a shop owner, in Lashkar Gah, Afghanistan.

August 31, 2005   A district governor, an election candidate, and three policemen are kidnapped and then murdered by Taliban terrorist near Kandahar City, Afghanistan.

August 31, 2005   Three mortars are fired at the Imam Kadhim Mosque in Baghdad when thousands of Shias are heading there, killing seven and wounding 36 others.

The mortar attack is claimed by Jaish al-Taifa al-Mansoura (Army of the Victorious Community), which has been linked to al-Qaeda. There are many more victims, about 950 killed and 800 injured, by crowds running to flee the scene when there are rumors of another suicide bomber about to detonate a bomb.

September 7, 2005   Sixteen civilians, including two children, are killed and 21 civilians are wounded when a car bomb is detonated by a suicide bomber at a restaurant in Basra, Iraq. No group claims responsibility.

September 14, 2005   More than 114 civilians are killed and 156 are wounded when a car bomb is detonated by a suicide bomber at a gathering of laborers looking for jobs in Baghdad. Elsewhere in Baghdad, 11 civilians are killed and 14 are wounded when a car bomb is detonated by a suicide bomber at a gas station. In a third incident, 15 civilians are killed and eight wounded when a car bomb explodes near a convoy in Baghdad. Al-Qaeda in Iraq claims responsibility for all three attacks.

September 16, 2005   Twelve civilians are killed and 24 are wounded when a car bomb is detonated by a suicide bomber near a mosque in Tozkhurmato, Iraq. No group claims responsibility.

September 17, 2005   Thirty are killed and 38 are wounded when a car bomb explodes at a Shiite market in Nahrawan, Iraq. No group claims responsibility.

September 27, 2005   A Spanish court sentences Imad Eddin Barakat Yarkas, alias "Abu Dahdah," a Syrian-born man, to 27 years in prison for conspiring with al-Qaeda.

September 29, 2005   Some 102 are killed and 150 wounded when three car bombs are blown up by suicide bombers ten minutes apart in a crowded public area in Balad, Iraq. Al-Qaeda in Iraq claims responsibility. On November 1, 2005, it is announced that a Moroccan terrorist who lives in Syria, Muhsen Khayber, a member of Ansar al-Islam organization, is responsible for this attack.

September 30, 2005   Twelve people are killed and 41 are injured when a car bomb is detonated at a vegetable market in Hilla, Iraq. Al-Qaeda in Iraq claims responsibility.

October 3, 2005   Twelve people are killed and six are wounded when an improvised explosive device is detonated in a restaurant in Hilla, Iraq. No group claims responsibility.

October 5, 2005   Thirty-six civilians are killed and 95 are wounded when a car bomb is detonated by a suicide bomber in a mosque in Hilla, Iraq. No group claims responsibility.

October 6, 2005   In Uthaim, Iraq, five Oil Ministry guards are killed as they are driving. No group claims responsibility.

October 11, 2005   Thirty civilians are killed and 45 are injured when a car bomb is detonated by a suicide bomber at a vegetable market in Tal Afar, Iraq. Al-Qaeda in Iraq claims responsibility.

October 15, 2005   Two bombs explode at a shopping mall in Ahvaz, Khuzestan, in Iran, killing six and wounding 100. It is not clear which group is responsible. Fifteen days later, Iranian officials announced that they had arrested some 30 suspects for the attack and the earlier one in June.

October 23, 2005   Twelve Iraqi construction workers are killed and one is kidnapped when their construction site is attacked by gunmen in Jorf al-Sakhr, Iraq. No group claims responsibility.

October 24, 2005   Some 20 are killed and 40 injured when they are attacked by militants using rocket-propelled grenades, mortars, and three vehicle-borne improvised explosive devices detonated by suicide bombers targeting two Baghdad hotels used by foreign journalists and a police checkpoint. Al-Qaeda in Iraq claims responsibility.

October 29, 2005   Thirty civilians are killed and 42 are wounded when a car bomb is detonated by a suicide bomber at a market in the Shiite town of Howaider. No group claims responsibility.

November 2, 2005   Twenty-nine civilians are killed and 62 others are wounded when a car bomb is detonated in front of a Shiite mosque in Musayyib, Iraq. No group claims responsibility.

November 5, 2005   Twelve members of a Kurdish Shiite family near Baghdad are killed and two wounded when their vehicle is ambushed by unknown terrorists.

November 9, 2005   Three suicide bombers set off explosive devices simultaneously at three hotels in Amman, Jordan, killing 63 people and injuring about 115. Al-Qaeda in Iraq claims responsibility.

November 10, 2005   Thirty-five are killed—seven police officers and 28 civilians—and 25 are wounded when an explosive device is detonated by a suicide bomber at a restaurant in Baghdad. Al-Qaeda in Iraq claims responsibility.

November 18, 2005   Two suicide bombers kill 77 and wound 80 when they blow themselves up in two Shiite mosques in the town of Khanaqin. A third suicide bomber is prevented from detonating his device after he is arrested by police. No group claims responsibility. In Baghdad, three suicide car bombs are detonated in a coordinated attack targeting two hotels used by foreign journalists, killing 20 and injuring 40. All three blasts are claimed by al-Qaeda in Iraq.

November 19, 2005   Between 35 and 50 civilians are killed and between 40 and 80 are wounded when a suicide bomber attacks a funeral tent in Abu Saydah, Iraq. No group claims responsibility. In Haditha, 15 civilians and one U.S. soldier are killed and two U.S. soldiers are wounded when an improvised explosive device is detonated and leads to an exchange of gunfire. No group claims responsibility. In Baghdad, 12 civilians and three police officers are killed and 20 civilians are wounded when a vehicle-borne improvised explosive device is detonated at a busy market. No group claims responsibility.

November 24, 2005   Between 11 and 14 civilians are killed and between 17 and 23 are wounded by a suicide bomber at a crowded marketplace in Hilla, Iraq. It is the first attack by a group calling itself Partisans of the Sunni, which targets Shiites.

November 26, 2005   Four aid workers—two Canadians, a Briton, and an American—are kidnapped in western Baghdad. Their captors claim that the aid workers are spies working under the cover of a Christian organization. The American is later found dead, and the rest of the hostages are released. The attack is claimed by a group calling itself the Swords of Righteousness Brigades, which is believed linked to the Islamic Army.

December 8, 2005   Thirty-two civilians are killed and 44 are wounded by a suicide bomber on a bus en route from Nasiriyah to Baghdad. No group claims responsibility.

December 23, 2005   Four security guards and one police officer are killed and eight are wounded when a bomb is detonated by a suicide bomber at a Shiite mosque in Balad Ruz, Iraq. No group claims responsibility.

December 29, 2005   Fourteen family members are kidnapped and killed by gunmen in Mahmudiya, Iraq. No group claims responsibility.

January 1, 2006   Two people are killed and six are wounded when attackers open fire on worshippers outside a Shiite mosque in Baghdad. No group claims responsibility.

January 3, 2006   Two people are killed and three are wounded when gunmen attack mourners at the funeral of a Shiite political activist in Baghdad. The likely target is the activist's boss, Abdul Aziz al-Hakim, head of the leading Shiite political party in Iraq, who escapes injury. No group claims responsibility.

January 4, 2006   A bomb, intended for a police patrol, explodes in an outdoor Baghdad market, killing seven people and wounding 15. No group claims responsibility. In Muqdadiyah, Iraq, 36 people are killed and 42 are wounded when mortars and a suicide bomb detonate at a funeral for the nephew of Ahmed al-Bakka, a prominent Shiite politician. No group claims responsibility.

January 5, 2006   In Karbala, Iraq, 63 people are killed and approximately 120 are wounded when the Imam Hussein Shrine, a major Shia pilgrimage site, is attacked by a suicide bomber with an explosive belt. Al-Qaeda in Iraq claims responsibility. In Baghdad, three coordinated car bomb attacks kill two people and wound six. No group claims responsibility.

January 7, 2006   A reporter for the *Christian Science Monitor,* Jill Carroll, is taken hostage while on assignment in Baghdad by Sunni Muslim terrorists. Her interpreter is killed. On February 28, Iraqi Interior Minister Bayan Jabr Solagh accuses the Islamic Army of Iraq of kidnapping Carroll. Carroll is freed on March 30 after 82 days in captivity.

January 15, 2006   Six Sunni terrorist groups announce that they are forming the Mujahideen Shura Council. The groups are: Tanzim Qa'idat al-Jihad fi Bilad al-Rafidayn (al-Qaeda in Iraq), Jaish al-Taifa al-Mansoura, al-Ahwal Brigades, Islamic Jihad Brigades, al-Ghuraba Brigades, and Saraya Ansar al-Tawhid. The group's purpose is "to liberate Iraq from occupation, to unite and direct all mujahideen efforts and to raise the flag of Islam and Sunnah."

January 17, 2006   Seven civilians supplying food to the Iraqi army are killed when gunmen attack them in Baghdad. No group claims responsibility.

January 18, 2006   Three drivers and seven security personnel are killed when gunmen attack their convoy in Baghdad. No group claims responsibility.

January 19, 2006   Sixteen people are killed and 21 are injured when an improvised explosive device is detonated by a suicide bomber in a Baghdad restaurant. Seconds later, a second explosion is aimed at a group of policemen at a nearby restaurant, and kills an additional seven people and wounds another five. No group claims responsibility.

January 22, 2006   A home of a policeman in Balad Ruz is hit by a grenade, which misses him but kills five of his relatives, including his four children, and wounds his wife. No group claims responsibility.

January 29, 2006   In a Shiite neighborhood of Iskandariyah, Iraq, 11 people are killed and five are wounded when a bomb explodes near a candy shop. No group claims responsibility.

January 29, 2006   Three people are killed and 17 are injured in six bombings at churches across Baghdad and Kirkuk. No group claims responsibility.

February 1, 2006   Eight people are killed and 50 are injured when a bomb explodes near a group of laborers outside a Sunni mosque in Baghdad. No group claims responsibility.

February 2, 2006   Eleven people are killed and 70 are injured when two vehicle-borne improvised explosive devices are detonated by an unidentified suicide bomber within 20 minutes of each other, one in an outdoor market and one in a gas station in Baghdad.

February 5, 2006   In Madain, Iraq, five persons are killed and six are injured when unidentified terrorists detonate several roadside bombs.

February 7, 2006   Seven people are killed and at least 20 are injured in two bombings aimed at Shias in Baghdad. No group claims responsibility.

February 10, 2006   Nine people are killed and 28 are injured when a vehicle-borne improvised explosive device is detonated outside a Sunni mosque in Baghdad. No group claims responsibility.

February 13, 2006   In Baquba, Iraq, five members of the Supreme Council for the Islamic Revolution in Iraq (SCIRI) are killed when their car is attacked by gunmen. No group claims responsibility. Ten people are killed and 40 are injured when an improvised explosive device is detonated by a suicide bomber outside a bank in Baghdad. No group claims responsibility.

February 14, 2006   Unknown assassins near Balad kill 11 Shias, including their target, the tribal chieftain of the Hayalin tribe, and injure four others. No group claims responsibility.

February 16, 2006   Six people are killed and 13 are injured when a vehicle-borne improvised explosive device is detonated in a market in Baghdad. No group claims responsibility.

February 20, 2006   In Mosul, Iraq, five people are killed and 21 people, including ten policemen, are injured when an improvised explosive device is detonated in a restaurant. The Brigades of Abu Dajana al-Ansari, the suicide brigade of the Mujahideen Shura Council, claims responsibility. Meanwhile in Baghdad, four construction workers are killed and 19 are injured when a bomb explodes near Liberation Square in Baghdad. No group claims responsibility. Also in Baghdad, 12 people are killed and 15 injured when an unidentified suicide bomber detonates himself aboard a bus in a Shiite neighborhood.

February 21, 2006   Twenty-two people are killed and 28 are injured when a vehicle-borne improvised explosive device is detonated in a marketplace in Baghdad. No group claims responsibility.

February 22–23, 2006   The golden dome of the Askariya shrine in Samarra, one of the holiest sites for Shia Muslims, is destroyed by Sunni terrorists. In retribution, Shia groups carry out about 168 attacks on Sunni mosques and kill about ten Sunni imams.

February 23, 2006   Unknown terrorists gun down 47 people after they force cars to stop at a phony checkpoint between Samarra and Baghdad. The victims are both Shias and Sunnis returning from protesting the bombing of the Askariya shrine, a holy site for Shiites, in Samarra.

February 25, 2006   In Karbala, a bomb at a market frequented by Shias detonates and eight people are killed and 31 are injured. No group claims responsibility. Meanwhile, in Buhruz, Iraq, 13 people are killed when gunmen break into their home. No group claims responsibility.

February 26, 2006   Unknown terrorists kill 15 people and injure 45 when mortars are fired at a joint Sunni-Shiite demonstration in Baghdad. No group claims responsibility.

February 27, 2006   Four people are killed and 15 are injured when two bombs explode simultaneously outside a Sunni mosque in Baghdad. No group claims responsibility.

February 28, 2006   Five bodyguards of a defense ministry advisor are killed and seven others are injured when a bomb explodes near the advisor's convoy. The Mujahideen Shura Council claims responsibility.

February 28, 2006   Several separate attacks are staged at different mosques in the country. Twenty-three people are killed and 55 are injured when a vehicle-borne improvised explosive device is detonated by unknown terrorists near a Shiite mosque in Baghdad. No group claims responsibility. Six people are killed and 16 are injured when a suicide bomber detonates an explosive near another Shiite mosque. No group claims responsibility. Also in Baghdad, three people are killed and 11 are injured when a bomb explodes near a Sunni mosque in Baghdad. No group claims responsibility.

February 28, 2006	The chief of the Shiite al-Atayfat tribe and eight of his relatives are killed in Tarfaya, Iraq. No group claims responsibility.
February 28, 2006	Twenty-three people are killed and 51 are injured when an improvised electronic device is detonated by a suicide bomber at a gas station in Baghdad. No group claims responsibility.
March 1, 2006	Three civilians are killed and 15 are wounded when a vehicle-borne improvised explosive device is detonated near a bus stop in Baghdad. No group claims responsibility.
March 2, 2006	Twenty-seven workers are killed when gunmen attack two brick factories and a power station in Nahrawan, Iraq. No group claims responsibility.
March 2, 2006	In Karbala, Iraq, 106 are killed and 233 are injured when between four and nine bombs are detonated by a suicide bomber outside a Shiite mosque. In another attack on a Shiite mosque, this one in Baghdad, 65 people are killed and 320 are injured when three bombs are simultaneously detonated by three suicide bombers. In both attacks, no group claims responsibility, but police suspect a group linked to al-Qaeda in Iraq.
March 2, 2006	Five people are killed and ten are injured when a bomb is detonated on a minibus in Baghdad. No group claims responsibility.
March 2, 2006	A bombing by unknown terrorists in Karachi, Pakistan, kills four, including a U.S. diplomat.
March 3, 2006	In Baghdad, seven people are killed and 15 are injured after bombs are detonated by two suicide bombers outside the Interior Ministry. Al-Qaeda in Iraq claims responsibility.
March 6, 2006	Six people are killed and 23 are injured when a car bomb explodes in a market in Baquba, Iraq. No group claims responsibility.
March 8, 2006	Seven workers are killed and seven others are injured when gunmen attack their minibus in Baghdad. No group claims responsibility.
March 9, 2006	Five civilians are killed and 12 are injured when a vehicle-borne improvised explosive device is detonated near a Sunni mosque in Baghdad. No group claims responsibility.
March 10, 2006	Fifty-three people are killed and 100 are injured when a bomb is detonated by a suicide bomber near a funeral in Mosul, Iraq. The Soldiers of the Prophet's Companions claims responsibility.
March 12, 2006	Fifty-eight people are killed and 200 are injured when two markets are attacked by vehicle-borne improvised explosive devices and mortars in a Shiite neighborhood of Baghdad. No group claims responsibility.
March 14, 2006	Fifteen Sunni men are shot and killed in Baghdad. No group claims responsibility.

March 23, 2006	Seven people are killed and 22 are injured when a vehicle-borne improvised explosive device is detonated in a market near a Shiite mosque in Baghdad. In Khalis, Iraq, five people are killed and 17 are injured when a bomb explodes near a Sunni mosque. No group claims responsibility for either attack.
March 27, 2006	Seven people are killed and 35 are injured when rockets are fired at the offices of two Shia political parties—the Dawa Party and the Fadhila Party—in Baghdad. No group claims responsibility.
March 29, 2006	Eight employees of a trading company in Baghdad are killed and six security guards are injured by assassins. No group claims responsibility.
March 30, 2006	In Baiji, Iraq, gunmen ambush a vehicle and kill eight employees of an oil refinery. No group claims responsibility.
March 31, 2006	A Shia tribal leader and five members of his family are killed when unknown gunmen ambush their car on the way home from a funeral in Balad Ruz, Iraq.
April 3, 2006	Targeting a Shiite mosque in Baghdad, ten people are killed and 38 are wounded by a truck bomb detonated remotely by unknown terrorists.
April 4, 2006	A car bomb in a Shiite neighborhood of Baghdad kills ten people and wounds 28. No group claims responsibility.
April 6, 2006	Fifteen people are killed and 30 are wounded when a car bomb is detonated near a Shiite shrine in Najaf, Iraq. No group claims responsibility.
April 7, 2006	Ninety people are killed and 164 are wounded when three suicide bombers dressed in traditional female attire, two of them actually men, detonate their explosive belts in a Shiite mosque in Baghdad. The target is likely Sheikh Jalaluddin al-Saghir, the imam of the mosque and a member of parliament from the Shiite United Alliance, who was not injured in the attack. No group claims responsibility.
April 8, 2006	Six people are killed and 21 are wounded when a car bomb is detonated at a Shiite shrine in Musayyib, Iraq. No group claims responsibility.
April 11, 2006	Five people—two civilians and three police officers—are killed and 13 people are wounded when a car bomb explodes outside a restaurant in Baghdad. No group claims responsibility. In a separate incident in Baghdad, three people are killed and nine are wounded when a bomb explodes on a bus. No group claims responsibility.
April 12, 2006	In another attack on a Shiite mosque, this one in Howaider, 31 people are killed and at least 70 are wounded by a suicide car bomber. No group claims responsibility.
April 12, 2006	One police officer and three civilians are killed and four people are wounded when a bomb explodes in Baghdad. No group claims responsibility. In Tal Afar, three people are killed and seven are wounded when a suicide car bomber attacks a vegetable market. No group claims responsibility.

April 13, 2006   Fifteen people are killed and 22 are wounded when a car bomb detonates in a market in a Shiite neighborhood in Baghdad. Meanwhile, in Basra, seven people are killed when a Sunni family is attacked by unknown gunmen. No group claims responsibility for either attack.

April 14, 2006   Eleven construction employees are killed after being kidnapped in Basra, Iraq. No group claims responsibility.

April 15, 2006   Seven people are killed and 24 are wounded when a car bomb explodes outside a restaurant in Baghdad. No group claims responsibility.

April 16, 2006   A car bomb is detonated near a Shiite mosque in Mahmudiya, Iraq, killing 11 and wounding 23. No group claims responsibility.

April 16, 2006   Four people are killed and seven are injured when a car bomb explodes in a market in Baghdad. No group claims responsibility.

April 16, 2006   In Mosul, seven workers doing construction work on a police station are killed by unknown gunmen No group claims responsibility.

April 18, 2006   Seven people, including three police officers, are killed and 20 people are wounded when a bomb explodes inside a restaurant in a Baghdad. No group claims responsibility.

April 19, 2006   Fourteen Sunnis are killed by unknown terrorists in Baghdad. Unknown terrorists also kill five street cleaners in Baghdad, targeting these workers because they are predominantly Shias and are perceived to be spies for the U.S. government.

April 23, 2006   Seven people are killed and three are wounded after a mortar attack outside the Defense Ministry building in Baghdad. In a separate incident, six Shiites are killed by kidnappers. No groups claim responsibility for either attack.

April 24, 2006   Three people are killed and 25 are wounded when a suicide car bomber attacks the Ministry of Health building in Baghdad. In a separate incident, five people are killed and 25 are wounded when a car bomb detonates near Mustansiriya University in Baghdad. It is not clear which group is responsible for either attack.

April 24, 2006   Bombings at three locations in a tourist area in Dahab, Egypt, kill 20 Egyptians and three foreigners while injuring 62 others. Tawhid wal Jihad group, an Islamist group composed of Bedouins who live in the Sinai, is believed responsible. One of the group's leaders, Nasser Khamis al-Mallahi, who masterminded the Dahab attack, is killed on May 9, 2006, in a shoot-out with police.

April 25, 2006   Ibrahim al-Hindawi, a senior judge in Baghdad, is killed by gunmen. No group claims responsibility. Judges are frequent targets of assassinations in Iraq.

April 26, 2006   Four people are killed and two are injured when a bomb explodes on a minibus in Baghdad. No group claims responsibility.

April 27, 2006   Three people are killed and ten are wounded when a bomb explodes inside a restaurant in Baquba, Iraq. No group claims responsibility. In another attack in Baghdad, Mayson Ahmed al-Hashimi, the sister of Vice President Tariq al-Hashimi, is killed along with her bodyguard and escort. No group claims responsibility. On April 28, two members of the al-Qaeda–linked cell led by Abu Musab al-Zarqawi are arrested in connection with the attack.

April 30, 2006   Twelve Sunnis are found dead in Baghdad. No group claims responsibility.

May 4, 2006   Ten people are killed and 52 are injured when a bomb is detonated by a suicide bomber outside a courthouse building in Baghdad. No group claims responsibility.

May 5, 2006   Six Sunnis are gunned down outside a grocery store in Baghdad. No group claims responsibility.

May 7, 2006   Twenty-one people are killed and 52 are injured when a vehicle-borne improvised explosive device is detonated by a suicide bomber outside a government building in Karbala, Iraq. No group claims responsibility.

May 8, 2006   Five people are killed and ten are wounded when a vehicle-borne improvised explosive device is detonated near a courthouse in Baghdad. No group claims responsibility.

May 8, 2006   A bomb in a public square in Baghdad kills five and wounds ten. No group claims responsibility.

May 9, 2006   Twenty-four people are killed and 134 are injured when a vehicle-borne improvised explosive device is detonated by a suicide bomber in a crowded market in a Shiite neighborhood of Tal Afar, Iraq. No group claims responsibility.

May 10, 2006   In Baquba, Iraq, 11 employees of Diyala Electronics Company are killed and six are wounded when gunmen attack a minibus carrying them home from work. No group claims responsibility.

May 11, 2006   A bomb detonated by a group of street cleaners in Baghdad kills five of them. No group claims responsibility. Five people are killed when a bomb is detonated in a market in Baghdad. No group claims responsibility.

May 14, 2006   Fourteen people are killed and six are injured when two vehicle-borne improvised explosive devices are detonated by suicide bombers near a checkpoint in Baghdad. No group claims responsibility. The attack may have targeted the convoy of Electricity Minister Abd-al-Hassan Shalash that was close to the checkpoint at the time, but he is not injured in the attack.

May 14, 2006   Terrorists detonate a bomb in a market in Baghdad killing five people and injuring 15. No group claims responsibility.

May 15, 2006   Six members of the same family are killed by gunmen in Baghdad. One policeman is killed and two people are injured when a bomb is detonated as police responded to the first attack. No group claims responsibility. In Balad Ruz, unknown gunmen gun down four teachers.

May 16, 2006   Nineteen people are killed in a coordinated attack near a market in a Shiite neighborhood in Baghdad. Gunmen first attack and kill five Shiite guards in the parking lot. Soon after, a car bomb, strategically parked near an oil tanker, detonates, causing the tanker to explode, killing 14 others and wounding 37. The terrorists are unknown.

May 18, 2006   Seven car mechanics and a driver are killed when their vehicle is attacked by gunmen in Baghdad. No group claims responsibility.

May 20, 2006   Five people are killed and ten are injured when a vehicle-borne improvised explosive device is detonated by a suicide bomber in Qaim, Iraq. No group claims responsibility. In Baghdad, 19 people are killed and 58 are injured when a bomb is detonated near a crowd of people looking for work in a Shiite neighborhood. No group claims responsibility.

May 21, 2006   Thirteen people are killed and 17 are injured when an explosive device is detonated by a suicide bomber in a crowded restaurant in Baghdad that is popular with policemen. No group claims responsibility. The attack is claimed by the Mujahideen Shura Council.

May 23, 2006   Eleven people are killed and nine are injured when a vehicle-borne improvised explosive device is detonated outside a Shiite mosque in Baghdad. No group claims responsibility.

May 26, 2006   Nine people are killed and 30 are injured when a bomb is detonated in a market in Baghdad. No group claims responsibility.

May 29, 2006   Seven people are killed and 20 are injured when a vehicle-borne improvised explosive device is detonated near a market in Baghdad. No group claims responsibility. In another incident in Baghdad, nine people are killed and 25 are injured when a vehicle-borne improvised explosive device is detonated near a Sunni mosque. No group claims responsibility.

May 30, 2006   In Iraq, nine people are killed and ten are injured when a bomb is detonated outside a bakery in Baghdad. No group claims responsibility. In Hilla, 12 people are killed and 32 are injured when a vehicle-borne improvised explosive device is detonated near a car dealership sales center. No group claims responsibility. In Husseiniya, 25 people are killed and 65 injured when a vehicle-borne improvised explosive device is detonated near a crowded market. No group claims responsibility.

May 31, 2006   Five people are killed and three are injured when their minibus is attacked by gunmen in Baquba, Iraq. No group claims responsibility.

June 1, 2006   Two people are killed and 18 are wounded when a bomb explodes in Tayaran Square in Baghdad. No group claims responsibility.

June 2, 2006   Five people are killed and 57 are wounded when two bombs explode by a pet market in Baghdad. No group claims responsibility. In another incident, two people are killed and five wounded when a bomb explodes close to a Shiite mosque. No group claims responsibility.

June 3, 2006

In Basra, 28 people are killed and 62 are wounded when a suicide car bomber attacks a market.

June 4, 2006

Twenty-one people, most of them ethnic Turkomen and many of them high school students, are killed and one is wounded in Ain Laila, Iraq, when terrorists make a fake checkpoint and force passengers off three buses.

June 5, 2006

A local politician in Baghdad and his driver are killed when his car is attacked in the city. Also in Baghdad, 11 people, all of them students, are killed when their bus is attacked by gunmen. No group claims responsibility for either attack.

June 6, 2006

Two people are killed and seven are wounded when the Interior Ministry is attacked by mortar fire in Baghdad. No group claims responsibility. Also in Baghdad, a city council member and two of his bodyguards are killed when his car is attacked by gunmen. No group claims responsibility. In a third incident in Baghdad, four people are killed and 18 are wounded when a car bomb is detonated at a Shiite funeral. No group claims responsibility.

June 7, 2006

Abu Musab al-Zarqawi, the leader of al-Qaeda in Iraq, is killed while attending a meeting at an isolated house north of Baquba, Iraq, when two U.S. jets drop bombs on the building. Six others are also reportedly killed, including al-Zarqawi's wife and child. Meanwhile, two people are killed and 17 are wounded in Baghdad when a bomb explodes at a market. No group claims responsibility.

June 8, 2006

Thirteen people are killed and 29 are wounded when a bomb explodes at a fruit market in Baghdad. No group claims responsibility. In another incident, seven people are killed and 17 wounded when a bomb explodes in a Shiite neighborhood. No group claims responsibility. In a third incident, six people are killed and 13 wounded when a bomb explodes in a market in eastern Baghdad. No group claims responsibility. In another incident in a Shiite area in Baghdad, nine people are killed and 42 are injured when a car bomb explodes. No group claims responsibility.

June 10, 2006

Nine people are killed and 23 are wounded when a car bomb explodes outside a Shiite mosque in Baghdad. No group claims responsibility. In another attack, four people are killed and seven are wounded when gunmen fire at a minibus. No group claims responsibility. In a third incident, three people are killed and 28 wounded when a bomb explodes at a market. No group claims responsibility.

June 11, 2006

Six people are killed and 42 are wounded when a car bomb explodes in Baghdad. No group claims responsibility.

June 12, 2006

Six employees of the Iraqi Industry Ministry are killed and 12 are wounded when a bomb explodes near a minibus in Baghdad. No group claims responsibility. In a second incident in Baghdad, six people are killed and 41 are wounded when a car bomb explodes at a market in a Shiite neighborhood. No group claims responsibility. Meanwhile, in Tal Afar, Iraq, four people are killed and 40 are wounded when a suicide car bomber attacks a gas station. No group claims responsibility.

June 13, 2006
Six bombing and suicide attacks occur throughout Kirkuk, Iraq, killing 13 and wounding approximately 17. The attacks are aimed primarily at police and government targets and are claimed by the Mujahideen Shura Council.

June 15, 2006
Three people are killed and 14 are wounded when a car bomb detonated by unknown terrorists explodes outside a bakery in Baghdad. In Baquba, a gunman attacks a bus and kills ten passengers, all of them Shiite men. No group claims responsibility. In Tikrit, four people are killed and 15 are wounded when a Sunni mosque is attacked. No group claims responsibility.

June 16, 2006
Al-Qaeda in Iraq is suspected of being behind the suicide bombing of a Shiite mosque in Baghdad that kills 13 people and wounds 28.

June 17, 2006
In another bombing of a minibus, four people are killed and seven are wounded in a Shiite neighborhood in Baghdad. No group claims responsibility. In another incident in Baghdad, six people are killed and 25 are wounded when a bomb explodes at a market. The Mujahideen Shura Council claims responsibility.

June 17, 2006
Two people are killed and 24 are wounded when a bomb explodes at an outdoor market in Baghdad. No group claims responsibility.

June 18, 2006
Four people are killed when a bomb explodes on a minibus in Baghdad. No group claims responsibility.

June 20, 2006
Seven people are killed and 18 are injured when a bomb explodes at a market in Sadr City, a predominantly Shiite section of Baghdad. No group claims responsibility. In a second attack in Baghdad, two people are killed and 28 are wounded when a bomb explodes in one of the city's commercial districts. In a third attack, five people are killed and 11 are wounded when a car bomb explodes in western Baghdad. No group claims responsibility. In Basra, two people are killed and five are wounded when a suicide bomber attacks a group of senior citizens. No group claims responsibility.

June 21, 2006
Two people are killed and eight are wounded when a car bomb explodes in the Sadr City area of Baghdad. No group claims responsibility. In Taji, Iraq, 11 employees of government factories are killed after being kidnapped. Of the workers initially taken from the factories, about 30, mostly Sunnis and women, are released by the hostages, and 17 are freed by a police raid. It is not clear which group is responsible.

June 22, 2006
A bomb in Baghdad detonates on a motorcycle killing two people and wounding 25. No group claims responsibility. Also in Baghdad, two people are killed and five wounded when a car bomb explodes near a movie theater. No group claims responsibility.

June 23, 2006
Five people are killed and 18 are wounded when a car bomb explodes in Basra, Iraq, near a gas station and market. No group claims responsibility. In Hibib,

Iraq, 12 people are killed and 20 wounded when a bomb explodes near a Sunni mosque. No group claims responsibility. Meanwhile in Baghdad, two people are killed and four are wounded after some Shiites demonstrating against an earlier suicide bombing are gunned down. No group claims responsibility.

June 25, 2006   Three people are killed and seven are wounded when a bomb explodes in a market in Baghdad. No group claims responsibility. Also in Baghdad, two people are killed and five are wounded when a bomb explodes on a minibus. No group claims responsibility.

June 26, 2006   Twenty-five people are killed and 33 are wounded when a bomb explodes in the Shiite village of Kharnabat, Iraq. No group claims responsibility. In the Shiite city of Hilla, Iraq, 15 people are killed and 56 wounded when a bomb explodes at a market. No group claims responsibility.

June 27, 2006   Three people are killed and ten are wounded when a car bomb explodes at a market in Baghdad. No group claims responsibility. In Kirkuk, Iraq, an unknown suicide bomber targets a gas station and kills three people and wounds 21.

June 28, 2006   Three people are killed and 12 are wounded by a suicide car bomber near a Sunni mosque in Baquba, Iraq. No group claims responsibility.

June 29, 2006   Seven people are killed and 27 are wounded when a suicide car bomber attacks a funeral for a Shiite soldier in Kirkuk, Iraq. No group claims responsibility.

June 30, 2006   Three people are killed and seven are wounded when a bomb explodes close to a bus near Kirkuk, Iraq. No group claims responsibility. In the village of Daliqiya, Iraq, a group of Sunnis, who are trying to leave after being threatened by Shiites, are attacked by Shiite gunmen. Six people are killed and three are wounded After Iraqi police become involved, terrorists kill the head of the police force, Colonel Sami Abbas Hassan, and two of his bodyguards. U.S. and Iraqi forces then jump into the fray killing three terrorists and wounding another three, and arresting four.

July 1, 2006   Sixty-six people are killed and 144 are injured when a vehicle-borne improvised explosive device is detonated in an outdoor market in Baghdad. The attack is claimed by Ansar al-Sunna Army Supporters. But three days later, Iraqi officials announce they have killed a terrorist linked to al-Qaeda who assisted in the attack.

July 5, 2006   Six people are killed and 17 are injured when a vehicle-borne improvised explosive device is detonated near a Shiite mosque in Baghdad. No group claims responsibility.

July 6, 2006   Twelve people, including eight Iranian Shiite pilgrims, are killed and 39 people, including 22 Iranians, are injured when a vehicle-borne improvised explosive device is detonated by a suicide bomber outside a Shiite holy site in Kufa, Iraq. It is not clear which group is responsible.

July 7, 2006   Five people are killed and one is injured when gunmen attack their car near Kirkuk, Iraq. No group claims responsibility. In Tal al-Banat, nine people are killed and 59 are injured when a vehicle-borne improvised explosive device is detonated outside a Shiite mosque. No group claims responsibility.

July 9, 2006 Forty-two Sunnis are killed when Shiite gunmen storm their neighborhood in Baghdad. No group claims responsibility. In a second incident, five people are killed and two are injured by another bomb. No group claims responsibility. In a third attack, also in Baghdad, 17 people are killed and 38 are injured when two vehicle-borne improvised explosive devices are detonated simultaneously near a Shiite mosque. No group claims responsibility.

July 10, 2006 Five people are killed and 12 are injured when a vehicle-borne improvised explosive device is detonated by a suicide bomber near the office of the Patriotic Union of Kurdistan Party in Kirkuk, Iraq. No group claims responsibility. In Baghdad, eight people are killed and 41 injured when two bombs are detonated outside a shop. No group claims responsibility. In a Sunni area of the city, six passengers and a driver are killed when gunmen attack their bus. No group claims responsibility.

July 11, 2006 Sixteen persons are killed and 13 people are injured after a car bomb and two suicide bomb explosions near a restaurant in Baghdad. The car bomb portion of the attack is claimed by the Islamic Army in Iraq and the two suicide bombers are claimed by the Mujahideen Shura Council. In another incident, eight people are killed and three are injured when their company is attacked by gunmen. No group claims responsibility. On the road between Baghdad and Najaf, ten mourners on their way to a funeral are killed when they are attacked by gunmen. No group claims responsibility. Back in Baghdad, five people are killed and 17 are injured when a vehicle-borne improvised explosive device is detonated. No group claims responsibility.

July 12, 2006 Eight people are killed and 30 are injured when a bomb is detonated by a suicide bomber in a restaurant in Baghdad. No group claims responsibility. In a second incident in Baghdad, six people are killed when they are attacked by gunmen. No group claims responsibility. In Muqdadiyah, Iraq, unknown gunmen attack a bus station. They separate the Shias from the crowd, take them captive, and later shoot them. No group claims responsibility.

July 13, 2006 Six people are killed and three are injured when a vehicle-borne improvised explosive device is detonated by a suicide bomber outside the village council headquarters in Abu Saida, Iraq. The Mujahideen Shura Council claims responsibility. In Baghdad, five street cleaners are killed and two are wounded when a bomb is detonated near them. No group claims responsibility. In Mosul, two policemen and three civilians are killed and two policemen and three civilians are injured when a vehicle-borne improvised explosive device is detonated by a suicide bomber. No group claims responsibility.

July 14, 2006 In Mosul, Iraq, two policemen and three civilians are killed and four people are injured when a vehicle-borne improvised explosive device is detonated by a suicide bomber near a police patrol. No group claims responsibility. In Baghdad, eight people are killed and ten are injured when a bomb is detonated and mortars are fired near a Sunni mosque. No group claims responsibility. Meanwhile, on the road between Kut and Karbala, Iraq, five people are killed when their bus is attacked. No group claims responsibility.

July 15, 2006	Six people are killed and 11 are injured when a bomb is detonated near a market in Baghdad. No group claims responsibility.
July 16, 2006	A Mujahideen Shura Council suicide bomber detonates a bomb at a cafe in Tuz Khormato, Iraq, killing 26 and wounding 22.
July 17, 2006	Fifty people are killed and 90 are injured—most of them Shiites—when they are attacked by mortars, automatic weapons, and rocket-propelled grenades in a market in Mahmudiya, Iraq. The attack is claimed by a new group calling itself Supporters of the Sunni People which said it sought to revenge attacks on Sunnis by Shias.
July 18, 2006	Fifty-nine people are killed and 105 are injured when a vehicle-borne improvised explosive device is detonated by a Mujahideen Shura Council suicide bomber in a crowd of laborers in Kufa, Iraq.
July 19, 2006	In Kirkuk, Iraq, five people are killed and 16 are wounded when a bomb is detonated outside a cafe. No group claims responsibility. In Basra, five people are killed and five are injured when their throats are slit by unknown attackers. No group claims responsibility. In Baghdad, five people are killed and 17 are injured when two bombs are detonated in a crowd gathered because of an earlier explosion. No group claims responsibility. Finally, in Rasheed, Iraq, three people are killed and 11 people are injured when gunmen attack a market. No group claims responsibility.
July 20, 2006	Ten people are killed and seven are injured when a vehicle-borne improvised explosive device is detonated in a gas station in Baiji, Iraq. No group claims responsibility. In Mosul, five people are killed. No group claims responsibility.
July 21, 2006	Seven people are killed when gunmen attack them in Mahmudiya, Iraq, a Shiite area. No group claims responsibility.
July 22, 2006	Seven workers are killed and one is injured when gunmen attack their home in Baghdad. No group claims responsibility.
July 23, 2006	Seventeen people are killed and 30 are injured when a vehicle-borne improvised explosive device is detonated in a market near a courthouse in Kirkuk, Iraq. No group claims responsibility. In Baghdad, 34 people are killed and 72 are injured when a vehicle-borne improvised explosive device is detonated by a suicide bomber in a market in Baghdad. Two hours later, eight people are killed and 20 are injured when a second bomb is detonated. No group claims responsibility.
July 25, 2006	Terrorists from the 1920 Revolution Brigades attack two fuel trucks traveling from Kirkuk to Baghdad with grenades, killing both drivers.
July 27, 2006	Five members of Saddam Hussein's Baath Party are killed in al-Diwaniyah. No group claims responsibility. Thirty-one people are killed and 150 are injured when at least one vehicle-borne improvised explosive device is detonated, two rockets hit, and two mortar shells explode in a predominantly Shiite neighborhood of Baghdad. No group claims responsibility.

July 30, 2006

Unidentified terrorists ambush a car in Hawija, Iraq, and kill the five passengers, four of them policemen.

August 1, 2006

Five civil servants are killed and six are injured when gunmen attack their minibuses in Baghdad. No group claims responsibility. Five people are killed and four are injured when gunmen attack their bus on an agricultural road between Rasheed and Yussefiya. No group claims responsibility.

August 2, 2006

Sixteen people are killed and 14 are injured when two bombs are detonated at a soccer stadium in Baghdad. No group claims responsibility.

August 3, 2006

Ten people, including three policemen, are killed and 15 people are injured when a vehicle-borne improvised explosive device is detonated by a Mujahideen Shura Council suicide bomber at a soccer game in Hadhra, Iraq. In Baghdad, 12 people are killed and 29 are injured when a bomb is detonated in a market. No group claims responsibility.

August 4, 2006

A suicide car bomber strikes a market in Kandahar, Afghanistan, killing 21 people. The Taliban is probably responsible.

August 6, 2006

At least ten people are killed and 18 are injured when a bomb is detonated by a suicide bomber at a funeral in Tikrit, Iraq. No group claims responsibility.

August 7, 2006

The owner of a barbershop and four customers are killed when gunmen attack the shop in Baghdad. No group claims responsibility.

August 8, 2006

Nine people are killed and eight are wounded when a bomb is detonated at a bus station in Baghdad. No group claims responsibility. Also in Baghdad, ten people are killed and 50 are injured when two bombs are detonated in a market. No group claims responsibility.

August 9, 2006

Five people are killed and two injured by gunmen at a market in Baghdad. No group claims responsibility.

August 10, 2006

Thirty-five people are killed and 122 injured by a suicide bomber at a checkpoint near a mosque in Najaf, Iraq. The Soldiers of the Prophet's Companions claim responsibility. In Baghdad, six people are killed and four injured by a bomb detonated in a restaurant. In Muradiya, Iraq, five people are killed. No group claims responsibility.

August 10, 2006

A bomb plot targeting several airplanes from Heathrow Airport near London that are headed for the United States is stopped by authorities. The would-be bombers, whose group was infiltrated, include Pakistan-born British citizens and converts to Islam with links to al-Qaeda.

August 11, 2006

Sixty-three people are killed and 140 injured when four car bombs are detonated near a market in Baghdad. No group claims responsibility.

August 15, 2006

Ten people are killed and 41 injured by a suicide bomber in a car outside the offices of the Patriotic Union of Kurdistan in Mosul, Iraq. The Mujahideen Shura Council claims responsibility.

August 16, 2006	Eight people are killed and 28 injured by a bomb near a crowd of laborers in Baghdad. Also in Baghdad, 14 people are killed and 55 injured by two bombs on a busy street. No group claims responsibility.
August 17, 2006	Seven people are killed and 15 injured when a car bomb blows up at a market in Baghdad. No group claims responsibility.
August 19, 2006	Seven pilgrims are killed when gunmen attack them near a mosque in Baghdad. No group claims responsibility.
August 20, 2006	Twenty-two pilgrims are killed and ten injured by gunmen near a mosque in Baghdad. No group claims responsibility.
August 21, 2006	Eight fruit traders are killed by having their throats cut in Madain, Iraq. No group claims responsibility.
August 22, 2006	Five people, including two children, are killed when gunmen attack their home in Mosul, Iraq. No group claims responsibility.
August 27, 2006	Nine people are killed and 22 injured when a suicide bomber detonates a car bomb at a checkpoint and by a suicide bomber outside the house of a police commander in Baghdad. Also in Baghdad, nine people are killed and 18 are injured when a bomb is detonated on a public bus. No group claims responsibility. In Basra, seven people are killed and ten injured by a car bomb at a market. No group claims responsibility. In Khalis, six people are killed and 12 injured by a bomb on a crowded street. Also in Khalis, 12 people are killed and 25 injured by gunmen at a market. No group claims responsibility.
August 28, 2006	Sixteen people, including ten police, are killed and 47, including 18 police, injured when a suicide bomber blows up a car bomb at a checkpoint outside the Interior Ministry in Baghdad. The Mujahideen Shura Council claims responsibility.
August 29, 2006	Five people are killed by gunmen in Baquba, Iraq. No group claims responsibility.
August 30, 2006	Twenty-four people are killed and 35 injured by a bomb in a market in Baghdad. No group claims responsibility.
August 31, 2006	Sixty-eight people are killed and 300 injured by car bombs and mortar shells in Shiite areas in Baghdad. No group claims responsibility.
September 1, 2006	Fourteen South Asian Shiites are killed when gunmen ambush a bus on its way to Karbala, Iraq. Ansar al-Sunna claims responsibility for the attack.
September 2, 2006	Three people are killed and eight wounded by gunmen attacking a bus of Shiite pilgrims traveling to Karbala, Iraq. In Baghdad, two people are killed and 21 wounded by a bomb in the city's center. No group claims responsibility.
September 3, 2006	Four people are killed and 19 wounded by a bomb at a market shop in Khalis, Iraq. No group claims responsibility.

September 5, 2006   Three people are killed when gunmen attack Shiite pilgrims travelling through Baghdad. In Samarra, three people are killed and six wounded by a bomb near a fuel tanker. No group claims responsibility.

September 7, 2006   Thirteen people—the attacker and 12 policemen—are killed and 39 wounded when a suicide car bomber attacks a fuel depot in Baghdad. In southern Baghdad, two people are killed and six wounded by a bomb near a minibus. Also in Baghdad, six people are killed by two bombs at a market. In all of these attacks, no group claims responsibility.

September 8, 2006   Three people are killed and 22 wounded when mortars are fired at a road leading to Karbala, Iraq, often used by Shiite pilgrims. Meanwhile, in southern Baghdad, two people are killed and 15 wounded when a bomb explodes near a mosque. No group claims responsibility for either attack.

September 9, 2006   Three people are killed and 14 wounded by a bomb in Kirkuk, Iraq. A second bomb explodes as police and medical personnel arrive, killing one policeman and wounding two others. No group claims responsibility.

September 10, 2006   Three people are killed and 15 wounded by a bomb at the Haraj market in Baghdad. No group claims responsibility.

September 11, 2006   Seven people are killed and three wounded by mortars, rifles, and explosives in an attack on a Shiite mosque in Bani Saad, Iraq. No group claims responsibility.

September 12, 2006   Four people are killed and 24 wounded by a bomb at a market in Muqdadiyah, Iraq. No group claims responsibility.

September 13, 2006   Twelve bystanders are killed and 34 wounded by a bomb in eastern Baghdad. The Mujahideen Shura Council claims responsibility. Also in Baghdad, 19 people are killed and 62 wounded by a bomb in a parking lot. No group claims responsibility.

September 14, 2006   Nine people are killed and 17 wounded by a car bomb near the Iraqi passport office in central Baghdad. Also in Baghdad, six people are killed by gunmen attacking a Shiite house in a Sunni area. In a third incident, nine are killed and 26 wounded by a car bomb in the Karrada district of Baghdad. No group claims responsibility in any of these attacks.

September 15, 2006   Four people are killed and six wounded by a bomb at a soccer field in Falluja, Iraq. No group claims responsibility.

September 17, 2006   Two people are killed and eight wounded by a bomb at a market in central Baghdad. In Kirkuk, eighteen people are killed and 55 wounded by a truck bomb near the offices of two Kurdish political parties. No group claims responsibility.

September 18, 2006   Twenty-one people are killed and 17 wounded by a suicide bomber at a market in Tal Afar, Iraq. No group claims responsibility.

September 18, 2006   In Somalia, in an assassination attempt by Islamist revolutionaries on President Abdallah Yusuf Ahmed, 11 people are killed, including the president's brother and six of the attackers.

September 19, 2006	Twenty-one people are killed and 50 wounded near an army base in Sharqat, Iraq, by a car bomb and suicide bomber attack. Meanwhile, in Baghdad, two people are killed and 25 wounded when a car bomb explodes near a gas station. No group claims responsibility.
September 20, 2006	Twenty-two people are killed and 24 are wounded by a suicide bomber at a market in Tal Afar, Iraq. No group claims responsibility.
September 21, 2006	Five people are killed and 14 wounded in two incidents when bombs explode in Shiite neighborhoods of Baghdad. No group claims responsibility.
September 23, 2006	Thirty-eight people are killed and 42 wounded when a bomb explodes near a group of people crowding around a kerosene truck in Sadr City, a Shiite district of Baghdad. The Soldiers of the Prophet's Companions claim responsibility.
September 24, 2006	Four people are killed and 14 people wounded when a car bomb explodes near a Christian church in Baghdad. No group claims responsibility.
September 26, 2006	One person is killed and six wounded by a car bomb at a fuel station in Kirkuk, Iraq. In Baghdad, three people are killed and 21 wounded when two bombs explode in close succession. In Mahmudiya, Iraq, seven people are killed and 11 wounded when a series of explosions occur near an apartment building of mainly Shiite Muslims. No group claims responsibility.
September 27, 2006	Ten people are killed and 11 wounded by a gunman at a Sunni mosque in north-west Baghdad during a prayer service. Also in Baghdad, five people are killed and eight wounded by a car bomb near a market in a predominately Shiite area. In a third incident, five people are killed and 15 are wounded when a suicide bomber attacks the Iraqi Communist Party headquarters. No group claims responsibility.
September 28, 2006	Five people are killed and 34 wounded when two car bombs explode near a restaurant in Baghdad. No group claims responsibility. As police and rescue personnel arrive another car bomb explodes.
September 29, 2006	Members of Dhi Qar Organization, a pro-Saddam Hussein group, kill seven men, including two close relatives of Muhammad al-Uraybi, the judge in the trial of former Iraqi leader Saddam Hussein.
September 30, 2006	Three people are killed and 30 wounded by a suicide car bomber at a market in Tal Afar, Iraq. No group claims responsibility.
September 30, 2006	A suicide bomber detonates explosives outside the interior ministry in Kabul, Afghanistan, killing 12 and wounding more than 40.
October 3, 2006	Seven policemen, including Brigadier Shaaban al-Obeidi, are killed when a bomb targeting al-Obeidi is detonated in Baghdad. In Baquba, four family members and their driver are killed when gunmen attack their home. Also in Baquba, eight people are killed when they are attacked by gunmen. No group claims responsibility.
October 4, 2006	Five people are killed and six injured by gunmen at a cafe in Baghdad. In an attack on the convoy of Industry Minister Fawzi al-Hariri, 18 civilians and three

bodyguards are killed, and 63 civilians, 15 policemen, and 11 bodyguards are injured when at least two bombs are detonated in Baghdad. No group claims responsibility.

October 8, 2006   Five people are killed by gunmen in Haditha, Iraq. No group claims responsibility.

October 9, 2006   Thirteen people are killed and 46 injured by a car bomb at a market in Baghdad. No group claims responsibility.

October 10, 2006   Six policemen are killed and four injured by a car bomb as they respond to a report of a body found in a car. The Islamic State of Iraq, the new name of Mujahideen Shura Council, claims responsibility. Also in Baghdad, ten people are killed and four are injured by a bomb detonated outside a bakery. No group claims responsibility.

October 11, 2006   Five people are killed and six injured by a bomb at a busy intersection in a Shiite area of Baghdad. It is not clear which group is responsible for the attack.

October 12, 2006   Eleven people are killed and two injured when gunmen storm a TV station in Baghdad. The victims include the founder and director of al-Shabbiya Television in Baghdad, Abdul Rahim Nasralla al-Shameri. He is also a leader of the Justice and Democratic Development Party, a secular political party. It is not clear which group is responsible. Also in Baghdad, five people are killed and 11 injured by a car bomb in a public square as rescuers arrive after the explosion of an earlier such device. No group claims responsibility.

October 13, 2006   Six Shiite women and two children are killed when gunmen attack them while they are buying vegetables in Baghdad. No group claims responsibility.

October 14, 2006   Eight people are killed when a bomb is detonated by a suicide bomber in a market in Qaim, Iraq. No group claims responsibility.

October 15, 2006   Seven people are killed and five injured when two bombs blow up targeting the convoy of Halah Shakir, undersecretary for financial affairs at the Iraqi Interior Ministry. The Islamic State of Iraq claims responsibility. In Kirkuk, five people are killed and ten injured by a suicide bomber near a Facilities Protection Service convoy. In Tal Afar, five people are killed by a suicide bomber. At least 31 people are killed by gunmen across Baghdad. In al-Latifiyah, eight people are killed when gunmen attack the home of a Shiite family. No group claims responsibility.

October 16, 2006   Ten people are killed and 20 are injured when a car bomb blows up near a bank in a market in Suwayra, Iraq. In Baghdad, 20 people are killed and 27 injured by a suicide bomber at a funeral. In Mahmudiya, Iraq, five members of a Shiite family are killed when gunmen attack their home. No group claims responsibility.

October 17, 2006   Five people are killed when gunmen attack their home in Balad Ruz, Iraq. No group claims responsibility.

October 19, 2006   Ten people are killed and 20 injured by a bomb at a market in Khalis, Iraq. No group claims responsibility.

October 20, 2006	Nine members of a Shiite family are killed when gunmen attack their home in Aziziyah, Iraq. No group claims responsibility.
October 21, 2006	Nineteen people are killed and 60 injured by car bombs and mortar shells at a market in Mahmudiya, Iraq. Meanwhile, in Baghdad, five people are killed and 25 injured by a suicide bomber on a bus. No group claims responsibility.
October 22, 2006	Fifteen people are killed and 25 injured by a bomb and gunmen in Muradiya, Iraq. No group claims responsibility.
October 25, 2006	Six people are killed by a bomb near a bus in Balad Ruz, Iraq. No group claims responsibility.
October 27, 2006	Five people are killed and five are injured when gunmen attack a bus filled with Shiites near Khalis, Iraq. It is not clear which group is responsible.
October 28, 2006	Five people are killed and 20 injured by a bomb near a residential complex in Iskandariyah, Iraq. No group claims responsibility.
October 30, 2006	Twelve people are killed and 38 injured when four car bombs are detonated in Shiite neighborhoods, a currency exchange office, and a bus in Baghdad. Also in Baghdad, 31 people are killed and 50 are injured by a bomb at a street corner. No group claims responsibility.
October 31, 2006	Twenty-three people are killed and 19 injured by a car bomb at a wedding party in Baghdad. No group claims responsibility.
November 2, 2006	Seven people are killed and 45 injured by a car bomb at a market in Baghdad. In Baquba, five people are killed when gunmen attack fuel trucks. No group claims responsibility.
November 3, 2006	Five guards are killed and two injured by several bombs on the Baghdad-Kirkuk Highway near a convoy of President Jalal Talabani's guards. It is unclear if the attack was an assassination attempt, since Talabani was abroad at the time. Meanwhile, in Baghdad, two civilians and four gunmen are killed when gunmen attack a mosque and are killed by an army platoon. No group claims responsibility.
November 7, 2006	Seventeen people are killed and 20 injured by a suicide bomber at a cafe in a Shiite neighborhood of Baghdad. No group claims responsibility.
November 8, 2006	Six people are killed and 26 are injured by a car bomb at a crowded market in Mahmudiya, Iraq. No group claims responsibility.
November 9, 2006	Seven people are killed and 27 injured by a car bomb in a crowded area of Baghdad. Also in Baghdad, nine people are killed and 27 injured by a suicide bomber in a crowd of people at a spare parts market. In the Karrada district of downtown Baghdad, a suicide car bomber crashes his vehicle into a group of people at a spare parts market, killing nine people and wounding 27 others. Also in Baghdad, five people are killed and six are injured by a suicide bomber outside a mosque. No group claims responsibility.

November 11, 2006　　Eight people are killed and 38 injured by two bombs under parked cars in Hafidh al-Qadhi Square in Baghdad. Near Baghdad, ten people are killed and several others kidnapped when militants set up a fake checkpoint on a Sunni part of the highway south of the city. No group claims responsibility.

November 13, 2006　　At least 11 people are killed and 18 wounded by a bomb on a minibus in Baghdad. Also in Baghdad, five employees of Iraq's state-owned oil company are killed by gunmen. No group claims responsibility.

November 14, 2006　　Ten people are killed and 25 injured by a bomb in a market in Baghdad. Near Fakhmaya, Iraq, on the Iranian border, seven people are killed when gunmen attack a bus. No group claims responsibility. Terrorists disguised as Iraqi police commandos infiltrate the Iraqi Ministry of Education in Baghdad and kidnap dozens of employees and drive toward Shiite neighborhoods. Most are reported released, but it not clear how many are killed. Moqtada al-Sadr's Mahdi Army is likely responsible.

November 15, 2006　　Eleven people are killed and 33 injured when a car bomb blows up near a fuel station in Baghdad. No group claims responsibility.

November 16, 2006　　Nine people are killed and two injured by gunmen in a bakery in Baghdad. No group claims responsibility. Attacks on bakeries are frequent in Iraq and often have sectarian motivations because bakers are traditionally Shias.

November 19, 2006　　Twenty-two people are killed and 44 are injured by a a suicide bomber in a crowd of day laborers in Hilla, Iraq. Three men, two Egyptians and an Iraqi, are arrested. In Baghdad, 11 people are killed and 51 injured by two bombs at a bus station. In Sadiya al-Jabal, eight people are killed and two are injured when gunmen attack their minibus. No group claims responsibility.

November 21, 2006　　In Afghanistan, a Kandahar provincial councilwoman's husband is assassinated in Kandahar. It is not known which group is responsible.

November 21, 2006　　Seven people are killed when gunmen attack a minibus taking children home from school in Baghdad. In Iskandariyah, Iraq, seven people are killed and one is injured by a bomb. No group claims responsibility.

November 21, 2006　　Pierre Gemayel, Lebanon's industry minister, an outspoken critic of Syrian control over Lebanon, is killed in a car bomb in a Beirut suburb. Syria is suspected of being responsible.

November 23, 2006　　Terrorists detonate at least five car bombs and fire mortars on Sadr City, a Shiite area of Baghdad, killing at least 215 people and wounding 257. In response, Shiite terrorists fire mortars at Sunni neighborhoods and mosques which kill one and wound 14. The perpetrator is unknown.

November 24, 2006　　Twenty-three people are killed and 43 injured by two bombs outside a car dealership in Tal Afar, Iraq. In Baghdad, six people are killed after being kidnapped at a mosque and set on fire. No group claims responsibility.

November 26, 2006   A bomb detonates in a restaurant in Afghanistan's Paktika Province, killing 15 and injuring 25 others. The Taliban claims responsibility for the attack.

November 27, 2006   A cell phone store owner is killed when gunmen attack the store in Muqdadiyah, Iraq. After the assasination, another bomb is detonated inside the store, killing four more people and wounding 35. In Baghdad, six people are killed and three are injured when gunmen open fire on a crowded street. No group claims responsibility.

December 2, 2006   Six people are killed when gunmen open fire on a crowd in Gamra, Iraq. In Baghdad, 68 people are killed and 121 are injured by three car bombs detonated in a market. No group claims responsibility.

December 5, 2006   Sixteen people are killed and 25 injured by three car bombs outside a gas station in Baghdad. Also in Baghdad, 15 people are killed and seven injured when their minibus is attacked. No group claims responsibility.

December 9, 2006   Six people are killed and 44 injured by a suicide bomber outside a Shiite shrine in Karbala, Iraq. No group claims responsibility.

December 10, 2006   Five people, including one policeman, are killed when gunmen storm their home in Baghdad. No group claims responsibility.

December 12, 2006   At least 71 people are killed and 236 wounded when a car suicide bomber, posing as a prospective employer, blows up his truck amidst a group of day laborers in central Baghdad. No group claims responsibility.

December 13, 2006   Eleven people are killed and 27 wounded by a car bomb near a Shiite mosque in Baghdad. In a mostly Shiite Baghdad neighborhood, four people are killed and 14 wounded when two car bombs explode. Meanwhile, in Yarmouk, a Sunni area of the city, two people are killed and three wounded by a car bomb. In Hasna village, Iraq, nine people are killed when gunmen attack a Shiite family in their house.

December 20, 2006   Four people are killed and seven wounded by a car bomb in the Adhamiya neighborhood of northern Baghdad.

December 22, 2006   Nineteen people are killed by a suicide bomber in Baghdad.

December 24, 2006   One person is killed and 20 wounded by two roadside bombs in Khanaqin, Iraq.

December 25, 2006   Three people are killed and 20 wounded when a suicide bomber attacks a minibus in Baghdad. Also in Baghdad, nine people are killed and 11 wounded by a car bomb in a marketplace.

December 26, 2006   Twenty-six are killed and 54 wounded by three car bombs in western Baghdad. Also in Baghdad, 17 people are killed and 35 wounded by a car bomb near the Sunni Abu Hanifa mosque.

December 27, 2006   Fifteen people are killed and 20 wounded by a car bomb in northeastern Baghdad.

December 28, 2006   Seven people are killed and 35 wounded by two bombs in a Baghdad market. In another attack, ten people are killed and 35 wounded by a bomb near a crowd waiting in line for heating fuel at a stadium in Baghdad.

December 29, 2006   Nine people are killed and 15 wounded by a suicide bomber near the home of the sheikh of a Shiite mosque in Khalis, killing the cleric, his brother, and seven others.

December 30, 2006   After being found guilty of the murders of 143 Shias in 1982 when he was head of Iraq, Saddam Hussein is hanged at the Iraqi army base Camp Justice in Kadhimiya, Iraq. Thirty-one people are killed and 58 wounded by a car bomb at a fish market in Kufa, Iraq. In Baghdad, two car bombs kill 36 people and wound 77.

Glossary

Abu Nidal Organization (ANO): Palestinian group that split from the Palestine Liberation Organization (PLO) and worked as a mercenary group at various times for Iraq, Syria, and Libya.

Abu Sayyaf Group (ASG): Islamist revolutionary group in the southern Philippines.

Action Directe: An urban terrorist group in France during the 1960s.

Action for National Liberation (ALN): A splinter group from the Brazilian Communist Party, led by Carlos Marighella, and the People's Revolutionary Vanguard (VPR), created by radical students.

Al-Aqsa Martyrs Brigades: A military formation within Fatah organized by grassroots elements, mainly in the West Bank, under the leadership of Marwan Barghouti.

Al-Gama'a al-Islamiyya (IG): An Egyptian Islamist group which split off from the Muslim Brotherhood, used mass organizing techniques, and then turned to terrorism in the 1990s. Many imprisoned leaders later declared the decision to begin armed struggle was a mistake.

Al-Ittihad al-Islami (Islamic Union): The largest Somalian Islamist group; has ties to al-Qaeda.

Allied Democratic Forces (ADF): A partnership between Islamists and the National Army for the Liberation of Uganda (NALU).

All-Tripura Tiger Force (ATTF): Nationalist terrorist group in northeast India seeking independence for all tribal areas within the state of Tripura and expulsion of Bengali-speaking immigrants.

Al-Qaeda: International coalition of Islamist terrorist groups established by Osama bin Laden.

Al-Qaeda in Iraq (Tanzim Qa'idat al-Jihad fi Bilad al-Rafidayn): The representative of al-Qaeda in Iraq and leading force in the insurgency there. It was created by a merger in October 2004 between al-Qaeda and Abu Musab Zarqawi's earlier insurgent group in Iraq, Tawhid and Jihad.

Al-Umar Mujahideen (AuM): Islamist group seeking to make the Indian state of Jammu and Kashmir part of Pakistan.

Anti-Salvadoran Liberation Action Group: Nationalist terrorist group seeking to kill Salvadorans who take jobs from Guatemalans.

Argentine Anti-Communist Alliance: Right-wing Argentinian group.

Armed Islamic Group (GIA): Radical Islamist terrorist group in Algeria, affiliated with al-Qaeda.

Armed Revolutionary Nuclei: A group that split from the Italian right-wing group Ordine Nuovo. Also known as NTA, Nuclei Territoriali Antimperialisti.

Armenian Genocide Justice Commandos (JCAG): Armenian nationalist terrorist group seeking revenge against Turkey and the annexation to Armenia of parts of eastern Turkey.

Armenian Secret Army for the Liberation of Armenia (ASALA): A left-wing Armenian nationalist terrorist group seeking the annexation to Armenia of parts of eastern Turkey.

Army of God: A tiny U.S. organization committed to the use of violence to stop abortions.

AUC (United Self-Defense Forces of Colombia): An alliance of Colombian right-wing paramilitary groups fighting left-wing revolutionaries.

Aum Shinrikyo: A Japanese religious cult seeking world domination which used poison gas in the Tokyo subway.

Basque Fatherland and Liberty: *See* Euskadi Ta Askatasuna (ETA).

Black Panthers: Black nationalist group in the United States.

Black September: Front group for the Palestinian Fatah during the 1970s.

Bodo Liberation Tiger Force (BLTF): A nationalist group seeking a separate state of Bodoland in northeast India.

Communist Party of Nepal-Maoist (CPN-M): Social revolutionary terrorist group in Nepal.

Democratic Front for the Liberation of Palestine (DFLP): Neo-Marxist nationalist Palestinian group which split from the Popular Front for the Liberation of Palestine (PFLP).

EGTK (Tupac Katari Guerrilla Army): Bolivian group seeking a government controlled by native Indian peoples.

ELN (National Liberation Army): Colombian social revolutionary group.

ELN-R (National Liberation Army Reborn): Peruvian social revolutionary group.

ERP (People's Revolutionary Army): Marxist social revolutionary group in Argentina.

Euskadi Ta Askatasuna (ETA): Known in English as Basque Fatherland and Liberty, a Basque nationalist terror group fighting Spain for an independent Basque state.

FALN (Armed Forces for National Liberation): Puerto Rican nationalist terrorist group operating in the United States.

FAR (Rebel Armed Forces): Revolutionary group in Guatemala that later became a part of the umbrella organization Guatemalan National Revolutionary Unity (URNG).

FARC (Revolutionary Armed Forces of Colombia): Military wing of the Colombian Communist Party.

Fatah: Palestinian group, which frequently used terrorism, and the leading faction in the Palestine Liberation Organization (PLO).

First of October Anti-Fascist Resistance Group (GRAPO): Spanish left-wing terrorist group.

Force-17: Elite section of Palestinian organization Fatah, originally the personal guard for Yasir Arafat, which engaged in terrorism.

FPL (People's Liberation Forces): Marxist group in El Salvador.

FPMR (Manuel Rodriguez Patriotic Front): Revolutionary social group in Chile associated with the Communist Party.

Free Aceh Movement: Separatist nationalist group in Indonesia.

Free Islamic Revolutionary Movement: Name used by Hezbollah in Lebanon for attacks on Western military forces in the 1980s.

Free Papua Movement (OPM): Nationalist revolutionary group seeking to separate West Papua from Indonesia.

Front de Libération du Québec (FLQ): A left-wing nationalist terrorist group that sought to separate Québec from Canada.

GIA: *See* Armed Islamic Group.

God's Army: A splinter group of the Keren National Union, which seeks an independent Keren state in Myanmar.

Guatemalan National Revolutionary Unity (URNG): An umbrella group of Guatemalan terrorist groups formed by ELN, ORPA, and other organizations.

Guerrilla Army of the People-Free Fatherland and the Joaquin Murieta Extremist Movement: Left-wing Chilean social revolutionary group.

Guerrilla Army of the Poor (EGP): A Communist terrorist group seeking to overthrow the government of Guatemala.

Hamas: Palestinian Islamist group using terrorism.

Harakat ul-Mujahideen (HUM): Pakistani Islamist group trying to separate Jammu and Kashmir from India to become part of Pakistan.

Harakat ul-Jihad-I-Islami (HUJI): An Islamist group that began fighting the Soviets in Afghanistan during the 1980s, then switched to attacking India, trying to make Jammu and Kashmir part of Pakistan.

Hezbollah: A Lebanese Shia Islamist group.

Hizbul Mujahideen (HM): Pakistani group trying to separate Jammu and Kashmir from India to become part of Pakistan.

Hmar People's Convention-Democracy (HPC-D): Nationalist group seeking self-government for Hmars in northeast India.

Irish Republican Army (IRA): Nationalist revolutionary group which originally sought the independence of Ireland and later sought to unite Northern Ireland with the Republic of Ireland.

Islamic Jihad: A name used by several different Islamist groups, notably an Egyptian and a Palestine one.

Islamic Movement of Uzbekistan (IMU): Islamist revolutionary group in Uzbekistan.

Italian Social Movement (MSI): Italian neo-fascist party which had terrorist elements.

Jaish-e-Mohammed (JEM): Islamist revolutionary group seeking to detach Jammu and Kashmir from India and join it to Pakistan.

Jammu and Kashmir Liberation Front: Islamist group seeking to detach Jammu and Kashmir from India and annex it to Pakistan.

Jemaah Islamiya Organization (JI): Malaysian-based Islamist group seeking to create an Islamist state in all of Southeast Asia.

Kach: Extremist Jewish nationalist group founded by U.S.-born radical Rabbi Meir Kahane.

Kamtapur Liberation Organisation (KLO): Nationalist group seeking an independent state in India in the West Bengal–Assam area.

Kurdistan Workers' Party (PKK): Left-wing nationalist movement of Kurds in Turkey which used terrorist tactics. Includes the People's Liberation Army of Kurdistan (ARGK).

Lashkar-e-Jhangvi: Islamist group seeking to detach Jammu and Kashmir from India and join that area to Pakistan.

Lashkar-e-Tayyiba: Islamist group seeking to detach Jammu and Kashmir from India and attach that province to Pakistan.

Liberation Tigers of Tamil Eelam (LTTE): Tamil nationalist terrorist group seeking to carve out a separate Tamil state in northern Sri Lanka.

Lord's Resistance Army (LRA): Radical Christian social revolutionary group in Uganda.

Loyalist Volunteer Force (LVF): Protestant terrorist group in Northern Ireland.

Maoist Communist Center (MCC): Leftist terrorist group in West Bengal, India.

Moro Islamic Liberation Front (MILF): Islamist group seeking to create a separate state in the southern Philippines.

Manuel Rodriguez Patriotic Front (FPMR): Revolutionary social group in Chile associated with the Communist Party.

Moroccan Islamic Combatant Group (GICM): Islamist group in Morocco.

Movement of April 19: Revolutionary group in Colombia.

MRTA (Tupac Amaru Revolutionary Movement): A Marxist-Leninist revolutionary movement in Peru derived from the Movement of the Revolutionary Left.

Mujahideen-e Khalq (MEK): Leftist group with a philosophy combining Marxism and Islam, seeking to take over Iran.

Muslim Brotherhood: Islamist group with independent branches in many countries, especially Syria, Jordan, and Egypt.

National Army for the Liberation of Uganda: Social revolutionary group in Uganda.

National Democratic Front of Bodoland (NDFB): Nationalist group seeking a separate state for the Bodo people of India's Assam area.

National Liberation Army (ELN): Colombian social revolutionary group.

National Liberation Army Reborn (ELN-R): Peruvian social revolutionary group.

National Liberation Front of Tripura (NLFT): Nationalist terrorist group in India seeking independence for all tribal areas within Tripura and expulsion of Bengali-speaking immigrants.

National Socialist Council of Nagaland-Isak-Muivah (NSCN-IM): Maoist group seeking to create a Naga state in India.

New People's Army (NPA): Left-wing social revolutionary group formed by the Communist Party of the Philippines.

Ordine Nuovo: An Italian fascist group.

Oromo Liberation Front (OLF): Nationalist group seeking to create an Oromo state from Ethiopia.

Palestine Liberation Front (PLF): A name used by several small Palestinian nationalist terrorist groups sponsored by Iraq, Libya, and Syria.

Palestine Liberation Organization (PLO): An umbrella organization led by Fatah which approved of terrorist tactics and whose members often used them.

Pattani United Liberation Organization: A nationalist and Islamist group seeking separation of Muslim areas in southern Thailand.

People's Liberation Forces (FPL): Marxist group in El Salvador.

People's War Group (PWG): A Maoist terrorist organization, seeking a Communist state in India.

Popular Boricua Army: Successor to the Puerto Rican FALN, seeking an independent state.

Popular Front for the Liberation of Palestine (PFLP): Palestinian group with a pan-Arab nationalist ideology that often used terrorism.

Popular Front for the Liberation of Palestine-General Command (PFLP-GC): Syrian-controlled Palestinian group outside the PLO that often used terrorism.

Popular Resistance Committee: Small ultraradical Palestinian group with possible ties to al-Qaeda.

Popular Struggle Front: Small Palestinian nationalist terrorist group.

Red Army Faction (RAF): German social revolutionary terrorist group, often called the Baader-Meinhof Gang.

Red Brigades: Social revolutionary terrorist group in Italy.

Revolutionary Armed Forces of Colombia (FARC): Military wing of the Colombian Communist Party.

Riyad us-Saliheyn Martyrs Brigade: Chechen group committed to establishing an independent Islamic state in Chechnya and other Muslim areas of Russia.

Salaf Group for Preaching and Combat (GSPC): Algerian Islamist group that split from the GIA.

17 November Group: Small social revolutionary terrorist group in Greece.

Shining Path (also known as SL by its Spanish name, Sendero Luminoso): Radical social revolutionary group in Peru combining Maoist politics with nationalism for the tribal peoples and using a heavily terrorist-oriented strategy.

Sipah-e-Sahaba Pakistan (SSP): Islamist terrorist group in Pakistan.

Socialist Patients Collective (SPK): German group that turned to terrorism and which argued that mental illness is the product of capitalist society and the only way to cure it is through Marxist revolution.

South Moluccan Suicide Commando: Terrorists seeking independence for the South Moluccan Islands in Indonesia.

Students Islamic Movement of India (SIMI): Islamist group in Uttar Pradesh, India.

Tawhid and Jihad (Jama'at al-Tawhid wa'al-Jihad): A group established by Jordanian-born Abu Musab al-Zarqawi in Iraq after the U.S. invasion in 2003 and which later affiliated with al-Qaeda.

Tupac Amaru Revolutionary Movement (MRTA): A Marxist-Leninist revolutionary movement in Peru derived from the Movement of the Revolutionary Left.

Tupac Katari Guerrilla Army (EGTK): Bolivian group seeking an Indian government.

Tupamaros: A left-wing Uruguayan urban social revolutionary group.

Turkish Communist Party/Marxist-Leninist (TKP/ML): A terrorist group seeking a Communist revolution in Turkey.

Turkish Nationalist Movement Party (MHP): Turkish nationalist group which originally was pan-Turkist and has a paramilitary arm, the Grey Wolves.

Ulster Defense Association (UDA): Protestant nationalist group in Northern Ireland, including the Ulster Freedom Fighters (UFF), which carries out terrorist attacks.

United Liberation Front of Assam (ULFA): Seeks an independent state of Assam in India.

United People's Democratic Solidarity (UPDS): A group, created by the merger of the Karbi National Volunteers and Karbi People's Front in India, seeking a separate Karbi-Anglong nation in Assam, India.

United Self-Defense Forces of Colombia (AUC): Alliance of Colombian right-wing paramilitary groups fighting left-wing revolutionaries.

Weathermen: Left-wing terrorist group in the United States. Also known as the Weather Underground Organization (WUO).

West Nile Bank Front: A terrorist group in Uganda that sought the return of dictator Idi Amin.

Selected Bibliography

This bibliography represents a selection of some of the most useful books for research and further reading. Of course, there is a massive literature on terrorism, specific groups, and the conflicts or ideologies that have spawned terrorism. This list is offered as a starting point.

Abuza, Zachary. *Militant Islam in Southeast Asia: Crucible of Terror.* Boulder, CO: Lynne Rienner Publishers, 2003.

Adams, James. *The Financing of Terror.* New York: Simon & Schuster, 1986.

Alexander, Yonah. *ETA: Profile of a Terrorist Group.* Ardsley, NY: Transnational Publishers, 2001.

Anderson, Sean. *Historical Dictionary of Terrorism.* Lanham, MD: Scarecrow Press, 2002.

Aston, Clive C. *A Contemporary Crisis: Political Hostage-Taking and the Experience of Western Europe.* Westport, CT: Greenwood Press, 1982.

Barkun, Michael. *Religion and the Racist Right: The Origins of the Christian Identity Movement.* Chapel Hill, NC: University of North Carolina Press, 1997.

Brogan, Patrick. *World Conflicts.* Lanham, MD: Scarecrow Press, 1998.

Clark, Robert P. *The Basque Insurgents: ETA, 1952–1980.* Madison: University of Wisconsin Press, 1984.

Coates, James. *Armed and Dangerous: The Rise of the Survivalist Right.* New York: Hill & Wang, 1995.

Collin, Richard Oliver, and Gordon L. Freedman. *Winter of Fire: The Abduction of General Dozier and the Downfall of the Red Brigades.* New York: Dutton, 1990.

Combs, Cindy C. *Terrorism in the Twenty-First Century.* Upper Saddle River, NJ: Pearson/Prentice Hall, 2000.

Crenshaw, Martha, and John Pimlott, eds. *Encyclopedia of World Terrorism.* Armonk, NY: M.E. Sharpe, 1997.

Crothers, Lane. *Rage on the Right: The American Militia Movement from Ruby Ridge to Homeland Security.* Lanham, MD: Rowman & Littlefield, 2003.

De Cataldo Neuburger, Luisella. *Women and Terrorism.* New York: St. Martin's Press, 1996.

Delong-Bas, Natana J. *Wahhabi Islam: From Revival and Reform to Global Jihad.* New York: Oxford University Press, 2004.

Demaris, Ovid. *Brothers in Blood: The International Terrorist Network.* New York: Scribner, 1977.

Emerson, Steven. *American Jihad: The Terrorists Living Among Us.* New York: Free Press, 2003.

Emerson, Steven, and Brian Duffy. *The Fall of Pan Am 103: Inside the Lockerbie Investigation.* New York: Putnam, 1990.

English, Richard. *Armed Struggle: The History of the IRA.* New York: Oxford University Press, 2003.

Feldman, Noah. *After Jihad: America and the Struggle for Islamic Democracy.* New York: Farrar, Straus & Giroux, 2003.

Ford, Franklin L. *Political Murder: From Tyrannicide to Terrorism.* Cambridge, MA: Harvard University Press, 1985.

Friedman, Norman. *Terrorism, Afghanistan, and America's New Way of War.* Annapolis, MD: Naval Institute Press, 2003.

Gold, Dore. *Hatred's Kingdom: How Saudi Arabia Supports the New Global Terrorism.* Washington, DC: Regnery, 2003.

Graysmith, Robert. *Amerithax: The Hunt for the Anthrax Killer.* New York: Berkley Books, 2003.

Hacker, Friedrich. *Crusaders, Criminals, Crazies: Terror and Terrorism in Our Time.* New York: Norton, 1976.

Hoffman, Bruce. *Recent Trends and Future Prospects of Iranian Sponsored International Terrorism.* Santa Monica, CA: Rand, 1990.

Hoffman, Bruce. *Recent Trends and Future Prospects of Terrorism in the United States.* Santa Monica, CA: Rand, 1988.

Hoffman, Bruce. *Right-wing Terrorism in Europe.* Santa Monica, CA: Rand, 1982.

Hoffman, Bruce. *Right-wing Terrorism in Europe Since 1980.* Santa Monica, CA: Rand, 1984.

Hoffman, Bruce. *A Strategic Framework for Countering Terrorism and Insurgency.* Santa Monica, CA: Rand, 1992.

Hoffman, Bruce. *Terrorism and Weapons of Mass Destruction: An Analysis of Trends and Motivations.* Santa Monica, CA: Rand, 1999.

Israeli, Raphael. *War, Peace and Terror in the Middle East.* London: Peter Cass, 2003.

Jenkins, Brian Michael. *Combatting Terrorism.* Santa Monica, CA: Rand, 1981.

Jenkins, Brian Michael. *Rand's Research on Terrorism.* Santa Monica, CA: Rand, 1977.

Juergensmeyer, Mark. *Terror in the Mind of God: The Global Rise of Religious Violence.* Berkeley: University of California Press, 2000.

Karawan, Ibrahim. *The Islamist Impasse.* Oxford and New York: Oxford University Press, 1997.

Kassimeris, George. *Europe's Last Red Terrorists: The Revolutionary Organization 17.* New York: New York University Press, 2001.

Al-Khattar, Aref M. *Religion and Terrorism: An Interfaith Perspective.* Westport, CT: Praeger, 2003.

Kinzer, Stephen. *All the Shah's Men: An American Coup and the Roots of Middle East Terror.* Hoboken, NJ: Wiley, 2003.

Kisala, Robert. *Religion and Social Crisis in Japan: Understanding Japanese Society Through the Aum Affair.* Basingstoke, UK, and New York: Palgrave, 2001.

Kushner, Harvey W., ed. *The Future of Terrorism: Violence in the New Millennium.* Thousand Oaks, CA: Sage Publications, 1998.

Laqueur, Walter. *The Age of Terrorism.* Boston: Little, Brown, 1987.

Laqueur, Walter. *A History of Terrorism.* New Brunswick, NJ: Transaction, 2001.

Lentz, Harris M. *Assassinations and Executions: An Encyclopedia of Political Violence, 1865–1986.* Jefferson, NC: McFarland, 1988.

Lentz, Harris M. *Assassinations and Executions: An Encyclopedia of Political Violence, 1900 through 2000.* Jefferson, NC: McFarland, 2002.

Lesser, Ian O. and others. *Countering the New Terrorism.* Santa Monica, CA: Rand, 1999.

Lewis, Bernard. *What Went Wrong?: Western Impact and Middle Eastern Response.* New York: Oxford University Press, 2002.

MacArthur, John. *Terrorism, Jihad, and the Bible: A Response to the Terrorist Attacks.* Nashville, TN: W Publishing Group, 2001.

McClintock, Cynthia. *Revolutionary Movements in Latin America: El Salvador's FMLN & Peru's Shining Path.* Washington, DC: U.S. Institute of Peace Press, 1998.

McKittrick, David. *Making Sense of the Troubles: The Story of the Conflict in Northern Ireland.* Chicago: New Amsterdam Books, 2002.

McKittrick, David, Brian Feeney, Seamus Kelters, David McVea, and Chris Thornton. *Lost Lives.* Edinburgh, UK: Mainstream, 1999.

Michel, Lou. *American Terrorist: Timothy McVeigh & the Oklahoma City Bombing.* New York: Regan Books, 2001.

Mickolus, Edward F. *Terrorism, 1980–1987: A Selectively Annotated Bibliography.* New York: Greenwood Press, 1988.

Mickolus, Edward F. *Terrorism, 1988–1991: A Chronology of Events and a Selectively Annotated Bibliography.* Westport, CT: Greenwood Press, 1993.

Mickolus, Edward F. *Terrorism, 1992–1995: A Chronology of Events and a Selectively Annotated Bibliography.* Westport, CT: Greenwood Press, 1997.

Mickolus, Edward F. *Terrorism, 1996–2001: A Chronology.* Westport, CT: Greenwood Press, 2002.

Millard, Mike. *Jihad in Paradise: Islam and Politics in Southeast Asia.* Armonk, NY: M.E. Sharpe, 2004.

Mullins, Wayman C. *A Sourcebook on Domestic and International Terrorism: An Analysis of Issues, Organizations, Tactics, and Responses.* Springfield, IL: C.C. Thomas, 1997.

Murphy, Paul J. *The Wolves of Islam: Russia and the Faces of Chechen Terror.* Washington, DC: Brasseys, 2005.

National Counterterrorism Center. *A Chronology of Significant International Terrorism for 2004.* Washington, DC: U.S. Government Printing Office, 2005.

O'Ballance, Edgar. *Islamic Fundamentalist Terrorism, 1979–95: The Iranian Connection.* New York: New York University Press, 1997.

O'Day, Alan. *Terrorism's Laboratory: The Case of Northern Ireland.* Aldershot, Hants, UK, and Brookfield, VT: Dartmouth Publishing, 1995.

Pape, Robert Anthony. *Dying to Win: The Strategic Logic of Suicide Terrorism.* New York: Random House, 2005.

Piszkiewicz, Dennis. *Terrorism's War with America: A History.* Westport, CT: Praeger, 2003.

Rand Corporation. *Recent Trends in Palestinian Terrorism.* Santa Monica, CA: Rand, 1984.

Rand Corporation. *Right-wing Terrorism in West Germany.* Santa Monica, CA: Rand, 1986.

Reeve, Simon. *The New Jackals: Ramzi Yousef, Osama Bin Laden and the Future of Terrorism.* Boston: Northeastern University Press, 1999.

Ressa, Maria. *Seeds of Terror: An Eyewitness Account of Al-Qaeda's Newest Center of Operations in Southeast Asia.* New York: Free Press, 2003.

Ruane, Joseph, and Jennifer Todd. *The Dynamics of Conflict in Northern Ireland: Power, Conflict and Emancipation.* Cambridge, UK, and New York: Cambridge University Press, 1996.

Robins, Robert S. *Political Paranoia: The Psychopolitics of Hatred.* New Haven, CT: Yale University Press, 1997.

Rubenstein, Richard E. *Rebels in Eden; Mass Political Violence in the United States.* Boston: Little, Brown, 1970.

Rubin, Barry, and Judith Colp Rubin, eds. *Anti-American Terrorism and the Middle East: A Documentary Reader.* New York: Oxford University Press, 2002.

Sanchez, Gonzalo, Charles W. Bergquist, and Ricardo Penaranda, eds. *Violence in Colombia: The Contemporary Crisis in Historical Perspective.* Wilmington, DE: SR Press, 1992.

Schanzer, Jonathan. *Al-Qaeda's Armies: Middle East Affiliate Groups & The Next Generation of Terror.* New York: Specialist Press International, 2005.

Schweitzer, Glenn E., and Carole C. Dorsch. *Superterrorism: Assassins, Mobsters, and Weapons of Mass Destruction.* New York: Plenum Trade, 1998.

Shafritz, Jay M. *Almanac of Modern Terrorism.* New York: Facts On File, 1991.

Sivan, Emmanuel. *Radical Islam: Medieval Theology and Modern Politics.* New Haven, CT: Yale University Press, 1990.

Stern, Kenneth S. *A Force Upon the Plain: American Militia Movement and Politics of Hate.* New York: Simon & Schuster, 1996.

Stickney, Brandon M. *"All-American Monster": The Unauthorized Biography of Timothy McVeigh.* Amherst, NY: Prometheus Books, 1996.

Tanter, Raymond. *Rogue Regimes: Terrorism and Proliferation.* New York: St. Martin's, 1998.

Taylor, Robert. *History of Terrorism.* San Diego, CA: Lucent Books, 2002.

Thackrah, John Richard. *Dictionary of Terrorism.* New York: Routledge, 2004.

Wardlaw, Grant. *Political Terrorism: Theory, Tactics, and Counter-measures.* Cambridge, UK, and New York: Cambridge University Press, 1989.

Watson, Francis M. *Political Terrorism: The Threat and the Response.* Washington, DC: R.B. Luce, 1976.

Weinberg, Leonard. *Political Parties and Terrorist Groups.* London and New York: F. Cass, 1992.

Weinberg, Leonard, and Ami Pedahzur. *Political Parties and Terrorist Groups.* London and New York: Routledge, 2003.

White, Jonathan R. ed. *Terrorism: An Introduction.* Belmont, CA: Thomson/Wadsworth, 2003.

Wilkinson, Paul. *Political Terrorism.* New York: Wiley, 1974.

Woodworth, Paddy. *Dirty War, Clean Hands: ETA, the GAL and Spanish Democracy.* Crosses Green, Cork, Ireland: Cork University Press, 2001.

Zulaika, Joseph, and William A. Douglass. *Terror and Taboo: The Follies, Fables, and Faces of Terrorism.* New York: Routledge, 1996.

Periodicals

Arquilla, John and others. "Information-Age Terrorism." *Current History,* April 2000, pp. 179–185.

Badolato, Edward V. "Iran: The Real Terrorist Threat." *Journal of Counterterrorism & Security International,* Spring 1998, pp. 8–10.

Bahgat, Gawdat. "Iran and Terrorism: The Transatlantic Responses." *Studies in Conflict and Terrorism,* April–June 1999, pp. 141–152.

Bodansky, Yossef. "Italy Becomes Iran's New Base for Terrorist Operations." *Defense & Foreign Affairs Strategic Policy,* Vol. 26, no. 4–5 (April–May 1998), pp. 5–9.

Bowers, Stephen R., and Kimberly R. Keys. "Technology and Terrorism: The New Threat for the Millennium." *Conflict Studies,* No. 309 (May 1998), pp. 1–24.

Bruce, James. "Arab Veterans of the Afghan War." *Jane's Intelligence Review,* April 1995, pp. 175–179.

Bruce, James. "The Hunt for Middle Eastern Terrorists— Part 2." *Jane's Intelligence Review,* October 1995, pp. 458–461.

Chalk, Peter. "Low Intensity Conflict in Southeast Asia: Piracy, Drug Trafficking and Political Terrorism." *Conflict Studies,* No. 305/306 (January–February 1998), pp. 1–36.

Chalk, Peter. "Political Terrorism in South-East Asia." *Terrorism and Political Violence,* Summer 1998, pp. 118–134.

Emerson, Steven. "Inside the Osama Bin Laden Investigation." *Journal of Counterterrorism & Security International,* Fall 1998, pp. 16–26.

Emerson, Steven. "Osama Bin Laden's Special Operations Man." *Journal of Counterterrorism & Security International,* Fall 1998, pp. 28–29.

Emerson, Steven. "Terrorism in America: The Middle Eastern Connection—Domestic Groups That Support Middle Eastern Terrorism." *Journal of Counterterrorism & Security International,* Spring 1998, pp. 13–15.

Emerson, Steven. "The Tucson Connection." *Journal of Counterterrorism & Security International,* Fall 1998.

Enders, Walter, and Todd Sandler. "Is Transnational Terrorism Becoming More Threatening?" *Journal of Conflict Resolution,* June 2000, pp. 307–332.

"Enemies and Assets." *New American,* Vol. 13, no. 4 (March 3, 1997).

Hoffman, Bruce. "The Confluence of International and Domestic Trends in Terrorism." *Terrorism and Political Violence,* Summer 1997, pp. 1–15.

Howard, Roger. "Entertaining Osama: Testing the Limits of Taliban Hospitality." *Jane's Intelligence Review,* November 1998, pp. 14–16.

Kutschera, Chris. "Iran: A Network of Terror." *Middle East,* No. 266 (April 1997), pp. 17–18.

Leader, Stefan. "Cash for Carnage: Funding the Modern Terrorist." *Jane's Intelligence Review,* May 1998, pp. 42–46.

Leader, Stefan. "Osama bin Laden and the Terrorist Search for WMD [weapons of mass destruction]." *Jane's Intelligence Review,* June 1999, pp. 34–37.

Leader, Stefan, and David Wiencek. "Drug Money: The Fuel for Global Terrorism." *Jane's Intelligence Review,* February 2000, pp. 49–54.

Lukin, Anthony A. "History in the Headlines: The Meaning of the Mohammed Rashid Case." *Journal of Counterterrorism & Security International,* Summer 1998, pp. 45–47.

Lupsha, Peter A., and John Fullilove. "Beyond State Terror: The 'Grapes of Wrath.'" *Low Intensity Conflict & Law Enforcement,* Winter 1996, pp. 301–332.

Medd, Roger, and Frank Goldstein. "International Terrorism on the Eve of a New Millennium." *Studies in Conflict and Terrorism,* Vol. 20, no. 3 (July–September 1997), pp. 281–316.

"The Modus Operandi of Militant Islamic Extremist Groups on American Soil." *Journal of Counterterrorism & Security International,* Spring 1998, pp. 20–22.

Pringle, Caleb. "Terrorist Organizations' Use of Information Age Capabilities." *Defense & Foreign Affairs Strategic Policy,* Vol. 27, no. 1 (1999), pp. 9–12.

Ranstorp, Magnus. "Interpreting the Broader Context and Meaning of Bin-Laden's 'Fatwa.'" *Studies in Conflict and Terrorism,* October–December 1998, pp. 321–330.

Richardson, Louise. "Terrorists as Transnational Actors." *Terrorism and Political Violence,* Winter 1999, pp. 209–219.

Rosenau, William and others. "Transnational Threats and US National Security." *Low Intensity Conflict & Law Enforcement,* Winter 1997, pp. 144–161.

Simon, Steven, and Daniel Benjamin. "America and the New Terrorism." *Survival,* Vol. 42 (Spring 2000), pp. 59–75.

Smith, William D. "Principal Rogue Nations Are Unrelenting in Their Efforts to Export Terrorism." *Sea Power,* January 1997, pp. 51–58.

U.S. Department of State. *Patterns of Global Terrorism,* annual, Washington, DC (1983–2003).

Venter, Al J. "Iran Still Exporting Terrorism to Spread Its Islamic Vision." *Jane's Intelligence Review,* November 1997, pp. 511–516.

Waller, Robert. "The Libyan Threat to the Mediterranean." *Jane's Intelligence Review,* May 1996, pp. 225–229.

Wiencek, David. "Drug Money: The Fuel for Global Terrorism." *Jane's Intelligence Review,* February 2000, pp. 49–54.

Zanini, Michele. "Middle Eastern Terrorism and Netwar." *Studies in Conflict and Terrorism,* July–September 1999, pp. 247–256.

Internet Sites

International Policy Institute for Counter-Terrorism: www.ict.org.il/

Israel Ministry of Foreign Affairs: www.mfa.gov.il/mfa/home.asp

The MIPT Terrorism Knowledge Base: www.tkb.org/AboutTKB.jsp

Rand Corporation: www.rand.org/research_areas/terrorism/

South Asia Terrorism Portal: www.satp.org/satporgtp/site.htm

Terrorism Research Center: www.terrorism.com

Malcolm Sutton, *Bear in mind these dead . . . An Index of Deaths from the Conflict in Ireland 1969–1993.* Books published in 1994; revised and updated excerpts at: http://cain.ulst.ac.uk/sutton/book/index.html

Index

About the Authors

Barry Rubin is director of the Global Research for International Affairs (GLORIA) Center, a professor at the Interdisciplinary Center, and editor of the *Middle East Review of International Affairs (MERIA) Journal, The Truth About Syria; The Long War for Freedom: The Arab Struggle for Democracy in the Middle East; The Tragedy of the Middle East; The Transformation of Palestinian Politics; Revolution Until Victory: The Politics and History of the PLO; Cauldron of Turmoil: America in the Middle East; Modern Dictators; Secrets of State: The State Department and the Struggle over U.S. Foreign Policy; Paved with Good Intentions: The American Experience and Iran; The Arab States and the Palestine Conflict; Islamic Fundamentalism in Egyptian Politics;* and *The Great Powers in the Middle East, 1941–1947.*

Judith Colp Rubin is a veteran journalist and author of *Women in the Middle East: Veils and Protests* and *Religions in the Middle East: The Root of Identity*. She is co-author with Barry Rubin of *Hating America: A History; Yasir Arafat: A Political Biography; Loathing America;* and *Anti-American Terrorism and the Middle East.*